The
Student Pilot's
Flight Manual

From First Flight to Pilot Certificate

10th Edition

Original text by William K. Kershner

Edited by William C. Kershner

Aviation Supplies & Academics, Inc.
Newcastle, Washington

William K. Kershner began flying in 1945 at the age of fifteen, washing and propping airplanes to earn flying time. By this method he obtained the private, then the commercial and flight instructor certificates, becoming a flight instructor at nineteen. He spent four years as a naval aviator, most of the time as a pilot in a night fighter squadron, both shore and carrier based. He flew nearly three years as a corporation pilot and for four years worked for Piper Aircraft Corporation, demonstrating airplanes to the military, doing experimental flight-testing, and acting as special assistant to William T. Piper, Sr., president of the company. Bill Kershner held a degree in technical journalism from Iowa State University. While at the university he took courses in aerodynamics, performance, and stability and control. He held the airline transport pilot, commercial, and flight and ground instructor certificates and flew airplanes ranging from 40-hp Cubs to jet fighters. He is the author of *The Student Pilot's Flight Manual, The Instrument Flight Manual, The Advanced Pilot's Flight Manual, The Flight Instructor's Manual,* and *The Basic Aerobatic Manual.* Kershner operated an aerobatics school in Sewanee, Tennessee using a Cessna 152 Aerobat. He received the General Aviation Flight Instructor of the Year Award, 1992, at the state, regional and national levels. The Ninety-Nines awarded him the 1994 Award of Merit. In 1998 he was inducted into the Flight Instructor Hall of Fame, in 2002 was installed in the Tennessee Aviation Hall of Fame, and in 2006 was inducted into the International Aerobatic Club Hall of Fame. William K. Kershner died January 8th, 2007.

Editor William C. Kershner received his early flight training from his father, William K. Kershner. He holds Commercial, Flight Instructor and Airline Transport Pilot certificates and has flown 22 types of airplanes, ranging in size from Cessna 150s to Boeing 777s, in his 10,000+ flight hours. He works as an airline pilot and lives with his wife and two sons near Sewanee, Tennessee.

The Student Pilot's Flight Manual: from first flight to pilot certificate
William K. Kershner
Illustrated by the Author

© 2006–2010 William K. Kershner and Elizabeth Ann Kershner as trustees (or their respective successors as such trustees) of the William K. Kershner Trust, dated August 16, 2001. Previous editions © 1960–2001 William K. Kershner.
First edition published 1960 by Iowa State University Press. Tenth Edition 2010 published by Aviation Supplies & Academics, Inc. All rights reserved. No part of this book may be reproduced in any form or by any electronic or mechanical means, including information storage and retrieval systems, without permission in writing from the publisher, except for brief passages quoted in a review.

Aviation Supplies & Academics, Inc. • 7005 132nd Place SE • Newcastle, WA 98059
Email: asa@asa2fly.com • Internet: www.asa2fly.com

Cover photo: William K. Kershner flies his Cessna 152 Aerobat, N7557L, near his home of Sewanee, Tennessee. This photo was taken by Mike Fizer on March 14th, 2000 for the 2001 AOPA calendar. Dad had over 7,000 separate spins of between 3 and 25 turns in his 22 years teaching aerobatics in this airplane. Two months after his death in January 2007, my son, Jim, and I were honored to deliver 57L to Dulles International Airport for display at the National Air and Space Museum's Steven F. Udvar-Hazy Center. — *William C. Kershner*

Photo credits: Front cover, courtesy of AOPA; photo under Dedication, page v, and Chapter 24 cross-country photos, courtesy of Elizabeth Motlow; start of Part 1 "Before the Flight," Adam Korzekwa/istockphoto; start of Part 2 "Presolo," George Jurasek/istockphoto; start of Part 3 "Postsolo Maneuvers" and Part 6 "Syllabus," Ken Babione/istockphoto; start of Part 4 "Cross Country and Night Flying," photo © Smithsonian Institution, used with permission of National Air and Space Museum; start of Part 5 "The Knowledge and Practical (Flight) Tests," skyf/fotolia.

Printed in the United States of America

2015   2014   2013   9 8 7 6 5 4

ASA-FM-STU-10
ISBN 978-1-56027-719-4

Library of Congress Cataloging-in-Publication Data:
Kershner, William K.
        The student pilot's flight manual / William K. Kershner.—10th ed.
        p.   cm.
Includes bibliographical references and index.
        1. Airplanes—Piloting—Handbooks, manuals, etc. 2. Airplanes—Piloting—Examinations—Study guides. I. Title.
TL710 .K42 2001
629.132' 52—dc21
        2001016995

Contents

Dedication, *v*

Acknowledgments, *vi*

Preface, *vii*

Part One
Before the Flight

1 Starting to Fly, *1-1*

2 The Airplane and How It Flies, *2-1*

3 Cockpit—Instruments and Systems, *3-1*

4 Preflight Check, *4-1*

5 Starting the Airplane, *5-1*

6 Taxiing, *6-1*

7 Pretakeoff or Cockpit Check, *7-1*

Part Two
Presolo

8 Effects of Controls, *8-1*

9 The Four Fundamentals, *9-1*

10 Elementary Precision Maneuvers, *10-1*

11 Elementary Emergency Landings, *11-1*

12 Stalls and Slow Flight, *12-1*

13 Takeoffs and Landings, *13-1*

Part Three
Postsolo Maneuvers

14 Advanced Stalls, *14-1*

15 Emergency Flying by Reference to Instruments, *15-1*

16 Postsolo Precision Maneuvers, *16-1*

17 Special Takeoff and Landing Procedures, *17-1*

18 High-Altitude Emergencies, *18-1*

Part Four
Cross-Country and Night Flying

19 The Navigation Idea, *19-1*

20 The Chart and Other Printed Aids, *20-1*

21 Using the Radio, *21-1*

22 Weather Information, *22-1*

23 The Cross-Country—Knowing Your Airplane, *23-1*

24 Navigation Planning, *24-1*

25 Flying the Cross-Country, *25-1*

26 Introduction to Night Flying, *26-1*

Part Five
The Knowledge and Practical (Flight) Tests

27 The Knowledge Test Review, *27-1*

28 The Practical (Flight) Test, *28-1*

Part Six
Syllabus

Private Certificate Syllabus, *S-1*

Appendixes

A *Airport/Facility Directory* Excerpts and Legend, *A-1*

B Added Notes on Engines and Other Systems, *B-1*

C Sport Pilot—Airplane, Single-Engine Land (ASEL), *C-1*

Bibliography and Printing History, *Bib-1*

Index, *I-1*

Sectional Chart, *back of book*

Dedication

The 10th Edition of the *Student Pilot's Flight Manual* is dedicated to my parents:

Elizabeth Ann Deyo Kershner   1933-2009

William K. Kershner   1929-2007

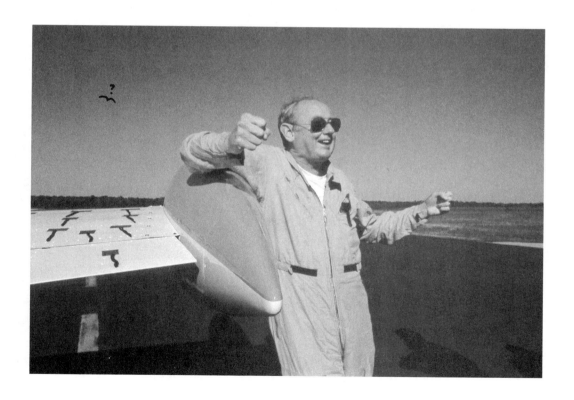

Acknowledgments for the Tenth Edition

Thanks go to my wife Donna and sister Cindy for their help and encouragement.

My editors at ASA, Jennie Trerise and Jackie Spanitz, showed me great patience and offered invaluable advice. Sarah Hager, graphic designer at ASA, did an outstanding job with the layout of the book and the redesign of the cover. Rebecca Gibson, flight instructor and airport manager at Sewanee, gave me useful perspective on judgment and aspects of cross-country flying.

And my special thanks go to flight instructor Genie Rae O'Kelley for her help with my aviation career and the careers of so many others.

The acknowledgments for the 1st through 9th Editions are found with the bibliography.

Preface to the Tenth Edition

This book is written to cover the fundamentals of light-plane flying, and emphasizes flying skills and knowledge that will cover a wide range of airplane types and sizes. For instance, crosswind landing techniques effective in a Cessna 152 can also work well in a Boeing 777 or Bandeirante turbo prop. And although technology has changed dramatically over the years, the basics of flying and good judgment have not.

This manual is not intended to just help the reader "squeak by" the FAA knowledge (written) test and practical test (flight test or checkride), but to lay a foundation of solid knowledge for use in the everyday process of learning to fly airplanes. Even after thousands of hours in the air, most pilots still learn something on every flight.

The flight maneuvers are written in the probable order of introduction to the student. The spin is included to give the student pilot an idea of what the maneuver entails and the dangers involved in an inadvertent low-altitude spin.

Although this book was originally written for the individual working toward the private pilot certificate, ASEL (airplane, single-engine, land), it includes all the information necessary for the slightly more restrictive sport or recreational pilot certificates. For example, the sport pilot applicant will not require training in emergency instrument flight (Chapter 15) or night flying (Chapter 26). The already certificated pilot can use this book in preparing for the Flight Review (14 CFR 61.56—required every 24 months). Referencing Chapters 27 and 28, along with a review of 14 CFR Parts 61 and 91, will bring the pilot back up to speed on subjects perhaps not touched on in awhile.

The student pilot will notice the almost total lack of technology used on the knowledge and flight test. The training for these first certificates is fixed on the basic skills of flying: controlling the airplane, using good judgment in choosing a course of action, and navigating with landmarks and a chart.

This manual is, of necessity, written in general terms, as seen in the (often changing) areas of information and weather services. Because airplanes vary from type to type in the use of flaps, carburetor heat, spin recovery and other procedures, the *Pilot's Operating Handbook* or equivalent source is the final guide for operation of your specific trainer. Of course, all of the performance and navigation charts in this text are for reference and example only.

Pilots should have ready access to a few other important resources. I have found the bare minimum to be the *Aeronautical Information Manual* (AIM), Federal Aviation Regulations (Title 14 of the Code of Federal Regulations), *Aviation Weather Services* (FAA Advisory Circular 00-45), and *Aviation Weather* (AC 00-6A). The *Advanced Pilot's Flight Manual* (Kershner) is a good source for more detail on aerodynamics and for transition to more complex airplane types.

I will welcome any feedback offered on the 10th Edition of *The Student Pilot's Flight Manual*. Please contact me through ASA (email: feedback@asa2fly.com).

Flying is one of mankind's most rewarding and challenging endeavors. Every flight is different and most experienced pilots can tell of wonders they've seen that no ground-bound person will ever know.

William C. Kershner
Sewanee, Tennessee

Part One
Before the Flight

1

1

Starting to Fly

There are many reasons why people want to start flying. Maybe you are a younger person who wants to make it a lifetime career or maybe you are a slightly more senior citizen who always wanted to fly but until now haven't had the money. Whether a man or woman, young or old, you still may have a few butterflies in your stomach while worrying about how you will like it or whether you can do it. That's a natural reaction.

What can you expect as you go through the private pilot training course? You can expect to work hard on most flights and to come down from some flights very tired and wet with perspiration, but with a feeling of having done something worthwhile. After others, you may consider forgetting the whole idea.

Okay, so there will be flights that don't go so well, no matter how well you get along with your instructor. The airplane will seem to have decided that it doesn't want to do what you want it to. The situation gets worse as the flight progresses and you end the session with a feeling that maybe you just aren't cut out to be a pilot. If you have a couple of these in a row, you should consider changing your schedule to early morning instead of later afternoon flights, or vice versa. You may have the idea that everybody but you is going through the course with no strain at all, but every person who's gone through a pilot training course has suffered some "learning plateaus" or has setbacks that can be discouraging.

After you start flying, you may at some point decide that it would be better for your learning process if you changed instructors. This happens with some people and is usually a no-fault situation, so don't worry about a change or two.

It's best if you get your FAA (Federal Aviation Administration) medical examination out of the way very shortly after you begin to fly or, if you think that you might have a problem, get it done before you start the lessons. The local flight instructors can give you names of nearby FAA aviation medical examiners.

How do you choose a flight school? You might visit a few in your area and see which one suits you best. Watch the instructors and students come and go to the airplanes. Are the instructors friendly, showing real interest in the students? There should be pre- and post-flight briefings of students. You may not hear any of the details, but you can see that such briefings are happening. Talk to students currently flying at the various schools and get their opinions of the learning situation. One good hint about the quality of maintenance of the training airplanes is how clean they are. Usually an airplane that is clean externally is maintained well internally, though certainly there are exceptions to this.

What about the cost? It's a good idea to have money ahead so that you don't have to lay off and require a lot of reviewing from time to time. Some flight schools give a discount if you pay for several hours ahead of time.

You are about to set out on a very rewarding experience; for an overall look at flight training and future flying you might read the following.

The Big Three

As you go through any flight program, particularly in a military flight program, you will hear three terms used many times: *headwork, air discipline,* and *attitude toward flying.* You may be the smoothest pilot since airplanes were invented, but without having a good grip on these requirements, you'll last about as long as a snowball in the Amazon River.

Headwork

For any pilot, private or professional, the most important thing is good headwork. Nobody cares if you slip or skid a little or maybe every once in a while land a mite harder than usual, but if you don't use your head—if you fly into bad weather or forget to check the fuel and have to land in a plowed field—you'll find

Figure 1-1. Headwork is remembering to put the landing gear down.

people avoiding you. Later, as you progress in aviation and lead flights or fly passengers, it's a lot more comfortable for all concerned if they know you are a person who uses your head in flying. So as the sign says—THILK, er, think.

Air Discipline

This is a broad term, but generally it means having control of the aircraft and yourself at all times. Are you a precise pilot or do you wander around during maneuvers? Do you see a sports car and decide to buzz it? Air discipline is difficult at times. It's mighty tough not to fly over that good-looking member of the opposite sex who happens to be sunbathing right where you are doing S-turns across the road—but be firm!

More seriously, air discipline is knowing, and flying by, your own limitations. This means, for instance, holding down for bad weather and not risking your life and your passengers' lives. It also means honestly analyzing your flying faults and doing something about them. In short, air discipline means a mature approach to flying.

Attitude

A good attitude toward flying is important. Most instructors will go all out to help someone who's really trying, even a complete bungler. Many an instructor's favorite story is about ol' Joe Blow who was pretty terrible at first, but who kept at it until he got the word, and is now flying rockets for Trans-Galaxy Airlines. With a good attitude you will get plenty of help from everybody. More students have failed in flying because of poor headwork and attitude than for any other reason. This doesn't imply "apple polishing." It does mean that you are interested in flying and study more about it than is required by law.

2

The Airplane and How It Flies

The Four Forces

Four forces act on an airplane in flight: *lift, thrust, drag,* and *weight* (Figure 2-1).

Lift

Lift is a force exerted by the wings. (Lift may also be exerted by the fuselage or other components, but at this point it would be best just to discuss the major source of the airplane's lift, the wings.) It is a force created by the "airfoil," the cross-sectional shape of the wing being moved through the air or, as in a wind tunnel, the air being moved past the wing. The result is the same in both cases. The "relative wind" (wind moving in relation to the wing and airplane) is a big factor in producing lift, although not the only one (Figure 2-2).

Lift is always considered to be acting perpendicularly both to the wingspan and to the relative wind (Figure 2-3). The reason for this consideration will be shown later as you are introduced to the various maneuvers.

As the wing moves through the air, either in gliding or powered flight, lift is produced. How lift is produced can probably be explained most simply by Bernoulli's theorem, which briefly puts it this way: "The faster a fluid moves past an object, the less sidewise pressure is exerted on the body by the fluid." The fluid in this case is air; the body is an airfoil. Take a look at Figure 2-4, which shows the relative wind approaching an airfoil, all neatly lined up in position 1. As it moves past the airfoil (or as the airfoil moves past it—take your choice), things begin to happen, as shown by the subsequent numbers.

Figure 2-2. The airfoil.

Figure 2-1. The four forces. When the airplane is in equilibrium in straight and level cruising flight, the forces acting fore and aft (thrust and drag) are equal, as are those acting at 90° to the flight path (lift and weight, or its components).

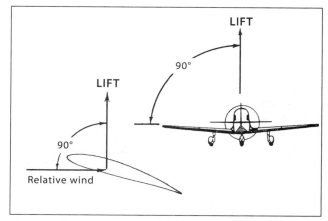

Figure 2-3. Lift acts perpendicular to the relative wind and wingspan.

Figure 2-4. Airflow past the airfoil.

The distance that the air must travel over the top is greater than that under the bottom. As the air moves over this greater distance, it speeds up in an apparent attempt to reestablish equilibrium at the rear (trailing edge) of the airfoil. (Don't worry, equilibrium *won't* be reestablished.) Because of this extra speed, the air exerts less sidewise pressure on the top surface of the airfoil than on the bottom, and lift is produced. The pressure on the bottom of the airfoil is normally increased also and you can think that, as an average, this contributes about 25 percent of the lift; this percentage varies with "angle of attack" (Figure 2-5).

Some people say, "Sure, I understand what makes a plane fly. There's a vacuum on top of the wing that holds the airplane up." Let's see about that statement.

The standard sea level air pressure is 14.7 pounds per square inch (psi), or 2,116 pounds per square foot (psf). As an example, suppose an airplane weighs 2,000 pounds, has a wing area of 200 square feet, and is in level flight at sea level. (The wing area is that area you would see by looking directly down on the wing.) This means that for it to fly level (lift = weight) each square foot of wing must support 10 pounds of weight, or the wing loading is 10 pounds psf (2,000 divided by 200). Better expressed: There would have to be a difference in pressure of 10 pounds psf between the upper surface and the lower surface. This 10 psf figure is an average; on some portions of the wing the difference will be greater, on others, less. Both surfaces of the wing can have a reduced sidewise pressure under certain conditions. However, the pressure on top still must average 10 psf less than that on the bottom to meet our requirements of level flight for the airplane mentioned. The sea level pressure is 2,116 pounds psf, and all that is needed is an average difference of 10 psf for the airplane to fly.

Assume for the sake of argument that, in this case, the 10 psf is obtained by an *increase* of 2.5 psf on the bottom surface and a *decrease* of 7.5 psf on the top (which gives a total difference of 10 psf). The top surface pressure varies from sea level pressure by 7.5 psf. Compared to the 2,116 psf of the air around it, this is certainly a long way from a vacuum, but it produces flight!

Note in Figures 2-2 and 2-4 that the airflow is deflected downward as it passes the wing. Newton's law, "For every action there is an equal and opposite reaction," also applies here. The wing deflects the airflow downward with a reaction of the airplane being sustained in flight. This can be easily seen by examining how a helicopter flies. Some engineers prefer Newton's law over Bernoulli's theorem. But the air *does* increase its velocity over the top of the wing (lowering the pressure), and the downwash also occurs. The downwash idea and how it affects the forces on the horizontal tail will be covered in Chapters 9 and 23.

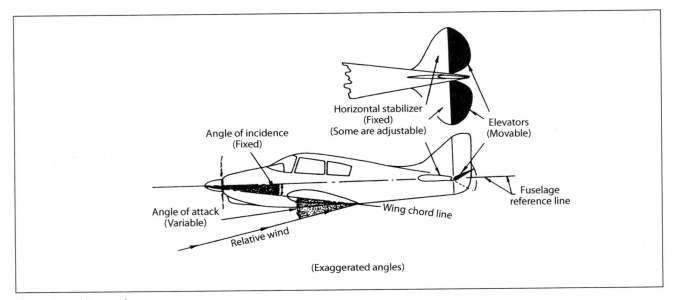

Figure 2-5. Nomenclature.

Angle of Attack

The angle of attack is the angle between the relative wind and the chord line of the airfoil. Don't confuse the angle of attack with the angle of *incidence*. The angle of *incidence* is the fixed angle between the wing chord line and the reference line of the fuselage. You'd better take a look at Figure 2-5 before this gets too confusing.

The pilot controls angle of attack with the elevators (Figure 2-5). By easing back on the control wheel (or stick) the elevator is moved "up" (assuming the airplane is right side up). The force of the relative wind moves the tail down, and because the wings are rigidly attached to the fuselage, (you hope) they are rotated to a new angle with respect to the relative wind, or new *angle of attack*. At this new angle of attack the apparent curvature of the airfoil is greater, and for a very short period, lift is increased. But because of the higher angle of attack more drag is produced, the airplane slows, and equilibrium exists again. (More about drag later.)

If you get too eager to climb and *mistakenly* believe that the reason an airplane climbs is because of an "excess" of lift (and so keep increasing the angle of attack), you could find that you have made a mistake. As you increase the angle of attack, the airplane slows and attempts to reestablish equilibrium, so you continue to increase it in hopes of getting an "excess" of lift for more climb. You may make the angle of attack so great that the air can no longer flow smoothly over the wing, and the airplane "stalls" (Figure 2-6).

It's not like a car stalling, in which case the engine stops; the airplane stall is a situation where the lift has broken down and the wing, in effect, is no longer doing its job of supporting the airplane in the usual manner. (The engine may be humming like a top throughout the stall.) There is still some lift, but not enough to support the airplane. You have forced the airplane away from the balanced situation you (and the airplane) want to maintain. For the airplane to recover from a stall, you must decrease the angle of attack so that smooth flow again occurs. In other words, point the plane where

Figure 2-7. Pitch attitude, climb angle (flight path), and angle of attack.

it's going! This is done with the elevators, the angle of attack, (and speed) control (Figure 2-5). For most lightplane airfoils, the stalling angle of attack is in the neighborhood of 15°. Stalls will be covered more thoroughly in Chapters 12 and 14.

At first, the student is also confused concerning the *angle of attack* and airplane *attitude*. The attitude is how the plane looks in relation to the horizon. In Figure 2-7 the plane's attitude is 15° nose up, but it's climbing at an angle of 5°, so the angle of attack is only 10°.

In a slow glide the nose attitude may be approximately level and the angle of attack close to that of the stall. Later in your flying, you'll be introduced to the attitude of the wings (wing-down attitude, etc.), but for now only nose attitudes are of interest.

The coefficient of lift is a term used to denote the relative amounts of lift at various angles of attack for an airfoil. The plot of the coefficient of lift versus the angle of attack is a straight line, increasing with an increase in the angle of attack until the stalling angle is reached (Figure 2-8).

Lift depends on a combination of several factors. The equation for lift is:

$$L = C_L S \frac{\rho}{2} V^2, \text{ or } L = C_L \times S \times \frac{\rho}{2} \times V^2$$

where L = lift, in pounds

C_L = coefficient of lift (varies with the type of airfoil used and the angle of attack). The coefficient of lift, C_L, is a dimensionless product and gives a *relative* look at the wings' action. The statement may be made in groundschool that, "At this angle of attack, the coefficient of lift is point five (0.5)." Point five what? "Just point five, and it's one-half of the C_L at one point zero (1.0)." Just take it as the relative effectiveness of the airfoils at a given angle of attack. Later, the coefficient of *drag* will be discussed.

Figure 2-6. The stall.

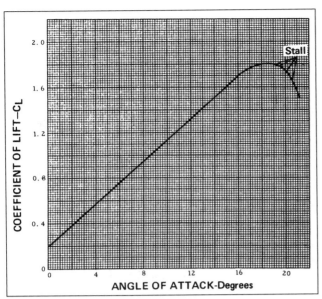

Figure 2-8. Relative lift increases with angle of attack until the stall angle is reached.

S = wing area in square feet

$\frac{\rho}{2}$ = air density (ρ) divided by 2. Rho (ρ) is air density, which for standard sea level conditions is 0.002378 slugs per cubic foot. If you want to know the mass of an object in slugs, divide the weight by the acceleration of gravity, or 32.2. (The acceleration caused by gravity is 32.2 feet per second per second at the earth's surface.)

V^2 = velocity in feet per second squared

When you fly an airplane, you'll be working with a combination of C_L and velocity; but let's talk in pilot terms and say that you'll be working with a combination of angle of attack and airspeed. So lift depends on angle of attack, airspeed, wing area, and air density. For straight and level flight, lift equals weight. Assuming that your airplane weighs 2,000 pounds, 2,000 pounds of lift is required to maintain level flight. This means that the combination of the above factors must equal that value. The wing area (S) is fixed, and the air density (ρ) is fixed for any one time and altitude. Then C_L (angle of attack) and velocity (airspeed) can be worked in various combinations to maintain the 2,000 pounds of lift required. Flying at a low airspeed requires a high angle of attack, and vice versa. As the pilot you will control angle of attack and, by doing so, control the airspeed. You'll use power (or lack of power) with your chosen airspeed to obtain the desired performance.

While the factors of lift are being discussed, it might be well to say a little more about air density (ρ). The air density decreases with increased altitude and/or temperature increase. Airplanes require more runway to take off on hot days or at airports of high elevation because of decreased air density. You can see in the lift equation that if the air is less dense, the airplane will have to move faster through the air in order to get the required value of lift for flight—and this takes more runway. (The airspeed mentioned is called "true airspeed" and will be discussed in more detail in Chapter 3.) Not only is the lift of the wing affected, but the less dense air results in less power developed within the engine. Since the propeller is nothing more than a rotating airfoil, it also loses "lift" (or, more properly, "thrust"). Taking off at high elevations or high temperatures can be a losing proposition, as some pilots have discovered after ignoring these factors and running out of runway.

Interestingly enough, you will find that lift tends to remain at an almost constant value during climbs, glides, or straight and level flight. *Don't* start off by thinking that the airplane glides because of decreased lift or climbs because of excess lift. *It just isn't so.*

Thrust

Thrust is the second of the four forces and is furnished by a propeller or jet. The propeller is of principal interest to you at this point, however.

The theory of propellers is quite complicated, but Newton's "equal and opposite reaction" idea can be stated here. *The propeller takes a large mass of air and accelerates it rearward, resulting in the equal and opposite reaction of the plane moving forward.*

Maybe it's time a few terms such as "force" and "power" should be cleared up. Thrust is a *force* and, like the other three forces, is measured in pounds. A *force* can be defined as a tension, pressure, or weight. You don't necessarily have to move anything; you can exert force against a very heavy object and nothing moves. Or you can exert a force against a smaller object and it moves. When an object having force exerted upon it moves, *work* has been done.

Work, from an engineering point of view, is simply a measure of *force* times *distance*. And while at the end of a day of pushing against a brick wall or trying to lift a safe that won't budge, you feel tired, actually you've done no *work* at all. If you lift a 550-pound safe 1 foot off the floor, you'll have done 550 foot-pounds of *work* (and no doubt strained yourself in the bargain). If you lift a 50-pound weight to a height of 11 feet, you'll have done the same *work* whether you take all day or 1 second to do it—but you won't be developing as much *power* by taking all day. So the *power* used in lifting that 50 pounds up 11 feet, or 550 pounds up 1 foot, in 1 second would be expressed as:

Power = 550 foot-pounds per second

Obviously, this is leading somewhere, and you know that the most common measurement for power is the term "horsepower." One horsepower is equal to a power of 550 foot-pounds per second, or 33,000 foot-pounds per minute (60 seconds × 550). Whether the average horse of today can actually do this is not known, and unfortunately nobody really seems to care.

The airplane engine develops horsepower within its cylinders and, by rotating a propeller, exerts thrust. In straight and level, unaccelerated, cruising flight the thrust exerted (pounds) is considered to equal the drag (pounds) of the airplane.

You will hear a couple of terms concerning horsepower:

Brake horsepower—the horsepower developed at the crankshaft. In earlier times this was measured at the crankshaft by a braking system or absorption dynamometer known as a "prony brake." *Shaft* horsepower means the same thing. Your airplane engine is always rated in brake horsepower, or the power produced at the crankshaft. Brake horsepower and engine ratings will be covered more thoroughly in Chapter 23.

Thrust horsepower—the horsepower developed by the propeller in moving the airplane through the air. Some power is lost because the propeller is not 100 percent efficient, and for round figures, you can say that the propeller is at best about 85 percent efficient (the efficiency of the fixed-pitch propeller varies with airspeed). The thrust horsepower developed, for instance, will be only up to about 85 percent of the brake horsepower.

If you are mathematically minded, you might be interested in knowing that the equation for thrust horsepower (THP) is: THP = TV ÷ 550, where T is thrust (pounds) and V is velocity (feet per second) of the airplane. Remember that a *force* times a *distance* equals *work*, and when this is divided by time, *power* is found.

In the equation above, *thrust* is the force, and velocity can be considered as being distance divided by time, so that TV (T × V) is power in foot-pounds per second. Knowing that 1 horsepower is 550 footpounds per second, the power (TV) is divided by 550 and the result would give the horsepower being developed—in this case, *thrust horsepower.* (*See* Chapter 9.) THP = TV mph ÷ 375, or TV knots ÷ 325 (more about "knots" later).

For light trainers with fixed-pitch propellers, a measure of the power (brake horsepower) being used is indicated on the airplane's tachometer in rpm (revolutions per minute). The engine power is controlled by the throttle. For more power the throttle is pushed forward or "opened"; for less power it is moved back or "closed." You'll use the throttle to establish certain rpm (power) settings for cruise, climb, and other flight requirements.

Torque

Because the propeller is a rotating airfoil, certain side effects are encountered. The "lift" force of the propeller is the thrust used by the airplane. The propeller also has a drag force. This force acts in a sidewise direction (parallel to the wing span or perpendicular to the fuselage reference line).

The propeller rotates clockwise as seen from the cockpit, causing a rotating mass of air to be accelerated toward the tail of the airplane. This air mass strikes the left side of the vertical stabilizer and rudder. This air mass, called "slipstream" or "propwash," causes the airplane to veer or "yaw" to the left. Right rudder must therefore be applied to hold the airplane on a straight track (Figure 2-9). This reaction increases with power, so it is most critical during the takeoff and climb portion of the flight. The slipstream effect is the biggest factor of torque for the single-engine airplane.

Figure 2-9. The slipstream effect makes the airplane want to yaw to the left.

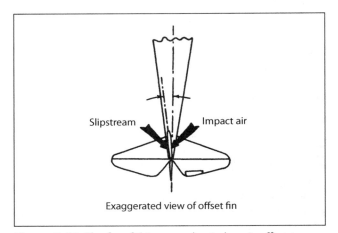

Figure 2-10. The fin of this example airplane is offset to balance the yawing forces at cruise.

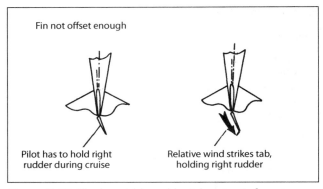

Figure 2-11. The bendable rudder tab corrects for minor yaw problems at cruise. Some airplanes have a rudder tab that is controllable from the cockpit. (*See* Chapter 8.)

An offset fin may be used to counteract this reaction. The fin setting is usually built in for maximum effectiveness at the rated cruising speed of the airplane, since the airplane will be flying most of the time at cruising speed (Figure 2-10).

The balance of forces at this point results in no yawing force at all, and the plane flies straight with no right rudder being held.

Sometimes the fin may not be offset correctly due to tolerances of manufacturing, and a slight left yaw is present at cruising speed, making a constant use of right rudder necessary to hold the airplane straight. To take care of this, a small metal tab is attached to the trailing edge of the rudder and is bent to the left. The relative air pressure against the tab forces the rudder to the right (Figure 2-11).

On many lightplanes this adjustment can be accomplished only on the ground. The tab is bent and the plane is test flown. This is done until the plane has no tendency to yaw in either direction at cruising speed.

Assuming that you have the tab bent correctly and the plane is balanced directionally, what happens if you vary from cruising speed? If the same power setting of 2,400 rpm, for instance, is used, the arrows in Figure 2-12 show a simplified approach to the relative forces at various airspeeds.

In a climb, right rudder is necessary to keep the plane straight. In a dive, left rudder is necessary to keep it straight.

In a glide there is considered to be no yawing effect. Although the engine is at idle and the torque effect is less, the airspeed is lower and the effect of the offset fin is also less.

Some manufacturers use the idea of "canting" the engine slightly so that the thrust line of the propeller (or crankshaft) is pointing slightly to the right. The correction for a left-yawing tendency at cruise is taken care of in this way rather than by offsetting the fin. In such installations, however, right rudder is still necessary in the climb and left rudder in a dive under the conditions shown in Figure 2-12.

Figure 2-12. A comparison of forces at various airspeeds (constant rpm).

Another less important contributor to the "torque effect" is the tendency of the airplane to rotate in an opposite direction to that of the propeller (for every action there is an opposite and equal reaction). The manufacturer flies each airplane and "rigs" it, making sure that any such rolling tendency is minimized. They may "wash in" the left wing so that it has a greater angle of incidence (which results in a higher angle of attack for a particular nose attitude) than that of the right wing. This is the usual procedure for fabric-covered airplanes, resulting in more lift and more drag on that side. This may also contribute very slightly to the left yaw effect. In some airplanes, a small metal tab on one or both of the ailerons can be bent to deflect the ailerons as necessary, using the same principle described for the rudder tab (the tab makes the control surface move). The controls and their effects will be discussed in Chapter 8, and you may want to review this section again after reading that chapter. Figure 2-13 shows the ailerons and aileron tab.

Two additional factors that under certain conditions can contribute to the torque effect are gyroscopic precession and what is termed "propeller disk asymmetric loading" or "P factor." Gyro precession acts *during* attitude changes of the plane, such as those that occur in moving the nose up or down or yawing it from side to side. Gyro precession will be discussed in Chapters 3 and 13. Asymmetric loading is a condition usually encountered when the plane is being flown at a constant, positive angle of attack, such as in a climb or the tail-down part of the tailwheel airplane takeoff roll (Chapter 13). The downward-moving blade, which is on the right side of the propeller arc as seen from the cockpit, has a higher angle of attack and higher thrust than the upward-moving blade on the left. This results in a left-turning moment.

Actually the problem is not as simple as it might at first appear. To be completely accurate, a vector system including the propeller angles and rotational velocity and the airplane's forward speed must be drawn to get a picture of the exact angle of attack difference for each blade. In other words, if the plane is flying at an angle of attack of 10°, this *does not* mean that the downward-moving blade has an effective angle of attack 10° greater than normal and that the upward-moving blade has an effective angle 10° less than normal, as might be expected.

From a pilot's standpoint, you are only interested in what must be done to keep the plane straight. *When speaking of "torque," the instructor is including such things as the rotating slipstream, gyroscopic effects, asymmetric disk loading (P factor), and any other power-induced forces or couples that tend to turn the plane to the left.*

Drag

Anytime a body is moved through a fluid (such as air), drag is produced. Drag acts parallel to and in the same direction as the relative wind. The "total" drag of an airplane is composed of two main types of drag, as shown by Figure 2-14.

Parasite drag (Figure 2-15)—the drag composed of (1) "form drag" (the landing gear and radio antennas, the shape of the wings, fuselage, etc.), (2) skin friction, and (3) airflow interference between components (such as would be found at the junction of the wing and fuselage or fuselage and tail). As the word "parasite" implies, this type of drag is of no use to anybody and is about as welcome as any other parasite. However, parasite drag exists and it's the engineer's problem to make it as small as possible. Parasite drag increases as the square of the airspeed increases. Double the airspeed and parasite drag increases *four* times. Triple the airspeed and parasite drag increases *nine* times.

Figure 2-13. Your trainer may have a bendable tab on the aileron(s).

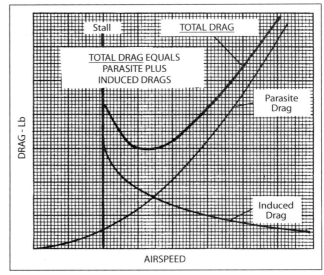

Figure 2-14. The total drag of the airplane is made up of a combination of parasite and induced drag.

Figure 2-15. Parasite drag.

Induced drag—the drag that results from lift being produced. The relative wind is deflected downward by the wing, giving a rearward component to the lift vector called *induced drag* (the lift vector is tilted rearward—*see* Figure 2-16). The air moves over each wing tip toward the low pressure on the top of the wing and vortices are formed that are proportional in strength to the amount of induced drag present. The strength of these vortices (and induced drag) increases radically at higher angles of attack so that the *slower* the airplane flies, the *much greater* the induced drag *and* vortices will be (Figures 2-14, 2-16, and 2-17).

Figure 2-16. Induced drag.

Figure 2-17. Wing tip vortices.

Weight

Gravity is like the common cold, always around and not much that can be done about it. This can be said, however: Gravity always acts "downward" (toward the center of the earth). Lift does not always act opposite to weight, as you will see in Chapter 9.

3

Cockpit — Instruments and Systems

Figure 3-1. The controls, radios, and instruments for a "composite" general aviation trainer. Some trainers have a "glass cockpit," where the flight instruments are combined and shown on a screen. These trainers also have Global Positioning Systems on the right side of the panel. This book is aimed at the basics, however.

Figure 3-1 shows controls and instruments for a "composite" airplane. The seats and control wheels have been "removed" for clarity. Chapter references indicate where more information may be found concerning each item. If there is no reference, the item is covered in this chapter. (Glass cockpits are touched on at the end of this chapter.)

1. *Airspeed indicator* (ASI).
2. *Attitude indicator.*
3. *Altimeter.*
4. *Turn coordinator.*
5. *Heading indicator.*
6. *Vertical speed indicator* (VSI).
7. *Clock.*
8. *Magnetic compass.*
9. *Audio Console.* This contains the transmitter selector (the black knob) that, in this installation, allows you to select the number one transmitter (item 10) or the second transmitter (item 11). You can also choose whether you want to listen to a selected set on the cabin speaker or through the earphones (also noted in item 37). *See* Chapter 21.
10. *NAV/COMM* or *COMM/NAV set,* a combination of communications equipment and VHF omnirange (VOR) receiver and indicator (also called a "one-and-a-half" set). The left side of the equipment, or the "one," is the communications *transceiver* (transmitter/receiver); the right side is a navigation *receiver* (the "half"). *See* Chapter 21.
11. The second *NAV/COMM control* and *VOR indicator.*
12. *Transponder* (Chapter 21).
13. *Automatic direction finder* (ADF) control box and indicator (Chapter 21). It's unlikely that your "primary" trainer has all the aviation electronics (avionics) equipment shown here; it will more likely have a NAV/COMM and possibly an ADF and/or transponder. You'll get familiar with more complex avionics as you progress to higher certificates and ratings.
14. *Tachometer* (indicates engine rpm).
15. *Ammeter.*
16. *Suction gauge,* the instrument that indicates the drop in inches of mercury created by the engine-driven vacuum pump. The vacuum pump provides the suction to operate the gyro horizon, directional gyro, and in some cases, the turn and slip indicator. (In most cases the turn coordinator or turn and slip is electrically driven as a backup.)
17. *Primer* (Chapter 5).
18. *Parking brake.*
19. *Rheostat* to control the brightness of the instrument panel and radio dial lights (Chapter 26).
20. *Engine instrument cluster,* which may include fuel quantity, fuel pressure, oil pressure, and oil temperature gauges. High-wing trainers that depend on gravity for fuel feeding do not have a fuel pressure gauge. Low-wing airplanes have an engine-driven fuel pump (something like that in your car) and must have an electrically driven pump as a standby, so a fuel pressure gauge is required (Chapters 5 and 7).
21. *Carburetor heat* (Chapter 4).
22. *Throttle* (Chapters 2, 5, and 7).
23. *Mixture control* (Chapter 5).
24. *Electric flap control.* You move the handle down to the indentations (notches) to preselect, for instance, 10-degree, 20-degree, or 30-degree of flap deflection (Chapter 13).
25. *Cabin heat control* (Chapter 4).
26. *Cabin air control.* A combination of cabin air and cabin heat may be used to control the temperature and flow rate in the cabin.
27. *Map compartment* (used to hold most everything except maps).
28. *Master switch,* which, as will be discussed later in this chapter, is a "split" switch to control both the alternator and the battery.
29. *Electrically driven fuel pump* (low-wing airplanes) mentioned in item 20. This is turned ON as an aid in starting (for some airplanes) and as a safety standby for takeoff and landings if the engine-driven fuel pump should fail (Chapter 7).
30. *Ignition switch.* The airplane has left (L) and right (R) magnetos to furnish ignition. The airplane is flown with the key in the BOTH position, using both magnetos. To start the airplane, the key is turned past the BOTH position to the spring-loaded START. After starting, the key is released and moves back to BOTH (Chapter 4).
31. *Electrical switches.* These will be for navigation (position) lights, wing tip strobes, and a red rotating beacon on the top of the fin. There will also be a taxi and landing light switch for most airplanes.
32. *Circuit breaker panel* for the items that depend on the electrical system, such as radios and lights. These circuit breakers (fuses are used for various items in some airplanes) are designed to stop any overloading of circuits and are "safety cutoffs" to prevent fire or damage to the system.
33. *Aircraft papers.* The Airworthiness Certificate must be *displayed* (*see* end of chapter).
34. *Toe brake* (left) (Chapter 6).
35. *Rudder pedal* (Chapters 6 and 8).
36. *Elevator* or *stabilator trim wheel and indicator.*
37. *Microphone.* For receiving, the speaker (usually located on the cabin ceiling) is often used; however,

your trainer may have earphones. Many planes have both a speaker and earphones, and the pilot selects whichever method of receiving is preferred. *See* the right side of item 9.

38. *Fuel selector valve.* This example airplane has a tank in each wing and is selected to use fuel from the left wing tank. The OFF selection is very seldom used, but the selector valve should *always* be checked before starting to make sure the fuel selector is on an operating (and the fullest) tank (Chapter 23).

39. *Manual flap control.* The flap handle is operated in "notches," giving various preset flap settings. The button on the end of the handle is used to unlock the control from a previous setting. Your trainer will probably have one of the two types (items 24 and 39) shown here, but not both. Or your trainer may not have flaps (Chapter 13).

Required Instruments

Altimeter

The altimeter is an aneroid barometer with the face calibrated in feet instead of inches of mercury. As the altitude increases, the pressure decreases at the rate of about 1 inch of mercury for each 1,000 feet of altitude gain. The altimeter contains a sealed flexible diaphragm, correct only at sea level standard pressure (29.92 inches of mercury) and sea level standard temperature (59°F or 15°C). Indicating hands are connected to the diaphragm and geared so that a small change in the diaphragm results in the proper altitude indications. The altimeter has three hands. The longest indicates hundreds of feet and the medium-sized hand, thousands of feet. Another pointer indicates tens of thousands of feet, but it is doubtful if you will have a chance to use this one for a while.

A small window at the side of the face allows the altimeter to be set to the latest barometric pressure as corrected to sea level. As you know, the atmospheric pressure is continually changing and the altimeter, being a barometer, is affected by this.

Barometric Scale

Setting Knob

Altimeter set at field elevation of 720 feet

Figure 3-2. Altimeter setting.

Suppose that while you're flying, the pressure drops at the airport (maybe a low-pressure area is moving in). After you land, the altimeter will still be "in the air" because of the lower pressure. The instrument only measures the pressure and has no idea where the ground is unless you correct for pressure changes. The altimeter is usually set at field elevation so that a standard may be set among all planes. In other words, pilots fly their altitude with respect to sea level. The elevations of the airports around the country vary, and if the altimeters were set at zero for each field there would be no altitude standardization at all. The altitude you read when the altimeter has been set to the present corrected station barometric pressure is called "mean sea level" (MSL) or indicated altitude. Remember that this does not tell you how high you are above the terrain at a particular time. As an example, assume your field elevation is 720 feet. Set the altimeter at 720 feet with the setting knob, as shown in Figure 3-2.

If you want to fly at 2,000 feet above the local terrain, your indicated altitude will be 2,720, or 2,720 feet above sea level (Figure 3-3). If you were asked your altitude by a ground station (or another plane) you'd answer, "2,720 feet MSL."

With the altimeter set to sea level you can call FAA Flight Service Stations or towers in the vicinity of the destination airport and get the altimeter setting. They'll give their barometric pressure in inches of mercury,

Altimeter reads 2,720 ft.

1,400 ft.   2,200 ft.

2,720 ft.

Sea level

Figure 3-3. *Absolute altitude* is the height above the surface. *True altitude* is the height above mean sea level. *True altitude* is a constant 2,720 feet here.

corrected to sea level. You'll set this in the small barometric scale on the altimeter and this will correct for any pressure difference between your home field and the destination. The altimeter should read the destination field's elevation after you land. If not, there's an altimeter error.

Airplanes used for instrument flying must have had their altimeter(s) and static pressure system (*see* Figure 3-5) tested and inspected to meet certain minimums, within the past 24 calendar months by the manufacturer or a certificated repair facility.

Figure 3-4. Finding the density-altitude when altimeter setting and temperature are known. Another example:

Assume an altimeter setting of 29.80 and an outside air temperature of 21°C at an indicated altitude of 4,000 feet. What is the density-altitude as found by this chart?

First, correct the indicated altitude to the pressure altitude by *adding* 112 feet (*see* the conversion factor above for 29.80). The pressure-altitude is 4,112 feet (it's higher than indicated altitude because the pressure is *lower* than the standard of 29.92 inches of mercury).

You move up and to the right on the pressure altitude at 4,112 feet (A) until intersecting the 21°C outside air temperature (B) to get a density-altitude of approximately 5,800 feet — sure, it's hard to read that closely on the graph; a calculator gave an answer of (C) 5,734 feet. Try reading *that* on the graph! (FAA-CT-8080-2E)

When you fly from a high- to a low-pressure area, the altimeter reads too high: H to L = H. When you fly from a low- to a high-pressure area, the altimeter reads too low: L to H = L. In other words, when you fly from a high-pressure region into one of lower pressure, the altimeter "thinks" the plane has climbed and registers accordingly, when actually your altitude above sea level may not have changed at all. Since you will be flying in reference to the altimeter, this means that you will fly the plane down to what appears to be the correct altitude and will be low. If the outside temperature at a particular altitude is lower than standard, the altimeter will read higher than the airplane's actual altitude if not corrected. HALT (**H**igh **A**ltimeter because of **L**ow **T**emperature). Higher than standard temperature means an altimeter that reads low. Figure 19-12 shows how to correct for a nonstandard temperature.

As an example of flying from a high- to a low-pressure area, suppose you take off from an airport where the altimeter setting is 30.10 inches (corrected to sea level) and fly to one with an actual altimeter setting of 29.85 (corrected to sea level). If you forget to reset the altimeter before you land, the altimeter would read approximately 250 feet higher than the actual field elevation. In other words, sitting parked at the new airport's field elevation of 1,000 feet, the altimeter would read 1,250 feet, and "thinks" you're still 250 feet above the airport.

At lower altitudes, for approximately each 1.0 inch of mercury change, the altimeter (if not reset for the new pressure) would be 1,000 feet in error. The actual atmospheric pressure change was from 30.10 down to 29.85, a value of 0.25 inches, or the altimeter "climbed" 250 feet during your flight. The barometric scale in the setting window follows the needle movement as you use the setting knob, and vice versa. If you use the knob to *decrease* the 1,250-foot reading to the field elevation of 1,000 feet, the window will indicate 29.85. Or, if when approaching the airport, you were given the correct altimeter setting by radio, you would *decrease* the window setting to 29.85 and thereby *decrease* the altimeter indication by 250 feet and be right on the field elevation when you land.

Pressure-altitude is shown on the altimeter when the pressure in the setting window is set at 29.92, meaning that this is your altitude as far as a standard-pressure day is concerned. Unless the altimeter setting on the ground is exactly 29.92 and the pressure drop per thousand feet is standard, the pressure altitude and indicated altitude will be different. Pressure altitude computed with temperature gives the density-altitude, or the standard altitude where the density of the air at your altitude is normally found.

Density-altitude is used for computing aircraft performance. In your flying, you will use indicated altitude or the altitude as given by the actual barometric pressure corrected to sea level. Figure 3-4 is a chart for computing density-altitude if pressure altitude and temperature are known.

As an example, the altimeter setting is 29.92, (which is the standard), the pressure altitude is 2,000 feet, and the outside air temperature is 70°F (21°C). From the temperature, move up until the 2,000-foot pressure altitude line is intersected. Running horizontally from that point, a density-altitude of about 3,200 feet is found. In other words, the warmer than standard temperature has lowered the air density so that the airplane would operate as if it was at 3,200 feet, when it's actually 2,000 feet above sea level.

Note that there is a pressure altitude conversion factor in Figure 3-4 to be used if the altimeter setting is not the standard 29.92. You would calculate the density-altitude by correcting the pressure altitude with the conversion factor and then finding the density-altitude as before.

For instance, the altimeter setting is 29.5 (29.50), the field elevation is 2,900 feet, and the outside temperature is 80°F (27°C). First, you'd correct the pressure altitude by adding 392 feet (the altitude correction at 29.5 inches of mercury) to get 3,292 feet of pressure altitude (call it 3,300). Draw a line up the vertical line from 80°F to intersect this pressure altitude value and then move horizontally from this point to read a density-altitude of about *5,300 feet*. Although the airplane is sitting at an airport at 2,900 feet above sea level, because of the lower atmospheric pressure and higher temperature (making the air "thin") it will only perform as if it's at 5,300 feet above sea level. *The runway might not be long enough for a safe takeoff under these conditions.* The computations seem to be a little complicated right now, but come back and look at Figure 3-4 again after you've read Chapter 17.

Airspeed Indicator

The airspeed system is composed of the pitot and static tubes and the airspeed indicator instrument (Figure 3-5). The pitot-static system measures the dynamic pressure of the air. As the airplane moves through the air, the relative wind exerts a "ram" pressure in the pitot tube. This pressure expands a diaphragm that is geared to an indicating hand. This pressure is read as airspeed (in miles per hour, or knots) rather than pressure. In short, the pitot-static system measures the pressure of the relative wind approaching the wings (and the entire plane, for that matter). A pitot tube alone would not tell the pilot how much of this pressure was the

Figure 3-5. Typical general aviation trainer airspeed indicator and pitot-static system. The airspeed, altimeter, and vertical speed indicators rely on the static tube for the ambient static pressure. In addition, the airspeed needs the pitot tube for the entrance of dynamic pressure into the diaphragm. As shown, the pitot tube also contains static pressure, which is "cancelled" by the static pressure in the static tube and inside the case.

dynamic pressure giving the wings their lift. The static tube equalizes the static pressure within and without the system, leaving only the dynamic pressure or airspeed being measured. You will check the pitot tube and static vent openings during the preflight inspection, as will be covered in Chapter 4.

Let's discuss *airspeed* and *groundspeed* while we're on the subject. Once a plane is airborne, it is a part of the air. The airplane moves through the air, but the air itself may move over the ground. The plane's performance is not affected by the fact that the entire mass is moving. It is only affected by its relative motion to the mass.

At a certain power setting for a certain attitude, a plane will move through the air at a certain rate, this rate being measured by the airspeed indicator. Figure 3-6 shows the idea, using "true" airspeed or its real speed in relation to the air moving past the airplane.

Groundspeed is like walking on an escalator. If you're walking against the escalator at its exact speed, you make no progress. By walking with the escalator,

Figure 3-6. The airplane's true airspeed is 100 mph; its groundspeeds are 80 and 120 mph, as shown.

your speed is *added* to its speed. Chapter 10 goes into more detail on this.

Lightplane airspeed indicators are calibrated for standard sea level operation (59°F and 29.92 inches of mercury). As you go to higher altitudes, the air will be less dense and therefore there will be less drag. The plane will move faster, but because of the lesser density, airspeed will register less than your actual speed. This error can be corrected roughly by the rule of thumb: "Add 2 percent per thousand feet." This means that if your "calibrated" airspeed is 100 mph at 5,000 feet, your "true" airspeed is 5 × 2 = an additional 10 percent = (.10)(100) = 10 mph + 100 mph = 110 mph. This works generally up to about 10,000 feet, but for closer tolerances and altitudes above this, a computer should be used.

The computer takes into consideration any deviation of temperature and pressure from the "normal lapse rate." *The standard temperature at sea level is 59°F (15°C). The normal lapse rate, or temperature drop, is 3½°F (2°C) per thousand feet.* The "2 percent per thousand feet" rule of thumb uses this fact and does not take into consideration any change from the normal lapse rate or from standard conditions.

The calibrated airspeed mentioned above is the corrected indicated airspeed, so in order to find the true airspeed the following steps would apply:

1. *Indicated airspeed (IAS) + Instrument and position error = calibrated airspeed (CAS).*
2. *Calibrated airspeed plus pressure altitude and temperature correction (2 percent per thousand feet, or use a computer) gives the true airspeed (TAS).* (Most lightplanes have IAS correction information, but for others, assume IAS to equal CAS.)

Looking back at the lift equation in Chapter 2 you'll see in it the expression $(\rho \div 2) \times V^2$. This is the dynamic pressure that contributes to the wing's lift and is measured by the airspeed indicator, as discussed earlier. For instance, at an indicated 100 mph the dynamic pressure is about 25.5 psf. Your airspeed indicator is made so that when dynamic pressure of that value enters the pitot tube, the hand will point to 100 mph. At sea level air density, your motion relative to the air will actually be 100 mph when the airspeed indicates this amount (assuming that the instrument is completely accurate).

As you know, the air density decreases with altitude. When you are at 5,000 feet and are indicating 100 mph (25.5 psf), the airspeed indicator doesn't reason that the plane is actually moving faster in relation to the air and making up for the lower density in the dynamic pressure equation. All the indicator knows is that 100 mph worth of dynamic pressure is being routed into it

and leaves it up to you to find the "true" airspeed, or the plane's actual speed in relation to the air mass at the higher altitude.

If your plane indicates 50 mph at the stall at sea level, it will indicate 50 mph at the stall at 5,000 or 10,000 feet (assuming the same airplane weight and angle of bank; in Chapter 9 you'll see why such a condition is made). This is because a certain minimum dynamic pressure is required to support the airplane, and for your plane it happens to be an indicated 50 mph (or about 6.4 psf).

Another airspeed you may hear about is equivalent airspeed (EAS). At higher airspeeds and altitudes, compressibility errors are induced into the system. Looking back at Figure 3-5, you see that there is static pressure in the *instrument case*, which (theoretically, anyway) cancels out the static pressure in the *diaphragm* (let in through the pitot tube). At high speeds where compressibility is a factor, the effect is that of "packing" and raising the pressure of the *static* air in the pitot tube and diaphragm. The static air in the *case* doesn't get this effect, so that indicated (and calibrated) airspeeds are shown as *higher* than the actual value. A correction is made to obtain the "correct" CAS; this is called the *equivalent* airspeed. EAS would then be used to find the TAS. For high-speed airplanes the correction would be:

1. IAS plus (or minus) instrument and position error = CAS.
2. CAS minus compressibility error = EAS.
3. EAS corrected for pressure altitude and temperature = TAS.

You won't have to cope with compressibility errors for the airplane you are training in, but you should be aware that such factors do exist.

The calibrated airspeed is the "real" airspeed affecting the flying of the airplane and is the dynamic pressure $[(\rho/2)V^2]$ in pounds per square foot (psf). If you want to find the dynamic pressure working on the airplane at, say, 100 knots (more about knots shortly), you use the equation V^2 knots/295. At 100 knots, the result is 33.9 psf (call it 34 psf).

You'll note that examples of true airspeed in this section used statute miles per hour. While flying, you'll use the nautical mile (6,080 feet) and knots (1 knot equals 1 nautical mile per hour). Also, 1 nautical mile equals 1.152 statute miles. This book will follow the data as produced in the *Pilot's Operating Handbooks* and use knots (K) for speed and nautical miles (NM) for distance, with a few exceptions to be noted in later chapters. While this will seem strange at first, you'll soon get accustomed to thinking in these terms in flying.

Tachometer

The lightplane tachometer is similar in many ways to a car speedometer. One end of a flexible cable is attached to the engine and the other is connected to the instrument. The rate of turning of the cable, through mechanical or magnetic means, is transmitted as revolutions per minute (rpm) on the instrument face. The average lightplane propeller is connected directly to the engine crankshaft so that the tachometer registers both the engine and propeller rpm. The propeller is usually geared down in larger planes, and in that case the ratio of engine speed to propeller speed can be found in the *Airplane Flight Manual*. At any rate, you always use the engine rpm for setting power because this is what is indicated on the tachometer in the direct drive or geared engine.

Most tachometers have a method of recording flight hours, based on a particular rpm setting (say, 2,300 rpm). This means that the engine is not "building up time" as fast when it's at idle or at lower power settings. The time indicated on the recording tachometer is used as a basis for required inspections and overhauls, and the reading is noted in the logbooks whenever such work is done on the airplane and/or engine.

Oil Pressure Gauge

Every airplane is equipped with an oil pressure gauge (Figure 3-7), and to the majority of pilots it is the most important engine instrument (the fuel gauge runs a close second). Some oil pressure gauges have a curved Bourdon tube in the instrument. Oil pressure tends to straighten the tube, and through mechanical linkage a hand registers the pressure in pounds per square inch. The move now is toward using electrical transmitters and indicators, particularly for more complex engine installations.

Oil pressure should reach the normal operating value within 30 seconds after the engine starts in temperate conditions. The instrument should be checked about every 5 minutes in flight, since it is one of the first indicators of oil starvation, which means engine failure and a forced landing. If the oil pressure starts dropping, land at an airport as soon as safely possible.

There have been many cases of the instrument itself giving bum information. After you notice the falling (or low) oil pressure, keep an eye on the oil temperature gauge for a rising temperature as you turn toward an airport or good landing area. Pilots have depended solely on the oil pressure gauge and landed in bad places when the engine was getting plenty of oil (and the oil temperature stayed normal).

Figure 3-7. Oil pressure gauge.

Oil Temperature Gauge

The vapor-type temperature gauge is used for older lightplanes. The indicating head or instrument contains a Bourdon tube and is connected by a fine tube to a bulb that contains a volatile liquid. Vapor expansion exerts pressure, which is read as temperature on the instrument. Most trainers do not have a cylinder head temperature gauge, so the oil temperature gauge is the only means of telling if the engine is running hot. Most airplanes now use the principle of electrical resistance change for measuring oil temperature. Figure 3-8 shows general aviation oil temperature gauges.

Section 2 of the *Pilot's Operating Handbook* for your airplane will contain the limits of operation and markings for the engine instruments (*see* Figure 3-30).

Compass

The airplane compass is a magnet with an attached face or "card" that enables you to read directions from 0° to 360°.

The magnet aligns itself with the Magnetic North Pole, and the plane turns around it.

Every 30°, the compass has the number of that heading minus the 0. For instance, 60° is 6 and 240° is 24 on the compass card. It's broken down further into 10° and 5° increments. The compass card appears to be backward in the diagram, but as the plane actually turns around the compass, the correct reading will be given.

In a shallow turn, the compass is reasonably accurate on headings of East and West but leads ahead of the turn as the plane's heading approaches South and lags behind as it approaches North. If you are on a heading of *North* and make a turn in either direction, the compass will initially roll to a heading *opposite* to the bank. On a heading of *South* when the turn is started, the compass will initially roll to a heading indication *exceeding* that actually turned (**N**orth–**O**pposite, **S**outh–**E**xceeds, or NOSE). The amount of lead or lag depends on the amount of bank and the latitude at which you are flying. Knowing the amount of lead or lag in the compass you are using will be helpful in rolling out on a heading.

Figure 3-8. (A) Engine instrument cluster with cylinder head and oil pressure and temperature gauges. (B) Another engine instrument cluster arrangement. (Courtesy of Castleberry Instruments and Avionics, Inc.)

Figure 3-9 is a simplified drawing of the magnetic compass. The magnets tend to point parallel to the earth's lines of magnetic force. As the compass is brought nearer to the Magnetic North Pole, the magnets will have a tendency to point toward the earth's surface.

If directly over the Magnetic North Pole, the compass would theoretically point straight down, causing a great deal of confusion to all concerned. The magnetic compass is of little use close to the pole, so other methods of navigation are used in this area.

The suspension of the compass card causes certain problems. For instance, if you are flying on a generally easterly heading and accelerate, the compass will turn toward a northerly heading even though the plane has not turned. This occurs on a westerly heading as well.

If on these headings the plane decelerates, a southerly indication is given under these conditions, as can be seen by referring to Figure 3-9. The following can be noted:

Acceleration—The compass indicates a more northerly heading.

Deceleration—The compass indicates a more southerly heading.

One way of remembering what happens is ANDS (**A**cceleration–**N**orth, **D**eceleration–**S**outh).

Acceleration/deceleration errors are not considered a factor in North and South headings.

When the plane is climbed, dived, or banked (particularly a bank of more than 15°–20°), inaccuracies result. Notice in a climb or glide (on an east or west heading) that the compass inches off its original indication because of the airplane's attitude (assuming that you have kept the nose from wandering). The compass card and magnets have a one-point suspension so that the assembly acts as a pendulum and also will tilt in reaction to various forces and attitudes of flight (acceleration, banks, nose attitudes, etc.). This tilting action is also a major contributing factor to the reactions of the compass. The "floating" compass as described here is used for reference rather than precision flying (Figure 3-10). In turbulence the compass swings so badly that it's very hard to fly a course by it. It's a good instrument for getting on course or keeping a general heading between checkpoints on cross-country, but never blindly rely on it. There will be more about this instrument in later chapters.

Figure 3-11 is a newer type of magnetic compass with a vertical card. The small airplane is fixed; the card turns in a more easily readable way and is like the new faces on the heading indicator in Figure 3-22. Chapter 15 goes into more detail on use of the magnetic compass.

Figure 3-9. Magnetic compass.

Figure 3-10. The lubber line and instrument case are fastened to the aircraft, which turns around the free-floating compass card and magnets.

Figure 3-11. Vertical card magnetic compass. (Courtesy of Hamilton Instruments, Inc.)

Additional Instruments

The instruments discussed in the earlier part of this chapter are all that are required for daytime VFR flight, but the instruments discussed below will also be used in your training. Federal Aviation Regulations require that emergency recovery from a loss of visual references (such as accidentally flying into clouds or fog) be demonstrated on the private flight test. There have been a large number of fatal accidents caused by pilots overestimating their abilities and flying into marginal weather. It can be easily demonstrated that flying by the seat of your pants when you have lost visual references is a one-way proposition—*down.*

The instruments discussed earlier are used for your day-to-day flying under the VFR (visual) type of flying; for instrument flying (and your instruction in emergency flying using the instruments) more equipment is needed. The FAA requires that on the practical (flight) test the airplane be equipped with "appropriate flight instruments" for checking the pilot's ability to control the airplane by use of the instruments. It's very likely that your trainer will be equipped with all of the instruments covered in this chapter, but techniques are given in Chapter 15 for using only the turn coordinator or turn and slip (plus airspeed and altimeter) to maintain control of the airplane under simulated or actual instrument conditions.

Gyro Instruments in General

Gyro instruments work because of the gyroscopic properties of "rigidity in space" and "precession."

If you owned a toy gyroscope or top in your younger days, the property of "rigidity in space" is well known to you. While the top was spinning, it could not be pushed over but would move parallel to its plane of rotation (on the floor) in answer to such a nudge. The gyroscope resists any effort to tilt its axis (or its plane of rotation) (Figure 3-12). This property is used in the attitude indicator and heading indicator.

The property of "precession" is used in the turn and slip indicator. If a force is exerted against the side of a rotating gyro, the gyro reacts as if the force was exerted at a point 90° around the wheel (in the direction of rotation) from the actual place of application (Figure 3-13).

Figure 3-12. The gyro maintains rigidity in space.

Figure 3-13. Precession

Turn and Slip Indicator (Needle and Ball)

The turn and slip indicator is actually two instruments. The slip indicator is merely a liquid-filled, curved glass tube containing an agate or steel ball. The liquid acts as a shock dampener. In a balanced turn the ball will remain in the center, since centrifugal force offsets the pull of gravity (Figure 3-14).

In a slip there is not enough rate of turn for the amount of bank. The centrifugal force will be weak, and this imbalance will be shown by the ball's falling down toward the inside of the turn (Figure 3-15). (You experience centrifugal force any time you turn a car—particularly in an abrupt turn at high speed as you tend to move to the outside of the turn.)

The skid is a condition in which there is too high a rate of turn for the amount of bank. The centrifugal force is too strong, and this is indicated by the ball's sliding toward the outside of the turn (Figure 3-16).

The slip and skid will be discussed further in "The Turn," in Chapter 9.

The turn part of the turn and slip indicator, or "needle" as it is sometimes called, uses precession to indicate the direction and approximate rate of turn of the airplane.

Figure 3-17 shows the reaction of the turn and slip indicator to a right turn. Naturally, the case is rigidly attached to the instrument panel and turns as the airplane turns (1). The gyro wheel (2) reacts by trying to rotate in the direction shown by (3), moving the needle in proportion to the rate of turn (which controls the amount of precession). As soon as the turn stops, the precession is no longer in effect and the spring (4) returns the needle to the center. The spring resists the precession and acts as a dampener, so the nose must actually be moving for the needle to move. The ball may be off to one side even though the needle is centered.

For instance, in a side or forward slip (to be covered later) the airplane may be in a bank with the pilot holding opposite rudder. The ball will be in a more extreme position than that shown in Figure 3-15.

Some turn and slip indicators are calibrated so that a "standard-rate turn" of 3° per second will be indicated by the needle's being off center by one needle width (Figure 3-17). This means that, by setting up a standard-rate turn, it is possible to roll out on a predetermined heading by the use of a watch or clock. It requires 120 seconds (2 minutes) to complete a 360° turn. There are types of turn and slip indicators calibrated so that a double-needle-width indication indicates a standard-rate turn. These have a "doghouse" to

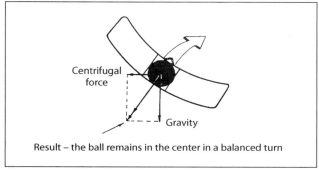

Figure 3-14. A balanced right turn.

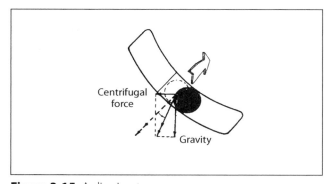

Figure 3-15. A slipping turn.

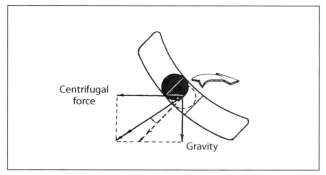

Figure 3-16. A skidding right turn.

Figure 3-17. (A) Turn and slip indicator (vacuum-driven). Newer instruments are electrically driven. (B) The gyro wheel in the turn and slip is attached in the instrument so that when it reacts to yaw, it can only tilt around the long axis of the instrument (X-X). It is limited in its tilt action by stops. The gyro wheel in the turn coordinator moves (in reaction to precession) around an axis 30° from the long axis of the instrument and so reacts to both roll and yaw inputs. Since precession acts while a force is being *applied*, the turn coordinator only reacts to yaw (rate of turn) once the bank is established.

indicate a standard-rate turn (Figure 3-18 left). If your heading is 070° and you want to roll out on a heading of 240°, first decide which way you should turn (to the right in this case). The amount to be turned is 240 − 70 = 170°. The number of seconds required at standard rate is 170 ÷ 3 = 57. If you set up a standard-rate turn, hold it for 57 seconds, and roll out until the needle and ball are centered, the heading should be very close to 240°. You will have a chance to practice these timed turns "under the hood" (by instruments alone) during your training.

One of the most valuable maneuvers in coping with bad weather is the 180° turn, or "getting the hell out of there." It is always best to do the turn *before* you lose visual contact, but if visual references are lost inadvertently, the 180° turn may be done by reference to the instruments.

The advantage of the turn and slip over other gyro instruments is that the gyro does not "tumble" or become erratic as certain bank or pitch limits are exceeded (*see* "Attitude Indicator").

A disadvantage of the turn and slip is that it is a rate instrument, and a certain amount of training is required before the student is able to quickly transfer the indications of the instrument into a visual picture of the airplane's attitudes and actions.

The gyro of the turn and slip and other gyro instruments may be driven electrically or by air, using an engine-driven vacuum pump or an outside-mounted venturi. (Some airplanes use an engine-driven *pressure* pump.) The venturi is generally used on older light-planes because of its simplicity; it is nothing more than a venturi tube causing a drop in pressure and drawing air through the instrument past the vanes on the gyro wheel as the plane moves through the air (Figure 3-17).

Turn Coordinator

The turn coordinator also uses precession and is similar to the turn and slip in that a standard rate may be set up but, unlike that instrument, it is designed to respond to roll as well.

Note that the gyro wheel in the turn and slip (Figure 3-17) is vertical and lined up with the axis of the instrument case when yaw forces aren't acting on it. In the turn coordinator the gyro wheel is set at approximately 30° from the instrument's long axis, allowing it to precess in response to both yaw and roll forces (Figure 3-17). After the roll-in (or roll-out) is complete, the instrument indicates the rate of turn. Figure 3-18 compares the indications of the two instruments in a balanced standard-rate turn (3 per second) to the left. Note that the turn coordinator also makes use of a slip indicator (ball).

Figure 3-18. A comparison of a standard-rate turn as indicated by the turn and slip and the turn coordinator. The "2 MIN" indicates that if the wing of the miniature airplane is placed on the reference mark, it will take 2 minutes to complete a 360° turn (3° per second).

Attitude Indicator

The attitude indicator (Figure 3-19) or gyro horizon (older name — artificial horizon) depends on the "rigidity in space" idea and is a true attitude instrument. The gyro plane of rotation is horizontal and remains in this position, with the aircraft (and instrument case) being moved about it. Attached to the gyro is a face with a white horizon line and other reference lines on it. When the instrument is operating correctly, this line will always represent the actual horizon. A miniature airplane, attached to the case, moves with respect to this artificial horizon precisely as the real airplane moves with respect to the real horizon. This instrument is particularly easy for students to use because they are able to "fly" the small airplane as they would the large airplane itself.

There are limits of operation on the less expensive attitude indicators and these are, in most cases, 70° of pitch (nose up or down) and 100° of bank. The gyro will "tumble" above these limit stops and will give false information as the gyro is forced from its rotational plane. The instrument will also give false information during the several minutes required for it to return to the normal position after resuming straight and level flight.

"Caging" is done by a knob located on the instrument front and is useful in locking the instrument before doing aerobatics, which include the spin demonstration discussed later. Because it is possible to damage the instrument through repeated tumbling, this caging is a must before you do deliberate aerobatics. Most of the later attitude indicators do not have a caging knob. Figure 3-20 compares two types of attitude indicators (older type is on the left).

The more expensive attitude indicators have no limits of pitch or bank, and aerobatics such as rolls or loops can be done by reference to the instrument. These are used in jet fighters and are generally electrically driven rather than air driven, as in the case of the older type gyros, because of the loss of efficiency of the air-driven type at high altitudes. Attitude indicators have a knob that allows you to move the miniature airplane up or down to compensate for small deviations in the horizontal-line position.

The attitude indicator is more expensive than the turn and slip but allows the pilot to get an immediate picture of the plane's attitude. It can be used to establish a standard-rate turn, if necessary, without reference to the turn coordinator or turn and slip indicator, as will be shown.

An airplane's rate of turn depends on its velocity and amount of bank. For any airplane, the slower the

Figure 3-19. Attitude indicator. Shown is a nose-up, left-wing down (5° bank) attitude. Although it appears to indicate a shallow climbing turn to the left, a check with other instruments is needed to confirm this.

Figure 3-20. Attitude indicators (caging and noncaging types).

Figure 3-21. The turn and slip, turn coordinator, and attitude indicator indications in a standard-rate turn at 100K. Setting up the thumb rule for the bank angle only works for the balanced turn (no slip or skid).

velocity and the greater the angle of bank, the greater the rate of turn. This will be evident as soon as you begin flying and is probably so even now.

A good rule of thumb to find the amount of bank needed for a standard-rate turn at various airspeeds (mph) is to divide your airspeed by 10 and add 5 to the answer. For instance, airspeed = 150 ÷ 10 = 15; 15 + 5 = 20° bank required. This thumb rule is particularly accurate in the 100–200 mph range.

Figure 3-21 compares the indications of the turn and slip, turn coordinator, and attitude indicator in a standard-rate turn to the right at 100 K *true airspeed*. (True airspeed would be the proper one to use in the rule of thumb, but indicated or calibrated airspeed is okay for a quick result.)

A rule of thumb for finding the required bank for a standard-rate turn when you are working with knots is to divide the airspeed by 10 and multiply the result by 1½. As an example, at an airspeed of 156 K you'd get 15.6° (call it 16°). One and one-half times 16 is 24° required.

Heading Indicator

The heading indicator functions because of the gyro principle of "rigidity in space" as did the attitude indicator. In this case, however, the plane of rotation is vertical. The older heading indicator has a compass card or azimuth scale that is attached to the gyro gimbal and wheel. The wheel and card are fixed and, as in the case of the magnetic compass, the plane turns about them.

The heading indicator has no "brain" (magnet) that causes it to point to the Magnetic North Pole; it must be set to the heading indicated by the magnetic compass. The instrument should be set when the magnetic compass is reading correctly, and this is done in straight and level flight when the magnetic compass has "settled down."

You should check the heading indicator against the compass about every 15 minutes in flight. More about this in Chapter 25.

The advantage of the heading indicator is that it does not oscillate in rough weather and it gives a true reading during turns when the magnetic compass is erratic.

Figure 3-22. Three types of heading indicator presentations.

A caging/setting knob is used to cage the instrument for aerobatics or to set the proper heading.

A disadvantage of the older types of heading indicators is that they tumble when the limits of 55° nose up or down or 55° bank are reached. Newer heading indicators have higher limits of pitch and bank and have a resetting knob rather than a caging knob. Figure 3-22 compares the faces of the old and new types.

More expensive gyros, such as are used by the military and airlines, are connected with a magnetic compass in such a way that this creep is automatically compensated for.

The greatest advantage of the heading indicator is that it allows you to turn directly to a heading without the allowance for lead or lag that is necessary with a magnetic compass.

Figure 3-23 shows the schematic of the engine-driven vacuum system of a popular trainer. The air filter is on the firewall under the instrument panel.

Figure 3-23. Engine-driven vacuum pump system.

Vertical Speed Indicator

This is an instrument that is useful in maintaining a constant rate of climb or glide.

It is a rate instrument and depends on a diaphragm for its operation, as does the altimeter. In the rate of climb indicator the diaphragm measures the change of pressure rather than the pressure itself, as the diaphragm in the altimeter does.

The diaphragm has a tube connecting it to the static port (*see* Figure 3-5), or the tube may just have access to the outside air pressure in the case of cheaper or lighter installations. This means that the inside of the diaphragm has the same pressure as the air surrounding the plane. Opening into the otherwise sealed instrument case is a capillary, or very small tube. This difference in the diaphragm and capillary tube sizes means a lag in the equalization of pressure in the air within the instrument case as the altitude (outside pressure) changes.

Figure 3-24 is a schematic diagram of a vertical speed indicator. As an example, suppose the plane is flying at a constant altitude. The pressure within the diaphragm is the same as that of the air surrounding it in the instrument case. The rate of climb is indicated as zero.

The plane is put into a glide or dive. Air pressure inside the diaphragm increases at the same rate as that of the surrounding air. However, because of the small size of the capillary tube, the pressure in the instrument case does not change at the same rate. In the case of a glide or dive, the diaphragm would expand—the

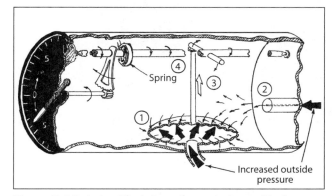

Figure 3-24. A simplified view of a vertical speed indicator. As the plane descends, outside pressure increases. The diaphragm expands immediately (1). Because of the small size of the capillary tube (2), pressure in the case is not increased at the same rate. The link pushes upward (3) rotating the shaft (4), which causes the needle to indicate 400 fpm down as shown. The spring helps return the needle to zero when pressures are equal and also acts as a dampener. The instrument here is shown proportionally longer than the actual rate of climb indicator so that the mechanism may be clearly seen.

amount of expansion depending on the difference of pressures. The diaphragm is mechanically linked to a hand, and the appropriate rate of descent, in hundreds (or thousands) of feet per minute (fpm), is read on the instrument face.

In a climb the pressure in the diaphragm decreases faster than that within the instrument case, and the needle will indicate an appropriate rate of climb. The standard rate of descent in instrument work is 500 fpm (Figure 3-25).

Because in a climb or dive the pressure in the case is always "behind" the diaphragm pressure, a certain amount of lag results. The instrument will still indicate a vertical speed for a short time after the plane is leveled off. For this reason the vertical speed indicator is not used to maintain altitude. On days when the air is bumpy, this lag is particularly noticeable. The vertical speed indicator is used, therefore, either when a constant rate of ascent or descent is needed or as a check of the plane's climb, dive, or glide rate. The more stable altimeter is used to maintain a constant altitude.

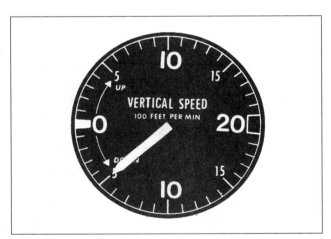

Figure 3-25. Standard rate of descent.

Summary of the Additional Instruments

Gyro instruments and the vertical speed indicator are not covered in detail as would be done in a training manual for an instrument rating. The calibrations and procedures used by instrument pilots are not covered for obvious reasons. For the noninstrument-qualified private pilot or the student, these instruments are to be used in an emergency only as a means of survival. Even the most expensive instruments cannot compensate for lack of preflight planning or poor headwork in flight.

Electrical System

Since most trainers these days have electrical systems for starting and for lights and radios, Figure 3-26 is included to give an idea of a simple system.

The battery stores electrical energy, and the engine-driven alternator (or generator) creates current and replenishes the battery, as necessary, as directed by the voltage regulator or alternator control unit.

The ammeter (item 15, Figure 3-1) indicates the flow of current, in amperes, from the alternator to the battery or from the battery to the electrical system. When the engine is operating and the master switch (item 28, Figure 3-1) is ON, the ammeter indicates the charging rate of the battery. If the alternator isn't working or if the load is too great, the ammeter will show the discharge rate of the battery.

Note in Figure 3-26 that the system has a split master (electrical) switch (upper left-hand corner). The right

Figure 3-26. Electrical system. If you don't have a background in electricity, these diagrams can seem very complicated. Your job as pilot will be to know what system is affected by a loss of electrical power. You'll need to know what components are protected by circuit breakers or fuses and where the breakers (or fuses) are in the cockpit. This diagram shows the electrical items.

half of the switch (BAT) controls all electrical power in the airplane. The left half (ALT) controls the alternator. For normal operations both switches should be ON so that the system (BAT) is working and the alternator is "replenishing" the electricity used by the various components, as is the case for your automobile (except the airplane doesn't depend on the battery/alternator for ignition, but more about this shortly). If the alternator started acting up, you'd turn it off and rely on the battery (for a while, anyway), conserving electricity by turning off all unnecessary electrical equipment. You should not, in this particular system, turn off the battery switch when the alternator is operating.

If the battery is completely dead, hand starting (propping) the airplane (Chapter 5) may get the engine running, but the alternator needs some electrical power to energize it to start charging. It won't be building up the battery, even after the engine is running. An outside source of electricity (with jumper cables, for instance) is necessary for beginning the charging process by the alternator. Let the pros at the airport do it.

Circuit breakers or fuses are installed to protect the electrical circuits (item 32, Figure 3-1). The circuit breakers "pop out" or the fuses burn out when an overload occurs, breaking the connection between the item causing the problem and the alternator-battery system. The circuit breakers may be reset, but a 2-minute cooling period is usually recommended. Most pilots figure that if a breaker pops two times in a row, it's best to leave it out. In the case of a system using fuses, spare fuses are sometimes carried in clips in the map compartment.

The ignition system is shown in Figure 3-26, but it is self-sustaining and independent of the alternator-battery system. An airplane engine does not need an alternator-battery system to operate. In fact, for many years most did not have one; the engine was started by hand. The magnetos are run by the engine and in turn furnish the spark for combustions — a sort of "you rub my back and I'll rub yours" arrangement that works very well. The magnetos will be covered again in following chapters.

Aircraft Documents

Every aircraft must carry three documents at all times in flight: (1) Certificate of Aircraft Registration or ownership, (2) Airworthiness Certificate (this must be displayed), and (3) Airplane Flight Manual or equivalent form containing an equipment list and limitations. Look in your plane and know where these documents are.

Certificate of Aircraft Registration

The Certificate of Aircraft Registration (Figure 3-27) contains the name and address of the owner, the aircraft manufacturer, model, registration number, and manufacturer's serial number. When a plane changes owners, a new registration certificate must be obtained.

Airworthiness Certificate

The Airworthiness Certificate (Figure 3-27) is a document showing that the airplane has met the safety requirements of the Federal Aviation Administration and is "airworthy." It remains in effect as long as the aircraft is maintained in accordance with the Federal Aviation Regulations. This means that required inspections or repairs are done and notice of this is entered in the aircraft and/or engine logbook.

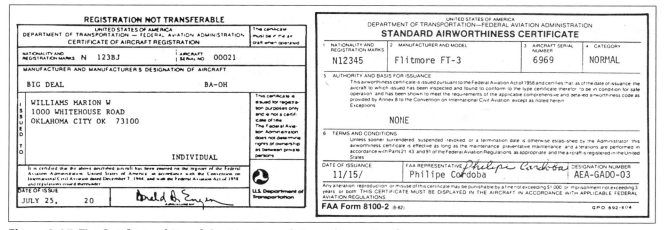

Figure 3-27. The Certificate of Aircraft Registration and Airworthiness Certificate.

Airplane Flight Manual or *Pilot's Operating Handbook*

The *Pilot's Operating Handbooks* (POH) for general aviation airplanes are laid out as follows for standardization purposes:

Section 1: General—This is a general section and contains a three-view of the airplane and descriptive data on engine, propeller, fuel and oil, dimensions, and weights. It contains symbols, abbreviations, and terminology used in airplane performance.

Section 2: Limitations—This section includes airspeed limitations such as shown in Figure 3-28.

The primary airspeed limitations are given in knots and in both indicated and calibrated airspeeds (although some manufacturers furnish mph data as well), and the markings are in knots and indicated airspeeds.

The maneuvering speed, which is the maximum indicated airspeed at which the controls may be abruptly and fully deflected without overstressing the airplane, depends on the stall speed, which decreases as the airplane gets lighter. More about this in Chapter 23. Figure 3-29 shows the airspeeds from Figure 3-28 as they would appear on the airspeed indicator.

Included in this section are power plant limitations—engine rpm limits, maximum and minimum oil pressures, and maximum oil temperature and rpm range to be used (Figure 3-30). Weight and center of gravity limits are included for the particular airplane.

Maneuver and flight load factor limits (also to be discussed in Chapter 23) are listed, and operation limits (day and night, VFR, and IFR) are found here. Fuel limitations (usable and unusable fuel) and minimum fuel grades are covered in this section. An airplane may not be able to use some of the fuel in flight and this is listed as "unusable fuel." For example, one airplane has a total fuel capacity of 24 U.S. gallons with 22 U.S. gallons being available in flight (2 gallons unusable).

Section 3: Emergency procedures—Here are checklists for such things as engine failures at various

AIRSPEED LIMITATIONS

	SPEED	KCAS	KIAS	REMARKS
V_{NE}	Never Exceed Speed	141	141	Do not exceed this speed in any operation.
V_{NO}	Maximum Structural Cruising Speed	104	107	Do not exceed this speed except in smooth air, and then only with caution.
V_A	Maneuvering Speed: 1600 Pounds 1450 Pounds 1300 Pounds	 95 90 85	 97 93 88	Do not make full or abrupt control movements above this speed.
V_{FE}	Maximum Flap Extended Speed	89	85	Do not exceed this speed with flaps down.
	Maximum Window Open Speed	141	141	Do not exceed this speed with windows open.

AIRSPEED INDICATOR MARKINGS

MARKING	KIAS VALUE OR RANGE	SIGNIFICANCE
White Arc	42 - 85	Full Flap Operating Range. Lower limit is maximum weight V_{S_0} in landing configuration. Upper limit is maximum speed permissible with flaps extended.
Green Arc	47 - 107	Normal Operating Range. Lower limit is maximum weight V_S at most forward C.G. with flaps retracted. Upper limit is maximum structural cruising speed.
Yellow Arc	107 - 141	Operations must be conducted with caution and only in smooth air.
Red Line	141	Maximum speed for all operations.

Figure 3-28. Airspeed limitations and airspeed markings as given in a *Pilot's Operating Handbook*. Note the stall speeds (V_{S1} for flaps up, and V_{S0} for landing configuration) are given for maximum certificated weight. Compare the airspeed limitations with the indicator markings here. V_{NO} is the maximum structural cruising speed (or max speed for *Normal Operations*).

Figure 3-29. Important airspeed markings. For most airplanes manufactured before the 1976 models, the values were given in miles per hour and calibrated airspeed; 1976 and later models will have the airspeed markings as indicated airspeed in knots. (1K = 1.152 statute mph—*see* Chapter 19.) Your instructor will give you the word about this for the airplane you are using.

POWER PLANT INSTRUMENT MARKINGS

INSTRUMENT	RED LINE MINIMUM LIMIT	GREEN ARC NORMAL OPERATING	RED LINE MAXIMUM LIMIT
Tachometer	- - -	2000 - 2750 RPM	2750 RPM
Oil Temperature	- - -	100° - 240°F	240°F
Oil Pressure	10 psi	30 - 60 psi	100 psi

Figure 3-30. Power plant limitations.

portions of the flight; forced landings, including ditching; fires during start and in flight; icing; electrical power supply malfunctions; and airspeeds for safe operations.

There are amplified procedures for these "problems" including how to recover from inadvertently flying into instrument conditions and recovering after a vacuum system failure, spin recoveries, rough engine operations, and electrical problems.

Section 4: Normal procedures — This section also covers checklist procedures from preflight through climb, cruise, landing, and securing the airplane. It's followed by amplified procedures of the same material. Recommended speeds for normal operation are summarized, as well as being given as part of the amplified procedures. Environmental systems for the airplane and other normal procedures are also included.

Section 5: Performance — Performance charts (takeoff, cruise, landing) with sample problems are included with range and endurance information, airspeed calibration, and stall speed charts.

Section 6: Weight and balance and equipment list — Airplane weighing procedures are given here, with a loading graph and an equipment list with weights and arms of the various airplane components.

Section 7: Airplane and systems descriptions — The airframe, with its control systems, is described and diagrammed. The landing gear, engine and engine controls, etc., are covered in this section. Also, fuel, brake, electrical, hydraulic, and instrument systems are laid out in detail. Additional systems such as oxygen, anti-icing, ventilation, heating, and avionics are covered here.

Section 8: Airplane handling, service, and maintenance — Here is the information you need for preventive maintenance, ground handling, servicing and cleaning, and care for that particular airplane.

Section 9: Supplements — This is devoted to covering optional systems with descriptions and operating procedures of the electronics, oxygen, and other nonrequired equipment. You should be well familiar with the *Pilot's Operating Handbook* of your airplane.

Logbooks

The Federal Aviation Regulations require that the registered owner or operator keep a separate maintenance record for airframe, engine(s), and propeller(s).

Airplanes must have had an annual inspection within the preceding 12 calendar months to be legal. There are some exceptions for special flight permits or a progressive (continuing) inspection procedure, but the vast majority of airplanes fall under the requirements of an annual inspection. You might check with your instructor about your airplane. The annual inspection must be done, even if the airplane has not been flown during that time.

In addition, if the airplane is operated carrying persons for hire (charter, rental, flight instruction, etc.), it must have had an inspection within the past 100 hours of flying (tachometer time or other approved method of noting the time). The 100-hour limitation may be exceeded by not more than 10 hours if necessary to reach a place at which the inspection can be done. The excess time must be included in the next 100 hours of time in service.

If your airplane has had any major repairs or alterations since its manufacture, a copy or copies of the major repair and alteration form must be aboard the airplane (normally it's attached to the weight and balance information for convenience). This lists the airplane make and model, registration number, manufacturer's serial number, and the owner's name and address; it may also have that particular airplane's latest empty weight, the empty center of gravity location in inches from the datum, and the useful load of the plane. The useful load includes the weight of usable fuel, occupants, and baggage. The maximum weight minus the empty weight equals the useful load. (Use actual passenger weights.) The gas weight is 6 pounds per gallon, and the oil, $7\frac{1}{2}$ pounds per gallon. When you are loading the baggage compartment, do not exceed the placard weight, even if you have plenty of weight left before reaching the maximum for the airplane. You may overstress the compartment as well as adversely affect the position of the center of gravity of the plane. (Chapter 23 covers this subject in more detail.) Any major repairs or additions of equipment such as radios, etc., that would affect the position of the center of gravity are noted on this form.

On the back of the major repair and alteration form is a description of the work accomplished. The person authorized for such work signs the form and gives the date that the repair or alteration was completed.

The 100-hour inspection can be completed and signed by a certificated airframe and power plant mechanic, but the annual inspection must be supervised by an A and P mechanic or facility holding inspection authorization. If you get the 100 hours done by such mechanics or facilities, it can count as an annual inspection. If an annual inspection is done anytime in, say, the month of May (which means that it is good until the end of the following May) and it's necessary to get a 100-hour inspection in August, this 100-hour inspection, if done by the same people who did the annual, can count as a new annual inspection — which means that the next annual is due by the end of the following *August*, not the next May. The inspectors will note the date and recorded tach time (or other flight time), and the type of inspection will be noted in the logbooks.

The logbooks are not required to be in the plane at all times, as are the first three documents discussed, but they must be available to an FAA inspector if requested. This means that if you're operating away from the plane's normal base, it would be wise to take the logbooks with you.

Radio Equipment

The instructor may explain the use of the radio equipment before the first flight, particularly if you are flying from an airport with a control tower or a Flight Service Station (FAA radio station). You will have a chance to watch and listen to the instructor for the first few flights and will soon be asking for taxi instructions and takeoff and landing clearances yourself, under supervision. If you are flying from an airport where a radio is required, you might also look at Chapter 21 soon after you start flying.

Most small airports have a "UNICOM" or aeronautical advisory station for giving traffic information and wind and runway conditions to pilots operating in the vicinity of the airport. You may get an early start in the use of radio while operating out of an airport so equipped.

Glass Cockpit

Although systems vary, flat panel displays or electronic flight information systems (EFIS) usually consist of two electronic screens, one showing primary flight information (Primary Flight Display or PFD) and one showing navigation and engine information (Multi-Function Display or MFD). The flight information is usually derived from solid-state attitude reference units (aircraft attitude and acceleration), air data units (airspeed, altitude and rate of climb) and magnetometer (heading). Navigation data usually comes from a GPS receiver and is displayed on the multi-function second screen along with the engine instruments. Backup or standby instruments are included along with the 2 LCDs; these normally include a conventional airspeed indicator, mechanical attitude indicator, and an altimeter.

The PFD is not just a representation of the basic mechanical instruments, but the aircraft's attitude surrounded by the other flight information in various formats. Airspeed is often shown as a movable tape on the left side of the display, altitude as a tape on the right side next to a vertical speed scale with a moving pointer. The

traditional "ball" indication can be shown as a movable base of the "sky-pointer" arrow that always points away from the ground. The base of the pointer slides out to show uncoordinated flight. Heading is sometimes shown on both the flight and navigation display.

Navigation data is often depicted as a moving map with aircraft position, weather information (either from onboard or downloaded radar), traffic, terrain and closest airports.

Advantages to this instrument system are excellent (or better) in-flight situational awareness and the ability to somewhat tailor the displayed information. Maintenance personnel are able to update the system software and more easily troubleshoot problems than with traditional instruments.

The complexity and flexibility of EFIS means a great deal of training should be accomplished on the ground. Using computer simulation or cockpit practice dramatically reduces frustration in-flight. For safety, a pilot must avoid the temptation of being "heads down"

Figure 3-31. Conventional "steam gauge" flight instruments (top) and glass cockpit PFD depiction of flight instruments.

for any length of time in flight or on the ground with the engine running. Transitioning to an aircraft with standard instruments and navigation may feel quite awkward after using EFIS.

Summary

Don't expect to have all the information in this chapter and the following four chapters down cold before you start flying. Read them over and then use them for review purposes after you've been introduced to the various subjects (the cockpit, preflight check, starting, and taxiing) by the instructor. This is a workbook and is intended to be used both before and as you fly. Remember, too, that your instructor and the *Pilot's*

Operating Handbook will have recommendations as to what is best for your particular airplane and operating conditions.

As a review of the effects on non-standard temperatures on the accuracy of the altimeter as noted earlier in the chapter, take a look at Figure 3-32.

Figure 3-33 shows the effect of flying from a high-pressure area to a low-pressure area without resetting the altimeter. There are several questions on the knowledge test about temperature and pressure change factors of the altimeter, but you should know that information for practical purposes as well.

For more-detailed information on the systems discussed in this chapter, read Appendix B in the back of this book.

Figure 3-32. HALT. There is a **H**igh **A**ltimeter because of **L**ow **T**emperature. The altimeter *indicates* higher than the *actual* aircraft altitude. This will be of even more importance when you start working on that instrument rating and are concerned about traffic and terrain clearance when solely on instruments.

Figure 3-33. Flying from a high-pressure area to a low-pressure area without resetting the altimeter results in the altimeter indicating erroneously high.

Preflight Check

An organized check is the best way to start a flight. The best way to proceed is to make a clockwise (or counterclockwise, if you like) check starting at the cockpit and getting each item as you come to it. Don't be like Henry Schmotz, student pilot, who checked things as he thought of them. He'd check the prop, then the tailwheel and run back up front to look at the oil, etc. One day Henry was so confused that he forgot to check the wings (they were gone — the mechanic had taken them off for recovering) and tried to take off. He wound up in dire straits in the middle of a chicken farm right off the end of the runway. After he cleaned himself up, the first thing he did was to set up an organized preflight check and has had no trouble since.

One of the biggest problems the new student (and the more experienced pilot too) has is knowing what to look for in the preflight check. The first few times you look into the engine compartment and see that maze of wires, pipes, plates, etc., it seems that you wouldn't know if anything was out of place or not. The airplane engine assembly is compact and sealed. What's meant by this is: (1) There should be no evidence of excess *fluid leaks* (oil, brake fluid, or other fluids) in the compartment or on the engine. You may expect a certain small amount of oil, etc., to be present; but if in doubt about the "allowed amount," ask someone. (2) There should not be any loose wires or cables. Every wire or cable should be attached at both ends. If you find one dangling loosely, ask your instructor or a mechanic about it. Don't feel shy about asking questions.

Look at the inside of the bottom cowling to check for indications of fluid leaks. Some airplanes have cowlings that require a great deal of effort to remove — it's a bit impractical to remove what appears to be several hundred fine-threaded screws to check the engine before each flight. This is a bad design by the manufacturers, since the preflight check is definitely more than just checking the oil.

Discussed here (and shown in Figure 4-1) is a clockwise check of a typical high-wing general aviation airplane with side-by-side seating. The *Pilot's Operating Handbook* for your airplane has a suggested preflight check and you and your instructor may want to use it, referring to the *Handbook* or a checklist as you do the check. As you walk out to the plane, look at its general appearance; sometimes discrepancies can be seen better at a distance. Start the actual check at the cockpit.

Your instructor will point out the following items and note the things to look for on your particular airplane:

1. *Switch off.* You'll be checking the propeller so make sure the magneto switch is in the OFF position. This does not guarantee that the ignition is off, but you will double check the magnetos themselves later (in some airplanes). Better yet, the key should be *out* of the ignition, if the airplane is so equipped.

Lower the flaps fully so that the hinges and operating rods may be examined more closely. If the flaps are electrical, before you turn the master switch ON make sure that the propeller area is clear. In rare cases, if the starter solenoid or other components are malfunctioning the starter might automatically engage of its own accord (the key is not even in the starter switch) and could be a real hazard to people or animals near the propeller. Be sure that the master switch is OFF after the flaps are down. Remove control locks.

For some planes with an electric stall warning horn, you may want to turn the master (electrical) switch ON and move the tab on the wing to hear the horn. For other airplanes with a stall warning light (no horn) and the stall warning tab well out on the wing, have somebody else move it while you watch the light on the instrument panel. Make sure the master switch is OFF after either type of these checks is completed. Chapter 12 goes into more detail on the principle of stall warning devices.

Nearly every nut on the airplane is safetied by safety wire, an elastic stop nut, or a cotter pin; there *are* a few exceptions, so if in doubt about a particular item, ask your instructor.

Figure 4-1. The preflight check.

2. *Tires and brakes.* The tires should be inspected for fabric showing or for deep cuts. Roll the airplane a foot or so to see all sides of the tire. (Obviously, if this was a jet airliner it would be quite a job to roll it back and forth, but this book was written for lightplanes.) Check the brakes and brake lines for evidence of hydraulic leaks. Check the landing gear struts for damage and for proper inflation of the oleo strut if the plane has this type of shock absorber.

3. *Look for wrinkles* or any signs of strain or fracture along the sides of the fuselage near the landing gear. If the plane has been landed hard, this will be the first place to show it. Check for pulled or distorted rivets in a metal airplane.

4. If the aircraft has *wing tanks, visually* check the one on this side at this point; don't rely on tank gauges. You should drain fuel from the tank into a clear container (commercially available) to check for dirt and/or water. Hold the container up to the light (or sun) to get a better look. If contaminants are found, the fuel should be repeatedly drained and checked until it is clear. As a student pilot, however, the presence of foreign matter in the fuel should call for a discussion with your instructor and an extra check before flying. One disadvantage of holding the fuel up to the sky is that a full container of water or jet fuel (!) will appear blue, or the color of 100 Low Lead aviation fuel. Some instructors suggest that the container be held against the side of a white area of the fuselage to check its true color. Jet fuel, which can cause a fatal crash if used in a reciprocating engine, smells like kerosene, and a quick sniff of the fuel could avoid a bad problem.

It's best to fill the fuel tanks in the evening after the last flight; this keeps moisture from condensing on the sides of the tank during the cooler night temperatures and so decreases the possibility of water in the fuel.

Some pilots make up a crude tank dipstick from a 12-inch wooden ruler or wooden dowel so that they can get a look at the relative amount of fuel in the tank; they calibrate the sticks by filling the tanks a gallon or two at a time and marking them. One caution is that rubberized tanks may be punctured by a *sharp* stick. Calibrated fuel dipsticks are available for various airplanes through aviation supply houses.

5. *Engine compartment.* Open the cowling on the pilot's side and check:

a. *Ignition lead ("leed") wires* for looseness or fraying. There are two magnetos, each firing its own set of plugs (two separate leads and plugs for each cylinder). The dual ignition system is for safety (the engine will run on either magneto alone), and each magneto will be checked during the pretakeoff check at the end of the runway. The magnetos are self-supporting ignition and have nothing to do with the battery. The battery-alternator system only furnishes power to the starter and other electrical equipment.

b. *Each magneto* has a ground wire on it. When the ignition switch is turned to RIGHT or LEFT, the ground wire is electrically disconnected on that magneto, and it is no longer "grounded out" but is ON. You may do the same by a physical disconnection of the ground wire on a magneto. It may also vibrate loose, and that magneto will be ON even though the switch inside says OFF. It may vibrate off inside the magneto where it can't be seen, so it is best to always consider the prop as being "hot" even after checking the switch and ground wires. *Check both magneto ground wires at this point* if possible.

c. *Look at the carburetor heat and cabin heat muffs for cracks.* These are shrouds around the exhaust that collect the heated air to be routed to the carburetor or cabin heater.

Carburetor heat is necessary because float-type carburetors are very effective refrigerators. The temperature of the air entering the carburetor is lowered for two reasons: (1) The pressure of the mixture is lowered as it goes through the venturi (narrow part of the throat), which causes a drop in temperature. (2) The evaporation of the fuel causes a further drop in temperature. The result is that there may be a drop of up to 60°F

Figure 4-2. Carburetor heat system.

below the outside temperature in the carburetor. If there is moisture in the air, these droplets may form ice on the sides of the venturi and on the jets, resulting in loss of power. If the situation gets bad enough, this can cause complete stoppage of the engine. That's where carburetor heat comes in. In a plane with a fixed-pitch prop (no manifold pressure gauge), the usual indication of icing is a dropping back of rpm with no change in throttle setting. There may be only a small amount of ice in the venturi and the effects may not be noticeable at full or cruising throttle, but when the throttle is closed to the idle position, all outside air may be shut out and the engine literally strangles. *So...before you close the throttle in the air, pull the carburetor heat; give it about 10 seconds to clear out any ice before pulling the throttle back.* (See item 21, Figure 3-1.)

Carburetor icing boils down to this. It isn't the heat, or the lack of it, it's the humidity. At very low temperatures (say about 0°F) the air is so dry that carburetor icing is no problem. A wet cloudy day with a temperature of 50–70°F is the best condition for carburetor icing to occur.

As you pull the carburetor heat control knob in the cockpit, a butterfly valve is opened, allowing the prewarmed air from around the exhaust to mix with the outside air coming into the carburetor. This prevents ice from forming or melts ice already formed. (Figure 4-2 shows a *full* hot setting.)

Here are some of the indications of carburetor icing. The rpm starts creeping back slowly. Being a normal pilot, you'll probably open the throttle more to keep a constant rpm setting. A few minutes later (or sooner if icing conditions are bad), you'll have to open the throttle farther. Finally, realizing there is ice about, you'll pull the carburetor heat and get a shock. There'll be about a 100-rpm drop plus some soul-shaking reactions from the engine for a few seconds before the ice melts and power returns to near normal.

If there's a lot of ice, here's what happens. The ice melts and becomes a deluge of water into the engine. A little water helps compression (World War II fighters used water injection for bursts of power), but you can get too much of a good thing. Some pilots recommend partial heat in this situation, but the best answer is to use full heat as soon as signs of icing appear and continue using it as long as necessary, realizing that some power is lost because of the warmer, thinner air. When using full carb heat in cruise, leaning the mixture will regain most of the lost power. Check with your instructor about the best procedure for your airplane.

As part of the pretakeoff check, pull on the carburetor heat with the engine running at 1,800 rpm (or whatever rpm the manufacturer may ask for) and watch for a drop-off of about 100 rpm. It will vary from plane to plane, but this is about the normal drop. The heated air going into the engine is less dense than an equal volume of the outside cold air, and the engine will suffer a slight loss in power. In other words, if there's no drop-off, you're not getting heat to the carburetor, and it would be wise to find out what's up before flying.

The air coming through the carburetor heat system is not filtered, as the normal outside air coming to the carburetor is (*see* item 8), so it's possible to pick up dust and dirt when the carburetor heat is used on the ground. It's best to avoid extensive use of carburetor heat on the ground, particularly when taxiing, which may "stir up the dust."

Carburetor heat richens the mixture (the warmer air is less dense for the same weight of fuel going to the engine), so that using carburetor heat with the mixture full-rich at higher altitudes makes the engine run rough unless the mixture is leaned. Chapter 5 covers the use of the mixture control.

The fuel injection system is becoming more popular because of better fuel distribution to the cylinders and a lesser tendency to icing problems, but the carburetor will still be used for quite a while.

Most lightplane cabin heaters operate on the same principle of using hot air from around the exhausts. Pulling the cabin heat control opens a valve and allows the hot air to come into the cockpit. The effectiveness of the carburetor (and cabin) heat depends on the temperature of the air in the shroud(s), and this depends on the power being produced. If on a cold day you've been descending for some time at a low power setting with carb and cabin heats on and suddenly find that your feet are getting cold, you can be sure that the carburetor heat is becoming as ineffective as the cabin heat. Get plenty of power back on to assure effectiveness of the carb heat and also to warm the engine, or you shortly may have trouble getting the engine to respond. Larger planes will have the more efficient and more expensive gasoline cabin heaters.

d. The *fuel strainer drain* (not just for the fuel tanks) is located at the bottom of the airplane near the firewall. (The firewall separates the engine compartment from the passenger compartment.) Drain the fuel into a clear container, as noted in item 4, and check for contaminants. Some airplanes have more than one fuselage fuel drain.

e. While you're browsing in the *engine compartment*, your instructor will show you how the *engine accessories* should look. (Is that wire that's dangling there normal?) Since you probably don't have experience as an airplane mechanic, many things will just have to *look* right. Know the preflight check so thoroughly that anything not in its place will stick out like a sore thumb.

f. If the oil tank cap is on this side, *check the oil*. In most planes of this type, the oil is on the right, but don't count on it. The minimum allowable amount will vary from plane to plane. The instructor will give you this information. Most lightplanes of the 100-hp range hold 6 quarts and have a minimum flyable level of 4 quarts. Make sure the cap is secured after you've checked the oil. If you add oil, be sure it is the recommended grade or viscosity for the season and your airplane. Know whether your airplane uses ashless dispersant oil or straight mineral oil (Chapter 23).

g. *Check the alternator* for good wiring and connections (if you can see it; some airplanes have alternators that are pretty inaccessible without taking the cowling off). To repeat from Chapter 3, the alternator serves the same purpose as the one in your car; it keeps the system up for starting and operating the electrical accessories such as lights and radios and some engine and flight instruments as noted earlier. The battery box (and battery) is located in the engine compartment in some airplanes and should be checked for security here.

Figure 4-3. Components of the engine and systems of a current trainer as discussed in this chapter.

Figure 4-3 shows the components of a current trainer using a Lycoming 0-235 L2C engine that develops 110 brake horsepower at 2,550 rpm. (You might review Chapter 2 about brake and thrust horsepower.) The propeller has been removed.

Looking at the various parts:

AB—alternator drive belt.

AL—alternator.

BB—battery box.

CB—carburetor.

CH—carburetor heat hose from the muffler shroud (CM).

CS—carburetor intake screen.

CX—the common exhaust outlet or stack.

CY—one of the four cylinders.

EP—external electric power plug (for use on those cold mornings when the battery is dead; this is optional equipment).

FC—filler cap (oil).

FS—fuel strainer.

HT—hose from the muffler shroud for cabin heat.

IM—intake manifold (route of the fuel-air mixture from the carburetor to the cylinder, there are four of them here).

ML—magneto (left).

MR—magneto (right).

OB—oil breather line, which releases pressure created in the crankcase by the hot oil vapors (when you go out to the airplane after it has just come down, you may see a small patch of light brown froth of oil or water on the ground under the outlet pipe. You can trace the route here from

the front of the crankcase to the outlet opening). In the winter, the breather hose (sticking down below the cowling) should be checked to assure that the moisture, condensed to water, has not frozen over and sealed the outlet. If the outlet is sealed by ice, the pressures could build up in the crankcase and damage it.

OC—oil cooler. The oil is routed from the engine-driven oil pump through this small radiator to the engine and finally to the sump (it's slightly more complicated than that).

OF—oil filter.

OL—oil line from the oil cooler.

OS—the oil sump or oil storage tank.

SP—spark plugs. Each cylinder has two plugs.

SW—spark plug (ignition) wire or lead.

VV—vacuum system overboard vent line. (*See* Figure 3-23.)

XM—exhaust manifold.

It's unlikely that you'll get the cowling this much off of your airplane during any preflight check, but you might quietly watch the mechanics working on an engine in the hangar or look at an engine in the process of being overhauled. (Don't move any propellers; the mechanic might not appreciate it and it could be dangerous.)

h. Make sure the *cowling* is secured.

i. On some trainers the *vent for the static system* is located on the left side of the fuselage just behind the cowling. The static system instruments are, as you recall, the altimeter, rate of climb indicator, and airspeed indicator (which also needs a source of ram pressure, the pitot tube). The designers have located the static pressure orifice at a point where the actual outside static pressure exists (without any ram or eddying effects), and the hole must be clear to ensure accurate readings of the three instruments. Other locations for the static opening are on the pitot tube (which would then make it a *pitot-static tube*) and on the side (or sides) of the fuselage between the wing and the tail assembly. Check with your instructor about the particular system for your airplane. (*See* Figure 3-5.)

6. *Check the propeller* for spinner security and for nicks. Propellers are bad about sucking up gravel and then batting it back against the tail. A sharp nick is called a "stress raiser" by engineers because stresses can be concentrated at the point of the nick, possibly causing structural failure and the loss of a propeller tip. (You may have used this same principle by notching a piece of wood to break it more easily.) Since the propeller is turning at 40 revolutions per second, an unbalanced propeller could literally pull the engine from its mount. If you have any doubts about prop damage when making the preflight check, you'd better have a mechanic or a flight instructor take a look at it. Figure 4-4 shows a method that mechanics use to eradicate comparatively small stress raisers. *Don't move the prop. The ground wire might be off inside the mag where you can't see it—or if the engine is hot, it may kick over if the prop is moved, even if the mags are working normally.*

7. *Look in the engine-cooling openings* for objects that might hinder air flow. Planes have hit small birds, and these have been jammed into the engine fins causing a hot spot, followed by the ruining of a cylinder. The fins are finely engineered and any obstruction cuts down the cooling efficiency. You may be able to check the alternator and its drive belt at this point in some airplanes. Birds like to build nests in there, too, and can do it overnight.

8. *Look at the carburetor intake screen.* The screen is there to stop bugs, dirt, and other foreign matter from going into the carburetor. Check for security and see if the screen is clogged.

9. *Check the oil radiator* for obstructions or damage.

10. *Step back to check alignment of the landing gear.* You'll never make a hard landing, of course, but that character who just flew the plane might have. Look behind before you step back. (One student stepped back and sat in a 5-gallon can of freshly drained oil.) This would be the point where you'd check the nosewheel tire and oleo for signs of wear or damage.

Figure 4-4. An exaggerated view of a "stress raiser" and the method of "dressing" the nick to eliminate this problem. A nick of this relative size usually means that the propeller is sent back to the manufacturer or discarded. (Enough nicks—and dressing—on one blade could cause a balance problem.) The shaded area shows removed material.

11. *Open the right side of the cowling.*
    a. *Check the ignition leads and the right magneto.* If the leads are frayed, bring this to the attention of the instructor.
    b. *Check the oil* if it's on this side—it probably will be.
    c. *Take a good look at the items that were hard to check from the other side.* Don't be like Oswald Zilch who checked only the side the oil was on. One day a mechanic took off two of the cylinders, and since Oswald never checked that side, he tried to take off and ran through the same chicken farm that Henry Schmotz, of no-wing fame, had recently vacated.
    d. *Secure the cowling.*

12. *Check the tire and landing gear strut.* Check the brake assembly.

13. *Check the strut fittings* at the fuselage for safetying (if they aren't covered by a fairing).

14. *Visually check the fuel quantity on this side.*

15. *Check the pitot-static tube*, if it's on this side, for obstructions.

16. *Look under the wing for tears or wrinkles* in the skin structure. A wrinkle means a strained member.

17. *Check the strut wing attachments* for safetying.

18. *Grasp the wing* in line with the two spars, if it is a fabric-covered trainer, and give it a brisk shake. Make sure the instructor is not standing under the other wing or you may knock him or her cockeyed. This is a bad way to start a flight. (On the other hand you may *want* to. Use your own judgment.)

    The reason for holding the wings in this manner is that you are putting a direct stress on the spars; if there has been any damage to these members or there are broken drag wires, the damage will show up by sound and/or by wrinkling in the skin.

The metal trainers with plastic wingtips are somewhat harder to check for damage in this manner because pressure exerted on these plastic tips may crack them. In that case, grasp the wing on the leading edge just inboard of the plastic tip. The main wing structure may consist of a single box spar with the metal airfoil shape built around attached ribs (with the ailerons and flaps added) rather than a two-spar and rib system. You should try to move it to check for wrinkles, but you also should look at the rivets in the wing to check for signs of overstress. Sometimes, but not always, this will be indicated by the paint being cracked around the rivet, or it may appear that certain rivets have moved slightly or seem elongated.

19. *Check the ailerons* for excessive play or slackness between the two. Look at the aileron actuating rod and hinge assembly for security. Check the aileron counterweights for security; these are weights placed ahead of the aileron hinge line to balance it for aerodynamic reasons.

20. *Check the flap hinges and tracks* for cracks or excessive wear. Look at the general condition of the flaps (no stretched rivets or cracks).

21. *Drain some fuel* from the right tank drain to check for water or other contamination. Some flight school operators advocate the check for water once a day rather than every flight. However, it's better to drain them every flight so that *you* can see that it's clear, rather than taking someone's word for it. (An expensive airplane and your neck are a pretty high price to pay just to avoid draining 15 cents worth of gasoline.)

22. *Look alongside the fuselage for tears or wrinkles or pulled rivets.* If the static vent is in this area, make sure it's clear of dirt. (Look under the belly, also.)

23. If the *stabilizer* is externally braced, look at the brace wires or struts and check for slack wire or loose attachments. Most stabilizers now are of cantilever construction and have no external bracing. Grasp the tip of the stabilizer and check for internal damage by exerting up and down forces on it. *Don't try to pick the tail up by the stabilizer tip. It's quite possible that you might damage it.* Many lightplanes have signs painted on the stabilizers warning against lifting the tail this way, but you can get a pretty good idea if things aren't up to snuff by shaking it. Better to find out now than at 500 feet. Some planes have an adjustable stabilizer instead of a trim tab. Some trainers have a "stabilator" (stabilizer-elevator combination), and the entire horizontal tail surface acts as the elevator.

24. *Move the elevators* up and down to check for full movement. Note any binding of the hinges and check for safetying on all hinge bolts. Look under the elevator and stabilizer for tears and wrinkles. If your plane has a stabilator (a one-piece "flying tail," *see* Chapter 8), check its movement and condition.

25. *Check the rudder* for binding and limits of operation. Look for fraying of the cables and safetying of the cable attachments at the rudder horn.

26. *Tailwheel.* If your airplane is the tailwheel type, naturally this would be the place to check the tailwheel. The rudder is connected to the tailwheel by coiled springs that absorb ground shocks to the rudder and also make for smoother directional control on the ground. Check these springs. Check the tailwheel attachment bolts for signs of wear or shear breakage. The last student may have landed slightly sideways, and this puts a large shear stress on the attaching bolts.

27. *Check the other stabilizer and elevator and look at the trim tab.* Is it set at nose up? Nose down? Neutral? Check the trim tab cables for wear if they are accessible. Make sure the tab does not have excessive play.

28. *Check this side for tears or wrinkles.*

29. *Check this fuel tank for water and other contamination.*

30. *Check this wing, aileron, flap, and strut. Check the pitot tube* if it is on this side.

31. *Check the strut fuselage attachments* for safety.

32. *You should now be back at the door, ready to get in.* If for some reason you are not back at the door, ask somebody how to get there.

A suggestion for the preflight check — make sure the switches are OFF and then check all of the fuel items at the same time. Note that there are *five* items that pertain to the fuel or fuel systems to be checked: the *two* tanks (should be checked visually) and the *three* drains (two wing tank drains and the main system drain). You might be less likely to overlook one of these items if you get them at the same time and then proceed with the clockwise check (starting from the cockpit as illustrated). If you use this system, make sure you don't pull a Henry Schmotz.

It's a good idea, for high wing airplanes in particular, to drain the wing tank drains first to get water or other contaminants that have settled to the tank bottom, then drain the main (lowest) drain.

It could happen that draining the main drain first would pull contaminants down into the line between the tank and the carburetor so that they would not show up in the wing tank fuel sample. The garbage might only make itself known at a very bad spot just after lift-off.

Some systems require that each tank be drained through the fuel strainer (lowest) drain. Your instructor will issue you a *Pilot's Operating Handbook* shortly after you start to fly, and discussions and your reading will make things much clearer about the systems of your airplane.

Another point about fuel checking: A mixture of 100LL (low lead, blue) and 80 octane (red) fuel of equal or near equal proportions will appear clear (as in water). If your airplane requires a *minimum* grade of 100LL and the fuel sampler shows clear contents, this could indicate that (1) 80 octane was mixed with the 100LL (and the engine might not like that), (2) the sampler is full of water, or (3) jet fuel has been put in the tanks, although the most common description of jet fuel is that it is "straw colored"—as noted earlier in this chapter, a sniff test would be an added check.

Aviation legend has it that there was a case of a jealous spouse who put sugar in the fuel tanks of a rival's airplane. The pilot-owner, who drained and checked the fuel *every flight*, caught the problem—table sugar does not dissolve in 80 octane or 100LL fuel—and the crystals gave it away. The story does not cover how, or if, the *domestic* problem was solved. Also, covered earlier in the chapter, *any* indication of an unusual condition during your fuel check should call for a discussion with an instructor or mechanic.

When you are flying solo, make sure that the other seat belt and shoulder harness is fastened so that there are no "loose ends" to hang out of the airplane. A seat belt and/or shoulder harness banging in the slipstream against the fuselage sounds like an engine malfunction. Pilots have put airplanes down in strange places and damaged them because it sounded as if the engine was blowing up. As will be said many times during your flight training, always maintain control of the airplane, *then* fix the problem.

After the complete check, the airplane is okay, and you are ready to get in, fasten your belt and shoulder harness and start the engine.

Your instructor will, on the first flight, have you adjust the seat height and position for best visibility and operation of the controls. You should use this setting for following flights so that your visual perception or control travel efforts aren't changed.

Starting the Airplane

The plane with a starter has one disadvantage against its many advantages. There is nobody out front cranking the prop and keeping people from getting hit by it. A dog or small child can easily get under the nose unseen and be killed or seriously injured when you start the engine. *Before you turn the master switch ON to start the engine, shout, "Clear?" and receive the acknowledgment, "Clear!" from somebody on the ramp who is in a position to see.* If you don't get this reply but go ahead and turn the master switch ON and push the starter button anyway, you may have reason to regret it the rest of your life.

Sure, if you holler, all of the airport personnel will get out of the way, but the visitors or kids won't know what the word means. Some pilots are criminal in their starting procedures; they shout, "Clear!" and before the word is out of their mouths are starting the engine. This is as bad as saying nothing. Get set up to start, get acknowledgment of your shout, then start the engine. The few seconds you wait between "Clear!" and starting the engine gives you one last look around the propeller area. On the other hand, don't check that everything is clear and then dawdle in the cockpit until somebody has a chance to stick a sawhorse or something under the prop.

General Procedure

(Use your *Pilot's Operating Handbook*)
1. *Preflight check complete.*
2. *Seat belts and shoulder harness fastened.*
3. *Controls move freely.*
4. *Fuel ON fullest tank.*
5. *Mixture rich.*
6. *Prime as needed.*
7. *Throttle cracked (open about ¼-inch).*
8. *Brakes ON.*
9. *Radios and other unnecessary electrical equipment OFF.*
10. *Make sure that the propeller area is clear, turn the master switch ON, and then turn the electrically-driven fuel pump ON* (if the airplane is so equipped) before starting to see if it's working. You can hear it and see the fuel pressure come up. You'll turn the electric pump OFF after the engine starts to check that the engine-driven pump is working. (*See* Chapter 7.)
11. *"Clear?"* After receiving acknowledgment, ensure that the master switch is ON and engage the starter (airplanes with no electrical fuel pump).

Cold Weather Starting

When the mercury is nudging down toward zero, the airplane's engine can get cantankerous to start. You want a rich mixture, or a high ratio of gasoline to air, during the cold weather start. Prime the engine well and leave the primer out, so you can give it a shot if needed after the engine starts. It's possible that you may have to keep it running with the primer until the engine starts to warm up. Once the engine is running on its own, push the primer in and lock it, or the engine will run rough, particularly at low rpm, because raw gas will be pulled into the engine, making the mixture too rich for a warm engine. Take a look ahead at Figures 23-17 and 23-18. There you'll see that the primer system is a separate source of fuel and injects the fuel directly into the cylinders, bypassing the carburetor.

Hot Weather Starting

The engine will run hot and stay hot a long time after being shut down in the summer. A hot engine has a tendency to "load up" or flood itself, and the fuel-air ratio should be comparatively low for best starting.

Suppose you come out to the airplane just after it has come down on a hot day. You run a preflight check and the prestart check is completed. The guys on the ramp give you a thumbs up and you push the starter. The prop turns over, and over, and over. If you've done the prestart procedure correctly, the chances are that the engine is loaded. One way to clear it out is to turn off all the switches, open the throttle wide, and have somebody pull the prop through several times. Then close the throttle and start the prestart procedure again. The reason for the open throttle is that as the engine turns over, the added air through the carburetor helps to clear the cylinders of excess fuel.

Another procedure is to open the throttle at least halfway as soon as you realize the engine is loaded and then continue the start. The engine will clear itself out and start. Of course, you'll have to pull the throttle back as soon as it starts, or everybody in the hangar will hear the noise and figure that you'll be coming through there any second.

If the engine is obviously loaded, you can open the throttle and have the mixture at idle cutoff as the start is continued. This is a more complicated approach for the inexperienced pilot, since the throttle must be retarded and the mixture control moved out of idle cutoff as the engine starts. This procedure is mentioned for later use.

It's possible during a start the engine will backfire, causing the fuel in the carburetor to be ignited. *If you suspect that there is a fire in the carburetor intake, keep the engine turning over. The fire will be sucked into the cylinders where it belongs.* A fire extinguisher may have to be used outside the airplane in some conditions. You may put the mixture to idle cut-off, turn the fuel off, and open the throttle as you keep the engine turning over with the starter. Review the *Pilot's Operating Handbook* for specific procedures.

After the fire is out, shut down the engine and have a mechanic inspect the carburetor and engine compartment for damage.

Accelerating Pump

While discussing the subject of starting, it might be well to mention that some trainers have an accelerating pump on the carburetor whereby a quick forward movement of the throttle results in an added spurt of fuel being injected into the carburetor throat. This is done so that if the pilot suddenly opens the throttle, the engine gets enough fuel to accelerate quickly and smoothly. The accelerating pump is also useful in starting the airplane and can often be used in lieu of the primer. By pumping the throttle, raw fuel is injected into the carburetor throat and an extra rich mixture is

pulled into the cylinders when the engine starts turning over. The primer is normally set up to send fuel *directly* to the cylinders rather than injecting fuel into the carburetor throat, as the accelerating pump does. *Because the accelerating pump puts fuel into the carburetor, overzealous use of it can mean fuel is pooled in the carburetor and carburetor air box (see Figure 4-2), and the chances of a fire can be greater than when using the primer.*

When the temperature is very low, using the primer is the most effective means of ensuring that sufficient fuel is available for starting. (Excessive priming tends to wash oil from the cylinder walls with resulting increased engine wear, but it's a necessary evil.) A method you may try in cold weather when you become more proficient is to use the primer as the engine is turning over. This tends to decrease the chances of loading up because the engine will usually start when conditions are "right" for it.

Mixture Control

The purpose of the mixture control is to allow the pilot to set the ratio of fuel-to-air mixture going to the engine. As a quick and dirty figure, a mixture of 1 pound of fuel to 15 pounds of air is about right to support combustion.

Assume that your airplane doesn't have a mixture control, but the carburetor has been set at sea level by a mechanic to give the amount of fuel to the engine to get this 1:15 ratio. As the airplane climbs, the air becomes less dense and weighs less per cubic foot. The carburetor, though, is sitting there fat, dumb, and happy, letting the engine get the same amount (weight) of fuel as it did at sea level, but now it is getting less than the correct amount (weight) of air. The mixture, which was just right for sea level, is now overly "rich" (too much fuel for the air available), combustion efficiency drops, and power is lost. You are also using more fuel than necessary. You may have run into this problem in driving to high elevations in your car.

Now suppose you do all of your flying from an airport high in the Andes, where the air is "thin." There still being no mixture control in the cockpit, the mechanic has adjusted the carburetor to get the magic 1:15 ratio of fuel to air at that high elevation. When you fly down to a sea level airport, you'll find that as you descend the engine starts to run rough, coughs a couple of times, and quits. Why? Because as you descend, the air becomes denser and the fuel that the carburetor had been metering to the engine at the high altitude is not enough to support a combustion mixture in the denser air. The engine is running too "lean"; in fact, it doesn't want to run at all.

Lest you think that the 1:15 ratio (or 15:1, whichever way you prefer to think of it) is the only mixture for an airplane to operate with, it might be added that combustion can occur in mixtures as widely divergent as 1:7 (very rich) to 1:20 (very lean), but these are the extremes. The mixture control in the airplane allows you to take care of such variations as necessary.

When the mixture control is full-forward, the setting is full-rich. This full-rich position is always set slightly richer than would give the best fuel-to-air ratio for full power. This is done to be on the safe side because a rich mixture aids in engine cooling and only a slight amount of power is lost. As the control is pulled out or moved aft, the mixture becomes progressively leaner until the "idle cutoff" position is reached at the full-aft or full-out position. The fuel is cut off completely in the idle cutoff position. This is the way an engine with a mixture control is shut down.

The mixture control is normally in the full-rich position for takeoff and other high-power conditions and for starting. However, you can see that for takeoffs from airports at high elevations, this could be too rich and power would be lost. Later, you'll learn the techniques for leaning the mixture for takeoffs under these conditions, but for now use full-rich unless the instructor says otherwise. You may never take off from an airport of an elevation (or density-altitude) where this leaning is necessary. In Chapter 13 ("After Landing/Taxi-In," on Page 13-28) more details will be given on cruise control (setting power and mixture) in flight.

Stopping the Engine

Occasionally, in hot weather the engine of older type trainers won't stop when the ignition is turned off (no mixture control). The engine is so hot that it is "preigniting," or setting off the fuel mixture without benefit of spark plugs. After you cut the switch, open the throttle wide as the engine runs down. This will send fuel and cool air into the cylinders, lowering the temperature and keeping preignition from occurring.

In some cases, the engine will kick backward after the switch is cut. This is a form of preignition, and opening the throttle will usually stop any tendencies toward this engine-punishing action.

The throttle is opened on the shutdown in the winter to send fuel into the cylinders to help the next start. This is particularly important if your primer isn't as good as it should be.

For airplanes equipped with mixture controls, the shutdown technique is to pull the throttle back to idle and pull the mixture all the way aft (to the idle cutoff position). The engine will quit smoothly. The beauty of using the mixture control rather than the ignition switch to shut down the engine is that the possibility of preignition is eliminated (there's no fuel left in the cylinders to be ignited). If the idle cutoff is improperly set, you might find that the engine tends to continue running at idle because some fuel is still getting through the carburetor. One method of shutting down in this case is to leave the control in idle cutoff and advance the throttle until the incoming air leans the mixture to a point where combustion can no longer be supported. (In extreme conditions you may have to turn the fuel selector off and wait it out.)

As will be noted in Chapter 7, the instructor may check the ignition switch for proper operation before stopping the engine normally with the mixture control.

Propping the Plane

Nearly all planes have starters these days, but the following is presented for your possible use. *If you plan on doing any propping (cranking the propeller by hand), you should receive instruction from someone with experience; it's an extremely risky business.* Another rule is to never prop an airplane without a competent pilot or mechanic, *who is familiar with the particular airplane,* at the controls. Propping a plane without a competent operator inside is asking for great excitement, tire tracks on your sports jacket, and loss of an airplane.

The idea of starting is the same as with an electric starter except you have manpower instead of electricity turning the prop. There'll be a little more conversation in this case.

Man out front: "OFF AND CRACKED!" (Meaning switch off and throttle cracked.)

You: (*After* checking to make sure that the fuel valve is ON, the mags are OFF, and the throttle is cracked) "OFF AND CRACKED."

Man out front: (After pulling the prop through several times to get the engine ready for start) "BRAKES AND CONTACT!"

You: Check the brakes and say, "BRAKES AND CONTACT," *before* turning the switch on. Notice that you're giving the benefit of the doubt in all cases.

He pulls the prop again and the engine starts. If in hot weather the engine loads up and doesn't start, the propper will have to clear the cylinders of the excess fuel. If he trusts you, he may say, "Keep it hot and give me half," meaning for you to leave the switch on and open the throttle halfway, adding that you are expected to hold brakes firmly and pull the throttle back as soon as the engine starts. He may push against the prop hub to see if you are holding the brakes, will then pull the prop through until the engine starts, and will be very, very unhappy if you forget to pull the throttle back and are not holding any brakes. One student chased a mechanic with an airplane for 50 yards one day. Of course, soon afterward the mechanic chased the student with a wrench.

In most cases with students, the person propping will say, "SWITCH OFF AND THROTTLE OPEN," and you will make sure the switch is off and the throttle is open. When the plane is ready to start, the propper will say, "THROTTLE CLOSED, BRAKES AND CONTACT." You'll close the throttle (he can hear it close from the outside), say, "THROTTLE CLOSED, BRAKES AND CONTACT," hold the brakes, and turn the switch on.

The whole idea in starting an airplane is safety. That prop is a meat cleaver just itching to go to work on somebody. Don't you be the one who causes it to happen, and don't be the one that it happens to.

"CONTACT!" may sound dramatic, but unlike "SWITCH ON!" which, on a noisy ramp may sound like "SWITCH OFF!" there is only one meaning to the word (the magnetos are, or are to be, *hot*). Besides, "CONTACT!" evokes memories of biplanes and barnstorming, helmets, and goggles. (Great!)

When You're Swinging the Prop

Always figure the switch is on, no matter what the person in the cockpit says. Push against the prop hub to see if the pilot is holding the brakes. He (or she) may be an old buddy but having no brakes can do you a lot of damage here, so don't take any chances.

Before you start to prop the plane, look at the ground under the prop. Is there oil, water, or gravel that might cause your feet to slip out from under you? If the ground doesn't look right, then move the plane—better a tired back than a broken one.

You: "OFF AND CRACKED."

Cockpit: (After checking) "OFF AND CRACKED."

A lot of nonpilots think that the prop is turned backward and "wound up" and released, but this is wrong. You will turn the prop in its normal direction—that is, clockwise as seen from the cockpit, counterclockwise as seen by you when standing in front of the plane. You're doing the same thing a starter does—turning the prop over until the engine starts. (Your car starter doesn't turn the engine backward and then let go to make it start.)

Figure 5-1. Propping the airplane.

Put both hands close together on the prop about halfway between the hub and the tip (Figure 5-1). Don't wrap your fingers around the trailing edge; just have enough of the tips there to pull the prop through, because if the engine should kick back, your fingers would suffer. (You may also be fired into orbit if you hang on tight enough.) Stand at about a 45-degree angle to the prop; this should have your right shoulder pointing in the general direction of the hub. Keep both feet on the ground but have most of your weight on the right foot. As you pull the propeller through, step back on the left foot. This moves you back away from the prop each time. Listen for a sucking sound that tells you the engine is getting fuel. This will be learned from experience; an open or half-open throttle does not have this sound.

When you think the engine is ready, step back and say, "BRAKES AND CONTACT." After the acknowledgment from the cockpit, step forward and give the prop a sharp snap. Then step backward and to one side as the engine starts.

The starting problems you may encounter have already been discussed.

Don't stand too far from the prop. This causes you to lean into it each time you pull it through.

If the prop is not at the right position for you to get a good snap, have the person in the cockpit turn the switch off. Then move the prop carefully to the position required. *As far as you are concerned, the switch is always on.*

After Starting

The oil pressure should come up to normal within 30 seconds in warmer weather. Any undue delay should cause you to shut the engine down. Your instructor will have advice for cold weather starts.

After the engine is running well, you should retract the flaps (they were down for the preflight), and (if electrically driven) you will want to wait until the alternator is in operation and helping the system.

6

Taxiing

Some students at first have more trouble taxiing the airplane than flying it, so you might want to take special note of this chapter.

Communications

At non-tower airports you'll set one of the communications transceivers to the UNICOM, or local advisory, frequency to coordinate your takeoff, pattern, and landing with other traffic in the area.

For instance, at small airports where you have to taxi on the runway (no taxiways) to get to the point of takeoff, it's customary to announce in the blind on UNICOM such statements as "SEWANEE-FRANKLIN COUNTY TRAFFIC, CESSNA SEVEN FIVE FIVE SEVEN LIMA, BACK TAXIING ON RUNWAY TWO-FOUR." This lets incoming traffic know that you're going to use Runway 24 and are taxiing on the runway itself the "wrong way" to get to the end for takeoff. Your airport may have different procedures, but your instructor will brief you on them.

At most controlled airports (with a tower), you will listen to ATIS (Automatic Terminal Information Service)—a continual broadcast of recorded noncontrol information concerning winds, ceiling, visibility, and runway(s) in use—and when you contact ground control for taxi instructions, you'll let them know that you have "Information Bravo" or "Charlie," the latest information (the recording is updated periodically and a new alphabet symbol assigned to it).

Your instructor will probably let you handle the radio after the first couple of flights. There is a condition known as "mike fright," in which a normally intelligent person forgets everything he or she was going to say on the radio as soon as a microphone is raised to their lips. Just about every pilot has had it, and even experienced pilots have had it when they did not think through what they were going to say. Those smooth-talking tower controllers also have run into it a time or two in their careers.

There's more detail on communications in Chapter 21.

Wind Indicators

Get in the habit of checking the wind indicators before getting into the plane so that you'll know which runway is in use. There are three main types of wind indicators (Figure 6-1): (1) the windsock, a cloth sleeve that has the advantage of telling both wind direction and velocity; (2) the wind tee, a free-swinging T-shaped marker

WIND

The windsock

The wind tee

The tetrahedron

Figure 6-1. Airport wind indicators.

that resembles an airplane; and (3) the tetrahedron (a Greek word meaning "four bases or sides"), a four-sided object that resembles an arrowhead when seen from the air.

Airplanes normally take off and land into the wind because the lower groundspeed shortens the ground run.

Some students remember the correct way to use the windsock at first by thinking of the plane as being blown from a trumpet. Think of the tee as an airplane. The way it's heading is the way you want to take off and land. The tetrahedron is an arrowhead pointing the way for you to take off and land.

Segmented Circle

The wind indicator is usually in a segmented circle to draw the pilot's attention to it from the air (Figure 6-2). The runways are shown as extensions from the circle. If one or more of the runways has a right-hand traffic pattern (the normal pattern is left-hand), this will be indicated by the extensions. Perhaps there is a hospital or town on one side of the airport, and it's best to keep the air traffic away from that area.

Take off and land with the other traffic even though this does not agree with the wind indicator. However, remember one thing: When solo, *you* are the pilot in command of your airplane. If some character is trying to break his neck by landing downwind (with the wind) in strong wind, or other such foolishness, you'd be better off to continue to circle until that mission is accomplished, and then you can land in the proper direction.

Incidentally, hard-surfaced runways are numbered by their magnetic headings to the nearest 10°. Runway 22 means that the plane's magnetic heading on this runway will be about 220° when taking off or landing. The actual heading may be 224°, but it is called 22. If the actual heading was 226°, then the runway would be 23, or considered to be 230°. The opposite direction on the same runway (22) would be called 4 (40°). (*See* Figure 6-3.) These numbers are painted on the runways. This

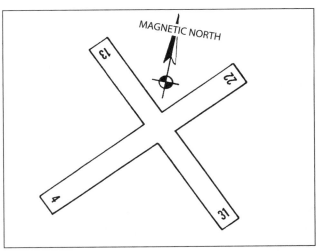

Figure 6-3. Runway numbering system.

enables transient pilots to pick out the active runway more easily from the air after the tower has given them landing instructions or UNICOM has given them an advisory.

The wind is not always right down the runway, so you'll use the runway that mostly coincides with the wind direction and the crosswind takeoff and landing techniques your instructor will show you. (*See* Chapter 13.)

Taxiing

The majority of the trainers used today are of the tricycle-gear type, which, if nothing else, has cut down on the number of taxiing accidents. In the older tailwheel types, the nose was high and obscured the view of the pilot, so continual "S-turning" was required to keep the taxi area ahead in sight. Sometimes the nose was swung just in time for the pilot to realize that the airplane was bearing down fast on a large, immovable, and/or expensive object. The lower nose of the nosewheel type makes it easier to see ahead at all times.

Also, the nosewheel steering is usually more positive and gives better control in strong wind conditions.

The airplane on the ground is out of its element. It lumbers and shakes and moves awkwardly. But in order to fly, you first must taxi, and you'll find that a certain degree of skill is required to move the airplane on the ground under varying wind conditions.

Most tricycle-gear airplanes are steered on the ground with the rudder pedals, which are connected to the nosewheel *and* rudder. Some airplanes have stiff connections between the rudder pedals and the nosewheel, while others have a softer-feeling spring-loaded bungee to transmit the pedal pressure to the nosewheel.

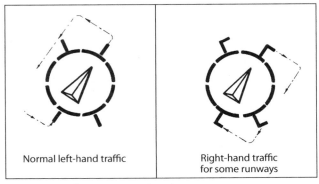

| Normal left-hand traffic | Right-hand traffic for some runways |

Figure 6-2. The segmented circle.

In any type, push the rudder pedal in the desired direction of turn. As will be noted later, brakes may be used in some cases to tighten the turn. Other airplanes have a free-castering type of nosewheel (not connected to the rudder pedals), with brakes being the primary steering control at low-speed taxiing.

Your probable tendency in the first taxiing session (and later ones, too) will be to grab that control wheel in front of you and try to use it to steer the airplane. Your past experience in driving cars can result here in what educators call "negative transfer"; turning the wheel does nothing but move those ailerons out on the wings, which are sometimes an aid in taxiing but won't help you avoid that million-dollar corporation jet you're headed for. The instructor may have you keep your hands off the wheel during the first couple of taxi periods so that you can break the car habit.

The taxi speed, which is controlled with the throttle, should be a fast walk out on the taxiway and much slower in a congested area such as the apron. Use the throttle as necessary to maintain the taxi speed.

Flight Controls in Taxiing

When taxiing downwind and the wind is strong, hold the wheel forward so that the wind strikes the down elevator and keeps the tail from rising.

When taxiing upwind (into the wind), hold the wheel back so that the wind force and propwash hold the tail down. At any rate, tailwheel or tricycle gear, always hold the wheel so that forces acting on the elevator will hold the tail down (Figure 6-4).

As noted earlier, the tricycle-gear airplane generally has more positive reactions in taxiing and doesn't tend to weathercock (turn into the wind) as easily as the tailwheel type. One problem with the latter is that a too-fast taxi, moving downwind, can be a hazard if sudden braking is required. The airplane may tend to nose over and, if the wheel or stick is pulled back (which is a usual reaction to "keep the tail down"), the tailwind gets under the elevators and magnifies the problem, sometimes at the price of a propeller or worse.

Under certain wind conditions the ailerons are useful in taxiing.

In Figure 6-5 the wind, coming from the side and behind, wants to make the plane weathercock or turn into the wind and is also trying to push the plane over. The elevators are down, and opposite rudder is needed to keep the plane from weathercocking. By turning the wheel to the right, the right aileron is up and the left is down as shown. The impact of the wind on the down left aileron helps fight the overturning tendency, and the added area of the down aileron works against the weathercocking force. The aileron control (wheel or stick) is held away from the wind in a quartering tailwind.

When the plane is taxiing into a quartering headwind, the aileron is held into the wind, the wheel is back to keep the tail down, and opposite rudder is used as needed to stop any weathercocking tendency. Hold the wheel as if to climb into the wind (Figure 6-6).

If the wind is directly from the side, the ailerons are of no assistance unless your taxi speed is high enough

Figure 6-4. Elevator handling — upwind and downwind taxiing (tailwheel type).

WIND FROM LEFT REAR
Right aileron
Right rudder as necessary
Down elevator

Figure 6-5. This applies to tricycle-gear airplanes also.

Figure 6-6. Control positions for a crosswind (tailwheel airplane).

to get a good relative wind against the ailerons; *if you are taxiing that fast, slow down.*

"In days of old, when men were bold" and planes were light and ailerons large, ailerons were used opposite to the turn. The drag of the down aileron helped the plane to turn. The planes are now heavier and the ailerons smaller, so ailerons have a negligible effect unless you happen to be doing at least 25 K or so and, again, this is taxiing too fast.

If there is a strong, quartering tailwind, it is possible to nose over a tricycle-gear airplane, especially if brakes are abruptly applied. What happens is that the plane "bows." The wind is able to get under the upwind wing and the stabilizer, and the plane may rotate around an imaginary line drawn between the nosewheel and the downwind main wheel. This reaction is aggravated if the elevators are in the *up* position. The same tendency is present, particularly in high-wing airplanes (where the center of gravity is farther above the wheels), when an abrupt turn is made while taxiing downwind in a strong wind. One memory aid is that when the wind is strong and behind the airplane (straight or quartering), hold the wheel as if diving away from the wind.

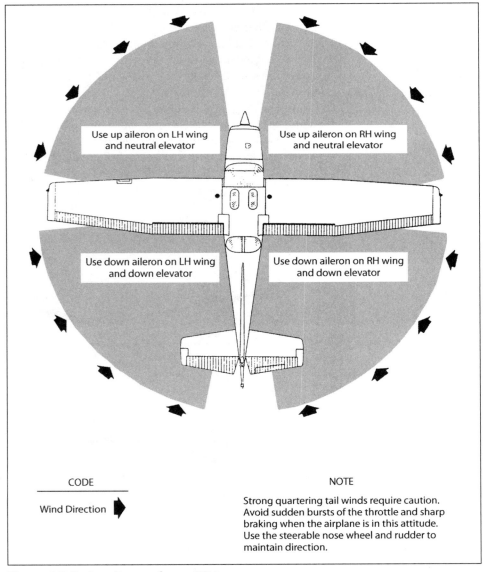

Figure 6-7. Taxiing diagram, from a POH.

Although the tricycle landing gear has made taxiing much safer and easier, you will still need to exercise caution at all times. Figures 6-5 and 6-6 show control deflections as they would apply to either landing gear type.

This matter of using controls in taxiing may be quite confusing at first, but just visualize what you want the wind to do when it strikes a particular control surface and go on from there. After a while it'll become second nature.

Figure 6-7 gives the control deflections as shown in a *Pilot's Operating Handbook*.

Taxi Signals

Figure 6-8 shows the signals you might get when being directed by a line attendant. The main thing is to keep the speed down very low when taxiing close to aircraft or other objects so that you can respond quickly to the signals (or stop on your own).

Another helpful hint, when taxiing a high-wing airplane among other high-wing airplanes while the sun is out and high, is to look down at the *shadows* of the two airplanes' wing tips to get a better picture of how far apart they are. It's pretty hard to look out directly at your and the other airplane's wing tips to judge the distance between them. If in doubt anytime before taxiing in tight quarters, shut the engine down and get a taxi director and/or people to "walk your wing" (walk with

Figure 6-8. Taxi signals. You should be well familiar with these signals, both as a director or directee. (From the *Aeronautical Information Manual*)

each wing tip as you start back up and taxi slowly, to watch for possible collision hazards). Sometimes, after a lot of car driving experience, people who are just starting to fly forget that there are 18- or 20-foot "projections" on each side of the cabin. You may decide to shut down and manually pull or push the airplane past the danger spot.

Brakes

Most airplanes have separately-controlled brakes for each main wheel. Your plane may have either heel brakes or toe brakes; that is, the pedal is operated by your heel or toe. The *toe brake* is a part of each of the rudder pedals and is applied by bending your foot so that the ball or your toes apply the pressure (Figure 6-9). You will taxi with your heels on the floor until the brake is needed. Then slide your foot up and apply brakes along with the rudder. The brakes are hydraulic, similar in action to those in your car except you aren't able to brake one wheel at a time in the car.

The *heel brake* is usually a cheaper, mechanical brake and is found only on older airplanes. The pedals are located under the rudder pedal and slightly toward the inside of the pedal. Instead of using hydraulic pressure to do the braking, the heel brake usually has a steel cable running from the pedal to its wheel. It is used by placing your heels on the pedals as shown in Figure 6-10 and applying pressure.

Don't use brakes for taxiing unless you have to. There will be days when you have to taxi crosswind in a tailwheel type for a long distance with the wind so strong that opposite rudder won't be enough (Figure 6-11). In many cases you can help steering by applying short bursts of power to help the rudder and tailwheel do the job. Obviously, any blasting of the rudder must be of short duration. You don't want to take off except on the runway. If none of these work, you may have to use downwind braking from time to time.

After continued usage, the brake may get hot and fade out completely, and you're worse off than when you started. If it's that windy, it would be best to use brakes or whatever else is needed to get back to the hangar and lock the plane in it.

The brakes are used for stopping the plane at slow speeds, holding it at a standstill, and making a tight turn.

If you have to make a tight turn, use full rudder and then apply brake. Never lock a wheel to turn the plane. This is hard on tires. If you get in a spot requiring a locked-wheel turn, stop the engine, get out, and push the plane around. An easy way to lose friends is to start the engine on the ramp, jam on full throttle, and brake to make a jazzy turn. The pilot whose plane is being blasted by your propwash and flying gravel is going to take a dim view of your taxi technique.

Figure 6-9. The toe brakes.

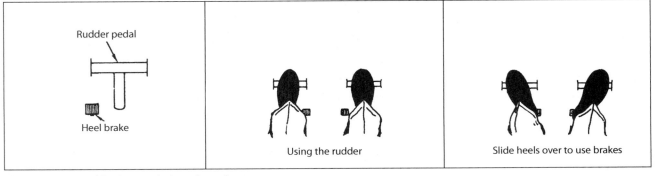

Figure 6-10. Heel brakes are being phased out.

Figure 6-11. Taxiing in a strong direct crosswind (tailwheel type).

Don't jam on both brakes quickly at the same time! You don't have to be an aeronautical engineer to figure out what would happen if you did. You may get away with it in a tricycle-gear plane, but even in this it could throw a great stress on the nosewheel assembly and slide the tires.

Don't depend on the brakes — they may fail when least expected. In a congested area, taxi so that the plane will slow down immediately when the throttle is closed. There's nothing more disconcerting than to come roaring up to somebody's $100,000 airplane at the gas pit, applying brakes, and feeling that sickening mushiness as they fail. This is a time when you wish you had a ceremonial sword to fall on — and as quickly as possible.

Don't taxi with a lot of power and use brakes to keep the speed down. The brakes will burn up very quickly. This seems to be one of the most common faults of students' taxiing. Many people flew for years before brakes became universal for airplanes, so don't become dependent on them.

Your plane will probably have a parking brake. The instructor will show you how to use it and will warn you that it is sometimes unreliable and that it is best to chock the wheels or tie the plane down if you have to leave it for any period of time.

A type of brake used on some older tricycle-gear airplanes consists of a hand brake that operates both brakes simultaneously when pressure is applied. This system, when used in conjunction with the steerable nosewheel, also allows small-radius turns. This system requires a short period of transition for pilots not accustomed to using a hand brake.

Some Important Notes

You should check the brake effectiveness immediately as power is added and the airplane starts to move out of the parking spot. You can see if they are working *before* picking up speed and boring into something expensive.

When approaching the airport for landing, briefly press the brake pedals to check for firmness. If the pedals feel mushy or one or both "go to the floor," you are warned about possible braking problems *before* you are on the ground and running out of runway. You may decide to go to another airport with longer runways.

Figure 6-12 is from the *Aeronautical Information Manual* (FAA) and shows holding position markings (sometimes called "hold short" lines). These mark the boundaries between the taxiway and the runway and shouldn't be crossed until you've ascertained that there is no traffic on the final approach (non-tower airport) or the tower has cleared you onto the active runway for the takeoff phase (controlled airport). Before flying into a controlled field, thoroughly review the airport signage in AIM Chapter 2, or review ASA's signage reference card.

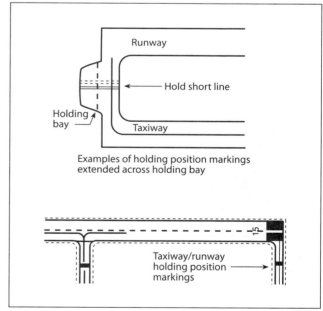

Figure 6-12. Taxiway holding position markings (arrows). The instructor will also review taxi, runway, and other signs, particularly at towered airports. (From the *Aeronautical Information Manual*)

7

Pretakeoff or Cockpit Check

The pretakeoff check is the last chance you'll have of finding something wrong with the airplane before the flight, so it should be a thorough one. In the preflight check on the line it was found that the airplane looked okay; here you will find out if the airplane *operates* okay (Figure 7-1). Following is a general look at a carburetor-equipped trainer, but you should always use the manufacturer's pretakeoff checklist for the airplane, whether carburetor or fuel injected.

Procedure

1. *Taxi to the warm-up spot by the runway and turn the plane into the wind.* The modern air-cooled engine is designed to operate in the air, and the less it runs on the ground the better off it is. It's better to turn into the wind when you operate it on the ground. Don't have your tail pointed across the runway when you make the run-up. Your propwash could give landing planes some problems.

2. *Run the engine up to about 1,000 rpm and leave it there while you check the controls.* This gives the engine a chance to be warming and smoothing while you run through the rest of the cockpit check. If you are flying a plane with an electrical system, it's a good idea to run the rpm up to where the alternator is effective, usually at about 800–1,200 rpm. The days are gone when a pilot sat on the end of the runway and took a lot of time warming up the engine. It's possible to damage an engine by prolonged ground runs. When you finish the cockpit check and the engine will take the throttle smoothly, take off.

3. *Check the ailerons by moving the wheel or stick to the left and say to yourself, "Wheel to the left, left aileron up, right aileron down."* Look at both ailerons. Move the wheel in the opposite direction and watch how the ailerons move. *DON'T JUST WIGGLE 'EM TO SEE IF THEY MOVE FREELY—MAKE SURE THEY MOVE IN THE RIGHT DIRECTION.* Aileron cable arrangements may have been reversed by mechanics who replaced them. If you take off with the ailerons reversed (turning the wheel to the left makes the plane bank to the right), a crash is almost certain to occur before you realize what's happening.

4. *Move the wheel through its full backward and forward range.* (Wheel back, elevator up, etc.) Look back at the elevators and check the elevator trim tab to see that it is neutral. Check the trim tab control setting in the cockpit to see that it coincides with

Figure 7-1. A thorough pretakeoff check is vital to a safe flight. (Sounds rather pompous, eh?) Do it anyway!

the actual setting of the tab. If your plane has an adjustable stabilizer, look back to check its actual setting with the stabilizer indication in the cockpit. For future reference (in case you are at a strange field and the indicator is broken) you might check the number of turns of the cockpit trim control from either full-up or full-down that is required to get the neutral position. Obviously this technique should be necessary only on a temporary basis; the indicator should be repaired at the earliest possible time. It's considered good practice by many pilots to roll the elevator tab or adjustable stabilizer control through its full travel (up and down) to check for possible binding (especially important in freezing weather); at any rate make sure it's in the correct setting for takeoff.

5. *You checked the rudder control while taxiing, but look back and move it again for full play*. In some tricycle-gear airplanes you will not be able (and shouldn't try) to move the rudder while the plane is stationary. But you should have some idea of rudder control reaction during the process of taxiing. For airplanes with controllable rudder trim, this would be the time to check the setting for takeoff.

6. *Check the flaps for operation and equal deflection if you haven't done so during the preflight check*. Of course, the trainer you're flying could easily be landed without them, but it's better to find out now that they don't work than to suddenly discover it when trying to land on the shortest runway in three counties. If your flaps don't pass the test, taxi back and get them fixed. If you wait to try them in the air for landing, you might find that only one will extend. (And no student pilot should be doing slow rolls on final approach.)

7. *Start on the left side of the instrument panel and check each instrument as you move from left to right*. There may be a slight variation of this order of checking for your particular airplane, and you may not have some of the instruments mentioned.

   a. The *airspeed indicator* should be reading zero, or well below the stalling speed.

   b. The *attitude indicator* small reference airplane should be set as close to the actual attitude of your airplane as possible.

   c. Set the *altimeter* and check *both hands* for proper field elevation setting. Too many pilots look only at the hundred-foot hand and set the altimeter wrong—particularly after a large change in atmospheric pressure. Notice that the short (thousand-foot) hand in Figure 3-2 also registers approximately 720 feet. This gives you a double check.

Figure 7-2. Use care in setting the heading indicator to the magnetic compass.

   d. When taxiing you should have noted the reactions of the *needle in the turn and slip* (left turn, needle to the left, etc.) or turn coordinator. This naturally assumes that the instrument is powered by an engine-driven vacuum pump or is electrically powered. If it is venturi-driven, it shouldn't be operating when you taxi because if it does, you've been taxiing quite a few knots too fast.

   e. The *heading indicator* is set with the *magnetic compass*. (Check that the compass is reading right for your approximate heading.) Some instructors recommend setting the heading indicator after the airplane is lined up with the runway on known runway headings; this can give a double check of the magnetic compass. Take a good look at Figure 7-2. The heading indicator has been set incorrectly because the pilot automatically set its lubber, or reference, line to relatively match that of the magnetic compass. The pilot thinks that the heading indicator was set to about 260° when actually it was about 280°. Say the compass reading to yourself and set *that* number on the heading indicator.

   f. The *vertical speed indicator* should be indicating a zero rate of climb.

   g. Check and set the *airplane clock*.

   h. The instructor will show you how to check the *radio* or radios if the plane has one or two and if you are in a position to receive. (In a controlled field you will have turned the radio transmitter-receiver on after start and contacted ground control for taxi clearance to your present position (*see* Chapter 21).

   i. The *tachometer* is holding steady. There are no excessive fluctuations of the instrument hand, and the engine sounds and feels okay.

   j. The *oil pressure* is in the normal operating range. (You checked it right after the engine started, and you want to make sure that it's holding.)

k. *Oil temperature* is okay. On a really cold day, you'll have a long wait if you wait for the oil temperature to come up to the operating range. Just look to see that it's not too high or whether it's beginning to move if the day isn't very cold.

l. If the airplane is a low-wing type with wing tanks, check to see if the *engine-driven fuel pump* is working properly with the *electric boost pump OFF*. The fuel pressure should stay in the normal range. Turn the electric pump ON again as an emergency standby for takeoff unless the *Pilot's Operating Handbook* specifically says otherwise. Its job is to aid in starting (for some airplanes) and to be as an emergency standby for takeoffs and landings in case the engine-driven pump fails (it, of course, would be turned on if the engine-driven pump failed anytime in flight). *After takeoff* you will normally turn it off after reaching a safe altitude. Watch the fuel pressure as you turn it off, the engine-driven pump may have failed and the electric pump may have been carrying the load. If, after shutting it off, the fuel pressure falls and the engine starts cutting out, turn the pump on and enter the traffic pattern for landing.

m. Check the *ammeter* for proper charge if the plane has an electrical system.

n. Note the *suction gauge* for normal value. (This instrument indicates the drop in atmospheric pressure—in inches of mercury—established for the vacuum-type gyro instruments by the engine-driven vacuum pump.) Most vacuum gauges in normal operation will indicate a drop in pressure of between 4 and 5 inches, but the instructor and/or *Pilot's Operating Handbook* will furnish the specifics for your airplane.

8. *Fuel* on fullest tank. Check the fuel gauges to see if the indications jibe approximately with the fuel amount shown in your visual inspection of the fuel quantity.

9. *Engine run-up:* Check *again* so that you won't blast another plane behind you, then run the engine up to 1,800 rpm or that recommended by the manufacturer and check *each magneto.* Turn the switch from BOTH to R (right magneto only). Watch the tachometer for an rpm drop. You are allowed a 75 to 125 rpm drop, depending on the airplane. (If the rpm drops more than is allowable, it's best to take the plane back to the hangar.) Turn the switch back to BOTH and watch it pick up. This gives you a double check on the rpm loss.

Turn the switch from BOTH to L, or left, and watch for the drop. Now turn back to BOTH and

watch the rise. Make sure the switch is on BOTH after you check the mags. Compare the rpm drops.

Pilot's Operating Handbooks give both a maximum allowable drop on each magneto and a maximum allowable difference between mag drops. For instance, one airplane cites a maximum drop of 150 rpm for each magneto or a maximum of 75 rpm drop differential between the two.

When you turn the switch to LEFT, the right magneto is grounded out and the engine is running on the left magneto only. Since one spark plug does not give the smooth burning of the mixture in a cylinder as that which occurs with both plugs firing, a drop in rpm is expected (and the limits are given by the manufacturer). If you switch to one of the mags and the engine does as well (no drop) as it did on BOTH, you are probably still running on both mags (a ground wire is off or the ignition switch is bad). Make sure this is reported so that no one can be hurt if they move the prop with the "hot" mag still in action. Remember, at these earlier stages, anything unusual on the preflight or pretakeoff check should be reported to an instructor or mechanic immediately. If you should inadvertently go to the OFF position while checking the mags, close the throttle (to prevent a backfire) before turning the switch back on. You'll usually have time to close the throttle *and* turn the switch on before the engine dies.

Occasionally, you'll have an excessive drop in rpm that is caused by fouled spark plugs. On some makes of engines, the left magneto is more susceptible to this problem than the right because it feeds the bottom plugs on *all* of the cylinders and the bottom plugs are more likely to be fouled by oil. (The right magneto fires all of the top plugs in these engines.) This plug problem is most likely to be present if the plane has been sitting idle for a long period or if the piston rings are worn. The scarcity of grade 80 fuel, necessitating the use of grade 100, has caused plug fouling by lead deposits. On other makes of engines, the right magneto fires the *left top* and *right bottom* plugs. (And, of course, the left magneto fires the *right top* and *left bottom*.) You might check with your instructor on the ignition setup for your particular airplane.

If your plane has a mixture control, it is often possible to clear a fouled plug by leaning the mixture during the run-up. This causes the temperature in the cylinder to rise enough to "burn out" the trouble. Needless to say, this treatment can be overdone from the engine's viewpoint. You are better off at your point of experience to taxi back to have a mechanic look at the problem.

Don't make your run-up over loose gravel because the propeller will pick it up and will be damaged. (If you doubt the "picking up" ability of a prop, watch when an airplane is sitting over a puddle of water with the engine running; a minor waterspout will result.)

10. While at 1,800 rpm, pull the carburetor heat ON. Watch for a drop of about 100 rpm, showing that the warm air is getting into the engine, cutting down its power, and that the carburetor heat is working. Leave the carburetor heat on for 10 seconds. If the rpm suddenly increases during that time, it means that you picked up carb ice since starting up and warns you that icing conditions exist for this flight. (The heat cleared it up—temporarily.) Push the heat OFF for the takeoff, since it will cut down on the power available. If carburetor icing conditions are bad, you can leave it ON until the throttle is full open for the takeoff. At fields of high elevation with the mixture in full-rich and carburetor heat full ON, you'll find that takeoff power is practically nonexistent. The actual high density-altitude (the air is less dense), plus a full-rich mixture setting, *plus* the even more lowered density of the warm air from the carburetor heat can cut down power drastically, as noted in Chapter 4. Under these conditions, you would need to lean the mixture before takeoff, per your POH.

11. Close the *throttle* and check the *idle rpm* with the carburetor heat ON to see if the engine operates properly in this condition, which may be the same as found on the latter part of the approach when the runway is "made." If the engine wants to quit or runs roughly, you should have it checked by a mechanic because the propeller will windmill in flight even when the engine is dead and would mask the problem. It would be a shock to need to add power to avoid that cow that just sauntered out on the runway and find that the engine had already quit when you closed the throttle and you have no power available. If the recommended landing procedure for your airplane is not to use carb heat, check the idle with it OFF. Idle rpm should be between 500 and 700 and the engine should idle without loping. If you didn't lock the primer after starting, the engine will draw raw gas through the primer system and will tend to load up and quit at idle. Check the primer control for security.

Push the carb heat OFF for takeoff for the same reasons noted in item 10.

Set the power to about 1,000 rpm to help keep the plugs from fouling with lead.

As noted at the beginning of the chapter, your airplane may have fuel injection so some of the comments and suggestions about carburetor heat may not apply. Again, the main thing is to always use the manufacturers checklist for either type of fuel system. For more details on fuel injection look at Appendix B, Page B-5.

12. If the field is short or if you so desire, hold *brakes* and make a *full-power run-up*. With experience (and word from the instructor) you'll be able to see what is normal for a "static" rpm indication (no windmill effects because of forward speed). (Don't do this over dirt, sand, or gravel.)

13. *Make sure the door(s) or canopy is closed and latched.* Quite a stir can be created by the sudden opening of a door just after lift-off. *Check with your instructor about possible procedures if this should occur.* (In addition to specifics for your airplane, the instructor will tell you that maintaining control of the airplane is *first, last,* and *always* when a door comes open.) Assure yourself that your seat is latched securely; you don't want to slide away from the controls at a critical point during the takeoff.

14. a. At tower (controlled) airports, switch to the tower frequency and, when you have finished the Pretakeoff check, advise them you are ready for takeoff. *Never* taxi onto a runway at a controlled airport without permission. Readback the tower's instructions using your airplane's registration and the runway number. Usually the instructions will be one of these three:

1) *Hold position* or *Hold short:* Which means you are not to cross the hold short line onto the runway (Figure 6-12). Reply example: "November Seven Five Five Seven Lima, holding short of runway two-four."

2) *Taxi into position and hold:* Which means taxi onto the runway, line-up and wait. Remember, you are not cleared for takeoff. This clearance is usually given because of other traffic or possible wake turbulence (Chapter 13).

3) *Cleared for takeoff:* You give a last check for traffic, open the throttle and takeoff.

Note: Always check the runway number before you taxi onto it and, since tower personnel can make mistakes, too, *always* check for traffic.

b. At uncontrolled (non-tower) airports, announce your intentions on the appropriate frequency (see Pages 21-7 through 21-9) and check for landing and departing traffic. Check for traffic *both* ways—someone might be landing or taking off downwind.

Part Two
Presolo 2

8

Effects of Controls

Most of your first flight will consist of finding out how the various controls affect the airplane. The instructor will climb the plane to a safe altitude (at least 1,500 feet above the ground) and demonstrate the use of each of the flight controls. You'll use the individual controls to learn how the plane reacts to each and see that they are most often used together in what is known as "coordinated" flight.

The instructor will also trim the airplane for straight and level flight and show you how the plane flies by itself, demonstrating its natural stability. During the flight the instructor will also show you the practice areas and point out outstanding landmarks and their reference to the airport.

Bumpy air on this first flight may cause you to be tense at first. The "bumps" are caused by uneven heating of the earth's surface. A plowed field reflects heat; a forest or water area absorbs it. As you fly over the terrain, the rising air currents are of different velocities, so the plane rises and drops slightly. As the air rises, it is cooled and soon becomes stable and smooth. The altitude at which this occurs varies from day to day, but on a hot summer day you may climb to 6,000 or 8,000 feet before finding smooth air.

Elevators

The elevators control the pitching motion of the plane and are your airspeed control (Figure 8-1). Under normal flying conditions (the plane is right-side up), pressing back on the wheel moves the elevators "up." The relative wind forces the tail downward, the nose moves up, and *if you started with sufficient power and airspeed*, the plane starts to climb. Conversely, if the wheel is pressed forward, the nose goes down and the plane dives. If the plane is inverted and you press the wheel back, obviously the plane will not climb but will dive.

The best way to look at elevator movement, however, is to think of it as follows: wheel (or stick) back, the nose moves toward you; wheel forward, the nose moves away from you. This works for all attitudes.

At a low airspeed you might still think you can climb, or climb at a greater rate, by pulling the nose up, but you find that the up-elevators don't "elevate" the airplane but just decrease the airspeed. The nose moves up, *but* the increased drag causes the airplane to climb less or even start sinking! Power makes the airplane climb.

Let's take a situation such as the one you'll face when you're first introduced to the normal climb.

Figure 8-1. Elevators control movement about the lateral axis (pitch).

You're flying along at cruise power and airspeed and want to climb. Back pressure is gently exerted on the wheel until the nose moves to the normal climb position relative to the horizon, as shown by your instructor. (You will also open the throttle to climb power.)

Okay, when you applied back pressure on the wheel, the elevators moved up. The relative wind moving past the elevators results in the tail moving downward (Figure 8-2). Since the wings are rigidly attached to the fuselage, they are rotated as well. This results in an increase in angle of attack (and drag), the plane starts slowing up to the speed for best rate of climb, you apply climbing power, and the plane climbs. *This is the technique for a steady climb.* You'll find you can "zoom" the airplane, that is, get a short-term climb by trading airspeed for altitude, using the momentum of cruise speed. In fact, because of this excess energy available at cruise speed, the airplane will start to climb as soon as you start to ease the nose up. (You will see that the airspeed will start decreasing immediately.)

The job of the elevators in the climb is that of airspeed control—to get to the speed at which the greatest excess horsepower is available, which is the speed for best rate of climb. As a rule of thumb for most trainers, this will be found at about 1.4–1.5 times the flaps-up, power-off stall speed. (This is for calibrated airspeed, or CAS. You might review this in Chapter 3.)

To repeat: The elevators control the angle of attack (and indirectly the airspeed) of the airplane. Because most lightplanes don't have angle of attack indicators, you'll be watching the airspeed indicator for the plane's reactions to your use of the elevators. Therefore, the elevators are considered to directly control the airspeed.

Power (or lack of it) gives the required performance. Suppose a light trainer uses the same airspeed for best rate of climb speed and recommended glide speed. You would maintain with the elevators the same airspeed for both maneuvers; the difference in performance (climb or glide) would be in the amount of power used (climb power or idle). Or you could fly straight and level at that same speed by using some power. So, one of the things you'll learn is that the "elevators" are really misnamed; everybody uses the term, though, so it's a little late to change it. Probably it started back in the early days of flying when it was believed that this was their function—to "elevate" the airplane.

The trainer you will be flying may have a "stabilator" or "flying tail" instead of a stabilizer-elevator combination. The entire horizontal tail of the plane moves and acts as a stabilizer or elevators, as required. The principle of operation is the same—the "stabilator" is an angle of attack and airspeed control and, like the elevator, has a trim tab to help the pilot correct for various airplane loadings and airspeeds.

Elevator Trim Tab

Elevator or stabilator trim tabs are used to hold elevator or stabilator pressure for the pilot. If an unusually heavy load was placed in a back baggage compartment, the tail would be heavy, the nose would want to rise, and you would have to hold forward pressure on the wheel to keep from slowing up. The trim tab is controlled from the cockpit, and during flight the plane can be trimmed for climb, glide, or straight and level. Some planes use an adjustable stabilizer for this purpose.

Larger planes require use of the trim tab or adjustable stabilizer when speed or power is changed, but your instructor probably will have you fly all maneuvers *at first* with the plane trimmed for straight and level so that the varying control pressures can be felt. Some students get in the habit of trimming the plane full nose-up for landing, but this can lead to difficulties if a go-around is required. The application of power may cause the nose to rise so sharply that the plane is stalled before the nose can be lowered. This will be discussed further in Chapter 14.

Returning to the example of a heavy load in the baggage compartment (Figure 8-3): The nose wants to go up; the pilot holds the nose at the proper position and trims the plane "nose down" until there is no pressure against the wheel. When the tab control is moved to the "nose-down" position, the tab on the elevator moves up. The relative wind strikes the tab, forcing the elevator down for the pilot. (This is strictly an example; you'll read later that the baggage compartment is not to be overloaded.)

Rudder

The rudder controls the yawing motion of the airplane (Figure 8-4). Push the left rudder pedal and the nose yaws to the left; push the right and the opposite occurs.

Figure 8-2. Relative wind at the instant of the plane's rotation.

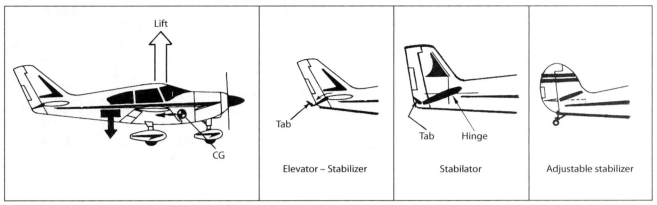

Figure 8-3. Pilot has to hold the wheel forward because the plane wants to nose upward. (Center of gravity is moved aft.) The trim tab or the adjustable stabilizer does it for you. "Nosedown" trim is set in all cases here.

The prime purpose of the rudder is to overcome the adverse yaw of the aileron. In certain maneuvers such as the slip and crosswind landing, ailerons and rudder are used opposite to each other, but 99.99 percent of the time they are used together in the air.

On tailwheel-type airplanes the rudder is connected to the tailwheel by coil springs, and this is the main factor in ground steering. The tricycle-gear types have a mechanical linkage between the rudder pedals and the nosewheel so that ground steering depends even less on the rudder. (In the tailwheel airplane, sometimes a blast of slipstream striking the rudder can help in turning; for tricycle-gear types it has little effect.) "Rudder" is another term that is misleading. A rudder of a boat is the main tool for turning. An airplane's rudder is not the primary control used for turning; in normal flight it is an auxiliary to the ailerons.

However, you'll find that by application of rudder in the air it is possible to turn. By pushing the rudder pedal you skid the airplane, causing one wing to move faster than the other (Figure 8-5). This added lift causes the airplane to bank and the rest of the turn is normal. It can be rolled out in the same manner, as will be demonstrated to you.

Rudder Trim

In Chapter 2, the "bendable" rudder tab was discussed; some of the later model trainers have a rudder bungee or tab that is controllable from the cockpit. You can adjust the rudder trim as necessary in flight to get the desired reaction. In these airplanes, one of your jobs during the pretakeoff check at the end of the runway will be to set the trim properly. (It's set to a "nose-right" indication to help you on that right rudder to overcome "torque" on takeoff and climb.)

Ailerons

The ailerons roll the airplane. If the stick is moved to the left (in an airplane with a wheel, the wheel is turned to the left), the left aileron moves up and the right aileron moves down. The relative wind strikes the control surfaces as shown and the airplane rolls to the left (Figure 8-6).

The aileron tab(s) for trimming the airplane laterally was discussed in Chapter 2 (Figure 2-13).

Figure 8-4. The rudder controls movement about the vertical axis (yaw).

The plane will continue to roll as long as the ailerons are deflected. In fact, this generally would be the way you'd do a slow roll—plus the use of other controls to aid the process.

Ailerons are used to bank the airplane. The airplane banks in order to turn. There's nothing in the world that gives less traction than air. When a rudder pedal is pushed, the nose yaws around, but the plane tries to continue in a straight line. True, it would gradually turn because the yawing would speed up one wing, giving it more lift and banking it, but it would be an inefficient and uncomfortable process. When the airplane is banked, the lift force acts as a centripetal, or holding, force as well and can be considered to be broken down into two parts—this is a legal assumption according to engineering mechanics (Figure 8-7).

The centripetal force (or horizontal component of lift) then helps the plane to stay in the turn. It is the force acting against the tendency of the airplane to continue in a straight line. *So in order to turn properly, the airplane must be banked.*

Figure 8-5. Banking the airplane by rudder alone.

Figure 8-6. The ailerons control movement about the longitudinal axis (roll).

Figure 8-7. In a turn, lift is broken down into the vertical component (lift working against weight) and the horizontal component (which turns the airplane).

9

The Four Fundamentals

During the first flight, after you are familiar with the effects of the controls, the instructor will introduce you to one or more of the Four Fundamentals: *the turn, the normal climb, the normal glide,* and *straight and level.* These are the basic maneuvers of flying. You'll be using them or a combination of them for the rest of your flying career, so get them down pat now.

The Turn

In the discussion of ailerons, it was found that the plane must be banked in order to turn in the air. Fine—all you have to do is jam the wheel over in the direction you want and you turn that way. *Not so fast!* There's more to it than that. Let's see what happens when you give it left aileron (that is, you turn the wheel or move the stick to the left).

The lift and drag vectors (Figure 9-1) show that although the wheel is turned to the left there's more drag on the right because of the down aileron. The plane rolls to the left but the nose yaws to the right. The plane will slip to the left and finally set up a balanced turn. The right yaw you got is called "adverse aileron yaw," and the rudder is used to correct for this. *The rudder is used any time the ailerons are used in a turn.* Most planes have a differential aileron movement

(the aileron moves farther up than down) and aileron designs that decrease this initial yaw effect.

To make a turn to the left, left aileron and left rudder are used smoothly together. As soon as the desired amount of bank is reached, the controls are neutralized. The wheel is moved smoothly back to the neutral position, the pressure on the control wheel is eased off, and rudder pressure is no longer needed. This is called "neutralizing" the controls—the relaxing of exerted pressure on them. This term will be used throughout this chapter. Air pressure should streamline the control surfaces when the control wheel and rudder pedal pressures are relaxed. If the controls are not neutralized, the turn will become steeper and steeper.

You're in the turn. If you let go of the controls the plane will turn indefinitely (or at least as long as the fuel lasts) *except for one small detail.*

Lift is considered to act perpendicularly to the wingspan. Consider an airplane in straight and level flight where lift equals weight. Assume the airplane's weight to be 2,000 pounds.

In Figure 9-2A everything's great—lift equals weight. If the plane is banked 60° as in Figure 9-2B, things are not so rosy. The weight's value or direction does not change. It's still 2,000 pounds downward. The lift, however, is acting at a different angle. The vertical component of lift is only 1,000 pounds, since the cosine of 60° is 0.500 (60° is used for convenience here; you certainly won't be doing a bank that steep in the earlier part of your training). With such an unbalance, the plane loses altitude. The answer, Figure 9-2C, is to increase the lift vector to 4,000 pounds so that the vertical component is 2,000 pounds. This is done by increasing the angle of attack. Back pressure is applied to the elevators to keep the nose up. To establish a turn to the left:

1. Apply left aileron and left rudder smoothly.
2. As the bank increases, start applying back pressure smoothly.

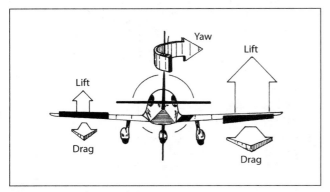

Figure 9-1. Adverse aileron yaw.

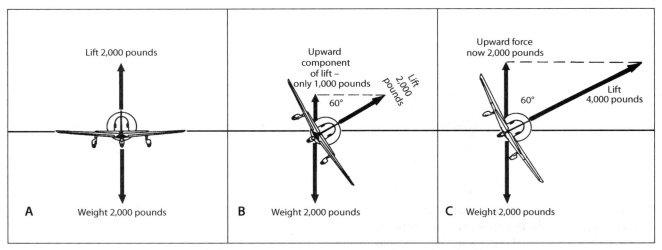

Figure 9-2. The vertical component of lift must be equal to weight in a constant-altitude turn.

3. When the desired amount of bank is reached, the ailerons and rudder are neutralized, but the back pressure is held as long as you are in the bank. Now you can turn indefinitely.

To roll out of the left turn:
1. Apply right aileron and right rudder.
2. As the bank decreases, ease off the back pressure.
3. When the plane is level, the ailerons and rudder are neutralized and there should be no more back pressure.

If the rudder and aileron are not coordinated properly, the plane will skid or slip. The skid occurs when *too much* rudder is used. You'll try to slide toward the outside of the turn as you do when a car turns a corner. The slip is a result of *too little* rudder, and you'll feel that you are sliding toward the inside of the turn. These errors can be felt and give you an idea of the expression "seat of the pants flying." Students have been known to wear out the seats of perfectly good pants, sliding around during the presolo phase.

If in our example of the 60° bank, you roll out level but don't get rid of the extra 2,000 pounds of lift you have, obviously the airplane will accelerate upward (the "up" and "down" forces will no longer be in balance). Maybe your idea of coordination is that demonstrated by a ballroom dancer, but it's necessary in flying too. Think of control *pressures* rather than movement. The smoother your pressures, the better your control of the airplane.

If you aren't particularly interested in the trigonometric approach to back pressure, Figure 9-3 gives another approach.

Load Factors in the Turn

The turn introduces a new idea. It is possible to bank so steeply that the wings cannot support the airplane. The lift must be increased so drastically that the critical angle of attack is exceeded, and the plane stalls. In the previous example at 60° of bank, it was found that our effective wing area was halved; therefore, each square

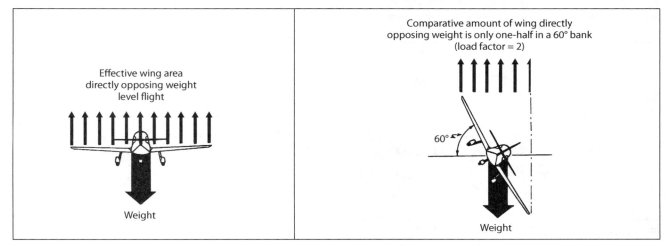

Figure 9-3. The effects of bank angle on the amount of lift that is directly opposing weight.

foot of wing area had to support twice its normal load. This is called a *load factor of 2*. A plane in normal, straight and level flight has a load factor of 1, or 1 "g." You have this same 1 g load on your body at that time. Mathematically speaking, the load factor in the turn is a function of the secant of the angle of bank. The secant varies from 1 at 0° to infinity at 90°; so to maintain altitude indefinitely in a constant 90° bank, an infinite amount of *lift* is required—and this is not available.

For those interested in the mathematics of the problem, the following is presented.

It is interesting to note that the stalling speed of the aircraft can be figured for each degree of bank. In the airplane weighing 2,000 pounds and having a wing area of 200 square feet, the wing loading is 10 pounds per square foot. With a load factor of 2, the wing loading is

$$20 \text{ pounds per square foot} = \frac{\text{weight}}{\text{wing area}} \text{ or } \left[\frac{W}{S}\right]$$

Using the equation

$$L = C_L S \frac{\rho}{2} V^2$$

and solving for V (stall), you find that the stall is at $C_{L MAX}$, so that value would be used in the equation:

$$V_{STALL} = \sqrt{\frac{L}{C_{L MAX} S \frac{\rho}{2}}}$$

But in level flight L = W so that

$$V_{STALL} = \sqrt{\frac{W}{C_{L MAX} S \frac{\rho}{2}}}$$

And since $C_{L MAX}$ (the maximum coefficient of lift), S and ρ are considered to be constants for a given situation, the new stall speed is directly proportional to the square root of the change in the wing loading W ÷ S. Then V_{STALL} is a function of the square root of the load factor. So the stall speed in a 60° bank is $\sqrt{2}$ times that of the stall speed in level flight. If the plane stalls at 50 K in level flight, its stall speed in a 60° bank is $50 \times \sqrt{2} = 50 \times 1.414 = 70.7$ K. *All of this is assuming that you hold enough back pressure to maintain level flight* (Figure 9-4). If no back pressure is held, the airplane will be in a diving turn, there is still a load factor of 1, and the stall speed is not increased. If you make this kind of turn, it is wise to have a lot of altitude. Needless to say, the Federal Aviation Administration frowns on such capers at low altitudes because you are likely to leave pock marks on surface structures when you hit.

Figure 9-4. Choose an angle of bank (in this case, 55°). Multiply the corresponding number (1.32) times the wings-level (normal) stall speed to get the stall speed at this angle of bank.

Simply stated—if you want to find the stalling speed of your plane in a level turn, either of the following will apply:

$$V_{STALL} \text{ in the turn} = V_{STALL} \text{ (level) } \sqrt{\text{load factor}}$$

or

$$V_{STALL} \text{ in the turn} = V_{STALL} \text{ (level) } \sqrt{\text{secant of the angle of bank}}$$

Figure 9-5 is a diagram of the increase of stall speeds with bank. The numbers have been rounded off, but note that the stall speed increase with bank for any flap setting increases at the ratio indicated by Figure 9-4. Gross weight (maximum certificated weight) is used, but for lighter weights, the multiplier for bank increase would be the same. (The airplane will always stall in a 60° bank at a speed of 1.414 times the wings-level stall speed whether it's given in mph or knots.)

Now back to the important, practical side of flying. Putting it simply: The stall speed goes up in the constant altitude turn; and the steeper the bank, the faster the stall speed jumps up, as can be seen in Figures 9-4 and 9-5. The load factors just discussed are "positive" load factors and are attained by pulling the wheel back, causing you to be pressed down in the seat. A negative

Figure 9-5. Stall speed increases with bank.

=Power Off= STALLING SPEEDS MPH — CAS				
Gross Weight 1600 lbs.	**ANGLE OF BANK**			
CONDITION	**0°**	**20°**	**40°**	**60°**
Flaps UP	55	57	63	78
Flaps 20°	49	51	56	70
Flaps 40°	48	49	54	67

load factor is applied if the control wheel is pushed forward abruptly, and in this case you feel "light" and tend to leave the seat. Lightplanes are generally stressed to take a maximum positive load factor varying from 3.8 to 6, and a negative load factor of between 1.52 and 3, depending on the make and model. Both you and the plane are able to stand more positive g's than negative. Positive or negative load factors can be imposed on the plane by sharp up or down gusts as well as by the pilot's handling of the elevators. (*See* Chapter 23.)

Review of the Turn

1. Apply aileron and rudder pressure in the desired direction of turn.
2. Begin back pressure.
3. When desired steepness of bank is reached, neutralize the ailerons and rudder but hold enough back pressure to keep the nose at the correct place on the horizon; turn until you get ready to roll out. Check the nose, wings, and altimeter for a smooth level turn.

The Rollout

1. Apply opposite ailerons and rudder. Gradually ease off the back pressure as the wings become level.
2. As the wings become level, neutralize the ailerons and rudder (the back pressure will be completely off at this point).

Ride with the turn. You'll have a tendency at first to lean against the turn. Remember that in a proper turn, the resulting forces will hold you upright in the seat.

If you are in a side-by-side airplane, the position of the nose seems different in left and right turns (Figure 9-6). You will be sitting to the left of the center line of the fuselage so that when the airplane is turning left the nose will seem high and the tendency is to lose altitude as you "correct" for this. In a right turn, the nose will appear too low and the tendency will be to gain altitude. Your instructor will demonstrate the proper nose position for climbs, glides, turns, and straight and level and may also demonstrate that elevator trim can be used to maintain back pressure in an extended turn situation (retrimming as the airplane rolls out). Figure 9-6 shows the views from the left seat during left and right constant altitude turns.

Coordination Exercises

After you are familiar with the idea of the turn, the instructor may have you do what is known as a coordination exercise. This consists of heading the plane at a point on the horizon and rolling from left to right bank, and so forth, without letting the nose wander from the point. It is a very good way to discover how much control pressure is needed to get the desired effect with the plane.

The beginning of the maneuver is like that of the beginning of the turn. Ailerons and rudder are used

Figure 9-6. Perspective in left and right constant altitude turns. Note that your reference (which is a point on the cowling *directly in front of you*, and not the center of the nose) is at the same position in relation to the horizon. Don't use the center of the cowling as a reference.

together. Then, before the nose has a chance to move, hold it on the point with opposite rudder. Apply opposite aileron and more opposite rudder and roll it to the other side, then repeat the process. You will find it difficult at first but will soon get the knack and be able to roll smoothly from one side to the other without the nose moving from the point.

Although in parts of the maneuver the controls are crossed and not coordinated as they are in the turn, you will find that your turns will profit by a short period of this maneuver.

The Normal Climb

Another of the Four Fundamentals is the normal climb, and at first you will practice starting it from normal cruising flight. To climb, the nose is eased up to the proper position relative to the horizon, the throttle is opened smoothly to the recommended climb power, and, as the airspeed starts to decrease, right rudder is applied to correct for torque. The recommended airspeed for best rate of climb is maintained.

You had a brief introduction to the climb in Chapter 8 when the elevators were discussed. There you noted that the elevators do not make the airplane climb; they are used to attain and maintain the *airspeed* at which the best rate of climb is found. That airspeed, engineers have found, is the one at which the greatest amount of excess horsepower is available at climb power for your airplane. (The rate of a steady climb depends on the amount of excess horsepower available.) An equation for determining rate of climb is:

$$\text{Rate of climb (fpm)} = \frac{33,000 \times \text{excess horsepower}}{\text{weight of plane}}$$

The horsepower in that equation is *thrust* horsepower, or the power being effectively developed through the propeller, as mentioned in Chapter 2. You also remember from that chapter that power is *force* times *distance per unit of time*, and 1 horsepower is equal to 550 foot-pounds per second, or 33,000 foot-pounds per minute. That's where the 33,000 in the equation comes in; it's set up for a rate of climb in *feet per minute*. By illustration, suppose your plane weighs 1,500 pounds, has an engine capable of developing 100 *brake* (or shaft) horsepower at the recommended climb power setting at a particular altitude, and the propeller is 85 percent efficient at the climb speed. This means there will be 85 *thrust* horsepower available at the climb speed. Suppose, also, that at that speed 55 *thrust* horsepower is necessary to maintain a constant altitude. This means that 30 thrust horsepower is available for use in

climbing. From the above equation we find the rate of climb to be 660 feet per minute:

$$\text{R/C (fpm)} = \frac{33,000 \times 30}{1,500} = 660 \text{ fpm}$$

So the excess thrust horsepower is working to raise a weight (the airplane) a certain vertical distance in a certain period of time (rate of climb). If no excess horsepower was available at the climb speed, the rate of climb would be zero. If you throttled back until the power being developed was less than that needed just to keep the airplane flying at a particular airspeed, a "negative" rate of climb would result; the airplane would descend at a rate proportional to your "deficit" power.

As a pilot you won't worry about excess horsepower, but you will use the recommended climb airspeed and power setting and let the rate of climb take care of itself.

The revolutions per minute of a fixed-pitch prop such as on a light trainer are affected by the airspeed. Assume you set the throttle for cruising at 2,400 rpm. If the airplane is dived, the added airspeed will give the propeller a windmilling effect and the rpm will speed up to, say, 2,500 or 2,600 rpm. If you pull the nose up for a climb, the airspeed decreases and the rpm drops below the cruising setting. Therefore, it is necessary to apply more throttle to obtain climb power (usually full open [forward] throttle for most trainers). Normal climb speed is about 1.4 to 1.5 times the stall speed and results in the best *rate of climb*. Your instructor will show you the correct climb attitude and airspeed for your particular plane (Figure 9-7).

To Climb

1. Ease the nose up to normal climb position and maintain back pressure to keep it there.
2. Increase the power to the climb value.
3. As speed drops, apply right rudder to correct for torque.
4. Don't let the nose wander during the climb or the transition to the climb.

To Level Off from the Climb

1. Ease the nose down to level flight position.
2. As speed picks up, ease off right rudder.
3. Throttle back to maintain cruise rpm.
4. Don't let the nose wander during the transition.

Probable Errors

1. Climbing too steeply—overheating the engine and actually decreasing the rate of climb.
2. Too shallow a climb—easy on the engine but not a good way to gain altitude.

Figure 9-7. The climb and level-flight attitudes. This doesn't necessarily mean that you are climbing or flying level. These are attitudes only. Power makes the difference.

3. Over- or undercorrecting for torque during the climb transition.
4. Rough transition to the climb or straight and level flight.
5. Not keeping the nose lined up on a reference point—letting it wander.

After you've gotten the feel of the controls for the climb well in hand, your instructor will have you trim the airplane for it. As you level off, the trim will have to be changed for straight and level cruising flight.

The Climbing Turn

This is a combination of the two fundamentals covered so far. It is, as the name implies, a turn while climbing.

For practice at first, the climbing turn will be executed from a straight climb; that is, establish a normal climb and then start your turn.

Make all your climbing turns very shallow (Figure 9-8). Steep banks require added back pressure (angle of attack) to keep the nose up, which sharply reduces the rate of climb because of greater drag (induced drag; *see* Chapter 2). *A 10° bank is plenty.*

Torque must be considered in making a climbing turn. *Anytime the plane is climbing, right rudder pressure or right rudder trim must be used.*

Suppose you are climbing and want to turn to the right. You are already holding right rudder, but as right aileron is applied more right rudder is needed to take care of aileron yaw, so the turn is something like the following.

Climb:
1. Back pressure.
2. Right rudder.

Figure 9-8. Keep the bank shallow in the climbing turn or else the climb will suffer.

Climbing right turn:
1. Right aileron and more right rudder—make the turn shallow.
2. More back pressure.
3. Neutralize the ailerons and return to enough right rudder to correct for torque.

Rolling out to resume the straight climb:
1. Left aileron and very little left rudder (in some planes, easing off the correction for torque may be all that is needed).
2. As the wings become level, neutralize the ailerons and get back on that right rudder.

Again, any time you make a turn it requires added back pressure.

The torque effect is as if slight left rudder was being held. In a left-climbing turn, torque will tend to skid you into a steeper bank. In a right-climbing turn, it will tend to skid you out of the turn.

When you have the climb and climbing turn idea well in mind and are able to control the aircraft in a reasonable manner, you should start the habit in your climbing turns of maintaining a constant bank and making definite 90° turns as you climb. (This will be your introduction to precision flying.)

It's best not to climb straight ahead for long periods because you can't see other airplanes over the nose. Make occasional shallow turns to each side of your "base course" or lower the nose briefly to check ahead.

The Normal Glide

The normal glide is a third fundamental and the least understood by the beginning student. The nose is not pushed *down* to glide as commonly believed, but, on the contrary, back pressure is needed to keep the glide from getting too steep.

In Figure 9-9A the airplane is trimmed for straight and level flight. The force caused by the slipstream and relative wind acting on the stabilizer just balances the force of the weight trying to pull the nose down. The plane is in balance. Pulling the throttle back to idle causes a lessening of the tail force by two factors: (1) The slipstream effect has dropped to nil because the propeller of an idling engine produces a very weak slipstream, and (2) the plane starts slowing immediately now that the drag is greater than the thrust—hence the relative wind speed decreases. (The decreased slipstream is by far the biggest factor in this nosing-down process, however. Item 2 mentioned above can be neglected for all practical purposes.)

The result is shown in Figure 9-9B. The plane noses down until the forces are balanced again. Your speed now may be higher than desired for the glide. If you want to glide at 70 K, you must slow the plane to that speed by holding back pressure so that the plane's glide attitude is something like that in Figure 9-10. Normal glide attitude in most lightplanes is only slightly

Figure 9-10. Level flight and glide attitudes.

more nose-down than the straight and level position (Figure 9-11).

Tailwheel-type airplanes are shown in Figure 9-9 and 9-10, but the tricycle-gear trainer reacts the same way.

The recommended normal glide speed gives you the most feet forward for altitude lost. For a fixed-gear trainer, the normal glide ratio is about 9:1, that is, 9 feet forward for each foot of altitude lost.

If you glide at a too-fast airspeed, the 9:1 ratio drops off to maybe only 5:1. You can tell the steep glide by sight (nose position, airspeed increase), sound (increase in pitch of sound of wind), and feel (the controls become firmer).

Trying to "stretch the glide" by pulling the nose up also causes the glide ratio to suffer. You can recognize the too-slow glide by sight (nose high), sound (decrease in wind noise), and feel (the elevator pressure feels "mushy"). You've increased the angle of attack to such a point that drag holds the plane back, but gravity is still pulling the plane down with the same force, resulting in a lower glide ratio. *So stick to that recommended glide speed.*

Figure 9-9. The airplane is designed to have a nosing down tendency when power is reduced.

Figure 9-11. Notice that the glide attitude is only slightly more nose down than that for straight and level flight.

Note: Pull the carburetor heat ON before closing the throttle in flight unless the Pilot's Operating Handbook *recommends otherwise.* Its use will be mentioned here each time the glide is covered, but your trainer and conditions may not always require it.

Assume that you are flying straight and level and want to glide:

1. Carburetor heat ON.
2. Close the throttle (to idle after 10+ seconds).
3. Hold the nose in the level flight position.
4. As the airspeed drops to normal glide speed, ease the nose down slightly to the normal glide position as shown by the instructor.
5. Clear the engine about every 200 feet of the descent. This means running the rpm up to about 1,500 and then back to idle.

You'll notice that quite a bit of back pressure is necessary to hold the nose up. The instructor may let you trim the plane for the glide. In that case, roll or move the trim until you feel no force against the wheel. Most instructors want you to get the feel of the plane and will probably only demonstrate trim in the glide at first.

To return to straight and level flight:

1. Apply power smoothly to cruise rpm as you simultaneously ease off the back pressure.
2. Push carburetor heat OFF after cruising flight is established.

With more experience you'll open the throttle up to about 100 rpm less than the cruise setting so that, when the carburetor heat is pushed OFF, the rpm will be at the cruise setting.

The altimeter appears to "lag" in the climb or glide, particularly in the glide. If you want to level off at a specific altitude, say 1,500 feet, it is wise to start the above procedure about 50 feet above that, or 1,550

feet. The plane has momentum downward that requires altitude to change—and maybe your reactions aren't perfect yet, so give yourself about 50 feet for recovery from the glide. Of course, the bigger the airplane and the faster you are descending, the more margin you'll use.

If the back pressure is not eased off as you open the throttle, the nose will rise sharply as the slipstream strikes the up-elevators. The elevators are comparatively ineffective in the glide, so you use a lot of up-elevator. When the prop blast hits all that surface, something's bound to happen.

Your instructor will later have you trim the airplane for the glide and you'll be pretty busy at first, readjusting the trim when you apply power to level off. The nose will want to rise with the addition of power, being helped very well by the nose-up trim, and in some airplanes you'll tend to underestimate the forward pressure required to keep the nose down while retrimming.

Common Errors

In starting the glide:

1. Not giving the carburetor heat enough time to work before closing the throttle.
2. Abrupt throttle movement—jerking it back to idle.
3. Holding the nose up too long, resulting in too slow a glide speed.
4. Letting the nose wander as the glide is entered.
5. Forgetting to clear the engine in the glide.

In recovery from the glide:

1. Opening the throttle abruptly.
2. Letting the nose wander.
3. Not releasing back pressure or changing trim in time the nose goes up and the plane climbs.

The carburetor heat is the first thing ON before, and the last thing OFF after, the glide.

If icing conditions are bad, the carburetor may ice enough to cause engine stoppage between the time you push the heat off and get around to opening the throttle, particularly if you are the fumbling-fingers type. Granted, this would be an unusual occurrence, but why take the chance? Do it correctly now until it becomes a habit.

Clear that engine! In the winter, the engine may cool so much after an extended glide without clearing that it won't take throttle. In the summer the engine may "load up" and quit. *If you want to see what an actual emergency landing is like, don't clear the engine.*

Your instructor will have you glide at various flap settings at the recommended landing-approach airspeed(s).

Gliding Turn

Like the climbing turn, the gliding turn is a combination of two of the Four Fundamentals. Combine the glide and the turn and you get a gliding turn. An extended steep gliding turn is called a spiral.

Probably the first thing you'll notice about the gliding turn is that the rudder seems to have lost much of its effect. Although the ailerons are ineffective in comparison with level flight, they still feel the same as they did in the climbing turn because the airspeed is approximately the same for climb and glide. The rudder, however, is suffering from lack of slipstream (Figure 9-12). Concentrate on coordination again. Use the controls so that the airplane reacts correctly.

Any time a turn is made, back pressure is required. If you have back pressure in the glide and make a turn, it will require more pressure. The principle is the same for climbing, gliding, or level turns. When the plane

Figure 9-12. The rudder and elevator get a slipstream during cruise and climb.

banks, the lift vector must be increased. If you use insufficient back pressure:

1. In the climbing turn—no climb, only turn.
2. In the level turn—turn plus a shallow dive.
3. In the gliding turn—turn plus a steeper dive.

In rolling into or out of a gliding turn, the rudder is not as effective as you've been used to because of the weaker slipstream.

Common Errors

1. Not enough back pressure in the turn—plane dives.
2. Not enough rudder on roll-in and roll-out.
3. Not easing off back pressure when rolling out—the nose comes up and the plane slows up.

Your instructor will have you make 90° gliding turns in each direction after you have a good idea of the procedure.

Straight and Level Flying

One of the most important of the Four Fundamentals is straight and level flying; some pilots have trouble even after years of experience. Nearly every student has difficulty keeping the wings level. The average student tends to stare out over the nose with the glazed gaze of a poleaxed steer. Don't try to keep the wings level by watching for the cant of the nose, because the nose line is so short that one of the wings can be down quite a way before the nose shows it. Correct straight and level flying means that you are directionally straight and longitudinally and laterally level (Figure 9-13).

The plane, if trimmed properly and left alone, will do a better job of flying than you are able to do. Many a student flies a low wing cross-country wondering about that nagging sliding sensation, then later notices a sore back.

This is what's happening. You are unconsciously holding the aileron one way or the other. A plane with a stick is flown with the right hand, and sometimes you allow the weight of your arm to pull the stick in that direction, resulting in a right slip. Because the wheel is flown with the left hand, sometimes the left aileron is slipped in.

The plane is banked and wants to turn, so you helpfully hold opposite rudder to keep the nose from moving and are now in a slip. In Figure 9-14, the resultant direction is downward and the plane starts losing altitude gradually. To stop this, you use back pressure to maintain altitude, and the controls are in the position shown in Figure 9-14. You are holding right aileron,

Figure 9-13. In straight and level flight, the airplane should be kept (1) directionally straight (no yaw), (2) longitudinally level (nose at the proper position with respect to the horizon), and (3) laterally level (the wings the same distance *above* the horizon for the high-wing craft, or the same distance *below* the horizon for the low-wing airplane).

left rudder, and up-elevator when you should be able to fly "hands off."

The instructor will show you how to trim the airplane for straight and level flight. Generally this is done as soon as you reach the assigned practice altitude. It consists of placing the nose at the correct attitude, leaving the climb power on until the expected cruise airspeed is reached (then set up cruise rpm), and trimming until the stick or wheel force against your hand is zero (the same technique as described in the normal glide).

Larger planes not only have controllable tabs for the elevators but have tabs for the rudder and ailerons as well. The pilot can trim the plane for the attitude or speed desired.

Some lightplanes have a bendable aileron tab similar to the one on the rudder as discussed in Chapter 2. If the plane has a tendency to fly wing-low at cruise, the pilot is able to bend the aileron tab so that this is corrected. The procedure is the same as used for the rudder tab. Bend the tab and fly. If further correction is needed, land, make the correction, and fly again.

Once you have established good straight and level flight, there's nothing to do but watch the plane to see that it keeps this attitude. Some students feel that they should do *something* and consequently the plane receives quite a workout.

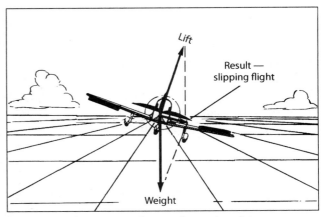

Figure 9-14. Exaggerated view of wing-low flying.

Try not to be tense, but if you are, don't worry about it. Flying is a strange experience at this point, and if you are completely relaxed you're one student in a million. However, if you are too tense the learning process slows down.

If a wing goes down momentarily, as may happen on a hot, bumpy day, bring it up with aileron and rudder together. As soon as the wings are level, neutralize the controls. If you try to use aileron alone, the plane will yaw from its heading.

Usually another "bump" will raise that wing, but this return to wings-level flight is not always immediate, so you can help the process. But don't overdo it because on bumpy days you'll be worn out in 30 minutes.

All through this book so far it has been stated that power controls altitude and that elevators are to be used to establish the proper airspeed for the maneuver involved. You will find, however, that in straight and level *cruising* flight, for minor altitude adjustments it's a lot simpler to use the elevators. For instance, if you are 50 feet low, you will exert (slight) back pressure on the wheel and regain the altitude rather than adding power, which from previous discussions would be the "proper" thing to do. (Use "energy effect.") However, you might also take a look at the tachometer to make sure that the altitude loss (or gain) wasn't caused by an improper setting.

Common Errors

1. Flying with one wing low.
2. Holding back pressure unconsciously, causing the plane to climb. (This is usually a sign of tenseness.)
3. Fighting the bumps. Every once in awhile release the wheel or stick to see if you have been working at it too hard.

Note: These are the Four Fundamentals. These and stalls will be the backbone of your presolo flying.

The Four Fundamentals and Instrument Indications
Private Pilot Certificate

The FAA requires that on the Private Pilot practical (flight) test you demonstrate the ability to recover from an emergency situation such as accidentally flying into clouds or fog. This means that you must be able to get out of such a situation through use of the flight instruments.

Tests have shown that students got better grades on the flight test when this training started early, that is, when flight with reference to instruments was integrated with the pre- and postsolo maneuvers. The FAA recommends that this integrated method be used in training all student pilots.

As in all of your flight training, the steps must be taken logically. When you are able to do the Four Fundamentals and feel at ease in the airplane, the instructor will have you go through these same maneuvers, directing attention to the instrument indications during the process of each. Later, you will use an extended visor cap, or "hood" that will restrict your vision to the instrument panel. At this point, however, it will be better to see the plane's attitude as well as the instruments so that you will be able to tie in the plane's actions with the instrument indications (and vice versa). In order to fly without outside visual references, you must be able to "see" what the plane is doing through the instruments.

Figures 9-15 through 9-20 show the Four Fundamentals (plus climbing and descending turns) as seen from the cockpit and by the instrument indications. The airplane is heading north at 4,000′ MSL at the start of the maneuver.

It will likely be at this stage that you will first note the idiosyncrasies of the magnetic compass. You will see for yourself that in actual flight the compass is affected by steep banks, attitude changes, and acceleration or deceleration of the airplane. In many cases the compass may initially show a change of direction of up to 30° as soon as the plane is banked for a turn; in some cases it may show a turn in the opposite direction at first. In any event, the various actions of the compass for each maneuver cannot be shown here; in Chapter 15 more information will be given about it. The heading indicator gives a true indication of the amount of turn, but the compass is accurate only when the plane is flying straight and level in balanced, unaccelerated flight.

During these maneuvers your attention will be on the instrument panel a large part of the time and the instructor will maintain a close watch for other airplanes.

14 CFR §61.109 (Private Pilot) requires that you have a minimum of 3 hours of flight training in a single-engine airplane on the control and maneuvering of the airplane solely by reference to instruments (*see* Chapter 15). The instructor will require that you be able to safely control the airplane by use of the instruments *before* you go on a solo cross-country. Precision instrument flight will not be required, but you will be expected to maintain control of the airplane by reference to instruments.

T-Tail Airplanes

Some airplanes have T-tails (the horizontal tail surfaces are on top of the fin and rudder). The horizontal tail is out of the slipstream (Figure 9-21), and changes in power don't cause the pitch changes discussed earlier in the chapter (Figures 9-9 and 9-10), or at least such changes are smaller. You might watch for the differences if you go from one type to the other (T-tail or standard) during your flying career.

Figure 9-21. The T-tail is usually out of the slipstream so that the pitch change with power is decreased.

Figure 9-15. A balanced constant-altitude turn (standard-rate). The airspeed is slightly less than cruise because of bank (and back pressure). The heading indicator shows a left turn, and the turn coordinator shows a balanced standard-rate turn. Altitude is constant.

Figure 9-16. Normal straight climb. The airspeed is steady at climb speed. The attitude indicator shows that the attitude is nose-up, wings-level. The heading indicator shows a constant heading; the turn coordinator indicates balanced straight flight. The altitude is increasing as shown by the altimeter and vertical speed indicator.

Figure 9-17. Climbing turn, standard-rate. The airspeed is steady at climb speed. The attitude indicator shows 11° bank, climb attitude. The heading indicator shows a left turn. The turn coordinator shows a standard-rate balanced turn. Altitude is increasing as indicated by the altimeter and vertical speed indicator. The climb rate is lower than the straight climb due to the bank angle.

Figure 9-18. Normal power-off glide (straight descent). The airspeed is steady at the proper glide speed. The attitude indicator shows a slight nose-low, wings-level attitude. The heading indicator shows a constant heading; the turn coordinator indicates straight balanced flight. The altitude is decreasing as indicated by the altimeter and vertical speed indicator.

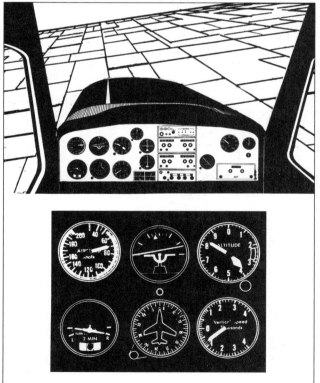

Figure 9-19. Balanced, standard-rate, gliding turn. The airspeed is steady at glide speed. The attitude indicator shows a slight nose-low, 10° bank. The heading indicator shows a right turn. The turn coordinator indicates a balanced, standard-rate right turn. The altitude is decreasing as shown by the altimeter and vertical speed indicator.

Figure 9-20. Straight and level flight. Airspeed steady at expected cruise value. Attitude indicator shows nose- and wings-level flight. Heading indicator shows a constant heading. Turn coordinator, straight and balanced flight. Altitude constant as shown by altimeter and vertical speed indicator.

Elementary Precision Maneuvers

Elementary precision maneuvers include steep turns and wind drift correction.

Steep Turns

The only difference between the steep turn and the normal turn is the steepness of bank. Many instructors have made this statement, and many students have nodded agreement but mentally noted that they didn't believe a word of it. The fact is that the techniques are the same with one or two minor additions.

A steep turn is one with a bank of over 30°. In Chapter 8 and "The Turn" in Chapter 9, you noted that in medium turns (15°–30° bank) you were able to take care of the need for increased lift by increasing back pressure. As the turn gets progressively steeper, you will find that the lift must be increased so much that you run out of angle of attack. In other words, the airplane stalls before you get enough lift to maintain altitude.

In the steep turn you may need increased power to maintain altitude because two things are happening: (1) The required added back pressure means a higher angle of attack and greater induced drag (*see* Chapter 2) and (2) the added load factor in the turn causes an increase in the stall speed. The added power serves to compensate for the added drag (which might otherwise finally result in an altitude loss), and it also helps lower the stall speed. You'll note in doing stalls that the stall speed is lower when power is used (Chapter 12).

The 720° Power Turn

The 720° power turn is a confidence-building precision maneuver that consists of 720° of turn with a coordinated roll-in and roll-out and a bank of 45°–60°. You will use added power and vary your bank as needed to maintain altitude (Figure 10-1).

Pick a point on the horizon or a road below as a reference point. The turns are done at an altitude of at least 1,500 feet above the surface. Look around for other traffic before starting the turn.

As you roll into the turn, open the throttle smoothly so that as the desired angle of bank is reached the power setting is approximately that of climbing power. Because of the great amount of back pressure needed after the turn is established, the angle of attack will be such that the airspeed will drop appreciably. You have a high power setting and low airspeed, so you will have to correct for torque effect.

Once the desired amount of bank is reached, the ailerons are neutralized, sufficient right rudder to correct for torque is held, and back pressure is held as needed to keep the nose at its proper place on the horizon. This nose position may be slightly higher than that in medium turns because of the required increase in angle of attack (added back pressure). A good rule of thumb is to have your bank and power established before you have made over 45° of turn.

You will find that the back pressure required is somewhat greater than you had anticipated.

If you see that the plane is losing altitude, the best method of bringing it back is to shallow the bank slightly. This will increase the vertical component of lift and the nose will return to the correct position. Then resume your steeper bank. Or if the plane is climbing, steepen up slightly and/or relax back pressure slightly.

The reason for not making the back pressure take care of all of the altitude variations is this: If you are in a 60° bank, the stall speed is increased 1.414 times that in level flight. If you try to climb or try to increase the lift at this bank, obviously you will run out of angle of attack. At 60° it takes 2 pounds of lift to get 1 pound of the vertical component. This is a losing proposition, and with steeper banks these odds jump sharply (*see* Figures 9-4 and 9-5).

Check your wings, nose, and altimeter as you turn. Watch for the checkpoint. Some students make three or four complete turns instead of two because they aren't watching for the point. After all, this is a precision maneuver.

A   Pick your reference point.

B   Smoothly apply power as you roll in.

C   Start the rollout about 45° before completion of the second turn.

D   The rollout is complete. The plane is at cruise power and altitude.

Figure 10-1. Elements of a 720° power turn.

After you've completed the first 360° of turn, if you held altitude, the plane may wallow or bump slightly as it flies through its wake turbulence. The more slipstream you hit on the second 360° the better your turn (though this could be argued). It's possible, however, to hit a bump even if the altitude ran wild.

The idea is not to start out, say at 3,000 feet, lollygag around from 2,800 to 3,200, and then feel proud because you happen to be back at 3,000 feet when you roll out.

While your instructor won't be too critical about your performance at this stage of the game, it's a good idea to learn the technique now. Then you won't have to sweat 720s later when you should be practicing advanced stalls or other maneuvers.

The second 360° is a continuation of the first; make corrections as needed. Watch for the checkpoint and start rolling out and throttling back about 45° before you are lined up with it. The roll-out should be smooth and timed so that the plane is in a straight and level attitude and at cruising power when the checkpoint is reached.

The hardest part about the roll-out is keeping the nose from coming up. It takes a lot of back pressure to hold it up in the turn, and it will take concentration in easing off that back pressure. During the first few times, it will seem that you don't relax back pressure—you press forward to get the nose down where it belongs.

To review the 720° turn:

The 720° power turn uses the same fundamentals as the shallow or medium turn. A steep turn requires only a longer period of deflection of the ailerons and rudder in order to obtain the steeper bank.

The reason right rudder may be needed is that the torque effects are caused by added power and slower airspeed, not the steepness of bank.

Power is used because (1) the angle of bank is such that the stall speed is increased, and (2) the required added angle of attack is increasing drag to the point where altitude may no longer be efficiently maintained by back pressure alone.

Some students get the idea that the nose can be held up by top rudder. The infinitesimal amount of the upward thrust angle doesn't compare with the great loss of efficiency suffered by slipping the airplane and slowing it down.

Probable Errors

1. Back pressure added too soon at the beginning of the turn—the nose rises and the plane climbs.
2. Applying full power or opening the throttle too soon—airspeed has not dropped yet and the engine overspeeds.
3. When the nose drops, trying to pull it up by back pressure alone, not shallowing bank—results in high stresses on the plane.
4. Failure to watch for the checkpoint. (Make a mental note as it goes by the first time. That way you won't make the instructor sick as you go around and around.)
5. Not releasing all of the back pressure on roll-out—the plane climbs.
6. Forgetting to throttle back as the plane is rolled out—also causes the airplane to climb.
7. The usual coordination problems of slipping and skidding.

Wind Drift Correction Maneuvers

The instructor will usually introduce you to the idea of wind drift correction by choosing a road or railroad that has a crosswind component and having you fly directly over it and then alongside it. You'll reverse course and fly in the opposite direction so that you can get practice in correcting for both a left and right crosswind. But first, let's take a look at the principle of wind drift correction.

You've seen lightplanes flying on windy days and noticed that they sometimes appeared to be flying sideways. In relation to the ground they were, but as far as the air was concerned the planes were flying straight as a string.

Suppose you wanted to cross a stream in a boat, paddling or motoring briskly from X to Y. The current is swift, so if you start out, as in Figure 10-2A, you can see what happens—there's much sweat but little progress toward your destination.

By pointing the nose directly across the stream at Y, you wind up at Z. In Figure 10-2B you play it smart. You point the boat upstream, how far up depends on the speed of the current, and you keep experimenting until you get the correct angle.

The same idea applies to the airplane (Figure 10-3). The wind is the current in this case. If you want to fly from X to Y with the wind as shown, you must angle into the wind, or set up a "crab."

If you start out pointing the nose at Y, you end up as shown in Figure 10-3A. So you correct for the wind by making a balanced turn and rolling out at the correction angle as shown in Figure 10-3B.

As shown in Figure 10-4, the balloon, you, and the rocket-plane are all part of the airmass and all will be found 20 NM south of course after one hour. You and

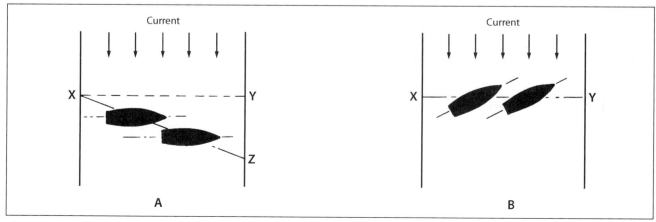

Figure 10-2. Boats and river currents.

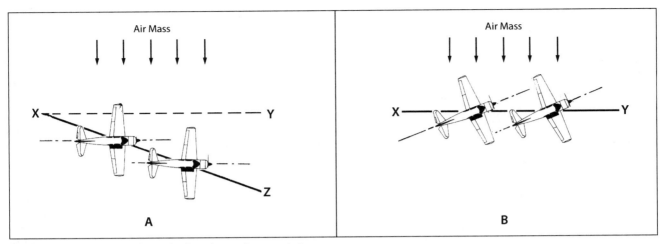

Figure 10-3. The principle applied to the airplane and air mass.

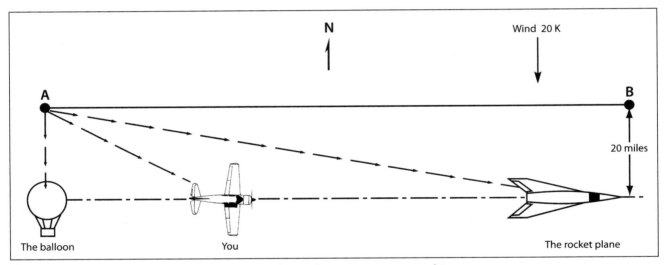

Figure 10-4. The air mass will move the three aircraft equally in a given amount of time.

the rocket-plane have the ability to smoothly roll into a crab, neutralize the controls and fly the ground track (course) you need to get you to your destination (B). You fly the crab in coordinated flight (not slipping or skidding) and are using some of your airspeed to offset the wind pushing you off course (*see* Figure 10-3). Due to its very high airspeed, the rocket-plane will have a much smaller crab angle than you. Only in one case do you use uncoordinated flight (a slip) to offset drift (Chapter 13).

The Rectangular Course

The purpose of the rectangular course is to give you a chance to fly the airplane while your attention is directed outside. As you learned the Four Fundamentals, you concentrated on the airplane and only noted its reference to the ground as a whole. Now you'll begin to use the plane and make it follow a definite path over

the ground. During the first few minutes you'll feel as frustrated as a one-legged man in a kicking contest.

This maneuver consists of flying a rectangular pattern around a large field or fields and is done for three reasons:

1. To get into the habit of flying the plane while dividing your attention between the cockpit and objects outside.
2. To learn to correct for wind drift in flying a straight course in preparation for cross-country flying.
3. To get practice in low precision flying in preparation for traffic pattern flying.

The rectangular course is done at 600 feet because mistakes are easily seen at that altitude, and it builds confidence to fly at a lower altitude.

The instructor will try to pick a field lying so that the wind is blowing diagonally across it. This will give you practice in wind correction on all four legs (Figure 10-5).

Procedure

Enter the pattern at a 45° angle, flying downwind (point 1). It is easier to set up your first correction downwind because drift can generally be seen more easily. This is just a human foible, but it works out that way. The turns around the field can be made either to the left or right. Assume in this case that the turns are to the left (Figure 10-5).

Roll out of the turn at what you think is the proper correction angle. The plane's distance from the field should be far enough away for the boundary to be easily seen and yet not so far away that your mistakes can't be seen. About 600–800 feet from the boundary would be a good distance for the average lightplane. Some students roll out parallel to the boundary and then make the correction, but it's advisable for you to get into the habit of making a correction as soon as possible.

Assume that at point 2 you undercorrected and the plane is drifting into the field. Make a balanced turn of a few degrees into the wind and see how things fare. If you are now holding your own and are not too close to the field to see the boundary without straining, fly the plane to the end of the field.

At point 3 you'll have to make a left turn. Since there is a quartering tailwind, it will tend to push you away from the field, particularly if a shallow turn is made (point 4). The best thing, then, is to make a fairly steep turn at this point. The steepness of bank will depend on the wind velocity—the greater the wind velocity, the steeper the bank. Roll out of the turn with whatever correction you think necessary (point 5). Don't count on having the same angle of correction as you had on the other leg. The wind probably won't be crossing this leg at the same angle. As shown in the diagram, the wind is more from the side here, so more correction is needed. The vector of the wind pushing you into the field on the first leg was not as great as the vector tending to move the airplane away from the boundary on this second leg.

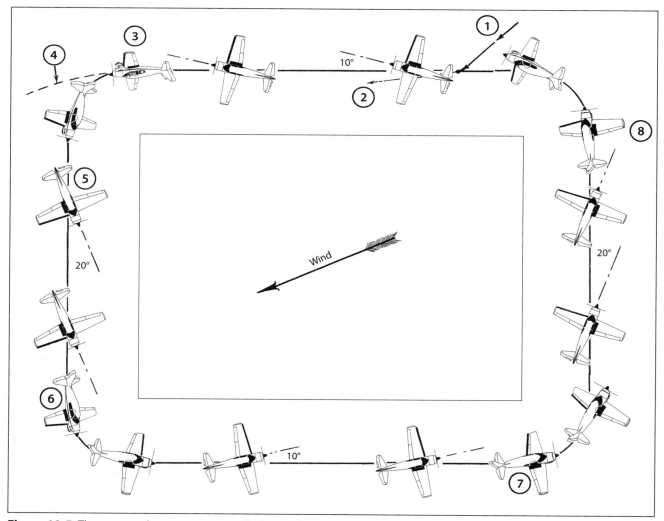

Figure 10-5. The rectangular course is normally done at 600–1,000 feet above the surface.

In the second leg, the wind is still somewhat behind the plane, so when you get to point 6 you can figure on another fairly steep turn. This turn will not be as steep as the one at point 3 because the wind component on your tail is not as great as it was at point 3.

Your angle of bank (the steepness of the turn) is directly proportional to your speed over the ground. So the bank at point 3 (Figure 10-5) is the steepest, and at point 7 is the shallowest.

Continue the rectangular course. At point 7 the bank must be shallow because you are flying into the wind (your groundspeed is low). At point 8 the first part of the turn is shallow, then it is steepened to keep the plane at the correct distance from the field.

Start the turn when you arrive even with the corner. (*You are looking directly down the line at the next side of the rectangular course as you start the turn.*) If you are crabbing (left or right), the lateral, or wing, axis will *not* be pointed down the next side at the point of turn. Make shallow or steep turns as necessary. (*See earlier discussion.*)

Probable Errors

1. Poor wind drift correction—not setting up correction soon enough.
2. Not recognizing drift or not making a firm correction after recognizing it.
3. Not maintaining altitude. Most students tend to climb in a rectangular course—there are a few rugged individualists who lose altitude.
4. Coordination problems. Some students who make perfect turns at higher altitudes get so engrossed in watching the field that their turns are awesome spectacles indeed.
5. Not anticipating the required angle of bank based on the current groundspeed. Using too much bank on the upwind turns and too little on the downwind turns.

S-Turns Across a Road

S-turns across a road, like the rectangular course, are good maneuvers for getting you used to dividing your attention between the airplane and the ground. The primary purpose, however, is to show you how to correct for wind in a turn. There was a brief introduction to this idea in the rectangular course, but S-turns give you a chance to acquire finesse.

S-turns are a series of 180° turns of about a quarter-mile radius using a road as nearly perpendicular to the wind as possible. (This is for planes of 90–95 K cruise. Faster planes will use a greater radius.)

The reasons for S-turns are:
1. To fly the airplane while dividing your attention between the cockpit and the ground.
2. To learn to correct for wind drift by varying the bank. This will come in handy later in circling and remaining near the same spot in a strong wind.
3. To get practice in precision flying in preparation for advanced maneuvers later.

S-turns are also done at 600 feet for the same reasons as those given for the rectangular course.

The object is to fly a series of semicircles of the same size, making smooth balanced turns and correcting for wind drift by varying the steepness of the bank. The plane should cross the road in a level attitude with the wings parallel to the road.

Procedure

A road that runs as nearly 90° to the wind as possible is picked. It is best to enter the S-turns downwind, because drift is more easily detected and corrected by the student if correction requires a steepening of the bank rather than shallowing it out. The first turn can be made in either direction.

As shown in Figure 10-6, the initial bank must be steep; otherwise, the wind would "push" the plane too far from the road before the turn is completed (point 1).

Assuming that you have set the correct steepness of bank, when point 2 is reached the bank must be shallowed or the plane would be turning at the same rate of turn in degrees per minute, but as it began to head into the wind, the groundspeed would drop. It would appear to "pivot" and would not follow the smooth curve of the semicircle but would end up at point 3.

The shallowing of the turn should be such that the wings are level as the plane crosses the road, still at 600 feet (point 4).

After you cross the road, the bank should be a shallow one in the opposite direction. If a steep bank is used, a path such as at point 5 would result.

When point 6 is reached, the bank must be steepened in order to have the turn completed as the plane crosses the road again. If the bank was not steepened at point 6, a path like that of point 7 would occur. The plane would not cross the road at the correct place nor would the wings be level or parallel to the road.

Continue the series until you get tired or run out of road. Remember: *The angle of bank is directly proportional to the groundspeed.* (The greater the groundspeed, the greater the angle of bank.)

Figure 10-6. S-turns across the road.

The angle of bank in S-turns must be constantly changing. The hardest part of trying to keep the maneuver smooth is at point 8, where you have to roll from a steep bank one way to a steep bank in the opposite direction.

If the wind is strong, many students do not have a shallow enough bank on the upwind side of the road, and the airplane drifts into the road. Strangely enough they are able to correct on the downwind side without much trouble. Many times in this situation the plane's path over the ground looks like Figure 10-7.

One problem with these maneuvers is that you may spend *all* of your time looking at the ground references. You should keep an eye out for other traffic as well. AIM Chapter 8 has some good information on collision avoidance procedures.

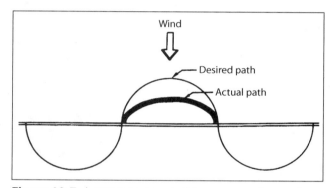

Figure 10-7. A common error in S-turns across the road.

Probable Errors

1. Failure to properly correct for drift.
2. Rolling out of the turn too soon or too late, resulting in crossing the road with wings not parallel to it.
3. Gaining or losing altitude.
4. Coordination problems in the turns (jerky or slipping and skidding).

In the S-turn you are interested in a definite path over the ground and therefore must correct for the movement of the air mass of which you are a part.

11

Elementary Emergency Landings

At some time during the period of rectangular courses or S-turns, your instructor will demonstrate an elementary emergency landing or "simulated emergency," as you may hear it called.

Engines nowadays are very reliable. Cases of engine failure are rare, but you will still be given emergency-landing practice because pilots still run out of fuel and leave oil caps off. It is still possible, too, that the engine could fail structurally, so it's better to be prepared.

The elementary emergency is given below 1,000 feet and requires a 90° gliding turn at most. The instructor will pull the carburetor heat and close the throttle at some point during the maneuvers and demonstrate the procedure.

If it is at all possible, you want to land into the wind. If the plane stalls at 50 K and you have a 15-K headwind, your groundspeed (or relative velocity to the ground) at touchdown will be 35 K. The advantages of this are obvious. However, sometimes a field may not be available for an upwind landing. Or if the field is steeply sloped, it's better to land uphill even if it's downwind. Obstacles may require that you land downwind.

Sometimes students who've been doing the rectangular course or S-turns for several minutes and have been correcting for a stiff wind forget the wind direction as soon as the throttle is closed for the simulated emergency.

Picking the right kind of field (at low altitude you don't have much time to shop around) comes with experience. If you've lived on a farm, you can spot a good field without much trouble.

Table 11.1 is a list and description of various types of fields with comments about each type.

Obviously there will be times when some of the landing spots labeled "poor" and "very poor" will be the only ones available. It then becomes the case of making the best of a bad situation. As one instructor put it, "Hit the softest, cheapest thing in the area as slowly as possible"—which pretty well covers it.

What to Do

In the case of an actual forced landing below 1,000 feet:

1. Establish the max distance glide airspeed.
2. Pull on the carburetor heat. You can do this simultaneously as you ease the nose up to conserve altitude and establish the proper glide airspeed. The

TABLE 11.1 Types of fields for emergency landings

Type of Field	Description	Comments
Good—pasture	Brown-green; may have live-stock or cow paths cross it	You can land in a pasture, but land in the part well away from the stock. Cows like to eat airplane fabric so don't be gone too long to telephone (unless you have a metal plane).
Good—freshly cut wheat, barley, oat fields, etc.	Brown grass but mower marks can usually be seen	Very good for emergency landing, if any place could be considered good for an emergency landing.
Fair—field of high grass, wheat, etc.	Rich green or golden	Not much landing roll, because field may be soft under camouflage of grass. Possibly plane will nose over.
Poor—high corn	Green. Or later brown	Field itself usually rough. Plane will probably be damaged.
Poor—freshly plowed field	Dark brown	If the field is soft the plane will nose over. If you must land in a plowed field, land parallel to the rows.
Poor—terraced field	Contour lines	Contour lines show that it is sloping. Never land across the contours.
Very poor—swamps, woods, etc.		Land as slowly as possible, but don't stall it in.

carburetor may have iced up and will clear out when heat is applied. Normally you will have some warning beforehand, such as the rpm dropping, but you may not have noticed. The carburetor heat should be pulled ON immediately because if the engine is dead, it will be cooling and any residual heat in the system will be dissipating rapidly. If you wait too long, there may not be enough heat left to clear out any ice (if that was the problem).

3. Pick your field and start the approach.
4. Switch to another fuel tank (if your airplane has more than one).
5. Electric boost pump ON (if equipped).
6. Mixture RICH.

Do not waste time trying other methods of starting. Do Items 4–6 after you have the field selected and the approach set up. Then get back to your approach. Don't try to use the starter.

The propeller usually windmills after an engine failure and will start again if the fault is remedied. If it does, climb to an altitude of 2,000 or 3,000 feet while circling the field. If you are sure of the reason for the failure (tank run dry, carburetor icing, etc.) and have remedied it, continue your flight. Otherwise keep your high altitude and pick a route of good terrain back to the airport.

Once you have selected a field, you have very little time to change your mind. Pilots have been killed trying to change fields in an emergency because they made turns too steep and stalled at low attitudes.

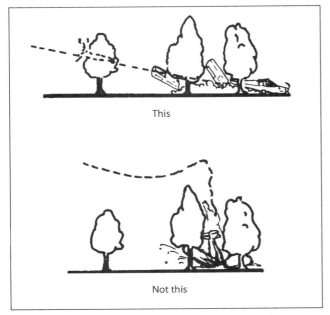

This

Not this

Figure 11-1. It's better to have control at impact than to stall or spin the airplane in.

A normal glide is a must for an emergency landing. If you are high and dive at the field, the airspeed goes so high that the plane "floats" and you still overshoot, or go past the field.

If you try to "stretch a glide," the rate of descent actually increases as the angle of attack gets into the critical range. It's better to hit something when you have control than to stall and drop in (Figure 11-1).

If you are going to land in trees, don't stall the plane above and drop in. Get as slow as possible, still having control, and fly into the trees.

It's impossible to list exact procedures for every situation, but you'll try to keep the airplane under control without stalling, and you'll try to pick a landing point that will allow the lowest deceleration (something soft like shrubs or weeds, rather than a stone wall or a solid tree trunk). As for when to turn off all switches before impact, your *Pilot's Operating Handbook* will have such information. Your primary goal is to keep the cockpit intact.

Sometime after you have had the simulated emergency demonstrated, the instructor will close the throttle and say, "Emergency landing." You will then go through the procedure. The instructor will let you glide to a reasonably low altitude or an altitude where you could see whether the field could be made, then will say, "I've got it," open the throttle, take the plane up, and point out any mistakes you may have made.

Review the *Pilot's Operating Handbook* for information on these procedures.

Probable Errors

1. Failure to establish a normal glide promptly.
2. Indecisiveness in selecting a field.
3. Trying to stretch the glide if low and to dive if high.
4. Making steep or uncoordinated turns close to the ground.

12

Stalls and Slow Flight

A stall is a condition in which the angle of attack becomes so great that the flow over the airfoil breaks down and the wings can no longer support the airplane. An airplane can be stalled at any speed, attitude, or power setting—as many a dive bomber pilot found out when he tried to pull out of a dive too quickly. He may have been doing 400 K, but the plane was stalled as completely as if he had climbed too steeply. What happens is shown in Figure 12-1.

With the knowledge that a stall is caused by too great an angle of attack, the proper recovery is always to decrease that angle of attack and get the air flowing smoothly again whether you are doing 40, 400, or 4,000 K.

You won't be doing accelerated stalls like that just discussed until later, but if you know what a stall is, the accelerated stall will be no different from the first elementary ones. The stalls in this phase will be done by gradually pulling the nose up and slowing the plane to the stalled condition.

In the earlier days of aviation, keeping the wings level during stalls was a problem. In the older planes, control effectiveness in the stall was lost in alphabetical order—AER. The **A**ilerons were the first to go,

followed by rapidly decreasing **E**levator effectiveness, and, last of all, the **R**udder. Generally, if power was used during the stall, the rudder was effective throughout.

In many cases, use of ailerons alone to raise a wing during a stall resulted in an opposite effect to that desired. When the aileron was applied, the down aileron on the low wing caused adverse yaw effects, resulting in a further slowing of that wing and causing it to stall first. This was disconcerting, to say the least, and led to some interesting wing-leveling techniques. Pilots found that it was possible, for instance, to raise the low wing during the stall by applying opposite rudder—which yawed the plane in that direction, speeded up the low wing, gave it added lift, and caused it to rise. Sometimes this opposite rudder was applied so enthusiastically that the high wing was slowed to the point that it abruptly exceeded the critical angle of attack and stalled first, thereby causing a great deal of adrenalin to flow in occupants of the plane.

Planes type-certificated under the Federal Aviation Regulations (as U.S. general aviation planes are now) must meet certain rolling (ailerons) and yawing (rudder) criteria throughout the stall. The Federal Aviation Administration, therefore, now encourages the use of

Figure 12-1. Pilot releases bomb, discovers that altitude is very low; pulls back stick abruptly. Plane changes attitude but momentum carries it down. Result—a high-speed stall. Lacking altitude for a smooth pull-out, plane strikes the ground.

coordinated controls to keep the wings level during the stall. While keeping the wings level is not critical at the altitudes where stalls will be practiced, it will be very important when you start landings, as will be shown later.

There is one very important point: Get the nose down (decrease the angle of attack) *first* before trying to level the wings. Once the angle of attack is below the stall value, the ailerons and rudder are less likely to get you into trouble in any airplane.

Several methods of design are used to aid lateral control throughout the stall. The idea in each case is to have the wing tips stall last. If a wing tip stalled first (and it is unlikely that both will stall at exactly the same time), a dangerous rolling tendency may occur as the stall breaks.

The tips may be made to stall last by "washout." The manufacturer builds a twist into the wing so that the tips always have a lower angle of incidence (and a resulting lower angle of attack) and will still be flying when the root area has stalled (Figure 12-2).

Another method of having the root stall first is the use of slots near the tip. The opening (Figure 12-3) near the leading edge allows the air to maintain a smooth flow at angles of attack that would result in a stall for the unslotted portion of the wing.

Still another method is that of stall strips (Figure 12-4), or spoiler strips, being placed on the leading edge of the root area of the wing, breaking the airflow and resulting in an earlier stall for this portion. Some airplane wings have higher lift-type airfoils at the tip, causing the wing tip to stall last. In some cases several of these design techniques may be combined.

Stalls as an Aid to Landings

As you'll see, a normal landing is nothing more than a stall. The average lightplane landing is begun at an altitude of about 15 or 20 feet from a normal glide. At this point you begin the landing transition, or start "breaking the glide." From here it becomes a matter of your judgment in trying to have the airplane completely stalled just as it touches. This means that you have the wheel or stick full back and the plane stops flying at the instant it contacts the ground.

The instructor will show you a series of straight ahead stalls that will be good preparation for landing practice later.

In practicing stalls, it's important not to stare blindly over the nose. Get an idea of the plane's attitude by looking out of the corners of your eyes. The instructor

Figure 12-2. Exaggerated view of wing tip washout. The ailerons are still effective even though the wing root is in the stalled condition.

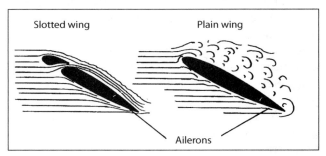

Figure 12-3. Plain and slotted wings at equal angles of attack.

Figure 12-4. The stall strip as a means of ensuring that the root section stalls first.

will probably have you practice landings from a normal glide at 2,000 or 3,000 feet above the ground. It's impossible to see the ground by looking over the nose of the average trainer when it's in the landing attitude; so as soon as you start the transition, switch your scan to along the left side of the nose, noting the plane's attitude out of the corner of your eye and keeping the wings level through coordinated use of the controls.

Once the nose is at the landing attitude (the instructor will show you the proper nose position), it becomes a matter of pinning it at that position by continued back pressure.

Approach to Stalls — Power-On or Power-Off

You'll practice these stalls in takeoff or climb configuration (power-on) or approach configuration (power-off), straight ahead, or in 20° banked turns. For the straight ahead stalls, be sure to "clear the area" by making two 90° turns in opposite directions because the nose will be in one place and form a blind area. Recover at least 1,500 feet above the ground.

Approach to stalls is so named because the airplane is not allowed to stall, but recovery is effected as soon as indications of a stall occur (buffeting or decay of control effectiveness).

Approach to a Stall — Power-Off

Procedure (Straight Ahead)
1. Clear the area.
2. Carburetor heat ON — throttle back to idle.
3. Apply gentle back pressure to raise the nose to about the landing touchdown attitude — don't let the nose wander off heading.
4. Hold the nose at this point by continued back pressure — keep the nose directionally straight by looking alongside it at a reference point on the horizon. The use of the elevators in approaching the stall can be likened to a vicious cycle. As the plane is slowed by the elevators, the nose tends to drop — requiring more up-elevator, which slows the plane further, requiring more elevator, etc. The point where the wheel or stick is all the way back and the nose drops is the stall "break." In the approach to a stall, the process does not go as far as the break (Figure 12-5).
5. Indications of the approaching stall are sensed by:
   a. Sight — check the attitude and airspeed indicator.
   b. Feel — the controls are ineffective and mushy. The airplane may shudder or vibrate as the stall approaches.

   c. Sound — the wind and engine noise level drops as the plane slows.

   Lower the nose to level flight and apply full power simultaneously. (Easy with that throttle — don't ram it open.)
6. Carburetor heat OFF.

The idea of this maneuver is for you to learn to recognize the approaching stall. You could recover easily by leaving the throttle back at idle; it just takes a little more altitude, that's all. Don't start thinking that power is the big thing in the recovery. *The change in the plane's attitude is the most important part.* Your instructor will also have you practice these stalls in 20° banked turns in each direction.

Approach to a Stall — Power-On

Use cruising power on this one (Figures 12-6 and 12-7). The technique is fundamentally the same except you'll have to raise the nose higher in order to speed up the approach to the stall. The plane wants to "hang on" longer when power is used. A thing to remember: At higher rpm you have torque effects as the plane slows, and the plane is less laterally stable because of gyroscopic effects; that is, you may have more trouble keeping the wings level.

Procedure
1. Clear the area.
2. Slow the airplane to approximately the climb speed or slightly below by throttling back and maintaining a constant altitude, then set the rpm to cruise.
3. Ease the nose slightly higher than for the power-off version, maybe 5° higher. (Your instructor will demonstrate the nose position.) Keep the wings level.
4. Keep the nose in line with a point on the horizon. Remember that torque will be acting on the plane.
5. As the approaching stall is noted (sight, sound, feel), lower the nose and open the throttle fully (Figure 12-7).

A Ease nose up to landing attitude.

B Watch for signs of approaching stall.

C Lower nose and apply full power.

Figure 12-5. Approach to a stall.

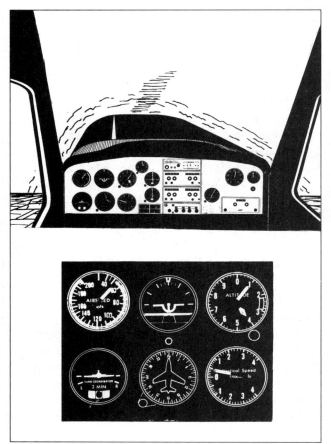

Figure 12-6. Power-on partial (imminent) stall. The airspeed is near stall. Heading indicator, no turn. Attitude indicator, nose high, wings level. Turn coordinator, straight balanced flight. Altitude, steady or increasing slightly.

Figure 12-7. Lower nose to level flight and open throttle at the same time. Airspeed increasing. Heading indicator, no turn. Attitude indicator, level flight. Turn coordinator, straight balanced flight. Altitude, constant or slightly decreasing.

Granted, you'll be practicing approaches to stalls at an altitude where the recovery will be no problem. Still, you might as well get in the habit of using full power and recovering with as little altitude loss as possible because someday you may be low and won't have time to reason, "Well, I'm pretty low so maybe I'd better use full power; on the other hand, possibly I should..." (CRUNCH).

You'll also get practice in power-on approaches to stalls in banks of about 20°.

Open that throttle each time unless you are called upon by your instructor or the FAA check pilot to demonstrate a power-off recovery. Again, the addition of power is to reduce the altitude loss during the recovery. Getting the control wheel or stick forward is the move that recovers the airplane from the stall.

Some Straight-Ahead Stalls

Normal Stall — Power-Off

Another step in the stall sequence is the wings-level normal stall. This is the one you'll use for landing practice at altitude. The first part of the stall is quite similar to the imminent stall. In this case, however, you continue increasing back pressure until the wheel or stick is full back or the stall breaks and the nose starts to drop. Recovery is effected by releasing back pressure and applying full power (easy with that throttle). Try to recover with a minimum altitude loss. Many students get eager to recover from the stall, release the back pressure, and immediately come back again with the wheel to minimize the altitude loss (they think). The plane stalls again (called a secondary or progressive stall) and the process of recovery must be redone. It is possible to do a series of secondary stalls (even the fifth stall is called a secondary stall) and, if the ground is close, you'll feel as nervous as a cat in a roomful of rocking chairs until the plane is flying normally again.

Recover firmly, but don't get rough with the airplane. Minimize your altitude loss, but don't get a secondary stall.

During your first series of stalls, the plane seems to have a mind of its own. The wings don't want to stay level. Maybe you push forward on the wheel a little harder than you mean to and your stomach comes up in your throat. Don't worry about it; there were several hundred thousand other people who felt the same way before you came along.

After several stalls you'll get the idea. (Do these stalls both clean and with landing-flap settings.)

Procedure

1. Clear the area.
2. Carburetor heat ON—close the throttle to idle.
3. Ease the nose up to the landing attitude.
4. Pin it at that position with continued application of back pressure. If you are preparing for landings, practice looking out the left side, keeping the wings level and the plane at the correct nose-up attitude by checking it from the corners of your eyes.
5. When the stall breaks, recover by lowering the nose, applying full power as you do so, minimizing altitude loss. (Flaps up in increments, if used.)
6. Carburetor heat OFF.

More about this idea of keeping the wings level: If a wing drops, the plane is banked and will turn. This doesn't matter at high altitudes, but runways are only a couple of hundred feet wide at best (some of them will be only 50 feet) and the plane will be off into the boondocks before you know it. Here's a good place to get the wings-level idea down pat. Then you won't have any trouble when landing practice starts.

If the wing drops slightly, use coordinated controls. Exact stall recovery techniques will vary from airplane to airplane, but the general principle is the same for all airplanes and airspeeds. *Get the air flowing smoothly over the wings with the minimum loss in altitude.*

If you are flying an older airplane, the ailerons may not be effective throughout the stall and use of rudder may be needed to stop rolling tendencies. Your instructor will demonstrate the best technique for maintaining lateral control during the stall for your particular airplane. However, the chances are that coordinated aileron and rudder usage will be the most effective means.

Normal Stall—Power-On

Fundamentally, this is the same as the stall just discussed. The nose position will be higher because of the power. As seen in Figure 12-8, when the plane uses power, its path is changed and the attitude will be more nose high, but the angle of attack at the stall will be roughly the same for a given flap-setting.

A plane will stall at a slightly slower airspeed with power on than it does with power off. The effect of the slipstream over the center section of the wing makes a slight difference. The more nose-high attitude also gives a vertical component to the thrust, which in effect lowers the wing loading. (Wing loading, you remember from Chapter 2, is the airplane weight or load that is supported by each square foot of wing area.)

Figure 12-8. The attitude is more nose-high than for the power-off version.

Procedure

1. Clear the area. (You're probably getting tired of hearing this by now, but do it anyway.)
2. Ease the nose up to a slightly higher position than that used for the power-off normal stall; your instructor will demonstrate.
3. Keep the wings level.
4. When the stall break occurs, lower the nose and open the throttle the rest of the way. Then level the wings with coordinated aileron and rudder if you fell asleep in item 3 (Figure 12-9).

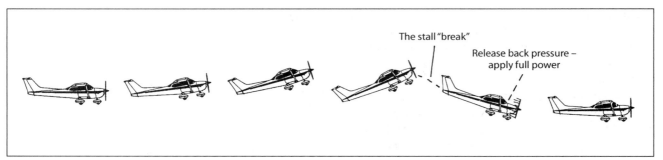

Figure 12-9. Power-on normal stall.

Complete or Full Stall — Power-On and Power-Off

This stall has little application other than as an exercise in keeping the wings level during the stall, but if you're having that problem, a few of these will help you see the light.

In earlier days this was sometimes referred to as a "rudder exercise stall" because the wings were kept level or bank corrections were made by using the opposite rudder to raise a wing, as mentioned at the beginning of the chapter.

Procedure — Power-Off
1. Clear the area.
2. Carburetor heat ON — throttle at idle.
3. Ease the nose up to an attitude of 30° above the horizon. Keep the wheel back until the nose falls to the horizon. Keep the wings level during the recovery.
4. As the nose crosses the horizon, effect a normal recovery. Release the back pressure and apply power. You will notice that the nose will be somewhat lower during the recovery from the complete stall compared to the normal stalls.
5. Carburetor heat OFF. The power-on complete stall is fundamentally the same except for the increased difficulty in keeping the nose straight and the wings level because of torque and gyroscopic effects.

Characteristic Stall

This stall is a good demonstration of the built-in stability of the airplane. It disproves the nonflyer's idea that the airplane is just waiting for a chance to "fall."

This stall can be done either with power on or off, as your instructor may want to demonstrate for you. For discussion purposes, assume that you are going to make a power-off stall. The idea is to start a normal power-off stall (trimmed for cruising flight), getting the break, but instead of recovering as usual, take your hands and feet off the controls. The nose will drop and the plane will make its own recovery. (You can go back up and get your stomach later.) In most lightplanes you will have to ease the plane out of the dive in the power-off characteristic stall. It would come out of the dive by itself, but the airspeed might be in the region of the red line, or "never exceed" speed, at the bottom of the first oscillation.

If the plane had cruising power throughout the maneuver, the initial dive would not be nearly as steep as the power-off one, and the recovery would be back to level cruising flight. Generally, it is not necessary to pull the plane out of the dive when you are using cruising power. The oscillations that result are called phugoid oscillations, which sounds very technical. Sometime during the course of an ordinary conversation, work the talk around so you can mention "phugoid oscillations" — it's quite impressive.

Put bluntly, the idea of this maneuver is to show that most of the trouble that occurs during stalls is caused by some heavy-footed, ham-handed pilot groping around in the cockpit. The characteristic stall is not required on the private practical (flight) test but is a good maneuver for building up your confidence in the airplane.

Procedure
1. Clear the area.
2. Start a normal power-on or power-off stall.
3. When the stall breaks, take your hands and feet off the controls.
4. Ease the plane out of the dive and return to level flight.

Common Errors
1. Not getting the stall break or having the wheel or stick back to the stop before releasing the controls.
2. Letting the airplane pick up excessive speed in the dive.

Elementary Turning Stalls

Takeoff and Departure Stalls — Climbing Turns

Many a pilot has taken off in front of friends on a bright Sunday afternoon and decided to give them a little extra show—a takeoff, followed by a steep climbing turn. The result—a little more show than bargained for, with a stall at the top of one of these colorful maneuvers.

Or suppose you are landing at a very short airport with trees at the far end. You are just about to touch down when you realize that you're almost out of runway. The trees are close. You open the throttle and try to climb and turn out of the way. What happens then? If you've practiced a few departure stalls, just what can happen will be evident and you will have learned a method of recovery. Better to have used headwork in the first place than to have gotten into such a predicament.

The takeoff and departure stall is designed to give you practice in recognizing and coping with such a situation. You will do these stalls both from straight flight and from moderately banked (20°) turns with recommended takeoff power. In both types, the climb will be initiated at lift-off speed and the angle of attack slowly increased until the stall occurs. Power-on, wings-level stalls have already been covered, so this section will only discuss the climbing-turn stall.

The climbing-turn stall is done by throttling back and slowing the plane as if on a landing approach. At about 5 K above the stall, open the throttle to recommended takeoff power and ease the plane up into a climbing turn of approximately a 20° bank in either direction. Continue to increase the angle of attack until the stall occurs. For the majority of airplanes, the higher wing will normally tend to stall first, particularly in a right-climbing turn because of torque effects,

and the plane will roll in that direction. Here's why the top wing tends to stall first: As you pull up into the stalled condition, the wings start losing lift and the plane mushes and starts to slip. In the right-climbing turn, torque is working to yaw the nose against the turn and aggravates the slipping condition.

As shown by Figure 12-10, the higher wing receives turbulence when a slip occurs, while the lower wing is comparatively free; consequently the high wing will stall first. When the break occurs, the airplane rolls in the direction of the high wing. In such a case the ball of the turn and slip (needle and ball) will indicate a slip just as the break occurs. The rigging of the wings of your particular airplane can affect its reaction. Also, if the plane is skidding at the stall break, the low or inside wing will be the first to go. If your plane has a needle and ball, you can note that the roll at the stall break is "away from the ball." (If the ball is to the right, the roll will be to the left; if the ball can be kept centered, any tendency to roll is minimized, but it still might roll in either direction, so be ready for it. The only problem is that with most airplanes, the rapid decay of rudder effectiveness as the stall is approached may not allow the pilot to keep the ball centered.)

When you are practicing these turning stalls, dual or solo, you might notice that the nose will usually drop at the stall break, an instant before the roll occurs. This follows the analysis shown by Figure 12-10.

Relax back pressure to recover. You already have a fair amount of power on throughout the maneuver, but you should increase it to maximum. But relaxing the back pressure is the main stall-recovery aid here, as always. In a few airplanes with good rudder effectiveness, by keeping the ball centered, the *right*-climbing turn can result in the low (right) wing dropping! This is, of course, the reason you practice these stalls—to see what *your* airplane will do.

A — Highest wing gets interference from fuselage.

B — Plane rolls toward high wing.

C — Recover to straight and level flight with coordinated use of controls.

Figure 12-10. A rolling moment may be set up as the plane stalls.

With more practice you'll be able to recognize the start of the roll and the break and recover in level flight by catching the stall at the right point.

The angle of bank must be moderate in order to get a good break. If you bank the plane too steeply, the nose may drop, tending to make the stall harder to attain because of the increase in airspeed. In many cases the nose will be low enough that the plane will merely mush, and you'll be turning in a tight circle, losing altitude with the plane shuddering but not getting a definite stall break. This too-steep bank will give you more trouble during solo practice of these stalls. It's a matter of stall speed being a function of wing loading. Without the instructor's weight, the wing loading is lower and the plane is harder to stall from an airspeed standpoint.

In doing these stalls, note the altitude at the point of assumed takeoff and compare it with the altitude on recovery.

Procedure

1. Since you will be turning, it is not necessary to make special clearing turns. Keep looking around during the approach to the stall.
2. Pull the carburetor heat ON (if required for your airplane), reduce the power, and slow down to liftoff speed.
3. When the airspeed drops to 5–10 K above the stall, apply recommended climb power (carburetor heat OFF) and attempt a comparatively steep climbing turn (the climb is comparatively steep; the bank is shallow) in either direction.
4. When a wing or the nose starts to drop and the break is definite, relax back pressure and apply full power.
5. Level the wings with coordinated controls after the recovery is started. (Don't just go by the airspeed; you should feel and hear this pickup in speed as well.)

Common Errors

1. Too steep a bank—the plane doesn't stall but mushes or spirals instead.
2. Too early a recovery—the plane does not get a chance to break before the recovery is started.
3. Too late a recovery—the plane may rotate too far before you get a recovery started.
4. Nose too low—the climb is not steep enough, the plane mushes.

Approach to Landing Stalls — Gliding Turn

This is the power-off version of the takeoff and departure stalls, and like them will be done from both straight glides and moderately banked (approximately 30°) gliding turns in landing configuration (full flaps and trim set). Power-off, wings-level stalls were covered earlier, so only the gliding-turn stall will be covered here (Figure 12-11).

You will notice that the rolling tendency is not nearly so great with the power off. The plane tends to mush and shudder and it is harder to get a sharp stall break, particularly if you are solo. It may require a faster rate of applying back pressure to get the break as compared with the departure stall. When you fly heavier planes, you will find that in most cases you don't have to work to make them stall. The faster planes will stall and generally give comparatively little warning. You are more interested in the technique of recovery than in the effort required to get into the stall. So don't get complacent about stalls.

Procedure

1. Carburetor heat ON. Set the plane up in the landing configuration. Establish a normal gliding turn in either direction.
2. Continuously add back pressure, raise the nose to about the landing position or slightly higher.
3. When the break occurs (or you have full up-elevator), stop any rotation and recover by releasing back pressure and applying full power.
4. Carburetor heat OFF.
5. Clean up the airplane (gear and flaps, as applicable) and climb to an altitude at least 300 feet above the altitude at which full control effectiveness was regained.

Figure 12-11. The approach to landing stall (gliding turn).

Probable Errors

1. Too steeply banked—plane mushes in a turn rather than stalling.
2. Nose not high enough—again the plane mushes with no definite stall break.
3. Improper throttle handling—too fast or too timid application of power.

Flaps and Stalls

Figure 12-12 shows the coefficient of lift versus angle of attack (also *see* Figure 2-8 and the discussion there) for a wing—clean and with landing flaps extended (20° in this case). Note that the maximum coefficient of lift is noticeably higher with flaps extended. Using, for example, the 0° angle of attack as a common starting point, you'd see that by slowly increasing the angle of attack, the flapped condition would reach its critical angle of attack (stall) well before the clean wing would have problems.

The point is this: Pilots tend to think that stalls can only occur with the nose well above the horizon. You can see that some airplanes with full flaps, approaching landing in a turn, might stall with the nose well below the horizon. This is because the airplane's "normal"

approach attitude is much lower, and the stall attitude will also be equivalently lower compared to the non-flapped condition (same power setting).

Flight at Minimum Controllable Airspeed (Slow Flight)

This is designed to show you how to recognize the stall and to help you get to know your airplane. Someday you may have to fly the plane close to the stall, and knowing how the plane flies in that region may save your neck.

Such flight (sometimes called "slow flight") is usually considered to be level, sustained flight at a speed close enough to the stall (about 5 K above) so that if power was chopped, or if the angle of attack or load factor is increased, you would get an immediate stall. You will be expected to demonstrate minimum-speed flying to the FAA examiner during the private practical (flight) test. You will be asked to make minimum-speed climbing, gliding, and level turns in various configurations and banks. The flight test tolerances in straight and level slow flight will be to maintain within 10° of heading and 100 feet of altitude.

Figure 12-12. Coefficient of lift and stall break attitudes for a fictitious airplane—clean and with landing flaps down.

Don't get the idea that the speed for slow flight (or minimum controllable airspeed) is always the same for your airplane. The *angle of attack* at the stall is always the same (for a given flap setting), but the airspeed at the stall varies with the *weight* of the airplane. The less a particular airplane weighs, the less its airspeed when that fixed maximum angle of attack is reached. The stall airspeed is also lowered by the lowering of *flaps*. Take a look back at Figure 9-5. The stall speeds given there are at the maximum certificated weight of 1,600 pounds and are power-off. Note that the stall speeds decrease with an increase in flaps for any condition of bank. For instance, looking at the effects of flaps at 0° bank (wings level), the stall speed decreases from 55 mph to 49 mph at 20° of flaps, and then down to 48 mph at the 40° flap setting. Note that the second 20° only lowered the speed by another 1 mph. Added drag is a greater factor than added coefficient of lift in this area (20°–40°) of flap setting.

Okay, take an airplane that stalls at 55 mph (no flaps) at 1,600 pounds with the *power at idle*. If you wanted to fly slow flight in this condition (idle), you would probably set up a speed about 5 mph faster, *or 60 mph calibrated airspeed* (CAS).

Now use 20° of flaps. At this same airplane weight you would add 5 mph to the stall speed (49 mph) and set up a descent at about 54 mph. For 40°, 53 mph (CAS) would be a good number.

At a *lighter weight* of 1,300 pounds you might use *55, 49,* or *48* mph respectively in slow flight, to have a 5 mph margin.

A little earlier in the chapter it was noted that the use of power decreased the stall speed (Figure 12-8) so that the airspeed, as an example, could be lowered another 3 mph for each condition. Now the new speeds would be *52, 46,* and *45* mph CAS, respectively, for slow flight in the three flap settings, at a lighter weight, *and using power.*

While numbers have been cited here to make the point that *flaps, lower airplane weights,* and *more power* will all *lower* the airspeed given for stall (and hence the required slow-flight speed if the same margin is kept), the idea is to *fly* the airplane by your feel and senses. Figure 9-5 and the discussion about it in this chapter use miles per hour as examples. The principle remains the same whether expressed in miles per hour or knots.

Procedure

1. Throttle back to a power setting much less than required to maintain level slow flight. After the first time, you'll have an approximate idea of what's needed. Maintain altitude as the plane slows. This means that the nose must be slowly raised. As the required speed is approached, start adding power as necessary to keep the altitude constant. You can see in Figure 12-13 that the power required to fly the airplane *increases* again after the airspeed is decreased from cruise down past a certain point.

2. Maintain your heading. You have power on and a low airspeed, and torque must be taken care of.

3. Notice that elevators and throttle are coordinated in maintaining airspeed and altitude. If you are losing altitude, add power and adjust the nose position to maintain the proper airspeed. If you are too slow but are maintaining altitude, ease the nose slightly lower and adjust your power to assure staying on that altitude. Keep checking the altimeter and airspeed. *You'll also be watching for other planes.*

4. Make a shallow turn in each direction. Maintain altitude in the turn. This will mean increased power and a slight raising of the nose.

5. Level the wings and gradually throttle back to idle as you lower the nose to maintain a glide at the minimum control speed of 5 K above the stall. Make 20°–30° banked turns in each direction.

6. Return to level, slow flight by applying power and easing the nose up. Try to keep the airspeed from varying during this transition. You'll note in slow flight, as in other phases of your flying, that an increase in power tends to make the nose rise, which will make it seem as if all you have to do as power is applied is to *think* about the nose easing up.

7. Increase the power and ease the nose up to a climb at minimum speed. Make shallow turns in each direction. (Don't climb too long, since the engine will overheat at low airspeed/high power.)

Making the transition from level flight to glide to climb, etc., without varying the airspeed more than 5 knots takes some heavy concentration, but when you can do it, you'll have an excellent feel for the aircraft.

The instructor will probably not do any more before solo than have you fly the plane at the minimum speed to get the feel of slow flight. You will not be required to maintain as close tolerances of altitude as later in your training. However, if you seem to get the hang of slow flight, you may go on with the transition to climbs and glides. You will probably review slow flight before going on the cross-country solo.

Remember that you should also be able to do slow flight by referring to the instruments. In this condition, you don't rely on your senses but on the instruments. The instructor will give you a chance to practice this, both hooded and with visual references during periods of dual.

You should get slow-flight practice in as many combinations of flaps and power as possible. If your trainer has retractable gear (it's doubtful), you should fly at minimum controllable speeds in cruise and landing configurations. You might repeat steps 1 through 7 in various flap configurations. (Don't try to climb very long at the low speed with the flaps extended.)

Your instructor may cover the airspeed indicator during the visual slow-flight practice so that you can fly the airplane by pitch attitude and power and may also cover the tachometer so that you will use power as needed to maintain altitude rather than staring at the rpm numbers.

Common Errors

1. Losing or gaining altitude in the transition from cruise to slow flight.
2. Poor speed control in the transitions.
3. Stalling the airplane.
4. Poor altitude control during the level portions of slow flight. (Slow flight is also called "maneuvering at critically slow airspeeds.")
5. Failure to hold heading due to high torque and reduced rudder effectiveness at low airspeeds.

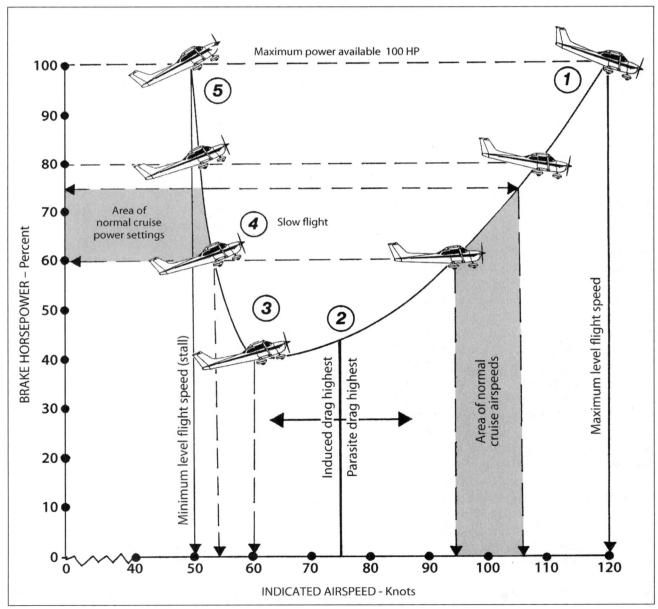

Figure 12-13. The power required to maintain a constant altitude (sea level) for a fictitious, very efficient light trainer at a particular weight (attitudes exaggerated).

Power versus Airspeed

You might be interested to know that in slow flight you will be operating in a condition that pilots call the "back side of the power curve." Figure 12-13 shows the attitudes and power required to maintain a *constant altitude* at various airspeeds for a typical light trainer at one particular weight at sea level. Other weights and/or altitudes would have separate curves. To simplify matters, Figure 12-13 is set for brake horsepower and indicated airspeed because these will be the two factors you'll be working with as a pilot. The engine of this plane is able to develop 100 brake horsepower at the altitude used here (sea level).

All the vehicles you've been operating before (bicycles, motorcycles, automobiles) always require *more power to go faster* at any particular road condition or grade; in your flying of the airplane in straight and *level cruising flight,* this has also seemed to be the case. The kicker is that the added power in the normal cruise area doesn't directly make the airplane go faster, but *allows it to go faster without losing altitude.* This is important to remember. The airplane in the example can go faster than the maximum speed shown but only at a cost of altitude. Road vehicles are supported by the ground and don't have to rely on producing lift, hence their horsepower is used basically only to overcome parasite drag.

The power curve gets its characteristic U shape because the airplane is subjected to *two* types of drag. Looking back to Chapter 2, you remember that *total drag* is composed of *parasite drag*, which increases with airspeed, and *induced drag*, which becomes much stronger as the airplane slows up. You've been doing all of your straight and level flying in that area of the power curve (normal cruise) where parasite drag is the big factor. Because you're more used to talking in terms of horsepower, Figure 12-13 shows the horsepower required to overcome a combination of the two types of drag throughout the speed range of the airplane.

Note in Figure 12-13 that the area of normal cruise power settings for the airplane in the example runs from 60 horsepower (60 percent power) to 75 horsepower (75 percent power). This is the normal range of cruise power settings for most airplanes—from *60 to 75 percent* of the normal rated power, the power the engine can produce continuously at sea level.

Point 1 shows the maximum level-flight speed of the airplane. It requires 100 horsepower to fly this airplane at a constant altitude (sea level) at this speed, and that's all that this particular engine has available. From that point, as the airplane flies at slower airspeeds, less horsepower is required to maintain a constant altitude; moving down the curve, point 2 is reached. This is the

point where parasite drag and induced drag are equal. Incidentally, this is the point of maximum cruise efficiency, or *maximum range*, of the airplane. You'll get more miles to the gallon while maintaining altitude at that speed, which is about 150 percent of, or 1.5 times, the stall speed (for trainers). This would be the airspeed at which to fly if you got in a bind for fuel and had to stretch it to make an airport some distance away. This 1.5 ratio is calibrated airspeed.

As you move back down the curve, point 3 is the airspeed at which the minimum power is required to maintain altitude. This would be the airspeed you'd use if you were looking for *maximum endurance*, or longest time airborne, and is roughly about 120 percent of the stall speed (or 1.2 times the stall speed, however you like to think of it).

Decreasing the airspeed below point 3 results in the power required to fly the airplane (at a constant altitude) starting to increase sharply; induced drag is beginning to make itself known. The part of the curve from point 3 back to the stall is called the "backside of the power curve," which implies that something unnatural is occurring. It's only unnatural if you don't have the full picture of what happens to drag at various airspeeds, and the term is a rather poor one (like "elevators"). Note that this airplane requires as much power (60 horsepower) for slow flight, 5 K above the stall (point 4), as it does to cruise at an airspeed of 94 K.

Finally, as the stall is approached at point 5, all of the power is needed to maintain altitude; if the angle of attack is increased further, the stall occurs even though full power is being used. (The attitudes of the airplane at the extreme ends of its speed range are exaggerated in Figure 12-13.)

Practice-flying at minimum controllable airspeeds is extremely important; it shows you what to expect when you are flying at speeds fairly close to the stall (as might be done on a power approach to a short field). If you find yourself too low and slow and close to the stall on the power approach, you would not pull the nose up. This would demand more horsepower and make you sink faster. You would instead add power and ease the nose lower. In less critical situations you wouldn't even have to add power but would just ease the nose down to pick up a slightly higher airspeed (where less power is required).

Notice also how steeply the curve goes up at the maximum level-flight speed, point 1. If this same airplane had another 30 horsepower, it wouldn't have a much greater top speed. In fact, an added 30 horsepower (an added 30 percent) would only mean an increase in top speed of about 10 percent. As a rule of thumb for high cruising speeds or top speeds, the increase in airspeed (percentage) is about one-third of the increase in power (percentage) for a particular airplane. Speed can be expensive.

Chapter 23 will go into more detail as to how to set up specific *cruise* power conditions for your airplane.

Spins

(Note: The spin recovery procedure in the POH for your airplane is, of course, the one you should memorize and use.)

While stalls are fresh in your mind, it's a good idea to discuss spins. The FAA does not require the demonstration of spins for any certificate or rating other than the flight instructor's certificate, but you'll have ground instruction for them and your instructor may demonstrate and have you practice spins in a properly certificated airplane. But sometime you may want to have a spin demonstration by an instructor; it's a good idea for anybody to know what they are and how to cope with them.

Spins are to be practiced in a properly certificated airplane, of course. Before getting a demonstration, you should have a good idea of what to expect. The spin is an aggravated stall resulting in autorotation. In short, it is a condition where one wing stalls first and the plane "falls off " in that direction. One wing has more lift left and it is chasing the other more stalled wing like a dog after its tail.

You've had experience with this in the departure and approach stalls. One wing stalls and the plane starts to rotate in that direction. If you had kept the wheel back, not recovering from the stall, and held rudder in the direction of rotation, a spin would have resulted. *If you relaxed the back pressure, at least in the first turn or so, the spin would have turned into a tight diving turn and you would know how to get out of that.*

Okay, so a spin occurs when you stall one wing before the other and continue to hold back pressure, not allowing the plane to recover from the stalled condition.

The normal spin procedure is to start a normal power-off stall (after clearing the area); just before, or as, the stall occurs, apply *full rudder* in the direction you want to spin. It's a good idea to begin no lower than 4,000 feet above the ground. A one-turn spin in the average lightplane takes about 1,000 feet of altitude from start to finish. Have enough altitude so that you will recover at least 3,000 feet above the ground. *Never deliberately spin with flaps down.* A spin to the left is covered below.

Procedure

1. Clear the area and start a normal power-off stall. Carburetor heat ON.
2. Just before the break occurs, apply full left rudder and continue to bring the stick or wheel full aft. The left wing stalls (Figure 12-14).
3. Hold the wheel fully back and keep that left rudder in. Sometimes it may be necessary to apply a burst of power to start the spin. The prop blast gives the rudder added effectiveness to yaw the plane. Because of the yaw created by your use of the rudder, the left wing "moves back" and has less relative lift. The right wing, being moved forward, has relatively higher lift. The result is a roll to the left, causing the left wing to increase its angle of attack (which was right at the stall, anyway), so the left wing has stalled and is now developing much less lift (and more drag) than the right wing. A spin can occur only if the airplane (or at least one wing) has passed the stall angle of attack and stays there. So the spin is created by a too-high angle of attack with yawing or rolling (the rolling can be induced by the yaw or other factors). For instance, look back to Figure 12-10. You're out practicing takeoff and departure stalls solo one day and are making a right-climbing turn entry as shown. The airplane rolls briskly to the left and you use full right aileron to stop the roll—before you release the back pressure. Also, maybe your feet were lazy and you didn't use rudder against the roll like you should have. The down-aileron acts as a flap and the left wing is suddenly shifted to the left-hand "flap" curve shown in Figure 12-12; in addition, the angle of attack on that down-moving wing is increasing. Things meet in the middle (at the stall) pretty fast, and the wing starts the autorotation part. You'll have to break it by closing the throttle, neutralizing the ailerons, using opposite rudder, and moving the wheel forward briskly. But let's get back to talking about a deliberate spin.

Figure 12-14. *Just before or as the stall occurs (depending on the airplane), apply rudder in the direction of spin.*

4. The nose drops, but the full up-elevator does not allow the plane to recover from the stall. The unequal lift of wings gives the plane its rotational motion (Figures 12-15 and 12-16).

The nose is not pointed straight down, though it will certainly appear this way to you during the first spin (Figure 12-17).

Figure 12-18 shows the developed spin as seen from the cockpit.

Figure 12-19 shows the spin as it may look to you from the cockpit that first time. Don't stare over the nose, but keep your eyes moving, checking different objects on the ground.

The plane's rotational motion tends to keep the imbalance of lift as seen in Figure 12-20.

As you can see, the relative wind caused by the plane's path toward the ground is the same speed and direction for both wings, and the relative wind caused by rotation is the same velocity but from an opposite direction for each wing—giving a great difference in the angles of attack of the wings.

Once the spin is established, you can maintain it as long as you like with full up-elevator and full left rudder.

Relaxing the back pressure will result in some airplanes going from the spin into a spiral.

A properly executed spin is not any harder on an airplane than a stall. The airspeed remains low. (If you get a chance during the demonstration, look at the airspeed indicator. It will be showing a speed in the vicinity of the normal stalling speed or even "zero" in some trainers.)

A sloppy recovery puts far more stress on the airplane than the spin itself.

Recovery

At this point we'll just look at the rudder and elevator use during the spin recovery. A full recovery procedure will be discussed later.

1. Apply full opposite rudder as needed to stop rotation. Opposite rudder alone would stop rotation on older, lighter trainers. Newer planes may require full opposite rudder and then brisk forward pressure before rotation will stop.

   If in an accidental spin you're confused as to the direction of rotation, use rudder opposite to the indications of the turn needle or the small airplane in the turn coordinator as shown in Figure 12-21B. These indicators are deflected to the left (a left spin), so opposite (right) rudder would be applied.

2. Relax the back pressure. Again, in older lightplanes you need only to relax the back pressure. *A later*

model may require the wheel or stick to be moved forward briskly and held there. But more about this shortly.

3. When the rotation stops, neutralize the rudder.

4. Ease the plane from the dive. You converted the plane's actions from a rotating stall to a straight dive. Don't wait too long to pull the plane out of the dive because the airspeed will be building up. On the other hand don't jerk it out, since you don't want to put undue stress on the airplane.

Figure 12-15. The airplane is rolling and yawing into the spin.

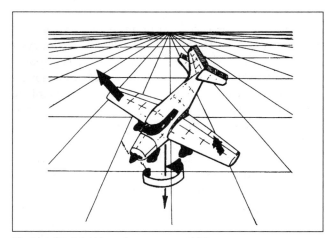

Figure 12-16. Wings have unequal lift.

Figure 12-17. One or both of the wings is stalled even though the airplane appears to be pointed nearly straight down. The angle of attack is the key.

Figure 12-18. The spin as seen from the cockpit.

Figure 12-19. The spin as it will probably be seen from the cockpit your first time. The ball in the turn coordinator is to the left side of the instrument, you will notice, not to the right as might be assumed by theory. (You are holding full *left* rudder, which under normal flying conditions would put the ball to the right—but not in a developed spin with the instrument mounted on the left side of the panel, as shown.)

Common Errors

1. Failure to get a clean spin entry—getting a spiral instead. (More about this shortly.)
2. Overenthusiasm on the releasing of back pressure, that is, pushing forward abruptly on the wheel and causing a negative load factor to be put on the plane.
3. *Not* releasing the back pressure enough. Some students get so eager to get out of the left spin, for instance, that they stop the rotation by full right rudder and forward wheel, then pull right back with the wheel to pull out of the dive. They are astounded to notice that they restalled the airplane and that the still held right rudder caused them to enter a spin to the right. This is called a progressive spin but is really the same as any other spin. In this case it requires that you start a new recovery procedure for a spin to the right. This is embarrassing unless you can convince the instructor that it was a deliberate demonstration of your skill. Flight instructors are pretty skeptical people.

In discussing spin recovery, it was noted that most older lightplanes need only a little relaxation of rudder or back pressure to ease them out of a spin. However, improper loadings may cause even a "docile" airplane (or maybe it's a type of light airplane that doesn't know it's supposed to get out so ridiculously easy) to surprise you. One recommended type of recovery would be to apply full opposite rudder, followed immediately by a brisk forward motion of the control wheel or stick, which is held until the rotation stops. If you've tried the "relaxation of control" type of recovery and the spin is continuing, go back to pro-spin controls and institute the type of recovery just cited to get a "running start."

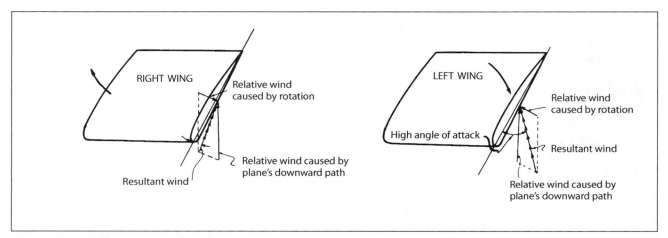

Figure 12-20. Differences in angles of attack in a spin.

In some cases how *fast* the wheel or stick is moved forward is almost as important as how *far* it's moved forward. You could get into an accidental spin at altitude during a stall, and you should also know that *closing the throttle helps the recovery.*

If you do accidentally get into a spin situation someday when you are at altitude practicing stalls, your initial instinct will be (as the airplane rolls and the nose drops to a very low pitch attitude) to hold the wheel or stick all the way back to pull the nose up. *Don't.* You'll need to get the wheel or stick forward to break the stall, and sometimes this is hard to make yourself do.

One instructor experienced in spins, when asked to recommend a "spin warner" (that is, when the airplane is being stalled and yaw or roll is being induced), answered that a boxing glove should come out of the instrument panel hitting the pilot and forcing release of the wheel or stick.

Summary of a Spin Recovery

If you think that during a practice stall things are going too far, as a general approach you should take the following steps:

1. Close the throttle. This makes initial recovery much easier for most airplanes.
2. Neutralize the ailerons. In some airplanes, ailerons *against* the spin make conditions worse; in others, ailerons *with* the spin make conditions worse. In the confusion you might use ailerons the wrong way and delay or preclude recovery, so keep the ailerons neutral.
3. Apply full rudder opposite to the roll or yaw.

4. Then when the rudder hits the stop, briskly move the stick or wheel forward to break the stall and help stop the rotation. Again, you'll automatically tend to hold back the wheel in an attempt to pull the nose up. *(Don't.)*
5. When rotation stops, neutralize the rudder and ease the airplane out of the dive.

Spins and Spirals

Some people have problems knowing the difference between spins and spirals. Figure 12-21A shows the airspeed, turn coordinator, and turn and slip indications in a spiral.

Spiral—This is nothing more than a steep diving turn. The airspeed is rising rapidly and the turn and slip (or turn coordinator) shows a moderate to high rate of turn in the well-developed spiral. The ball will probably be to the left in most airplanes because it takes left rudder in a dive to keep it centered; you've gotten into this situation unconsciously, so you aren't correcting for it. (Right rudder is needed at low speeds and high power settings to keep the ball centered.) The spiral is a low angle of attack/high-speed situation and the recovery procedure is to use *normal control pressures.* You'd level the wings with coordinated aileron and rudder and *then* ease the nose back to level. You'd also throttle back as soon as you realized the airspeed was picking up to keep the rpm under the red line (fixed-pitch prop). But the point is that the spiral is nothing more than an exaggerated combination of two of the Four Fundamentals—a turn and a descent—and the average 2-hour student should be able to recover from it.

A. Spiral   B. Spin

Figure 12-21. Instrument indications in a spiral and a developed spin (to the left, in both cases). For the spin recovery, you would apply full rudder opposite to the turn coordinator airplane or the needle. (Pay no attention to the ball.) The instruments shown here are on the *left* side of the instrument panel. The ball in a slip indicator on the *right* side of the instrument panel always went to the *right* in different side-by-side trainers spun by the author.

Spin—This is a high angle of attack/low-airspeed situation; the airspeed will be hovering somewhere down in the stall area (Figure 12-21B). The recovery requires an apparently unnatural use of the controls. You don't use aileron and rudder together to "level" the wings. You neutralize the ailerons just to keep from complicating matters, as noted earlier, and use rudder alone against the rotation. Instead of "naturally" getting the nose up by added back pressure, you'll have to try to push it even farther down to decrease the angle of attack and get out of the stalled condition. Then bring the nose up with back pressure after the airplane is out of the spin (rudder neutral) and in the dive.

Note that the ball is well to the left side of the two turn instruments in Figure 12-21B. It's assumed that this is a side-by-side trainer and those instruments are on the left side of the panel; this could well be the indications of the ball in a *left* spin. The ball (slip indicator) tends to go to the side of the panel it is mounted on, regardless of spin direction. Usually the rate of yaw and/or roll is much greater than in the spiral, with the indicators) pegged in the direction of spin. You, however, will have no comparison as shown by A and B in Figure 12-21, and the low airspeed (constant or oscillating in a low-speed range) will be the big clue for detecting a spin situation. *The ball is to be ignored as an indication of spin direction.*

So the spiral problem is that of a too-high airspeed. "Normal" control pressures are used to recover.

The spin problem is that of a too-low airspeed (too-high angle of attack). Mechanical control *movements* are used to initiate the recovery. The airplane is then flown normally out of the dive.

Summary of Elementary Stalls and Spins

The elementary stall recovery requires that you get the air flowing smoothly over the wing again. Control pressure or abruptness of control movements will vary between lightplanes and heavy planes and will even vary between different types of lightplanes. Whatever the type of plane, the required result is the same.

An airplane can be stalled at any speed and attitude.

The fact that spins were covered right after the elementary stalls does not necessarily mean that this is the phase in which you will practice spins. Your instructor will likely want to wait until after you solo or may not demonstrate them at all. It is a good idea to be able to recognize and recover from the spin and move on to other maneuvers after you have done this.

All "normal" category airplanes that are capable of spinning are placarded against spins, and if your trainer is so certificated you won't be doing them. Some "utility" category airplanes are also placarded against spins.

The airplane's attitude and heading will be changing rapidly during these maneuvers, and you'd better keep those eyeballs moving. The practice area is no place to "run into an old friend" (or anybody else, for that matter) (Figure 12-22).

A stall warning indicator may be an electrical or a reed type (sound). The electrical type is attached to a cockpit warning device such as a light or horn, depending on the make or model. A general idea is shown in Figure 12-23.

Figure 12-22. Other airplanes may be using "your" practice area.

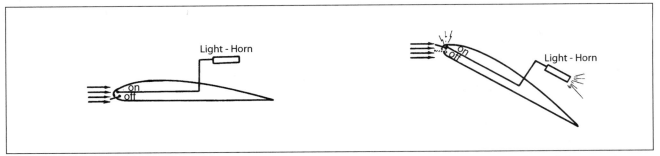

Figure 12-23. At normal angles of attack, the relative wind keeps the switch in the OFF position. As the airfoil approaches the critical angle of attack, the relative wind pushes the tab to ON. The horn or light operates as long as the critical angle of attack continues.

The tab is set at the correct angle for the particular airfoil being used. The indicator "warns" of any approaching stall. Generally, it is set slightly ahead of the stall so that under normal conditions, such as a landing, the pilot is warned 5–8 K before the stall. The warning may be given anytime the angle of attack becomes too great, regardless of the airspeed.

The pneumatic-type stall warning system used on some current trainers has an inlet on the leading edge of the left wing, connected by tubing to an air-operated horn within the pilot's hearing. The air pressure variations at changing, higher angles of attack draw air through the horn, giving warning of the impending stall several knots before the stall break occurs. The tone usually gets higher in pitch as the stall approaches. (If you notice that it's starting to play a hymn, you could be in a little trouble.)

The military uses angle of attack indicators for performance information, particularly for approaches. The advantage of this is that the airplane always stalls at the same angle of attack (for a given flap setting) regardless of weight or g forces acting on the airplane. The angle of attack indicator doesn't have general acceptance for light general aviation airplanes but may be used in the future.

A Few Last Notes on Spins

1. The *Pilot's Operating Handbook* and an instructor current in spins in that model are the final authorities on spins for a particular airplane.
2. *In an accidental spin with the flaps down, get them up as soon as possible for easier recovery and to avoid exceeding the flaps-extended airspeed,* V_{FE} *(Figure 3-28 and 3-29), in the postspin dive.*
3. *If you believe you are beginning to get into an accidental spin situation and have forgotten everything else you've read, been told, or practiced,* CLOSE THE THROTTLE AND GET THAT CONTROL WHEEL OR THE STICK FORWARD *to break the stall condition—and the sooner the better. This is not always the most efficient method of spin recovery, but it can stop an impending problem if done soon enough. However, there's absolutely no substitute for being familiar with the spin and recovery characteristics of your airplane as demonstrated by and practiced with a savvy instructor.*

14 CFR Part 61 requires that the applicant for a sport, recreational or private pilot certificate has had ground instruction in stall awareness, spin entry, spins, and spin recovery techniques. If you don't actually get to do spins, your instructor will give you such ground instruction so that you'll at least have an understanding of the factors involved. There are questions about spins in the Private and Sport Pilot Knowledge Tests.

13

Takeoffs and Landings

After you have about 5 or 6 hours and are proficient in the Four Fundamentals, stalls, wind correction maneuvers, and elementary emergencies, the periods of shooting takeoffs and landings will begin.

Maybe you feel that takeoffs and landings are the most important parts of flying, but as far as your training is concerned they are just another maneuver. Students may place even more weight on landings than takeoffs.

Takeoffs are not important, they think, but *LANDINGS* are. So with this attitude, they find themselves having plenty of trouble when it comes to getting the bird smoothly into the air.

Normal Takeoff

The instructor will have you follow through on the takeoffs during the first flight or two, and probably by the third or fourth flight you will be making the takeoffs yourself.

Most of the trainers being used today are the tricycle-gear type. As in taxiing, the lower nose position gives better visibility during the ground roll parts of the takeoff and landing.

Because the airplane is in level flight position, the takeoff becomes a matter of opening the throttle smoothly, keeping the airplane straight, and as the controls become firm, applying back pressure to ease the nosewheel up to attain the takeoff attitude, and letting the airplane fly itself off. As you found in taxiing, most tricycle-gear airplanes have nosewheel steering, and during the initial part of the ground roll, right rudder pedal pressure will be needed to take care of the left-turning tendency always existing in a low-speed, high-power situation. While the nosewheel is on the ground, the steering is divided between the nosewheel and the aerodynamics of the deflected right rudder; as the nosewheel is lifted, be ready to use more right rudder to compensate for the loss of nosewheel steering.

Tricycle-Gear Airplane Takeoff Procedure

1. See that no airplanes are landing. Taxi to the center line of the runway.
2. Line up with the center line or, if there isn't one (as on a grass strip), use a reference at the far end of the runway and keep scanning the surface between you and that reference.
3. Apply power smoothly to get rolling, then move on to full throttle. Keep your hand on the throttle and check the engine instruments.
4. As the controls become firm (particularly the elevators), use back pressure to obtain the proper angle of attack for takeoff. Be ready to add right rudder as the nosewheel lifts clear (Figure 13-1).
5. After the lift-off, relax back pressure slightly to assure that the nose maintains the proper climb attitude. Maintain that attitude and climb straight ahead, correcting for torque and keeping your hand on the throttle to make sure that it's at climb power. Ease the flaps up (if used) at a safe altitude (usually at 100–200 feet above the ground).

Common Errors

1. During the initial part of the roll, allowing (or "helping") the control wheel to move forward so that the elevators are slightly or well down. This could put too much weight on the nosewheel and could cause a delay in the takeoff or steering problems—called "wheelbarrowing" (to be covered later in the chapter).
2. The average student at first is usually timid in applying back pressure at the right time to ease the nose up to the takeoff attitude. This results in the airplane staying on the ground with too high an airspeed, thus wasting runway and possible getting some nosewheel "chatter." Some King Kong types give a mighty heave too early and pull the airplane abruptly into the air before it's quite ready to go. You'll find that after a couple of takeoffs you'll be

Figure 13-1. (A) Line up with the center line and apply power to start rolling, then smoothly go to full power for takeoff, keeping the airplane straight by smooth application of right rudder. (B) As the controls become firm, start applying more back pressure to ease the nose up to the takeoff attitude.

able to apply the right amount of back pressure at the right time.

3. Not relaxing back pressure after the lift-off (or continuing to hold the back pressure used to bring the airplane off) so that the airplane's nose rises sharply and doesn't maintain the best rate of climb speed (V_Y).

Figure 13-2 shows the side view of a takeoff for a tricycle-gear airplane.

Takeoff for Airplanes with Tailwheels

You are trying to leave the ground as smoothly and efficiently as possible. Taxi onto the runway, first making sure no other planes are on final approach, and line up with some object such as a tree at the far end (Figure 13-3). In most planes with tailwheel-type landing gear, it is difficult to see over the nose in the three-point attitude, so you must look at your object alongside the nose for the first part of the takeoff run. You may ask, "What if there's no tree?" Lacking a reference point at the end, watch the left side of the runway. The takeoff consists of three phases: (1) the initial or three-point position part of the run; (2) the roll on the front two wheels, in

which the plane is streamlined to pick up speed quickly; and (3) the lifting off, or transition to flight.

Phase 1
Open the throttle slowly to get the plane rolling then continue to apply full power smoothly.

The torque situation is this: You are now using full power, but the plane is barely moving. The rudder itself is comparatively ineffective, and the greater part of the steering must be done with the tailwheel. As the speed picks up, the rudder begins to get more effective and less right pedal pressure is needed. Don't worry about the change in rudder pedal pressures, just keep that tree lined up correctly. Of course, you will be watching the runway as well.

The best method of handling the elevators is to have them at neutral or slightly ahead of neutral. There's no need to force the tail up abruptly. In fact, holding the wheel full forward to get the tail up too soon might cause loss of directional control. If the tail comes up abruptly before you have effective rudder, the plane may turn to the left before it can be stopped with rudder. If the elevator trim tab has been set at neutral (and you saw that it was during the pretakeoff check), the tail will come up by itself when the time gets ripe. You can,

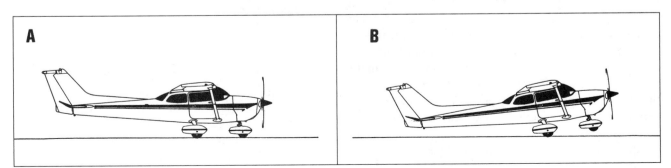

Figure 13-2. A side view of the initial roll (A) and lift-off (B) attitudes for a tricycle-gear airplane.

Figure 13-3. Pick an easy-to-recognize object to line up on.

however, help the process by exerting slight forward pressure on the elevators as the plane picks up speed.

Don't "walk" the rudder, hoping to average out the swing of the nose—you'll never get the feel of the takeoff that way.

Probable Errors in Phase 1

1. Abrupt throttle usage resulting in poor directional control at the beginning of the run.
2. Not keeping the plane lined up with the object at the end of the runway.
3. "Walking" the rudders.

Phase 2 — The Tail-Up Part of the Roll

Many students have trouble in the transition from phase 1 to phase 2. While the plane is rolling in the three-point position, you have both tailwheel steering and, in the latter part of phase 1, fairly effective relative air moving past the rudder. When the tail comes up, the tailwheel no longer helps and a further deflection of the rudder is required for torque correction. Students sometimes have trouble correcting for torque and keeping

the nose lined up. Their takeoffs are smooth rolls interrupted by a period of mad maneuvering because they use the rudder too enthusiastically. The plane weaves down the runway, putting great side stresses on the tires and landing gear. This type of rudder action slows the takeoff and, if it goes too far, may result in structural damage to the airplane.

Watch for any swinging of the nose and catch it early with the minimum of rudder pressure.

The tail slowly comes up and you are keeping the plane straight. The tree hasn't moved and now you can see the whole runway ahead (Figure 13-4).

Probable Errors in Phase 2

1. Getting eager to get the tail up and having steering problems.
2. Trying to force the airplane off too soon by excessive back pressure, resulting in slowing the airplane and delaying the takeoff.

A good demonstration of the effects of gyroscopic precession can be given by forcing the tail up suddenly

Figure 13-4. Now all you have to do is keep it straight and wait.

on takeoff. The rotating propeller acts as a gyro wheel. When the tail is raised, the rotational plane of the propeller is changed. As the tail comes up, the effect is that of a force being exerted against the top of the propeller arc from behind. You know that a gyro reacts as if the force had been exerted at a point 90° around the wheel (measured in the direction of rotation). The airplane reacts as if the force had been exerted at the right side of the arc, and this tends to turn the plane to the left. The faster the tail is raised, the more abrupt this left-turning action. This acts only as long as the plane's attitude is being changed. Once the takeoff attitude is reached and maintained, precession is not an important factor. You will not be worried so much about what causes certain effects on takeoff as about correcting them. If the nose veers to the left, no matter what the cause, you'll have to straighten it out. This is the most important thing to remember.

Phase 3 — Lift-Off

As the plane picks up speed, the controls become firmer. The attitude is that of a shallow climb. This makes it possible for the plane to lift itself off as flying speed is reached.

As the airspeed approaches the takeoff value, the plane will become "light" and may start skipping or bouncing. If this happens, use more back pressure and bring the plane off. The skipping or bouncing is an indication that the plane is ready to fly but there is not quite enough angle of attack to lift it off. Once the plane breaks free, keep it in the air. It doesn't help matters to hit again. If there is a crosswind, you may be drifting across the runway the next time you hit, thus putting a heavy side load on the landing gear.

After you are off the ground with no danger of hitting again, relax back pressure slightly so that the nose does not rise too steeply as the plane accelerates and the elevators become more effective (Figure 13-5). After this point it's no longer a takeoff but a normal climb, and you've been able to cope with that for some time.

As soon as the wheels leave the ground, the rudder no longer steers the airplane. Use coordinated aileron and rudder to turn until you get back on the ground again.

Procedure

1. See that no planes are landing. Taxi to the center line of the runway. Use all the runway available; that portion behind doesn't help you.
2. Line up with some object at the far end of the runway.
3. Apply power smoothly to get it rolling, then apply full throttle smoothly.
4. Keep the plane lined up with the object at the end of the runway.
5. As the tail comes up, be prepared for the need of added right rudder.
6. As controls become firm, bring in gentle back pressure, if necessary, to lift the plane off; when it is off, keep it off.
7. After takeoff, level off to pick up climb speed. Remember the takeoff speed is slightly above stall speed and well below proper climb speed.

If the runway is smooth and you use proper techniques, it should be hard to tell when the plane leaves the ground.

Normal Landing

The normal landing is nothing more than a normal power-off stall, with the stall occurring just as the plane touches the ground. Why stall the airplane? You can put a lightplane on the ground at 100 K, but this is hard on the plane (and on you) and also uses up more runway than is practical. The best idea is to land at the slowest speed possible and still have control of the airplane.

The first thing you want to learn is that the importance of landings is vastly overrated by the public (and probably by you too at this stage). If you make a

Relax back pressure slightly so that the plane does not climb too steeply as the airspeed increases

Figure 13-5. The normal takeoff (tailwheel type).

smooth landing, you're the greatest pilot alive to your passengers. There are several reasons for this: (1) Landings are always made at the airport (you hope) where everybody can see them and know what they are; (2) this flying is still somewhat mysterious to the average person, who figures it must take a high degree of skill to be able to come back down after defying gravity and the elements; and (3) the landing is a maneuver done close to the ground where the smallest mistakes may look like near crashes. At 3,000 feet you may skid a half mile, but since there are no references up there is doesn't show up.

This disease of sweating landings even strikes experienced pilots who should know better. It is interesting to note that the perfect landing is always made on a day when the airport is deserted. But bounce your way in on a sunny Sunday afternoon, with somebody special along for that first ride, and there'll be a fence full of jeerers as you try to park as inconspicuously as possible.

But speaking on a pilot's level, the idea of a landing is to get the plane on the ground without fanfare. *That's all that it is.*

Procedure

The landing is started from a normal glide at a height of about 20 feet (or about hangar height) above the ground. This starting height depends on the size of the airplane and is also affected by the rate of descent. Large planes may start the transition at 75 feet, but hangar height is about right for the lightplane. Start the landing transition or "break the glide" at hangar height by gradually easing the wheel or stick back to stall the airplane. About 19 of that 20 feet is used to change the airplane's attitude from that of the normal glide to the landing attitude.

Transition must be gradual. If you pull the wheel back abruptly, the plane will go up. This is called "ballooning." Ease the nose up to the landing attitude, disturbing the plane's flight path as little as possible. *This takes a certain amount of skill, as you will discover.* The plane is slowing up all this time as the angle of attack is being increased. By the time you are down to about a foot off the ground, the transition to landing attitude is complete and your job is to keep that attitude by using more and more back pressure. *The best way to make a landing is to try to hold the plane off as long as possible.* The faster the plane settles, the faster the rate of application of back pressure must be. The plane continues to settle and slow up. Remembering stalls, you know that the slower the plane gets, the more elevator is needed to hold its attitude, which slows it, etc. You should run out of elevator just as the plane touches the ground.

Thermals, gusts, or downdrafts affect the transition. Only in theory, or on a perfectly calm day, will the wheel be moved smoothly back at a nearly constant or predictable rate.

In other words, there may be times during the transition when you have to relax back pressure. Never *push* forward. Remember you are at a low speed and a high angle of attack. If you decrease the angle of attack suddenly, there will be a lag before the speed picks up. During this time, lift will be practically nothing and you might find that you've made a serious mistake. There may be times when the back pressure must be stopped where it is and other times when it seems that you must pull back rapidly on the wheel or stick at the last part of the landing process. Well, that's the way it is. But one thing is important—start the landing from a normal glide. Generally a poor approach means a poor landing.

Land the tricycle-gear plane so that the initial contact is made on the main wheels. Try to hold the nosewheel off so that the airplane's attitude causes aerodynamic drag and helps slow it down on the landing roll (Figure 13-6).

Later you'll find that there is an optimum time to ease the nosewheel down to get the maximum drag on the landing roll for each plane.

Figure 13-6. Landing the tricycle-gear airplane.

Figure 13-7. The three-point landing (tailwheel type).

The tailwheel airplane should be landed so that the tailwheel and main gear touch simultaneously (Figure 13-7), although for some airplanes (some pilots argue) the tailwheel should touch an instant early.

Where to Look

In order to know when and how much back pressure is to be applied, you must know where the plane is in relation to the ground (Figure 13-8). The nose will be coming up higher and higher as you approach the landing attitude. It will be impossible to see the ground over the nose in some airplanes in the last stage of the landing transition, as you will see during the landing demonstrations in the early part of your training. Some trainers have "low noses," and it's possible to look directly ahead during the landing. But getting into the habit of looking along the left side of the nose works for *all* airplanes. You will be sitting on the left in a side-by-side airplane; the stick and throttle arrangement in a tandem plane also makes it easier for you to turn your head to the left. So you will look out this side after the transition begins. (When you get to be a flight instructor and sit on the right, you'll naturally have to look out the *right* side and this is a tough problem at first for new instructors.)

So the best place to look is to the left, alongside of the nose and far enough ahead so that the ground is not blurred. Don't stare at one spot. Scan the ground; your depth perception depends on a lot of eye movement. If you look only straight down out the side window, the relative movement of the ground is great and you may have a tendency to stall the airplane while it's still a fair distance off the ground. The plane will "drop in" and could be damaged. If you look too far ahead, the error in your depth perception may cause you to fly the plane into the ground.

As you reach about 20 feet, or hangar height, begin the transition (Figures 13-9, 13-10, and 13-11).

Again, don't try to look over the nose. If you can see over the nose during the landing, in most airplanes you don't have the correct landing attitude and will fly into the ground. If you get the nose at the right position and stare blindly up at it, you won't have any idea where the ground is. You'll find out exactly where when you hear (and feel) the sickening thud.

Keep the plane lined up with the runway and have the wings level when you touch down. The stall warner should be making its presence known under normal conditions.

Figure 13-8. Maintain a constant attitude/airspeed during the latter (power-off) part of the approach.

Figure 13-9. After starting the transition at about 20 feet, continue to ease smoothly back on the wheel (altitude shown here about 15 feet).

Figure 13-10. Landing attitude is reached at a height of about 1 foot; continue back pressure to maintain this attitude.

Figure 13-11. The plane continues to settle as you keep easing back on the wheel and it touches in the correct landing attitude. Keep the wheel full back and maintain directional control with the rudder.

Ground Loops

In Figure 13-12 (tailwheel) and Figure 13-13 (tricycle-gear) you see that the momentum of the plane will act through the center of gravity, and the center of friction with the runway may be considered to act at a point midway between the wheels.

If the plane isn't pointed the way it's flying when it hits, a ground loop might result. A ground loop is an abrupt turning of the airplane on the ground. If the ground loop is violent enough, the plane may rock over and drag a wing. The best way to avoid a ground loop is to make sure the plane is lined up with the runway when the touchdown is made.

If the ground loop has started and a wing has dropped, don't get any ideas of bringing it up with rudder. This works in the air but makes matters worse on the ground. The plane rocks over because of the sharpness of the turn. Applying rudder to "speed up" that down wing in hopes of bringing it up only results in a sharper turn. Use all controls including the throttle to stop or slow down the ground loop. A burst of power coupled with prompt rudder and/or brake action against the turn is usually effective as a means of recovery.

If a wing is down during the landing transition, the plane will turn. You'll have to concentrate on keeping those wings level, the plane straight, and making the transition all at the same time. Later you'll be shown how holding a wing down and applying opposite rudder will help in a crosswind landing.

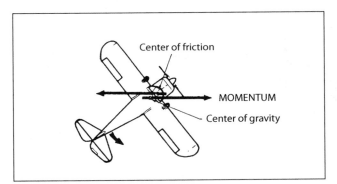

Figure 13-12. Center of gravity, momentum, center of friction (tailwheel plane).

Figure 13-13. The tricycle-gear plane tends to straighten out.

In moving the wheel back during the landing process, students sometimes pull *up* on the left side of the control wheel as well as moving it back (the wheel is generally held on the left side by the left hand). This means that aileron is being applied, the wing is lowered, and the airplane "drifts" toward the right edge of the runway. The stick control, being used by the right hand, is often pulled to the right with the same results.

When you're flying cross-country, a slightly lowered wing for a short time may mean that the plane's path will vary several hundred feet to that side. It's not noticeable up there, but because many runways aren't even a hundred feet wide, you may end up out in the gravel pits and tall grass alongside the runway.

One common error students make during the landing roll is to relax back pressure and allow the control wheel to move forward. In the tailwheel type, this doesn't keep that tailwheel down firmly enough on the ground for good steering; in the tricycle-gear airplane, it will allow too much weight on the nosewheel, causing "wheelbarrowing." Wheelbarrowing occurs when the added weight on the nosewheel causes it to become extra sensitive to rudder pedal pressures during the ground roll. Your correction for a slight nose movement on the rollout may be exaggerated and the airplane overreacts, abruptly turning toward the direction of that corrective rudder. In other words, relaxing of back pressure during the landing roll-out is bad for both types of airplanes.

The first hour of landings will keep both you and the instructor busy. You'll be worn out at the end of the hour but will discover that landings are both fun and interesting.

Shooting Takeoffs and Landings

Most students have 3 to 4 hours of takeoffs and landings before solo. Some may have 2 hours and others 6. This will be the most enjoyable part of your presolo work. You won't have to take the instructor's word for it if you foul up. You can see and feel it for yourself.

The Traffic Pattern

Now that you know the theory of takeoffs and landings, it's good to have an idea of how to go about practicing them.

The airport traffic pattern is established so that planes flying from that field will have some standard of operation for safety's sake.

A typical traffic pattern for a small airport is shown in Figure 13-14. Some airports have a right-hand pattern for some runways, as will be shown by their segmented circles. But the principle is the same.

Back in the olden days of flying, most lightplane approaches were made from a normal power-off glide so that if the engine quit during any part of the approach, the airplane could still make it to the runway. Nowadays, the aircraft engine is so reliable that this is an extremely minor factor; the recommended method of making the approach is to reduce power (as recommended by your instructor) opposite to the point of intended landing and make further reductions as the approach continues. You may have all the power off just after turning final, or you may have to carry power until reaching the runway—it depends on your situation. You'll also make some approaches from a power-off glide to learn your airplane's glide characteristics, but most of the time you'll make approaches with a gradual reduction of power all the way around. Power-off approaches will be covered later in the chapter.

You'll be introduced to the takeoff and landing series gradually. You've probably made the takeoffs without any help for the last two or three flights and have been following through on the controls during the last few landings. Generally, takeoffs and landings are started with the instructor demonstrating two or three at the end of a regular period, allowing you to practice more takeoffs and landings each time until the whole period is spent on these maneuvers.

The first couple of hours of landing practice will probably be full-stop landings. That is, you will let the plane slow down; then you'll turn off the runway and taxi back to make another takeoff. This is good practice in learning to control the airplane as it slows up on the landing roll, as well as smoothing out any taxiing problems. Later you'll probably shoot "touch-and-go's"—opening the throttle, pushing the carburetor heat off (if it was used throughout the approach; your instructor will have recommendations), raising the flaps, and taking off again. Touch-and-go's allow more landings during a practice period and are good for the student who only needs practice in the landing itself, but they should not be overdone.

Figure 13-14. An example traffic pattern. Shown is a "closed pattern" as used in shooting takeoffs and landings. Your instructor will demonstrate, and you will practice, departing and entering the pattern. (Substitute your own numbers.) The leg after takeoff, as you climb out tracking the runway center line, is the *departure leg*. When making a go-around and flying the pattern into the wind, the term is *upwind leg*. When making a go-around or aborted landing, fly to the *right* of the runway as you climb out, as shown at the top of Figure 13-39(A), so you can keep an eye out for airplanes taking off and climbing out. For a right-handed pattern go-around, it's particularly important that you watch for airplanes turning into your path. Also *see* Figure 20-2.

Figure 13-15. Varying the downwind leg position for different winds.

Figure 13-16. Variation of approach angle with wind. Constant glide attitude and airspeed (angles exaggerated).

Figure 13-17. Positions on the downwind and base leg.

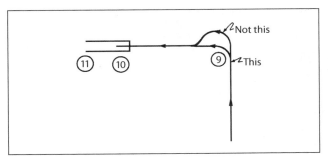

Figure 13-18. The turn onto the final leg and the last part of the approach.

The best way to get an idea of what happens during a typical takeoff and landing pattern is to take it step by step (Figures 13-15 through 13-18).

Assume that you are sitting at the takeoff end of the runway, the pretakeoff check is complete, there are no planes landing, and the wind is moderate (8–10 K) and right down the runway.

1. Taxi into position and make a normal takeoff.
2. Make a normal climb straight ahead to the altitude set by your local rules. Look back occasionally to see that you are climbing in line with the runway and not headed out cross-country.
3. When the turn altitude is reached, look behind again to make sure you aren't going to turn into a faster plane coming up from behind. Make a 90° climbing turn to the left. Actually, the turn should not be quite 90°, since you will have to compensate for the wind. Incidentally, don't make any turns inside the airport boundary. It's better to be at least 1,000 feet past the end of the runway before turning.
4. Make the second 90°, left-climbing turn whenever it is necessary in order to establish the correct distance from the runway on the downwind leg. The principle of establishing a distance from the runway is this: If the wind is strong, the approach angle is steep on the final approach for a particular power setting; therefore, more altitude is needed at point X (Figures 13-15 and 13-16). Maybe you say, "Why not stay the same distance from the runway for every wind velocity and just make that first turn sooner?" It can be demonstrated that you will be critically low at the point of the final turn if the wind is strong and also you'll have no "straightaway" or final to establish yourself for the landing.
5. Climb to 1,000 feet. Keep the plane flying parallel to the runway (Figure 13-17).

6. Pull the carburetor heat a few seconds before you reach the position directly opposite the intended landing spot. Give it a chance to clear out any ice before you start reducing power. The use of carburetor heat will depend on the airplane and conditions: (a) You may not use carburetor heat for certain airplanes if conditions preclude icing, (b) you may be told to apply carburetor heat on the downwind leg to check for icing and then push it off if no evidence of icing is found, or (c) you may use full carburetor heat throughout the approach.

7. Reduce power and set up the approach speed.

8. Make a slightly more than 90° turn to the left. Continue to reduce the power as necessary to control the approach path. One problem students have is making this turn too shallow, so the airplane is nearly over to the final leg before the first 90° of turn is completed. This would then require a steep 90° turn onto final, at a low altitude, to line up with the runway center line—a disconcerting and possibly dangerous practice. This is more likely to happen in a high-wing trainer because the down-wing may keep the runway hidden throughout the turn onto the base leg. You may not realize that you are moving so close to the final leg. This is particularly a problem if the airplane on the base leg has a tailwind component as shown in Figure 13-31. Most instructors prefer that the turn at point 8 (Figure 13-17) be slightly steeper than the one at point 9 (Figure 13-18) because (a) the steeper turn is done at the higher altitude, and (b) the turn will be completed soon enough so that the wings can be leveled for a straight base leg (and a good look at the runway). More about this later in the chapter.

9. Make the final turn as needed to line up with the center line of the runway. A common fault of students is overshooting the runway on the final turn. This happens when the final turn is not started soon enough and the plane must be turned back into the runway. Another error is making the final turn too soon, angling toward the runway. Shoot for at least a ¹/₂-mile final.

10. When your height above the ground is approximately 20 feet, begin the transition to the landing attitude. Keep the plane straight and the wings level. At about 1–2 feet, the landing attitude should be reached. Continue the back pressure, maintaining this attitude as the plane settles. The wheel or stick should reach its full back travel just as the wheels touch.

11. Keep the plane rolling straight down the runway. As it slows to taxi speed, turn off the runway and taxi back for another go.

Don't try to turn off the runway at too high a speed—you may ground loop.

Don't try to slow the airplane too quickly by using brakes. It's not good for a tricycle-gear-equipped plane, and you may nose over in a tailwheel-type plane; it takes experience to be able to apply brakes on the landing roll without nosing over. It's hard on tires too.

Figure 20-2 gives suggested traffic patterns as in the *Aeronautical Information Manual* and you might want to look it over as you prepare to fly to other airports during the cross-country portion of your flight training.

Flaps

You've seen the flaps during the preflight checks, and the instructor has shown you how to use them in the approach to landing stalls as well as during the approach demonstrations. But now take a closer look at how *you* are to use them during these takeoff and landing sessions and in future pattern work (Figure 13-19).

By extending the flaps you increase the camber (curvature) of the wing, which results in more lift *and* more drag for a certain nose position. This means you can have a steeper angle of descent to clear obstacles because of the drag, and you will land at a lower airspeed because of a higher coefficient of lift. There may be a pitch change with flap extension.

As the flaps are extended (lowered) in the approach, the nose must be lowered to maintain the normal glide speed. After the landing, the drag of the flaps helps shorten the landing roll.

For takeoff the flaps are set at the position recommended by the manufacturer. This may vary from no deflection for normal takeoff to 10 degrees or more for special procedures such as for soft- or short-field takeoffs. If your airplane has flaps, you'll be shown their use from the beginning.

Figure 13-19. A suggested use of a checklist and flap operations during the approach and landing portion of the traffic pattern. Your instructor and the airplane's *Pilot's Operating Handbook* may require a modification of this procedure. (From the *The Flight Instructor's Manual*)

The flap operation range is marked by that white arc on the airspeed indicator. The bottom of the white arc is the flaps-down, power-off stalling speed at the maximum certificated weight of the airplane. The high value (top of the white arc) is the maximum speed at which full flaps may be used at any weight. (For safety, think of this speed as the maximum at which *any* flaps may be used.) If the flaps are lowered at an *indicated* (calibrated) airspeed higher than noted at the top of the white arc, possible structural and trim problems could occur. Since the flaps add both drag and lift for any given airspeed, you will find that your angle of descent will be steepened by their use; you will also find that the landing speed is measurably lowered. Generally it's best *not* to combine slips and flaps; some airplanes don't like it. You might check this for your airplane at a safe altitude with an instructor (the *POH* will have information for this).

You'll get instruction on landing *without* flaps in an airplane equipped with flaps, unless the operations limitations prohibit no-flap landings. If you've been using flaps a lot lately, that first practice no-flap landing will give the impression that you're going to float all the way down the runway; you'll tend to let the airspeed get too great on final approach. For most airplanes the actual landing technique is easier without flaps; the nose can be eased up with less effort or trim. You should be familiar with how the airplane handles on landing both with and without flaps.

While flaps are a great aid to the pilot on approach and landing, they can be a problem when a sudden go-around is required. Flap drag eats up horsepower that could be used for needed climb. Someday you may have to make a go-around from a touchdown attitude with full flaps, starting at not more than a couple of feet above the runway. This would be about the most critical condition for a go-around; you're low and slow and the airplane is "dirty."

First, on any go-around *add full power before starting to clean up the airplane.* The power will stop or slow your rate of descent. Then start getting the gear and flaps up. You'll be surprised, but the change in stall speed from idle to full power almost offsets the difference in stall speed between flaps up and flaps down (it depends on the particular airplane). In other words, apply full power and figure on starting to get the flaps up right afterward. This doesn't mean that you instantly go from full flaps to no flaps, but get some flaps off as soon as full power is applied and continue to get them up as soon as safely possible. Many pilots have been warned so much about the danger of suddenly pulling the flaps up that they spend valuable time—and attention—just seeing how smoothly and slowly the flap cleaning-up process can be done. For some airplanes, the manufacturer recommends that flaps be brought up (in increments) *before* the landing gear for best go-around results. Most trainers have fixed gear anyway, so this is a decision you probably won't have to make—now.

Slip

The slip is a very important maneuver for airplanes not equipped with flaps and is used to increase the angle of descent without increasing the airspeed. If you are high on the final approach and dive the plane (Figure 13-20A), you will get down to the runway but will also have excess speed that will cause the plane to float down the runway. In the slip, the pilot turns the plane so that an unstreamlined shape is presented to the relative wind (Figure 13-20B). Airspeed will stay low even in a steep descent because of this drag.

There are two kinds of slips: the sideslip and the forward slip. The difference is a matter of the path over the ground. The idea is the same for both.

Take a slip in general. The technique is to use aileron in the direction of slip. When aileron alone is used, adverse yaw occurs, as you know from experience by now. If you give it left aileron, the plane banks to the left and the nose yaws to the right. Stop the nose at the peak of its yaw with right rudder. Continue to hold left aileron and right rudder and whatever back pressure is needed to maintain glide speed. The more aileron and opposite rudder used, the steeper the slip, which means a steeper angle of descent (Figure 13-21).

The steeper the slip, the more the airplane's path varies from the way the nose is pointing. Bank an

Figure 13-20. (A) Silhouette of the drag area of a plane in a dive. (B) Silhouette of the drag area of a plane in a slip.

Figure 13-21. A forward slip on final.

A The sideslip

B The forward slip

Figure 13-22. Aerodynamically, the airplane doesn't know the difference between a sideslip or forward slip. You'll set up the situation as necessary to get the proper path over the ground.

airplane 15° and notice the difference between the forward slip and the sideslip. *Remember, for a 15° bank the flight path of the airplane will vary from the way the nose is pointing by a certain number of degrees.* Assume, for instance, that in the case of a 15° bank the variation is 10° (Figure 13-22).

The forward slip is used to lose altitude while following your original flight path and is considered as a means of losing altitude faster without picking up excess speed, as would be done in a dive.

The sideslip is normally used to correct for wind drift (as you will see later in crosswind landings) *or to change the flight path of the airplane as you increase the angle of descent.*

Right now let's discuss the *forward slip*. It's a handy maneuver in a forced landing. After you are able to do slips, the forced landing becomes a matter of picking a field, making a slightly high approach, and slipping into the field. If you try to hit the field right on the nose, make an error in judgment and undershoot, you can never get that altitude back and will hit short of the field. You can always lose altitude, so make the approach slightly high and slip off the excess altitude as you need to.

If there is a slight crosswind on the runway that you are slipping into, always slip (bank) into the wind. This way you can make a slight sideslip so that your path is straight down the runway. Say, for instance, that for

Figure 13-23. Combining a forward slip and sideslip to correct for wind drift as you lose extra altitude.

a 30° banked slip the flight path is 20° from the nose. Just don't turn the nose so far from the wind (Figure 13-23).

Also, by slipping upwind, it's easier to convert the forward slip to a sideslip for wind drift correction on the landing (Figure 13-24).

If you slipped to the right with a left crosswind, it would be necessary in recovering to roll from a right bank to a left wing-down position. You would be

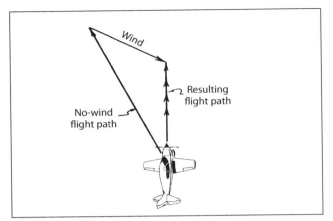

Figure 13-24. The slideslip as used to correct for wind drift on landing. (That's quite a crosswind shown here, and in such a real situation you'd be better off going to another airport with a runway more into the wind — but the example shows up better this way.)

drifting across the runway at a good clip by the time you got the wing lowered and drift correction set up.

A left slip means using left aileron. A right slip means the use of right aileron. The aileron is considered to be the main control in the slip, with the rudder used as an auxiliary, or "heading lock."

Procedure

For a forward slip to the right from a normal glide:
1. Right aileron is applied. As the nose yaws left, stop it at that position with left rudder. If added steepness of bank is needed, add more right aileron and left rudder.
2. Maintain normal glide pitch attitude.
3. When you are ready to recover, neutralize the controls and maintain normal glide speed with the elevators.

Common Errors in the Forward Slip

1. Yawing the plane so that the flight path is changed.
2. Letting the nose come up as the slip is entered, resulting in a low airspeed. Some airplanes require that you hold a slight forward pressure to keep the nose from coming up too high in the slip.
3. Picking up speed in the slip—nose too low.
4. Picking up speed on the recovery from the slip. *Don't slip too low, it takes altitude to recover.*

A Couple of Added Notes on the Slip

The slip will be fairly hard at first. You've been taught for several hours that aileron and rudder go together and now have to "uncoordinate." Many instructors don't allow their students to slip the airplane if they are high on one of the first solo approaches, and some don't instruct slips until sometime after solo. You can get into trouble if the airplane is allowed to get too slow

during the slip. It's always a good idea to practice at a safe altitude before using slips on a landing.

Some trainers have a static port only on the left side, as shown back in Figure 3-5. This can cause some errors of airspeed in slips. Take a good look at Figure 3-5. You can see that the static pressure in the static tube should exactly cancel the static pressure in the pitot tube (it says here), leaving the dynamic pressure to be properly indicated as airspeed. In a forward slip, or sideslip to the *left*, dynamic (or ram) pressure will be entering the static tube. The pressure in the airspeed instrument case will be higher than normal. This will tend to keep the diaphragm from expanding properly and the airspeed will read low. (Dynamic pressure coming in the "wrong way" tends to cancel out the "proper" dynamic pressure coming in the pitot tube.) In a slip to the right, a low-pressure area tends to be formed on the left side of the airplane, *lowering that static pressure* so that it doesn't "cancel" the static pressure in the pitot tube (and diaphragm). The airspeed indicator "thinks" that the airplane is going faster than it really is and so reads *high*. The point is, if you rely on the airspeed indicator rather than the airplane's attitude, you may be too fast in the slip and lose the benefit of the maneuver, or you may be too slow and have an abnormally high sink rate. Some airplanes have static ports on both sides, which tend to cancel out static pressure problems.

Interestingly enough, some *Pilot's Operating Handbooks* advise against slipping with the flaps down (apparently meaning a *forward* slip) but say nothing against using the wing-down crosswind landing, which is a sideslip. Again, for any given banked slip the aerodynamics are the same. (Crosswind landings will be covered shortly.)

Recoveries from Bad Situations During the Landing

As everyone knows, you will not always make perfect landings, so you will be shown the corrective procedure if you happen to foul up a little on an approach or landing.

Flying into the Ground

This is generally caused by your trying to look over the nose. Naturally you won't want to pull the nose up in the way when you're trying to look over it—the plane hits on the main wheels and bounces. You've probably seen planes hit on the wheels and go up 10 or 15 feet in the air and figured that the plane hit mighty hard to jump that high. Here's what happened. The plane hit the ground with quite a bit of flying speed left because

Figure 13-25. The bounce recovery.

the pilot hadn't gotten the nose up to slow the plane down. The wheels hit and the rebound forced the nose up suddenly, giving the wings added lift. The result was that most of the height of the bounce was caused by this lift—not by the bouncing rubber tires (tailwheel airplanes).

To recover, *ease* the nose over and if the height is 5 feet or more and you've gotten pretty slow it's a good idea to add power (Figure 13-25). If there's not enough runway left for landing, open the throttle full, push the carburetor heat OFF, and make another pattern and landing. And *this time don't bounce.*

Many students realize that they are about to hit and make a last ditch jerk on the stick or wheel just as the plane touches. This aggravates the situation considerably. It's also poor form to sit there doing nothing after the bounce, with the plane pointed up and the airspeed dropping.

Most bounces are minor—maybe only a foot or so. If this is the case it's generally not necessary to add power; reland, making sure the plane has the correct landing attitude when it touches again. Most instructors will forgive *one* bounce per landing but *not* two or three (or more).

Pilots have the problem of getting out of phase with the bounces, thus making matters worse. Even the tricycle-gear plane can produce a series of impressive actions when the pilot touches down on the nosewheel, yanks back on the wheel, and manages to be 180° out of phase with the airplane... *Land again, making sure the airplane has the correct landing attitude when it touches.*

Dropping the Plane In

When the plane is stalled too high above the ground, the resulting back-wrenching maneuver is called "dropping it in."

Students, after flying a plane into the ground, to the accompanying anguished screams of the instructor, may go to such efforts to keep from repeating this mistake on the next landing that they "drop it in." This usually results in even louder cries from the instructor.

Dropping in is caused by not knowing where the ground is. You are looking too close to the airplane and the ground is blurred. Your depth perception is poor, and you are perfectly happy landing 5 feet off the ground. Many a flight school owner has wished for a runway jack when seeing a favorite, shiny new airplane being stalled several feet above the ground (Figure 13-26).

Figure 13-26. Sometimes a runway jack is needed for the pilot who keeps landing up in the air.

It's very important that you be able to recognize the factors leading up to the drop-in.

As soon as you realize that you and the runway have not made connections and the plane is stalling, *apply power!* You won't have room to completely recover, but the power may slow the descent enough to soften the impact and keep the plane from being damaged.

Another cause of dropping in is ballooning (coming back on the wheel too abruptly) during the transition and then not relaxing back pressure, thus letting the speed get too slow. Being too low on the approach while trying to stretch the glide is another cause. You unconsciously pull the nose up as you see that it's going to be a pinch making the runway; by the time you start breaking the glide, the airspeed is very low (the angle of attack is very high), and you run out of airspeed and inspiration before the airplane reaches the ground.

In some cases of ballooning or bouncing the tendency is to add power while the airplane is *pointed up*, thereby dragging it up even higher at a too-low airspeed. The power is then cut, giving the airplane a further distance to "fall" than was the situation in the first place. The addition of power *at the wrong time* can aggravate an already bad situation. *Basically, power is added to decrease or stop a rate of descent, either immediately as the descent starts and/or during the process.*

Too Low in the Approach

There'll be quite a few times during the presolo part of your flying when you'll misjudge the approach and realize the plane is going to be short of the runway. Maybe it was caused by the downwind leg being too far out from the runway or because that first approach turn wasn't started soon enough or you chopped off all the power too soon. At any rate you're going to run out of altitude before reaching the runway. *Don't try to stretch the glide; power is needed.*

As soon as you realize that you are low, apply power. Don't wait until the plane is skimming over that cornfield a fourth of a mile from the runway before doing something about it.

Apply enough power to get to the runway and still maintain the normal approach speed. In applying the power you'll raise the nose slightly. A mistake some students make is forgetting to lower the nose again when they have the runway made and closing the throttle. With the nose up and power off, the plane loses airspeed quickly and the end result is that the student drops the plane in.

Another mistake made by some students is to apply full power and fly the plane to the runway at about cruising speed and then wonder, when the power is chopped off, why the plane won't land but floats to the far end of the runway.

The sooner you recognize the fact that you are low and do something about it, the more credit you'll be given for judgment.

Too High in the Approach

On a hot summer day a light airplane will be affected by updrafts and may end up too high to land; or you may have flown the downwind leg too close to the runway. With your inexperience, the only thing to do is open the throttle and take it around. Again, the sooner you recognize that a go-around (called a *balked landing*) is required and do something about it, the more credit you'll be given for headwork.

Later, as you become proficient in slipping the plane (or using more flaps), you'll be able to land under conditions that now require a go-around.

Once you've decided to go around, do it! Use full power. Sometimes a student forgets this simple rule and staggers out at partial power, nearly causing heart failure for himself, the instructor, and any spectators present. Open the throttle all the way, get the carburetor heat OFF (if used), and get the flaps up, using the procedure recommended by your instructor. The instructor will be watching your reactions during the latter stages of presolo landing practice, wondering, "Can I trust this student to do the right thing when bouncing or coming in too high or too low on the first solo?" How you take action when action is needed will help the instructor decide when you are ready to solo.

The *Pilot's Operating Handbook* for your airplane will give the best go-around or balked landing procedure for your airplane, and you should use that and the instructor's suggestions. As mentioned in the section on flaps, the general procedure is to apply full power to stop the descent (then carburetor heat OFF, if used) and get the flaps up in increments. If the airplane has retractable landing gear, don't be too hasty about getting it up because if the airplane is inadvertently allowed to contact the runway during the go-around process, it's better that the gear is down and locked. The landing gear poses comparatively low drag at that low airspeed and may be retracted after a safe altitude is reached.

Emergencies on Takeoff and in the Pattern

Right after takeoff is the worst time to have an engine failure and the most likely time for it to happen. You are climbing out after an extra good takeoff. Suddenly the engine starts kicking up and then quits cold. What now?

The worst possible move on your part would be to try to turn back to the runway. Sure, there's some pretty rough country right off the end of the runway. But you'll have a better chance for survival there than by trying to turn back to the field. Analyze what happens. The engine quits. The plane is in the climb attitude with no power. If you had time to think about it now, the situation would look like the first part of the normal power-off stall-and that's what it is. While you sit there, the airspeed is dropping fast. You realize what's happening and quickly whip the plane around to get back to the runway. A few seconds later you're sitting in a pile of junk wondering what happened. You gambled and lost. The plane was very slow, and when you turned it the speed was less than the stalling speed for that bank.

Experience has shown that an attempt to make a 180° turn to get back to the runway after engine failure on the climb-out is fraught with peril. It depends on the altitude at which the failure occurs, but statistics argue against trying to turn back. This doesn't mean that you have to just sit there when a shallow turn would let you miss that crockery factory. A rule of thumb for lightplanes is: Don't make 90° of turn at less than 400 feet and 45° of turn at less than 200 feet. Note that the rule of thumb is for lightplanes or the average two-place trainer, and heavier airplanes with higher stall speeds may require much more. Approach turns in the traffic pattern were done in a normal glide with the nose down and plenty of altitude. In the takeoff emergency, you start with the nose up and sit there for a while before you realize what's happened. The 400- and 200-foot limits mentioned above take this (and your probable nervousness and roughness in an actual emergency) into consideration.

Get the nose down as soon as possible after the engine failure and make as good a landing as possible under the conditions.

In case of a partial power failure after takeoff and there's no runway left for stopping, fly straight ahead and try to gain altitude without slowing the plane critically. Make all turns shallow. Don't try to turn back to the airport too soon. You're headed into the wind and, if the engine quits completely, will land at a much slower groundspeed this way.

In any actual emergency landing, once you are definitely committed, cut off the mixture, fuel, ignition, and master switches before you land. This will lessen chances of fire after impact if things don't work out as you plan.

Although you probably won't have much time for debating in this situation, it's probably better to turn the master switch off last so that communications and the flaps (if electrical) could be used during the last part of the approach.

One problem with students is that once they have opened the throttle for takeoff they feel the takeoff *must* be made. If you are rolling down the runway and things don't feel right to you (perhaps the engine does not sound like it should or the trim doesn't feel right), throttle back immediately and keep the airplane straight, hold the wheel back, use careful braking as necessary, and taxi back to find out what the problem is. *Don't be afraid to abort a takeoff.*

Your instructor may cover the airspeed indicator during the presolo landing sessions to let you see that you can make safe approaches by checking the airplane's attitude and power combinations as you complete the pattern. It could be that sometime you may neglect to check the pitot tube during the preflight and discover after you've lifted off that it's not working—mud daubers built a home in there. Or maybe water had gotten in and froze when the airplane was pulled out of a warm hangar to subfreezing conditions. You'll find after demonstration and practice that making an approach and landing without an airspeed indicator isn't as bad as you imagined. Remember also, once you get to the point of transition to landing, you won't be looking at the airspeed indicator anyway.

The instructor also may include a pattern or two with the altimeter covered as well to allow you to estimate the various pattern altitudes and airspeeds.

Crosswind Takeoffs and Landings

The wind may be directly down the runway on all of your presolo flying days. But the chances are slim that this will happen, so you'll doubtless get some instruction in crosswind landings during one of the presolo landing periods. At any rate, there'll be many times during your flying career when crosswind takeoffs and landings must be made.

Crosswind Takeoff

In review, look at Figure 13-27—of a tailwheel airplane sitting crosswind on the ground. Because all the weight is centered near the main wheels and because the fin and rudder present a large area and the tail is light, the plane wants to weathercock, or turn into the wind. Since the points of friction (the wheels) are low, the plane also tends to "lean over." These two actions must be taken care of any time the plane is on the

Figure 13-27. The airplane tends not only to lean away from the wind but also to turn into it (weathercock).

ground in a crosswind—the amount of compensation depends on the strength of the wind.

Procedure

Both types of airplanes are lined up with the center line of the runway as with a normal takeoff. Assume in this case a moderate (8 K) crosswind is from the left. As you smoothly apply power, hold full left aileron and be prepared to use enough rudder to correct for both torque and the weathercocking tendency. The controls for both types will look like Figure 13-28.

If the wind is directly across the runway, the ailerons will be ineffective until the plane picks up speed. At low speeds, any effect you get from the aileron will be comparatively small.

As the plane picks up speed, the ailerons and rudder will become more and more effective and less control deflection will be needed.

If you ease the nosewheel off early, the tendency to turn to the left will be much greater than usual because not only have you lost the nosewheel steering and now must depend on the rudder alone, but also, the

nosewheel friction no longer fights the weathercocking tendency.

The tailwheel airplane should have the tail lifted slightly higher than normal, and you should also be prepared to add even more right rudder than in a no-wind or no-crosswind condition. The tailwheel is free and its friction no longer opposes the wind's sidewise force. The tricycle-gear type, all other factors equal, has less tendency to weathercock during the early part of the run because of the greater weight on the (large) nosewheel. In a crosswind from the right, the two forces (torque and weathercocking) tend to counteract each other. You want to make sure of sufficient flying speed at lift-off so that the plane doesn't start skipping. As soon as the plane gets into the air, it will want to start drifting. If it hits the ground again, heavy side loads may be put on the landing gear. So, for the tailwheel type, raise the tail higher than usual and hold the plane on the ground longer.

Gradually ease off the aileron deflection as the ailerons become more effective. As soon as you are sure the plane is ready to fly, lift it off with definite, but not abrupt, back pressure. At the takeoff point there will be some aileron deflection to the left, and the plane will start to bank slightly in that direction after it leaves the ground. Apply left rudder as well and make a balanced turn to the proper drift correction angle. Level the wings, then continue a normal climb (V_Y). Look back at the runway during the climbout to see that you have the right amount of correction angle (Figure 13-29). At a controlled field, if you are instructed to "fly runway heading," you fly the heading of the runway and do not crab into the wind on climbout. The controller expects you (and everyone else) to drift downwind. Retract the flaps (and the gear, as applicable) at a safe altitude.

Figure 13-28. Starting the crosswind takeoff roll.

As soon as you are definitely in the air, set up the proper crab angle.

Figure 13-29. The crosswind takeoff.

You'll hear talk of "the crosswind component" from time to time. This is the component of the wind vector that is actually trying to push you sideways. A strong wind does not necessarily mean that there will be a large crosswind component. When pilots talk of a strong crosswind, they usually are referring to the fact that there is a large crosswind component. Check Figure 13-30.

Some manufacturers furnish crosswind component charts for their airplanes, and you can find whether a particular runway wind condition would exceed the

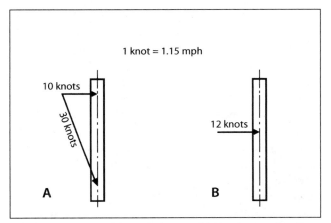

Figure 13-30. (A) Although the wind has velocity of 30 K, it has a crosswind component of only 10 K. (B) The wind velocity is 12 K, all of which is crosswind component.

demonstrated (for certification purposes) crosswind component for your airplane. Usually the maximum cited (at 90° to the runway) is 0.2 V_{S0}, or 20 percent of the stall speed with landing flaps.

A crosswind slightly complicates matters for all legs of the traffic pattern. This is where the rectangular course pays off (Figure 13-31).

Probable Errors

1. Not enough aileron into the wind at the beginning.
2. Pulling the airplane off before it's ready to fly—letting the airplane skip and drift.
3. Holding too much aileron at the latter stages of the takeoff so that the plane banks steeply into the wind as soon as the wheels leave the ground.
4. Not making a turn to set up a crab—holding the wing down and slipping after takeoff.
5. Not looking back at the runway occasionally on climbout—resulting in not flying in line with the runway.

Crosswind Landing

You know that the plane must be headed straight down the runway when it lands, and in normal landings it was just a matter of keeping the nose straight and the wings level. It's a different proposition if there is a crosswind. If the nose is kept straight and wings level on final, the plane may drift completely away from the runway

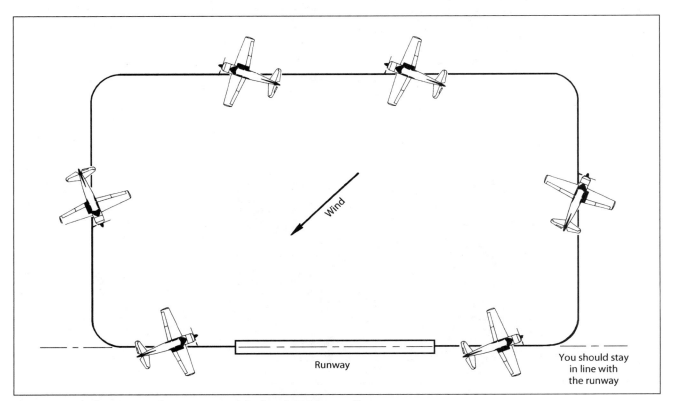

Figure 13-31. The rectangular course as applied to the airport traffic pattern.

before you have a chance to land. Or, at best, it will land drifting across the runway and put heavy stresses on the landing gear.

The plane will tend to ground loop because not only are the forces of the impact at work, but the plane wants to weathercock as well (Figure 13-32).

Crab Method of Correction

One way to correct for drift is to set up a crab on the final approach, then just before the plane touches, skid it straight with the runway using the rudder. True, the crab will compensate for drift, but it requires no small amount of judgment to know when to straighten the plane. You've had the experience during normal landings of thinking you're about to touch down and then a thermal or ground effect holds the plane up for a good distance down the runway. The same thing can happen in a crab approach. You may straighten out the plane. It starts drifting again and there you sit—too little time to set another crab—so the plane lands drifting. For the next few seconds you're as busy as a one-eyed cat watching two mouse holes.

Another common error is not straightening the plane soon enough and landing while still in a crab. This doesn't do the landing gear any good either. It's best, then, that the crab method be avoided at this point of experience.

Wing-Down Method

The simplest way for the student to make a crosswind landing is by the wing-down or slip correction method. This is accomplished by lowering the upwind wing and holding the opposite or downwind rudder. When the plane is banked, it wants to turn. The opposite rudder stops any turn and causes the plane to slip.

The procedure is this: As you roll out on final approach, lower the upwind wing the amount needed to correct for drift and apply opposite rudder to stop

any turn. Watch for any signs of over- or undercorrecting and adjust the bank and opposite rudder accordingly. *The lower the wing, the more drift correction is being applied and the more opposite rudder is needed* (Figure 13-33).

On gusty days you may be continually varying the bank as the crosswind's velocity changes.

Continue to hold the wing down as necessary throughout the landing. There's no need to try to raise the wing at the last second. As the plane slows during the landing process, more aileron and rudder deflection is needed because (1) the controls are less effective as the speed lowers, and (2) the actual bank should be steeper, since the ratio of wind speed to your speed is increasing (more correction is needed). For example, if you are approaching at 100 K, a 10-K crosswind means a fairly minor correction. But by the time the airplane touches down at 50 K, the 10 K of wind represents a high percentage of your speed. Of course, if your plane's normal stalling speed is 50 K, you have no business approaching at a speed as excessive as 100 K. But it makes a good example. Land on the one main wheel and the tailwheel. The other main wheel will touch immediately after. After you are on the ground, the controls are used in the same way as for the crosswind takeoff—ailerons into the wind and opposite rudder as needed to keep the plane straight. Land the tricycle-gear plane on the one main wheel also. Ease the nosewheel down immediately after the other main wheel touches for effective ground steering in the crosswind. This method is so simple and effective that it is the most popular way of correcting for drift during the approach and landing.

Some airplanes have nosewheels that "fall free" from the steering mechanism so that when there is no weight on the wheel (anytime it's off the ground), the wheel will be free to track along the ground path when

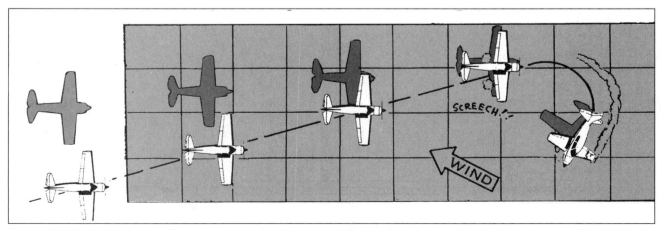

Figure 13-32. *Hoping* that you'll touch down before the wind drifts you off the runway is no way to take care of a crosswind. A ground loop could result.

Figure 13-33. A crosswind approach as seen from behind the airplane and from the cockpit. The slipping resultant (R) compensates for the crosswind component. If you had time to check it, the needle in the turn and slip indicator would show no turn, but the ball would show a slip.

it touches. In other words, in the wing-down crosswind approach the deflection of the rudder does not have the nosewheel "cocked" at touchdown. Other airplanes have a continual direct connection from rudder to nosewheel so that in a left crosswind (left aileron, right rudder), the airplane could have a tendency to veer to the right as the cocked nosewheel touches. Your instructor will discuss the best crosswind procedure for your airplane.

As you are slipping, a slightly steeper glide results, but this is of no great significance.

The only time that slipping is used to correct for a crosswind is on the final approach and landing. After shooting crosswind landings some students climb with a wing down after takeoff. All this does is cut down the rate of climb.

Probable Errors
1. Letting the plane turn when the wing is lowered.
2. Not recognizing drift.
3. Mechanical corrections—putting the wing down at a certain angle and not changing it, even though the crosswind varies.
4. Getting so wrapped up in the drift correction that the landing is forgotten.

If you bounce during a crosswind landing, remember that the plane will start drifting. Lower the wing and use opposite rudder as you reland the plane.

The crosswind landing technique is a form of sideslip. The sideslip, you remember, is a slip where the nose is pointed at an object (say, for instance, the runway) and the plane slips to one side—toward the lowered wing. In this case, the plane's movement to the side is counteracted by the wind. If you overcorrected

for drift or if there was no wind, the sideslip idea would be evident. In strong winds the two methods may be combined (crab and wing-down).

Crab Approach and Wing-Down Landing
You may like this idea better than the long slipping approach, which can be uncomfortable to both pilot and passengers.

As shown in Figure 13-34, this technique is to set up the proper crab angle (it will have to change as the wind changes on the approach) and maintain a straight path over the ground by this method until the point of round-out is reached. The airplane is then lined up with the runway, and the wing is lowered into the wind (and opposite rudder is used) as necessary to correct for drift as the landing is completed. It takes time getting used to making the transition, but with practice you'll probably find this method more to your liking than the long wing-down final.

You may have a problem getting the idea of the wing-down crosswind correction because in most cases you'll have this condition set up for only a few seconds during the very last of the final approach and the landing. Some instructors, for a training condition, will set up the landing approach 5 or 6 miles out on final, controlling the power themselves, and let the student see that the sideslip does work and, because of varying crosswinds, the correction may need to be changed throughout the approach. This technique is used to give the student more time to get used to the cross-control effect. After the idea is firmed up, the instructor will usually go back to the crab approach and wing-down landing (or you may prefer the wing-down method for all of the final leg).

Make the transition to a sideslip as the round-out height is reached.

Continue the landing— wing down, nose straight.

Wind

Figure 13-34. A crab approach with a wing-down landing.

Power-Off Approaches

Before you solo, your instructor will demonstrate and have you practice some approaches and landings with the power reduced to idle on the downwind leg as the airplane is abeam of the point of intended landing. (This is good experience in judging the flight path for landing on a prechosen spot without use of power. This doesn't mean that you can't add power to make the runway if you misjudged and are undershooting during one of the approaches; in fact, it's again strongly suggested that you don't get the airplane slow and cocked up trying to stretch the glide.)

Figure 13-35 shows a typical traffic pattern for engine-at-idle approaches.

Downwind Leg

In earlier days, the type of approach shown in Figure 13-35 was called the *180° accuracy approach* and was basically the "normal" approach for most light trainers.

Downwind and Base Keys

Two important points in the approach are the downwind key, where the power is reduced, and the base key, where the wings level after the turn onto the base leg. These are good locations for judging the progress of the approach.

Figure 13-36 shows how the power-off pattern may be played to compensate for a too-wide or too-close downwind leg. You'll also fly the pattern to cope for varying wind conditions.

If the wind is strong, the downwind leg should be closer to the runway; the wind effects on final will be greater because of the lower groundspeed and hence the airplane will spend a longer time in the headwind (or retarding) condition. In other words, a 30-second descending downwind leg (after the power is retarded

to idle) is not matched by a 30-second final leg. Because of the headwind on final, depending on its strength, the final leg might be 1 minute or more (as an example), with that extra time of retarding effects resulting in not making the runway unless power is used.

With experience you will be able to judge a proper distance from the runway (called "abeam distance") for these approaches, but some instructors use aids such as masking tape on the wing (low-wing airplane) or on the strut (Figure 13-37).

If there is a crosswind as shown in Figure 13-31, you will have to make corrections for wind on the crosswind, downwind, and final legs as well as that expected on base.

The first turn, onto base, should be (as mentioned earlier in the chapter) fairly steep (up to 30° bank), particularly in a high-wing airplane. The 90° (plus) of turn should be completed without delay so that you will arrive at the base key position with the wings level and a good view of the runway to check for needed corrections. On base *always look to the right* (in a left-hand pattern) *to check for airplanes that might be making a long straight-in approach.*

A problem instructors find on the base leg is that students often stare straight ahead over the nose, and not look at the runway until they *think* they are ready to turn onto final. This habit often leads to a late turn and flying past the runway center-line extension (Figure 13-38). This could lead to the dangerous situation of "cheating" on the turn with a cross-control stall resulting (*see* Chapter 14).

So it's better in most cases to make the turn onto the base leg with a fairly steep bank (up to 30°) and the turn onto final with a more shallow one (20° or less). *See* Figure 13-39.

Figure 13-40 shows the results of that too-shallow bank onto base, as seen from the cockpit.

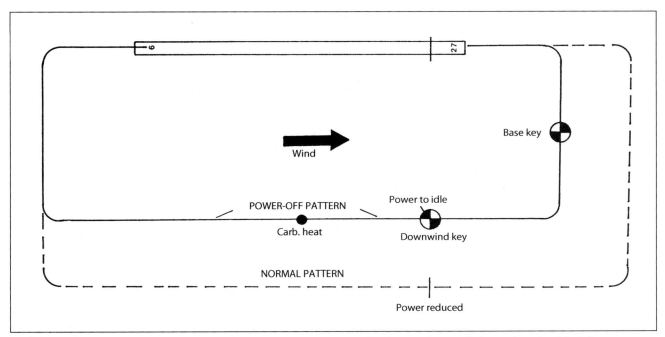

Figure 13-35. A power-off (engine at idle) approach. The exact use of carburetor heat will depend on the *Pilot's Operating Handbook* of the airplane and/or your flight instructor's suggestions, but here full carb heat is applied midway on the downwind leg and used throughout the approach.

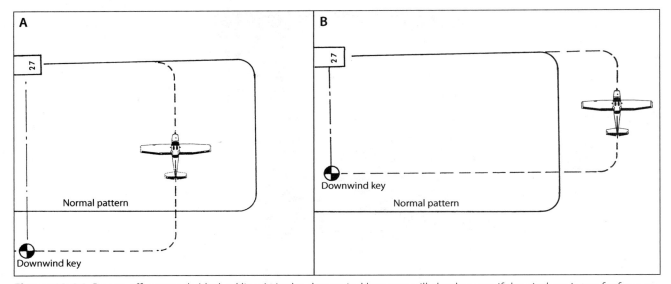

Figure 13-36. Power-off approach (dashed lines). At the downwind key, you will check to see if the airplane is too far from or too close to the runway.

(A) If the airplane is too far out from the runway, the descending part of the downwind leg could be shortened slightly to ensure making the selected touchdown point. (You should have at least one-fourth mile on final, though, because the final turn should not be at a too-low altitude.)

(B) If the airplane is too close to the runway at the downwind key position, the downwind leg is extended as necessary to ensure that the airplane is not too high on final.

The temptation is to make a *quick* turn to move in or out to get over to the normal abeam distance when on the downwind leg. It's best, however, not to make radical turns in the traffic pattern because of your airplane's blind spots and the possibility of a midair collision.

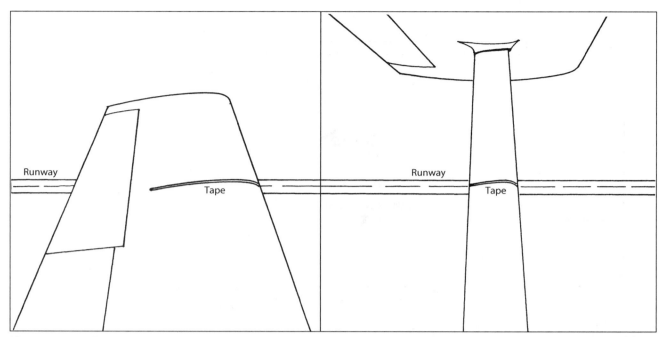

Figure 13-37. The instructor may put tape on the wing or strut if you're having problems finding the proper abeam distance. These references can change with various student heights (and the wings must be level each time). After some experience, you'll be able to judge the abeam distance without the tape.

Figure 13-38. Students (and other pilots) tend to stare straight over the nose while on base. Of course, you should check ahead here in case somebody is on an opposite base leg, but don't get locked on it.

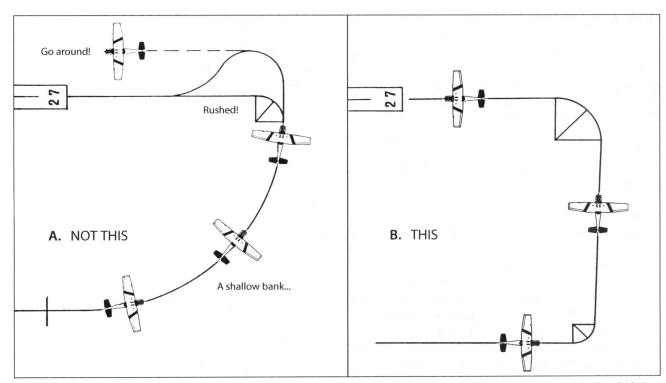

Figure 13-39. (A) The turn onto base is extra shallow, and the wing is obscuring the runway. When the wings are leveled, the pilot finds that either a very steep (and dangerous) turn onto final is required or it is necessary to make an S-turn (also a bad idea) in order to get lined up with the runway. A go-around may be necessary.

(B) The proper way is to make a comparatively steep balanced turn of about 30° bank so that the 90° of turn is completed fairly soon, the wings leveled, and the runway checked. A shallower (and less rushed) turn is then made at the proper point to roll out on final.

Figure 13-40. The problem of Figure 13-39 as seen from the cockpit.

(A) You're making that nice, very shallow, banked turn onto base. The runway is out there somewhere, but the wing is obscuring it.

(B) As you are rolling out of the turn on the base leg, you look for the runway to get set up for the turn onto final (uh-oh). A tailwind component on base (Figure 13-31) can make matters worse.

The Too-High Approach

If you see that you are high at the base key you have several options in an actual engine failure situation. You may (1) add flaps, if available, (2) deliberately S-turn past the center line of the landing area, or (3) slip the airplane after turning on final.

1. Assuming that you have flaps and are using them in increments (just before the turn onto base, more flaps on base, with last flap setting on final), you should be able to have a setting or two to spare if you are high at the base key position or on final.

2. Deliberately flying past the center line and S-turning back is not used on a "normal" approach, since it could put the airplane in a wrapped-up (steeply banked) turn at a low altitude. Later, as you gain experience, that procedure, when used with care, could be a valuable aid in a real engine-out situation, but your instructor will not want you to use it for the normal power-off approach at the airport.

3. When you're too high, slipping is the major aid for the airplane not equipped with flaps or if you have used up all the flaps. To repeat what was said in the section on Slips, the *Pilot's Operating Handbooks* of some airplanes warn against steep slips with flaps extended past a certain setting because of the effect of the disturbed airflow on the elevators.

A slipping turn to the final leg was used in earlier days in emergencies when the pilots saw on "base" that they were high and the final leg would be too short to allow time to set up a slip there. Your instructor will discourage use of the slipping turn in your normal practice sessions but may discuss it for emergency use during some of your ground sessions. Again, use of it will depend on pilot experience and the airplane (Figure 13-41).

The main thing in these practice sessions is not to get the airplane too wrapped up while turning final and to realize that, if you're feeling pushed or rushed, you have power available to make a go-around using the procedure discussed earlier.

Too Low

If you're too low in the power-off approach, the best and safest thing to do is to add power (as for the reduced-power approach discussed earlier in the chapter).

Gusty Air and Wind Gradients

If the velocity of the wind changes suddenly, it can affect your airplane. You know that it is possible to have different wind directions and velocities at different altitudes, so take the theoretical situation shown in Figure 13-42.

You are gliding at 70 K and the plane stalls at 50 K. Your speed in relation to the air is, of course, 70 K. But your speed in relation to the ground and to the calm wind is 70 minus 30, or 40 K. What happens as you suddenly fly into the area of calm air? The airspeed or speed relative to the calm air mass is only 40 K. The balance between lift and weight is broken (lift decreases suddenly) and the airplane accelerates downward, increasing the angle of attack to the point that the airplane stalls—which aggravates the situation.

The above illustration is exaggerated, but the principle applies on any gusty day. Many a pilot has been set for a landing on a gusty day and had the bottom drop out, then clambers from the wreckage and wonders why the airplane "fell." It's not unusual to have fluctuations of plus or minus 10 K on the airspeed indicator during an approach on a blustery day.

If there are gusty winds, fly your approach 5–10 K faster than normal. That way you won't be in such a bind when the wind speeds kick back and forth.

If you hit sudden turbulence on an approach, apply power first and then ask, "Was that a shear area? Was the wind dropping or picking up?" The chances are that the plane won't stall, but you may find the airspeed low with the ground coming up fast.

Wake Turbulence

Always be leery of taking off or landing close behind another plane. The bigger the plane, the more cautious you should be. Lightplanes always come out second best in a contest with an airliner's wing tip vortices. If the wind is calm, wake turbulence may hang over the runway for several minutes—even after the plane has gone out of sight. If you *have to* take off or land behind another plane, get on the upwind side if there is a crosswind (Figure 13-43). In light crosswinds, one vortex may stay over the runway.

Better yet—don't take off for a while. Always be prepared for wake turbulence if the wind is calm and big planes have taken off in the last few minutes. Lightplane wake turbulence is bad enough, but airliners and heavy aircraft can set up a fatal crash for you.

The wing tip vortices are shown in Figures 13-44 and 2-16. But not so well shown is the fact that the vortices descend after being formed, moving downward at 400–500 feet per minute, and tend to level off about 900 feet below the aircraft. Flying behind and below a large jet when it's clean and slow could cause big problems for you.

Don't fly at cruise speed directly behind and below a large aircraft or cross its flight path if you can avoid it. The turbulence may cause load factors so great as to cause structural failure of your plane.

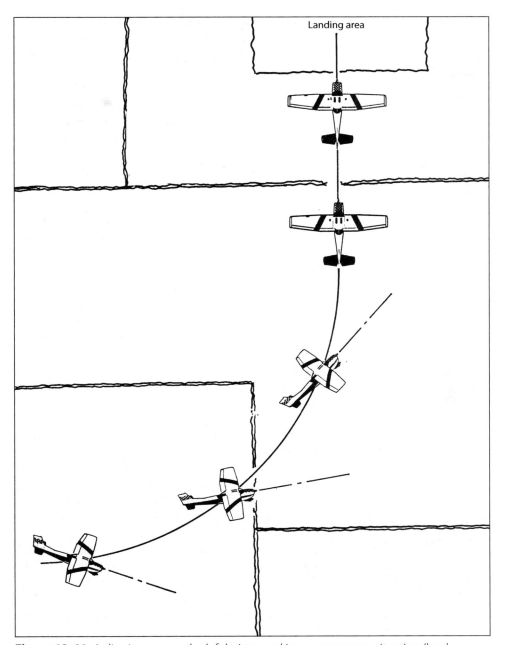

Figure 13-41. A slipping turn to the left being used in an emergency situation (bank exaggerated). The airplane is allowed to turn toward the lowered wing by using comparatively more (left) aileron deflection and less (right) rudder deflection than would be used to maintain a straight slip. At this point in your experience, the slipping turn is only *discussed* as *one* of the methods used in losing altitude on an approach, particularly in an emergency situation.

Figure 13-42. A shear area could cause problems on approach.

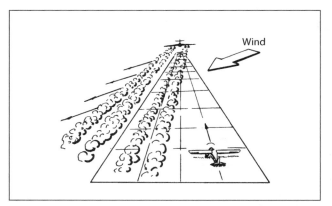

Figure 13-43. Take off or land on the upwind side of the runway if there is a crosswind.

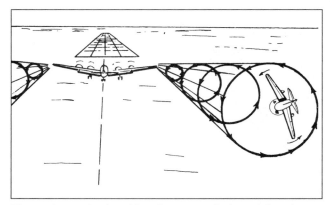

Figure 13-44. In the olden days, it was believed that "propwash" or the slipstream from the propeller(s) was the culprit, but then jets came out, causing the same problem, which couldn't be propwash! Later flight tests showed that the wing tips were the culprit and that the effects were much stronger than earlier considered.

Again, don't be proud—take it around if you think there'll be wake turbulence on landing. Wait a while longer before taking off if you're in doubt. (Don't sit on the runway; taxi out of the way.)

Read in the *Aeronautical Information Manual* Chapter 7, Section 3, which covers information you should know about wake turbulence. Look it over carefully to learn some facts that could save your neck someday.

After Landing/Taxi-In

Non-pilots may think the challenge is over once the airplane touches the ground, but the flight is not over until the airplane is tied down or in the hangar.

Rolling out on the runway, hold aileron into any crosswind. As mentioned earlier, this helps keep the upwind wing from being lifted and the aerodynamic drag from the down aileron on the downwind wing helps reduce weathercocking. Holding the yoke back will increase braking effectiveness in a tricycle gear airplane and give better steering in the tailwheel plane.

As you taxi back to the ramp, position the controls to offset the effects of the wind and reposition them anytime you turn (see Chapter 6). Check the brakes again as you approach the ramp and taxi slowly around people and airplanes. If you have to add power to maneuver in the ramp area, be aware of what your prop blast will hit.

Approaching the ramp, you may see your instructor pull the throttle to idle and momentarily move the mag switch to Off (then back to On). This is a check of the magneto ground wires (primary leads or P-leads). The engine should quit for the instant the switch is Off. If the engine keeps running, one of the P-leads is broken or the ignition switch is faulty and the mags are "hot" even with the key removed. This poses the danger of an inadvertent start if the propeller is moved, therefore notify a mechanic immediately and consider hanging a sign on the prop warning of the danger.

It's a good idea to remove the key after shutdown, ensuring the switch stays in the Off position. There may be a designated place for the key in the airplane or on a clipboard.

Most POHs have a shutdown or a securing the airplane checklist. It's important to use these checklists to avoid mistakes like leaving the master switch on and draining the battery, but you shouldn't spend much time at all on the ramp with the engine running and your head down looking at a checklist. Put a priority on getting the propeller stopped.

Solo

When you are able to make good takeoffs and landings and use good judgment in your flying, then you will solo. By this time you should have your medical certificate and student pilot certificate and have passed a written examination on 14 CFR Parts 61 and 91 and on your airplane and the local traffic rules.

Students, particularly in group training programs, get anxious to solo. (Jane or Joe Doe soloed in 12 hours, how come I have 16 hours and still haven't?) Don't worry, maybe their 6-hour slump wasn't as pronounced as yours or maybe they didn't have one. Very few students solo without hitting a slump somewhere along the line. It hits a large number of students at about the 6-hour point—and oddly enough it's called a 6-hour slump.

Usually it strikes after you've had an hour or two in the pattern and had a good first period of shooting landings. You feel pretty good and are all set to get these landings down pat and solo earlier than that Horace Numbskull who thinks he's such a hot pilot. Things don't go too well, and suddenly you can't find the ground with both hands. You're right in the middle of the 6-hour slump and feel lower than a whale's stomach.

You go on shooting landings, and it seems that, for a couple of hours, absolutely no progress is being made. Then suddenly one day you start landing like a pro; the instructor gets out—and you solo.

The instructor will tell you that the plane will get off quicker, climb better, and want to stay up longer with you alone—and so it will. You'll be so busy flying the plane that you won't notice that the other seat is empty. The first solo is the point where you suddenly discover that flying is pretty wonderful; when you get down and receive the congratulations of the people in the airport office, you're standing about a mile high.

The procedure for solo will generally be this: The instructor will get out and you'll shoot one landing and taxi back to where you started. The instructor may wave you on or stop you to discuss points of the solo takeoff and landing. In most cases you'll shoot three full-stop landings—for this reason: If you shoot one and then lay off for a few days, you'll probably start thinking, "That one good landing could have been luck…." If you shoot three you'll know it wasn't luck and won't talk yourself into a state of nervousness before the next solo flight.

Students sometimes worry about what the instructor will think if they have to take it around on that first solo approach. Traffic may require that you have to make a go-around during one or more of the first-solo approaches. So what? More than one first-solo student has had to circle (this writer did) while somebody else made an approach and landing. So don't worry about it. The instructor demonstrated, and you've practiced this enough so that you'll know what to do. The main thing is to not talk yourself into a dither if you have to go around. The instructor will think it's good judgment on your part, even if you lean to the cautious side. There will be plenty of times during your flying career when you'll have to take an airplane around, so do it now as necessary.

On a go-around, make a slight right turn and then parallel the runway so you can keep an eye on departing traffic as noted earlier in the chapter. If you think the final turn required is too steep, take it around as shown in Figure 13-39(A).

The instructor will probably ride around a couple of times the next time you fly and then turn you loose to shoot two or three periods of landings before taking you out to the area to introduce more advanced work.

Incidentally, students usually make their best landings during that first solo.

Don't get cocky and think you've learned it all, now that the first solo is behind you.

Don't ask when you will solo. You've bounced and jounced your instructor while causing a lot of aspirin chewing, for the past few hours. When you are ready, the instructor will be *more than glad* to get out. Seriously, it's as much a matter of pride for the instructor as it is for you.

Part Three 3
Postsolo Maneuvers

14

Advanced Stalls

Cross-Control Stall / Skidding

This stall is a perfect illustration of the dangers of abusing the controls. A typical case of a cross-control stall accident is this: A pilot sees in the turn onto final that it will require a sharper turn to line up with the runway. (Look at Figures 13-38, 13-39, and 13-40 again.) Pilots have always been told the dangers of banking too steeply at low altitude, so to avoid this and still make the turn, they do something much worse.

A small voice inside says, "Go on, use rudder, skid it around and you won't have to bank it."

So, the pilot skids it. As you know full well, when a plane is skidded, the outside wing speeds up, gets more lift than the inside one, and the plane starts to increase its bank. The pilot realizes this and unconsciously holds aileron against the turn. The down aileron on the inside of the turn helps drag that wing back more, slowing it up and decreasing the lift, which requires more aileron to hold it up—and so the cycle goes. As the plane is banked, use of bottom rudder and opposite aileron will tend to cause the nose to drop. The pilot helpfully holds more back pressure to keep the nose up. This, then, is the perfect setup for one wing to stall before the other. Figures 14-1 through 14-4 show the maneuver as seen from outside the airplane and from the cockpit.

The practice cross-control stall (at a safe altitude) is aimed at teaching you to recognize how such a stall occurs and giving you practice in effectively recovering from such a situation. The cross-control stall, like any other, can occur at any speed, altitude, or power setting.

The bad thing about this skidding stall is that the forces working on you as it is being approached are "normal." That is, you'll feel pushed to the outside of the turn (as is the case every time you make a turn in a car), so you may not be warned of impending trouble.

Figure 14-5 shows why the inside wing (with the down aileron) tends to stall first when, by "common sense," the down aileron should hold that wing up.

Looking back at Figure 12-12, you can see the effect on the coefficient-of-lift curve of extended flaps. Down ailerons will give the same general effect (although they're farther out on the wing). The up aileron (B) in Figure 14-5 gives the effect of the wing being twisted to a lower angle of incidence.

As you increase the angle of attack, as indicated by the arrow in Figure 14-5, the inside wing with the down aileron (C) will reach its "break" first and will stall. The question comes up: Shouldn't there be more lift on that wing and therefore no stall? By a bizarre arrangement of the controls to stop the airplane from rolling

Figure 14-1. Pilot sees that the plane will fly past the runway if the rate of turn is not increased.

Figure 14-2. The pilot doesn't want to make a steep bank at low altitude, knowing that the stalling speed increases with angle of bank, so applies rudder to cheat a little. Lift is greater on the outside wing because of its increased speed. The bank starts to increase because of the difference in lift. The pilot doesn't want the bank any steeper, so opposite aileron is applied.

Figure 14-3. The nose tends to drop because of rudder and aileron, so up-elevator is added. Down-aileron drags the wing back causing a steeper bank. More opposite aileron is applied, etc.

Figure 14-4. The inside wing stalls and the plane rotates abruptly toward the low wing. *The altitude is insufficient for recovery.*

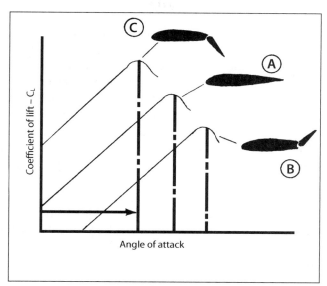

Figure 14-5. Coefficient of lift versus angle of attack for three conditions: (A) airfoil with no aileron or flap deflection, (B) the right wing (aileron up), and (C) the left wing (aileron down).

into a steeper bank, the pilot is assuring that the actual lift of each wing (in pounds) is equal to the other. And since angle of attack is the only criterion of the stall, that inside wing goes first.

Procedure — Power-Off

1. This is a turning stall, so the clearing turns are not necessary. Keep looking around during the stall.
2. Pull the carburetor heat ON and make a shallow gliding turn. (The direction of turn will be left up to you — practice them in both directions.)
3. Gradually apply more and more inside rudder to "cheat" on the turn.
4. Use opposite aileron as necessary to keep the bank from increasing.
5. Keep the nose up by increasing back pressure.
6. When the break occurs, neutralize the ailerons. Stop any further rotation with opposite rudder. Relax back pressure.
7. Roll out of the bank with coordinated controls.

The rotation toward that inside wing is so fast that it is quite possible that the bank will be vertical or past vertical before it is stopped.

In many ways the recovery from this stall is close to the recovery from a spin. The lift of the wings must be made equal. This is done by neutralizing the ailerons and stopping further rotation with rudder *at the same time* as back pressure is released. The neutralizing of the ailerons speeds the equalizing of lift.

Because of the low position of the nose when the rotation is stopped, the speed will build up quickly. Recover to straight and level flight with coordinated controls as soon as possible without overstressing the plane or getting a secondary stall.

Common Errors

1. Not neutralizing the ailerons at the start of the recovery.
2. Using too much opposite (top) rudder to stop rotation, causing the plane to slip badly during the recovery.
3. Waiting too long to roll out with coordinated control; too great an altitude loss.

Cross-control stalls, as such, are not required on the private practical (flight) test but were included here to show the hazards of trying to "cut corners" and the effects of neglecting coordination at critical times.

Your instructor may have you practice these stalls (dual only) using flaps or having the airplane in the clean configuration. Naturally if flaps are used, the instructor will be responsible for retracting them after the stall breaks to avoid exceeding the flaps-extended airspeed (V_{FE}) — the maximum value (top) of the white arc.

A suggested procedure is to make the turn onto base with a 30° bank. This gives an earlier roll-out on base that allows a check of the runway and for airplanes on straight-in approaches. A 30° bank raises the stall speed of *any* airplane by a factor of 1.07, or 7 percent.

Accelerated Stalls

The accelerated stall is a maneuver for proving that the stall is a matter of angle of attack, not airspeed. The accelerated stall is to be started no higher than 1.25 times the normal stalling speed because of extra stresses that may be put on the plane by stalling at higher speeds. The term "accelerated" means that the airplane is under forces of acceleration, or g forces, when the stall occurs.

Chapter 9 "The Turn" introduced the expression "load factor." In the 60° banked turn (constant altitude) the load factor was 2, or the airplane was subjected to 2 g's. As far as the wings were concerned, the airplane weighed twice as much. By working out the math it was shown that the stall speed was increased by the square root of the load factor, which turned out to be 1.414. In the 60° banked turn, the airplane stalled at a speed over

41 percent higher than normal stall speed. The same increase in stall speed effect would have occurred if you had loaded the plane to *twice* its normal weight and done an old-fashioned straight-ahead stall. (Don't load it that way!)

The pilot in Figure 14-6 can't understand why evidences of a stall show up when the airspeed is so high. (In a 60° banked constant-altitude turn, the stall speed is increased by a factor of 1.414, from 62 to 88 K. The pilot is feeling a load factor of 2 g's.)

You can also encounter positive acceleration forces when pulling up from dives or brisk pull-ups from straight and level; acceleration doesn't just happen in a turn, although in everyday flight, this is the most likely place to meet it. Of course, you could run into strong negative acceleration forces (or negative g's) if you were to shove the wheel forward abruptly at high speeds. (Don't do *that* either!) You've been used to thinking of acceleration in terms of increasing speed. This is not the type of acceleration of interest here.

Your elevators are not only the airspeed control but are also your g control. By rapidly pulling back on the wheel or stick, positive g forces are created. (They may be too positive at speeds well above the stall, and problems could result.) Pulling back abruptly means that excess lift is temporarily in existence. The airplane will start slowing immediately to reestablish the old lift

Figure 14-6. The stall is a function of angle of attack, not airspeed. This pilot is learning that the load factor is 2 g's and the stall speed in a 60° banked level turn is 1.414 times that of normal 1-g flight.

value (*the airplane always tends to remain in equilibrium as far as lift and weight are concerned*). You may, however, exceed the airplane's limit load factor (maximum allowed g's) before the airplane has a chance to slow and equilibrium can be established. Normal category airplanes are required to have a maximum limit load factor of 3.8 positive and 1.52 negative g's. Utility category planes have limit load factors of 4.4 positive and 1.76 negative g's. Your trainer will fall into one of these two categories. If you pulled hard enough to stall the airplane at twice normal stall speed, you'd pull 4 g's (2 squared is $2 \times 2 = 4$ g's). And this would be over the limit for a normal category airplane. (A more complete explanation of the various category requirements will be covered in Chapter 23.) If you pulled hard enough to stall the airplane at three times the normal stall speed, 9 g's would result (3 squared = 9), and you would be flying a wingless—or tailless—wonder.

The stalls you've done up to now have been at a normal load factor of 1 g. You *gradually* increased the angle of attack until the stall occurred.

The accelerated maneuver stalls will be done best from 45° banked turns with reduced power in cruising configuration. You'll increase the angle of attack smoothly in a level or slightly climbing turn until the stall occurs just above the normal stalling speed. Don't start increasing the angle of attack at a speed of more than 25 percent above the normal stall speed.

This stall is done in the turn for two reasons: (1) This is the position in which most pilots run into accelerated stalls when they try to "tighten the turn" by rapidly pulling back on the wheel or stick, and (2) it is done to keep from getting into a whip stall or "tail slide," as might happen if the pilot pulled the plane sharply up from a wings-level position. A whip stall occurs when the plane stalls in a vertical nose-up position—the plane slides backward before recovery can be effected. This puts a severe strain on the structure, particularly the elevators, and could cause structural failure. If the plane is banked, the position of the center of gravity and the effects of the fin and rudder won't allow the plane to get into such a predicament; the nose will fall to one side.

The stall break and recovery is fundamentally the same as the turning departure and approach stalls. The high wing will generally stall first unless you are skidding. Release back pressure, and after the recovery is started, return the plane to level flight with coordinated controls. The flight instructor may want you to recover (1) as soon as you recognize the stall and (2) after the stall develops and the nose falls down through the horizon.

In (1) the recovery can be simple and quick. Relaxing the back pressure at the right time will cause the plane to recover in straight and level flight if the high wing stalled first and you can effect a recovery just as the wings roll level.

In (2) the plane may have rolled over into a bank in the opposite direction and the nose will be low. Recover from the stall, *then* bring the plane to wings-level flight. Too many students try to do everything at once in this case and end up stalled again. The main thing is to get a complete and clean stall recovery with a minimum loss of altitude—the first time.

Bring the wheel back smoothly. Don't jerk the wheel back and put a lot of unnecessary stress on the plane. You will be expected to be able to recover from the accelerated stall both with and without application of power. Use power to recover unless specifically asked not to.

Procedure

1. At reduced power in cruise configuration, make a turn with about 45° of bank. Slow the airplane to 25 percent above normal power-off stall speed by slowly increasing the back pressure.
2. When a speed of less than 25 percent above normal stall is reached, increase the back pressure rapidly but smoothly until the stall occurs.
3. Release back pressure, open the throttle, and recover to straight and level flight using coordinated controls. Also practice recoveries without use of power.

Another procedure for an accelerated stall is to set up the 45° bank and *gradually* slow up the airplane at a constant altitude or a moderate rate of climb, reducing the power until the stall occurs at a higher-than-normal airspeed.

Common Errors

1. Jerking the wheel back—putting too much stress on the plane.
2. The other extreme—too slow in applying back pressure so that the stall isn't an accelerated one.
3. Too brisk a forward pressure on recovery so that negative load factors are applied.

Stabilator or Elevator Trim Tab Stall

When the elevator trim tab was discussed in Chapter 8, it was noted that the elevator trim tab or the stabilator trim could get you into trouble under certain conditions.

The combination of high power setting and full nose-up elevator (or stabilator) trim can result in a tendency for the airplane to assume some pretty impressive nose-up attitudes. (These spectacular reactions are most likely to occur accidentally when close to the ground.)

You saw the effects of power when you were first practicing recoveries to level flight from a glide. The nose wanted to rise as cruise power was applied, and it took a definite concentration on your part to keep it down where it belonged. You had the plane trimmed for level flight those times. Picture the situation if you had been using *full power* as would be done on a takeoff or a go-around with the trim in the *full nose-up* condition. Add to these problems outside distractions (plus the fact that you are at a low altitude), and you have a bad combination.

The instructor will demonstrate this stall at a safe altitude, as for all the other stalls. The conditions will be set up, and the instructor will apply full power and probably keep hands off the wheel to show you what the plane will do. (You guessed it; the nose will claw upward and the stall break, when it comes, will most likely be to the left because of torque effects.)

You'll then get a chance to practice recovering before things get out of hand. The main idea is to keep that nose down. For most light trainers the nose can be held down without too much trouble. The hazard is in the surprise associated with an actual situation. Practicing these stalls will give you quick recognition of the problem and the best means of recovery for your particular airplane. The following will generally apply:

1. *Recognize the problem immediately* (improper trim).
2. *Get the nose down to no higher than the normal climb position with whatever forward pressure is needed.* Then get the trim back to neutral as soon as practicable. If the forward pressure required is so strong as to require both hands on the wheel, keep them there and climb to a safe altitude before trying to get on the trim. Then you can use one hand intermittently to get the trim squared away.
3. *Do not chop the power after the nose has risen.* You'll be too low to clear the problem and add power again. If the situation has progressed, the chopping of power could cause an immediate stall.

Excessive Top-Rudder Stall

Rough usage of the controls during a slip is a good way to discover the excessive top-rudder stall. By using excessive top rudder in a slip or turn, the high wing is stalled and the stall is quite similar to the departure and approach stalls. As you remember, in these stalls the high wing stalled first because the plane started slipping and part of that wing's airflow was disturbed or blanked out. In the excessive top-rudder stall, you speed up the process by holding top rudder and causing the plane to slip. The high wing drops a little faster because of this "help," but the recovery is the same as for the departure or approach stall, or any stall for that matter. Relax back pressure as you apply coordinated control pressure to return to straight and level flight.

Excessive Bottom-Rudder Stall

This one is close to the cross-control stall except that, in the turn, rudder alone is used to stall the low wing. You skid the plane as back pressure is increased, and the high wing has more lift (and lower angle of attack—*see* "Spins" in Chapter 13) so that, when the plane stalls, the low wing is the first to go. Recovery is standard. Relax the back pressure as you stop further rotation with the rudder and return to level flight by coordinated control usage.

General Talk About Stalls

By now you should realize that the plane can be stalled flying straight down or straight up. You can make the high wing or low wing stall in a turn. You see that one thing has remained true in all stall recoveries—*get the air flowing smoothly over the wing*. This may mean relaxing the back pressure in a lightplane or using a brisk forward movement of the stick or wheel in a heavy plane.

The problem with any stall is that at the break the nose pitches down and your instinct is to hold back on the stick or wheel to bring it back up. At low altitudes in an inadvertent stall, this is even more the case. It may take some doing to move the control wheel or stick forward to recover from the stall. (You'll have to move the wheel back again to stop loss of altitude; but don't get a secondary stall.)

By the time you finish these advanced stalls you'll know a great deal more about the airplane and will be confident in your ability to fly it.

Emergency Flying by Reference to Instruments
Private Pilot

The idea of giving student pilots emergency instrument instruction was debated in aviation circles for several years before the ruling was made. Some argued that "a *little* knowledge is a dangerous thing" and felt that students or private pilots might get just enough confidence in their instrument flying ability to attempt to fly in marginal weather. Others said that it was up to the individual. Some might try it, but many more lives would be saved by this training than would be lost by student overconfidence.

These are emergency maneuvers like the low- and high-altitude emergencies and simulated engine failure on takeoff. You would not deliberately cut the ignition to practice those emergencies nor would you deliberately fly into conditions where flying by reference to instruments is necessary.

In requiring this training, the FAA still does not authorize actual instrument flying by anyone other than a properly instrument-rated pilot. If you accidentally fly into Class B, C, or D controlled airspace (*see* Chapter 21) when the weather is below visual flight minimums, the FAA will be interested in talking to you, since you would be a collision hazard for airplanes on authorized instrument flight.

Flying under actual instrument conditions is quite different from simulated instrument flying. If you foul up during the practice sessions, you can always pull the hood up and recover by looking out (if the instructor hasn't already recovered for you). "Practicing" actual instrument flying is like "practicing" actual parachuting. There's no practice about it—it must be done correctly each time. As the Navy would say, "This is no drill!"

To ensure that you have a good grasp of emergency instrument flying, you should get instruction on the following items:

1. Recovery from the start of a power-on spiral.
2. Recovery from the approach to a climbing stall.
3. Normal turns of 180° duration left and right to within 20° of a proper 180° heading.
4. Shallow climbing turns to a predetermined altitude and heading.
5. Shallow descending turns at reduced power to a predetermined altitude and heading.
6. Straight and level flight.

These will probably be introduced and practiced as definite exercises during the dual flights of the second or postsolo phase of the syllabus. A portion of each dual period will be spent on the above requirements as well as the strictly visual flight maneuvers as covered in Chapters 14, 16, 17, and 18.

One thing will be stressed at all times. *Fly the airplane in exactly the same manner as in normal flight. There are no gimmicks, shortcuts, or special techniques. The instruments "see" the plane's attitude and give you the information.* Instrument practice is to teach you to interpret the information given by the instruments and to make the plane respond in the desired manner by use of the indications.

The six maneuvers are based on the premise that you have just flown into worsening weather conditions and suddenly the ground has disappeared and there's nothing left but a gray mist. Which way is up? Or down? Even though for the first few seconds the plane may continue flying straight and level, your body may want to lie to you. The balance center in the middle ear may get a bum signal. (It's surprising how much that balance depends on sight.) You are convinced that the plane is in a left-climbing turn or right-diving turn or any other maneuver that may strike your fancy at the moment. The number of flying hours has no bearing on a pilot's ability to fly the plane by "feel" alone. *No pilot can do it.*

Nearly all trainers used today have a full panel of flight instruments as shown in Figure 15-1, but for training purposes some of the explanations will also assume that a heading indicator and attitude indicator are not available. *Coordinated use of the ailerons and rudder is needed, as always, and the turn indicator and ball should be thought of as working together.*

Figure 15-1. A diving spiral to the right.

The term "turn indicator," as used in this book, will mean either the needle in the turn and slip or the small airplane in the turn coordinator as applicable to your airplane. The wheel and throttle will also be coordinated throughout these maneuvers. Again, if the plane you are using for training has an attitude indicator and a heading indicator, you would use them in all of the following maneuvers.

Recovery from a Power-On Spiral

The power-on spiral is probably the most common result of trying to fly the plane under instrument conditions without proper training and/or instrumentation.

Many fatalities have been caused by pilots entering this flight condition when visual references are lost. The plane picks up speed rapidly in the diving turn; the pilot sees the airspeed increasing and tries to stop the descent by increasing back pressure, which actually tightens the turn and makes the situation worse. Two things usually happen with this type of recovery

attempt: (1) The plane strikes the ground while still in the spiral or (2) it comes apart in the air due to the high stresses imposed by the excessive back pressure (which, as you know, causes a high load factor). The maneuver is aptly named the "graveyard spiral."

You learned in the "720° Power Turn" in Chapter 10 that, if the nose started dropping in the steep turn, there was little use in trying to bring it up by back pressure alone. The situation was generally made worse instead of better. The bank had to be shallowed to stop the loss of altitude.

The bank in the power-on spiral under actual conditions may be approaching vertical. The "basic" instruments would indicate the following in the power-on spiral (Figure 15-1):

1. Turn indicator—shows a great rate of turn; the ball may or may not be centered. It is shown as not centered in the diagram. Knowing the effects at higher speeds, the ball is more likely to be to the left because of right yaw effects. *See* "Torque," Chapter 2.
2. Airspeed—high and increasing.
3. Altimeter—showing a rapid loss of altitude.

Recovery (Attitude and Heading Indicators Inoperative)

To recover from the condition as effectively as possible, do the following:

1. Reduce power to slow the airspeed increase and avoid overspeeding the engine.
2. Center the turn indicator and ball through coordinated use of ailerons and rudder. If the needle or small airplane is to the right, apply left rudder and aileron until the indicator is centered.

   This coordination is necessary because through harsh application of top rudder the turn might be stopped (the turn indicator centered) and the plane may stay in the bank, with the result that back pressure would still put stresses on the plane with little action toward recovery. A glance at the ball, however, would immediately show the imbalance.
3. Check the airspeed. As you roll out of the bank apply back pressure (easy!) to stop the increasing airspeed. A rough approximation is that in a spiral or dive recovery, at the instant the airspeed starts to decrease, the plane's nose is in the level flight attitude. When this is indicated, ease on forward pressure so that the nose is not pulled up into a steep climb or stall attitude. As the plane returns to steady, straight and level flight, the airspeed will continue to decrease until the cruise speed is attained (assuming the power is at cruise setting).

   The reason for applying back pressure only until the airspeed shows the change is that in trying to go any further toward recovery by watching the airspeed you may get the result shown in Figure 15-2. The nose will want to continue up past the level flight position because of the excess speed of the dive; forward pressure is needed to stop this. In fact, in most cases as the wings are leveled, the nose will tend to rise without back pressure from you, but you'll need to check this for your airplane.

   In the 130-K dive in Figure 15-2, the plane has a lot of energy to dissipate. If you pull the nose up (remembering that there's no outside visibility) or let the nose come up until cruise speed is reached, you will find that the attitude is quite nose high and the airspeed drops rapidly to the stall, requiring forward pressure or a stall recovery.
4. The fourth main step in the recovery is to "stop the altimeter." This is the finer adjustment to be made immediately after getting the plane to the approximate level flight attitude through use of the airspeed indicator. Little attention will be paid to the altitude of leveling other than recovering as smoothly and quickly as possible. You will find that stopping the altimeter, with the power setting at cruise, will

result in a stable cruise airspeed in a short while. Check the airspeed in your scan of the instruments, but realize that it will settle down shortly of its own accord. Don't try to rush it. After the plane is under control, altitude and directional adjustments may be made.

During the latter phases of the recovery the turn indicator must not be neglected, and a constant scan of all instruments is needed for a safe, firm recovery. The plane must be kept under control directionally while the descent (or ascent) is being controlled or stopped.

You will note that nothing was mentioned about heading in this case. It doesn't matter. Recover from the spiral, let the compass settle down, and make a timed turn back toward the good weather area. Timed turns will be discussed later in this chapter. (Reset the heading indicator as soon as feasible.)

One important thing should be mentioned. As you know, the fixed-pitch prop will windmill in a dive and the engine will overspeed. It is better if you throttle back at the start of the spiral recovery to avoid this abuse of the engine.

Figure 15-2. Don't chase the airspeed.

Summary of the Power-On Spiral Recovery

1. Retard power.
2. Center the turn indicator.
3. Start back pressure smoothly as needed. Check airspeed for the first indication of a change. Stop the back pressure.
4. Stop the altimeter (with forward pressure as needed).
5. Maintain the instrument scan throughout the recovery.
6. When the plane is under control, make adjustments in power, altitude, and direction as needed.

Figure 15-3 shows the steps used in the recovery from a power-on spiral. You should know how to effect a recovery by use of the basic instruments shown in Figure 15-3 but will, in most cases, have the use of an attitude indicator. (Of course, you could have tumbled it with your outrageous maneuverings while getting into this situation.) Figure 15-4 shows that the attitude indicator can be used to level the wings and bring the nose up to level flight. You would readjust the power as the airspeed approaches the cruise value.

Recovery from the Approach to a Climbing Stall

The climbing stall sometimes occurs when visual references are lost, or it may be a result of letting the nose rise too high in the spiral recovery. In either case the recovery technique is the same. You have had a chance to practice stalls visually, as well as noting the instruments during the maneuver. Assume that the attitude and heading indicators are inoperative for the first part of the discussion.

As a review, check the indications as the stall is approached (at cruising power) (Figure 15-5).
1. Turn indicator—may or may not be centered.
2. Airspeed—decreasing (probably rapidly).
3. Altimeter—increasing altitude, or steady in the last stage of stall approach.

Recovery

1. Relax the back pressure (or push forward if necessary) until the airspeed starts to increase.
2. Center the turn indicator.
3. Use the altimeter to level off. Lose a minimum of altitude but don't get a secondary stall; you may want to sacrifice another 100 feet of altitude to ensure that this does not happen.

| 1. Reduce power | 2. Center the needle and ball (or level the coordinator) | 3. Start back pressure smoothly. Check the airspeed for a change. Relax back pressure. | 4. Stop the altimeter |

Figure 15-3. The steps in recovery from a power-on spiral, using the basic instruments.

Figure 15-4. The attitude indicator gives a better picture of the spiral situation. You would retard the power, then simultaneously roll out as you bring the nose up to the level flight attitude. One disadvantage of the *simultaneous* roll-out pull-up is that high stresses may be put on the airplane at high speeds.

4. Maintain the instrument scan throughout the recovery. Keep the turn indicator centered.

5. After recovery to cruising flight is made, make power, altitude, and directional adjustments as needed.

Use of the airspeed for recovery from an approach to a stall follows the same general idea as that in the spiral. In this case, however, the airspeed starts *increasing* when the attitude of the plane is approximately level. To be on the safe side, this point should be passed so that the plane will be in a slightly nosedown attitude to ensure a definite recovery. This is more important when the stall breaks than in an approach where the plane still has some flying speed.

You will notice that, in the case of the stall recovery, the primary need is to get the airspeed back into a safe range, and any deviation in direction can be corrected after the recovery is made.

Again, the use of the attitude indicator makes things much easier; you can simultaneously lower the nose as the wings are leveled. If you are sure the attitude indicator is working properly, the following would apply:

1. Relax back pressure as full power is applied.

2. Ease the nose down (leveling the wings) to a pitch attitude below level flight.

3. As the airspeed approaches cruise value, ease the nose up to level, readjust power, and make altitude and heading corrections as necessary.

The reason for the lowering of the nose below the normal level flight attitude is to assure that no new stall is encountered by trying to stop it at the level flight attitude (Figure 15-6).

180° Turn

You had a chance to practice turns with reference to instruments during the presolo phase and will now have a chance to make turns using the turn indicator, airspeed, and altimeter as well as using the full panel for these maneuvers.

A heading indicator makes 180° turns (or any turn) simple (Figure 15-7); just turn and roll out when it reads correctly. (Your problem with the older type of instrument may be figuring out just *what* heading is 180° from the present one. *See* Figure 3-22.)

Figure 15-5. Approach to a climbing stall.

Figure 15-6. (A) The attitude indicator shows that the airplane is in a nose-high left turn. (B) Level the wings as you ease the nose below the normal level flight attitude until the airspeed approaches the normal cruise. Then bring the nose to the level position and adjust power.

Figure 15-7. With the most popular type of heading indicators, finding your reciprocal heading and turning to it is easy. Other methods of turning will be discussed anyway.

Timed Turn — Recommended Method

The recommended method of making a 180° turn if you don't have a good heading indicator is by timing the entire turn using the turn indicator (and, of course, your airspeed and altimeter). One advantage here is that the turns may be made in either direction without the necessity of making separate calculations for each. Another advantage is that you can merely set up a standard-rate turn and hold it for 60 seconds. A time-piece is needed.

Test programs showed that students had trouble with the timed turn in that they would forget the time the turn started. One other thing that may bother you—a minute can be a long time. Students some times lose track of the time and think that they have been turning a minute and 30 seconds instead of an actual 30 seconds. Or you may check the clock and continue the turn for 2 minutes instead of the 1 minute required.

In bumpy weather the needle or turn coordinator will oscillate, and you will have to fly the average position rather than trying to keep the indicator exactly at the standard-rate turn position.

Remember that the turn indicator is not the only instrument to be watched during this maneuver. Keep up your scan. If the airspeed and altitude start getting away, stop the turn, recover to straight and level flight, and after the plane is under control, continue the turn.

When you are flying cross-country, always have the reciprocal of your course in mind. *This is the heading you will want to turn to.* If the plane stays under control after entry into the weather, then a 180° turn is desired. On the other hand, if you have inadvertently turned while in the clouds or fog, a 180° turn could put you deeper into the weather. Here is an illustration.

You are on a heading of 120° and suddenly fly into a condition where outside visibility is lost. The plane enters a spiral and you recover to straight and level. After recovery, the plane's heading is 280°. You don't particularly notice the heading but mechanically set up a 180° turn, which will actually carry you further into the weather, when a turn of 20° to the right would put you on the desired reciprocal heading. Even holding the 280° heading would be accurate enough to leave the weather area (Figure 15-8).

Using the Four Main Directions

In a shallow-banked turn, the magnetic compass is fairly accurate on the headings of East or West. It lags by about 30° as the plane passes the heading of North and leads by about 30° as the plane passes the heading of South. (The exact lag or lead will have to be checked for your situation, which will include latitude and other variables. For illustration purposes here, it is assumed to be 30°.) This is called "northerly turning error" and affects the compass while the plane is turning.

Assume that you are flying on a heading of 120° and want to make a 180° turn. The desired new heading will be 300°. By turning to the right, you will have

Figure 15-8. (1) A power-on spiral is accidentally entered. (2) Recovery is effected on a heading of 280°. (3) Without thinking, the pilot mechanically makes a 180° turn. (4) The pilot would have been out of the weather in a short time.

a cardinal heading (West) reasonably close to the new heading. A standard-rate turn is made to the right, but no timing is attempted. You will be watching for West on the compass, and as the plane reaches that heading you will start timing. The desired heading is 30° (300° minus 270°) past this and will require 10 seconds at the standard rate. The timing can be done by counting "one thousand and one, one thousand and two," and so forth, up to ten, at which time the turn indicator is centered (Figure 15-9).

A turn to the left could have been made realizing that the nearest major compass heading (North) will be 60°, or 20 seconds short of the desired heading of 300°. In that case you will set up a standard-rate turn to the left and will not start timing until the compass indicates 030°. Remember that the compass will lag on a turn through North and will be behind the actual heading by about 30° (Figure 15-10).

When the 030° indication is given, the 20-second timing begins, either by the sweep-second hand of the aircraft clock or your watch or by counting.

There are several disadvantages to this system, the major one being that it requires a visual picture of the airplane's present and proposed heading—and mental calculations. You may not have time or may be too excited for a mental exercise at this point. Also,

in bumpy weather the compass may not give accurate readings on the four main headings.

The main advantage is that reasonably accurate turns may be made without a timepiece, as the new heading will never be more than 45°, or 15 seconds, away from a major heading. This method is presented as something to be filed away and used if necessary.

Shallow-Climbing Turns to a Predetermined Altitude

Perhaps you hit bad weather and start letting down but suddenly fly into an area where the ceiling is literally down on the ground. Altitude is needed, yet you don't want to fly further into the unknown territory as you climb. The shallow-climbing turn is the answer. You may have passed over some fairly high terrain or obstructions before letting down to sneak under and now need more altitude before flying back.

Figure 15-11 shows a typical climb attitude and airspeed indication for a trainer, as shown by the two flight instruments (climb power being used). Your instructor will probably cover the airspeed and attitude indicator at separate times to show how a proper climb can be set up by either instrument.

If you are using the full panel of flight instruments, the instructor may set up a spiral and require that after recovery you climb back up to a specific altitude and heading, as would be the case in a real situation. (You need to recover lost altitude; you also need to turn out of the bad weather.)

Suppose that at the end of a spiral recovery you are at 2,800 feet and your heading is 035°. You need 3,500 feet of altitude and a heading of 125° to get safely back to good weather. The airplane climbs at 700 fpm, and you'll be back up to the safe altitude in 1 minute. A 90° turn to the right is required, so using a standard-rate

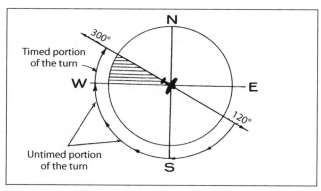

Figure 15-9. The 180° turn to the right.

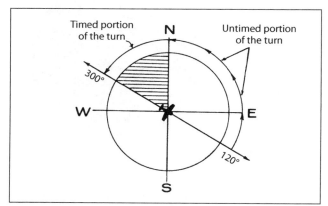

Figure 15-10. The 180° turn to the left.

Figure 15-11. At climb power a certain pitch attitude will give the correct climb airspeed. You should use this fact in initially setting up the climb. You may hear the expression, "Power plus attitude equals performance," among the instrument-rated pilots at the airport.

turn, you'll get there in 30 seconds. Fine. Set up your climb and turn. You'll be at your heading of 125 when you still have 350 feet of altitude to go. Roll out and make a straight climb until the required altitude is reached. *Keep an eye on that heading indicator during the straight climb.* Students sometimes get so interested in the altimeter that they let the airplane turn right on around—back into the imaginary, or actual, bad weather. ("Torque" sometimes is a culprit too.) So if you get to the heading first, maintain it as you climb; if you get to the altitude first, level off and continue the turn. The problem is not complete until you are at both the required altitude and heading (Figure 15-12).

The following explanation will assume that your heading and attitude indicators are temporarily out of action. One point: While the attitude indicator may be tumbled and out of action for several minutes (if you don't have an instrument with a caging knob), you can reset the *heading indicator* immediately and use it as an aid to keep your wings level (if you are getting indications of a turn to the right, that wing is down, etc.). You'll be surprised at how much aid the heading indicator can give you. Your first resetting of it with the magnetic compass will be a rough one, but you can reset it later after the compass has settled down.

Procedure (Basic Instruments)

Right rudder will be needed to keep the ball centered, as always in a climbing turn.

If climbing power is set, the turn kept shallow, and the airspeed is held at that of climb, the rate of climb will take care of itself. The rate of climb indicator is a very useful reference here. But "chasing" the vertical speed indicator will only result in a varying flight path. *Corrections must be smooth and deliberate.*

As in the case of the shallow-climbing turn with visual references, you will ease the nose up to the required position and apply climbing power. When you could see outside, the nose position, power setting, airspeed, and altimeter showed that the plane was in a normal climb. You found that by combining the proper nose position and power setting the altimeter and airspeed took care of themselves. Here you will use the airspeed and power setting to assure that the proper climb is maintained (take care of the airspeed and power, and the nose attitude will take care of itself as long as the other instruments are not neglected). It would be advisable to establish the climb first before the turn is started.

Figure 15-12. (A) Control of the airplane is recovered on the heading (035°) and altitude (2,800 MSL) shown. The desired heading is 125° and the required altitude is 3,500 feet. A standard-rate turn and a climb are started. (B) The heading is reached and the turn is stopped. A straight climb is continued to the required altitude. (C) The requirements are complete when the airplane is on both the required heading and altitude.

The idea of starting the level-off about 20 feet below the desired altitude still stands (for most light-planes). This allowance depends on the rate of climb; a fast-climbing jet may need several hundred feet to level off.

In visual flying, the leveling-off was accomplished by easing the nose over to the straight and level position, checking the altimeter, and, as the airspeed approached the cruise value, throttling back to cruise rpm and trimming the airplane. You paid little attention to the airspeed during the leveling process. The same applies here. If the altitude is kept constant and the power setting is at cruise, the airspeed will take care of itself and will soon settle down at the cruise value. It will still, however, be covered in the scan.

1. With the turn indicator centered, apply back pressure slowly to decrease the airspeed to the climb value. It will take a little time for the airspeed to drop to that of the climb. The best technique is to apply a certain amount of back pressure, let the airspeed stabilize, and apply more or less back pressure as needed. After you have practiced a few climb entries, this back pressure can be estimated. The trim tab can help maintain the climb, and you are encouraged to use it.
2. Apply climb power as the airspeed approaches the climb value.
3. After the climb is established with the airspeed and power setting (you've been keeping the wings level with the turn indicator), set up a standard-rate turn in the desired direction. At your plane's probable climb speed, the bank required for a standard-rate turn will be in the vicinity of 10°–15° so that the standard-rate turn is easy to maintain as well as giving the proper shallow bank required for a climbing turn.

Make all turns standard-rate. Later you may start the turn and climb at the same time. It may be desired to climb to a specific altitude and turn to a definite heading, so stop the turn but continue the climb, or vice versa, to get what you want.

Leveling-Off Procedure

1. At the proper distance below the chosen altitude start the leveling procedure. Relax back pressure to stop the climb.
2. Fly the altimeter; maintain the chosen altitude.
3. Center the turn indicator as you "stop the altimeter."
4. As the airspeed increases, throttle back to cruise power. Trim the airplane.
5. Make any heading corrections when the airplane is flying level (trimmed).

Shallow Descending Turns at Reduced Power to a Predetermined Altitude and Heading

A descent (or ascent) at a given airspeed can be controlled by the amount of throttle used. The simplest form of descent is one you have used in losing altitude by maintaining the cruise airspeed and throttling back until the desired rate of descent was obtained. You probably didn't measure the exact rate in feet per minute but used the controls to get what "looked good."

As in the other turns on instruments, you are advised to make these descending turns standard-rate. A steeper banked turn may get out of hand, and what started as a shallow descending turn may wind up as a graveyard spiral.

The descent could be made at any airspeed, but you wouldn't want to be slower than the normal glide or much faster than cruise because of the possibility of loss of control at the extremes of the airspeed range. The plane may be overstressed if turbulence is encountered at high speeds, or a stall might occur at the lower end of the airspeed range. The leveling-off process will be dependent on the rate of descent. For lightplanes, starting the level-off approximately 50 feet above the altitude will work for an average controlled descent of 500–800 feet per minute. You will be flying the turn indicator, airspeed, and altimeter (plus attitude and heading indicators, if available) for attitude, rate of turn, and descent.

After leveling off, the power will have to be increased to that of cruise in order to maintain altitude. Your instructor will have a recommended speed and power setting for descent available for your airplane. A 500-fpm descent is a good one to shoot for. It won't be so great as to risk loss of control (this is a "standard" rate of descent for instrument flying). For one high-wing trainer, a speed of 80 K is in the center of the green arc on the airspeed indicator (a good place to be), and a power setting of 1,900 rpm gives a 500-fpm descent. (You'll find that the rate of descent at your given airspeed and rpm will vary slightly with altitude and/or airplane weight, but the difference will not be enough to cause any problems.)

This exercise is complete when the airplane is on both the chosen altitude and heading.

Figure 15-13 shows the combination that might be used on descent on a partial, or emergency, panel.

Figure 15-13. (A) Power setting and airspeed of one trainer for a straight descent of approximately 500 feet per minute. (B) You would keep the wings level with the turn indicator and/or the heading indicator if you could get it back in action.

Straight and Level

Although you may have been practicing straight and level flying by reference to instruments for some time, it might be well to mention a few other points.

Talking about the full flight panel, it would seem that flying straight and level using attitude and heading indicators should be very easy. But the problem is that the student sees the means to keep a precise heading (the heading indicator) and so works too hard and overcompensates. You might have this problem: You see that the airplane has turned a few degrees off heading. You want to get back on the heading right away, so you roll into a bank to accomplish this. You find that you've overshot and now have to reverse the procedure. This game can go on as long as the instructor allows it—which is not too long. This is known as "S-turns across the route." The thing to keep in mind is that you will make *minor* corrections (more about that shortly)—and this will also apply later as you work on that instrument rating—and *ease* up (or down) to an airspeed, altitude, or heading if you've slipped off a little.

You may have to fly several minutes to get out of the weather. The ability to fly a straight and level path and not wander means a quicker return to a place where visual references are available. The turn indicator is the

primary indicator for keeping a fixed direction of flight if the other gyro instruments aren't available. Fly the turn indicator and use the compass for a cross-check. If the compass has settled down and shows that you are off heading, correct with a balanced turn in the proper direction. For minor variations from heading (up to 15°) a half standard-rate correction is preferred. If you are 10° off, make a one-half standard-rate turn ($1\frac{1}{2}°$ per second) for 7 seconds. In straight and level flying the student sometimes has a tendency to stare at the turn indicator, neglecting the rest of the scan. It's important that the instruments be continually crosschecked with each other.

You may get practice in flying straight and level using one or two of the instruments to show how a reasonable heading and altitude can be maintained. The procedure might be like this: You'll be under the hood, and the instructor will set up the airplane on a heading of, say, 090° and altitude of 3,500 feet. When everything has "settled down," the instructor will, for instance, cover all of the flight instruments except the attitude indicator and have you fly the airplane, keeping the proper pitch and wings-level position by this instrument only. After 2 minutes the instructor will uncover the altimeter and heading indicator, and you can see how close you are to the original requirements.

Combinations of instruments may be used to make the point that you can keep the airplane under control when ground references are lost. It's a good confidence-building exercise.

Straight Descents Using the Magnetic Compass

Suppose you've lost all three gyro instruments and need to let down through a cloud layer. As a last resort and if there is a good ceiling below, the magnetic compass may be used as a combination attitude indicator and heading indicator. The letdown should be made on a heading of South because the compass will react "normally" if a wing drops and a turn is started. In other words, on that heading the compass will show an increase in heading numbers if a right turn is starting or will show a decrease for a left turn. On a North heading, you recall that the compass will start moving the "wrong" way at the initiation of a turn—which could be fatally confusing. The South heading gives a quick and proper reference to keep the wings level. You might ask your instructor to demonstrate this on the way back from the practice area sometime.

Simulated Radar Advisories

If your airport traffic permits, your instructor on dual flights may bring you back from the practice area "on radar" several times. You'll go under the hood and the instructor will be "approach control radar" and direct you back into the traffic pattern and, perhaps, down to a few hundred feet on final. Then you will get problems that use the instrument training you've had. It will be good practice if you should later accidentally get into actual instrument weather and need radar service.

ASR—Airport surveillance radar is a nonprecision radar that allows the controller to vector you into the pattern and tell you what altitude you should be at various distances on final. (The controllers have no altitude information on you, just direction and distance.) Usually the weather minimums for ASR approaches are a 500-foot ceiling and 1 mile. Its primary purpose, however, is to expedite traffic flow in the terminal area.

PAR—Precision approach radar is used as a *landing* aid. The operator can check your approach path and advise whether the airplane is on course and/or on the glide path. This is the system used on the "Late Late Show" where the crippled jet has 5 minutes of fuel and the weather has just gone to zero-zero at the only airport available within several hundred miles. After much suspense (did they make it?), the jet taxies out of the fog. The minimums for the PAR approach are naturally lower than the ASR, but never as low as shown on the "Late Late Show." PAR systems are usually found on military/civilian joint-use airports.

Later you will also get practice in tracking to or from a VOR station or other navigation facilities and be able to communicate while doing so (*see* Chapter 21) and while flying the airplane by reference to the instruments.

Summary

The instruments give information on the plane's actions and attitudes and take the place of the horizon in visual flight. A certain amount of practice is needed to be able to see the plane's actions through the instruments. A plane's responses to the controls are the same under instrument conditions as under visual conditions; hence, no special control technique is used, but throttle and elevators, ailerons and rudder are coordinated as always.

If you can do the maneuvers cited in this chapter, you should have no trouble passing this area of the private practical (flight) test.

You may use the techniques discussed in this chapter to save your neck someday. If you should inadvertently find yourself in a situation of being on actual instruments, your worst enemy will be panic. You'll have practiced under the hood (dual) and will be able to keep control of the airplane *before* you go on that first solo cross-country. Take a couple of slow, deep breaths to slow yourself down, and remember the numbers (airspeeds, etc.) you've been taught. As will be covered later in this book and by your instructor, there are FAA people on the ground who can help, but you will have to fly the airplane and make the decisions (often the person on the ground is not a pilot).

Make a 180° turn before getting into the bad weather and save yourself some sweat.

Postsolo Precision Maneuvers

On every flight you'll have to cope with the wind (or lack of it), and these exercises are intended to help you compensate for drift so that *you* are in command of the airplane's path over the ground.

Another Basic Wind Drift Maneuver

Turns Around a Point

This maneuver is very close to the S-turn across a road because you're correcting for wind while in a turn. It is suggested that the steepest bank should be approximately 45° and the altitude should not be lower than 500 feet above the highest obstruction in the maneuver pattern. The idea of the turns about a point is to show the check pilot how well you can fly the plane when your attention is directed outside. Your check pilot will also want to find out if you understand wind drift correction principles (Figure 16-1).

Procedure

1. Pick a tree or some other small but easily seen object and set up the radius small enough so that the steepest bank is approximately 45°.
2. Enter the pattern downwind. Practice both left and right turns around the point. Many students only practice left turns and get a rude awakening when they are asked to make a turn around a point to the right on the check flight. The best altitude for keeping the point in sight is about 700 feet above the surface.
3. Vary the turn as needed to maintain a constant distance from the point—the greater the ground speed, the steeper the bank.
4. Maintain a constant altitude.
5. Keep your eyes open. This is a perfect place to have a low-altitude emergency thrown at you.
6. The check pilot may give you a free turn to get set up, but will keep up with the number of turns after the maneuver is started.

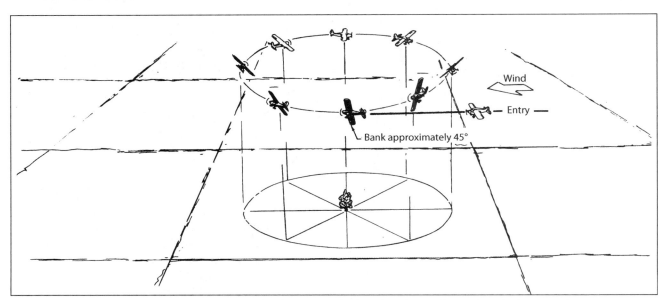

Figure 16-1. Turns around a point. The steepest bank is required when the plane is flying directly downwind.

Common Errors

1. Starting the maneuver with the plane too far from the point so that the steepest bank does not reach 45°.
2. Poor altitude control.
3. Pointing the wing at the tree—trying to keep the plane's attitude the same in relation to the point rather than having the plane's path constant, as it should be.
4. Failure to recognize wind drift or, if recognized, not doing anything about it.
5. Coordination problems. Students sometimes have trouble with this maneuver because they can't seem to convince themselves that the steepest bank is required when the airplane is headed *directly* downwind, as indicated in Figure 16-1.

Suppose an airplane is flying tangent (wings level) to the circle at the positions shown by A, B, C, and D in Figure 16-2. At A, the airplane is moving at its true airspeed *plus* the wind speed. This results in the highest relative speed to the reference point of any position around the circle. At C, its relative speed is the lowest because it is moving into a headwind. The arrow (vector) behind each airplane gives a picture of the relative speed at the four positions. The dashed lines show the comparative distances the airplane would be "away" from the circle for any given interval of time if no turn was made.

Figure 16-2. A comparison of rates of "leaving the circle" for an airplane flying at the same true airspeed at four positions on the circle.

The rate of turn, then, must be greatest at A if it is to "follow the circle." Since this is a coordinated maneuver, the bank must be greatest at that position (and the bank is most shallow at C). The banks at B and D will be comparable.

Vector Approach to the Maneuver

If you are interested in the mathematics of turns around a point, Figure 16-3 shows wind triangles for the airplane at eight points around the circle. As noted, the airplane's true airspeed is 100 K and the wind is from the top of the illustration (North) at 40 K. The solid thin arrow represents *groundspeed, or the airplane's path and speed with respect to the ground.* This groundspeed vector varies in size (speed) because of the wind, but at each of the eight points shown (or at *any* point on the circle) it must be tangent to the circle or else the plane would not be following the prescribed path; so this is the first consideration.

The true airspeed is indicated by the dashed arrows and is always 100 K for this problem. (Disregard slowing the airplane in the steeper banks.) The 100 K true airspeed vector, however, must be "pointed" in such a manner that the result of the plane's heading, plus the wind, makes the airplane's path tangent to the circle at any position. The wind is a constant velocity and direction.

Maybe you haven't done any work with the navigation computer yet, but you will, and you can come back to this later.

The circle can be thought of as an "infinite number of short, straight lines," and the airplane is flying "one leg" of a rectangular course for each one. In order to do this, the plane must be crabbed to fly the line tangent to the circle. The reason for the bank is to get the proper heading for the next "leg." The bank at point 1 must be steepest because the airplane is approaching the next "leg" at the greatest rate. At point 5 the opposite is true.

Of course, practically speaking, you fly the airplane and maintain the proper distance from the point by looking at it. But given the true airspeed and wind, you could work out on a navigation computer the required headings for each of the eight points given here. For instance, the course at point 1 is 180°. At point 2 the course would be 135°. At point 3 it would be 090°, etc., and you could find the wind correction angle. The required banks at each point could be obtained mathematically for the radius of the circle to be flown, using a turn equation similar to that given in Chapter 3 of the *Advanced Pilot's Flight Manual*. The maneuver could be theoretically flown "under the hood" once

Figure 16-3. The turns around a point maneuver when seen as a problem in vectors. You may want to come back to this one after you've done some work with the computer.

Figure 16-4. The views from the cabin of a high-wing airplane at points 1, 3, 5, and 7 in Figure 16-3. The pond would help you know the wind direction (*see* Figure 18-2).

the airplane is established in it. You would just match the proper banks to the various required headings you found for the eight (or more) points around the circle.

Maybe this approach to the maneuver doesn't interest you, and you can certainly do it well if you don't know a vector from a victor. But the main point here is that the rectangular course, S-turns across a road, this maneuver, and others are designed to teach you to fly the airplane on a certain path or track, correcting for wind.

Figure 16-4 shows what you might see from a high-wing airplane at points 1, 3, 5, and 7 in Figure 16-3.

Advanced Wind Drift Correction Maneuvers

The following maneuvers aren't required on the private or sport pilot practical test. You'll do the rectangular course, S-turns across a road, and/or turns around a point. (*See* Chapter 28.) They are given here for your information in case you and your instructor want to do some more complex wind drift correction.

Eights Around Pylons (Around-Pylon Eights)

Shallow Eights

This maneuver is closely akin to the turns around a point but, as the name implies, a figure eight is flown around *two* points, or pylons. The pylons are picked so that an imaginary line between them is perpendicular to the wind (Figure 16-5).

Shown in Figure 16-5 is a shallow around-pylon eight maneuver. The steepest bank should be approximately 30°. Your instructor will note that you may use the same pylons for steep or shallow pylon eights, using a straightaway portion between the pylons as shown. While at first you will enter downwind between the pylons, you will later enter from any point of the maneuver but will fly it so that the outer parts of the turns are made into the wind.

Note in Figure 16-5 that the entry is set up (point 1) and will be slightly wider from the pylon(s) than turns around a point (which required 45° maximum banks). You should be flying directly downwind and tracking to a position exactly between the pylons. When point 2 is reached, a turn is started in either direction (to the right, here). At this stage it's like the maneuver in Figure 16-3. (The bank will be steepest at point 2.) Note

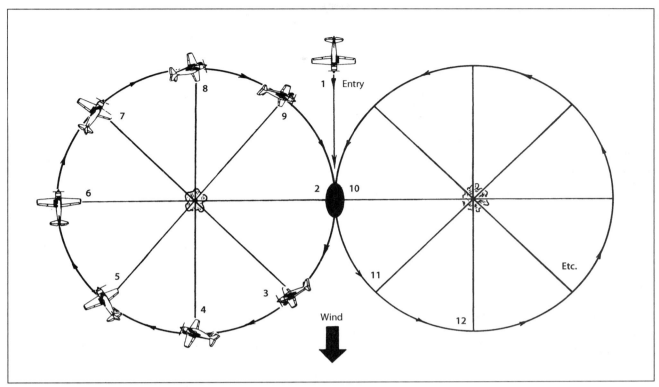

Figure 16-5. Shallow around-pylon eights. This maneuver is a more complicated version of turns about a point.

that at points 3, 4, and 5 the airplane is crabbed in the turn. Point 6 has the shallowest bank and points 7, 8, and 9 require crabbing. When point 10 is reached (or point 2 again), the airplane is rolled into a turn in the opposite direction and the second pylon is used (points 11, 12, etc.). *Not only should each circle be of constant radius, but both should be the same size.* One of the common errors students make is to have a too-wide turn on one pylon and a too-narrow turn on the other. Because of this tendency careful planning and orientation are needed to get back to the spot exactly between the two pylons. You may repeat the pattern any number of times, but usually four or five are the maximum done without a break.

The blacked-out ellipse in the center of the illustration might be called the "zone of confusion" because, even though the circles are supposed to be tangent, it's impossible for an airplane to be rolled from one turn to the other instantly. So in actual practice they can't be tangent, but you should make them as near tangent as *safely* possible.

Some common errors are:

1. Poor pylon picking (which will be covered shortly).
2. Coordination problems (slipping or skidding).

3. Altitude problems. The altitude should be the same as used for turns around a point and kept constant. The usual problem is a tendency to climb as the airplane is rolled from one bank to another, and then lose altitude as the new turn (steep bank) is established.
4. Orientation loss, or "losing" a pylon. You may continue well on past the point to roll in for the opposite turn. If you do this, you could make another 360° turn around the pylon, attempting to divert the attention of the instructor (or check pilot) by pointing out objects of local interest as you go around. (But you won't get away with it.)
5. Nonsymmetrical circles—the turn around one pylon steep, the other shallow. This, too, can usually be attributed to losing the other pylon as well as losing the center point of the pattern (point 2 or 10 in Figure 16-5).
6. Having too large an eight; the airplane is too far from the pylons and very shallow banks are required.

Steep Eights

Figure 16-6 shows the steep around-pylon eight maneuver. The turn pattern is closer to each pylon, and a straight leg is used to get set up for the other pylon. This maneuver uses wind drift corrections in straight

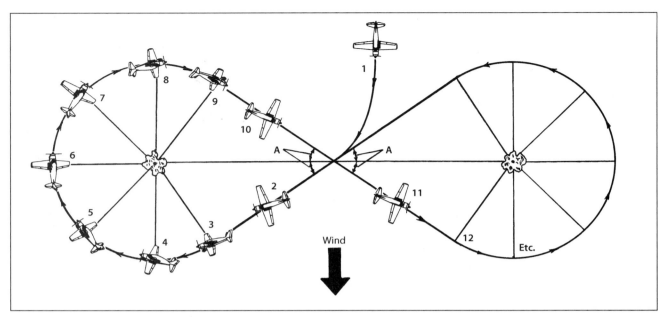

Figure 16-6. Steep around-pylon eights. Wind drift directions in both turning and straight flight are needed in this one.

flight and a turn. You'll have to plan the roll-out from one pylon so as to have the proper drift correction set up for the leg to the other pylon.

Note the steps at the following points in Figure 16-6:

Point 1. The airplane is in a position to enter the maneuver.

Point 2. Drift correction is set up in the straight leg.

Point 3. When the proper radius is reached, a turn is set up. Points 3 and 9 will require the steepest banks in this maneuver since the groundspeeds will be greatest at these positions.

Points 4–9. The bank is varied to maintain a constant radius. As point 9 is approached, the airplane is rolled out to set up the proper crab angle, points 10 and 11, to be at the required radius at point 12. This loop of the eight uses the same principle as the first.

The four angles indicated by the two A's may be those desired by the instructor. Later, you will pick the pylons and set the maneuver up so that each of these angles will be 45°. (You can figure that the steeper the bank around a given pair of pylons, the smaller these angles will be.)

Figure on encountering the same errors as listed for the shallow eights plus a couple that would especially apply to this maneuver:

1. The turn in the entry may be too soon or too late, making the first loop too tight or too wide. You'll find that at first you may take several patterns for each eight before settling down.

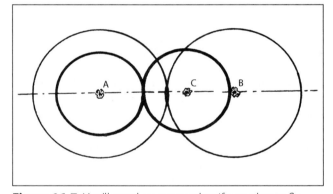

Figure 16-7. You'll need an extra pylon if you plan to fly both steep and shallow around-pylon eights "back-to-back." (Or you could pick an entirely new pair if you want a break.) A and B are the pylons for the shallow eights; A and C would be used for the steep ones.

2. Problems during the straight portions of the maneuver—poor wind drift correction so that the airplane is not at the proper distance from the pylon as the turn is started.

Another pylon should be selected if the "back-to-back" idea (no straightaway) is used for steep *and* shallow eights (Figure 16-7).

The principles involved are the same as for the other wind drift correction maneuvers discussed earlier. The turning portions of the eights follow the theory shown in Figure 16-3—the airplane is crabbing in the turn. The straight flight parts use the principles you learned when you first flew parallel to a road, correcting for a crosswind.

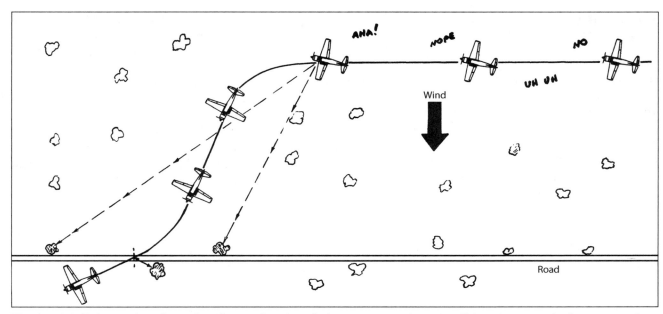

Figure 16-8. Picking pylons. Points beside a road are best for keeping your orientation. If there is no good reference exactly between the pylons, you should find the center with relation to some object, such as the tree shown here.

The eights are more complicated than turns around a point because you have another pylon to consider and must be planning your transition from one to the other, even while maintaining a constant radius around one pylon. It's easy to lose that other pylon by getting too involved in the one you are working with. It makes for a sinking feeling on a check flight when you roll out and don't see anything that looks like the other pylon you selected earlier. Picking your pylons is very important; isolated trees near roads or other outstanding landmarks are good references (Figure 16-8). Choosing one of several trees in a large field can lead to results you might imagine.

These maneuvers are done at the same altitude as you used for the other wind drift correction exercises.

The Perplexing Problem of Proper Pylon Picking

Probably one of your biggest problems is finding pylons the proper distance apart and oriented perpendicular to the wind. Students have gone on pretty good cross-country flights looking for pylons that were "just right," while the instructor or check pilot grew restless in that right seat. A good method of picking pylons is to fly crosswind, looking to the downwind side. As soon as a proper pair of pylons is spotted, the airplane can be turned downwind to enter. Picking pylons beside a road helps a great deal in orientation. (Pylons don't have to be trees, they can be other *immobile* objects; one student picked a cow for one and, needless to say, the pattern was affected as the animal walked across the pasture. An automobile that drives off is also considered a poor choice in most quarters.)

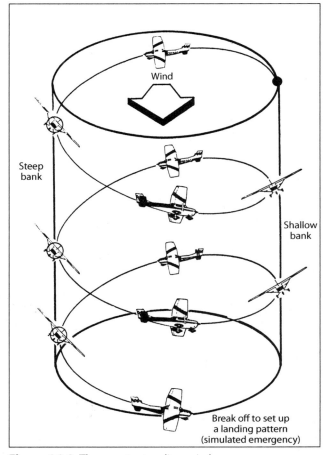

Figure 16-9. The constant-radius spiral.

Spirals (Constant-Radius Descending Turns)

This is a maneuver that uses the wind drift correction skills you learned in turns around a point; in this case, however, you're descending with power at idle (Figure 16-9). The practical aspect is that with practice you can spiral down around a particular point to set up a traffic pattern in the event of a power loss at altitude. (Figure 18-3 shows the idea also.) You'll get some practice with this during your pre- and postsolo dual when the flight instructor gives you simulated high-altitude emergencies.

The spiral is a little more difficult than turns around a point because the airplane will be getting closer to the reference as you descend and the perspective will be changing. (The bank is steepest when flying directly downwind and shallowest when headed upwind, as discussed in turns around a point.) Hold the maximum bank to 40°.

The main problem in a spiral is that the airspeed may tend to get away from you—the usual error is to be too fast. Hold the airspeed to within ±10 K of that desired.

Special Takeoff and Landing Procedures

Now you've done it! You're a victim of that old tried and true aviation saying, "You can land a plane in places where you can't get it out." The field seemed short when you landed, and now the wind has died and things look pretty grim. There are some 50-foot trees at the other end of the runway that you'll have to get over. A special type of takeoff is needed here. (*Or maybe you shouldn't take off.*)

Short-Field Takeoff

The short-field takeoff is a maneuver aimed at just such a situation. You must take off efficiently and make the steepest angle of climb that is safely possible after takeoff. As a rule of thumb, a plane's maximum angle of climb is at a speed of approximately 1.3 times the power-off stall speed, but check the *Pilot's Operating Handbook* for the exact figure. In the normal climb you are interested in the maximum altitude gain over a given length of time (and still not ruin the engine). The maximum angle of climb gives you more altitude for the distance traveled forward (Figure 17-1). *The situation obviously calls for a maximum angle of climb.*

Procedure

1. Start the takeoff at the extreme end of the runway. Set the flaps as recommended by the manufacturer. Hold the wheel back and smoothly open the throttle.

2. As soon as you are certain the engine is developing full power, and the plane is accelerating properly, proceed with a tail-low takeoff. This is to let the plane get into the air sooner than would be the case if the airplane is "held on." The plane will accelerate faster when airborne because of the lesser drag of the air. Don't try to rush the process, because this will slow the takeoff as explained in "Normal Take-off" (Chapter 13). The attitude of the plane during the takeoff will naturally vary among airplanes.

3. The plane will lift off when the minimum flying speed is reached.

   Some pilots suggest that the airplane should be held on the ground until V_X (the max angle of climb speed), but this can cause two possible minor problems: (a) If the field is rough, this can be hard on the landing gear; if the surface is soft or consists of taller grass, you'll take a lot of room to get V_X. (b) For some nosewheel airplanes, a shimmy

Figure 17-1. Exaggerated view of maximum *angle* climb (1) versus maximum *rate* of climb (2).

could develop at high speeds on the ground, even on smooth, firm runways. The instructor will have suggestions for your particular airplane.

4. Attain and maintain the recommended maximum angle climb speed. Keep the throttle wide open. If conditions require this sort of takeoff, they also require all the power you can get from the engine.

5. At about 100 feet above the ground assume a normal climb (V_Y) and use normal climb power.

For check-ride purposes, the obstacle to be cleared is considered to be 50 feet high and the field is considered to be firm. Use the takeoff flap setting as recommended by the Airplane Flight Manual or *Pilot's Operating Handbook*.

Some pilots argue for making a 90° rolling takeoff in preference to the straight-roll technique. The fixed-pitch propeller of the lightplane is inefficient at low speeds. This means comparatively slow acceleration as the plane starts rolling. But the added efficiency gained by the 90° rolling takeoff does not offset the chances of an inexperienced pilot losing directional control. Also, there have been instances where the sharp turn moved fuel away from a wing tank outlet (called "unporting") so that the engine suffered fuel starvation during the takeoff or initial climb.

Your instructor may demonstrate various techniques.

Common Errors

1. Poor directional control when the brakes are released.
2. Trying to hurry the plane off the ground—resulting in high drag and slowing the takeoff.
3. Letting the airspeed pick up past the best angle of climb speed after takeoff and not getting a maximum angle of climb.

Some Added Notes

The *max angle of climb airspeed* is not necessarily the same as the *best obstacle-clearance airspeed* for some airplanes. Without getting involved in the mathematics or aerodynamics, the two airspeeds would be the same in a fixed-gear airplane with no flaps. For airplanes with retractable gear and flaps or for fixed-gear airplanes with flaps, the best obstacle-clearance airspeed given in the *Pilot's Operating Handbook may be lower* than that cited for the best angle of climb in that same publication. The best rate and best angle of climb airspeeds are usually found, for the plane operating in the cleanest condition (flaps up and gear up, if possible), by the manufacturer through flight test and graphical representation. The manufacturer may find by flight

test that the use of some flaps can help in the short-term requirement of clearing a 50-foot obstacle. Also, in a retractable-gear airplane, the wheels are likely to still be down at the time the obstacle is cleared. The *main thing is to set up the airspeed and configuration recommended in the* POH *for the short-field or obstacle-clearing takeoff because that's the problem at hand.* For particular airplanes there may be other numbers given in the *Handbook* for the longer-term max angle climb (and there may not).

It may seem when practicing short-field takeoffs that you are using all of the available length, but for one popular trainer at sea level (density-altitude), the use *of another 12 feet of runway* length will have the result of clearing the *obstacle by another 1 foot*. At a takeoff at 5,000 feet density-altitude in that airplane, each extra 20 feet of runway used will give another 1 foot of clearance over the obstacle. This would be assuming constant outside factors and pilot skills.

Of course, you don't plan on cutting it this close, but maybe an *inch* or less obstacle clearance sometimes could mean the difference between a safe takeoff and an accident. There's the old aviation adage: "Runway behind you, altitude above you, and fuel back in the fuel truck are three very useless items indeed."

Short-Field Landing

More About Power Approaches

The approach you've been making by gradually reducing the power to make the runway is a crude version of the power approach. (Sometimes you had to add power again to make the runway after you were too hasty in reducing it.) Power is a means of controlling the airplane's path on an approach and makes it possible to land on a particular spot. In the presolo work, little effort was made to make a "spot landing" or landing at a chosen point on the runway, but now you'll start making precision landings.

The power approach is a general term. It doesn't say at what speed the approach is made, but only that power is used to control the glide path. There are two power approach speeds in which you will be particularly interested, however. These are the power approach at normal glide speed and the short-field approach with a speed of approximately 1.3 times that of the stall speed.

Before, you were able to tell fairly soon whether you were too high or too low to make the runway, but now you want to predict your landing place within a few feet—and land there. By controlling the airspeed, you will be able to estimate the point of landing. By controlling the airspeed *and* the rate of descent, you will be able to pick the point of landing.

On a day of steady wind in a normal power-off approach, your point of landing has already been determined. But you don't know what this point is. How do you tell? Assume that you are trying to land at a particular spot on the runway—maybe it's a big clump of grass or oil spot that is easily seen. You want to land there, so watch it. If the spot apparently moves toward the nose, you will glide over it. If it moves out away from the nose, the plane will be short of the point. So you say, "By controlling the airspeed, I can set up means of telling whether I'm overshooting or undershooting; now what?" You can slip, add flaps, or add power as needed to hit the spot (Figure 17-2).

You keep a perfect glide speed, and the approach is such that the oil spot or clump of grass doesn't move. As soon as you start breaking the glide, the nose will start moving up and the spot will move under the nose. Let it; you've done everything possible, so forget the spot and make the landing.

Allowing for round-off, your path will look something like Figure 17-3. The landing will be slightly past the spot.

You could hit the spot exactly if the plane followed its original path all the way to the clump of grass, but who wants to glide right into the ground? It's hard on

airplanes for one thing. When maneuvered properly, *the airplane will always land slightly past the spot because of the rounding-off of the landing. There's always a certain amount of float to a landing, even one made from a normal glide, because of ground effect.*

Ground effect becomes a factor when the airplane is about at one-half wingspan distance from the ground, or about 18–20 feet for most training airplanes. The downwash of the wing is changed with the result that induced drag (look back to Figures 2-14 and 2-16) is decreased by up to 48 percent in some cases. Since the induced drag makes up a considerable part of the total drag at the lower airspeeds at takeoff and approach/landing, there may be a noticeable decrease in total drag just above the runway and the airplane "floats." In effect, the glide (approach) angle gets shallower.

Ground effect can be a factor on takeoff as well, as pilots have found when trying to take off at a high elevation on a hot day (high density-altitude) in an overloaded airplane. The airplane may get off, but as it climbs to about one-half the wingspan above the runway, the induced drag rises sharply. There have been extreme cases of airplanes flying into obstacles after takeoff because they were unable to climb out of ground effect.

Your best bet is an approach speed that has a minimum amount of float plus a definite margin of safety. There is such a speed, and a rule of thumb gives it as

Figure 17-2. (A) If the spot appears to be moving toward the airplane, you will be too high to land at the spot. (B) If the spot is "gaining" on the airplane, you will land short of the spot.

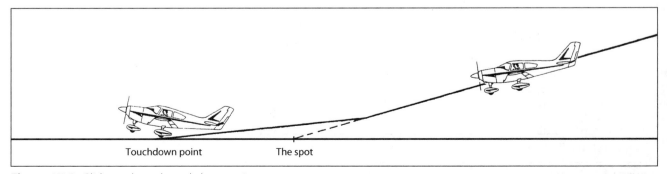

Figure 17-3. Glide angle and touchdown point.

about 1.3 times the power-off stalling speed (CAS). It's suggested that the airspeed on a short-field approach be *no greater* than this figure. For safety's sake, don't get too close to the stall speed—remember the gradient wind and gust effects. *There is no way of predicting the point of landing from a power-off approach on a gusty day.* Reviewing the wind effects, the plane's glide angle will be different for different wind strengths. The glide angle in relation to the ground may change from approach to approach or it may change several times during one approach (Figure 17-4). By making a power approach the pilot can compensate for wind variation and errors in judgment.

Short-Field Approach and Landing

The short-field approach is the most useful type of power approach. It allows the pilot to control the glide path and make a landing with a minimum of float; therefore, as the name implies, it is a good approach to make to short fields. The approach is made at a maximum speed of 1.3 times the power-off stall speed. (If your plane stalls at 50 K with landing flaps set, the maximum approach speed is 1.3 times 50, or 65 K.) At this speed the plane's glide path is particularly sensitive to

power adjustments because there is little excess airspeed to cause floating when power is removed. The 50-K and 65-K airspeeds used here are *calibrated* airspeeds (CAS).

The traffic pattern will be slightly wider and longer than normal. In essence you'll fly the pattern so that using a normal glide would cause undershooting of the runway; otherwise, if power is used in a normal pattern you'll overshoot.

Procedure

1. From a slightly wider downwind leg, start a power-off approach. Keep the airspeed at normal glide or slightly below.
2. After the first 90° turn, slow the plane to 1.3 times the stall speed and control the angle of descent with the throttle. Set final flaps.
3. Use power as needed to make the landing. It may be necessary to keep power on all the way to the ground if you get low and slow.

After the landing, hold the control wheel (or stick) full back as you apply braking. This helps put most of the weight on the main wheels of the tricycle-gear plane and makes for more braking efficiency. If it's not too

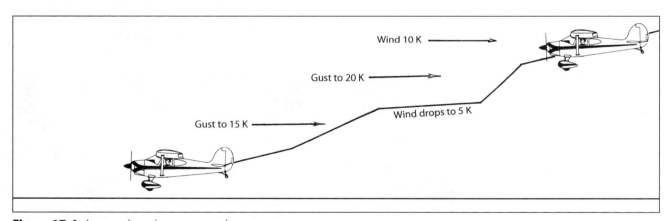

Figure 17-4. Approach path on a gusty day.

Figure 17-5. Only in smooth air, constant-wind conditions would the approach path be constant.

much of a distraction, upping the flaps will kill some of the residual lift and put more weight on the braking wheels. One problem, however, is that sometimes the pilots of retractable-gear airplanes have intended to pull up the flaps but moved the landing gear handle instead. Of course, an airplane on its belly will come to a stop in a reasonable distance—it's just a more expensive practice, that's all.

Common Errors

1. Gliding too fast in the normal part of the approach so that when the nose is raised to slow to the final approach speed, the airplane balloons and is too high to make a power approach.
2. Not keeping a constant airspeed during the power approach. Letting the speed pick up and drop as the power is increased or decreased.
3. Not establishing a constant angle of descent—either using full power or idle. You are free to use as much or as little power as needed, but it looks pretty bad on a check ride if you're a throttle jockey.
4. Closing the throttle while the plane is nearly staged and still off the ground—letting the plane drop in.

With more experience you'll be able to leave the throttle at a constant setting once the path is established. This is under constant wind and thermal conditions, of course (Figure 17-5).

Soft-Field Takeoff

In mud, snow, or tall grass, the drag on the wheels of the airplane tends to make acceleration suffer badly, and a special technique is required for taking off from a soft field.

The soft-field takeoff requires that the tail of the plane be held lower than normal for two reasons: (1) to lessen the chances of nosing over (tailwheel type) or the nosewheel digging in (tricycle-gear type) and (2) to have the angle of attack such that the weight is taken from the main wheels as soon as possible. This attitude will vary among planes, and you will have to have the

correct nose position shown to you. Wheel pants are easily clogged by mud or snow and are usually removed from planes operating under these conditions.

Procedure

Use flaps as recommended by the *Pilot's Operating Handbook.*

1. Taxi onto the takeoff area and keep the plane rolling—make a "rolling takeoff." On a soft field the plane will require a great deal of power to start it rolling again, and at high rpm on the ground the prop will pick up mud and gravel and be damaged.
2. Hold the wheel back to stop any tendency to nose over as you apply full power.
3. Put the nose in the proper attitude.
4. Lift the plane off as soon as possible without stalling.
5. As soon as the plane is flying, lower the nose and assume a normal climb. If obstacles are to be cleared, use V_X or the recommended obstacle-clearance airspeed.

The tailwheel airplane should be set up in a tail-low attitude as the takeoff run progresses (Figure 17-6).

Common Error

Not raising the tail on the tailwheel-type airplane—trying to take off in a three-point attitude.

Soft-Field Landing

The tendency for the nose to dig in on the soft-field landing is a problem, as on the takeoff from a soft field. On the takeoff the force trying to nose the plane over is normally not a sudden thing but may build up as the plane accelerates. As the plane lands, this force may be applied suddenly as the wheels take the weight of the plane. Although this effect will always be there, you can make it as small as possible.

Land the plane as slowly as possible. Use power to decrease the landing speed and to have as much

The airplane's attitude for a soft or rough field takeoff

The attitude for a normal takeoff

Figure 17-6. Soft or rough field and normal takeoff attitudes (tailwheel airplane).

nose-up attitude as safely possible at touchdown. Keep the tail down. Hold full back pressure.

The same principle applies on the soft-field landing for the tricycle-gear equipped plane. Land as slowly as possible and try to keep the nosewheel off. The drag of the main wheels will force it down, but you can keep as much weight off the nosewheel as possible by back pressure.

Gusty Wind Landings

Tricycle-Gear Procedures

The glide speed should be slightly higher to take care of the variance in wind velocity and, for some airplanes, the use of full flaps should be avoided for gusty conditions.

The airplane should be landed at a lower nose attitude than for smooth air, though you shouldn't land it on all three wheels at once (or the nosewheel first). The airplane will tend to rotate forward on the nosewheel at the landing impact; this decrease in angle of attack generally results in the airplane staying firmly on the ground—a decided advantage in gusty winds.

Wheel Landing— Tailwheel-Type Airplane

The wheel landing (Figure 17-7) is used when the wind is strong and/or gusty and gives you a means of having good control all the way down to the landing. The airplane is literally flown onto the ground, landing on the main wheels to keep a low angle of attack and stop any tendency for a sudden gust to pick the airplane off the ground, as might happen in a three-point landing under such conditions.

The technique at one time was to use power all through the landing, but this resulted in the pilot "juggling" the throttle, using up runway and fouling up the landing while trying to control the landing time with power (Figure 17-8).

Use only enough power to control your rate of descent and get to the position to make your power-off landing. Some pilots advocate using 1,300–1,600 rpm for a wheel landing, but you have found out that the average lightplane will maintain altitude at a power setting only slightly higher.

Use power only as needed to make the landing. The less used at touchdown the better. Without power the plane will land—not float halfway down the runway. *Elevators and throttle go together. Don't be mechanical with either one.*

True, the wind will be strong and the groundspeed will be low. This will keep the plane from using as much runway as it would under lesser wind conditions, but you can still eat up a lot of runway using poor techniques.

Procedure

The approach is made at an airspeed slightly faster than the normal glide, and the transition is made at a lower height for two reasons: (1) The plane must touch down at a higher speed, and (2) the attitude will be only

Figure 17-7. The wheel landing.

Figure 17-8. (1) You see that you are settling fast, add more power (oops, too much). (2) Now you throttle back. (3) Plane is now settling — add more power again, etc.

slightly tail-low, not three-point. Power is used to control the angle and/or rate of descent.

As the plane reaches the transition height, start applying back pressure to "round off" the glide path so that the plane will contact the runway with the main wheels in a slightly tail-low attitude. After the plane has touched, apply slight forward pressure to keep the tail up. This is to keep gusts from causing the plane to leave the ground again.

As the plane slows up, more and more forward pressure will be required to keep the tail up. When the wheel is all the way forward and the tail drops, move and hold the wheel completely back so that the up elevator will now hold the tail down. The reason for holding the tail up is to keep a low angle of attack as long as possible. When the elevators become ineffective, the plane's speed is slow enough that the wings have lost all lift. If you try to put the tail on the ground too soon after landing, you may find yourself several feet in the air, with very little airspeed. One disadvantage in keeping the tail up as long as possible is that directional control may be lost before the steerable tailwheel contacts the surface. However, generally the plane with this characteristic has a higher wing loading and is not as likely to be lifted by gusts during the landing roll. A suggested technique in this case is to maintain the forward pressure applied at touchdown, allowing the tail to lower gradually as the speed diminishes. The tailwheel will contact the runway before loss of rudder control occurs and at a speed allowing a smooth steady movement of the wheel to the full rear position without danger of becoming airborne again.

Too many students get impatient as the plane is skimming just above the ground and apply forward pressure to "put it on." This sets off a series of bounces that would make a kangaroo turn white. The trouble is that once you start bouncing, it usually gets worse until you take it around again or something (usually the landing gear) gives (Figure 17-9).

Another common mistake students make is to hold the plane off too long. The airspeed drops and the plane settles fast on the two front wheels. Result—more bouncing.

The crosswind correction for a wheel landing is the same as for the three-point landing. Lower the wing, hold opposite rudder as needed, and land on one wheel. The other wheel will come down immediately. Hold aileron into the wind and apply rudder as needed to keep it straight.

Common Errors
1. Too fast an approach—the plane floats.
2. Too slow an approach—the plane settles fast and bounces.
3. Getting impatient—shoving forward on the wheel "to make it stay on" (Figure 17-9).

If the plane starts bouncing, open the throttle and take it around and make a new landing.

Although wheel landings are best for gusty air, a good three-point landing can be made under these conditions if care is taken.

Dragging the Area

Before you go on a solo cross-country, the instructor will demonstrate how to drag the area, a procedure used in checking a strange field for landing. The idea is to pick a field and land before you run out of gas and have no choice.

Suppose that you become lost on a cross-country. You have about 15 minutes of gas left and there are no airports or recognizable towns in sight. Or maybe you locate yourself but realize there's no airport close enough to reach with the fuel remaining. Should you fly on to get as close to an airport as possible before the engine quits? Or should you pick a good field, look it over, and land there? Obviously this is a loaded question. You should pick a field.

Figure 17-9. Some people are bound and determined to land on the first approach.

Procedure

1. Pick a likely looking field and circle it at about traffic pattern altitude. Know the wind direction. Pick a field near a road or farmhouse if possible.
2. Set yourself up on the downwind leg and start a normal approach to the portion of the field you want to land on.
3. Fly at a height of about 100 feet, just to the right of the intended landing path.
4. Look for obstructions or hazards that could not be seen from traffic pattern altitude.
5. If the field is suitable, make another traffic pattern with a short-field approach.
6. After the landing, go to the farmhouse and ask if you may use the phone.

Dragging the area is done any time you feel that, for safety's sake, the plane should be on the ground and you aren't close to an airport. If the engine is in imminent danger of quitting, you may not have time to drag the area but must land immediately in the first likely looking field. This will be covered more thoroughly in "Problems and Emergencies," Chapter 25.

Takeoff and Landing Performance

It's very important to know the required takeoff and landing roll distances of your airplane plus the total distances required to clear a 50-foot obstacle. Figure 17-10 shows typical takeoff and landing performance charts. Look at the *Pilot's Operating Handbook* for your airplane and be able to use these and other performance charts (climb, cruise, etc.).

The airplane (and engine) is only aware of the *density-altitude* (standard), and this results from a combination of pressure altitude and temperature. (Pressure altitude is that shown on the altimeter when it is set to 29.92 inches of mercury—review Chapter 3.) The sea level standard temperature is 59°F (15°C) and the normal lapse rate, or normal temperature drop, is $3\frac{1}{2}$°F (2°C) per thousand feet. A higher temperature than normal would mean that the air density is less for that particular altitude. The air could be as "thin" as that found several thousand feet higher under standard conditions. The altimeter is only capable of measuring air pressure, not air density, so you must take variations from standard temperature into account.

In using the takeoff and landing charts (Figure 17-10) you may have to interpolate between values

given. For instance, assume that you will be taking off from a field with a pressure altitude of 3,000 feet with a 14-K headwind at a temperature of 15°C: First, you'd interpolate between 10° and 20°C at that pressure altitude for the ground run and total distances to clear a 50-foot obstacle. At 10°C the values are 935 and 1,780 respectively. At 20°C the distances are 1,010 and 1,915 feet, so you could expect them at 15°C to be 975 and 1,850 feet (rounded off). As the Notes in Figure 17-10 indicate, you should subtract 10 percent for each 9 K of headwind, so at 14 K (about 1.5 times 9 K) the reduction should be 15 percent for final figures of 830 and 1,575 feet (rounded off). The same idea would be used for the landing distance. *These distances are for a hard-surface runway; the takeoff run could be doubled by mud, snow, or high grass.* Also, these are "average" values; you can use a lot more runway with poor pilot technique.

Figure 17-11 is a climb chart for the airplane just discussed.

Figure 17-12 shows a graphical method of computing the ground roll required under different conditions.

Figure 17-13 (on Page 17-10) shows the takeoff distances (ground roll and to clear a 50-foot obstacle) for

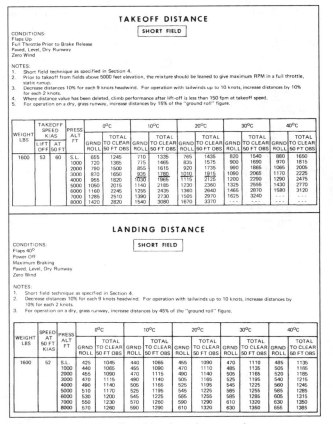

Figure 17-10. Takeoff and landing distance charts.

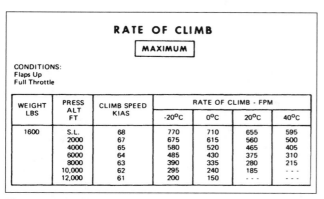

Figure 17-11. Maximum rates of climb chart.

a current trainer. Two propeller options are available for this airplane: (1) a climb propeller of lower (flatter) pitch, which is more efficient at lower airspeeds, and (2) a cruise propeller with a higher average pitch, which is not as efficient in lower-speed regimes but comes into its own at cruise speeds. Note that at a pressure altitude of 2,000 feet and a temperature of 20°C (at a weight of 1,600 pounds), the climb prop-equipped airplane uses less distance to lift off or to clear the 50-foot obstacle (arrows).

While the subjects of special takeoff and landing procedures and performance charts are being covered, it might be well to take a look at Figure 17-14.

The example shown gives an answer to 35-K headwind and 20-K crosswind components respectively. Looking at another problem, suppose an airplane has a manufacture-demonstrated crosswind component of 0.2 V_{S0} (*see* Figure 3-27) and its V_{S0} is 60 K. Can it legally land in a 30-K wind at a 25° angle to the runway? The actual value of the demonstrated crosswind is 0.2 × 60 = 12 K. Using Figure 17-14, you'll find that the crosswind component is 12.5–13 K, which is over the demonstrated limit. (The headwind component is about 27 K.) The problems you'll be given on the knowledge test will require that you find the angle ("you are landing on Runway 27 with a wind from 310° at 20 K") and then use the chart. The problems apparently assume that the runway is lined up exactly with 270°, and the wind and runway are both given in the same terms, magnetic or true directions (*see* Figure 6-3).

The manufacture-demonstrated crosswind component (0.2 V_{S0}) is that required by 14 CFR §23.233 (a) for certification of the airplane. Pilots experienced in a particular airplane may exceed this limit. (But, if there's a landing accident, there will be some discussion about 0.2 V_{S0}.)

Simulated High-Altitude Takeoffs

Before you get to the practical (flight) test, you should make a simulated high-altitude takeoff. The instructor will limit your power for takeoff, and you can see how the airplane would do (or not do) at some high altitude. The biggest problem you'll have is the very strong tendency to rush the airplane off. (This is also the tendency the first time you fly the airplane at maximum certificated weight from a comparatively short field.) The airplane seems to be dragging its feet, and you'll want to pull it off before it's ready. After you become airborne, don't pull the nose up "to get extra climb." You might put yourself in position 4 or 5 back in Figure 12-13, and performance will suffer even more.

Talking a little more about the density-altitude idea, every 15° (8½°C) above the standard temperature for your pressure altitude bumps the density-altitude up another 1,000 feet. Suppose you are going to take off at an airport at an elevation of 2,200 feet. The altimeter setting is 30.12 inches of mercury, which makes your pressure altitude right about 2,000 feet (1 inch of mercury equals approximately 1,000 feet of altitude). The pressure corrected to sea level is 0.20 inches of mercury higher than standard, so the pressure altitude is (0.20 × 1,000) = 200 feet lower than the elevation. The pressure altitude is 2,000 feet (which could also have been found by rolling 29.92 into the setting window).

The temperature is 82°F, which certainly is not unusual in the summer. The standard temperature for this pressure altitude is 52°F (59°F – [2 × 3½°F] = 52°F), since the normal lapse rate is 3½°F per thousand feet. The temperature (82°F) is 30°F above the standard. Since each added 15°F makes an additional 1,000 feet of density-altitude, your real density-altitude is the pressure altitude (2,000 feet) *plus* 2,000 feet, or *4,000 feet.* You think you're sitting at 2,000 feet, but the airplane knows that it is at 4,000 feet—and acts accordingly. If the temperature had been 97°F at that airport (entirely possible), another 1,000 feet would have been tacked on and the density-altitude would have been *5,000 feet.*

At an airport in the summer, it's not at all unusual for the temperature to be 15°F (or much more) above its "standard." The temperature, rather than atmospheric pressure changes, is the big factor. The not unusual temperature of 82°F in the example added 2,000 feet of density-altitude. To get that effect by pressure decrease (assuming a standard temperature) would mean that the pressure would have to be *2 inches* of mercury below normal, or the sea level pressure would be 27.92 instead

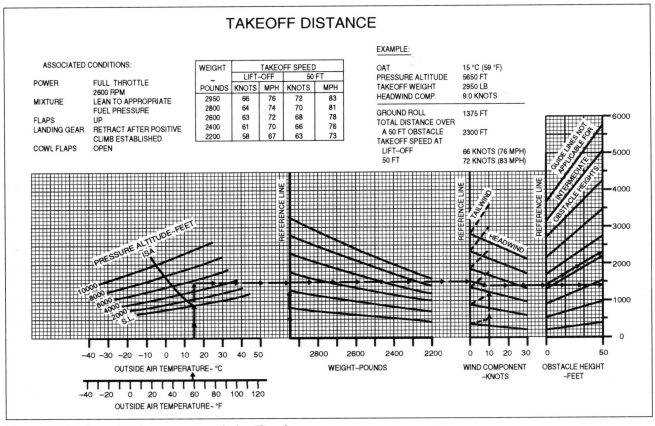

Figure 17-12. A graphical presentation of takeoff performance.

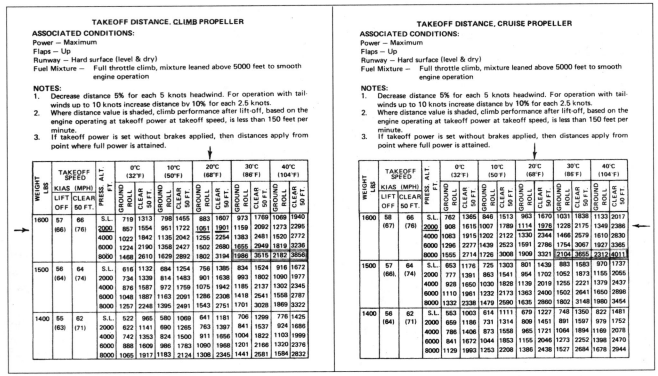

Figure 17-13. Takeoff distances for a two-place trainer for climb and cruise propellers. (Courtesy of Grumman American Aviation Corp.)

Figure 17-14. A crosswind–headwind component chart. (FAA)

of 29.92 inches of mercury. This *is* unusual, and such pressure conditions could only be found in the eye of a very strong hurricane.

Talking in terms of Celsius for the earlier example problem, the standard sea level temperature is 15°C, and the normal lapse rate is 2°C per thousand feet, so the following would apply: Standard temperature for the 2,000 feet is 11°C; the actual temperature is 28°C, or 17°C above standard. Since each $8\frac{1}{2}$°C adds another 1,000 feet of density-altitude, the answer is again 4,000 feet.

One thing that you may not have considered is that the *moist air is less dense than dry air* (all other factors equal), so the airplane will not perform as well in take-offs and climbs when the air is moist. (You might figure on up to about 10 percent less performance under wet conditions.)

One last thing about density-altitude: You may not know what it is at a particular time, but the airplane *always* does.

18

High-Altitude Emergencies

The high-altitude emergency gives you more time and a greater choice of fields. In earlier stages, however, this is a handicap, so practice is usually reserved for the postsolo period. The average student, when given a first high-altitude emergency, is as busy looking around as a one-eyed man watching a beauty contest. There are *too many* places to land. You may get confused and change your mind on the choice of a field several times and finally end up too low to do anything but land in the worst field within a 15-mile radius (Figure 18-1).

The high-altitude emergency requires that you do the following:

1. Set up the max distance glide. Start easing the nose up immediately to conserve altitude as well as to get to the best glide speed. At the same time:
2. Pull the carburetor heat ON (use it before the residual engine heat is lost).
3. Pick a field and head for it.
4. Find the wind direction.
5. Try to find the cause of the problem—carburetor ice, fuel tank run dry (switch tanks), etc. Set up a glide pattern so that you will hit a "key position" at

about the same point and at a slightly higher altitude above the ground than the point at which you closed the throttle to make a 180° power-off approach (the windmilling prop will hurt the glide).

This key position is chosen because by this time you've shot power-off approaches from this position. It's literally impossible to glide for a distant field from 2,000 or 3,000 feet above the ground and consistently hit it. It's been found to be easier to judge the glide angle if the approach involves a turn. (Review power-off approaches in Chapter 13.)

Let's take the emergency point by point as discussed below.

Telling Wind Direction

There are many ways of telling the wind direction when you are away from the airport: smoke, waves moving across a field of grain or waves on lakes, dust blowing, trees, etc. (Figure 18-2).

Figure 18-1. The instructor will discuss your errors on the forced landing.

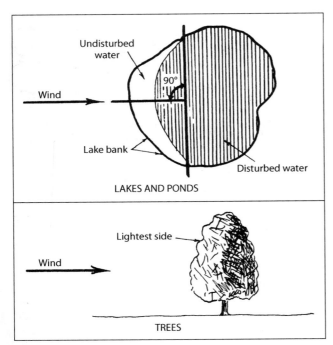

Figure 18-2. Lakes or ponds help you tell the wind direction, even if you are too high to see the actual wave movement; the bank on the windward side keeps the water undisturbed. The wind turns tree leaves over, showing their lighter side in the direction from which it is blowing.

Know the wind direction and approximate velocity at all times. Don't be like the student who didn't know the wind direction and stuck a hand out the plane window to find out (and figured that the wind was right on the nose at about 100 K).

It's better not to waste time trying to find out the wind direction *after* the emergency has occurred.

Picking Your Field

Know the types of fields in your part of the country. Has it been raining a lot lately? If so, that field of young wheat may be too soft to land on.

Look for electric or telephone poles across the field because you won't see the wires themselves from your altitude.

Look for fences across the middle of pastures. These are sometimes hard to see because the fields on both sides look alike.

If two fields are equally near and good for landing, pick the one closest to the highway or houses for several reasons. If the landing is a success (and with good planning it's bound to be), you will want to call the airport. If the plane is damaged or the engine is in bad shape (maybe there was an oil leak and the engine seized), the airport personnel may want to dismantle

the plane and haul it back. If the landing was not a success and you are injured, people will see the crash and come to your aid. The main thing is to get down without injury to you or (later) your passengers.

If your airplane has flaps, they'll be a great help in making the field. The idea is to add flaps in increments as necessary to hit the field. The usual student error in practice emergencies is to add flaps too soon (and full flaps at that) and sit there helplessly while the airplane starts to sink into the woods a quarter of a mile short of the chosen field. *If you have added flaps and start losing ground* (it looks as if the field is gaining on you), *get a notch or a few degrees of flaps up and watch things start improving. Then when you get to the proper position, put 'em back down again.*

The big misconception about flaps concerns the idea that once the flaps are down, they should never be retracted because the airplane will "fall" because of a loss of "lift." If you are close to the flaps-down stall speed and suddenly raise the flaps, you might find that the airspeed is *below* the flaps-*up* stall speed, and a stall could result. But if you are in a typical trainer at the normal glide speed and at a reasonable altitude (say, 300 feet or more), you'll be a lot better off in getting distance by easing off a notch or so of flaps (easy), even if that initial slight sink bothers you. As you ease off the flaps to extend the glide, you'll ease the nose up to maintain the required airspeed. Your instructor might have you practice power-off descents at altitude to see that the pitch attitude must be changed as the flap settings are varied in order to maintain a constant airspeed; more flaps, more nose down—less flaps, less nose down. Putting the flaps down in increments is the best way to do it to avoid flap juggling (up and down).

Procedure

1. When the engine stops, establish a normal glide. Carburetor heat ON. Pick the best field and turn to it (Figure 18-3). (Assume for this example that you can't correct the cause of the problem.) Maintain the normal glide speed throughout the exercise. This will give you the best glide ratio and the only means of knowing your glide path. If the speed is 70 K one minute and 50 K the next, who knows what the glide path will be?

   Figure 18-4 shows the maximum glide ratio of a current training airplane. As noted, from 6,000 feet above the surface a distance of approximately 8 NM may be covered with the conditions stated. Naturally, headwinds or tailwinds will affect these figures.

Figure 18-3. The key position helps to turn an unusual situation into one more familiar. Keep that glide speed constant.

2. Get over the field. Spiral to the key position or S-turn down. Try to find the problem.

3. Hit the key position at the traffic pattern altitude or slightly higher—better slightly high than too low at this point. Remember that a windmilling prop creates a great deal of drag, hence your glide ratio will suffer.

4. Plan your approach after the key position, thinking that a shallow slip or flaps may be required to make the field.

5. Once you have the field made, remember the landing is just like the one back at the airport (Figure 18-5). A normal landing will minimize the damage if the field is rougher than it looked from 3,000 feet.

6. The *Pilot's Operating Handbook* for your airplane has an emergency section in it (read it *now*—don't wait until you have a problem), and an emergency checklist is available in most current airplanes.

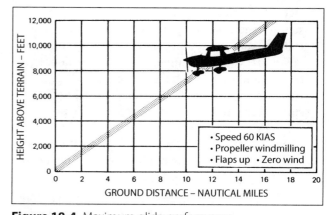

Figure 18-4. Maximum glide performance.

Figure 18-5. Well, it's no Dulles International Airport, but because you used proper techniques, you'll make it without any damage to the airplane or occupants.

Know where it is; a high-altitude emergency will probably give you time to look it over (if your hands aren't shaking so badly that the instructions are blurred). The shutdown procedure varies among airplane types and models, but you'll want to have the mixture, fuel, and ignition and master switches OFF before touchdown if you're definitely going to put it in a field. Even if the landing area looks fine, you don't want to take a chance on hitting an unseen hole or stump and having a fire result. As mentioned in Chapter 13, the master switch (electrical) may be the last thing turned OFF because you may be wanting to talk to someone on the radio (121.5 MHz is the emergency frequency monitored by the FAA and military facilities), and you may want to "squawk" 7700, the emergency code on the transponder. (More about radio frequencies and transponder codes in Chapter 21.) If your flaps are electrically operated, you may have to change the setting (increase or decrease) at the last moment. But be sure everything is OFF when you touch down. If you have time, unlatch the doors just before landing, to keep them from jamming.

7. After the plane is stopped and your knees have stopped shaking, see to the security of the plane. Set the parking brake if there is no tie-down kit in the plane, or better yet, chock the wheels with rocks or blocks. Get to the nearest phone and let the people at the airport know what happened.

An actual emergency is a nerve-wracking thing. You'll be scared, but if you've had practice in emergencies and have gone over the procedure in your mind, you'll make out fine, and it'll make good hangar talk after it's over.

Common Errors in Practice Emergencies

1. Changing fields too many times—if you see that the original field you picked has a big ditch or wires across the middle and there is another field within easy gliding distance, by all means take it. However, once you hit the key position at a field you're pretty well committed to it.
2. Not maintaining a constant glide speed—the result is usually that the field is missed and an airplane is "pranged."
3. Poor wind correction after the key position, that is, being too high or too low to make the field.

Discussion

After the field is "made," the instructor will take over and discuss the emergency with you.

Keep the engine cleared on the descent during a practice emergency. The high-altitude emergency means an extended glide and cooling of the engine, particularly in cold weather. Use carburetor heat as recommended by the manufacturer.

You will not practice emergencies solo. But while we're on the subject of extended glides, if sometime in cold weather you've glided from 3,000 feet down to 600 feet above the ground, the engine may cool and not want to take throttle at first. Don't ram the throttle open—open it slowly. Give the engine a shot of primer if it's particularly hard to get going again. One quick shot will usually do the trick. In hot weather, the engine tends to load up during an extended glide and will require careful clearing.

Emergency Descent

The *Pilot Operating Handbook*, or your instructor, will cover the emergency descent as it applies to your airplane. There are several situations where an immediate descent is required to save the airplane and occupants: (1) Loss of oxygen, or cabin decompression, at high altitudes (not likely a problem for the light general aviation trainer). (2) Engine fire. (3) Electrical fire. (4) Suspected carbon monoxide poisoning or the sudden critical illness of a passenger. (Don't make matters worse by a too-rapid rate of descent.) The point is that you should know and periodically review the procedure (which may require some fairly radical attitudes and airspeed) and always have a checklist available in the airplane.

Part Four 4
Cross-Country and Night Flying

The Navigation Idea

A flight is a success or failure before you leave the ground. Preflight planning is important at all times but particularly so before a cross-country flight. Too many pilots jump into a plane and head for distant airports with little thought of weather, the condition of the destination airport, or what kind of fueling or repair service can be obtained there.

There are several types of navigation used by pilots: (1) *pilotage*, or flying by reference to landmarks; (2) *dead* (deduced) *reckoning*, which is drawing vectors of the wind and your true airspeed and computing the heading, groundspeed, and estimated time of arrival at the destination; (3) *celestial navigation*, using a sextant to measure angles to heavenly bodies; and (4) *radio navigation*, or navigation through the use of radio aids, including GPS.

Pilotage is the major means of navigation for the student pilot, but radio navigation is coming into more use as trainers become better equipped.

Unfortunately, too many pilots rely on radio navigation and find themselves rusty in pilotage or use of the sectional chart if the radios go out.

Meridians, Parallels and Time

The earth is laid off in imaginary lines called meridians and parallels. The meridians run north and south and divide the earth like the sections of an orange (Figure 19-1). The prime meridian goes through Greenwich, England. All longitude (east or west measurements of position) is measured east or west from this line to the 180° meridian on the opposite side of the earth. Since the earth turns 360°, or a complete revolution, in 24 hours, each 15° of longitude means a difference of 1 hour as far as the sun is concerned. You can see this roughly in the time zones in the United States. The conterminous United States extends from about 67° west longitude to about 125° west longitude.

The earth is further divided north and south by parallels—so called because, instead of converging at two points as the meridians do, they are parallel to each other (Figure 19-1). The equator is the prime parallel, and latitude is measured north and south from it. The equator is 0° latitude and the United States runs from about 25° north latitude at the Florida tip to about 49° north latitude on the Canadian border. The North Pole is at 90° north latitude and the South Pole at 90° south latitude.

If someone said that a ship is at 15° west longitude, it would be almost impossible to locate. It could be anywhere on that meridian between the North and South poles. It would be much like telling a friend to meet you on 54th Street in New York City on a busy day. If you said instead, "Meet me at 54th and Blank Street," it would help matters considerably. You need both a latitude and a longitude to determine a position on a chart.

Each degree of latitude and longitude is broken down into 60 minutes, and each minute of *latitude* equals a nautical mile, or 6,080 feet. You can measure a distance on the map by laying the length to be measured north and south on the map and reading the minutes of latitude that it extends. This gives the distance in nautical miles; to convert these to statute or land miles, multiply the result by 1.15. In other words, a nautical mile equals 1.15 or about $1\frac{1}{7}$ statute (land) miles. (*See* Chapter 3.)

Don't measure distances between meridians this way because the equator would be the only place where 1 minute of longitude equals a nautical mile. The meridians converge as they get farther north or south, so while the distance between them in degrees is always the same, the distance in miles is not. Most aeronautical charts have a scale in statute and nautical miles, but all have nautical mile scales.

The meridians converge on the "true" North Pole so that any angle measured from a meridian is the angle from true North. If you were at a point on a map and

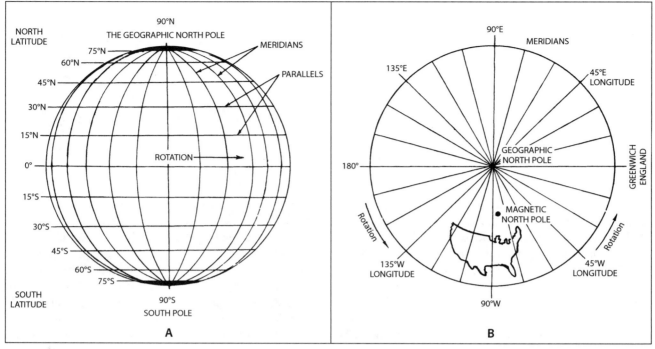

Figure 19-1. Navigation basics.

wanted to know the direction to another point, you would measure it as an angle clockwise from true North, using a meridian midway between the two points. The reason for choosing a middle meridian is because of the type of map you'll be using, as will be discussed later under "Plotter."

Then directions are measured clockwise from true North using 360° (a full circle). East is 90°, South is 180°, West is 270°, and North is 0° (or 360°). Northeast is 45°, Southeast 135°, etc. This means that the pilot can plan a course to the nearest degree.

The idea is to always use three digits in speaking or writing of directions; 90° should be 090°, pronounced "zero-nine-zero."

For navigational purposes, time is standardized to that at Greenwich. This coordinated universal time (UTC) is based on the 24-hour clock. Looking at Figure 19-1, you see that the earth rotates toward the "east." The day starts at 0000UTC or 0000Z (or 0000 Zulu), and since parts of the United States are from 67° to 125° "behind" Greenwich, as the earth rotates, our time will also be behind accordingly. If you are at 90° west longitude, your standard time will be 6 hours behind that of Greenwich (each 15° longitude = 1 hour of time). If the time is 0600 (6:00 A.M.) at your position, add 6 hours to obtain the Universal Time (1200 or 12:00 noon). If you are in the eastern standard time zone add 5 hours to get UTC (or Zulu) time, add 6 in the central standard time zone, and so on. For *daylight savings time*, you'd decrease the addition by 1 hour to

get Zulu time. (For central daylight time you'd add 5; for eastern daylight time you'd add 4 hours.)

The *Airport/Facility Directory* (to be discussed in the next chapter and also in Appendix A, which is the legend for the *A/FD—see* item 5 there) gives the proper conversions from Zulu (UTC) to local time or vice versa.

More About the Compass

Certain errors of the compass were discussed earlier in the introduction to the instrument and emergency flying by instruments. You know of the properties such as northerly turning error, which affect the compass in a turn, or the acceleration errors that affect it with speed changes. Other factors important in aircraft navigation should be considered in using the compass in straight, unaccelerated flight.

Variation

The fact that the Magnetic North Pole and the True North Pole are not the same means a little more work for you in navigating. The Magnetic North Pole is in Canada, and your compass points to this magnetic pole rather than the true one.

The angle between your direction to the True North Pole and the Magnetic North Pole is called variation. If at your position the Magnetic North Pole is 6° farther "east" than the True North Pole, you say that a 6°

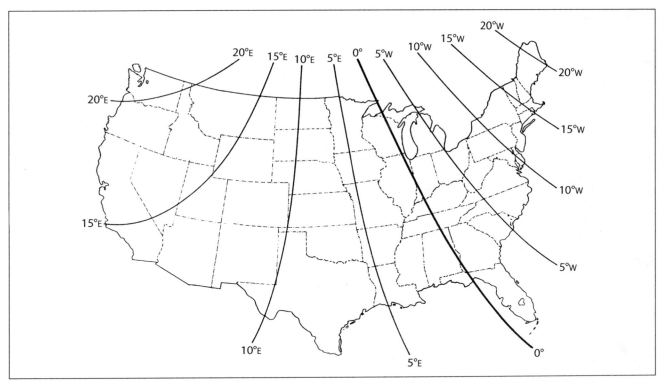

Figure 19-2. Approximate location of isogonic lines in the United States. The isogonic lines are continually changing.

east variation exists. The variation in the United States runs from about 22° West in Maine to about 20° East in Washington state. Isogonic lines, or lines of equal variation, are shown on the aeronautical charts and are given in 1° increments. If you are flying in an area where the two poles are "magnetically" in line, no correction for variation is needed. The isogonic line will show as 0° variation, or more properly, the 0° line is called the agonic line (Figure 19-2).

In plotting a course, you will measure the *true course* at a middle meridian (nearest to the midpoint of your course line). Because you will be referring to the compass, the course must be considered in relation to the Magnetic North Pole. You will add or subtract variation to accomplish this. *Remember: East is least and West is best.* This means that you will look at the isogonic or variation line that is nearest to the halfway point of your course and subtract 5° from the true course if the variation is 5°E or add 5° if the variation is 5°W. *Going from true to magnetic, subtract easterly variation and add westerly variation.* How much to subtract or add will depend on the value of the midpoint isogonic line.

The British have a saying, "Variation East, Magnetic Least; Variation West, Magnetic Best," which could also help you to remember.

If you measured the true course with a protractor and found it to be 120° and the midpoint isogonic

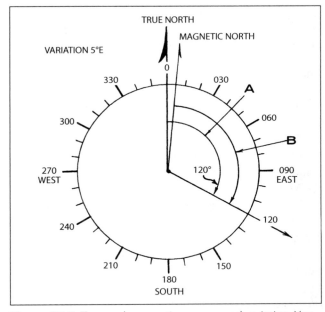

Figure 19-3. True and magnetic courses and variation. You measure the course from the map reference (True North Pole) and find that the angle is 120° (A). The Magnetic North Pole, in this example, is 5° "east" of the True North Pole, and your compass measures its angle from this and starts 5° "later" (B). The angle with reference to the Magnetic North Pole to the course line is 5° less than the true course and is 115° magnetic. This is the condition for *any* course in the geographic area of 5° E variation. If the problem had been for a place where the variation is 5° W, the magnetic North Pole would have been 5° "west" of the True North Pole and the 120° *true* course would mean a *magnetic* course of 125°.

Figure 19-4. An isogonic line (4° W) as depicted on a sectional chart.

line showed 5°E, your magnetic course would be 115° (Figure 19-3).

The terms "east" and "west" used for variation may be misleading to the newcomer. "East" and "west" might appear to have something to do with the direction the airplane is flying. *This is not the case at all.* Since the magnetic compass starts its measurements at the Magnetic North Pole, in Figure 19-3 it starts "counting" 5° later than your map reference (true North). This is the case whether you are flying on a course of 320°, 120°, or what have you. It might be better to speak in terms of "plus 5° variation" or "minus 5° variation," but the current method seems to be permanent. *Variation at a particular geographic position is the same for all types of airplanes, whether J-3 Cubs or 767s.*

Figure 19-4 is part of a sectional chart showing how variation is depicted.

Deviation

The compass will have instrument error called deviation, due in part to attraction by the ferrous metal parts of the plane. This error will vary between headings, and is usually noted for every 30° on a compass correction card, which is located on the instrument panel near the compass (Figure 19-5).

The compass is swung or corrected on a compass rose, a large calibrated circle painted on the hard-surfaced ramp or taxiway away from metal interference such as hangars. The plane is taxied onto the rose and corrections are made with a nonmagnetic screwdriver. Attempts are made to balance out the errors as much as possible. The engine should be running and radio and electrical equipment should be on to give a true picture of the deviation as it would be experienced in flight. To be completely accurate, the plane should be in level flight attitude (no problem with tricycle gear) with the tail supported by a sawhorse or short ladder (tailwheel type).

Suppose, for example, your magnetic course is 115°. This is not shown on the correction card, so some averaging will be necessary. Practically speaking, pick the reading on the card that is 120°. You see that for

FOR (MAGNETIC)	N	30	60	E	120	150
STEER (COMPASS)	O	26	58	87	118	150
FOR (MAGNETIC)	S	210	240	W	300	330
STEER (COMPASS)	183	214	243	275	303	332

Figure 19-5. A typical compass correction card.

120° you must fly 118° or subtract 2°. Subtract 2° from 115° and the compass course is 113°.

Unlike variation, which is a function of your geographic position, *deviation varies between individual airplanes* (and may vary in a particular airplane, depending on what electrical or radio equipment is currently in operation).

For the steps used to go from a true course (or true heading) to the course (or heading) with respect to the compass, remember that "True Virgins Make Dull Company":

1. *True* course (or heading)
2. Plus or minus *Variation* gives
3. *Magnetic* course (or heading)
4. Plus or minus *Deviation* gives
5. *Compass* course (or heading).

Remember that the "east is least..." idea is true only when going from a true course (or heading) to a magnetic course or heading. Working from magnetic to true, you would *add* easterly variation and *subtract* westerly variation. The normal procedure is to go from true to magnetic courses or headings, but knowledge tests have asked questions on the reverse procedure.

Plotter

The plotter is a small transparent plastic circle or semicircle marked from 0° to 359° (the semicircular plotter has a double row of figures at each point) to measure course angles on the map. Plotters have an attached plastic rule in scale miles for the sectional chart (1 inch equals about 7 NM) and other charts.

When you plan a cross-country, you'll draw a line between your departure airport and the destination airport and measure the true course with the plotter.

Measure the course at a midway meridian because the sectional chart is a Lambert conformal conic projection; that is, the meridians are closer together at the top of the map. By measuring from the middle meridian, a

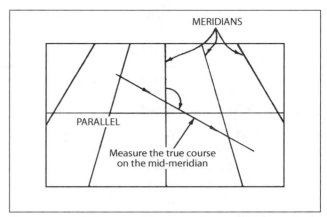

Figure 19-7. Exaggerated drawing of meridian convergence on a sectional chart.

more accurate course will be obtained. However, the error is so small that little trouble will be caused by not doing this — but, again, you might as well learn another good habit now (Figure 19-7).

It's possible to get confused when laying off a course by using a plotter, and students sometimes arrive at an answer that is 180° off. *Draw the course line and figure about what the direction is* (Jonesville is east-southeast of Smithtown, so you would figure somewhere between 90° and 135° true course). *Don't mechanically measure a course but think about what you're doing.* You'll soon be able to look at a course line on a map and guess within 5° of it. You should *read the plotter very carefully when checking the course.*

You will notice azimuth circles around each VOR station on the sectional chart. These are calibrated from 0° to 360° in 5° increments and are oriented on *magnetic* north. These are an aid to the pilot who is combining pilotage and radio navigation, as will be covered later. If you can't find your plotter and one of those omni roses is near your course line on the map, you may measure the magnetic course by laying a straight edge parallel to the course line and through the center of the circle (or use a parallel rule if you have one). The *magnetic* course is then read because of the orientation with magnetic north rather than a meridian, and you've saved the step of adding or subtracting variation.

Computer

A computer is a useful addition to any student pilot's equipment. It's a circular slide rule with the inside circle calibrated in time (hours and minutes) and the outside circle in velocity (miles per hour or knots) or gallons. With it you can check fuel consumption or speed. You learned in Chapter 3 that the 2 percent per thousand feet airspeed correction is only good for a standard day

Figure 19-6. Plotter with mileage scales and protractor for course measurement.

(59°F or 15°C at sea level) and for a normal temperature lapse rate, or drop, of 3½°F or 2°C per thousand feet. If you know the outside air temperature at your pressure altitude, the true airspeed can be readily found on the computer.

Finding True Airspeed

For navigation purposes you may want to check your true airspeed in flight. The steps are (as covered in Chapter 3) from indicated airspeed (IAS) to calibrated airspeed (CAS) to true airspeed (TAS). Remember that the IAS is not always correct. An airspeed correction table can be used to get the CAS (Figure 19-8).

Since the *calibrated* airspeed is the "correct" indicated airspeed, it is used to find the true airspeed. Assume that you are flying (flaps-up) at a pressure altitude of 4,500 feet (indicating 103 K), the outside air temperature is +5°C, and you want to find the TAS. Looking at Figure 19-8 you see that the IAS and CAS can be considered the same at 103 K. That takes care of the first step.

AIRSPEED CORRECTION TABLE
(Flaps Up)

IAS	40	50	60	70	80	90	100	110	120	130	140
CAS	51	57	65	73	82	91	100	109	118	127	136

(Flaps Down)

IAS	40	50	60	70	80	90	100				
CAS	49	55	63	72	81	89	98				

Figure 19-8. An airspeed correction table. The indicated airspeeds for normal cruise for this airplane will be in the vicinity of 100 K (depending on power setting and altitude). This is the most accurate area of the airspeed indications. (Example only.)

Figure 19-9 shows the method of getting the TAS.

Practically speaking, you'll seldom get your TAS in flight. You will be more interested in finding out your groundspeed. The cruise information in the airplane's *Pilot's Operating Handbook* is given as TAS for various power settings and altitudes (*see* Chapter

Figure 19-9. Finding the true airspeed. (1) The temperature (+5°C) and pressure altitude (4,500 feet) are set together; opposite the calibrated airspeed (2) of 103 K, the true airspeed (3) of 110 K is found.

23). However, you can check your TAS to see if you're getting the proper performance for your power setting and altitude or if the airspeed indicator has developed an error.

Some pilots use their indicated altitude instead of setting the altimeter to 29.92 for the pressure altitude to get the TAS. There is an error of about 2 percent for each thousand-foot difference between the indicated and pressure altitudes. Since this difference is generally much less than 1,000 feet, this method is considered accurate enough for practical use.

Getting the Groundspeed

You'll find that the computer is used most often in practical situations to find groundspeeds and estimated times of arrival.

The Knowledge Test for the private pilot's certificate contains questions that would concern a practical cross-country flight with multiple choice answers. A question might be: "You are over the center of the town of Jonesville at 1652 (4:52 P.M.) CST and over the center of Smithville at 1714 (5:14 P.M.) CST. What is your estimate of time and distance to the destination airport at Greenville?" Using the sectional chart issued to you for the examination, measure the distance between Jonesville and Smithville—it is 36 NM. So knowing that the distance from Jonesville to Smithville is 36 NM and flying time is 22 minutes, set up the problem as shown in Figure 19-10. Your groundspeed (or the speed over the ground between those towns) is 98 K. A distance of 59 NM from Smithville on to the airport would require 36 minutes. The estimated time of arrival (ETA) over the airport is 1750 CST. Your actual

Figure 19-10. Find the groundspeed. (1) Set up the time (22 minutes) opposite the distance traveled (36 NM) to get the groundspeed (98 K here) at (2). Once the relationship is established, the time required to fly other distances (59 NM in this case) can be found (36 minutes) as shown at (3). It is not necessary to actually know that the groundspeed is 98 K; you can go directly to (3). The estimated time of arrival over Greenville would be 1714 + 36 minutes, or 1750 CST.

time over the airport should be close to this unless you turn back, get lost, or the wind changes radically. This method is more accurate than working a wind triangle problem before the flight, since the wind information still may not be accurate for your area.

Notice also: In the area of point 3 in Figure 19-10 is the scale for converting nautical miles (or knots) to statute miles or miles per hour. Note that 40.5 NM equals 46.6 statute miles, although those numbers don't relate to this navigation problem. You would set the computer to whatever values you needed to convert.

Finding Fuel Consumption

Figure 19-11 shows how to find how much fuel you'll use flying from Smithville to Greenville. As Figure 19-10 shows, after checking the groundspeed as 98 K, you'd expect to take 36 minutes to fly the 59 NM. This typical light trainer uses 4.9 gallons an hour at 65 percent normal rated power. You would set up 4.9 (point 1 in the figure) on the outer scale opposite 60 minutes (speed index). Opposite 36 minutes you'll note that 2.94 gallons will be used (2). The 4.9 gallons per hour could have been 49 or even 490 if your airplane had this sort of fuel consumption (and the fuel consumed in

36 minutes would be 29.5 or 295 gallons respectively). The computer merely sets up ratios; you keep up with what the numbers really are (whether 4.9, 49, 490, or even 4,900).

Density-Altitude

Density-altitude, which is used for calculating aircraft performance, may be found on the computer. As an example, suppose you are flying at a pressure altitude of 4,500 feet and the outside air temperature gauge indicates +15°C. Figure 19-12 shows how to set up a problem.

Correcting Indicated or Pressure Altitude

Also shown on the computer is a *corrected altitude* function. The altimeter may read incorrectly because of a nonstandard temperature (which would affect the pressure working on it). Figure 19-13 shows how the altimeter can be corrected for this error, using 10,000' for the indicated altitude and -15°C for the temperature.

In this case, the altimeter goes through the same steps as the airspeed indicator (from indicated altitude,

Figure 19-11. Find fuel consumption.

Figure 19-12. Find density altitude: (1) Set up the pressure altitude (4,500 feet) opposite the temperature (+15°C) at that altitude. The density-altitude is approximately 5,500 feet as shown at (2). The standard temperature at 4,500 feet is +6°C so that the actual temperature for this problem (+15°C) is high. The warm air is "thinner" and the airplane is flying at a lower air density than would be shown by the altimeter alone and would be performing as if at an actual standard altitude of 5,500 feet, since performance depends on air density (among other things).

which is what the instrument actually reads, to *calibrated*, which would be the indicated altitude corrected for instrument and system error to "true" altitude after the effects of nonstandard temperature are taken into consideration). The standard temperature for 10,000 feet is -5°C, so the actual temperature of -15°C is 10°C lower than standard (1). The computer shows that the actual pressure altitude is approximately 9,600 feet, not the 10,000 shown by the altimeter (2). This would be of interest in clearing obstacles such as mountain ranges.

Wind Triangle

Flying cross-country requires application of the principles learned in the rectangular course. Instead of having a well-defined line such as a field boundary to follow, you must use the imaginary line between your home airport and the destination.

The wind triangle is a vector system. A vector is an arrow representing the direction and magnitude of a force, as seen in Chapters 8, 9, and 16. In the case of airplane navigation, these vectors are set up for a 1-hour period. On the earlier sample trip we found that the true course was 120°. Winds aloft are always given in true directions and in knots, and the altitudes given are above sea level. Rather than go through the steps to convert the true course to compass course, work the wind triangle with respect to true North and then convert the answer—your *true heading*—to compass heading, using corrections for variation and deviation.

Given:

1. The measured true course from Dover to Erin is 120°.

2. The Federal Aviation Regulations require that planes flying at 3,000 feet or more above the surface fly at indicated (MSL) altitudes of odd thousands plus

Figure 19-13. Correcting indicated or pressure altitude for nonstandard temperature conditions.

500 if the magnetic course to be flown is from 0° to 179° (3,500, 5,500, 7,500, etc.) and at even thousands plus 500 from 180° to 359° (4,500, 6,500, 8,500, etc.) (VFR—cruising altitudes). You see that the variation is 5°E, so just like Figure 19-3, the magnetic course is 115° (which is well within the eastern semicircle). Above 3,000 you must fly odd plus 500 feet. You checked the winds aloft at the National Weather Service Office or FAA Flight Service Station and found that the wind at 5,000 feet is from 220° true at 30 K. Because this gives you the best tailwind, you decide to fly at 5,500 MSL, which is the closest odd plus 500 altitude.

3. You've checked the *Pilot's Operating Handbook* and found that the TAS for this altitude will be 95 K.

On a blank piece of paper draw a line representing a true North line or meridian. Measure the true course with a plotter through some point on the true North line (Figure 19-14A).

This line is of indefinite length (1). Pick a scale and draw a wind vector in the correct direction and at the proper length from some point on the course line. The wind given for this altitude is in knots, so that length is drawn to scale and in the proper direction (2). We are assuming in this case that the wind is the same at 5,500 feet as that at 5,000. However, many times you can interpolate between altitudes if there is a large variation between the wind's direction and/or velocity. For instance, if the wind is 270° and 20 K at 5,000, and 310° and 30 K at 6,000, a reasonable assumption would be that the wind at 5,500 is halfway between these values, or 290° at 25 K.

From the wind arrow point, swing a line the length of your TAS (95 K) until it hits the course line (3) (Figure 19-14B). This gives you the vector picture (Figure 19-14C).

The line EW (earth-wind) represents the wind with respect to the earth. The line WP represents the movement of the plane with respect to the wind, and its length

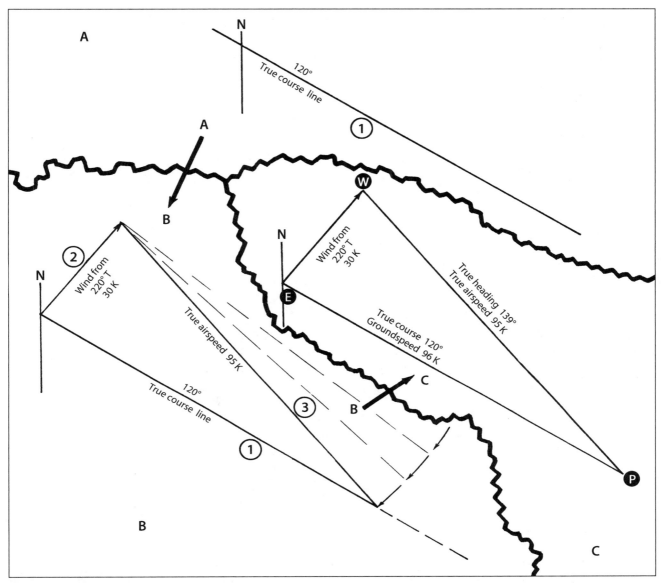

Figure 19-14. Working a wind triangle.

(the TAS) and angle (the true heading) tell you of the plane's movement and heading within the air mass.

The line EP (earth-plane) represents the plane's movement and speed with respect to the earth, and its direction is the true course you originally measured. The length of the line gives your groundspeed from Dover to Erin at 96 K. You could figure the return trip groundspeed and heading by extending the reciprocal course line through the point E and swinging another 95-K line from W to strike the course line, then reading the information as before.

Figure 19-15 shows another method of drawing the wind triangle for the Dover–Erin trip. For some people this makes the situation easier to see.

Figure 19-16 shows the Dover–Erin flight as applied to the airplane.

A point of interest: A plane does not make a round trip with wind in the same time as it can be done with no wind. It would seem that the plane having a head-wind one way and a tailwind the other would average the same as a plane making the round trip under no wind conditions—but it won't.

Assume a round trip of 100 NM each way. Both planes cruise at 100 K true airspeed. Plane A has a 20-K tailwind on the outbound leg and a 20-K headwind on the return trip. Plane B flies the same trip under no-wind conditions.

Plane A—Wind 20 K

Trip out—100 miles at 120 K =	50 min
Trip back—100 miles at 80 K =	1 hr 15 min
	2 hr 5 min

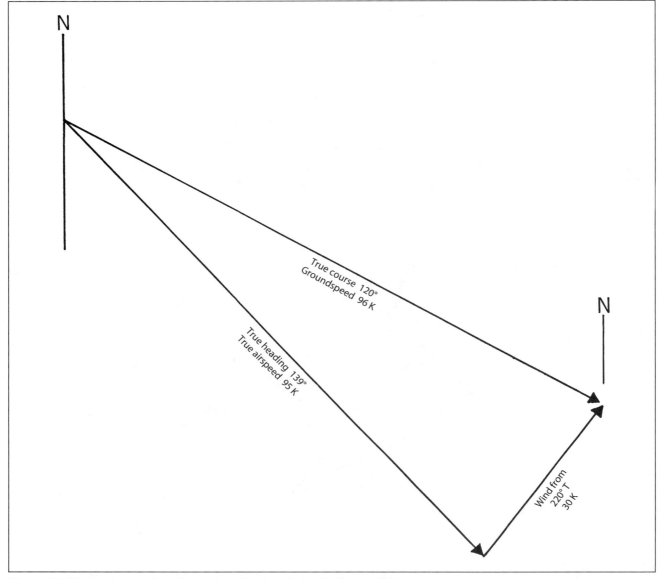

Figure 19-15. Another version of the wind triangle solution for Figure 19-14.

Plane B—Wind Calm

Trip out—100 miles at 100 K =   1 hr 0 min
Trip back—100 miles at 100 K =   1 hr 0 min
                                       2 hr 0 min

The stronger the wind as compared with the plane's cruise, the greater the divergence in time between the two conditions. The answer is that the plane with the wind flies longer in the headwind condition than the tailwind condition and loses the chance at equalization. Don't cut your fuel figuring too close under these conditions; *it won't average out.*

Remember any "course" (true, magnetic, or compass) deals with the plane's proposed path over the ground. Any "heading" (true, magnetic, or compass)

is a course with the correction for wind added or subtracted (Figure 19-15). The plane's "track" is its actual path over the ground.

Back to the wind triangle. You now convert the true heading to compass heading by correcting for *variation* to get *magnetic heading* and then adding or subtracting *deviation.*

Assume that the airplane in the problem is flying in an area where the variation is 4°E. Using that information and Figure 19-5, you would make the following steps:
   True heading = 139°
   Variation = 139° − 4° = 135°
   Deviation at 140° (Figure 19-5) = 0° (use nearest value)
   Compass heading = 135°

Suppose in another problem the true heading is found to be 235° in an area where the variation is 4°W.

The magnetic heading is 239°, and looking at Figure 19-5 at 240° magnetic (the nearest value), you would add 3° to get a compass heading of 239° + 3° = 242°. In cases where the magnetic heading is found to be between the values on the compass card, you may want to interpolate and split the difference in the addition or subtraction done to get the compass heading.

A Special Note

Most computers have a "wind side" for working out wind triangles (such as just discussed). Naturally, you won't be drawing wind triangles in the airplane because it's too complicated and the computer can do it much more quickly and easily. Each computer has its own manual and this book won't attempt to duplicate other efforts. *But* you should draw a couple of wind triangle problems on paper when you first get into the navigation business, and before using the computer, so that you can see the principles involved. Later, when you are using the computer to solve wind triangle problems, don't just insert a bunch of numbers and get an answer; *it may be wrong*. Have an idea of how the problem looks before setting it up on the wind side of the computer.

For instance, you have a problem as follows: true course, 090°; wind from 135° true. The true airspeed and wind velocity need not be available in order to know that the wind is from the right, and the true heading will be greater than 090° if a track of 090° is to result. (You will have a correction to the right.) You will have to correct right and "add" numbers to the true course if you are to track 090°. The *groundspeed* will be *less* than the *true airspeed* because there is a headwind

component also. Too many students mechanically use the computer and come up with wrong answers because they couldn't "see" the problem. If necessary when working practice wind problems on the computer at first, make a crude drawing of the wind direction and true course to get an idea of what to expect. The computer can be used to get exact answers. Later you won't need to draw the triangle.

Looking back at Figures 19-14 and 19-15, you can see that if you have the information on any two sides of the triangle the information on the third side may be found. The usual practical problem is as given in the earlier example of known wind (direction and velocity), true airspeed, and true course, and you are to find groundspeed and true heading (and magnetic and compass headings). The computer manual will also have sample problems such as how to find the wind direction and velocity if the other factors are known. You might get a question on the knowledge test requiring the finding of things other than groundspeed or true heading. In other words, you may get a problem that requires "working backward" to check on your knowledge of the principles involved. The point is to visualize the situation whether drawing a wind triangle on paper or using a computer.

Several electronic computers or calculators on the market are specifically designed for use in aviation, and problems may be worked on navigation, performance, weight and balance, and other requirements of flight. As mentioned a couple of paragraphs back, computers have their own manuals and sample problems, so this book won't go into detail on how to work them. If you have that type of talent, you can also set up a program for using the "ordinary" hand-held calculator in your flying. Electronic calculators can be used during the FAA Knowledge Test, subject to certain precautions.

When you start flying, or shortly thereafter, your instructor will suggest what type of computer and plotter you will need. Listen to that advice because you might otherwise buy cheap equipment that won't stand up or items that are more expensive or more complicated than you'll need.

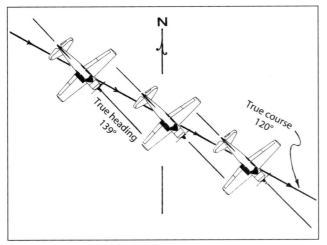

Figure 19-16. The wind triangle solution for Figure 19-14 as applied to the airplane.

The Chart and Other Printed Aids

These printed aids will assume more and more importance as you get out flying on your own. While you won't memorize the material, you should know what is contained in each publication—and where to find it.

Sectional Chart

The sectional chart, printed every six months, is the backbone of cross-country flying for the student and private pilot. It is printed by the National Oceanic and Atmospheric Administration and is extremely accurate. The scale is 1:500,000; that is, 1 inch on the chart equals 500,000 inches on the ground, or, as noted in the last chapter, the scale is about 7 NM to the inch. The chart contains such items as:

1. Aeronautical symbols used on the chart.
2. A map of the United States showing each sectional chart's coverage (named for a principal city on the chart such as Atlanta, Charlotte, etc.).
3. Topographical symbols—an explanation of the topographical or terrain symbols used on the chart.
4. Radio aids to navigation and airspace information plus data on obstruction symbols.
5. A list of the frequencies used by control towers in the area of the chart.
6. A list of prohibited, restricted, warning, and alert areas on the chart.

Figure 20-1 shows the sectional charts available for the 48 states portion of the United States.

Terminal areas of heavy air traffic concentration and complicated approach requirements (such as Chicago, Washington, Atlanta, etc.) publish VFR local area charts using the same typography and symbols as the sectional, but in more detail. These charts use a scale of 1:250,000. If you plan to go into such a congested area, you should have one of these up-to-date charts along.

Part of a sectional chart with a sample cross-country flight is reproduced in the back of this book.

Aeronautical Information Manual (AIM) — Official Guide to Basic Flight Information and ATC Procedures

The *AIM* contains instructional, educational, and training material—things that are basic and not often changed, some of which are discussed below (chapter references given are for *this* book).

Navigation aids—Backgrounds on aids to navigation such as the VHF omnirange, nondirectional beacon, and other aids to be covered in Chapter 21 of this book. There is also coverage of the Air Traffic Control Radar Beacon System, which you'll be using more and more as you gain experience.

Aeronautical lighting and airport marking aids—Includes the latest information on all types of runway lighting, airport rotating beacons, obstruction lighting, and runway markings.

Airspace—Controlled and uncontrolled airspace boundaries and altitudes are discussed, with notes on Class B, C, and D airspace (*see* Chapter 21). There's also coverage of special-use airspace such as military operations areas and restricted and prohibited areas. Airspace controlled by the tower (*see* Chapter 21) is covered in addition to information on temporary flight restrictions and other airspace requirements.

Air Traffic Control—There is a listing of services available to pilots, including Air Route Traffic Control Centers, towers, and Flight Service Stations (*see* Chapter 21) plus information on flying to and from controlled and uncontrolled airports. There's a section on radio communications with tips on radio techniques, the phonetic alphabet, and communications with the tower if you've lost part of your transmitting/receiving capability.

Operations at controlled and uncontrolled airports, plus traffic patterns, visual indicators (tetrahedrons,

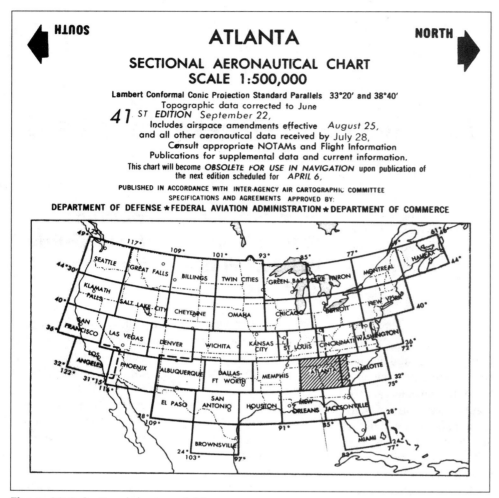

Figure 20-1. Sectional charts available.

wind socks, and segmented circles; Chapter 6), and traffic control light signals (Chapter 21).

You'll also get the word here on ATC clearances and separations required between airplanes in the airport environment.

Air traffic procedures—Preflight action, including flight plan filing and closing is included here. Departure, enroute, and arrival procedures are covered step by step in great detail. The pilot/controller roles and responsibilities are covered separately within this section.

Emergency procedures—Here the coverage pertains to your responsibility and authority as a pilot in an emergency: how to operate the transponder (Chapter 21), how to get found if you are "temporarily dislocated with respect to the preplanned route" (lost), and what to do if you are flying IFR and have a radio communications failure; this won't be a problem for you for a while.

This section also includes what to do under various emergency situations, search and rescue procedures

and visual emergency signals and codes, and radio communications failure procedures.

Safety of flight—Has good information on meteorology, including thunderstorms, wind shear, and microbursts (Chapter 22). There is a section on altimeter setting procedures with added information on altimeter errors. Wake turbulence is discussed in detail.

Birds and other potential flight hazards are discussed and the admonition is given to not fly under unmanned balloons. (Not covered there, but also to be considered, is that you probably should not fly under large birds either.)

Medical facts for pilots—This chapter has very good coverage of the physiological aspects of flying. You should be familiar with your responsibilities as a pilot.

Aeronautical charts and related publications—Here you'll find out what charts and publications are available and how to obtain them.

En route IFR—The VOR airways systems and special control areas. (*See* Chapter 21.) Communications and operating procedures enroute (instrument flight plan). Diagrams of cruising altitude requirements VFR and IFR).

Arrival IFR—The use of approach control, approach procedures, radar-controlled approaches, and IFR weather minimums.

General—Airports of entry and departure, and procedures. ADIZ (Air Defense Identification Zone) procedures.

This is only part of the useful information to be found in the AIM. You should have a copy in your library for reference. ASA's *FAR/AIM* has a useful Suggested Study List for various pilot certificates to go along with the Federal Aviation Regulations (14 CFR) and the AIM.

Figure 20-2 is from the AIM and shows recommended traffic patterns at nontower airports.

Airport/Facility Directory

This publication is available in seven subscriptions, each for a certain part of the United States (Figure 20-3). The small ($5\frac{3}{8} \times 8\frac{1}{4}$ inches) size and compactness make it handy to carry in the airplane.

The *A/F Directory* also includes VOR receiver checkpoints for the states covered in that particular section of the country and major changes in aeronautical

(sectional) charts. There are Special Notices including telephone numbers for Flight Service Stations and National Weather Offices.

Appendix A of this book is the legend and information on the Sewanee (Tennessee), Columbia–Mount Pleasant (Tennessee), and Huntsville (Alabama) airports. These airports will be used in the sample cross-country discussed in Chapters 24 and 25.

Notices to Airmen

By regulation, you are responsible for all factors that could affect the safety of your flight (14 CFR §91.103), and a knowledge of the Notices to Airmen (NOTAMs) that affect the route and destination of your flight is required. NOTAM information is classified into three categories:

1. NOTAM (D)—These are considered the "distant" NOTAMs and are given for all navigational facilities that are part of the National Airspace System (NAS), all IFR airports with approved instrument approach procedures, and for those VFR airports listed as such in the *Airport/Facility Directory* (*see* item 2 in the Appendix A legend). (NOTAM (L): These have been reclassified as NOTAM (D).)

2. FDC (Flight Data Center) NOTAMs—These can be considered as furnishing information that is

Figure 20-2. Recommended traffic patterns. (From the *Aeronautical Information Manual*). Also *see* Figure 13-14 in this book.

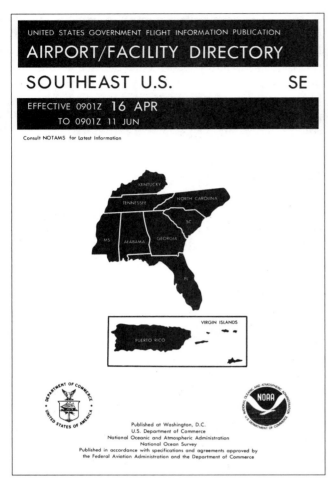

Figure 20-3. The *Airport/Facility Directory.*

DIRECTORY LEGEND
TABLE OF CONTENTS

General Information .... Inside Front Cover
Abbreviations 1
Legend, Airport/Facility Directory 2
Airport/Facility Directory 11
Heliports 248
Seaplane Bases 251
Notices 253
FSS and National Weather Service Telephone Numbers 262
Air Route Traffic Control Centers 267
GADO and FSDO Addresses/Telephone Numbers 269
Preferred IFR Routes 270
VOR Receiver Check 274
Parachute Jumping Areas 280
Aeronautical Chart Bulletin 284
Tower Enroute Control (TEC) 290
National Weather Service (NWS) Upper Air Observing Stations 304
Enroute Flight Advisory Service (EFAS) .... Inside Back Cover

regulatory in nature and contain such things as amendments to published instrument approach procedures and other current aeronautical charts.

3. TEMPORARY FLIGHT RESTRICTIONS—TFRs are implemented to restrict traffic from specific areas for a limited time. They are distributed as FDC NOTAMs and will have lateral and vertical dimensions, so over-flight of the TFR is sometimes possible.

TFRs may be issued to prevent flight near an accident or incident on the ground. This serves to protect overflying aircraft from a hazard or to protect people or aircraft involved in rescue/relief operations, such as forest fire suppression. The restriction may be placed to reduce collision risk between sightseeing aircraft at an incident site.

Presidential/VIP travel or security concerns around an event such as a national political convention will trigger restrictions.

TFRs will be issued for aerial demonstrations, space flight operations and major sporting events. There are standing restrictions around large stadiums when in use and around some landmarks, military facilities and power plants.

Current TFRs near your route of flight can be obtained from FSS. If you know you will fly near one, it's advisable to get updates en route.

An integral part of the NOTAM system is the biweekly *Notices to Airmen* publication. Data is included in this publication to reduce congestion on the telecommunications circuits. Once this is published, the information is not provided during pilot weather briefings unless specifically requested by the pilot. This publication contains two sections:

1. The first section has notices that are primarily distant (D) notices (and expected to remain in effect for an extended period) along with current FDC NOTAMs.

2. The second section contains special notices that are too long for the first section or affect a wide or unspecified geographic area.

Again, *you* as a pilot are responsible for knowing about NOTAMs that will affect your flights. You should inquire about those that will affect your flight when talking to the FSS during the preflight briefing for your cross-country flying.

Note: There are frequent changes in sectional chart symbols or items or presentations in the *AIM* and *A/FD.* Your instructor will be sure that you have the latest printings of aids available.

Using the Radio

Nowadays few airplanes are not equipped with radio communications and navigation equipment; chances are that you'll be introduced to it very soon after you start flying. The FAA has set up an extensive system of communications and navigation facilities. The personnel at those facilities are there for only one reason, to *help the pilot*, and you'll find that they can save you a lot of trouble (and perhaps help you out of a bind someday after you've messed up).

Frequencies

Your AM radio dial has a range of from 550 to about 1600 kilohertz (kHz), and you dial the frequency (station) you want. The FM band uses frequencies of from 88 to about 107 megahertz (MHz). The AM is MF (medium frequency) and is more likely to get interference from nearby thunderstorms than the FM stations, which broadcast on VHF (very high frequencies). The following listing gives an idea of the frequency bands in use now:

Very low frequencies (VLF)	10–30 kHz
Low frequencies (LF)	30–300 kHz
Medium frequencies (MF)	300–3000 kHz
High frequencies (HF)	3–30 MHz
Very high frequencies (VHF)	30–300 MHz
Ultra high frequencies (UHF)	300–3000 MHz

At the HF band the term megahertz (MHz) is introduced (1 megahertz = 1,000 kilohertz). This is done to keep things from getting too cumbersome as would be done by going on with the kilohertz idea. The term "hertz" is named after Heinrich Hertz, German physicist, and stands for "cycles per second." In your aviation radio work you'll be working mostly with VHF, LF, and MF.

Radio Navigation Aids

Radio Beacon

Radio beacons or nondirectional radio beacons (NDB) are assigned broadcast frequencies between 190 and 535 kHz, which makes them LF/MF facilities.

Each station continually transmits its particular assigned three-letter identifier in code except during voice transmissions.

Low-powered radio beacons called compass locators are used in conjunction with instrument landing systems (ILS). The compass locators have a two-letter identification and a range of at least 15 miles. The enroute or "H" (homing) facilities may have a range of up to 75 miles for the more powerful installations. The *Aeronautical Information Manual (AIM)* gives more details on designations and ranges for radio beacons and compass locators.

You will use an ADF (automatic direction finder) in the airplane to navigate with the radio beacon (Figure 21-1). You would select REC (receive) for better audio reception and set in the proper frequency for the desired radio beacon or broadcast station. Some sets have a selection of ANT (antenna) for this purpose. After the station is coming in loud and clear, you'd switch to the ADF setting.

The needle of the ADF points to the station you have selected and gives a relative bearing to that station. Always make sure that the station has been properly identified—it would be embarrassing on the flight test if you homed in on the wrong station. It can happen!

Figure 21-2 shows some magnetic headings and relative bearings to fictitious radio beacons. (Assume no deviation for these illustrations.)

(A) Shows that the magnetic heading is 060°, and the relative bearing is 060°, for a magnetic bearing to the station of 120° (60° + 60°).

(B) Indicates a magnetic heading of 290° with a relative bearing of 240°. You can find the magnetic bearing

Figure 21-1. The automatic direction finder needle points to the radio beacon or commercial broadcast station (if properly tuned).

to the station in two ways: You can add the two values and subtract 360 from the answer (290° + 240° = 530°; 530° − 360° = 170° to the station); or you note that the needle is pointing 120° to the left of the nose, so you can subtract this amount from the heading (290° − 120° = 170°). If the addition results in a number greater than 360°, subtract 360° from the result.

(C) The heading is 135° with a relative bearing of 195°. You can add the two numbers (135° + 195° = 330°) to the station. If you wanted to "visualize" the situation, you could say that the reciprocal of your heading is 315° and the station is 15° "farther around," so this would also give a result of 330°.

Looking at the lower part of Figure 21-2, you'll see a different presentation as found in newer ADF sets. The knob marked HDG (heading) is used to mechanically turn the card to set the airplane's heading under the indicator or lubber line. The needle then indicates the actual bearing to the station.

In (A) the airplane is heading 060°; this is set up on the card and the needle shows that the bearing to the station is 120°. This answer was found in the top illustration (A) by addition.

(B) Indicates that the bearing to the station is 170°.

(C) The bearing to the station is 330° as found before.

This presentation is an improvement over the addition and subtraction method required by the first type, but you have to be sure that the number you set in on the card is the same as the heading indicator shows. Anytime you change the airplane's heading, the ADF card has to be mechanically reset to that new figure if you want to have an accurate relative bearing to the station.

It would be good if this could be done automatically for you, so the RMI (radio magnetic indicator) was designed. It's a combination of heading indicator and ADF and VOR pointers. The heading indicator can be slaved to a remote magnetic compass so that precession is continually being corrected. You'll probably use an RMI when you start working on that instrument rating.

You "home" into a station by turning the airplane until the ADF needle points to a relative bearing of 000° (the station is straight ahead) and by keeping the needle in this position. A crosswind will result in a curved path (Figure 21-3). This is the simplest but not the most efficient way of getting to the station.

As you pass the station, the needle will swing and point to the rear (180° position on the dial). Later you will learn how to track into the station, setting up the proper wind drift correction that would result

Figure 21-2. Finding magnetic bearings to the station.

Figure 21-3. A curved path results if there is a crosswind during "homing" (the nose is kept pointed to the station). The effect shown is exaggerated for purposes of illustration.

in a straight flight path (the same principle covered in "Wind Triangle" in Chapter 19).

Your ADF set is able to pick up stations in the frequency range of 190–1750 kHz, which means that you can also home into AM commercial broadcasting stations. While those stations are normally more powerful than the radio beacons or H facilities, they have the disadvantage of not having continuous identification. You may have to suffer through several minutes of bad music before learning that you've been tuned to the right (or wrong) station.

Because the ADF operates in the LF/MF bands, it is subject to the troubles of the regular AM home radio when thunderstorms are in the vicinity. Precipitation static and thunderstorms may make reception difficult or impossible. Precipitation static is the result of static electricity generated when the airplane flies through rain, snow, etc.

The radio beacon has one advantage over VHF navigational equipment; it is not "line of sight." You can pick up the signals even when you are low and the station is over the horizon (just like the home radio).

If your trainer does not have an ADF, you might ask your instructor for a ground checkout on the operation of that equipment in one of the other planes on the field.

VOR

The most useful of the enroute radio navigation aids, other than GPS, is the VHF omnirange, or VOR as it is sometimes called. The VOR frequency band is from 108.00 to 117.95 MHz and uses the principle of electronically measuring an angle. The VOR puts out two signals. One is all-directional (or omnidirectional) and the other is a rotating signal. The all-directional signal contracts and expands 30 times a second, and the rotating signal rotates clockwise at 30 revolutions per second. The rotating signal has a positive and a negative side.

The all-directional or reference signal is timed to transmit at the same instant the rotating beam passes *magnetic north*. These rotating beams and the reference signal result in radial measurements.

Your omni receiver picks up the all-directional signal. Some time later it picks up the maximum point of the positive rotating signal. The receiver electronically measures the time difference, and it is indicated in degrees as your *magnetic* bearing in relation to the station (Figure 21-4). For instance, assume it took a minute instead of $\frac{1}{30}$ of a second for the rotating signal to make one revolution. You receive the all-directional signal and 20 seconds later you receive the rotating signal. This means that your position is $\frac{20}{60}$ or $\frac{1}{3}$ of the

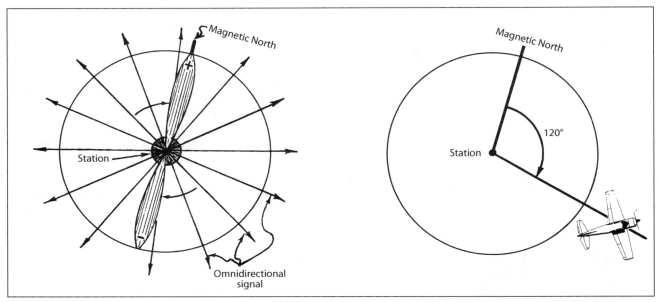

Figure 21-4. Principle of the VOR.

Figure 21-5. A VOR receiver. (Courtesy of Narco Avionics)

way around. (One-third of 360° is 120° and you are on the 120 radial.) The VOR receiver does this in a quicker, more accurate way.

The aircraft VOR receiver presentation is composed of four main parts: (1) a dial to select the frequency of the station you want to use; (2) an azimuth or omni bearing selector (OBS) calibrated from 0 to 360; (3) a course deviation indicator (CDI), a vertical needle that moves left or right; and (4) a TO-FROM indicator. Figure 21-5 is one type of VOR receiver.

Suppose you want to fly to a certain VOR, say, 30 miles away. First you would tune the frequency and

identify the station. You should have some idea where you are in relation to the station, but if not, turn the azimuth or direction selector until the deviation indicator or needle is centered, and the TO-FROM indicator says TO. Read the OBS. This is your course TO the VOR. If you turn on that magnetic course and keep the needle centered, you'll fly right over the VOR. If the TO-FROM says TO and you are going to the station, fly the needle. If the needle moves to the left, the selected bearing is to the left and you will turn the plane in that direction and fly until the needle is centered again. You will have to correct for wind to stay on the selected bearing (Figure 21-6).

In this case your position from the VOR looks something like that shown in Figure 21-6A.

While your bearing to the station is 300°, *you are on the 120 (one-two-zero) radial.* (The radials are like spokes from the VOR.) (*See* Figure 21-6A.) The radials are numbered from 0 through 359, so if the station asked where you were, you'd say, "I'm inbound to the station on the 120 (one-two-zero) radial." For example, if there's a westerly wind, the plane may drift from the selected bearing as shown in Figure 21-6B, and the LEFT-RIGHT needle would look like Figure 21-7.

The angle of correction or the "cut" you'll take will depend on the amount that you've drifted from course. Usually 30° would be the maximum even at some distance from the station. It may take some time for the needle to center again if you're far out. After the needle returns to center, turn back toward the original heading, but this time include an estimated wind correction on your compass or heading indicator. Watch the needle and make further corrections as needed.

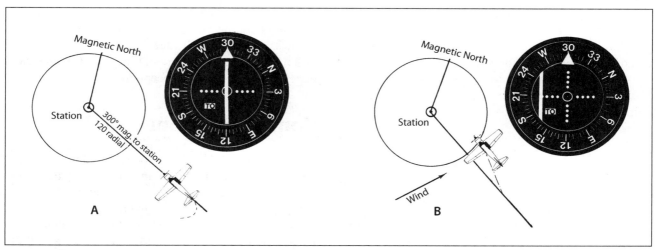

Figure 21-6. Using a VOR receiver to track to the station.

Figure 21-7. A heading indicator and two types of VOR indicators. The selected radial is to the left.

When you cross over the station, the TO-FROM indicator will oscillate, then fall to FROM. The receiver now says that you are on a bearing of 300° FROM the station. Always make sure your OBS is set close to your compass heading. This way the needle always points toward the selected radial. If you turned around and headed back to the station after passing it on a course of 300° and did not reset the bearing selector to coincide with your heading, the needle would work in reverse. *Always set your OBS to the course to be followed; then the needle senses correctly.*

The sensing is incorrect if you correct toward the needle, and the needle moves farther away from the center as you fly.

But, back to the station passage: The TO-FROM says FROM and your plane is on a course of 300° FROM the VOR, so the needle is correct. Continue to fly the needle as you did before the VOR was reached.

Most omni needles are set up so that a full deflection from center is 10° or more. If the needle is deflected

halfway, you can figure that you are about 5° from your selected bearing.

VORs are identified by Morse code and/or by the automatic recorded voice identification ("Airville VOR").

The accuracy of the VOR ground facility is generally ±1°, but some stations in mountainous terrain may have errors greater than this for some radials or may be unusable below certain altitudes; this is duly noted in the *Airport/Facility Directory*.

Summary

Frequency Band—108.0–117.95 megahertz.

Use—Navigation and instrument approaches. (A few don't have voice facilities. *See* the *Aeronautical Information Manual* and *Airport/Facility Directory*.)

Identification—Continual code or code and voice.

Advantages—(1) Very high frequency; not as affected by weather as LF/MF facilities. (2) Omni or all-directional signals.

Disadvantages—Line of sight; cannot be picked up if the plane is low (Figure 21-8).

The check pilot will require that you be able to tune, identify, and fly a VOR radial on the practical test.

Appendix A contains the various classifications of VORs and other navigational aids and their effective altitudes and ranges.

Figure 21-8. The VOR is line of sight.

Distance Measuring Equipment (DME)

The DME set in the aircraft sends out, at a specific spacing, interrogating pulses that are received by the specially equipped VOR station. The ground station then transmits a paired pulse back to the aircraft at a different pulse spacing and on a different frequency. The time required for the round trip of this signal exchange is measured by the DME unit in the aircraft and is indicated on a counter or dial as nautical miles from the aircraft to the station.

DME operates on frequencies between 962 and 1213 MHz (UHF), but because each DME frequency is always paired with an associated VOR frequency, the selector of the set may be marked in terms of the omni frequency band. All you have to do is to know the frequency of the associated VOR and set up the selector of the DME on this number, rather than having to remember the various DME frequencies or "channels."

VORTAC stations are combinations of two components: the VOR, giving azimuth information, and the TACAN (tactical air navigation) equipment, giving distance (DME) information. TACAN is a military innovation being used in FAA facilities. Note in the sectional chart in the back of this book that Huntsville has a VORTAC (named *Rocket*), and you would set up 112.2 MHz on the VOR set and the same on the DME equipment and get directions, groundspeeds, and distances from that station. The "Channel 59" is for TACAN equipment, and all VORs in the United States having the frequency 112.2 MHz would have a

channel 59 assigned. (*See* Appendix A.) Note also on the chart that Shelbyville has a VOR/DME that is used in the same way as indicated for the VORTAC, but the ground equipment is different. Like the VOR, the DME depends on line-of-sight reception.

Communications

Figure 21-9 is a COMM/NAV (communications and navigation) set. In the communications part of the equipment, you would set up the desired frequency that would allow you to transmit *and* receive.

The console (A) consists of the transceiver (this is insider talk for transmitter-receiver) set at 123.00 MHz for communications. (You'd transmit and receive with a UNICOM on this setting-more about UNICOM shortly.) The right half (NAV) is set at 115.95 MHz here to pick up a VOR station. The NAV receiver shown can pick up VOR/LOC (localizer) signals for navigation *and* approaches. The receiver range is from 108.00 to 117.95 MHz.

The localizer is used for instrument approaches (you can also use it in good weather if you like) and utilizes the *odd* frequencies (tenths, or hundredths, depending on the precision of your receiver) from 108.10 to 111.95 MHz (108.10, 108.15, 108.30, etc.). The localizer has a 3-letter Morse Code identifier preceded by I(••).

In Figure 21-9, (B) is a VOR/LOC indicator and (C) is a VOR/LOC with a GS (glide slope) needle added. As a student pilot you will normally use only the vertical needle of this indicator. Note that this is COMM 1 and NAV 1, which would usually be the uppermost

Figure 21-9. A NAV/COMM set (Courtesy of Bendix/King Radio Corp.)

set on the instrument panel. (*See* Figure 3-1.) This bottom COMM/NAV (or NAV/COMM) set is cited as "No. 2."

Your instructor will check you out on the COMM/NAV equipment for your airplane.

UNICOM

UNICOM, or aeronautical advisory, is an aid to the pilot operating into smaller airports with no tower. The UNICOM frequencies are the "private pilot's frequencies" and you can call into an airport so equipped and get the surface wind, traffic, and other information. You can also call in and get transportation if needed.

UNICOM is merely an advisory service by the airport operator. It cannot give traffic clearances to take off or land as would be done by a control tower.

The primary UNICOM frequencies in use are:

1. For airports *without* an operating control tower—122.7, 122.8, and 123.0 (or 122.700, 122.800, and 123.00 MHz, depending on how far you want to carry the zeroes). Other frequencies at these airports that are being brought into use are 122.725, 122.975, 123.050, and 123.075 MHz.

2. Airports with a control tower or FSS use the UNICOM frequency 122.950 MHz. Make sure that you aren't on UNICOM frequency asking for a cab when you should be listening and talking to approach control or the tower.

3. MULTICOM—This is a frequency (122.900 MHz) used to announce yourself (and your intentions) at airports without UNICOM, a Flight Service Station, or a tower. You (and other airplanes) would keep up with each other's actions using this frequency around and on the airport. It is also used for Search and Rescue.

4. *Air-to-air frequency*—122.750 MHz is to be used if you and your friend in that other airplane need to talk to each other. (This frequency is often abused with long-winded conversations.)

Incidentally, frequencies given in this book are subject to change, so you should keep up-to-date, checking the *AIM* and the *Airport/Facility Directory* for the latest frequencies assigned to the various facilities.

Flight Service Station (FSS)

The Flight Service Station has several functions in its job of assisting the pilot (you).

Flight plan service—You file all flight plans with an FSS in person, by telephone, or by radio. (If possible, avoid filing by radio; it ties up the frequencies too much.) A discussion of flight plans and how to file

them will be covered in more detail in Chapter 24, which covers navigation planning.

Pilot briefing service—You may obtain preflight briefing on weather (existing and forecast) along your route and information on the operating status of navigation aids and airport conditions either in person or by phone. Incidentally, when getting flight weather information by phone from either Flight Service Stations or Weather Service Offices, always tell them that you are a pilot, give the aircraft identification, and also note the approximate departure time, route, and expected time enroute to your destination. Also request a "standard briefing" if you haven't received a previous briefing or haven't gotten information from other FAA sources. Your briefing will normally cover the following information: (1) adverse weather, (2) current weather at the departure point, destination, and enroute; (3) forecasts for the points just mentioned, and (4) advisories, pilot reports (PIREPs) (*see* Chapter 22), winds aloft along the route, and NOTAMs (notices to airmen) plus military training routes within 100 NM of the FSS. About NOTAMs: ask for them every time. Ask for a *weather briefing* when you talk to the facilities, rather than taking it upon yourself to just request information on individual stations along your route. The briefer may use the phrase "VFR flight is not recommended" if he or she thinks conditions are not good enough for VFR (visual flight rules) flying. The latest telephone numbers for Weather Service and Flight Service Stations can be found in the *Airport/Facility Directory*. Tell the FSS people what you need and let them help you from there.

For in-flight briefing call the FSS on the proper frequency and let them know on which frequency you'll be listening. It is suggested that you call Flight Service Stations on 122.1 MHz (which is a one-way frequency *from* aircraft to them) and listen to one of the VOR frequencies on which they can transmit. This practice cuts down interference from other stations. Don't be impatient, because the people in the FSS could be tied up on another frequency. Also let them know that you are a student pilot; they'll appreciate the information and will give you extra consideration. (This goes for contacting approach controls and towers also.)

Assume you are on a cross-country and the weather ahead doesn't look too good. You can give a call to the nearest FSS and get the latest weather and the forecast for your destination.

You: "BLANKTOWN RADIO, THIS IS CESSNA SEVEN FIVE FIVE SEVEN LIMA, STUDENT PILOT, LISTENING JONES VOR, OVER." (This is not official, but you might repeat the station name twice on the initial call; such as, "BLANKTOWN, BLANK-TOWN RADIO... "The reason for this is that the station name would sometimes be missed by the FSS personnel and they might only hear "...RADIO." This would mean that the personnel in every FSS within reception distance of your transmitter think that you're calling them and time is wasted until the matter is straightened out.)

Blanktown radio: "CESSNA SEVEN FIVE FIVE SEVEN LIMA, THIS IS BLANKTOWN RADIO, OVER." (Notice that you'll make an initial contact, letting them know who you are and on what frequency you'll be listening for their reply. The FSS has identified itself to you and by saying "over" has handed the ball back. You should *always* let the FSS know on which frequency you expect a reply because the stations can transmit on several frequencies and may have to transmit simultaneously on all of them to make sure they get you. This causes interference with other stations and other aircraft. Keep in mind that some Flight Service Stations have jurisdiction over several VOR stations, so if you are listening on a VOR frequency, tell them which one.)

You: "THIS IS FIVE SEVEN LIMA, I'M ABOUT FIVE MILES EAST OF BLANKTOWN AT FOUR THOUSAND FIVE HUNDRED (4,500 feet), ENROUTE TO JONESVILLE. I'D LIKE THE LATEST JONESVILLE WEATHER AND THE FORECAST FOR THE NEXT TWO HOURS, OVER."

(Once you have established contact, it is not necessary to use your full number each time unless there might be confusion of close numbers/letters between two airplanes.)

Blanktown: "FIVE SEVEN LIMA, WAIT, OUT." (The "out" is to let you know that a reply to this transmission is not expected.)

Blanktown: THE LATEST JONESVILLE WEATHER IS... "(gives the Jonesville weather and forecast plus the Blanktown altimeter setting).

You: "FIVE SEVEN LIMA, THANK YOU. OUT."

You acknowledge receipt of transmissions or instructions by the last three digits (and/or letters) of your registration number.

Although it's not required, you should give your position and altitude when contacting an FSS, even if you're not on a flight plan because later, if you don't show up at the destination, your friends may start checking. The FSS will have on file a record of having talked to you at such-and-such a time, at such-and-such a position and altitude, and the search can start from there. You might as well get in the habit of giving your position and altitude in each contact.

En route services—You can report your position at any time to an FSS whether on a flight plan or not. If you are on a VFR flight plan the Flight Service Stations are the facilities to which you would normally make your position reports. In a bind you could report to a tower and they would relay the message.

Another en route service available from Flight Service Stations is that of giving aid in emergencies arising in flight. The personnel are trained to help in situations such as orienting the lost pilot (using radar, direction finding, omni receiver manipulation, or their knowledge of prominent landmarks reported by the pilot). If you have a problem, call the FSS and let them worry. (Of course, you are allowed to worry also if you like.) Emergency frequencies are discussed in the AIM.

Local Airport Advisory—This is provided by Flight Service Stations at airports not served by a control tower, or if the tower is not in operation.

For local airport advisory service (AAS) you would normally make initial contact with the FSS about 15 miles out and transmit and receive on 123.6 MHz.

Remember that it's only an advisory service. No airport control can be as complete as a control tower. Such information as wind, favored runway, field conditions, and *known* traffic will be given to you. If you have two-way radio, it's a good idea to maintain communications with the FSS within 10 statute miles of such airports. If you only have a receiver, you can maintain listening watch on the appropriate frequency when within 10 statute miles of the airport. You could also call them when taxiing out for departure. (AAS is not mandatory.)

Broadcast service—Continuous weather broadcasts are made over selected navigation aids. (Chapter 22 goes into more detail.)

Pilot weather reporting service—The FSS acts as a clearinghouse between pilots for exchanging information concerning turbulence, significant weather encountered, or other pertinent information. These pilot reports, or PIREPS, will be passed on by the FSS to other pilots in the area by direct communication or through the Teletype and scheduled weather broadcasts.

Check the latest *Airport/Facility Directory* for frequencies, since the sectional chart data may be out of date. Note that not all Flight Service Stations have all of the same frequencies (Figure 21-10).

> Civil Communications Frequencies—Civil communications frequencies used in the FSS air/ground system are now operated simplex on 122.0, 122.2, 122.3, 122.4, 122.6, 123.6; emergency 121.5; plus receive-only on 122.05, 122.1, 122.15, and 123.6.
>
>   a. 122.0 is assigned as the Enroute Flight Advisory Service channel at selected FSS's.
>   b. 122.2 is assigned to most FSS's as a common enroute simplex service.
>   c. 123.6 is assigned as the airport advisory channel at non-tower FSS locations, however, it is still in commission at some FSS's collocated with towers to provide part time Airport Advisory Service.
>   d. 122.1 is the primary receive-only frequency at VOR's. 122.05, 122.15 and 123.6 are assigned at selected VOR's meeting certain criteria.
>   e. Some FSS's are assigned 50 kHz channels for simplex operation in the 122-123 MHz band (e.g. 122.35). Pilots using the FSS A/G system should refer to this directory or appropriate charts to determine frequencies available at the FSS or remoted facility through which they wish to communicate.
>
> Part time FSS hours of operation are shown in remarks under facility name.
>
> Emergency frequency 121.5 is available at all Flight Service Stations, Towers, Approach Control and RADAR facilities, unless indicated as not available.
>
> Frequencies published followed by the letter "T" or "R", indicate that the facility will only transmit or receive respectively on that frequency. All radio aids to navigation frequencies are transmit only.

Figure 21-10. Flight Service Station frequencies. (From the *Airport/Facility Directory*)

Common Traffic Advisory Frequency (CTAF)

The common traffic advisory frequency is a service frequency designed for the purpose of airport advisories at uncontrolled airports. The CTAF may be a UNICOM, MULTICOM, FSS, or tower frequency and is identified in appropriate aeronautical publications.

Figure 21-11 shows how the CTAF might be presented in the *Airport/Facility Directory* airports with different facilities. Note that Muscle Shoals (Ala.) has both an FSS and a UNICOM, but for traffic advisories the FSS frequency is suggested. At the Sewanee–Franklin County (Tenn.) Airport, only UNICOM is available, so this is the CTAF.

Control Tower

If you've never been into a controlled field, you'll face the prospect with some misgiving. It's best if you have a brief idea as to the various functions of the tower so that things won't be so confusing the first time. You can think of operations of the tower as being divided into five main services:

1. *Local control*—The function that pilots think of as "The Tower." Local control has jurisdiction over the aircraft taking off and landing and, to quote the *Aeronautical Information Manual* (*see* Chapter 20 again), is "established to provide for a safe, orderly, and expeditious flow of traffic on and in the vicinity of an airport. When the responsibility has been so delegated, towers also provide for the separation of Instrument Flight Rules aircraft in the terminal area."

Towers are established in Class B, C, and D airspace (Figure 21-12).

A simpler explanation of the tower might be that the tower controls the traffic pattern entry and the traffic pattern itself, including takeoffs and landings. Local controllers are in the glassed-in top level of the tower because their control depends on visual identification of aircraft for takeoffs and landings.

```
MUSCLE SHOALS REGIONAL   (MSL)   1 E   UTC–6(–5DT)   N34°44.72' W87°36.61'                    ATLANTA
550    B    S4   FUEL 100LL, JET A   TPA—See Remarks   ARFF Index A                          H-4H, L-14G
RWY 11-29: H6693X150 (ASPH-GRVD)   S-59, D-98, DT-160   HIRL                                 IAP
   RWY 11: REIL. VASI(V4R)—GA 3.0°TCH 51'. Tree.        RWY 29: MALSR. Tower.
RWY 18-36: H4000X100 (ASPH)   S-30, D-50   MIRL
   RWY 18: Tree.
AIRPORT REMARKS: Attended continuously. Flocks of birds on and in vicinity of arpt. Turtles; deer; coyotes; and other
   wildlife on and in vicinity of rwys and taxiways. HIRL Rwy 11–29 and MIRL Rwy 18–36 opr dusk–0500Z‡. After
   0500Z‡ ctc MUSCLE SHOALS FSS—CTAF. TPA—1550 (1000) light acft 2050 (1500) turbo prop and jets. REIL
   Rwy 11 controlled by FSS. During calm winds preferred rwy is 29. Fuel avbl ngts call 205–383–2270 or
   205–386–7597. No general aviation parking on air carrier ramp.
COMMUNICATIONS: CTAF 123.6   UNICOM 122.95
   FSS (MSL) on fld. 123.6 122.4 122.2. LC 383–6541. NOTAM FILE MSL.
   MEMPHIS CENTER APP/DEP CON 120.8
RADIO AIDS TO NAVIGATION: NOTAM FILE MSL. VHF/DF ctc FSS.
   (L) VORTACW 116.5   MSL   Chan 112   N34°42.41' W87°29.49'   290° 6.3 NM to fld. 580/01E.
   ILS 109.7 I-MSL Rwy 29


SEWANEE
FRANKLIN CO     (UOS)   1 E   UTC–6(–5DT)   N35°12.24' W85°53.92'                            ATLANTA
1950    B    FUEL 80, 100LL                                                                 L-14H
RWY 06-24: H3300X50 (ASPH)   S-20   LIRL.
   RWY 06: SAVASI(S2L)—GA 3.5°TCH 28'. Trees.    RWY 24: VASI(V2L)—GA 4.0° TCH 31'. Trees.
AIRPORT REMARKS: Attended dalgt hours. For svc after hours call 615–598–0745. Sporadic crosswinds and
   turbulence. Deer on and in vicinity of rwy.
COMMUNICATIONS: CTAF/UNICOM 122.8
   NASHVILLE FSS (BNA) TF 1–800–WX–BRIEF. NOTAM FILE BNA.
RADIO AIDS TO NAVIGATION: NOTAM FILE BNA.
   SHELBYVILLE (L) VOR/DME 109.0   SYI   Chan 27   N35°33.72' W86°26.35'   130° 34.1 NM to fld.
      810/01W.
   SEWANEE NDB (MHW) 275   UOS   N35°12.26' W85°53.75'   at fld. (VFR only).
```

Figure 21-11. The CTAF of two different facilities.

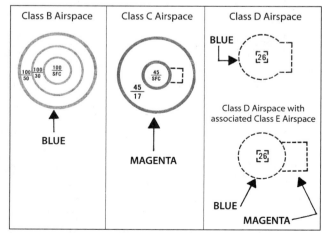

Figure 21-12. Class B, C, and D airspace as depicted on a sectional chart (all have operating control towers). The pilot and equipment requirements are most rigid for B and C and each will be discussed later in this book.

ALABAMA

HUNTSVILLE
HUNTSVILLE INTL—CARL T JONES FLD (HSV) 9 SW UTC−6(−5DT)   ATLANTA
 N34°38.43′ W86°46.39′   H−4H, L−14H
 629 B S4 **FUEL** 100LL, JET A   OX 1, 2, 3, 4   LRA   ARFF Index C   IAP
 RWY 18L−36R: H10000X150 (ASPH−GRVD)   S−90, D−200, DT−350, DDT−850   HIRL
  RWY 18L: MALSR. PAPI(P4R)—GA 3.0° TCH 70′. Pole.
  RWY 36R: REIL. VASI(V4L)—GA 3.0° TCH 55′. Thld dsplcd 200′. Trees. Rgt tfc.
 RWY 18R−36L: H8000X150 (ASPH−GRVD)   S−90, D−200, DT−350, DDT−850   HIRL   CL
  RWY 18R: ALSF2. TDZL. Rgt tfc.   RWY 36L: MALSR
 RUNWAY DECLARED DISTANCE INFORMATION
  RWY 18L: TORA−10000   TODA−10000   ASDA−9800   LDA−9800
  RWY 36R: TORA−10000   TODA−10000   ASDA−10000   LDA−9800
 AIRPORT REMARKS: Attended continuously. Migratory birds wild life refuge S and W of arpt. Twy X and Twy 'ONAN'
  CLOSED indef. Approximately 300 ft of Twy J south of the terminal; southeast portion of Twy G where it enters
  the air carrier apron; and approximately 75 ft of Twy E between Twys E5 and E6 are not visible from the twr.
  Intersection of Twy J and svc road is uncontrolled. 24 hr PPR for unscheduled air carrier ops with more than 30
  passenger seats call arpt manager 256−772−9395 extension 265. Flight Notification Service (ADCUS) avbl.
 WEATHER DATA SOURCES: ASOS (256) 772−8074. LLWAS. ————————**2**
 COMMUNICATIONS: CTAF 127.6   ATIS 121.25   UNICOM 122.95
  ANNISTON FSS (ANB) TF 1−800−WX−BRIEF. NOTAM FILE HSV.
  RCO 122.2 (ANNISTON FSS)
5 ®APP CON 125.6 (360°−179°) 118.05 (180°−359°)118.75 (1200−0600Z‡)
  ®DEP CON 125.6 (359°−179°) 118.05 (180°−358°) 120.35 (1200−0600Z‡)
  MEMPHIS CENTER APP/DEP CON 120.8 (0600−1200Z‡)   **4**   **3**
1—TOWER 127.6 (1200−0600Z‡, other times by NOTAM)   GND CON 121.9   CLNC DEL 120.35
 AIRSPACE: CLASS C svc 1200−0600Z‡ other times CLASS E.
 RADIO AIDS TO NAVIGATION: NOTAM FILE DCU.
  DECATUR (L) VORW/DME 112.8   DCU   Chan 75   N34°38.90′ W86°56.37′   094° 8.3 NM to fld. 590/01W.
   HIWAS.
  CAPSHAW NDB (MHW) 350   CWH   N34°46.42′ W86°46.74′   179° 8 NM to fld. NOTAM FILE HSV.
  ILS 109.3   I−HSV   Rwy 18R.
  ILS 108.5   I−ELL   Rwy 36L.
  ILS 111.9   I−TVN   Rwy 18L.
  ASR

Figure 21-13. Communications and other information for the Huntsville International Airport. (From the *Airport/Facility Directory*) See text explanation for numbers 1–5.

The local control (tower) frequencies are in the *Airport/Facility Directory* (*see* Figure 21-13).

2. *Automatic Terminal Information Service* (ATIS)— ATIS is the continual broadcast of recorded noncontrol information for certain *high-activity* airports. For instance, Sewanee–Franklin County Airport (*see* Figure 21-11) does *not* have ATIS.

Information such as the time of the latest weather sequence, ceiling, visibility (if the ceiling is above 5,000 feet and visibility is 5 miles or more, this information is optional), obstructions to vision, temperature, dewpoint (if available), wind direction (magnetic) and velocity, altimeter setting, other pertinent remarks, instrument approach, and runways in use is continuously transmitted on the voice feature of the VOR/VORTAC located on or near the airport or on a particular, separate VHF/UHF frequency.

Pilots of arriving aircraft are expected to tune into ATIS to get the just-mentioned information plus the appropriate approach control frequencies to be used. You'll also be expected to listen to ATIS before taxiing at an ATIS airport.

At the beginning and end of each broadcast, you'll be reminded that the information given is (was), for example, "Information Delta." When the information changes (the wind shifts, etc.) the broadcast data will be given as "Information Echo."

Let Clearance Delivery, Ground Control, or Approach Control (as applicable) know that you have "Information Delta" (or the latest information) upon *initial* contact.

3. *Clearance Delivery*—This is a separate frequency used for pretaxi clearances, either VFR or IFR. At busy airports, contact Clearance Delivery after listening to ATIS. Clearance Delivery will give you frequencies and instructions necessary to depart the busy terminal area. After you have the information given by CD and read it back correctly, you'll be told to change to the ground control frequency for taxi instructions.

4. *Ground Control*—Regulates traffic moving on taxiways and the runways not being used for takeoffs and landings. (Ground Control will coordinate with the tower if you have to cross a "hot," or active, runway.) It is on a different frequency than that of

Figure 21-14. Facilities near Huntsville. (1) The Capshaw radio beacon — indentification CWH, frequency 350 kHz. The line under the "350" indicates that there is no voice facility on that frequency. (2) The Rocket VORTAC site and its frequency box. (3) The airport information for the Huntsville International — Carl Jones Field. The frequency for the tower is 127.6 MHz; the frequency for the Automatic Terminal Information Service (ATIS, just discussed) is 121.25 MHz. The airport elevation is 630 feet above mean sea level (MSL), it has lights, the longest runway is 10,000 feet, and there's a UNICOM on the airport (122.95 MHz). (4) The boundaries of the 2,000- to 4,600-foot (MSL) portion of the Class C airspace (Class C airspace extends from the airport to the outer circle). Note that the smaller portion of the airspace, east of the airport, has altitude limits of 2,400–4,600 feet MSL. There is a wildlife refuge south and southwest of the airport, and you are expected to remain at least 2,000 feet above the surface in such an area.

the tower because you can imagine what radio clutter would result if some pilots were asking for taxi direction to Ace Flying Service while others were calling in for landing instructions.

For simplification and summary of local (tower) and Ground Control duties, note that local control has jurisdiction of aircraft in the process of landing and taking off. This includes aircraft while in the pattern and on the active runway. Ground Control is used for ground traffic on the airport *other than on the active runway during the takeoff or landing process.* The ground controller will be in the tower

beside the local controller. (And in some cases the same person may talk to you in both capacities, but on a different frequency, of course.)

5. *Approach/Departure Control* — The busier controlled airports have another position called "Approach/Departure Control." This may be a radar or nonradar setup. For a nonradar setup, the approach controller is in the glassed-in portion of the tower with the other two positions. The primary duty is to coordinate IFR traffic approaching the control zone, but the controller may coordinate IFR and VFR traffic during marginal VFR conditions as

Figure 21-15. Class B airspace at St. Louis Lambert Field. The heavier-lined circles are the boundaries of the various altitude limits. The thin-lined circle ("Mode C, 30 NM") is the outer limit of the 10 miles of "veil" around the airspace with the veil extending *generally* from a 20-NM to a 30-NM radius from the major airport (1). You may *not* enter Class B airspace without an air traffic control clearance but may fly in and through the veil portion without talking to anyone, as long as your airplane has an operating transponder with altitude reporting capabilities. (More about transponder operation later in the chapter.)

The Class B airspace is in the form of an inverted wedding cake, with some modifications as necessary for expediting traffic.

The "box" around the St. Louis area (2) indicates that there is an area chart with more details available (one inch equals 250,000 inches).

well as coordinating VFR traffic at busy terminals, even in CAVU (ceiling and visibility unlimited) conditions. The circled "R"s in Figure 21-13 indicate that Huntsville has radar.

Approach/departure controllers using radar are usually in an IFR room that is located in the tower building but not necessarily in the glassed-in portion. Approach controllers work directly with the tower and their duties are rotated between tower and IFR room positions.

Class C Airspace

Figure 21-14 shows the Class C airspace at and around the Huntsville International Airport. You must establish two-way radio communications with ATC (approach control or other required facilities) before entering Class C airspace.

You may not have a chance to enter Class C airspace until after getting your private certificate, but you should have some idea of the procedure for entering.

Being in Class C airspace or being radar vectored *does not relieve you of the responsibility to avoid other traffic. Also, keep in mind that the radar controller may not know the weather conditions in your vicinity and could vector you into conditions where visual references would be lost.* You are responsible for maintaining visual flight conditions and must notify the controller of a marginal situation. Remember that when you are solo you are the pilot in command. The final responsibility for safety is yours. ATC people and FSS personnel are conscientious, but they can make mistakes. Don't hesitate to speak up or deviate from their instructions if it looks as if your safety is involved. Keep them posted on your plans, though. Figure 21-15 is a look at *Class B* airspace.

When the weather is less than that required for VFR operations in Class B, C, and D airspace (*see* Figure 21-12 again), you, as a VFR pilot, may request and be given a clearance to enter, leave, or operate within it. This, of course, depends on traffic and non-delay of IFR operations (Special VFR—§91.157) *and is not available to student or sport pilots* (14 CFR §§61.89 and 61.315). You'll get a clearance from a tower, or if it is Class E (without a tower), a clearance may be obtained from an FSS, the nearest tower, or an Air Traffic Control Center. The minimum visibility requirements are 1 mile flight visibility for operations in the control zone and 1 mile ground visibility for takeoffs and landings. You'll stay clear of clouds, but remember that you might end up so low that you fracture the FAR concerning clearance from ground objects. Only instrument-rated pilots and IFR-equipped airplanes can get a Special VFR clearance at night.

Some airports have too much traffic to allow Special VFR, and they have a notation on the sectional chart to this effect (NO SVFR) next to the airport name box (*see* item 3 in Figure 21-15).

The Special VFR clearance may allow you to legally get into an airport as the weather is deteriorating, but to use it to get out in marginal conditions on a VFR flight should be rejected. You could get into worse weather and lose control of the airplane. Wait for better weather before departing; spend that ground time studying for the instrument rating, so that you can safely use more and more of the air traffic control facilities as you get experience.

Suppose you are approaching Huntsville from the northwest and plan to land at Huntsville International Airport (Figure 21-14):

1. Listen to *ATIS* to get the information on active runway(s), wind, and other information as covered earlier (item 2, Figure 21-13).
2. *Contact Approach Control* (item 5, Figure 21-13) on one of the frequencies cited in the ATIS or as shown in the *Airport/Facility Directory*. Note that since you are approaching from the northwest (*from about 315°*), the frequency to be used is 118.05 MHz, since you are approaching in the Huntsville sector between 180° and 359°. Tell them your position, altitude, type of aircraft, that you are landing at Huntsville International, and have *"Information Foxtrot"* (or whatever). If you have a transponder, they will have you select a discrete code (you'll be the only one using it at this particular time), which you will dial in. (*See* Figure 21-20 and accompanying text about transponder operation.)
3. The *tower* (item 1, Figure 21-13) is to be contacted when Approach Control wants to hand you over and, as you can see from Figure 21-13, the frequency is 127.6 MHz. After landing, you will be asked to switch to *Ground Control after* clearing the active runway (item 4, Figure 21-13). You can ask for taxi directions if you are new to the airport. The sample cross-country in Chapter 24 will go through the steps of approaching, landing, and taxiing at Huntsville International (it's one of the two stops) plus the steps required for getting out and on your way again. But now let's take a quick look at your probable steps in approaching and leaving a busy airport.

Approaching

1. *ATIS*—Listen and get the pertinent information.
2. *Approach Control*—Call Approach Control at about 20 miles out after you have that information, giving your position, altitude, and type of aircraft

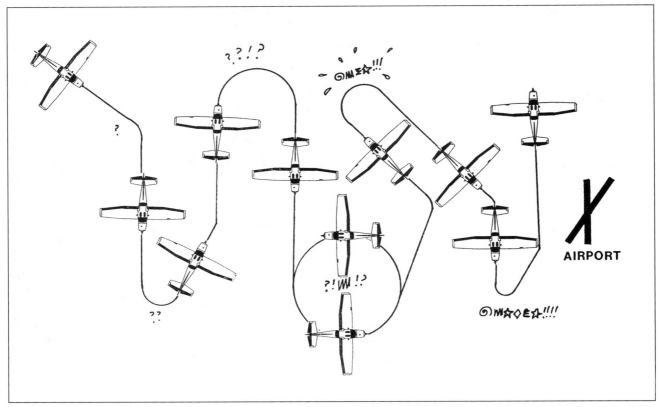

Figure 21-16. Sometimes it appears as if approach control is trying to help you build flying time, or gain meaningful aeronautical experience. (There are other airplanes out there to be considered.)

Figure 21-17. Elevation (side) view of the Class A, B, C, D, E, and G airspace. (The United States does not have a Class F airspace as do other countries.) The Class G airspace (shaded) on the left side of the illustration, extending up to 14,500 feet MSL, is uncontrolled airspace in the western United States. (From the *Aeronautical Information Manual*)

Airspace Features	Class A	Class B	Class C	Class D	Class E	Class G
Operations Permitted	IFR	IFR and VFR	IFR and VFR	IFR and VFR	IFR and VFR	IFR and VFR
Entry Prerequisites	ATC clearance	ATC clearance	ATC clearance for IFR. Radio contact for all.	ATC clearance for IFR. Radio contact for all.	ATC clearance for IFR. Radio contact for all IFR.	None
Minimum Pilot Qualifications	Instrument rating	Private or student certificate	Student certificate	Student certificate	Student certificate	Student certificate
Two-way Radio Communications	Yes	Yes	Yes	Yes	Yes for IFR	No
VFR Minimum Visibility	N/A	3 statute miles	3 statute miles	3 statute miles	*3 statute miles	**1 statute mile
VFR Minimum Distance from Clouds	N/A	Clear of clouds	500' below, 1,000' above, and 2,000' horizontal	500' below, 1,000' above, and 2,000' horizontal	*500' below, 1,000' above, and 2,000' horizontal	**500' below, 1,000' above, and 2,000' horizontal
Aircraft Separation	All	All	IFR, SVFR, and runway ops	IFR, SVFR, and runway ops	IFR and SVFR	None
Conflict Resolution	N/A	N/A	Between IFR and VFR ops	No	No	No
Traffic Advisories	N/A	N/A	Yes	Workload permitting	Workload permitting	Workload permitting
Safety Advisories	Yes	Yes	Yes	Yes	Yes	Yes

* Different visibility minima and distance cloud requirements exist for operations above 10,000' MSL

**Different visibility minima and distance from cloud requirements exist for night operations, operations above 10,000' MSL, and operations below 1,200' AGL.

Figure 21-18. A summary of the airspace classes and the requirements and limitations of each. There is no Class F airspace in the United States as found in other countries. (Courtesy of Phyllis Duncan, *FAA Aviation News*)

(plus "Information Delta," etc.). They may have you squawk a certain transponder code.

3. *Tower*—Contact the tower at Approach Control's instructions.

4. *Ground Control*—Contact Ground Control after clearing the active runway, at the tower's instructions.

Departing

1. *ATIS*—Get the information on runways in use, wind, etc.

2. *Clearance Delivery*—Contact Clearance Delivery and tell them you have "Foxtrot" or whatever. Get departure instructions, transponder "squawk," and Departure Control frequency. Write it down.

3. *Ground Control*—Tell them your position on the airport and request taxi clearance.

4. *Tower*—When you're ready for takeoff, say so and give your full aircraft number.

5. *Departure Control*—Contact Departure Control when told to by the tower, using the frequency given by Clearance Delivery.

If you are going back the way you came, note that the Departure Control frequency is the same as you used with Approach Control on the way into the airport. Note that coming *from* or departing *to* the northwest

the frequency is 118.05 MHz for Huntsville (Figure 21-13).

Sometimes it seems that the Approach Control is vectoring as shown in Figure 21-16.

Figure 21-17 is a side view of the various classes of airspace just discussed, plus Class A (above 18,000 feet MSL and not likely a factor for you as a student or private pilot just yet) and Class G (uncontrolled airspace, found only below 700 feet or 1,200 feet in most of the eastern portions of the continental 48 states).

Note that Class B airspace (the top view shown in Figure 21-15) may be multi-layered; Class C is two-layered and Class D is a cylinder with some extensions for approaches.

Figure 21-18 shows the requirements and limitations of the various classes of airspace just discussed.

Figure 21-19 shows the basic visual flight rules (VFR) minimums as shown in 14 CFR Part 91.

Transponder

Basically the transponder is a radar "transceiver" that picks up interrogations of the Air Traffic Control radar beacon systems and transmits or "replies." The two modes of operational types of equipment you'll be encountering are "A" (which is a straight reply type) and "C" (which replies and, through special encoding

Airspace	Flight Visibility	Distance from Clouds
Class A	Not Applicable	Not Applicable
Class B	3 statute miles	Clear of Clouds
Class C	3 statute miles	500 feet below 1,000 feet above 2,000 feet horizontal
Class D	3 statute miles	500 feet below 1,000 feet above 2,000 feet horizontal
Class E Less than 10,000 feet MSL	3 statute miles	500 feet below 1,000 feet above 2,000 feet horizontal
At or above 10,000 feet MSL	5 statue miles	1,000 feet below 1,000 feet above 1 statute mile horizontal
Class G 1,200 feet or less above the surface (regardless of MSL altitude)		
Day, except as provided in section 91.155(b)	1 statute mile	Clear of clouds
Night, except as provided in section 91.155(b)	3 statute miles	500 feet below 1,000 feet above 2,000 feet horizontal
More than 1,200 feet above the surface but less than 10,000 feet MSL Day	1 statute mile	500 feet below 1,000 feet above 2,000 feet horizontal
Night	3 statute miles	500 feet below 1,000 feet above 2,000 feet horizontal
More than 1,200 feet above the surface and at or above 10,000 feet MSL	5 statute miles	1,000 feet below 1,000 feet above 1 statute mile horizontal

Figure 21-19. VFR visibilities and cloud clearances for the various classes of airspace (Part 91). Student pilots are further limited to 3 miles (day) and 5 miles (night), even in Class G airspace. Also *see* 14 CFR §§91.155 and 61.89.

altimeter equipment, allows the ground controller to read off your altitude on the radarscope). Figure 21-20 shows a transponder control panel.

The IDENT selection in Figure 21-20 makes an airplane stand out on the controller's radarscope and is used momentarily to identify one target among many to ATC. The reply lamp flashes when the transponder replies to each interrogation from the ground station.

Primary radar depends on the reflection and return of its impulses; the transponder in the airplane is triggered by these impulses and, in effect, boosts them back for a better target indication on the ground radar.

For VFR flying (and when not in voice contact with a radar facility) you would set up 1200 on the transponder and present a clearer target as you fly—for *their* traffic-avoidance purposes.

For instance, if you were lost but in contact with an FSS or other nonradar FAA facility, they would probably have you switch frequencies to talk to a radar-equipped facility that would ask you to "squawk" a certain setting on your transponder. They could readily locate you among the many targets and vector you to an airport.

The emergency code is 7700; if you're in bad trouble in flight, this setting will get the attention of every radar facility in the area. (It's best to talk to the people, but if you can't, 7700 will get you help.) The lost communications code, used primarily for IFR problems, is 7600. There's even a code you'd use if someone is hijacking your Cessna 152, or whatever. Your instructor will discuss and demonstrate the use of the transponder (if the airplane has one) before you go solo cross-country.

The transponder is "line of sight" like the VOR and DME.

A Mode C transponder (a transponder that also gives altitude information to Air Traffic Control [ATC]) is required to fly in the "veil" of Class B airspace as noted earlier. They are also required when operating above the altitude of the ceilings and within the lateral boundaries of Class B or Class C airspace. So looking at Figure 21-14, if you want to fly *over* the Huntsville Class C airspace (above 4,600 feet MSL) or if you needed to fly *over* the St. Louis Class B airspace (above 8,000 feet MSL—*see* Figure 21-15), you have to be using a Mode C even though you are not actually penetrating that particular airspace. In addition, at an altitude at or above 10,000 feet MSL in the 48 continental United States, a *working* Mode C is required.

Light Signals

There may be a time when the airplane's radio is inoperative and you have to land at a controlled airport. You should know the light signals used by the control tower for planes not equipped with radio. The tower controller uses a portable light and is able to single out a particular aircraft for instructions. The signals are shown in Figure 21-21.

Figure 21-20. Transponder control panel. (Courtesy of Bendix/King Avionics Division)

Visual Approach Slope Indicator (VASI)

The VASI is located at some airports to provide a visual light path within the approach zone; the two-light system is set at 3°, although this may be higher at some airports to give proper obstacle clearance.

The simplest VASI system has two-light systems at different distances on the sides of the runway near the approach end with the glide slope reference line being between the two light units.

Each unit projects a beam of light with a white color in the upper part and a red color in the lower part. The indications would be:

Above glide slope	White	White
	White	White
On glide slope	Red	Red
	White	White
Below glide slope	Red	Red
	Red	Red

Some smaller airports have two units on the left side of the runway only.

When on the proper glide slope, the airplane in the system described here is in effect overshooting the bars at the threshold and undershooting the bars farther down. You will see the upper half (white) of the closer bars and the lower half (red) of the far set.

VASI can normally be seen from 3 to 5 miles out on the final approach.

The *AIM* gives details on the more complex VASI systems in use.

Color and Type of Signal	Movement of Vehicles, Equipment and Personnel	Aircraft on the Ground	Aircraft in Flight
Steady green	Cleared to cross, proceed or go	Cleared for takeoff	Cleared to land
Flashing green	Not applicable	Cleared for taxi	Return for landing (to be followed by steady green at the proper time)
Steady red	STOP	STOP	Give way to other aircraft and continue circling
Flashing red	Clear the taxiway/runway	Taxi clear of the runway in use	Airport unsafe, do not land
Flashing white	Return to starting point on airport	Return to starting point on airport	Not applicable
Alternating red and green	Exercise extreme caution	Exercise extreme caution	Exercise extreme caution

Figure 21-21. The light signals used by local control.

Emergency Locator Transmitter (ELT)

The ELT is required by Federal Aviation Regulations for all aircraft *except* those training within a 50-mile radius of the airport used for that training, flight test aircraft, new aircraft being ferried, and other special uses listed in 14 CFR §91.207. It's likely that the airplane you are using now has one, and the instructor may point out its location and antenna. (It may be so located in the airplane that the antenna is the only part you can see without removing panels.)

Basically, an ELT is a self-contained two-frequency transmitter with its own battery power. An impact resulting in 5 g's or more (or 5 times the acceleration of gravity) activates the unit, which automatically starts transmitting on 121.5 MHz (civilian international distress frequency) and 243.0 MHz (military).

The ELT, being VHF like the VOR, is line of sight and has the same advantages and disadvantages of that frequency range.

The ELT is designed to aid in locating downed airplanes, and pilots in flight often turn their receiver to 121.5 to check for an ELT signal. If one is heard, the nearest FAA facility should be advised so that a search for the transmitter can be started. ELTs may be triggered by hard landings or lightning strikes or in airplanes with a need for attention while just quietly sitting on a ramp or hangar. It sets off quite a frustrating search when a signal is heard in the midst of 100 or more tied-down aircraft (with many of the owners out of town with the keys).

The sets usually have three switch settings:
1. ON—activates the transmitter immediately. It's used for testing or if the "g" function is not working. The pilot may activate it manually in an emergency such as a "soft" landing in an inaccessible spot when rescue is needed.
2. ARM—is the normal setting, which would start the signals under an impact.
3. OFF—is used for shipping and storing (and after the St. Bernard with the keg gets there).

An ELT is tested *only* within the first 5 minutes past the hour and for only three audio sweeps, so that a massive Search and Rescue effort is not launched.

14 CFR §91.207 also covers replacement requirements of the batteries in an ELT.

Global Positioning System — GPS

The GPS is a United States satellite-based radio navigational, positioning, and time transfer system operated by the Department of Defense. GPS provides highly accurate position and velocity information and precise time on a continual global basis to users who are properly equipped, and it is unaffected by weather.

GPS is based on ranging and triangulation from a group of satellites in space that act as precise reference points. The GPS receiver measures distance from a satellite using the travel time of a radio signal (at approximately 186,000 statute miles per second). Each satellite has its own code, and the receiver puts those signals together to obtain a location. (The system might be considered a 21st century version of celestial navigation.)

The GPS constellation of 30 satellites is designed so that a minimum of five satellites are always observable by a user anywhere on earth. The receiver uses data from a minimum of four satellites above the mask angle (the lowest angle above the horizon at which it can use a satellite).

The GPS receiver needs at least four satellites to yield a three-dimensional position (latitude, longitude, and altitude) and time solution. The GPS receiver computes navigational values such as distance and bearing to a waypoint and groundspeed by using the aircraft's known latitude/longitude and references these to a database built into the receiver.

Your instructor will show you the basics of piloting and simple radio navigation during your training as a student, and he will emphasize the use of the sectional chart with radio navigation as a back-up. You may decide to get a GPS receiver to aid in those cross-countries after you get the sport or private certificate.

LAHSO

This sounds like something a cowboy would use for capturing livestock, but if you are going into an airport with a control tower, you should be aware of "Land and Hold Short Operations." These operations include landing and holding short of an intersecting runway, an intersecting taxiway, or some other designated point on a runway other than an intersecting runway or taxiway (Figure 21-22).

At controlled airports, air traffic may clear a pilot to land and hold short. You may accept such a clearance provided that you determine that the aircraft can safely land and stop within the Available Landing Distance (ALD). ALD data may be found in the special notices section of the *Airport/Facility Directory*.

Student pilots or pilots not familiar with LAHSO should not participate in the program.

The pilot in command has the final authority to accept or decline any land and hold short clearance. The safety and operation of the aircraft remain the responsibility of the pilot. Pilots are expected to decline a LAHSO clearance if they determine it will compromise safety.

While as a student pilot you aren't to participate in LAHSO, you should be aware of the program so you won't be caught by surprise after you get that pilot certificate and fly into those large, controlled airports in your personal jet.

Figure 21-22. Holding patterns for Land and Hold Short Operations (LAHSO). (From the *Aeronautical Information Manual*)

22

Weather Information

You're well ahead of the student pilots of pre-TV days as far as weather knowledge is concerned because you've been seeing the frontal systems and weather patterns on your screen every day. For instance, you know of the existence of high- and low-pressure areas and warm and cold fronts and the effects of circulation, but maybe a little review is in order.

Weather Patterns

Pressure

The standard sea level pressure is 29.92 inches of mercury (abbreviated Hg). The approximate drop in pressure is about 1 inch of mercury per 1,000 feet of altitude. (This is valid up to about 10,000 feet; the decrease in pressure is less as the altitude increases. In the 18,000- to 20,000-foot levels, for instance, the drop in pressure is only about 0.60 inch per thousand feet.)

The pressure may also be given in millibars, and at standard sea level conditions, the value is 1,013.2 millibars (a millibar is a unit of pressure based on the metric system). Since the standard pressure in inches of mercury is 29.92, it would follow that 1 inch of mercury pressure is equal to about 34 millibars—if you should need to convert from one to the other system. In the United States the altimeter settings are given in inches of mercury. Although the pressure is also given in millibars on the hourly sequence reports, it is not reported on the continuous weather *broadcasts*.

Standard sea level pressure may be given in the following ways: (1) 29.92 inches of mercury, (2) 1,013.2 millibars (also called "hectoPascals"), (3) 14.7 pounds per square inch, or (4) 2,116 pounds per square foot.

Pressure Areas

If the pressure stayed the same everywhere, the weather wouldn't be very interesting—and people would have a hard time making conversation.

Figure 22-1 shows the circulation around high- and low-pressure systems in the Northern Hemisphere. The opposite circulation occurs in the Southern Hemisphere; the earth's rotation (sometimes called the Coriolis force) causes this.

A high-pressure area *usually* means good weather (except for the circulation problem just covered), and low-pressure *usually* means bad weather, but you'll want to get more information from all possible sources (which is the purpose of the last part of this chapter). An elongated high-pressure area is a "ridge"; the equivalent low-pressure shape is a "trough."

Frontal Systems

A front is defined as a "zone of transition between two air masses of different densities."

The National Weather Service publishes charts of observed weather, and Figure 22-2 shows the symbols used to depict the various types of fronts (plus squall lines) on the charts.

You may set up your own memory aids to remember the symbols (cold is blue and sharp, etc.).

Cold Front

The cold front is usually characterized by a comparatively narrow weather band and by more violent weather than is associated with the warm front. The worst part of the cold-front weather is normally less than 100 miles from beginning to end. Cumulus (vertically developed clouds), heavy precipitation, and turbulence are usually associated with it. Fast-moving cold fronts may have squall lines, or a line of thunderstorms, 50 to 300 miles ahead and roughly parallel to the front. Your move, if encountering a squall line, is to get out of its area as expeditiously as possible.

After the cold-front passage there will usually be rapid clearing, with lower temperatures and strong gusty winds on the surface; this applies particularly to a fast-moving cold front. The wind will shift from the southwest or the west to come from the northwest or north (about a 90° wind shift) as the front passes.

Figure 22-3 shows the circulation about a frontal system. Note that the "typical" system is "pivoting" around a low-pressure system.

Isobars are lines joining points of equal pressure. The closer the isobars are together the steeper the pressure gradient and the stronger the winds in that area. You might keep this in mind when you look at a surface weather chart in a Weather Service Office.

The cold front moves faster than the warm front associated with the system, which can lead to a situation known as an occlusion (which will be covered later).

Figure 22-4 shows the cross section of an "average" cold front as it would appear if you sliced through the front as shown by A-A in Figure 22-3. (You are looking the way the arrows are pointing.)

The average cold front moves at a speed of 15–20 K but may under extreme conditions move at 50 K or more. It seems to move at a much higher speed than that if you happen to be in a 90-K trainer trying to outrun it.

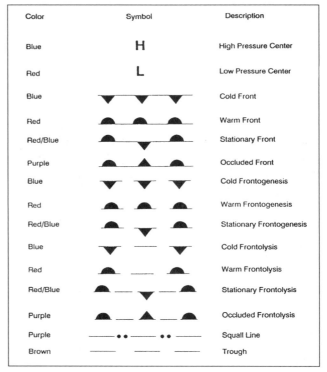

Figure 22-2. Front symbols used on a weather chart.

Figure 22-1. High- and low-pressure areas and circulation. While most of our weather is considered to be caused by frontal systems, circulation can bring warm, moist air into cool areas, causing fog, low stratus clouds, and precipitation. The Coriolis force, a result of the earth's rotation, causes deflection of the winds to the right in the Northern Hemisphere (and finally parallel to the isobars) at altitudes out of surface friction effects. The Coriolis force is directly proportional to the wind speed.

Figure 22-3. Circulation in the vicinity of a frontal system.

Warm Front

The warm front usually produces a much wider band of weather consisting of stratus-type clouds, with widespread areas of low ceilings, rain, and fog. However, if the warm air is unstable, cumulus-type clouds and thunderstorms may be found in the stratus layer. Many instrument pilots have had unexpected excitement flying through what they thought was going to be stable, smooth air. This, of course, is only of academic interest to you as a student pilot, since one of your primary aims is to avoid getting within *any* type of cloud.

The warm front usually moves at about one-half the speed of the cold front and this, plus the wider spread weather area, can sometimes mean a number of days when the birds are walking at your airport.

Figure 22-5 shows the cross section of an "average" warm front as indicated by the slice B-B in Figure 22-3.

While you won't be planning on flying within the clouds, the fall or wintertime warm fronts may pose problems in addition to low ceilings, as can be seen by Figure 22-6.

You can be flying well below the cloud level and suddenly encounter freezing rain. It's a very serious situation because ice can cover the windshield (and the entire airplane) in a very short time. A student pilot has no business flying if there is any possibility of freezing rain. (And this also applies for private and commercial pilots.) If you start running into freezing rain, get back out of the area as quickly as possible. You may find that climbing to just below the clouds will keep you in air that is warm enough that the rain hasn't started to freeze. Remember, though, that you may have to go back down through the freezing levels for landing, which can be a hazardous operation.

Occluded Front

The occluded front generally contains weather of both warm and cold fronts. Since the cold front moves faster than the warm front, it often catches up with the warm front. The occluded front contains all the disadvantages of the two types, with widespread stratus, low ceilings and poor visibilities with build-up, and thunderstorms within the frontal area. Figure 22-7 shows the occluded front.

Figure 22-8 shows the cross section of an occluded front as indicated by C-C in Figure 22-7. There are two types of occlusions, and Figure 22-8 shows the warm type. If the air in front of the system is colder (and denser) than the air behind the cold front overtaking the warm front, it will move up over the cold air as shown. Most of the weather will be found ahead of the surface front.

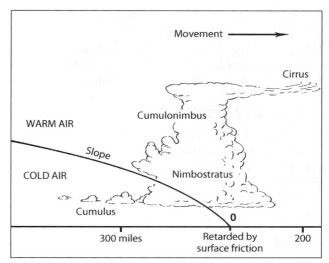

Figure 22-4. Cross section of a typical cold front. The slope varies from 1:50 to 1:150 and averages about 1:80.

Figure 22-5. Cross section of a typical warm front with the warm air stable. The slope of the warm front may vary from 1:50 to 1:200, the average being about 1:100.

Figure 22-6. Freezing rain associated with a warm front.

The cold-type occlusion is a situation in which the air behind the cold front is colder than that ahead of the system. The colder air slides under the cool air as shown by Figure 22-9. Most of the weather for this type of occlusion will be found near the surface front.

Stationary Front

The stationary front is so named because it is stationary, which makes pretty good sense when you stop to think about it. The weather associated with the stationary front is similar to that found in a warm front but usually not as intense. The problem is that the bad weather hangs around until the front moves out or dissipates.

Cloud Types

In discussing the weather indicated on the weather map, it would be well to take a general look at cloud types you'll expect to encounter when flying.

Clouds are broken down into four families: high, middle, and low clouds and clouds with large vertical development. The clouds are further described as to their form and appearance. The puffy or billowy-type clouds are "cumulus," the layered types are "stratus." The term "nimbo" (rain cloud) is added to clouds that would be expected to produce precipitation.

Figure 22-10 shows some representative types of clouds.

Normally, when flying near clouds of stratus-type formation, you would expect fairly smooth air. Cumulus clouds by their very nature are the product of air conditions that indicate the presence of vertical currents.

Clouds are composed of minute ice crystals or water droplets and are the result of moist air being cooled to the point of condensation. The high clouds (cirrus, cirrostratus, and cirrocumulus) are composed of extremely fine ice crystals. The biggest puzzle to the average person is that, if they are composed of ice, why don't they fall? For that matter, since the lower clouds are composed of water droplets, why don't they fall also? The answer is, of course, that the moisture is comparatively less dense than the ambient air. When the water droplets become a certain size, rain results (or snow or sleet, depending on the conditions). Hail is a form of precipitation associated with cumulonimbus-type clouds and is the result of rain being lifted by vertical currents until it reaches an altitude where it freezes and is carried downward again to gain more moisture; the cycle or recirculation may be repeated, giving the larger hailstones their characteristic "layers," or strata.

Clouds may be composed of supercooled moisture, and the impact of your airplane on these particles causes them to immediately freeze on the airplane. (Stay out of *any* clouds until you get that instrument rating later.)

Figure 22-8. A warm-type occlusion.

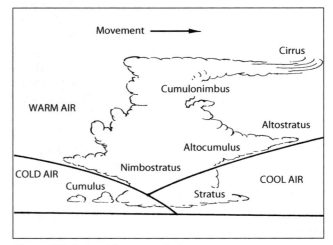

Figure 22-9. A cold-type occlusion.

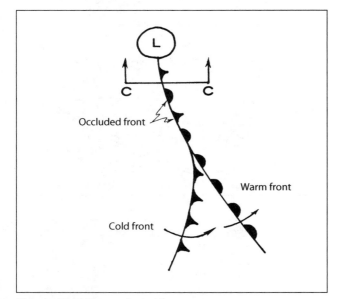

Figure 22-7. The occluded front.

As discussed, clouds are formed by moist air being cooled to the point of condensation, and this leads to the subject of lapse rates.

For air, the dry adiabatic lapse rate is $5\frac{1}{2}°$F per thousand feet. (Adiabatic describes a process during which no heat is withdrawn or added to the system or body concerned.) The normal lapse rate of "average" air is $3\frac{1}{2}°$F (2°C). The moist adiabatic lapse rate is produced by convection in a saturated atmosphere such as within a cumulus cloud. At high temperatures it will be in the vicinity of $4-5°$F. The dewpoint lapse rate is about 1°F per thousand feet.

For cumulus-type clouds that are formed by surface heating, the base of the clouds may be estimated by the rate at which the dry lapse rate "catches" the dewpoint. (Dry lapse rate is 5.4°F and dewpoint drop is 1°F per thousand, so the temperature is dropping 4.4° faster than the dewpoint per thousand feet.) Assume the surface temperature is 76°F and the dewpoint 58°F, a difference of 18°F. Dividing this number by 4.4, you find that the temperature and dewpoint make connections at about 4,000 feet—the approximate base of the clouds. This only works for the type of cloud formed by surface heating.

Hazards to Flight

Freezing rain and hail were briefly covered earlier, but you'll encounter other weather problems as you gain flying experience.

Thunderstorms

Thunderstorms are a triple threat: (1) There are clouds, so an inexperienced or noninstrument-rated pilot could lose control because of loss of outside references, but that's usually the least of the problems because of (2) the extreme turbulence that could cause loss of control by even the most experienced instrument pilot, as well as the possibility of the airplane being overstressed and coming apart, and (3) there is danger of aircraft structural icing and hail encounters.

The turbulence may also be so great that your head is being jolted so fast and hard that the instruments become difficult or impossible to read. It was once noted that an "average" thunderstorm (whatever that is) was continually releasing the energy of 50 Hiroshima-type nuclear weapons. Whether this was ever confirmed is not known, but most people wouldn't like to fly into the energy of *one* Hiroshima-type bomb.

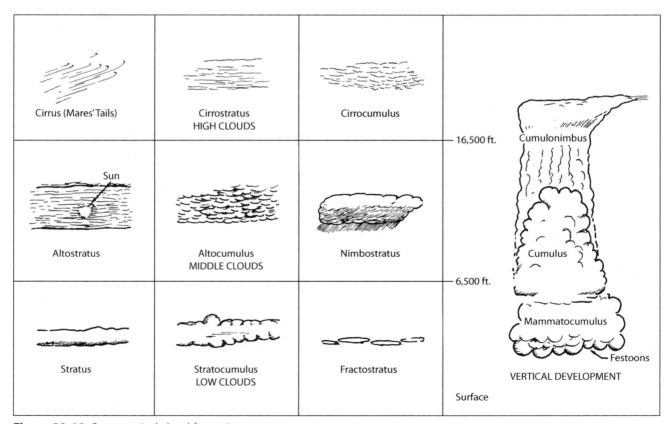

Figure 22-10. Some typical cloud formations.

Your lifetime project will be to avoid thunderstorms—whether you have an instrument rating or not. They can cause airliners to crash, and smaller aircraft could be pulled apart and *then* crash—the end product being the same.

Take a look at an "average" thunderstorm from start to finish: There are generally three stages, as noted by the book *Aviation Weather*:

1. *Cumulus stage*—The thunderstorm begins as a cumulus cloud. An updraft is the key part of the thunderstorm. The cumulus may be growing at a rate of 3,000 feet per minute, and you won't be able to outclimb it in a light aircraft to go over the top.

   The water droplets at this stage are small but are lifted past the freezing level, so icing could be a problem. As the raindrops get bigger, they fall and the rain creates a cold downdraft coexisting with the updrafts. When this occurs, the thunderstorm has entered the second stage.

2. *Mature stage*—When precipitation starts falling out of the base, the mature stage is reached. The downdraft may exceed 2,500 feet per minute; it spreads outward at the surface and may be felt there as the "first gust." Meanwhile, updrafts may be moving up at 6,000 feet per minute, and the shear area with its turbulence at the edge of these divergent drafts is better imagined than experienced.

   All thunderstorm hazards are worse during the mature stage.

3. *Dissipating stage*—Don't get the idea that the dissipating stage means that all is fine for penetration. This stage is indicated by the anvil head (Figure 22-10) and is now mostly downdrafts. However, since there is no defined line between the stages, the anvil may be seen while there are still updrafts, and hail may fall out of the anvil into the clear air below. A rule of thumb would be to stay at least 10 miles away from a thunderstorm.

Don't fly under a thunderstorm. Hail and turbulence could cause bad problems. It looks clear under there and you can see 15 miles, but go around anyway, giving yourself plenty of distance from it (at least 10 miles).

Remember again that squall lines are lines of thunderstorms, multiplying the problems.

Icing

Freezing rain or drizzle is the only structural icing you should get into "legally" as a student pilot or noninstrument-rated pilot. You are flying along "in the clear" (under the clouds) in rain when ice begins collecting on the airplane; you'll get out of it as soon as possible, perhaps climbing to just below the clouds and/or making a 180° turn as noted earlier.

You won't get the other types of structural icing unless you are in the clouds and, unless you have an instrument rating, you shouldn't be in clouds. Maybe you will inadvertently get into a cloud when on a cross-country in deteriorating weather and will be in there as long as it takes to make a 180° turn, but your job won't be to identify what type of ice is being picked up; you'll want to get back out of the cloud as safely and expeditiously as possible (Chapter 15).

As a private pilot, after getting back out and wiping those sweaty palms, you could say to your passenger(s), "We picked up some rime (or clear) ice, back there." This could tend to establish your credentials as a "weather" pro to them, but that's about all.

Clear ice—Formed by large droplets of moisture such as that found in rain or cumuliform clouds. It is hard and glossy and difficult to remove. It's the type of ice you'd find in ice cubes—solid.

Rime ice—Formed by small droplets such as those found in stratiform clouds or drizzle. There's air trapped in the ice, and its appearance is close to that of the ice forming on the trays or the inside walls of a freezer. It's comparatively easy to remove. You may feel tempted later, when flying IFR, to ask that particularly obnoxious passenger (the one who keeps asking, "Where are we?") to go out and remove it—in flight.

Frost

You've left the airplane tied down in the fall or winter and find very early in the morning that it is covered with a very thin layer of frost. You figure that the weight of the frost is certainly negligible, and it's so extremely thin that there will be no problems aerodynamically, so you load up everybody and go—for a while. You find yourself (and airplane) roaring down the street of a housing development off the far end of the runway. (Housing developments are always built in that location immediately after the runway is completed.) After untangling the airplane from fences and playground equipment (fortunately nobody was out yet) and surveying the damage and the problems of getting the airplane back for repair, you wonder if maybe that little frost hasn't cost you a lot of money.

Even thin frost disrupts the airflow over the wings and degrades lift. Don't take off with frost on the wings or horizontal tail surfaces; you may not get off.

Fog

While the other hazards are more readily avoided, fog can be one of the greatest dangers to any pilot because it may rapidly cover wide areas and develop while you are airborne and are concentrating on other matters. As you do more night flying, fog will become a factor to be very seriously considered under certain meteorological conditions.

Fog, according to FAA and Weather Service publications, is a surface-based cloud of either water droplets or ice crystals. Fog may form by cooling air to its dewpoint or by adding moisture to air near the ground.

Radiation fog—A shallower fog; one type is called "ground fog." You'll see ground fog from the air as a gray-white sea with taller objects sticking up through it. The top half of the hangar and the wind sock with towers may be quite visible, but the runway and surrounding area are covered. This fog usually occurs at night or in early morning with a clear sky, little or no wind, and a small temperature–dewpoint spread. The lack of overcast allows the ground to lose heat; the cooler (or cold) ground cools the highly moist air next to it, lowering the temperature to the dewpoint, and visible moisture is formed.

In addition, nuclei from industrial exhausts hasten the production of fog; an airport in a river bottom or on a lake shore near industrial emissions usually has a higher number of mornings with ground conditions of zero visibility. This fog will usually burn off before noon on clear days.

Wind may disperse the fog or increase its depth, depending on the velocity.

Radiation fog is formed over land because land cools rapidly as compared to water.

If you are shooting landings and the runway lights begin to have haloes (at night) or the runway or other ground objects start becoming slightly less distinct in outline, you'd better consider terminating the flight early, unless you have a good alternate airport in mind.

Advection fog—Formed when moist air moves over colder ground or water. If you are flying in the west coast area of the United States, you are well aware of how "sea fog" can form and move inland at times. Wind may also move fog up into the United States from the Gulf of Mexico during the winter.

These fogs look alike from the air, but advection fog may be found under an overcast, unlike radiation fog. If you ever have to race advection fog to an airport, you'll see how fast it can spread.

Upslope fog—When moist air is moved up a slope, cooling it, this type of fog is formed. The Sewanee (Tenn.) Airport, the point of origin for the example cross-country in this book, is on the edge of a plateau. When warm moist air is moved up the slope under certain wind conditions, Sewanee can be fogged in solid on some winter days—the victim of upslope fog.

Ice fog—The temperature has to be very cold for this fog to form because the water vapor sublimates directly to ice. It's mostly an arctic problem but can happen in very cold spots in the United States.

Precipitation fog—You've seen this fog when it's raining, or has been, and the moisture falls into cool air. When you're flying in light rain and look down to see fog forming (particularly in the wooded areas where the trees hold moisture), you'd better plan on getting to an airport. Warm fronts are usually the causes, and widespread areas of very dense fog can be formed in a short while. Also, if you're flying over a layer of scattered clouds, and rain is falling out of an overcast above, you'd better watch for that scattered layer to very soon become broken and then overcast. There's nothing like flying along without a care in the world and looking down to discover that the undercast is nearly total—and you don't have an instrument rating!

Recommended books for you to read on weather theory and Weather Services are *Aviation Weather* and *Aviation Weather Services*, available from the U.S. Government Printing Office. (*See* the Bibliography in the back of this book.) As you progress in aviation, you'll be branching out into areas of weather knowledge that may not apply to you now as a student pilot. Your job will be to assure that you don't stop the learning process.

Weather Information Sources

The most important thing is for you to know about weather and where to get information about it and how to understand what's being said about it. You can get the latest forecasts or hourly reports from either the FAA Flight Service Stations or the National Weather Service Offices.

You aren't expected to analyze and forecast the weather, but you must be able to use the services. If you can't read hourly reports or forecasts, all of that expensive weather-watching system will be of small value to you. The people in the Flight Service Stations and Weather Services Offices are always willing to help. They will explain the symbols and will give the weather in everyday language if you request it. You're better off if you know how to read the information yourself, since you can browse through the data at your leisure and compare the various reports. You can then ask more concise and worthwhile questions.

When you contact these agencies, tell them you're a pilot and give them your time of departure, route (if you aren't going direct), destination, and expected time of arrival.

Hourly Weather Report (METAR)

The METAR (Meteorological Aviation Routine Report) is available each hour at Flight Service Stations and Weather Service Offices. The list of abbreviations on this page is used in interpreting the surface observations and forecasts. Advisory Circular AC 00-45F, *Aviation Weather Services,* has a more extensive list under "Contractions and Acronyms."

Figure 22-11 shows actual METARs for Nashville, Tennessee, and Huntsville, Alabama, starting at the 1300Z weather for the 13th of the month.

Look at the Nashville information: (1) The hourly report is for Nashville (KBNA) and is issued for the 13th at 1253Z (131253Z). The wind at 3 knots is variable in direction (VRB03KT). Visibility is 5 statute miles (5SM) in haze (HZ). The ceiling is broken clouds at 7,500 feet (BKN075) and at 9,000 feet (BKN090). The lowest broken or overcast cloud level is the ceiling. The temperature is 25°C [Celsius] and the dewpoint is 21°C (25/21). The altimeter setting is 29.96 inches of mercury ["Hg] (A2996). Remarks (RMK): The information is an automated observation (AO2) with a precipitation discriminator (rain/snow). [*See* the abbreviations.] The sea level pressure is 1013.7 hectoPascals (SLP137) [known earlier as millibars]. For the use of selected stations, the temperature and dewpoint are given to the nearest 0.1°. The temperature is 25.1°C and the dewpoint is 20.6°C (T02510206). [The "zeros" after the "T" and before the "2" indicate the temperature is positive. A "1" in this place would indicate a negative temperature. Example: T00221011 is temperature +2.2°C, dew point -1.1°C.]

(2) This METAR for KBNA was issued at 1353Z. The wind [always in true directions] is from 230° at 5 knots (23005KT. Visibility is 6 statute miles (6SM) in haze (HZ). There is a broken layer [ceiling] of clouds at 7,500 feet (BKN075). The temperature and dewpoint are 26°C and 21°C (26/21), respectively, and the altimeter setting is 29.96"Hg (A2996). Remarks (RMK): The information is an automated observation (AO2) with a precipitation discriminator, the sea level pressure is 1013.8 hectoPascals (SLP138), and the temperature and dewpoint are 26.1°C and 20.6°C (T02610206).

(3) This is a Nashville METAR issued at 1453Z. The wind is from 230° at 7 knots (23007KT). Visibility is 9 statute miles (9SM). The clouds are few [0 to 2/8 sky coverage] at 15,000 feet (FEW150) and broken at 25,000 feet (BKN250). The temperature and dewpoint are 27°C and 21°C (27/21). The altimeter setting is 29.97"Hg (A2997). Remarks (RMK): The

Abbreviations		Descriptors	
AO1	Automated Observation without precipitation discriminator (rain/snow)	BC	Patches
		BL	Blowing
AO2	Automated Observation with precipitation discriminator (rain/snow)	DR	Low drifting
		FZ	Supercooled/freezing
AMD	Amended forecast (TAF)	MI	Shallow
BECMG	Becoming (expected between 2-digit beginning hour and 2-digit ending hour)	PR	Partial
		SH	Showers
		TS	Thunderstorm
BKN	Broken 5-7 octas (eighths) cloud coverage	**Weather Phenomena**	
CLR	Clear at or below 12,000 feet (ASOS/AWOS report)	BR	Mist
COR	Correction to the observation	DS	Dust storm
FEW	>0-2 octas cloud coverage	DU	Widespread dust
FM	From (4-digit beginning time in hours and minutes)	DZ	Drizzle
		FC	Funnel cloud
LDG	Landing	+FC	Tornado/water spout
M	In temperature field means "minus" or below zero	FG	Fog
		FU	Smoke
M	In RVR listing indicates visibility less than lowest reportable sensor value (e.g., M0600)	GR	Hail
		GS	Small hail/snow pellets
NO	Not available (e.g., SLPNO, RVRNO)	HZ	Haze
NSW	No significant weather (Note: NSW only indicates obstruction to visibility or precipitation previously noted has ended. Low ceilings, wind shear, and other weather conditions still may exist.)	IC	Ice crystals
		PL	Ice pellets
		PO	Dust/sand whirls
		PY	Spray
		RA	Rain
OVC	Overcast 8 octas cloud coverage	SA	Sand
P	In RVR indicates visibility greather than highest reported sensor value (e.g., P6000FT)	SG	Snow grains
		SN	Snow
P6SM	Visibility great than 6 SM (TAF only)	SQ	Squall
PK WIND	Peak wind	SS	Sandstorm
PROB40	Probability 40 percent	UP	Unknown precipitation (Automated Observations)
R	Runway (used in RVR measurement)		
RMK	Remark	VA	Volcanic ash
RY/RWY	Runway		
SCT	Scattered 3-4 octas cloud coverage	**Cloud Types**	
SKC	Sky clear	CB	Cumulonimbus
SLP	Sea level pressure (e.g., 1,001.3 reported as 013)	TCU	Towering Cumulus
SM	Statute mile(s)	**Intensity Values**	
SPECI	Special report	–	Light
TEMPO	Temporary changes expected (between 2-digit beginning hour and 2-digit ending hour)	no sign	Moderate
		+	Heavy
TKOF	Takeoff		
T01760158, 10142, 20012, 401120084 In remarks, examples of temperature information			
V	Varies (wind direction and RVR)		
VC	Vicinity		
VRB	Variable wind direction when speed is less than or equal to 6 knots		
VV	Vertical visibility (indefinite ceiling)		
WS	Wind shear (in TAFs, low level and not associated with convective activity)		

AO2 still indicates an automated observation, and the sea level pressure is 1,014.0 hectoPascals (SLP140). The temperature is 27.1°C and the dewpoint is 20.6°C (T02710206).

Looking at Huntsville (KHSV):

(4) Issued at 1256Z on the 13th, the wind is from 160° true at 3 knots (16003KT). Visibility is 3 statute miles (3SM) in mist (BR). [BR is an abbreviation for *brouillard*, the French word for mist.] There are a few clouds [0 to 2/8 coverage] at 2,800 feet (FEW028), scattered clouds at 7,000 (SCT070), and a broken layer at 10,000 feet (BKN100). The temperature and dewpoint are 22°C each (22/22), and the altimeter setting is 30.01″ Hg (A3001). Remarks (RMK): AO2 is an automated observation. The sea level pressure is 1,015.4 hectoPascals (SLP154), and the temperature and dewpoint are 22.2°C and 21.7°C (T02220217).

(5) At 1356Z the wind at Huntsville is calm (00000KT). Visibility is 3 statute miles (3SM) in mist (BR). There are scattered clouds [3/8 to 1/2 sky coverage] at 3,000 feet (SCT030) and broken clouds [5/8 to 7/8 coverage] at 10,000 feet (BKN100). Both the temperature and dewpoint are 22°C (22/22). The altimeter setting is 30.01″Hg (A3001). Remarks (RMK): AO2, and the sea level pressure is 1015.4 hectoPascals (SLP154). The temperature and dewpoint are 22.2°C and 21.7°C (T02220217).

(6) At 1456Z the wind at KHSV is from 190° true at 3 knots (19003KT). Visibility is 4 statute miles (4SM) in light rain (-RA) and mist (BR). There are a few clouds [0 to 2/8 coverage] at 800 feet (FEW008). The temperature and dewpoint are 24°C and 22°C (24/22). The altimeter setting is 30.02″Hg (A3002). Remarks (RMK): AO2 [again], and the rain began at 48 minutes past the last hour (RAB48). The sea level pressure is 1,015.9 hectoPascals (SLP159), and the temperature and dewpoint are 23.9°C and 21.7°C (T02390217).

Obtaining the hourly reports should trigger a reminder to check the NOTAMs (Notices to Airmen) for that station and enroute facilities. (Review Chapter 20, Notices to Airmen.)

Weather Forecasts

TAF

TAF stands for Terminal Aerodrome Forecast, or a forecast for a terminal point rather than for an area. [The area forecast will be covered later.] The TAF contains a definitive forecast for specific time periods and is issued at 0000Z, 0600Z, 1200Z, and 1800Z for each 24- or 30-hour time period. 30-hour TAFs are issued at international airports for the benefit of long-haul airlines.

TAF KBGF 161141Z 1612/1718 would be the header of a TAF for the Winchester, Tennessee airport (the name comes from the nearby **B**oiling **F**ork Creek) issued at 1141Z on the 16th of the month, valid from 1200Z on the 16th until 1800Z on the 17th, a 30-hour period. The folks at the airport will be on the lookout for that first 747 arrival.

Any timespans in the body of the TAF would include the date—"TEMPO 1623/1701" would be 2300Z on the 16th to 0100Z on the 17th.

The following is an explanation of a TAF for Pittsburg, Pennsylvania International Airport (a "TAF AMD" is an "amended forecast" which supersedes and cancels the original TAF):

TAF AMD KPIT 091730Z 0918/1018 22020KT 3SM –SHRA BKN020

   FM 092030 30015G25KT 3SM SHRA OVC015 TEMPO 0920/0922 1/2SM TSRA OVC008CB

   FM 100100 27008KT 5SM –SHRA BKN020 OVC040 PROB40 1004/1007 00000KT 1SM –RA BR

   FM 101000 22010KT 5SM –SHRA OVC020 BECMG 1013/1015 20010KT P6SM NSW SKC

---

(1) METAR KBNA 131253Z VRB03KT 5SM HZ BKN075 BKN090 25/21 A2996 RMK AO2 SLP137 T02510206

(2) METAR KBNA 131353Z 23005KT 6SM HZ BKN075 26/21 A2996 RMK AO2 SLP138 T02610206

(3) METAR KBNA 131453Z 23007KT 9SM FEW150 BKN250 27/21 A2997 RMK AO2 SLP140 T02710206

(4) METAR KHSV 131256Z 16003KT 3SM BR FEW028 SCT070 BKN100 22/22 A3001 RMK AO2 SLP154 T02220217

(5) METAR KHSV 131356Z 00000KT 3SM BR SCT030 BKN100 22/22 A3001 RMK AO2 SLP154 T02220217

(6) METAR KHSV 131456Z 19003KT 4SM -RA BR FEW008 24/22 A3002 RMK AO2 RAB48 SLP159 T02390217

Figure 22-11. Actual METARs for Nashville and Huntsville issued for the 13th of the month.

The original TAF:

**TAF KPIT 091730z 0918/1018 22020KT 3SM
–SHRA BKN020**

    **FM092030 30015G25KT 3SM SHRA OVC015
WS015/30045KT TEMPO 0920/0922 1/2SM
TSRA OVC008CB**

    **FM092300 27008KT 5SM –SHRA BKN020
OVC040 PROB 1004/1007 00000KT 1SM
–RA BR**

    **FM101000 22010KT 5SM –SHRA OVC020
BECMG 1013/1015 20010KT P6SM NSW SKC**

What It Means
TAF AMD is an amendment to the previously released
TAF covering the same period.

Where:
KPIT is the ICAO (International Civil Aviation Organization) airport identifier. The 3-letter identifiers are
preceded by a "K" for the contiguous United States
as is the case for METARs. Alaska and Hawaii use
4-letter identifiers beginning with "PA" and "PH,"
respectively.

When:
091730Z is the forecast for the 9th day of the month
with an issuance time of 1730Z (or UTC). This is a
2-digit date and 4-digit time.

0918/1018 is the valid period from the 9th day of the
month at 1800z (the "18") until the 10th day of the
month at 1800z. Midnight is referenced two ways in
TAFs: if a time period starts at midnight Zulu, it is written as 00 or 0000; if a period (or the whole TAF) ends
at midnight, it's written as 24 or 2400. See the 24-hour
TAF in Figure 22-12 for an example of the 00/24.

Wind:
22020KT is the direction (220 degrees true) and the
speed in knots as in a METAR.

    Note that the TAF AMD has deleted the forecast for
windshear. **WS015/30045KT** means at **1,5**00 feet we
expect wind to be **300** degrees at **45** KT. This indicates
low-level windshear, not associated with convective
activity.

Time periods, etc.:
FM092030 means from 2030Z on the 9th.
TEMPO 0920/0922 means temporary changes expected
between 2000Z and 2200Z on the 9th.
FM092300 from 2300Z on the 9th.
PROB40 1004/1007 means there is a **40-49%** probability of this condition occurring between 0400Z and
0700Z on the 10th. **PROB30** would mean **30-39%**
probability.

FM101000 from the 10th at 1000Z.
BECMG 1013/1015 is conditions becoming as
described between 1300Z and 1500Z on the 10th.

    Note that the TAF AMD removed the forecast
for windshear *and* delayed by 2 hours (**FM092300**
amended to **FM100100**) the call for "27008KT 5SM
–SHRA BKN020 OVC040."

Once the specific time periods can be discerned, the
sequence of **wind, visibility, significant weather,
cloud cover and cloud height** follows and is repeated
for each time block. The only exception is after quali-
fiers such as **PROB40, TEMPO,** and **BECMG** where
some of the components may be omitted if these are
not expected to change. Notice that, after **TEMPO
0920/0922,** there is no wind given and, after **PROB40
1004/1007,** there is no cloud cover listed. Note: When
No Significant Weather **(NSW)** appears, it only indicates obstruction to visibility or precipitation previously noted has ended. (*See* Abbreviations on Page
22-8.)
    Figure 22-12 is a TAF for Nashville.
    The forecast for Nashville (KBNA) was issued at
2333Z on the 12th (122333Z) and covers the 13th from
0000Z to 2400Z (130024).

TAF KBNA 122333Z 1300/1324 20003KT P6SM SCT040 BKN250
   FM 130600 00000KT 5SM BR BKN250
   FM 131400 24007KT P6SM SCT040 BKN250
   FM 131700 24010KT 5SM HZ SCT045CB BKN250
     PROB30 1317/1324 3SM TSRA BR OVC045CB

Figure 22-12. An actual TAF for Nashville on the 13th of the
month from 0000Z to 2400Z (or 0000Z on the 14th).

Taking the rest of Figure 22-12 step by step:
    At the start of the TAF, the wind is forecast to
be from 200° [always a true direction] at 3 knots
(20003KT), the visibility is greater than 6 statute miles
(P6SM) [think of the "P" as plus, or greater], clouds are
scattered at 4,000 feet (SCT040) and broken at 25,000
feet (BKN250).
    From (FM) the 13th at 0600[Zulu], the forecast is
for calm winds (00000KT) with visibility of 5 statute
miles (5SM) in mist (BR) and broken clouds at 25,000
feet (BKN250).
    From (FM) the 13th at 1400[Zulu], the forecast is
for winds from 240° at 7 knots (24007KT), visibility
is greater than 6 statute miles (P6SM), and there are
scattered clouds at 4,000 feet (SCT040) with a broken
layer at 25,000 feet (BKN250).
    From (FM) the 13th at 1700[Z], the forecast is for
a wind from 240° at 10 knots (24010KT), visibility
is 5 statute miles (5SM) in haze (HZ), with scattered

clouds at 4,500 feet, plus cumulonimbus (SCT045CB), and broken clouds at 25,000 feet (BKN250). There's a 30 percent probability (PROB30) between 1700[Z] and 2400[Z] (1317/1324) of a visibility of 3 statute miles (3SM), with thunderstorms with rain (TSRA), mist (BR), and an overcast at 4,500 feet with cumulonimbus clouds (OVC045CB).

Area Forecast

The Area Forecast (FA-Forecast, Area) covers several states and the coastal waters of those states, as required. Discussed here is an FA for the Salt Lake City (SLC) area, which covers the area as shown by Figure 22-13. Note that there are also five other areas with issuances cited in Miami (MIA), Dallas (DFW), San Francisco (SFO), Chicago (CHI), and Boston (BOS).

Area forecasts are normally issued 3 times daily for the six areas shown but may be at different times for different parts of the country.

Figure 22-14 is an area forecast for the Salt Lake City area as given in *Aviation Weather Services*.

Reviewing Figure 22-14 line by line, the heading indicates that the report is from Salt Lake City (SLC), it contains a clouds and weather forecast [the added C],

and it's an area forecast (FA) issued on the 14th of the month at 1045Z (141045).

The SYNOPSIS AND clouds and weather are for VFR (VFR CLDS/WX).

The SYNOPSIS is VALID UNTIL 0500Z on the 15th (150500).

The clouds and weather (CLDS/WX) forecast is VALID UNTIL 2300Z on the 14th (142300). The outlook (OTLK) is VALID from 2300Z on the 14th to 0500Z on the 15th (142300−150500).

SYNOPSIS—The HIGH pressure (PRES) over (OVR) northeastern (NERN) Montana (MT) will be continuing (CONTG) to move eastward (EWD) gradually (GRDLY). LOW pressure (PRES) over (OVR) Arizona (AZ), New Mexico (NM), and western (WRN) Texas (TX) will be remaining (RMNG) generally (GENLY) stationary (STNRY). Aloft (ALF), the trough (TROF) that extends (EXTDS) from western (WRN) Montana (MT) into southern (SRN) Arizona (AZ) will be remaining (RMNG) stationary (STNRY) for the valid period.

Idaho (ID) and Montana (MT)—SEE AIRMET SIERRA FOR mountain (MTN) obscuration (OBSCN) information.

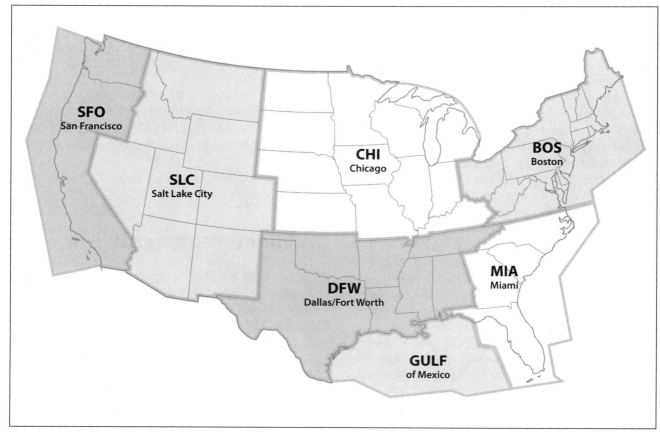

Figure 22-13. Area forecast locations. (From *Aviation Weather Services*)

```
SLCC FA 141045
SYNOPSIS AND VFR CLDS/WX
SYNOPSIS VALID UNTIL 150500
CLDS/WX VALID UNTIL 142300...OTLK VALID 142300-150500

SYNOPSIS...HIGH PRES OVR NERN MT CONTG EWD GRDLY. LOW PRES OVR
AZ NM AND WRN TX RMNG GENLY STNRY.  ALF...TROF EXTDS FROM WRN
MT INTO SRN AZ RMNG STNRY.

ID MT
SEE AIRMET SIERRA FOR MTN OBSCN.
FROM YXH TO SHR TO 30SE BZN TO 60SE PIH TO LKT TO YXC TO YXH
SCT-BKN070-090 TOPS 120-150. WDLY SCT SHRA.  TOPS SHWRS
FL180.  OTLK...VFR.
RMNDR AREA...SCT100-120.  ISOLD SHRA MNLY ERN PTNS AREA.
OTLK...VFR.

UT NV
NRN...SCT080. WDLY SCT SHRA.  TOPS SHWRS FL180. 15Z SKC.
18Z SCT100
OTLK...VFR.
```

Figure 22-14. An area forecast for the Salt Lake City area.

Locations FROM Medicine Hat, Alberta, Canada (YXH), TO Sheridan, Wyoming (SHR), TO 30 miles southeast (30SE) of Bozeman, Montana (BZN), TO 60 miles southeast (60SE) of Pocatello, Idaho (PIH), TO Salmon, Idaho (LKT), TO Cranbrook, British Columbia (YXC), back TO Medicine Hat (YXH) outline the area in question.

In the area outlined, conditions are forecast to be scattered to broken clouds at 7,000 to 9,000 feet (SCT-BKN070-090) mean sea level [MSL] with TOPS of clouds at 12,000 to 15,000 feet (120–150). There will be widely (WDLY) scattered (SCT) rain showers (SHRA). The TOPS of the showers (SHWRS) are at the flight level of 18,000 feet (FL180). The outlook (OTLK) is for VFR weather. [Note above that the outlook is from 142300Z to 150500Z.]

The remainder (RMNDR) of the AREA has forecast conditions of scattered clouds at 10,000–12,000 feet (SCT100–120). Isolated (ISOLD) rain showers (SHRA) are expected mainly (MNLY) in the eastern (ERN) portions (PTNS) of the AREA. The outlook (OTLK) is for VFR conditions.

Utah (UT) and Nevada (NV)—The northern (NRN) portion will have scattered clouds at 8,000 feet (SCT080). There's a forecast for widely (WDLY) scattered (SCT) rain showers (SHRA). The TOPS of the showers (SHWRS) will be at flight level of 18,000 feet (FL180). After 1500Z (15Z), the sky will be clear (SKC).

After 1800Z (18Z), the forecast is for scattered clouds at 10,000 feet (SCT100).

The outlook (OTLK) is for VFR conditions.

The *Categorical Outlooks* are as follows:

VFR (Visual flight rules)—Ceiling greater than 3,000 feet and visibility greater than 5 miles; includes sky clear.

MVFR (Marginal VFR)—Ceiling 1,000–3,000 feet and/or visibility 3–5 miles inclusive.

IFR (instrument flight rules)—Ceiling 500 feet to less than 1,000 feet and/or visibility 1 mile to less than 3 miles.

LIFR (Low IFR)—Ceiling less than 500 feet and/or visibility less than 1 mile.

In-Flight Weather Advisories

The National Weather Service (NWS) issues inflight weather advisories designated as AIRMETs (WA), SIGMETs (WS), Convective SIGMETs (WST), Center Weather Advisories, and Severe Weather Alerts. The advisories most useful to you as a student or low-time pilot will be AIRMETs, SIGMETs, and Convective SIGMETs.

Weather phenomena that are potentially hazardous to the aircraft require the issuance of an AIRMET.

1. AIRMET SIERRA—This is to alert the pilot checking the area forecast (FA) that, in the state or states

listed, there may be a problem with IFR conditions such as low ceilings (less than 1,000 feet), low visibility (less than 3 miles over 50 percent of the area at one time), or extensive mountain obscuration. In other words, when you see this, be prepared to check further for these phenomena.

2. AIRMET TANGO—This designator is given in the flight precautions in the FA to warn the pilot that there may be a problem with turbulence or sustained winds of 30 K or more in the area cited.

3. AIRMET ZULU—This alerts the pilot to information concerning icing and freezing problems in the FA states or areas.

AIRMETs may be issued between the normal release times if conditions warrant. Check with the National Weather Service or Flight Service Stations for the current normal times of issuance. The alphabet letters S, T, and Z are reserved for use only in AIRMETs.

Figure 22-15 is an AIRMET issued on the 30th at 0800Z for the Chicago area (CHIS), and the added "S" [SIERRA] indicates that ceilings and visibilities are involved.

Looking at the figure, the AIRMET SIERRA FOR IFR is VALID UNTIL 1400Z on the 30th (301400).

AIRMET IFR for Iowa (IA) and Missouri (MO) goes as follows:

FROM Fort Dodge, Iowa (FOD), TO Cedar Rapids, Iowa (CID), TO Columbia (COU), Missouri, TO Kansas City, Missouri (MKC), back TO Fort Dodge (FOD).

Ceilings (CIG) will be below (BLO) 1,000 feet (010) AND visibilities (VIS) below (BLO) 3 statute miles (3SM) in snow (SN). Conditions (CONDS) will be continuing (CONTG) beyond (BYD) 1400Z AND spreading (SPRDG) over (OVR) eastern (ERN) Iowa (IA), eastern (ERN) Missouri (MO), and Illinois (IL).

The IFR outlook (OTLK) is VALID from 1400Z to 2000Z (1400–2000) for Iowa (IA), Minnesota (MN), Wisconsin (WI), and Illinois (IL). Ceilings (CIG) below (BLO) 1,000 feet (010) AND visibilities (VIS) below (BLO) 3 statute miles (3SM) in snow (SN) will be spreading (SPRDG) INTO northeastern (NERN) Iowa (IA), southern (SRN) Minnesota (MN), southwestern (SWRN) Wisconsin (WI) AND northwestern (NWRN) Illinois (IL) between (BTWN) 1600Z AND 2000Z and will be continuing (CONTG) beyond (BYD) 2000Z.

SIGMETs are issued to cover weather phenomena considered to be of greater danger to aircraft than those situations listed above. The first issuance of a SIGMET is identified as an urgent weather SIGMET (UWS), and any that follow are given as plain WS. Items covered are

1. Severe icing not associated with thunderstorms.
2. Severe or extreme turbulence or clear air turbulence (CAT) not associated with thunderstorms.
3. Duststorms, sandstorms, or volcanic ash lowering surface or in-flight visibilities to below 3 miles.
4. Volcanic eruption.

Figure 22-16 is a SIGMET issued for the Dallas/Ft. Worth area (DFW). (*See* Figure 22-13 again for the area covered.) Let's look at the SIGMET.

This was the first issuance from the Dallas/Ft. Worth area at 051700 (DFWP UWS 051700). It's SIGMET PAPA 1 and VALID UNTIL 2100Z on the 5th of the month. [The nonconvective SIGMETs now have alphabetic designators that run from November (N) through Yankee (Y), excluding the AIRMET designators SIERRA (S), TANGO (T), and ZULU (Z), which were covered earlier.] Continuing through the figure:

Arkansas (AR), Louisiana (LA), and Mississippi (MS)—the area covered is FROM Memphis, TN (MEM), TO 30 miles north (30N) of Meridian, MS

```
CHIS WA 300800
AIRMET SIERRA FOR IFR VALID UNTIL 301400

AIRMET IFR...IA MO
FROM FOD TO CID TO COU TO MKC TO FOD
CIG BLO 010 AND VIS BLO 3SM SN.  CONDS CONTG BYD 1400Z AND
SPRDG OVR ERN IA ERN MO AND IL.

IFR OTLK VALID 1400-2000...IA MN WI IL
CIG BLO 010 AND VIS BLO 3SM SN SPRDG INTO NERN IA SRN MN SWRN
WI AND NWRN IL BTWN 1600Z AND 2000Z CONTG BYD 2000Z.
```

Figure 22-15. An AIRMET for Iowa and Missouri.

```
DFWP UWS 051700
SIGMET PAPA 1 VALID UNTIL 052100
AR LA MS
FROM MEM TO 30N MEI TO BTR TO MLU TO MEM
MDT TO OCNL SVR ICG ABV FRZLVL XPCD.  FRZLVL 080 E TO 120 W.
CONDS CONTG BYD 2100Z.
```

Figure 22-16. An initial SIGMET (UWS) issued for the Dallas/Fort Worth area.

(MEI), TO Baton Rouge, LA (BTR), TO Monroe, LA (MLU), and back TO Memphis (MEM).

There is moderate (MDT) TO occasionally (OCNL) severe (SVR) icing (ICG) above (ABV) the freezing level (FRZLVL) expected (XPCD). The freezing level (FRZLVL) is 8,000 feet (080) in the eastern (E) portion TO 12,000 feet (120) in the western (W) portion of the area.

The conditions (CONDS) will be continuing (CONTG) beyond (BYD) 2100Z.

The first time a SIGMET is issued for a phenomenon associated with a particular weather system, it will be given the next alphabetic designator in the series and will be numbered as the first for that designator (e.g., PAPA 1). Subsequent advisories will retain the same alphabetic designator until the phenomenon ends (PAPA 1, PAPA 2, etc.). In the conterminous United States, that phenomenon will retain that designator as it moves within an area or into one or more other areas. (Note: Alaska/Hawaii naming differs slightly.)

Convective SIGMETs are issued in the 48 conterminous states for any of the following phenomena:
1. Severe thunderstorms due to:
   a. surface winds greater than or equal to 50 K.
   b. hail, at the surface, greater than or equal to $\frac{3}{4}$ inch in diameter.
   c. tornadoes.
2. Embedded thunderstorms.
3. A line of thunderstorms more than 60 miles long.
4. Thunderstorms greater than or equal to VIP level 4 affecting 40 percent or more of an area at least 3,000 square miles.

There's a tie-in between the radar echo intensity and the turbulence in a thunderstorm (Called VIP levels).

Level 1—weak.
Level 2—moderate.
Level 3-strong.
Level 4—very strong.
Level 5—intense.
Level 6—extreme.

Your job will be to give *all* thunderstorms a wide berth of several miles.

Figure 22-17 is a sample Convective SIGMET for the *central* U.S. region.

Taking the figure line by line, Kansas City has issued a CONVECTIVE SIGMET. Its designator is 20C. It is VALID UNTIL 2055Z.

North and South Dakota (ND SD)—FROM 90 miles west of Minot, ND (90W MOT), to Grand Forks, ND (GFK), to Aberdeen, SD (ABR), to Rapid City, ND (RAP), to 90 miles west of Minot (90W MOT):

There is an intensifying (INTNSFYG) AREA of severe (SVR) thunderstorms (TSTMS) moving (MVG) FROM 250° [true] at 30 knots (25030KT). The TOPS are above (ABV) the flight level of 45,000 feet (FL450).

A TORNADO was reported (RPRTD) at 1820Z at 50 miles southwest (50SW) of Dupree, South Dakota (KDPR). There is HAIL up TO $\frac{1}{2}$ inch diameter (1/2IN). WIND GUSTS TO 45 knots (45KT) have been reported (RPRTD). TORNADOES, HAIL TO 1 inch (1IN), and WIND GUSTS up TO 65 knots (65KT) are possible (PSBL).

```
CONVECTIVE SIGMET 20C
VALID UNTIL 2055Z
ND SD
FROM 90W MOT-GFK-ABR-RAP-90W MOT
INTSFYG AREA SVR TSTMS MOVG FROM 25030KT.  TOPS ABV FL450.
TORNADO RPRTD 1820Z 50SW KDPR. HAIL TO 1/2IN...WIND GUSTS TO 45KT
RPRTD.  TORNADOES...HAIL TO 1 IN...WIND GUSTS TO 65KT PSBL.
```

Figure 22-17. A Convective SIGMET issued for North and South Dakota.

When you first start reading area forecasts and AIRMETs/SIGMETs, the sentence structure seems that of an ex-Luftwaffe pilot with punctuation problems, but with practice *yu cn rd thm without mch trbl.*

Transcribed Weather Broadcasts (TWEBS) — *No longer available.*

Wind Information

Figure 22-18 is part of an actual winds aloft forecast. The altitudes given are above *mean sea level*; some of the western stations may not issue the winds at 3,000 or even 6,000 feet because of the elevation (*see* DEN—Denver in Figure 22-18). Winds aloft information is given to the nearest 10° true and in knots. Temperatures are *Celsius.*

Looking at the forecast winds at Raleigh–Durham (RDU) and Richmond, Va. (RIC), at 3,000 feet, the winds are forecast to be light and variable (5 K or less) as given by the digits 9900. (No temperatures are given for any station at 3,000 feet as you can see.)

At 6,000 feet MSL at Nashville (BNA) the wind is forecast to be from 220° true at 46 K and the temperature is +5°C.

At Dubuque (DBQ) the forecast wind at 30,000 feet is from 740° at 4 K and...*hold it!* The compass only includes 360°, but this is no misprint. When the wind is over 100 K, 50 is added to the direction (this way they can keep the number of digits down to six for wind and temperature), and 100 is subtracted from the wind velocity, given as 4 (04) K here. So you would subtract 50 from the 74, which gives a direction of 24 (240° true), and add 100 to the force to get 104 K. The temperature is a cool -48°C at that altitude.

Winds Aloft Chart

The National Meteorological Center plots and transmits wind data obtained from observations and is given as 12-hour prognostics twice daily.

The winds aloft chart is a map of the continental United States for each particular altitude (or pressure level) of interest with an "arrow, barb, and pennant" presentation at selected stations to show the wind direction and velocity and the temperature (in degrees Celsius) for that altitude.

Figure 22-19 shows the "arrow, barb, and pennant" idea. Each pennant is 50 K, a full barb is 10 K, a half barb is 5 K. Remember that winds aloft are given in true directions and knots.

The numbers associated with the arrows are the middle digit of the direction from which the wind is coming. The "6" in the left-hand arrow system in Figure 22-19 confirms that the wind is from 260° true. (You could guess by the arrow that it is west-southwest but now know it's 260°.) The right-hand arrow in the figure has a "0" noting that the wind is from 300° true.

Figure 22-19. Barb and pennant presentation for the winds aloft chart. The wind is blowing the way the arrow is going. The temperatures are –30°C and –9°C. The levels covered for the winds aloft charts are (thousands of feet MSL) 6, 9, 12, 18, 24, 30, 34, and 39.

```
FD KWBC 151640
Based on 151200Z DATA
VALID 151800Z FOR USE 1700-2100Z. TEMPS NEG ABV 24000
```

FT	3000	6000	9000	12000	18000	24000	30000	34000	39000
BHM	1928	2231+07	2437+05	2539-02	2541-14	2756-26	267140	277749	288159
BNA	2043	2246+05	2346+03	2446+02	2448-15	2559-28	267842	268451	278561
RDU	9900	2207+05	2310+04	2612-01	2931-18	3047-31	316644	317352	317260
RIC	9900	2109+04	2314+02	2513-03	2926-19	3039-32	316145	316653	316360
ROA	1917	2220+03	2226+03	2328-03	2738-18	2850-30	296644	297453	297562
DBQ	2139	2341-02	2343+00	2353-04	2370-19	2382-32	740448	740756	750161
DEN			3126-13	3234-21	3136-31	3157-37	318244	309051	298955

Figure 22-18. Part of an actual winds aloft forecast for several selected stations, based on 1200Z data for the 15th of the month, valid at 1800Z on the 15th and for use from 1700–2100Z on that date. As noted, all temperatures (which are Celsius) are negative above 24,000 feet to save the space of putting a minus (–) in each case.

Pilot Reports

One of the most valuable sources of information is pilot reports, or PIREPs. These are on-the-spot reports *in the air* and are not forecasts or information based on observations from the ground. Figure 22-20 is an actual PIREP. One way to remember the symbol for pilot reports is that it is an **U**p in the **A**ir (UA) report. UUA is an *urgent* pilot report.

Other Services

There are some other weather services available to you:

1. TIBS—This is a recording of meteorological and aeronautical information available by phone. Depending on user demand, METARs, TAFs, winds aloft, and other information may be provided. For more detailed flight briefings, talk to an AFSS (automated flight service station) specialist. Phone numbers are found in the *Airport/Facility Directory*.

2. *FLIGHT WATCH* (Enroute Flight Advisory Service—EFAS)—This service will provide timely weather information in flight and is available throughout the conterminous United States along prominent and heavily traveled flyways. You should be able to get the service at 5,000 feet above the ground level within 80 miles from a FLIGHT WATCH outlet. Selected Flight Service Stations will provide the service, using remote communications facilities, as necessary. (FLIGHT WATCH is not intended for flight plan filing or position reporting, but for weather information only.)

   FLIGHT WATCH will use 122.0 MHz and you would call the particular FSS controlling the FLIGHT WATCH in the area. ("CHATTANOOGA FLIGHT WATCH. THIS IS ZEPHYR SIX FIVE FOUR FOUR TANGO," etc.) If you don't know which FSS controls the service, just call FLIGHT WATCH and give your position relative to the nearest VOR; they will contact you.

   Figure 22-21 shows the EFAS facilities in the southeastern United States.

3. *Hazardous In-Flight Weather Advisory Service* (HIWAS)—This is a continuous broadcast of in-flight weather advisories including AWW (Severe Weather Watch Bulletins and Alerts), SIGMETs, CWAs (Center Weather Advisories), Convective SIGMETs, AIRMETs, and urgent PIREPs. HIWAS is not a replacement for preflight or in-flight briefings or real time updates from Flight Watch (EFAS).

These other services are covered briefly so that you will have an idea of what is available. As you gain experience you'll make more and more use of these aids.

Weather Charts

Surface Analysis Chart

The surface analysis chart is the basis for the classic "weather map" and is issued every 3 hours beginning at 00Z. Isobars, pressure systems, and fronts are indicated on the chart as mentioned earlier in the chapter and as shown in Figures 22-2 and 22-3 (on Page 22-2).

This chart is a good first reference when you go to a Weather Service Office, FSS, or online for a check of the general layout of the weather. Since weather in the United States moves generally from west to east, you can check fronts or pressure systems to the west of your route and get a general idea of what might be a factor later.

After you've seen the chart, take a look at the hourly sequence reports along the route and compare them with what had been forecast. The presence of a cold or warm front nearly always means some kind of ceiling and visibility restrictions, but occasionally "dry" fronts will move through an area. By looking at the chart only, you might decide to "cancel because of the front."

Remember that the chart may be 2 or 3 hours out of date before you get to it, and you'll have to take the weather movement into consideration.

Figure 22-22 (Page 22-18) is an example of a surface analysis chart with the isobars spaced at 4-millibar intervals and labeled somewhere within their length (*see* the "1020" just south of the Florida panhandle). The Highs and Lows are shown with the extreme pressure (millibars) underlined, as shown on the chart with the 1025 over Kentucky and the 995 for the Low over southern Nevada. Fronts are shown with movement in the direction of the points (cold front) or bulges (warm front). Note that stationary fronts don't know which way to go.

Symbols ("station models") show weather at some of the stations used in making the chart. Station models originate from land stations, ships, buoys, coastal and maritime platforms. The key to the station models reports can be found in *Aviation Weather Services* (FAA Advisory Circular (AC) 00-45), but looking at the latest METARs along your route would give more recent conditions.

ICT UA/OV SLN /TM 0450 /FL060 /TP C172 /TA +10 /TB MDT AT 040 LGT BLO 030 /RM at 30 TEMP +2

Figure 22-20. A pilot report (UA) released by Wichita (ICT). The aircraft was over Salina (SLN). Time (TM) is 0450, flight level (FL060), type (TP) Cessna 172 (C172), temperature of the air (TA) +10°C. There is no report of sky cover (SK), flight visibility and weather (WX), or wind velocity (WV). The pilot does report turbulence (TB) as being moderate at 4,000 feet (MDT AT 040) and light below 3,000 feet (LGT BLO 030). RM stands for remarks. The temperature at 3,000 feet is +2°C (at 30 TEMP +2). An *Urgent* pilot report is UUA.

Figure 22-21. Enroute Flight Advisory Service stations in the southeastern United States. (From the *Airport/Facility Directory*)

Figure 22-22. The major value of the surface analysis chart is to give an overall view of fronts and pressure systems. It's issued every 3 hours.

Weather Depiction Chart

This chart is useful for getting a good look at restrictions to visibility and low ceilings that would not actually be shown on the surface analysis chart.

Cross-hatched or shaded areas indicate IFR conditions (ceiling less than 1,000 feet and/or visibility less than 3 statute miles). MVFR (marginal VFR) areas are enclosed within smooth contoured lines and indicate weather conditions of ceilings between 1,000 and 3,000 feet and/or visibility of 3–5 statute miles. No contours indicate VFR areas with ceilings greater than 3,000 feet and visibility greater than 5 statute miles.

Figure 22-23 is a weather depiction chart for the lower 48 states and it has an enlarged excerpt centered on Wyoming. Four reporting stations are decoded here (A, B, C, and D in the excerpt). The circular (dot) symbol represents sky cover and ranges from an empty circle showing clear skies to a solid black disk representing overcast skies (a circled "x" indicates sky obscured). If a lightly-written number is to the left of the sky cover, it is visibility in statute miles (no number if the visibility is greater than 5 miles). The heavier

number below the sky cover is the ceiling in hundreds of feet. The symbols for precipitation or obstruction to visibility are usually to the left of sky cover, but may be placed above it when two reporting stations are close together on the map, as in the case of Stations A and B (see excerpt in Figure 22-23). The complete list of symbols and terminology is found in *Aviation Weather Services.*

Station A: 2,000′ ("20") overcast (solid disk), 2 miles visibility ("2") in light snow (**, two "snowflakes"). This station is in the cross-hatched IFR area due to visibility less than 3 miles.

Station B: 1,300′ ("13") overcast (solid disk), 4 miles visibility ("4") in haze (the horizontal "8" or infinity symbol). This station is in the MVFR area because visibility is between 3 and 5 miles and ceiling is between 1,000′ and 3,000′. Either of these would trigger the MVFR label.

Station C: sky obscured (circled x, therefore no defined ceiling) and visibility ¾ mile in light snow (**).

Station D: 6,000′ ("60") broken (3/4 disk) ceiling with visibility greater than 5 miles (no visibility

Figure 22-23. Weather depiction chart. Shaded areas — IFR with ceilings less than 1,000 feet and/or visibility less than 3 statute miles. Contoured without shading — VFR areas with ceilings greater than 3,000 feet and visibility greater than 5 miles.

number). This station is in the VFR area due to ceiling greater than 3,000′ and visibility more than 5 miles.

Radar Summary Chart

Figure 22-24 is part of an actual radar summary chart. The shading shows radar echo areas and the contours outline intensities. For instance, over north central Alabama, the intensities are building toward the center of the area with tops at 32,000 (*320*). Bases would be designated with a bar over the height value (in hundreds). Note also that there may be a squall line in that area as indicated by the solid line. The direction and velocities of movement of areas and lines are shown by pennants (that Alabama line is moving east-southeast at 20 K).

There is a rain shower area of increasing intensity (RW +) south of the Florida panhandle, with tops at 15,000 feet (*150*). There is an area of thunderstorms and rain showers (TRW) south of Pensacola moving south (arrow) at 5 K (05).

NE means "no echoes" and OM indicates that a station is out for maintenance.

There is an area with rain and rain showers (tops at 23,000 feet) moving northeast at 25 K (arrow) in the Atlanta area.

The radar summary chart is especially valuable in showing intensities and movements of significant precipitation.

Weather Prognostic Chart

The low-level prognostic chart would be of the most value to you as a student or new pilot. Like the other charts, the weather areas are superimposed on a map of the United States. The low-level prog chart is composed

Figure 22-24. Radar summary chart.

of four panels. The top two panels of the chart show *significant weather* forecasts for 12 and 24 hours with scalloped or smooth lines, respectively, indicating MVFR or IFR areas of the country. The other two are for 12- and 24-hour forecasts of fronts and pressure centers (surface prog). The movement of each pressure center is indicated by an arrow and number showing direction and speed in knots. The surface prog also outlines areas of forecast precipitation (smooth lines) and/or thunderstorms (dot-dash lines _._._). If precipitation will affect half or more of an area, that area is shaded. Absence of shading indicates more sparse precipitation (less than half in that area).

Figure 22-25 is a sample of the charts just discussed.

The weather charts just covered plus actual reports, checked against terminal and area forecasts, will give you a look at the weather from several directions for your cross-country planning.

Figure 22-25. U.S. low-level significant weather prognostic chart (surface — 400 millibars). (From *Aviation Weather Services*)

Figure 22-26. Characteristics of "typical" warm and cold fronts. The vertically developed clouds may produce clear ice, whereas the stratus type (stable air) clouds, usually associated with warm fronts, may produce rime icing at or above the freezing level.

Summary

Your probable first reaction to this chapter on weather is that it is impossible to know everything about what is available to you as far as weather services are concerned. You don't have to remember that the terminal forecast is available at such and such a time. You do need to have some idea that sequence reports, winds aloft forecasts, area forecasts, and terminal forecasts *are available* to you through either a National Weather Service Office or FSS. Tell them that you're a (student) pilot and you're planning to fly from A to B, leaving A at such and such a time and expecting to get to B at about so and so. Will they give you the word? The specialists will help every way they can, so don't expect to understand weather facilities like those who spend 8 hours a day working at it.

This chapter is aimed for practical use by you as a student, sport or noninstrument-qualified private pilot. You'll learn more weather and high-altitude theory when you start working on that instrument rating.

The weather information sources and NOTAM services are in a continuing state of flux. Your flight instructor will be the major source for the latest changes.

If you are in doubt about the weather before takeoff—*don't go.* It's much better to be down here, wishing you were up there, than up there wishing you were down here. If you are in doubt about the weather ahead when you're flying—*make a 180° turn before you are* also in doubt about the weather behind you.

Figure 22-26 is another comparison of warm and cold fronts and their weather systems.

The Cross-Country — Knowing Your Airplane

Before planning the navigation for the trip, you must be introduced to facts about operating the airplane, which will be of particular importance now that you will be making extended flights away from the home airport. On the cross-country you will be more likely to encounter adverse weather, including flying in areas of moderate to severe turbulence, perhaps for extended periods of time. You should know about setting exact power and conserving fuel, a minor or nonexistent problem for local flying.

When you are off by yourself at a strange airport, you'll have added responsibility and will have to know more about your airplane systems than is needed at home base where your instructor is available to answer questions.

The following information is both for your present cross-country planning and for future reference. For instance, it's unlikely that you'll have problems with weight and balance of the airplane on your solo cross-country. But later, after you get that private certificate and decide to fly on vacation with your family or friends, and their baggage, knowledge of this area of flying will be of vital interest to you.

Airplane Papers

In Chapter 3 you noted that the airplane must have certain documents on board at all times. Make sure that these are in the aircraft before you leave the home airport.

1. The *Certificate of Aircraft Registration* must be current.
2. The *Airworthiness Certificate* must be *displayed* so that it can be easily read. Your airplane will have a *Standard Airworthiness Certificate*, because it will meet either "normal" or "utility" airworthiness requirements. (Airplanes can meet both requirements, but this will be covered a little later.) "Aerobatic" and "transport" category airplanes also have a Standard Airworthiness Certificate, but it's unlikely that as a student pilot you'll be flying these last two categories.

    A Standard Airworthiness Certificate is used in aircraft that carry people and property for compensation or hire.
3. The *Airplane Flight Manual*, or *operations limitations form*, must be aboard; the airplane weight and balance information (and equipment list) are a part of these documents. Check to see that the major *repair and alteration forms* (if any) are with the weight and balance information. These forms show *major* repairs. Their effects on empty weight and center of gravity of the airplane are indicated in the aircraft logbook.

When flying away from the home base, you'd better have the *aircraft and engine logbooks* along. (There's a separate book for the airframe, each engine, and each propeller.) *Make sure that the logbooks are up to date.* Your instructor, however, may prefer to keep them at the home base, with the understanding that the books can still be available to FAA or NTSB representatives within a reasonable time.

Airplane Categories and Load Factors

The airplane you will be flying will be of the normal or utility category, as mentioned in the last section. The primary difference between the two categories is that the normal category airplane normally has "limit load factors" of 3.8 positive g's and 1.52 negative g's, and the utility category airplane has limit load factors of 4.4 positive and 1.76 negative g's. Intentional spins are prohibited for normal category airplanes but may be done in some airplanes in the utility category. (Some airplanes are certificated as being "characteristically incapable of spinning.")

The term "g" is a unit of acceleration based on that of gravity, as discussed in Chapter 9 in "The Turn." The airplane in straight and level flight and unaccelerated glides and climbs has 1 g acting upon it (and so do you). In the utility category airplane, you can create positive acceleration forces up to 4.4 times its weight without exceeding safe limits (if the airplane hasn't been previously damaged). If you should encounter an upward gust during your 4.4-g maneuver, the lift is increased even more sharply, and instead of 4.4 g's, you may suddenly have a load factor of 6 or 7. Airplanes get bent this way.

Some airplanes are certificated in both categories. At the maximum certificated weight, the airplane is in the normal category and must be held to a load factor of 3.8 positive and 1.52 negative g's, or less. At a specified lighter weight, it can be flown as a utility category airplane and can safely cope with a load factor of up to 4.4 positive g's (and 1.76 negative g's). This can be seen by an example: One airplane having a maximum certificated weight of 2,300 pounds is classed as normal category at that weight; when it is flown at a reduced weight of 2,000 pounds, it can be operated as a utility category airplane. The maximum force acting on the wings would be approximately the same in both cases. At a weight of 2,300 pounds, a load factor of 3.8 g's (normal category limit) would be 3.8 × 2,300, or 8,740 pounds. At 2,000 pounds, a load factor of 4.4 g's (utility category limit) would result in a force of 8,800 pounds. Very nearly the same force would be supported by the wings, and 8,800 pounds would be the maximum they would be expected to carry without showing signs of permanent deformation. Not all airplanes would work out this close in total force but would have been checked out to sustain the maximum force expected from either of the two categories. The wings are not the only structures subject to failure; the horizontal tail or other components might break first if you exceed the limit load factor.

The load factors just mentioned are the total g's imposed. You start at 1 g, so only 3.4 g's more are needed to reach the positive limit load factor of 4.4. As far as the negative load factors are concerned, the normal positive 1 g is to the good; you'll have to go farther to get to the negative limit load factor. The airplane can go up to 2.76 g's on the negative side (from +1g) without permanent deformation.

Knowing that vertical gusts (up or down) can impose g loads on the airplane, you should be aware of several points. Take a look at your airspeed indicator markings and review the discussion of the airspeed indicator in Chapter 3. The green arc is the *normal operating range*, and the lower limit is the flaps-up, power-off stall speed at maximum certificated weight. The upper limit (where it meets the yellow) is called the *maximum structural cruising speed*. The yellow arc is the caution range and, of course, the red line speaks for itself. Even if the air is only mildly turbulent, keep the airspeed in the green area. Although your airplane at normal cruise will be indicating in the green, on descents you will have a tendency to let it slip up into the yellow, and the sudden encounter with turbulence at those speeds could result in excessive load factors. Figure 23-1 shows what happens when an up-gust is encountered.

In (A) in Figure 23-1, the airplane is flying in normal cruising flight at a certain required angle of attack. (You wouldn't know the angle but would have the proper cruise power setting and would be maintaining a constant altitude.) In (B) a sharp up-gust of 20 K is encountered. The vector diagram in (B) shows that the angle of attack has been sharply increased and lift is at a much higher value than normal. *A high positive load factor is imposed.* A measure of the load factor is the ratio of lift to weight. You remember that in the steep turn at 60° of bank, you had to double the lift in order to maintain a constant altitude, which resulted in a load factor of 2.

The airplane would quickly return to the original lift-to-weight ratio of 1, since drag would also rise sharply, but in the meantime the load factor would have already been at work.

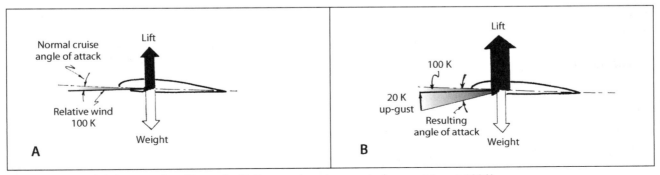

Figure 23-1. Airfoil showing the effects of a 20-K upward gust on an airplane cruising at 100 K.

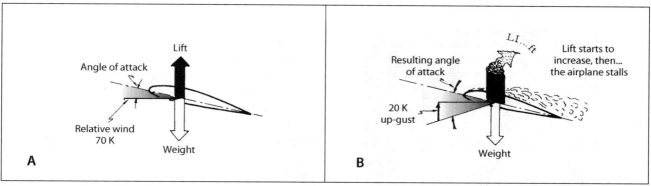

Figure 23-2. Effects of a 20-K upward gust on the airplane cruising at 70 K.

Figure 23-2 shows what would happen if the airplane was flying at a much lower airspeed when it encountered the same 20-K upward gust.

You'll note in (A) that the angle of attack is higher to maintain this lower airspeed of 70 K. (The lift-to-weight ratio is still 1, or lift equals weight, as before.) At (B) the 20-K up-gust results in the stalling angle of attack being reached; the lift starts to increase radically, but the airplane stalls before the limit load factor is reached. The gust in both cases would have the same effect—as if you had suddenly increased back pressure. The stall resulting from the situation in Figure 23-2 would be momentary, and the airplane would soon return to equilibrium. (The stall and recovery would be so fast that it would be unlikely that you would have time to even start your own recovery procedures.) Such a stall situation would be very bad on a low, slow approach on a gusty, turbulent day. You would make the approach several knots faster to lower the chances of an inadvertent stall at a critical point. This was also covered in "Gusty Air and Wind Gradients" in Chapter 13. Because of the comparatively low speeds used in the approach, the stall, rather than high load factors, is the problem encountered. At cruise and higher speeds, the possibility of overstress is the major factor; as everyone will agree, it's better to have a temporary stalled condition than to overstress the airplane, so in very turbulent air, you would slow the airplane to assure that it would stall before this could occur. The speed that divides the stall area from the area of possible overstress is called the "maneuvering speed" and has the designation V_A. The maneuvering speed varies from approximately twice the stall speed, as given by the gross weight calibrated stall speed (at maximum certificated weight), to about 1.6 times that figure at minimum flyable weight for most lightplanes. As an all-around figure when encountering moderate to severe turbulence, slow the airplane to indicate 1.6 times the calibrated stall speed *at all weights*. This will mean that the airplane will stall momentarily rather than

exceed the limit load factor; it will also mean an easier ride for you. Pilots' ideas of "moderate" and "severe" turbulence vary widely. Avoid such turbulent conditions if possible—check for Convective SIGMETs, SIGMETs, and AIRMETs before you go.

If you had "maneuver" and "gust" envelope diagrams for your airplane, you could pick out a range of speeds within which the airplane would neither stall nor be overstressed by expected maximum gusts, but since these are not normally available, you may have to use rules of thumb and stay on the safe side. Vertical gusts don't just affect the airplane in cruise; they work during climbs, glides, or any other maneuvers.

Summary

1. In light turbulence or if you expect that you may encounter it, keep the airspeed in the green arc.
2. In moderate to severe turbulence, slow the airplane to 1.6 times the flaps-up stall speed as given in the *Pilot's Operating Handbook* (calibrated airspeed). If you have more detailed information from the manufacturer on gust penetration speeds, use that (calibrated airspeed). Remember that the 1.6 figure is aimed only at assuring that the airplane will stall rather than be overstressed. Stalls at low altitudes are dangerous also.
3. Check Convective SIGMETs, SIGMETs and AIRMETs, and avoid areas of turbulence if possible.

Weight and Balance

It's very important that you have an understanding of airplane loading. Some pilots have only a hazy conception of what can happen when the maximum allowable weight and/or center of gravity limits are exceeded.

The "center of gravity" (CG) is the point at which the airplane's entire weight is assumed to be concentrated. The manufacturer sets limits on weight and the

Figure 23-3. Weight and balance envelope.

CG location so that the airplane will not be in a dangerous condition. Figure 23-3 shows a weight and balance envelope for a two-place trainer certificated in both normal and utility categories. The weight and CG must stay within the envelope.

You see that the airplane has closer limits in both weight *and* rearward CG location in the utility category. The less-rearward CG limit is present because this particular airplane in the utility category is not restricted against intentional spinning. The less-rearward CG limit assures that the airplane will retain good spin recovery characteristics. If the airplane's weight and balance fall outside the dashed line envelope, it is no longer in the utility category and intentional spins are prohibited. Figure 23-3 is taken from the airplane's *weight and balance form.* (The arrow shows a point to be discussed later.)

The term "moment" will become important when you start working with airplane loading. A moment is a measure of a force (or weight) times an arm and is normally expressed in pound-inches or pound-feet. For airplane weight and balance computations, moments are

discussed in terms of pound-inches. Figure 23-4 shows how two equal moments acting in opposite directions can cancel each other so that equilibrium exists.

You've applied the principle of moments by using a long pole in levering. Figure 23-5 shows the lift and weight moments acting on an airplane in straight and level cruising flight.

The forces and moments must be in balance for equilibrium to exist. A tail-down force normally exists in flight. To simplify matters, rather than establish the moments from the center of gravity (which is the usual case), for this problem they will be measured fore and aft from the center of lift. Assume for now that the lift force is a string holding the airplane "up"; its value will be found later.

The airplane in Figure 23-5 weighs 1,500 pounds and the CG is 5 inches ahead of the center of lift. This results in a *nose-down* moment of 7,500 pound-inches (5 × 1,500). To balance this, a moment acting in the opposite direction is required and will be furnished by a tail-down force. The center of "lift" (down-acting) of the horizontal tail is 150 inches behind the wing center of lift, so in order to have an equal *nose-up* moment, a tail-down force of 50 pounds is necessary (50 × 150 = 7,500 pound-inches). The airplane nose does not tend to pitch either up or down; the weight and tail-down moments are balanced. This is a simplified approach; there are other moments in existence (the wing has a moment of its own, which was neglected here). The tail-down force varies with CG position and/or airspeed.

Earlier in this book it was stated that in straight and level flight lift equals weight. This was done to keep from complicating the issue in the introduction to flight and the Four Fundamentals. The vertical forces working on the airplane must be equal. Looking at Figure

Figure 23-4. A system of two equal moments.

Figure 23-5. Lift and weight forces and moments acting on an airplane in flight at a particular weight and CG position.

23-5, you'll note that the down forces are weight, 1,500 pounds, and the tail-down force, 50 pounds. In order to fly straight and level, the total up force (lift) must equal these down forces. Hence lift must be 1,550 pounds, not 1,500 pounds as would be expected from the weight of the airplane. But in flight you don't worry about this. You make the airplane do its job by varying the tail force as necessary to obtain the desired angle of attack—and airspeed. You use trim or wheel pressure as necessary (plus power) to attain the end performance. There are thrust and drag moments also existing in flight, but these are comparatively minor and were neglected for this problem. So as far as flying the airplane and the g-force discussion are concerned, the tail-down force could be considered as weight and is important to the stability of the plane.

The position of the CG has an effect on the stall speed for a given weight because the higher the tail-down force (as would be required at a forward CG position), the greater the total load carried or the more the airplane "weighs." Look at Figure 23-5 to see that if the CG is moved far enough forward so that the taildown force increases to, say, 150 pounds total, the wings would have to support 1,650 pounds, not 1,550. The stall speed increases as the square root of the "weight" increases (actual or aerodynamic down load, as is the case for the example here). The stall speed marked on the airspeed indicator is based on maximum certificated weight at the most forward CG which gives the highest stall speed, a conservative approach.

If you place a lot of weight too far aft, a condition known as "longitudinal instability" could arise. First, look at the correctly loaded airplane; you know that the airplane, as you have flown it to date, has been inherently stable. That is, you can trim it at airspeeds from just above the stall to just below the red line and it tends to stay at that speed. You also know that if you trim it for cruise, for instance, slowing it down requires more and more back pressure as the speed decreases. Conversely, to increase the speed above the trimmed speed requires more and more forward pressure. This is the "weigh" it should be.

If you load it so that the CG is too far aft, the required tail-down force decreases. If you move the CG to a certain point, the requirement for a tail-down force may disappear completely. In effect, the airplane's nose may be displaced up or down with little or no effort on your part. In extreme cases, if offset by bumpy air, the nose could pitch up (or down) at an increasing rate, and an extremely dangerous situation would be in effect. In short, the airplane would tend not to return to its trim speed and would not want to maintain any particular airspeed.

If you observe the rearward CG limits as shown on the weight and balance envelope of your airplane, you'll avoid this condition.

Notice in Figure 23-3 that there is a forward CG limit on the envelope; this is to be observed also. However, just from the general characteristics of most light trainers, this one is sometimes hard to exceed, simply because there's just too little space up front to put baggage and other excess weight. (However, there are always those who will manage to put an anvil or two under the pilot's feet or pull some other unlikely stunt.) The main reason for the forward CG limit is that of control rather than stability. The CG may be so far forward that you don't have enough up-elevator to get the nose up to the proper position on landing—and end up bending something.

You'll notice that the airplane's baggage compartment is placarded for maximum weight. This is done for two reasons: (1) to prevent the center of gravity from being moved outside approved limits, which could be the case if the compartment was overloaded, and (2) structural considerations. The baggage compartment floor will be able to take its placarded weight up to the positive limit load factor, but suppose instead of putting in 100 pounds as placarded, you put in *200 pounds*. This would mean that at 3.8 g's, 760 pounds would be exerted instead of the 380 pounds it was designed to take. You just might have a new observation window where the baggage compartment floor used to be. *Observe all placards in the airplane.*

Running a Weight and Balance

The next step is to assure yourself that your airplane will stay within approved CG limits.

The "datum" is the point from which all measurements are taken for weight and balance computations. It may be a point on the airplane or it may be well in front of the airplane. Figure 23-6 shows a high-wing trainer with the datum located 60 inches in front of the leading edge of the wing. It is standard practice to establish the datum at a fixed distance ahead of a well-defined part of the airplane, or in some cases the front side of the firewall may be used. For trainers so equipped, the reference point is the straight leading edge.

Suppose that the empty weight CG is required. This is determined initially at the factory but may change if equipment is added. In such an event it would be duly noted in the logbook by the mechanic who makes the change.

The airplane is weighed in a level attitude with a scale under each wheel. The illustrated airplane's empty weight is a total of the three scale weights, or

Figure 23-6. The datum, with weighing point locations, and weights. The arms have been rounded off here.

982 pounds. The empty weight CG is found by using the datum and summing up moments.

The nosewheel center line is 23.9 inches aft of the datum, so its moment is 23.9 × 327 = 7,815 pound-inches. The two main wheel center lines are 91.5 inches aft of the datum, so 91.5 × (329 + 326) = 91.5 inches × 655 pounds. The moment of the two main wheels is 59,932 pound-inches. The total moment is 59,932 + 7,815, or 67,747 pound-inches. To find the position of the CG, the total moment is divided by the total weight, which gives the position where the *center of the total empty weight is acting to create the total moment*. This works out to be 69 inches (rounded off) (67,747 ÷ 982). (Actually, if you worked it out on a calculator, the answer would be 68.988798 inches, but you don't measure points that closely.) Hence, the empty center of gravity is 69 inches aft of the datum, or 9 inches behind the leading edge of the wing. The basic empty weight of an airplane includes fixed ballast, unusable fuel, full oil, full engine coolant (naturally, not applicable to air-cooled engines), and hydraulic fluid. The unusable fuel

for this particular airplane was negligible and did not add any weight to the empty weight "as weighed." If the airplane had not yet been painted at the time of the weighing, the weight of the paint (this may be from 5 to 20 pounds, depending on the size of the airplane) plus unusable fuel (if applicable) would have to be added to get the basic *empty weight* and CG. This is a favorite subject for questions on the Private Pilot Knowledge Test, and the student usually forgets that *unusable fuel and full oil are included in the basic empty weight*. Item 1 in Figure 23-7 (for a different trainer) gives the basic empty weight. Included in that item is 3.5 gallons of unusable fuel (the total tank capacity is 26.0 gallons with 22.5 usable).

Back to our original trainer, you could compute the effects of adding fuel, pilot, passengers, and baggage (Figure 23-6). The following would be a computation as given in the example airplane's weight and balance form. The arms here are rounded off to the nearest inch and would be given on the form.

Item	*Weight*		*Arm*		*Moment*
			(aft of datum)		*(pound-inches)*
Basic empty weight					
(includes full oil)	982	×	69	=	67,747
Usable Fuel (36 gal)	216	×	84	=	18,144
Pilot	180	×	81	=	14,580
Passenger	160	×	81	=	12,960
Baggage	100	×	101	=	10,100
	1,638				123,531

(You may find a slight error in the total pound-inches because the empty CG was rounded off.)

Again, dividing the *total moment* (123,531 pound-inches) by the *total weight* (1,638 pounds), it is found that the CG is located at 75.4 inches aft of the datum. Looking back to Figure 23-3, the weight and balance

SAMPLE LOADING PROBLEM	SAMPLE AIRPLANE		YOUR AIRPLANE	
	Weight (lbs.)	Moment (lb.-ins. /1000)	Weight (lbs.)	Moment (lb.-ins. /1000)
1. Basic Empty Weight (Use the data pertaining to your airplane as it is presently equipped. Includes unusable fuel and full oil)	1125	36.6		
2. Usable Fuel (At 6 Lbs./Gal.) Standard Tanks (22.5 Gal. Maximum)	135	5.7		
Long Range Tanks (35 Gal. Maximum)				
Reduced Fuel (As limited by maximum weight)				
3. Pilot and Passenger (Station 33 to 41)	340	13.3		
4. Baggage - Area 1 (Or passenger on child's seat) (Station 50 to 76, 120 Lbs. Max.)				
5. Baggage - Area 2 (Station 76 to 94, 40 Lbs. Max.)				
6. TOTAL WEIGHT AND MOMENT	1600	55.6		
7. Locate this point (1600 at 55.6) on the Center of Gravity Moment Envelope, and since this point falls within the envelope, the loading is acceptable.				

BAGGAGE LOADING AND TIE-DOWN

UTILITY SHELF

BAGGAGE AREA MAXIMUM ALLOWABLE LOADS

AREA ① = 120 POUNDS
AREA ② = 40 POUNDS
AREAS ① + ② = 120 POUNDS

✱ TIE-DOWN NET ATTACH POINTS

✱ A tie-down net is provided to secure baggage in the baggage area. The net attaches to six tie-down rings. Two rings are located on the floor just aft of the seat backs and one ring is located two inches above the floor on each cabin wall at the aft end of area ①. Two additional rings are located at the top, aft end of area ②. At least four rings should be used to restrain the maximum baggage load of 120*.

If the airplane is equipped with utility shelf, it should be removed prior to loading and tying down large baggage items. (Slide the tab of the locking clips on each end of the shelf to disengage the shelf from the aircraft structure.) After baggage is loaded and secured, either stow the shelf or, if space permits, install it for storing small articles.

Figure 23-7. A sample loading problem. If the airplane had been weighed at the factory without full oil or unusable fuel, this would have been "added" mathematically to get the basic empty weight of 1,125 pounds.

envelope for this airplane, you see by the dot (arrows) that the CG is within limits for the normal category (you have 12 pounds to spare in weight and about 0.8 inch in CG range). The airplane as loaded in this problem is outside the utility category envelope, so intentional spins would be prohibited.

You could work out combinations of pilot, fuel, baggage, and passengers to allow the airplane to be operated in the utility category.

The method used earlier to find the empty weight CG is not the shortest way to arrive at the proper answer; the weight and balance form will give simple preset equations to arrive at the answer. The method used here shows the principle. (Also, some of the figures were rounded off for simplicity.)

The FAA considers fuel to weigh 6 pounds per gallon and oil 7½ pounds per gallon. In practice you'd use actual passengers' weights to be accurate. (Naturally, you'd better not be flying nonrated persons until you get that private or sport pilot certificate.)

Other airplanes use a slightly different approach to the weight and balance problem. Figures 23-7, 23-8, and 23-9 show the steps as would be applied to a Cessna 150.

The sample problem in Figure 23-7 shows that the loaded airplane weighs 1,600 pounds and has a moment of 55,600 pound-inches. This would place it in the envelope, as shown in Figure 23-9.

Note in Figure 23-7 that the total baggage capacity of the airplane is 120 pounds. You can either put it all in area 1, or 80 pounds in area 1 and 40 pounds (its maximum allowable) in area 2.

Figure 23-8 shows how the various moments were obtained. The shallower the slope of the line, the more effect each pound has in increasing the moment. As an example, 100 pounds of baggage in area 1 furnishes the same moment (6,500 pound-inches) as a 167-pound pilot or front-seat passenger.

Figure 23-8. A loading graph.

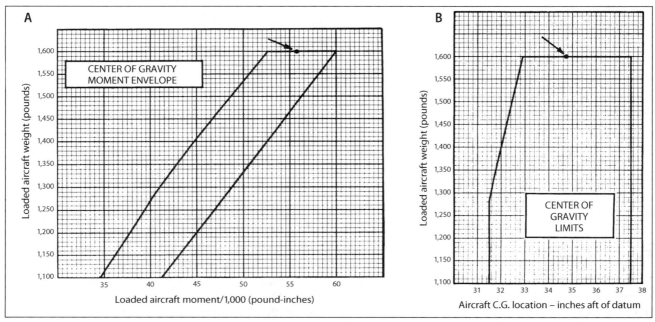

Figure 23-9. Center of gravity moment envelope and CG limits envelope for the sample airplane in Figure 23-7. The datum for that airplane is the front firewall. In this arrangement, weights rearward of that point have "positive" arms; weights forward would have "negative" arms, and this is basically the same idea as that shown in Figure 23-4. The total of the "negative" moments would be subtracted from the total of the "positive" moments to get some answer with the CG as (A), a positive moment acting "behind" the datum, or (B), the weight and CG in inches aft of the datum (firewall) as shown by the arrows in the two envelopes. To find the location of the CG, divide the total moment (55,600) by the total weight (1,600 pounds) as indicated by the arrow (B) to get a position of 34.75 inches aft of the datum.

Don't try to beat the system by overloading the airplane (and having it in a critical aft CG condition) and thinking that you'll "just get it a foot or so off the ground and if it doesn't feel right, I'll put it back on." An interesting phenomenon is that an airplane for a given weight and CG position is more stable in ground effect; that is, it doesn't want to nose up abruptly as it might up at altitude at a rearward CG. Also, as discussed in Chapter 17, ground effect starts to make itself known on approach and landing at a height of about one-half wingspan above the ground and becomes stronger as the airplane descends. The "downwash" from the wing is altered in ground effect; the direction of the flow at the horizontal tail is changed, and the effect is more of a tendency for the nose to stay lower, or the airplane feels more stable. This could fool a pilot who is *taking off*, the airplane may be marginal as far as stability is concerned in the ground effect; but as it moves upward after lift-off, the stabilizing influence is lost, the nose rises higher and higher, and a stall—and accident—occurs. This problem often occurs when people are leaving on vacation and "need" all that gear in the back seat and baggage compartment.

Also, you'll find that overloading affects takeoff performance radically. (A 10 percent increase in weight means at least a 21 percent increase in takeoff run distance.) The overloaded airplane manages to get off with the aid of ground effect, which reduces the induced drag, but is unable to climb more than a few feet. Obstructions at the far end of the runway could mean a hasty end to the flight. With the aid of ground effect, the airplane's performance is marginal, and when it starts to move upward, the increase in induced drag stops any further climb. Too many accidents are caused by the pilot trying to beat aerodynamic laws.

Fuel and Oil Information

When you refuel at a strange airport, it will be your responsibility to see that the proper grade of fuel and oil are used.

Fuel

Never use fuel rated below the minimum grade recommended for your airplane. You may go above as a temporary arrangement, but even then, stay as close to the recommended grade as you can.

The numbers are the antiknock quality of the fuel—the higher the number, the better the antiknock qualities. For instance, 80/87: The first number (80) is the minimum antiknock quality of the fuel in the lean mixture; the last (87) is the minimum antiknock quality in the rich mixture.

Grade 80 is becoming very rare in the United States. Some operators are stocking only one grade, 100 Low Lead, for use by airplanes requiring as a minimum either 80/87 or the 100/130 grade higher-leaded fuel.

You'll hear aviation fuel referred to as, for instance, grade 80 or grade 100, without the qualifying second figure (80/87). This term use was recommended by the American Society for Testing and Materials (ASTM) for simplification purposes, but the rich and lean antiknock ratings still stand.

The various octanes and performance-numbered fuels contain dyes of different colors to aid in identification.

The colors are valid in the United States but may not be the same in foreign countries.

Grade	Fuel Color
80/87	Red
100LL	Blue

In planning the cross-country, check in the *Airport/Facility Directory* to be sure that at least the minimum rated fuel for your engine is available at any place you intend to refuel.

Oil

The viscosity of oil will be indicated in one of two ways. You are probably most familiar with the SAE (Society of Automotive Engineers) numbers.

SAE Number	Commercial Aviation Number
40	80
50	100
60	120
70	140

Notice that in every case the commercial aviation number is exactly twice the SAE "weight." To get the SAE equivalent, divide the aviation number by two.

Know what type of oil your airplane has been using. You'll hear the terms "detergent" and "nondetergent," but the oil primarily used in airplane engines today is one of two types: (1) *mineral oil* (called nondetergent), which is plain oil with no additives, and (2) *ashless dispersant* (AD) *oil* (often mistakenly called "detergent"), which is mineral oil with additives that give better wear qualities and multiviscosity and also pick up small particles (contamination), keeping them suspended in the oil so that sludge and carbon deposits aren't formed. The old detergent oils could wash out carbon if added to an engine that had been using straight mineral oil and cause sludge problems in filters.

There are many multiviscosity oils available and your airplane may use one of these. Check before using cross-brands of this type of oil too.

Know and add *only* the brand and type of oil the airplane has been using. Some brands or types may not mix, but some oil manufacturers say that adding straight mineral oil to AD oils is normally all right if you feel you really need the oil to get home safely.

Cruise Control

Probably the term "cruise control" brings to your mind a vision of a vast array of knobs and dials requiring continual monitoring on your part. Cruise control actually means that in cruising flight you know such things as the amount of power being carried (used) and the fuel consumption. This section is based on the premise that your trainer uses a fixed-pitch prop.

Up to now you've probably paid little attention to what power has been carried or the specific fuel consumption, but you have used your instructor's recommendations for tachometer settings for various maneuvers; and, of course, you always checked to make sure you had more than enough fuel to make those local flights. (And if asked for the fuel consumption, you probably could answer vaguely "five or six gallons an hour, or somewhere in there.")

On extended flights it is vital that you know how much fuel you are using and how to plan use and conserve fuel if necessary.

Back in Chapter 5 the mixture control was introduced, but it could be that for local flying you haven't been checked out on mixture leaning techniques and have flown the airplane in the full-rich setting.

Figure 23-10 is a time, fuel, and distance to climb tabulation for a particular airplane. Pressure altitudes and standard temperatures are given. Suppose the elevation of your airport is 1,000 feet (and the pressure altitude and temperature are standard). You want to depart on a cross-country to cruise at 5,500 MSL. Your problem might be worked out like this: You would interpolate between 5,000 and 6,000 feet and get totals of 10 minutes from *sea level,* 1.45 gallons of fuel (call it 1.5 gallons), and a distance of 11.5 NM (call it 12 NM). However, you're starting from 1,000 feet so you would subtract those values (2 minutes, 0.2 gallons, and 2 NM) from the 5,500 figure and get an answer of *8 minutes, 1.3 gallons, (add 0.8 gallons for start, taxi, and takeoff for a total of 2.1 gallons of fuel for climb to 5,500 feet), and 10 NM to climb from your airport at 1,000 feet elevation to the cruise level of 5,500 MSL.*

Note that for each 8°C above standard for the altitudes you would add 10 percent to the three values of time, fuel used, and distance.

TIME, FUEL, AND DISTANCE TO CLIMB

MAXIMUM RATE OF CLIMB

CONDITIONS:
Flaps Up
Full Throttle
Standard Temperature

NOTES:
1.   Add 0.8 of a gallon of fuel for engine start, taxi and takeoff allowance.
2.   Increase time, fuel and distance by 10% for each 8°C above standard temperature.
3.   Distances shown are based on zero wind.

WEIGHT LBS	PRESSURE ALTITUDE FT	TEMP °C	CLIMB SPEED KIAS	RATE OF CLIMB FPM	FROM SEA LEVEL		
					TIME MIN	FUEL USED GALLONS	DISTANCE NM
1600	S.L.	15	68	670	0	0	0
	1000	13	68	630	2	0.2	2
	2000	11	67	590	3	0.5	4
	3000	9	66	550	5	0.7	6
	4000	7	65	510	7	1.0	8
	5000	5	65	470	9	1.3	10
	6000	3	64	425	11	1.6	13
	7000	1	64	385	14	1.9	16
	8000	-1	63	345	17	2.3	19
	9000	-3	63	305	20	2.7	23
	10,000	-5	62	265	23	3.2	27
	11,000	-7	62	220	27	3.7	32
	12,000	-9	61	180	33	4.3	38

Figure 23-10. Time, fuel, and distance to climb chart.

The distances shown are based on zero wind conditions. Wind would only affect distance (assuming that turbulence isn't hurting your climb performance), since the airplane would require the same amount of time and fuel to get to a certain altitude. Headwind or tailwind components would affect the number of miles covered in that time. (More about that in Chapter 24.)

Setting Power

In Chapter 12 you had a brief encounter with cruise control when it was mentioned that airplanes cruised at 75 percent of the rated power or below (65 and 75 percent are the most popular settings and 65 percent is a lot easier on the engine, for only a very small loss in airspeed).

To review some theory of airplane performance: Figure 23-11 shows a performance chart for a light trainer with a fixed-pitch prop.

Point (1) is the top speed of the airplane. For airplanes with unsupercharged engines, the *top speed is always found at sea level* because this is the place where the engine develops its maximum power. As altitude increases, the air becomes less dense and power is lost so that the maximum possible airspeed decreases. (You lose power faster than TAS is gained.)

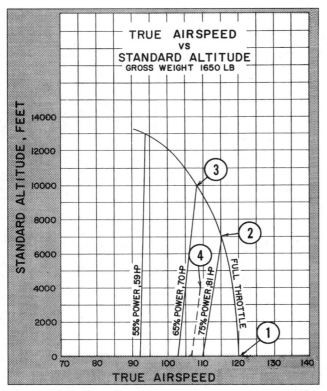

Figure 23-11. True airspeed versus standard (density) altitude for a light trainer.

At point (2) you'll note that the power has dropped off so that only 75 percent of the sea level power is being developed. Because 75 percent is the maximum legitimate cruising power setting, you'd get the most true airspeed per horsepower for extended operations at about 7,000 feet (standard, or density-altitude). If your airplane has a fuel consumption of, say, 7 gallons per hour at 75 percent power, you'll do better at that power by cruising at 7,000 feet (115) than at sea level (110). This is, of course, taking winds, ceiling, and other outside factors into consideration.

If you are a believer in the use of 65 percent as a cruise power setting, you can see that point (3) is best for this setting as far as getting the maximum TAS is concerned. An altitude of 10,000 feet is the highest at which you will be able to develop 65 percent of the sea level power.

Notice that TAS is gained with altitude at 65 and 75 percent—until you run out of throttle. You'll have to open the throttle as you increase altitude to maintain the same percentage of power. (You'll need a higher rpm to get 75 percent at 7,000 feet than at sea level.) Obviously, the first thought is that, if you are carrying more throttle (rpm), you must be burning more fuel at the higher altitudes. That's where cruise control comes

in. Because of the decrease in air density, the mixture can be progressively leaned with altitude increase so that 75 percent power at the higher altitudes results in fuel consumption no higher than that same power setting at sea level.

Next comes the question as to how to obtain the various power settings; the *Pilot's Operating Handbook* will help you out here. Figure 23-12 shows a graphical method of setting up power for various altitudes.

If you wanted to carry 70 percent power at 4,000 feet, it would require 2,500 rpm and the airplane would have a TAS as shown in Figures 23-11 and 23-12.

A careful took at Figure 23-12 shows that a power setting of 2,410 rpm is required for 70 percent at sea level, and 2,500 rpm at a standard (density) altitude of 4,000 feet. This means an increase of 90 rpm, which works out to be approximately 1 percent increase in rpm per 1,000 feet. For airplanes having rpm settings for cruise at sea level of 2,300–2,500 rpm you could, as a rule of thumb, add 25 rpm per 1,000 feet to maintain the sea level percentage of power. As an example, if 70 percent power at sea level requires 2,410 rpm, you'd be very close to the *Pilot's Operating Handbook* figure for *4,000 feet* by adding 100 rpm (4 × 25) to the sea level figure. This comes out to be 2,510 rpm, as compared to the 2,500 rpm in Figure 23-12. (It's extremely difficult to read a difference of 10 rpm on the tachometer, anyway.) Obviously, it is always better to use the manufacturer's figures, but if you know the sea level rpm for the desired power setting you can get within the ballpark for your altitude if you don't have a power setting chart along. You will be limited by the maximum allowable rpm at any time or altitude. (Don't exceed the red line on the tachometer at any time.)

Figure 23-12. True airspeed and rpm versus standard (density) altitude.

Leaning the Mixture

How do you know your fuel consumption? Figure 23-13 is a fuel consumption graph for the airplane just discussed. The mixture control can make quite a difference in fuel consumption. At 2,500 rpm there is a difference of about 1.1 gallons; in this case you'd burn about 16 percent more fuel in the full-rich setting than in best lean. (Nonturbocharged, direct drive engines can normally be leaned at any altitude in cruise at 75 percent power and below.)

There are several techniques, some of which include the use of cylinder-head temperature gauges or even special gauges designed specifically for use in leaning. For your present situation, however, the following technique, while not as accurate as some, is simple to use.

After you have reached the desired altitude, let the airplane establish the cruise airspeed and set the power. Then slowly move the mixture control aft until the engine begins to roughen slightly. Move the mixture control forward *just enough* to smooth out the engine again.

As the airplane climbs, the air becomes less dense, and less fuel is needed for a proper mixture as you increase altitude. If the engine starts running rough as altitude is gained (it will normally require at least 5,000 feet density-altitude for this problem to make itself known), lean the mixture until smooth operation

occurs. Use a full-rich mixture for climbs unless your instructor or the *Pilot's Operating Handbook* gives specific procedures for leaning in the climb.

Because of the loss of power involved with an overly rich mixture, at airports at higher elevations you may need to lean to obtain the best power for takeoff. Do this at full throttle at static run-up. Lean the mixture until maximum rpm occurs. Richen the mixture slightly from this maximum rpm setting to ensure proper cooling. (Don't do this over sand or gravel.)

One of the problems you may encounter on one of the solo cross-countries is forgetting to richen the mixture when descending from cruising altitude. You'll probably be so engrossed in getting into the traffic pattern and watching for other airplanes (plus maybe having a little stage fright about going into a controlled field) that the need for richening the mixture on the descent doesn't occur to you. The engine may start running rough—or even quit momentarily—to remind you of this oversight. *Use a checklist.*

Figure 23-14 is a cruise performance chart for a current trainer. You can interpolate between altitudes, horsepower, and temperatures to get the conditions you're flying in. For instance, you're flying at a pressure altitude of 5,500 feet and the temperature is 5°C above normal for that altitude. You want to carry 69 percent power and so would go through the following process: You'd start with the standard temperature numbers. At 4,000 feet, use 69 percent to get a TAS of 100 K and fuel consumption of 5.2 gallons per hour. At 6,000 feet (standard temperature) the values are 102 K and 5.2 gallons per hour (again interpolated between 73 and 64 percent brake horsepower).

So the values at 5,500 feet would be three-fourths of the difference between 4,000 and 6,000, or 101.5 K and 5.2 gallons per hour. (Practically speaking, you could get the information for 6,000 feet and be very close.) Further checking by interpolation of the effect of the addition of about 5°C above standard would show a small addition of about 1 K.

One point should be brought out: The airplane will use basically the same amount of fuel for, say, 70 percent power at any altitude, assuming that the mixture has been leaned properly in each case, but the advantage of altitude (once you get there) is that you are getting more miles to the gallon because of increased TAS. Take a look under the *standard temperature column* at 65 percent power at 2,000 feet and at 8,000 feet. At 2,000 feet pressure altitude, the TAS is 96 K at a fuel consumption of 4.9 gallons per hour. Interpolating to get 65 percent at 8,000 feet, the same fuel consumption (4.9 gph) is found but with a TAS of 101+ K. Note that the chart is given to the nearest knot and 0.1 gallon.

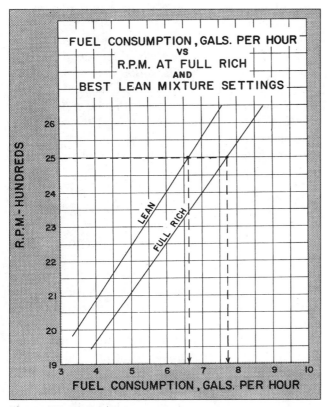

Figure 23-13. Fuel consumption versus rpm.

CRUISE PERFORMANCE

CONDITIONS:
1600 Pounds
Recommended Lean Mixture

PRESSURE ALTITUDE	RPM	20°C BELOW STANDARD TEMP			STANDARD TEMPERATURE			20°C ABOVE STANDARD TEMP		
		% BHP	KTAS	GPH	% BHP	KTAS	GPH	% BHP	KTAS	GPH
2000	2650	- - -	- - -	- - -	78	103	5.9	72	102	5.4
	2600	80	102	6.0	73	101	5.5	68	100	5.1
	2500	70	97	5.3	65	96	4.9	60	95	4.6
	2400	62	92	4.7	57	91	4.3	53	91	4.1
	2300	54	87	4.1	50	87	3.9	47	86	3.7
	2200	47	83	3.7	44	82	3.5	42	81	3.3
4000	2700	- - -	- - -	- - -	78	105	5.8	72	104	5.4
	2600	75	101	5.6	69	100	5.2	64	99	4.8
	2500	66	96	5.0	61	95	4.6	57	95	4.3
	2400	58	91	4.4	54	91	4.1	50	90	3.9
	2300	51	87	3.9	48	86	3.7	45	85	3.5
	2200	45	82	3.5	42	81	3.3	40	80	3.2
6000	2750	- - -	- - -	- - -	77	107	5.8	71	105	5.3
	2700	79	105	5.9	73	104	5.4	67	103	5.1
	2600	70	100	5.2	64	99	4.8	60	98	4.5
	2500	62	95	4.7	57	95	4.3	53	94	4.1
	2400	54	91	4.2	51	90	3.9	48	89	3.7
	2300	48	86	3.7	45	85	3.5	42	84	3.4
8000	2700	74	104	5.5	68	103	5.1	63	102	4.8
	2600	65	99	4.9	60	99	4.6	57	98	4.3
	2500	58	95	4.4	54	94	4.1	51	93	3.9
	2400	52	90	4.0	48	89	3.7	45	88	3.5
	2300	46	85	3.6	43	84	3.4	40	82	3.2
10000	2700	69	103	5.2	64	102	4.8	59	102	4.5
	2600	61	99	4.6	57	98	4.3	53	97	4.1
	2500	55	94	4.2	51	93	3.9	48	92	3.7
	2400	49	89	3.8	45	88	3.6	43	87	3.4
12000	2650	61	100	4.6	57	99	4.3	53	98	4.1
	2600	58	98	4.4	54	97	4.1	50	96	3.9
	2500	52	93	4.0	48	92	3.7	45	91	3.5
	2400	46	89	3.6	43	87	3.4	41	84	3.3

Figure 23-14. Cruise performance chart. Note, as mentioned earlier, that the power required for a specific horsepower must be increased by 25 rpm per 1,000 feet of altitude. The underlined figures for 54 percent power for 4,000, 8,000, and 12,000 feet show this (2,400, 2,500, and 2,600 rpm respectively).

Figure 23-15 includes range and endurance profile charts. Note (1) in each chart indicates that the chart allows for the fuel used for engine start, taxi, takeoff, and climb distance (range profile), and climb time (endurance profile) as would be taken from the time, fuel, and distance to climb chart (Figure 23-10).

You could use Figures 23-10 (for climb) and 23-14 (for level cruise) to make your own graphs.

Looking at Figure 23-15 you can see some interesting points.

Range is not so much affected by altitude (at lower altitudes) as endurance is. The range stays constant with altitude until certain altitudes are reached and then decreases with altitude. This is because the time and fuel required to climb to higher altitudes cut down on the total range available. (The miles covered during the climb are considerably less than those covered in straight and level flight—and at higher fuel consumption.)

Note that endurance is greatest at sea level and starts dropping immediately with altitude increase.

Maximum endurance is found at lower altitudes and at power settings of 40–45 percent power for this airplane (look at Figure 23-15).

As an example, using the range profile, you would expect to have a range of 400 NM (including climb) at 7,000 feet density-altitude (standard pressure and temperature at that altitude) at 55 percent power (94 KTAS) in zero wind. At sea level at 45 percent power, you could expect a range of 440 NM at 81 K (TAS).

A point you might notice by checking Figure 23-15 is that the maximum range (miles) for the various altitudes is found at a power setting of 45 percent of the rated brake horsepower. Looking back at Figure 12-13, you note that this is the area indicated by point (2) for maximum range conditions. The thumb rule cited for maximum range was a calibrated airspeed of 1.5 times the power-off, flaps-up stall speed. The stall speed for this example airplane (flaps-up, etc.) is 47 K. Converting the true airspeeds for the various altitudes, you would find that the thumb rule is close to optimum.

Figure 23-16 shows another method of computing fuel, time, and distance to climb.

The example shows how you would work a problem from an airport of 1,100 feet pressure altitude at 8°C temperature for a climb to 3,300 feet. A quick way to see how the graph works is to assume that the climb is from sea level to 8,000 feet (standard temperatures). You'll see that approximately 2.2+ gallons are used, with 17 minutes and 21 NM (no wind) required to reach that altitude.

Another point: Look back at Figure 23-10. To climb from sea level to 9,000 feet would require 20 minutes and 2.7 gallons of fuel. This works out to be 8.1 gallons per hour used in the climb, or more than a 65 percent higher rate of consumption than is found at 65 percent power at cruise and leaned (4.9 gph). The point is that if you have to do a lot of climbing, your fuel consumption (and hence fuel remaining) may fool you if *POH* figures aren't available.

Fuel Management

If your plane has selectors for two tanks, cross-country flying will likely be your introduction to switching tanks in flight.

If your airplane has two separate fuel tanks, one may be listed as the "main" tank and the other the "auxiliary." The manufacturer in this case will recommend use of the main tank (both may have the same fuel capacity) for takeoff and landing and use of the auxiliary only in level flight. A recommended procedure in this case would be to use the main tank until cruising flight is established, then switch to the other one. This will give you a check as to whether fuel can

Figure 23-15. Range and endurance profile charts for the airplane or use Figures 23-10 and 23-14.

Figure 23-16. Graphical presentation of fuel, time, and distance to climb.

be gotten from that second tank. There's no law that says you couldn't use most of the fuel in one tank and *then* switch to the other for the first time, *but* if the system of that second tank has a malfunction and won't feed, you'll have used nearly all of the available fuel and might not have enough left to make it to an airport. If you switch tanks right after cruise is established and the tank does have a malfunction, you can switch back to the good one and have sufficient fuel to turn around and get back to the airport.

It's important that the run-up before takeoff be done on the tank to be used for takeoff. If you make the run-up on one tank and at the last second decide to use another one, run the engine on the new tank for at least a minute at fairly high power settings (at 1,500 rpm or above). You might switch to that new tank, immediately start your takeoff, and learn the hard way that it won't feed. (Roughly speaking, you'll find that there'll be just enough fuel left in the carburetor to get you to exactly the worst point to have the engine quit.)

Figure 23-17 shows the schematic of a simple fuel system for a current high-wing trainer. The engine is gravity fed (the tanks are in the wings). The fuel from both tanks simultaneously moves to the fuel shutoff valve, which has two positions, OFF and ON.

Figure 23-18 is a fuel system schematic for a current low-wing trainer. Because the fuel tanks in the wings don't give gravity feed, an engine-driven fuel pump must be a part of the system. An electrically driven fuel pump also is installed as a safety standby for takeoff and landing, or at any time that the engine-driven pump should fail. Some *Pilot Operating Handbooks* recommend turning the electrical fuel pump ON when switching tanks if one has run dry. The pump was discussed briefly in Chapter 7. Since a fuel pump is used, a fuel pressure gauge is added to the system. This particular airplane uses fuel from either the left or right tank (you don't have a setting to use both tanks simultaneously). There is also an OFF position on the fuel selector valve.

An important factor is the amount of usable fuel in the tank. If a tank has a capacity of 20 gallons yet only 18 gallons are usable, you'll have to do your planning on the basis of 18 gallons, no matter what it says on the tank caps.

Have an idea ahead of time about how long you can expect to run on each tank at the planned power setting. Fuel gauges can and do fail.

If at all possible, when the airplane is being fueled at *any* time, you should personally oversee it. This is particularly important when at a strange airport. There have been cases of jet fuel being put in the tanks of an

Figure 23-17. Fuel system schematic for a high-wing trainer.

airplane with a reciprocating engine. If undetected, this will almost certainly cause a crash. While your small airplane is not likely to be mistaken for a jet or turboprop, fuel in service trucks has been inadvertently switched. In checking the fuel during the preflight of the airplane, *smell* it. You might be able to pick up the kerosene-like smell of jet fuel in the tanks.

There have been instances of fuel being put in the wrong tanks of an airplane; the pilot tells the line service people to "fill up the mains," and they fill up the auxiliary tanks with the result that the airplane may run out of fuel in the main tanks on takeoff or another critical point. (*But* the pilot should have checked the fuel level in the mains during the preflight.)

There have also been situations in which the "proper" fuel was put in *another airplane*! The pilot, not checking the fuel level before the flight, took off, figuring that "the gauges are wrong," and the flight was shorter than anticipated.

The problems just mentioned can be avoided if you oversee the fueling and check the fuel level visually (with a dipstick) during a thorough preflight check.

Notes on Constant-Speed Propeller Operation (Nonturbocharged Engines)

A study has shown that the vast majority of flight schools use only smaller trainers with fixed-gear and fixed-pitch propellers for their students and that most pilots are introduced to constant-speed propellers well after receiving the private certificate. However, a brief discussion should be given here so that if you get a chance to fly an airplane so equipped, you will have some background.

An analogy might be that the propeller pitch control is the "gear shift" and the throttle is the "foot pedal" of an automobile.

The prop control is moved forward for low pitch (high rpm) for takeoff and other high-power requirements and would be the equivalent of first or low gear. The engine would be revving up, developing higher horsepower. When the control is moved aft, the rpm decreases (the pitch or angle of attack *increases*) and less horsepower is being developed; also, the propeller is more efficient at cruise airspeeds at lower rpm. The constant-speed propeller acts as if you were automatically changing fixed-pitch props as needed.

Since, within the constant-speed operating range the propeller automatically maintains the rpm set by the pilot, checking the mags in that range would mask any drop. (The propeller would automatically flatten pitch to maintain constant rpm, even with the slight power loss of running on one mag.) In the pretakeoff check,

the mags are normally checked below 2,000 rpm so that the prop reacts to the rpm drop like the fixed-pitch trainer you've been flying.

Taking a typical flight, after checking the mags, you would "exercise" the prop by moving the control rearward and then forward a couple of times. This is done to ensure that it's responding properly and to recirculate the oil in the prop dome in systems using engine oil as a method of changing pitch.

Before the takeoff you'd make sure that the prop control was in the full-forward (high rpm) position and the mixture was full rich (or leaned as necessary for density altitude effects—*see* Chapter 5), then, after checking that the area was clear, you would open the throttle fully.

Sometime during the climbout you would, as the manufacturer requires, throttle back to a specific manifold pressure setting, *then ease* the prop control back to get recommended climb rpm (usually leaving the mixture rich until a particular density altitude is reached).

After reaching the chosen altitude, climb power would be left on until cruise speed is reached, then the procedure for reducing power would be to (1) ease the throttle back to the cruise setting, (2) move the prop control back to reduce the rpm to the cruise setting, and (3) lean the mixture.

Note that this is the safe way to do it. The throttle is moved back first because a lot of fuel/air mixture pressure (manifold pressure) and low rpm could cause a rise in pressure in the cylinders to such a point that damage could occur. (Figure what would happen if you were in fourth gear in a very powerful car and jammed

Figure 23-18. Fuel system schematic for one low-wing trainer.

on the gas to try to burn rubber.) The mixture is leaned last as a safety procedure when power is reduced.

If you suddenly had to climb, you would reverse the procedure just discussed to avoid detonation and damage. To *increase power:* (1) mixture—rich, (2) prop rpm—increase, and (3) throttle—open. To *decrease power:* (1) throttle—back, (2) prop control—back, and (3) mixture—lean (as desired).

For further reading on the subject you might check *The Advanced Pilot's Flight Manual*, Chapter 12, and *The Flight Instructor's Manual*, Chapter 17.

Now look at a couple of questions.

01. When adding full power in an airplane with a constant-speed propeller, the order of control usage would be

1—Throttle forward, mixture rich, propeller control forward.
2—Mixture rich, throttle forward, propeller control forward.
3—Throttle forward, propeller control forward, mixture rich.
4—Mixture rich, propeller control forward, throttle forward.

02. When reducing power with a constant-speed propeller, which of the following procedures should be used?

1—Throttle back, reduce rpm, and set (lean) the mixture.
2—Reduce rpm, throttle back, and set (lean) the mixture.
3—Lean the mixture, reduce rpm, and throttle back.
4—Richen the mixture, reduce rpm, and throttle back.

(Answers: 01, 4; 02, 1)

Summary

You should be familiar with the following airplane systems before going solo cross-country:

Fuel system—Total capacity, usable fuel, minimum grade of fuel, recommended order of tank usage (if pertinent).

Oil—Proper brand and grade for the engine and season (ashless dispersant or straight mineral oil).

Electrical—Location of the circuit breakers and other systems that would be affected by electrical power loss; battery capacity and location.

Many airplanes are equipped with outlets for use with *external power* sources so that the engine can be started if the battery is dead. As noted in Chapter 3, some electrical systems (alternator) need a certain amount of electrical power to start the process of battery charging again. If the battery is completely dead and the engine is hand propped (not using an external power supply to "energize" the system), the alternator won't charge the battery. While the engine will run very well, electrical components (radios, lights, etc.) will still not be available. Check on this as it pertains to your airplane. *Don't* prop the airplane unless you have had thorough instruction in the art, and a competent operator is in the airplane. Someone can fly to get you if necessary. Better that than an accident.

Radios—Ability to transmit and receive on all of the equipment; a knowledge of required frequencies, plus light signals used by the tower; how to use the radio to obtain aid in an emergency.

Power plant and cruise control—Engine operating limitations, setting up proper rpm for the power required, fuel consumption at various power settings, use of mixture control, use of carburetor heat.

24

Navigation Planning

The cross-country portion of flight training is both fun and challenging: you learn to navigate using landmarks and a sectional chart and get to land at strange and exotic (at least to a new pilot) airports. When you are ready for the private pilot flight test, you will have had at least 3 hours of dual and 5 hours of solo cross-country with each flight having a landing more than 50 NM from your starting point. One of your trips will be more than 150 NM total distance (at least 3 legs) with one point of landing more than 50 NM from your origin. All of the landings have to be full-stop and you will also have logged 3 full-stops at an airport with an operating control tower (14 CFR §61.109).

If you are working on your sport pilot certificate, your requirements for the flight test are to have had at least 2 hours of dual cross-country and 1 solo cross-country flight of more than 75 NM, with a full-stop landing more than 25 NM from point of origin. This solo flight only requires 2 legs and the controlled field landings are not required for the flight test, but is an additional sign-off before a sport pilot can fly into B, C or D airspace (14 CFR §§61.313 and 61.325).

14 CFR §61.93 gives complete details, but basically before you will be allowed to fly solo out of the local area, you must be familiar with flight planning (plotting courses, estimating times enroute and fuel required, and obtaining and evaluating weather reports). You'll have had flight instruction in crosswind and short- and soft-field takeoffs and landings as well as cross-country navigation by reference to aeronautical charts and to the magnetic compass. You'll also be checked out on emergency situations such as marginal visibility (and estimating visibility), deteriorating weather, getting lost, flying by reference to the instruments, and using radio aids and radar directives. Make sure you know about collision avoidance, wake turbulence precautions, and windshear avoidance. You'll have the word on the proper use of two-way radio communications and VFR navigational procedures and techniques plus traffic-pattern procedures.

Check back to Chapter 21 and be familiar with the various air space and clearance-from-clouds requirements.

Map Work

Your first cross-country flight will be with your instructor. After you've proved on the dual cross-country that you can do the job, your instructor will endorse your student pilot certificate for solo cross-country flights. This doesn't mean that you're now free to go anywhere, anytime the whim hits you. Your instructor will supervise all of your solo cross-country planning *and* flying because you aren't a pro just yet.

Most instructors will go dual with you on a specific route as discussed here, then have you fly the same route solo, so that you won't have the added pressure of flying by yourself in "unknown" territory. Later you'll make solo flights (with proper briefing) to airports that you haven't flown into dual. Speaking of planning, there are a few things you should make sure to cover.

The chart in the back of this book is set up for a flight from Franklin County Airport (Sewanee, Tenn.), to Maury County Airport (Columbia–Mount Pleasant, Tenn.), to the Huntsville International (Carl T. Jones) Airport (Ala.), and back to Sewanee. It's intended as an example and some symbols may be changed on an actual Sectional before you read this.

Each 10 NM of the route has been marked off to aid in checking distances and enroute times. This probably won't be needed after the first few trips.

1. *Check the Airport/Facility Directory* for the facilities of the airports at which you plan on landing. This material is always more up-to-date than the charts in this matter.

When you check the weather and file the flight plan with the Flight Service Station (personally or by phone), get the latest NOTAMs for the facilities and airports that you'll either be using or that will affect some phase of the flight (TFRs, for example).

Check Appendix A for this information on the airports and facilities to be used.

2. *Check the weather*, present and forecast, for the routes you'll be flying. This means also to check the forecast weather for the area of the home airport. You may get off and not be able to get back. (Pilots with friends of the opposite sex in other towns have been known to accidentally overlook this last point, and almost invariably get "weathered in" at one of the towns in question.)

3. *On the chart draw course lines between the airports.* Convert the true courses to magnetic and write this and the distance by each course line on the map. If the courses lie close to omni "roses" on the chart (the calibrated circles around each VOR station), you can save the step of converting the true course to a magnetic course by laying off a straight edge through the omni rose parallel to the course line and find the magnetic course directly (VOR stations are oriented with magnetic north, you remember). The chart in the back of the book is a reduced presentation of this cross-country as drawn on a sectional chart. [The scale at the top of the sample chart is reduced also so that you can use it to lay off distances with the edge of a sheet of paper.] Fold out and refer to that chart as you read this chapter.

4. Using the expected true airspeed of your plane, compute the approximate flight time involved in making the trip. The *Pilot's Operating Handbook* gives the range for your airplane as well as covering the fuel consumption in gallons per hour. Always allow yourself at least 45 minutes of fuel reserve—an hour is even better. Your instructor will have some suggestions; the POH also gives the amount of fuel used to climb to particular altitudes (along with recommended airspeeds and resulting climb rates at the various altitudes), as shown back in Figures 23-10 and 23-16.

Always, when planning a cross-country of this type, look over the entire route generally to become familiar with landmarks on the map and to check on special-use airspace and possible hazards.

Taking each leg of the example here, you might check the following.

Some of the checkpoints of the legs discussed next have been photographed from an airplane flying the route. Carefully compare the numbered checkpoint on the chart with its accompanying photograph. (Point 1 on the chart matches Figure 24-1; point 2 is shown in Figure 24-2, etc.) The points on the numbers on the chart are indicating the direction you would be looking

Figure 24-1. A "close-up" view of Estill Springs. The road and railroad run northwest to Tullahoma.

Figure 24-2. Approximately 24 miles from Sewanee: The town of Lynchburg is 3 miles down the road to the left (south). The junction of the highways to Shelbyville and Tullahoma is just to the left of course. Note the stream to the west side of the road to Lynchburg and that it crosses just north of town (chart and photo). The secondary road between the highway and the stream is not shown on the sectional chart. Small streams usually can be picked out by the trees along the banks.

at the checkpoint from the airplane. Sometimes railroads or streams are hard to see from the airplane, and you should compare different topographical features before jumping to conclusions about the checkpoint. For instance, maybe the town you see down there has a railroad running through, but there's no fair-sized river west of town, so it's not Jonesville, after all. You may want to remove the chart from the back of the book so that you can rotate it to get a better comparison of photos and chart.

Leg 1 — Sewanee to Maury County Airport (4,500 Feet MSL)

All of the distances noted on this flight are nautical miles and are rounded off to the nearest mile.

8 miles — You will cross a highway and power line and note that the town of Decherd is about 2 miles to your left and that Woods Reservoir is about 4 miles off to your right.

11 miles — The town of Estill Springs (and bridges) is below and slightly to the right as you cross a part of Tims Ford Reservoir (Figure 24-1).

19 miles — There are two inlets of Tims Ford Reservoir to the left, and the town of Tullahoma and Tullahoma Regional Airport are approximately 4 miles to the right.

24 miles — The course crosses a major highway just north of a road junction and the town of Lynchburg with its distillery and storage warehouses is 3 miles to the left (Figure 24-2).

30 miles — There is an antenna or communications tower right on your course line about 2 miles before you cross a highway (Figure 24-3).

32 miles — You will cross a major highway 1 mile south of where it is crossed by a transmission line.

41 miles — The route goes directly over the village of Belfast, intersecting a highway and railroad combination, and goes on from there to Lewisburg.

44 miles — The town of Lewisburg is below and to the right. Outstanding landmarks are a quarry just north and east of town (note the crossed-picks symbol on the chart) and the perimeter highway and airport north of town (arrows). You'd see a stream running generally north-south through town (Figure 24-4).

50 miles — You will cross Interstate I-65 approximately 1 mile north of an intersection. You would see the intersection on your dual flight and would use it as an important landmark on your solo on this leg to Maury County Airport. A power line crosses the interstate about 2 miles north, and you'll cross another north-south powerline about $1\frac{1}{2}$ miles after crossing I-65 (Figure 24-5).

56 miles — You will cross a railroad and highway (the highway is merged with the railroad on the chart) about a mile north of Culleoka.

59 miles — A major highway is crossed (Figure 24-6). Maury County Airport is in sight 6 miles ahead. The airport is centered in an area of mining. The *Airport/Facility Directory* (Appendix A) indicates that UNICOM is available and you should give a call at this point for wind, runway, and traffic information. Note that the main runway is 5-23, which is hard surfaced and 5,000 feet long; there is a shorter grass runway. Figure 24-7 shows the airport as seen from about 3 miles out. Note the mining areas.

Figure 24-3. You'll fly over (or very close to) an antenna at 30 NM from Sewanee.

Figure 24-4. Lewisburg, with the quarry on the northeast edge and the airport seen off to the north of town (arrow). You'd see on the actual cross-country that a railroad runs through the western edge of the town (photo arrow and chart).

Figure 24-5. An intersection to I-65 and a secondary road 1 mile to the left (south) of the course. Note the stream in the right side of the photo (the secondary road crosses it). The stream (arrows) is not shown on the chart, but, again, you'd see it on the dual flight and make a mental note for your solo trip.

Figure 24-6. Crossing a highway due south of the city of Columbia, which can be seen off to the right (north) at about 5 miles. The curves in roads and highways are not shown in great detail on sectional charts but are general representations. You'll note that the curve shown in the photograph appears to be slightly sharper than that on the chart. Part of this is due to perspective, but the chart cannot follow the sharper, smaller curves exactly.

Figure 24-7. Approaching Maury County Airport. The town of Mount Pleasant is in the upper left corner of the picture.

Check on the layout of the airports you'll be flying into both as a student pilot and in your future flying as well (Figure 24-8).

When looking at each leg, check the airports that can be used if you need to divert because of weather or other problems. On this route are Winchester, Tullahoma, Shelbyville, and Lewisburg airports. Arnold Air Force Base could be used in an emergency (it's normally restricted to military traffic except by prior permission), but you could get to either Tullahoma or Winchester more easily during that portion of the trip. For instance, if visibility was sharply restricted when you were south of Tullahoma, you would turn north and fly until you saw either a highway and railroad (in which case you'd turn left to follow them to the city of Tullahoma and the airport), or a highway alone running east-west (and you'd turn right to find the airport). Roads and railroads can be "brackets" to funnel you into a town. In other words, don't cross over these references, but use them to bring you to a prechosen point if visibility is down. You can look at the chart before going to see what would be a sure way to get to each of the airports, but more about that in the next chapter.

Be sure to have a good idea beforehand of the position of the airport relative to the town and other prominent landmarks. This is very important for airports having only grass landing areas; they are sometimes very hard to find.

Leg 2 — Maury County Airport to Huntsville International Airport (5,500 Feet MSL)

3 miles on course—A lake and dam should be about a mile off to your right.

9 miles—The route crosses a secondary road and power line, with a settlement about $1/2$ mile to the left.

A secondary road will be to the right, more or less paralleling the course line. A larger highway will be converging with the course from behind and to the left; it's about 4 miles left at this point. Look for the antenna just north of a settlement there.

18 miles—You'll cross two streams and a railroad and then intercept a major highway. There's an electric substation about a mile to the right. The city of Pulaski will be in sight 4 miles ahead.

22 miles—The route crosses the eastern edge of Pulaski and will "parallel" the railroad for a few miles. Abernathy Airport will be a little over 2 miles to the right as you pass it (Figure 24-9). Confirm that this is Pulaski by the road and railroad patterns out of the city. In very poor visibility if you get off course, it's possible that you might, for instance, confuse Lawrenceburg with Pulaski at first glance. One railroad runs directly through Lawrenceburg, but another skirts the west edge of Pulaski after it passes the airport. There is an outdoor movie at Pulaski west of town. Lawrenceburg has no outdoor movie.

30 miles—Rivers and stream bends make good checks; look at the system in the vicinity of the 30- to 35-mile distances. There's a railroad with a tunnel off to the right, but it may be hard to see. The railroad is

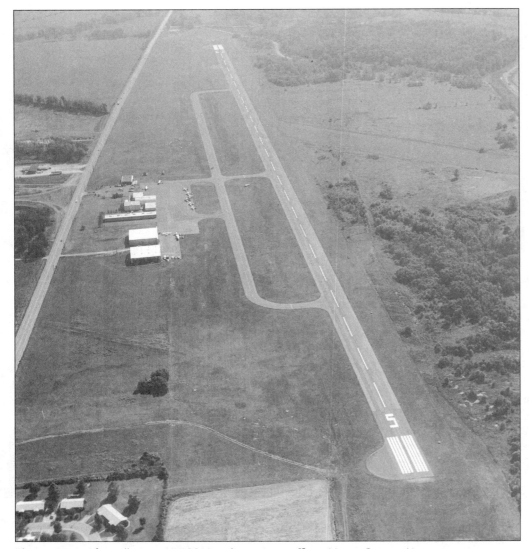

Figure 24-8. After talking to UNICOM and entering traffic at Maury County Airport, you are circling and are on the crosswind leg (heading 140°); a 90° turn will be made shortly to get on the downwind leg for Runway 23. (You are looking to the east-northeast here.) Check the layout of an unfamiliar airport as you circle. The wind is across the runway, but UNICOM has noted that traffic is using Runway 23. Note: This is still the crosswind leg of the pattern, even if the tetrahedron in the photo (just this side of the center short taxiway) indicates you're flying "upwind" at this point.

Figure 24-9. Looking southwest (to the right) at the Pulaski Airport (Abernathy Field) from over the city. Compare the sectional chart with the view here. Note on the chart that there is a road fork about a mile north of the airport (arrow). There is a quarry just off the approach end of Runway 33; it can be seen in the upper left of the photo. The quarry is not shown on the sectional chart. The airport remarks for Abernathy Field in the *Airport/Facility Directory* indicate, "Advance notice given to airport when explosives are scheduled at rock quarry approx. 1,000′ from RWY 33." This is not a factor for you on this trip but shows that having an up-to-date copy of the *A/FD* on hand is a good idea. You would note a railroad and well-defined stream just east of the airport.

Figure 24-10. At 33 miles from Maury County Airport, a railroad crosses the Elk River 3 miles off to the right (west) of the course. Compare the distinctive bends in the river (photo and chart).

Figure 24-11. Over the railroad after crossing the interstate. Athens (Alabama) is 7 miles south-southwest.

more or less "paralleling" the course and is off to the right (Figure 24-10).

40 miles—You'll cross Interstate I-65 at a curve just north of where the railroad running from Athens to Ardmore goes under the highway. Figure 24-11 looks down the railroad to the southwest shortly after the interstate is crossed.

45 miles—The city of Athens is about 5 miles off to the right of your course, and you should listen to ATIS (121.25 MHz) and then contact Huntsville approach control on 118.05 MHz with your position information as indicated by the *Airport/Facility Directory* or the information on the sectional chart. (*See* the box on the bottom of the chart, southwest of the town of Decatur.)

You will be asked to "squawk" a certain transponder code and probably to "ident." If your airplane doesn't have a transponder, you'd say so and may be given a turn or turns for identification. You'd then be vectored as necessary to avoid other traffic. You may be cleared straight in if wind and traffic permit (Figure 24-12).

Let approach control know if you are changing altitude, because this would affect other traffic at your new level. You'll be switched to the tower frequency about 5 miles out, and after clearing the active runway, you will contact ground control for taxiing.

You may be shy about getting taxi directions the first time or two that you go into a large airport. An "I'm a stranger here; could you direct me to _____," will always get you the right help.

Leg 3 — Huntsville to Sewanee (5,500 Feet MSL)

There's a lack of checkpoints on this leg, and you can figure before you even start that, about halfway along a leg like this in poor visibility, you might decide that you are "lost" and maybe ought to circle to try to find a recognizable checkpoint. *DON'T*. Look at the route; you'll see that the railroad and road(s) on the left (west) of the course can form one side of a bracket; the railroad and road coming up from the south through Stevenson (right edge of chart) to Sewanee will be the other side

Figure 24-12. Getting set up for a straight-in approach to Runway 18 Left at Huntsville – Madison County Jetport. It would be best to move over to the left from here in order to have about a 1-mile straightaway to check for wind drift and not angle all the way to the touchdown point.

and will be enough to get back to familiar territory. (In other words, in this particular case, if you are "temporarily disoriented with respect to the preplanned route" and off to either side of the course, flying in a northerly direction up a railroad will take you either to Cowan or Winchester and you can locate yourself if you haven't already done so on the way.)

Always in planning a flight by pilotage, look for such brackets. Spend a lot of time looking over sectional charts; you'll be surprised at the amount of information available.

Use the whole sectional chart. (One student cut out the piece of the sectional chart that pertained to his flight but discovered that strong winds had caused him to drift off that little patch of chart. He had to finally pick a field and land when fuel ran low.) Along these same lines, if one of your routes is close to the edge of the sectional chart, better take along the adjacent chart as well.

Huntsville International Airport has Automatic Terminal Information Service (ATIS), and you'd listen on 121.25 MHz before contacting clearance delivery on 120.35 MHz (Figure 21-13). You'd make contact with clearance delivery and then tell them your aircraft number and type, indicating that you have "Information Delta" (or whatever—*see* ATIS in Chapter 21). You'd also give your on-course heading (approximate) and cruising altitude (exact).

Clearance delivery would give a clearance such as "MAINTAIN RUNWAY HEADING" (after takeoff), "DEPARTURE CONTROL" (frequency) "on 125.6"

(MHz), and "SQUAWK 0134" (if you have a transponder). You'd read it back, and if it was correct, you'd hear:

Clearance delivery—"READBACK CORRECT. CONTACT GROUND CONTROL ON 121.9" (MHz). You would then contact ground control (121.9 MHz, Figure 21-13, and Appendix A) and get taxi instructions to the takeoff runway. If you need to, ask for specific taxi directions to the runway.

After taxiing to the run-up area (at Runway 18 Left for this example) and completing the run-up, switch to tower frequency (127.6 MHz) and request takeoff clearance. Before you're cleared for takeoff, you first may be told to hold or to taxi into position and hold. After you're airborne and about ½ mile past the end of the runway, the tower will tell you to switch to departure control. (No frequency will be given; you got that earlier, although you may ask if you forgot.) You'll get a radar vector ("Heading 020") to avoid the Redstone Restricted Area. After clearing the area, you'll be told to resume normal navigation and can track to the VOR and thence fly to Sewanee.

The VOR is on top of a knoll 12 NM from the airport, and you may have flown slightly more than this distance, depending on the radar vectors.

16–17 miles—You'll cross Highway 231 and then pass about 1 mile south of the North Huntsville Airport (Figure 24-13).

24 miles—The town of New Market, Ala., is directly below. Note that the highway crosses a railroad

Figure 24-13. Just after crossing Highway 231 after passing the VOR enroute to Sewanee (looking south). You'll cross Highway 231 about a mile north of where it bends slightly toward the west. The secondary road that forms a V with Highway 231 is not shown on the sectional. Looking to your left, you'll fly about ¹⁄₂ mile south of Huntsville (North) Airport.

Figure 24-14. After you pass New Market, the terrain ahead and to the right becomes more rugged (looking south-southeast).

just south of town and then recrosses it on the north edge.

31 miles—The town of Elora is 3 miles to the left (note the railroad junction). After passing New Market, the terrain in this area to the right of your course is rugged and rises rapidly from the flatlands, as evidenced by the warning (Figure 24-14).

36 miles—The course line crosses a secondary road, and the town of Huntland is 3 miles to the left. Visibility permitting, you should see that you are "paralleling" a highway (U.S. 64) and a railroad about 3–4 miles to the left (Figure 24-15).

42 miles—The village of Belvidere is 4 miles to the left. The railroad track is south of the road and swaps sides going through the town. (Historical note: Davy Crockett's first wife, Polly, is buried just southwest of Belvidere.) You'll likely be seeing Tims Ford Lake and Winchester and Decherd by now.

48 miles—Decherd and Winchester are about 5 miles to the left, and Winchester Airport is 3 miles to the left (Figure 24-16).

50 miles—Cowan is 1 mile to the left, and the town of Sewanee and Franklin County Airport will be

Figure 24-15. The town of Huntland, 3 miles to the left of course. Not much detail here, but if you've been keeping up with checkpoints, you'll know it's Huntland.

Figure 24-17. Cowan is 1 mile to the left of course. Check the railroad running to the northwest through town. Note the quarry south of town as seen here. Quarries and mines are indicated by crossed picks on the chart.

Figure 24-16. Winchester Airport, with the city of Winchester and Tim's Ford Lake in the upper left of the photo.

in sight (Figure 24-17). At 5,500 feet MSL you can figure on starting the descent at 500 fpm before getting to Cowan, since the traffic pattern at Sewanee is 2,800 MSL (elevation 1,950), a descent of 2,700 feet, or about 5½ minutes, is required. Don't be letting down in the pattern, so start a little sooner.

Computing Time and Fuel for the Legs

The trip, as shown on the sample chart, covers a total distance of 66 + 58 + 56 = 180 NM. An estimate of *flying* time at 96 K shows that 1 hour and 52 minutes would be *required just to fly the legs themselves*; another 10 minutes must be allowed at each stop for entering and leaving traffic and takeoff and landing, for a total of 2 hours and 12 minutes. The fuel to be used, based on this quick and dirty look at things, would be 10.8 gallons. It's a good idea to add another 30 percent, giving a final figure of about 14 gallons.

Plan on a *minimum* of 15 minutes on the ground at Maury County Airport and 30 minutes at a controlled field like Huntsville International, or figure that the example trip would take a minimum of 2 hours and 57 minutes (call it 3 hours).

Okay, for practice, plan the trip from Sewanee to Columbia–Mount Pleasant to Huntsville and back to Sewanee. You're using the numbers as given as an example in Figure 24-18.

The weather at Nashville, Huntsville, and surrounding areas is clear with 15 miles visibility; it is forecast to be good VFR for the next 12 hours.

The winds-aloft forecast for the area is
3-1914 (at 3,000 MSL, from 190° true at 14 K)
6-2312
9-2614
Assume standard temperatures.

Sewanee to Columbia – Mount Pleasant

You'll fly to Columbia–Mount Pleasant at 4,500 MSL and to Huntsville and Sewanee at 5,500 MSL using 65 percent power. Stops will be made at Columbia–Mount Pleasant and Huntsville.

Work out on a computer the groundspeed and true heading for the first leg (true course 288°). It's to be flown at 4,500 feet, so you'd split the wind directions and velocities between 3,000 and 6,000 feet and get an "average" at 4,500 feet of 210° true at 13 K.

The wind side of your computer shows that, for a TAS of 98 K (65 percent power at 4,500 feet at

standard temperature—*see* Figure 24-18), a groundspeed of 94 K and a true heading of 281° results. Note on the sectional chart that the isogonic (1°W variation) line crosses the course, so the magnetic heading will be 282°. *Use 1° W variation for all three legs.* Looking at Figure 24-18 as the compass card for this trip and interpolating, you'd see that for this heading you'd add 4°, so the compass heading would be 286°. Note that this is for the cruise part of the flight. If you worked out the climb portion also (Figure 24-18), you'd find that during the climb at 66 K (average TAS 69K), the groundspeed would be 70 K, the true heading 276°, and the compass heading 281°. (Use the 3,000-foot wind as "average.") You'd set this up on the compass and have no worries on the trip. *Nonsense.* You'll find in actual flying, for instance, that (1) the wind was not forecast accurately, (2) the wind has changed, (3) the compass hasn't been swung or the card corrected since Montgolfier's balloon flight, or (4) you added variation or deviation when you should have subtracted—or vice versa. *You'll watch those checkpoints and make heading corrections as necessary.*

The time, fuel, and distance required to climb from Sewanee (assume a 2,000-foot elevation) to 4,500 feet will be *5 minutes, 0.6 gallons, and 5 NM* (Figure 24-18—no wind).

Your groundspeed (assuming you take off and immediately head on course) for the first 5 minutes during the climb will be 70 K and you'll cover 6 miles. The cruise part of the trip, or the remaining 60 miles, will be at an estimated groundspeed of 94 K, so the time required to get there will be (5 + 38) = 43 minutes.

The letdown to Maury County Airport may be made at the same indicated airspeed as you had at cruise, and you would reduce the power to get a 500 fpm descent. You'll be letting down from 4,500 to 1,500 feet (elevation here is 676, and an 800-foot traffic pattern would be used for an altitude of 1,476 feet—call it 1,500). A 3,000-foot descent at 500 fpm would take 6 minutes. Six minutes from your estimated, or recomputed, time of arrival you'll set up the descent. Since the last 6 minutes enroute will be at reduced power, the fuel consumption would be slightly less, but to be on the conservative side, assume it to be the same as at cruise.

Fuel to be used then would be the start, taxi, and takeoff allowance (0.8 gallon) and climb (0.6 gallon) plus the 38 minutes at 4.9 gph (3.1 gallons), which gives a total for the leg of 4.5 gallons. Admittedly, this is carrying calculations pretty far, but later you may want to try out for the U.S. Proficiency Flight Team, or if you're in a college that is a member of the National Intercollegiate Flying Association, such computations could help you to be top pilot in various air meets.

TIME, FUEL, AND DISTANCE TO CLIMB

MAXIMUM RATE OF CLIMB

CONDITIONS:
Flaps Up
Full Throttle
Standard Temperature

NOTES:
1. Add 0.8 of a gallon of fuel for engine start, taxi and takeoff allowance.
2. Increase time, fuel and distance by 10% for each 8°C above standard temperature.
3. Distances shown are based on zero wind.

WEIGHT LBS	PRESSURE ALTITUDE FT	TEMP °C	CLIMB SPEED KIAS	RATE OF CLIMB FPM	FROM SEA LEVEL		
					TIME MIN	FUEL USED GALLONS	DISTANCE NM
1600	S.L.	15	68	670	0	0	0
	1000	13	68	630	2	0.2	2
	2000	11	67	590	3	0.5	4
	3000	9	66	550	5	0.7	6
	4000	7	65	510	7	1.0	8
	5000	5	65	470	9	1.3	10
	6000	3	64	425	11	1.6	13
	7000	1	64	385	14	1.9	16
	8000	-1	63	345	17	2.3	19
	9000	-3	63	305	20	2.7	23
	10,000	-5	62	265	23	3.2	27
	11,000	-7	62	220	27	3.7	32
	12,000	-9	61	180	33	4.3	38

CRUISE PERFORMANCE

CONDITIONS:
1600 Pounds
Recommended Lean Mixture

PRESSURE ALTITUDE	RPM	20°C BELOW STANDARD TEMP			STANDARD TEMPERATURE			20°C ABOVE STANDARD TEMP		
		% BHP	KTAS	GPH	% BHP	KTAS	GPH	% BHP	KTAS	GPH
2000	2650	- - -	- - -	- - -	78	103	5.9	72	102	5.4
	2600	80	102	6.0	73	101	5.5	68	100	5.1
	2500	70	97	5.3	65	96	4.9	60	95	4.6
	2400	62	92	4.7	57	91	4.3	53	91	4.1
	2300	54	87	4.1	50	87	3.9	47	86	3.7
	2200	47	83	3.7	44	82	3.5	42	81	3.3
4000	2700	- - -	- - -	- - -	78	105	5.8	72	104	5.4
	2600	75	101	5.6	69	100	5.2	64	99	4.8
	2500	66	96	5.0	61	95	4.6	57	95	4.3
	2400	58	91	4.4	54	91	4.1	50	90	3.9
	2300	51	87	3.9	48	86	3.7	45	85	3.5
	2200	45	82	3.5	42	81	3.3	40	80	3.2
6000	2750	- - -	- - -	- - -	77	107	5.8	71	105	5.3
	2700	79	105	5.9	73	104	5.4	67	103	5.1
	2600	70	100	5.2	64	99	4.8	60	98	4.5
	2500	62	95	4.7	57	95	4.3	53	94	4.1
	2400	54	91	4.2	51	90	3.9	48	89	3.7
	2300	48	86	3.7	45	85	3.5	42	84	3.4
8000	2700	74	104	5.5	68	103	5.1	63	102	4.8
	2600	65	99	4.9	60	99	4.6	57	98	4.3
	2500	58	95	4.4	54	94	4.1	51	93	3.9
	2400	52	90	4.0	48	89	3.7	45	88	3.5
	2300	46	85	3.6	43	84	3.4	40	82	3.2
10000	2700	69	103	5.2	64	102	4.8	59	102	4.5
	2600	61	99	4.6	57	98	4.3	53	97	4.1
	2500	55	94	4.2	51	93	3.9	48	92	3.7
	2400	49	89	3.8	45	88	3.6	43	87	3.4
12000	2650	61	100	4.6	57	99	4.3	53	98	4.1
	2600	58	98	4.4	54	97	4.1	50	96	3.9
	2500	52	93	4.0	48	92	3.7	45	91	3.5
	2400	46	89	3.6	43	87	3.4	41	84	3.3

FOR (MAGNETIC)	N	30	60	E	120	150
STEER (COMPASS)	0	26	58	87	118	150
FOR (MAGNETIC)	S	210	240	W	300	330
STEER (COMPASS)	183	214	243	275	303	332

Figure 24-18. A composite of Figures 19-4, 23-10, and 23-14 for use in planning the sample trip. (Do not use for actual flight planning.) Assume IAS = CAS in the climb and that the magnetic variation is 0°.

Columbia – Mount Pleasant to Huntsville

The climb portion will be from 676 feet to 5,500 feet for this leg (you might want to use 3,500 feet as a cruising altitude in an actual situation for a short trip like this). A quick estimate would be to assume a climb from 500 feet to 5,500 feet. Interpolating in Figure 24-18 between sea level and 1,000 feet, you'd need 1 minute, 0.1 gallon of fuel, and 1 NM. You'd then subtract this from the result of the interpolation between 5,000 and 6,000 feet, which is 10 minutes, 1.5 gallons (rounded off), and 12 miles. The difference would be 9 minutes, 1.4 gallons of fuel, and 11 miles (no wind).

The wind at 5,500 could be interpolated (and rounded off) to be from 225° at 12 K; you would use

that for your computer numbers. Using the wind at 6,000 feet would be accurate enough, since there is only a 500-foot difference. Again, the time required to climb and the fuel used would not be affected by wind (except for turbulence, which might cut down performance), but the distance would be, so working it out on the computer:

Wind—190° true at 14 K (average wind in the climb)

True course—160°

TAS (average in climb—*see* Figure 24-18) for an IAS of 66 K–69 K

Groundspeed in climb—57 K

True heading—166°

Magnetic heading—167°

Compass heading—168° (Figure 24-18)

The time required to climb has already been found to be 9 minutes, which at 57 K would be found on the computer to cover 8.6 NM (call it 9 miles).

The level and descent portion of the trip would cover 49 NM, so by looking at the cruise performance chart (Figure 24-18), you'd interpolate to find that, at 5,500 feet (standard temperature) at 65 percent power, the TAS would be 99 K (rounded off).

Working the last 49 miles at 99 KTAS (and not worrying about computing the average TAS and groundspeed in the descent), the wind is interpolated to be 225° true at 12 K, the computer indicates that the true heading is 166° (compass heading is 167°), and the groundspeed is 93 K.

The time required to fly the 49 NM leg is 32 minutes and the fuel used will be 2.6 gallons (again rounded off). The total fuel and time required for this leg will be:

> Start, taxi, takeoff—0.8 gallon
> Climb—1.4 gallons and 9 minutes
> Level—2.6 gallons and 32 minutes
> *Total—4.8 gallons and 41 minutes*

Huntsville to Sewanee

Altitude to be flown—5,500 feet MSL

Winds aloft—225° true at 12K at 5,500 feet (the winds may have changed since the first part of the trip, but assume that this is still a correct interpolation).

Average wind in the climb—190° true at 14 K.

Climb—no-wind climb information in Figure 24-18 from 500 feet MSL to 5,500 feet is the same as for the last leg.

Count on 9 minutes in the climb at an average TAS of 69 K and a fuel consumption of 1.4 gallons. The groundspeed and true heading, after using the computer, turn out to be 81 K and 041° respectively. The magnetic heading will be 042° and the compass heading 039° (Figure 24-18). The distance covered in the 9 minutes of climb at 81K is 12 NM.

> TAS at 5,500—99 K at 65 percent power
> True course (climb) to VOR—036°
> VOR to Sewanee—057°
> Compass heading for cruise—056°
> Groundspeed—111 K

Time and fuel required to fly 44 miles will be 23.8 minutes (24 minutes) and 2.0 gallons of fuel.

This leg will require 0.8 gallon for start, taxi, and takeoff, 1.4 gallons for climb, and 2.0 gallons for cruise, or a total of 4.2 gallons and a time of 33+ minutes. The flight log shows a total of 34 minutes, the result of rounding off the time between each checkpoint to the nearest minute.

The total flying time and fuel required for the three legs: 1 hour and 58 minutes and 13.5 gallons.

The climb takes more fuel than generally considered. For instance, looking at the climb chart portion of Figure 24-18, you'd see that to climb from sea level to 6,000 feet would require 11 minutes and 1.6 gallons of fuel. To fly at 6,000 feet at 65 percent power for 11 minutes (at 4.9 gph) would require 0.9 gallon. The climb fuel consumption is, for that example, nearly twice as much as for cruise consumption at 65 percent. The relative amount of fuel used in the climb part of a trip depends on a ratio of climb to cruise for that trip. The example here had short legs at comparatively high altitudes (maybe *too* high for a practical application in smooth air, but it gave more time for example purposes).

As noted earlier, you normally won't go into such detail on a short pilotage flight but, with experience in a particular airplane, will be able to estimate the fuel and time required to climb to various altitudes and the fuel consumption at, say, 65 and 75 percent power.

As a rule of thumb, for cruise (leaned) fuel consumption for airplanes with fixed-pitch props, multiply the actual brake horsepower being used (at 65 percent power in the 100-hp engine used in the example you'd be using 65 hp) by 0.075 to get gallons of fuel per hour being consumed. Multiplying 0.075 by 65 would give a number of 4.875 gph, which is "pretty close" to the 4.9-gph cruise consumption found on the chart (Figure 24-18). Of course you will have some different horsepower engines to deal with (now or later), for example, one rated at 150 hp. If you wanted to find the gallons per hour consumed at 65 percent power (leaned) in this engine, you'd multiply 150 by 0.65 to find the number of horsepower (which works out to be 97.5—call it 98 hp) and multiply this by the constant 0.075 to get 7.35 gph at cruise (call it 7.4 gph). You'll find that this works out close to the *Pilot's Operating Handbooks* for most light aircraft reciprocating engines.

Flight Log

In making up the flight log and planning the flight, remember to take into consideration the rule that on *magnetic courses* of 0°–179° inclusive, the airplane is to fly at an odd altitude plus 500 feet (3,500, 5,500, etc.) and on *magnetic courses* of 180°–359° inclusive, even altitudes plus 500 feet (4,500, 6,500, etc.). Although this must be followed if the airplane is flying 3,000 feet or more above the surface, it may be used at lower altitudes.

AIRCRAFT N 7557L			WEATHER		Reported _KHSV 18010KT 15 SM CLR_				BNA WINDS		
DATE _June 29_			Time		Forecast _18010KT P6SM FEW_				3 - 1914		
PILOT _S.G. Dickson_			0815 CDT		Reported _KBNA 19008KT 15 SM SKC_				6 - 2312		
					Forecast _22015KT SCT 050_				9 - 2614		

CHECK POINT	TC	MC	TAS	TH	MH	CH	DIST. / Rmdr.	EST. GS	ETE	EST. FUEL	TIME OVER	ATE	AGS	Notes, T.O. Time, Alt., Actual Fuel Used, etc.
ROAD & POWERLINE	288°	289°	69/98	276°/281°	277°/282°	282°/286°	8 / 58	70/94	6	1.5				FUEL INCLUDES TAXI, T.O. CLIMB, SHORT CRUISE (0.1)
ESTILL SPRINGS			98ᵏ	281°	282°	286°	4 / 54	94	3	↑				T.O. TIME _____
ROAD/ LYNCHBURG							12 / 42		8					
BELFAST							18 / 24		11					
CROSS HWY							18 / 6		11					
MAURY CO. AIRPORT	↓	↓	↓	↓	↓	↓	6 / 0	↓	4	3.0				TOTAL CRUISE FUEL — 3.1 TAXI, T.O. & CLIMB — 1.4
									43	4.5				TOTAL MINUTES AND GALLONS — LEG 1
ROAD & POWERLINE	160°	161°	69ᵏ	166°	167°	168°	9 / 49	57ᵏ	9	2.2				FUEL INCLUDES TAXI, T.O. & CLIMB - 2.2 GALLONS
CROSS RR STREAMS			99ᵏ				9 / 40	95	6	↑				T.O. TIME _____
CROSS INTERSTATE							22 / 18		14					
CROSS 4 LANE HWY							10 / 8		7					
HUNTSVILLE INTL AP	↓	↓	↓	↓	↓	↓	8 / 0		5	2.6				TOTAL CRUISE FUEL 2.6 GALLONS
									41	4.8				TOTAL MINUTES AND GALLONS — LEG 2
HUNTSVILLE (ROCKET) VOR	036°	7°	69ᵏ	041°	042°	039°	12 / 44	81ᵏ	9	2.2				FUEL INCLUDES TAXI, T.O. AND CLIMB - 2.2 GALS
CROSS HWY N. HSV AIRPORT	056°	057°	99ᵏ	057°	058°	056°	5 / 39	111ᵏ	3					T.O. TIME _____
NEW MARKET							7 / 32		4					
ELORA							7 / 25		4					
HUNTLAND							5 / 20		3					
COWAN							14 / 6		8					
SEWANEE FRANKLIN CO. AIRPORT	↓	↓	↓	↓	↓	↓	6 / 0	↓	3	2.0				CRUISE FUEL 2.0 GALLONS
									34	4.2	←			TOTAL MINUTES AND GALLONS - LEG 3
									1:58	13.5	←			TOTAL TIME AND GALLONS - ALL 3 LEGS

NOTAMS/Airspace Restrictions

HUNTSVILLE
R 2104 A/c - To 30,000
R 2104 B - To 2400

COMM/NAV Frequencies

MAURY CO. 122.8 MHz, NDB 365 kHz - PBC
HSV - APPROACH (FROM MAURY CO.) - 118.05
TWR - 127.6, GROUND 121.9, DEPT 125.6
VOR - RQZ - 112.2, ATIS 121.25
CD 120.35

Figure 24-19. A flight log for the three legs of the sample cross-country. Minutes have been rounded off and time for climb has been added at the first part of each leg. Later you won't use so many checkpoints on the flight log (but will still keep up with all of the checkpoints). Sometimes it's pretty discouraging to work out a complex and lengthy flight log only to discover that the wind information was all wet and your estimated groundspeeds and estimated headings have no resemblance to what you have during the flight. The main idea is to follow that line on the chart. Anyway, making out a flight log is a good way to ensure that you've checked the route and is an aid in getting ready for the Knowledge Test. Note that the checkpoints chosen are not necessarily those in the photos shown earlier.

Figure 24-20. VFR flight plan from Huntsville, Alabama, to Sewanee, Tennessee.

If you have made wind triangles or used the wind side of your computer, the *original* time estimates will be based on estimated groundspeed; otherwise use your cruise TAS. During the flight the actual groundspeed as checked on the computer will generally vary slightly because of changing wind velocities, as well as the fact that you will probably round off the time (minutes) between checkpoints.

Figure 24-19 is the flight log for the trip. The distances are between checkpoints and also the accumulation for each leg. ETE is the estimated time enroute and ATE is the actual time enroute. You'll work out the estimated groundspeed (EST GS) before leaving. AGS is actual groundspeed. The columns Time Over, ATE, and AGS are done in flight. Assume a magnetic variation of 1°W.

Filing a Flight Plan

The following are the types of flight plans available to the pilot:

VFR—A VFR flight plan, like the other types of flight plans, is filed with the nearest Flight Service Station in person or by phone. (Filing a flight plan by radio is frowned upon because it ties up needed frequencies, but it can be done.) The VFR flight plan is the simplest; basically, you follow these steps when filing.

You file the flight plan with a Flight Service Station using the format shown in Figure 24-20. It will be held by the FSS for 2 hours after the proposed departure time.

The "T" following the aircraft type (C-150/T) indicates that your airplane has a transponder *without* altitude-reporting capabilities.

If the airplane was equipped with Mode C (altitude-reporting capability) the "U" would be the letter to use there. The *Aeronautical Information Manual* has a listing of letters used to show special equipment (or lack thereof) on board when filing a flight plan.

The VFR flight plan does not require such information as altitude changes enroute or alternate airports. You can use the remarks section of the flight plan for pertinent information such as "will close by phone after landing at Sewanee" or other data; you may use this space to list the names of your passenger(s) after you get that pilot certificate. Closing a flight plan by radio is perfectly acceptable because it requires only a short transmission. (More about this in Chapter 25.) If you have no vital information for the remarks section, you may want to use this space to write some stirring line such as "Don't give up the airplane."

If your flight is terminated before reaching the destination, be sure to contact the nearest Flight Service Station and have them pass this information to the FSS responsible for the destination airport. If a flight plan is not closed within ½ hour of the estimated time of arrival, queries are sent to determine the location of the aircraft. If this and further checking down the line fail to locate the aircraft, Search and Rescue people are alerted 1½ hours after your ETA. (And if you want to get into a real jam, just be the guy who gets Search and Rescue alerted by forgetting to close a flight plan!)

If it looks like headwinds or other factors are going to result in a delay in arriving at your destination, you'd better get on the radio and tell the nearest FSS to pass this information along.

DVFR—The Defense VFR flight plan is necessary if you are going to fly in an ADIZ (Air Defense Identification Zone). It is a little different from the VFR, in that filing in the air is not just frowned upon, but doing so is to invite possible interception for positive identification. (This is an interesting experience, to say the least.) If you look suspicious, the interceptors could go further, but it's mighty hard to look suspicious in a trainer that cruises at 90 K or so, although perhaps looking at the interceptor pilots with a dark scowl or wearing a false red beard would help. The *AIM* gives details on procedures for filing and flying a DVFR flight plan.

IFR—The IFR flight plan is not for you yet and won't be covered here. Later, as you work on the instrument rating, you will be checked out on the procedures of filing and flying an IFR flight plan.

Summary

Be sure before you go that you have the proper (and current) charts, flight log, simple computer, a protractor or plotter (preferably with a straight-edge ruler as a part of it), a pencil, note paper, and a watch (if the airplane doesn't have a reliable clock).

In your flight planning, remember that 14 CFR §91.151 requires that, during the day, there is enough fuel to fly to the first point of intended landing, assuming normal cruising speed, and to fly after that for at least 30 minutes; at night, after reaching the first point of intended landing, you need enough fuel to fly at normal cruising speed for at least 45 minutes. It would be well for you as a student pilot to plan on having enough fuel to fly at least twice this amount of time.

For private pilot applicants, it's suggested that you fly at least one local area dual night session before starting on the cross-country phase of your flying. (*See* Chapter 26 of this book.) You'll feel a lot more comfortable if, on one of your solo cross-countries, a delay causes you to land at home (or elsewhere) after sunset. You and your instructor should plan those flights so that there is plenty of fuel, and daylight, reserve. It can be pretty uncomfortable when you realize that darkness is coming on and you're still in strange territory—with no night flying experience.

25

Flying the Cross-Country

You've planned the trip and checked the weather and the plane. You know how to operate the radios, know the light signals, and have checked the destination airports, so there's nothing left to do but go.

Departure

There are two ways to get established on course:
1. You may leave traffic and turn on course.
2. You may climb to altitude and fly back over the airport on course.

The first method is most commonly used, but you must realize that you'll be slightly off course in the beginning of the trip. Students generally have the most trouble at the first checkpoint. They haven't had time to set up a heading. Use the compass (and heading indicator) as a reference to get you headed in the right direction. Set the heading indicator with the magnetic compass at least once during each leg (Figure 25-1). There may not be winds-aloft information available, so fly the first few miles of the course with an estimated drift correction held. As soon as the first couple of checkpoints are passed, you will have some idea of the amount of correction needed.

En Route

After takeoff if you've filed a flight plan and have a radio, let the FSS know of your takeoff time (and write it on your log). Once you have leveled off and established the cruise power setting (making sure that you are at the proper altitude for your course if above 3,000 feet above the surface) switch tanks, if applicable, and lean the mixture.

When you are established on course and the first checkpoint is where it is supposed to be, note the compass heading.

Figure 25-1. Set your heading indicator with the magnetic compass *at least once* each leg of the cross-country (every 15 minutes would be a good interval). Students have set the heading indicator before leaving the home airport and *not* compared it with the magnetic compass further during the flight. After a couple of landings and engine shutdowns at other airports (the heading indicator may well be off because of this), the homeward-bound leg is often very interesting and gives the student experience in using orientation, or lost aircraft procedures.

Hold the map so the course line on the map is parallel to the course you're flying in the airplane (Figure 25-2). This way the towns will lie in their proper places. Sure, you have to read the names of towns upside down if you're headed south, but this is better than getting a checkpoint's relative position fouled up when you try to turn the map around in your mind.

As you come to each checkpoint, look on the map to see how far it is from the course line. If you're more than a mile off course, better make a correction because you'll probably be even farther off course by the time you get to the next checkpoint. *Keep up with the checkpoints.* Run a groundspeed check when you get to the prechosen checkpoint.

If there are scattered or broken clouds near your altitude, you can get a rough idea of the wind direction and velocity by observing the movement of the cloud shadows on the ground.

Figure 25-2. Hold the map so that the course on it is parallel to the course you are flying.

Watch your altitude and heading. (Airplanes sometimes ease off heading while you're checking the map.)

Don't bury your head in the cockpit; keep an eye (or two) out for other airplanes.

Be sure to check the engine instruments at least every 5 minutes (checking more often is a lot better). See each time if the fuel gauge is showing about the right reading for the time you've been flying.

On a longer cross-country, you should contact the nearest FSS for the current altimeter setting.

If you decide to make a position report enroute, use the PTA (**P**osition, **T**ime, and **A**ltitude) system. Tell them what kind of flight plan you're on and from *where* to *where*. For instance you might call an FSS as follows:

You: "JONESVILLE RADIO, THIS IS CESSNA NINE EIGHT EIGHT ZERO JULIET, STUDENT PILOT, LISTENING JONESVILLE VOR, OVER."

After Jonesville Radio has acknowledged your call, you might say the following:

You: "CESSNA EIGHT ZERO JULIET, (POSITION) GEORGETOWN AT (TIME) THREE TWO, (ALTITUDE) FOUR THOUSAND FIVE HUNDRED (4,500 feet), VFR FLIGHT PLAN FROM PALMYRA TO CUMBERLAND CITY, OVER."

Jonesville Radio will acknowledge and give you the altimeter setting, as well as any other information they feel would be of assistance.

You'll want to contact the nearest FSS if you're on a flight plan and decide to change your destination or return to the point of departure.

Destination Airport

To students on their first cross-country, the new airports are strange indeed. It seems that the sky is filled with planes, and at noncontrolled fields the airport personnel seem to have hidden the wind indicator. The wind indicator will be in a hard place to spot—not put in a clear place like your airport's indicator is. (Of course, the students going into your airport have the same thought.)

Start the letdown some distance out so you won't be diving into the traffic pattern. If you have a mixture control, don't forget to richen the mixture because, as noted in Chapter 23, when you descend into the denser air, the mixture, as leaned at altitude, will become too lean and the engine may run rough and/or quit. (If this happens, move the mixture control to rich and give yourself about 5 minutes for your pulse rate to normalize.) Use your prelanding checklist. If it's a controlled airport, give Approach Control a call about 20 miles out or as indicated in the *Airport/Facility Directory* (Chapter 20). If the field has a Flight Service Station, the personnel can only give information such as surface wind and altimeter setting and known traffic. You should contact the FSS for Local Airport Advisory service (LAA) 10 miles out. (UNICOM can be used also at a non-FSS airport.)

Airport advisories also provide NOTAMs, airport taxi route, and traffic patterns. When you're ready to taxi at an airport having LAA, you should call the Flight Service Station and let them know your intentions. (Give your aircraft number, type, location on the airport, and type of flight plan, if any.) They'll give you the recommended runway and other necessary information. LAA is not mandatory and no traffic control

Figure 25-3. Some runway markings as published in the *Aeronautical Information Manual* (AIM) "Airport Marking Aids and Signs" section. You should be familiar with the most common markings as shown in AIM, with particular emphasis on hold short (of the runway), the runway identifier (sometimes complicated at large airports with Left, Right and Center), and the closed runway or taxiway marking — the large "X" at each end.

is exercised, but you should take advantage of this service whenever possible. (The frequency 123.6 MHz is first choice for LAA, but you may use any of the other FSS frequency combinations if you choose.)

Check the field elevation on the chart. Add the traffic pattern altitude at which you want to fly to this and use the result as your indicated altitude around the airport.

Figure 25-3 shows two of the most common types of runway markings. AIM Chapter 2 Section 3 has the wide variety of markings you may encounter. The important thing is, no matter how complex the markings, identify the runway before you land on it and don't land over any X's.

It's an interesting point that pilots tend to be too high at a strange airport. Keep this in mind and make a slightly wider pattern than at home base.

Look the airport over as you circle. See how the taxiways are laid out. It's mighty easy to get lost on the ground at big airports.

After landing, as you taxi in to the ramp, locate the parking areas. If there is the slightest doubt in your mind about fuel — *gas up.*

Since you probably won't know where to park, line service may direct you to a parking place. You should be familiar with the taxi signals before going on the cross-country (Figure 6-8). The taxi director does not have to stand directly in front of the airplane to direct it, but may stand well to one side, pointing to the wheel that needs braking, and put you in the proper spot.

Follow directions; the director has a reason for putting you in a parking place, even if you don't see the point as you taxi in. Park there and discuss it after the engine shutdown if you want another spot. Most student pilots don't give taxi directors trouble. It's the more experienced pilots who tend to argue — while the engine (and prop) is running in a congested area. Some operations ask on UNICOM, while you are still in the air, if you will need service so that they'll know where to park you.

Tie the plane down. Don't go off and leave it untied, for several reasons: (1) Even if the wind is calm, it could pick up suddenly. (2) In the summer dust devils, or whirligigs as they are sometimes called, quite often suddenly move across the airport ramp. Some are strong enough to pick up a lightplane. (3) Propwash from other planes, particularly from big planes, can move your plane into other planes or into the side of the hangar. Later, when you have that pilot certificate and fly to an airport to spend the night or several days in the area, don't set the parking brake, if you are going to lock the airplane. The folks at the airport may need to move the airplane and this can't be done in that case. Make sure the airplane is well chocked and tied down with the *parking brake OFF.*

Take your logbook on solo cross-countries and have somebody sign it, attesting that you were at that airport.

Don't forget to close your flight plan. Sometimes you'll find it more convenient to contact the FSS and close it just after making the initial call to the tower. Or you may prefer to wait until you are on the ground and close it by phone.

It's an outside chance, but it has happened that pilots have closed their flight plans well before reaching their destination and had engine problems before contacting the tower (or landing at an uncontrolled airport), and Search and Rescue was delayed. You'll want to give yourself and your passengers the best protection, so you could cancel with the nearest FSS after initially contacting approach control or the tower, getting their permission to leave the tower frequency for a minute or so. If you had problems, approach control or the tower would wonder why you didn't call back or show up and could get things moving faster to find you. The tower will not automatically close your flight plan.

If you are on a solo cross-country and something happens that will delay you at an airport for a length of time (say, 30 minutes or more), also call the home airport and let them know what's happening. They have figured approximately when you should get home, allowing for time on the ground and average flight time, so don't make them have to call to find out what happened.

Problems and Emergencies

Getting Lost

If you encounter a problem, it will be most likely that of getting off course and/or losing checkpoints. The expression "and/or" is used because students (and experienced pilots) sometimes lose checkpoints even while *on course*. This is particularly true on parts of the trip where checkpoints are sparse or visibility is somewhat restricted. Being at a low altitude aggravates the problem.

When this happens, don't start circling or heading off into what you think might be the "new" right direction. Check your heading indicator with the magnetic compass, maintain the compass heading that you were doing okay with earlier, and try to identify other checkpoints. Pilots have missed a checkpoint and figured they were lost, but by continuing on their original heading found they were right on course, and checkpoints began to show up again.

If you are off course and *know it*, take a cut that will get you back to the course line at the next checkpoint (watch for it). Later when you have more experience, you won't be so hasty about getting back on course, but for now it's best that you get back to the preplanned route fairly soon (or else you might continue to drift farther off).

For the sake of argument, let's say that you've been flying for a long time and nothing looks as it should. You should have reached the destination airport several minutes ago, and because of low visibility, you believe (and your groundspeed estimates tend to confirm this) that you have missed it. It wouldn't be wise to continue blindly on, but you would set up definite means of locating yourself. First you'd climb, if the ceiling permits, to be able to see farther and to get better radio reception.

If the destination airport has an associated VOR and you have a working VOR receiver in the airplane, your problem is a small one. You'd look at the sectional chart (better yet, the *Airport/Facility Directory*) and get the VOR frequency. You'd turn on the set, *identify the station,* and rotate the omni bearing selector (OBS) until the needle was centered and the TO – FROM indicator showed TO. Then you'd track into the station using the OBS indicator as the base course.

If the destination airport doesn't have an associated VOR, your omni receiver can still help locate you. Look on the sectional chart and pick a couple of VOR stations in the *area* where you are. Pick some fairly outstanding landmark such as a river bend, road fork, or railroad junction and stay near it. Tune in one of the VOR stations, *identify it,* and turn the OBS until the needle centers and the TO – FROM indicator says FROM. Draw a line on the map from the chosen VOR along the bearing indicated on the OBS. Then tune in the other VOR and repeat the procedure.

You are in the *area* where the lines intersect. The term *area*, rather than *point*, is used because both your VOR receiver and the VORs may be slightly inaccurate. Find the outstanding checkpoint that you are circling by looking in the area of the intersecting lines on the map. This method of locating yourself by cross bearings is particularly interesting in turbulent air, and you may rest assured that at some time during the process you will drop (1) the pencil, (2) the straight-edge, (3) the map, or (4) all three at once.

Suppose you are on the Sewanee to Columbia-Mount Pleasant leg, the visibility has deteriorated, and you don't know where you are. You've made a couple of corrections and suspect that you may be south of course but aren't sure at all anymore. There's a very small town with a railroad track running north and south through it just ahead and you circle it as you work out the cross bearings.

1. You set up the Shelbyville VOR (109.0-SYI) on your receiver and *identify it*. Turn the OBS until the needle is centered and the TO – FROM indicator says FROM. You see that you are on the 250 radial of SYI. Continuing to circle the small town,

you note that there is a two-lane highway running north and south, just west of town, but continue your cross-bearing check.

2. Set up Graham VOR (111.6-GHM) and *identify it.* With the needle centered and the TO−FROM indicator reading FROM, you see that you are on the 140 radial of Graham. The *precise* line intersection of the two bearings shows that you are over the two Tennessee towns of Waco and Lynnville (and have an extraordinarily accurate VOR in this example).

Note on the chart that the two towns are quite close and Lynnville has a railroad running north-south through it.

Now that you have located yourself, you note that the visibility is worse now to the south and east and your best move is to go on to Maury County Airport rather than try to find the Lawrenceburg or Pulaski airports.

Okay, the visibility is poor and you don't have an ADF. How would be the best way to get there? If you fly directly for it, there's a possibility that you might pass to the left or right of the airport and miss it. (And after deciding you had missed it—were you to the right or the left?)

Shown in Figure 25-4 are two ways of getting to Maury County Airport. Regardless of the great accuracy of dead reckoning and other types of navigation as indicated by novels and movies, roads and railroads are still very good ways to get to a point in a pinch. Notice that using route A you are going to intercept the highway well south of the airport—and will *know* which way to turn. You'll turn right, staying on the right side of the highway. It is an unwritten rule that airplanes following a highway always stay to the *right*. This makes it easier to see the highway from the left seat, and if everybody stays on the right there will be less chance of midair collisions. You would follow the highway north and call UNICOM about 5 miles out.

Route B is another possibility. In this one you are staying over the original highway, following it north and turning to intercept the "airport highway" north of

Figure 25-4. Using VOR cross bearings to help locate yourself.

the airport. You would then follow that highway south to the airport, contacting UNICOM. Following a highway if you are caught in bad weather is one way of getting to a safe place. Note the relationship of railroads and highways to each other if they are running side by side. Make sure that, for instance, the railroad is west (or east, etc.) of the highway as it should be. (You may be following the wrong highway.) Look for good checkpoints along the highway such as bridges, power line crossings, and other references. Watch for television or radio towers as shown on the chart.

Best of all, when you check the weather before the flight, if it looks like it will be deteriorating—don't go. It's better to be sitting in an airport office wondering why you didn't go than to be flying with a tense stomach in rapidly decreasing visibility—wishing you were back in the airport office.

Assume for this example that the radio beacon is on the airport, so (getting back to your imaginary problem with Maury County Airport) if you have an ADF on board, you may tune in the radio beacon, *identify it,* and *home* into the airport (Figure 25-5). (You'll probably have a curving path because of wind, as indicated by Figure 21-3, but that's all right.) You could also use the ADF to help you in the highway—following process as discussed earlier. On route B you could follow the highway north from Waco–Lynnville until the ADF needle points well behind the left wing and then make your turn west to intercept the "airport's highway."

You may have to divert to an alternate airport because of weather or engine problems (such engine problems will be discussed shortly) and should have

Figure 25-5. Using the ADF to home into Maury County Airport after locating yourself over the towns of Waco–Lynnville. You could home into the station at the airport by changing the heading as necessary to keep the ADF needle on the 0° position in the indicator.

a good idea of the procedure before going on a solo cross-country. Your instructor, or the check pilot, may require that you leave the preplanned route for another airport on a dual flight or the check ride.

You should pinpoint your present position, if possible, estimate the heading (check the time), and then further work out heading and distances with a plotter—enroute.

Figure 25-6 shows that a nearby VOR can be an aid in finding an alternate airport in poor visibility. You could find the radial that the airport is on, fly over to that radial, and fly—from TO or FROM the station (as applicable)—to get to the airport. Remember to look on both sides as well as straight ahead when looking for the airport. You may not have set up the exact radial and your VOR receiver also could be a couple of degrees off.

Suppose nothing has worked so far and you still have no idea of your location (and no GPS to fall back on): Better make up your mind to get help before things get too far out of hand and you run out of fuel.

The FAA suggests the use of the "FOUR Cs" in such a situation:

Confess—Admit to yourself that you have a problem and confess it to the nearest ground station.

Climb—Altitude enables you to see farther and makes for better communications (ceiling permitting).

Communicate—You have a complex system of emergency aid no farther away than your microphone. Use 121.5 MHz if the other frequencies don't get any results.

Radar can also give you a hand. After you've called for help, the nearest radar facility may pick you up. The FSS or tower may have you switch to another frequency for radar help and you'll be requested to make various turns for radar identification or to set up a particular transponder code if you have the equipment. They will then vector you to an airport and will probably keep an eye on you to keep you on the straight and narrow.

Comply—Do what you're told by the aiding facilities.

Conserve—This is a fifth "C" that is also very important. *Conserve fuel!* You'll be needing it. Don't grind around aimlessly at 75 percent power and rich mixture when you could be using half the gas. For a situation where maximum endurance is needed (you are in communication and are being located and want to stay aloft as long as possible), a thumb rule would be to set up a speed of about 1.2 times the flaps-up, power-off stall speed as shown at the bottom of the green arc on the airspeed indicator (if it is shown as CAS), then adjust your power to maintain a constant altitude and lean the mixture. If your airplane has a calibrated stall

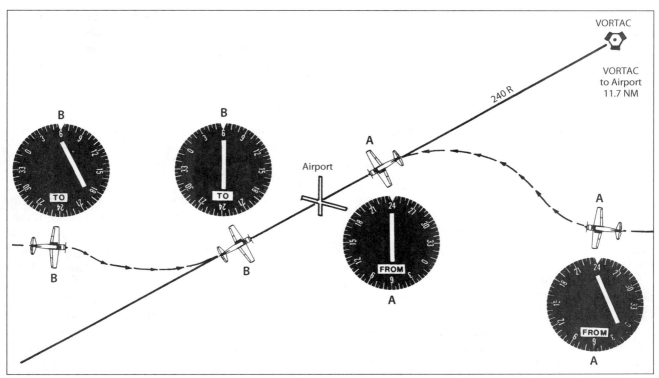

Figure 25-6. Using a VOR to help find an airport, which for the example is on the 240 radial of the VORTAC. The pilot of airplane A would set up 240 FROM on the VOR receiver and turn toward the radial and fly until the needle is centered. The pilot of plane B would set 060 TO on the VOR receiver and fly over to the radial, keeping the needle centered while looking for the airport. Both pilots would keep their eyes looking out of the cockpit, with only an occasional glance at the VOR receiver and heading indicator. DME equipment in the airplanes would make it easier too.

speed of 50 K (flaps up) the maximum endurance speed would be at about 60 K (CAS). This would roughly give the most *time per gallon.*

For maximum range (*miles* per *gallon*) another thumb rule is to set up an airspeed of 1.5 times the calibrated stall speed (clean). (The plane stalls at 50; 1.5 × 50 = 75 K for maximum distance per gallon.) This would be important over bad terrain or water when it is questionable whether or not you have the fuel left to get back to decent terrain. (Lean the mixture.)

Airplanes manufactured in 1976 and after have the airspeed indicators marked in knots and *indicated* airspeeds. The older airspeed indicators were marked in *calibrated* (or corrected indicated) airspeeds, and that's what these rules of thumb are based on. For the newer airplanes you would check Part 5 of the *Pilot's Operating Handbook* and get the calibrated airspeed for the bottom of the green arc and multiply *that* number by the 1.5, or 1.2, as just given. You then might have to reconvert from the calibrated number you got by the multiplication back to indicated airspeed for more accurate flying.

Cool, keeping your—This sixth "C" is probably the most important of all the items listed. *Take it easy.* If you have to, you can follow a road or railroad to a town and try to recognize it from the chart by landmarks such as racetracks, factories, and road and railroad complexes. The name of the town may be on a water tank, and some towns have their names painted on the roofs of large buildings. One student with a great opinion of the accuracy of VOR cross bearings, argued with the instructor: "That couldn't be Sewanee, the VOR bearings show us to be 5 miles north of there" (while looking at Sewanee prominently displayed in yellow on the roof of one of the buildings). This goes back to the idea that a VOR cross bearing is a good check of the *area* you are in. *Do not blindly depend on your navigation equipment when supposedly flying a cross-country by pilotage.*

All right, so you haven't been able to contact anybody, the ceiling is too low to pick up any help on the radio, or you have no radio and fuel is about gone. You'll have to make the decision to land the airplane before the engine quits from fuel starvation and you have no choice of fields. This is where dragging the area is a useful maneuver (Chapter 17). You'll pick the most likely looking field in the area and look it over. You've had practice in short- and soft-field landings, so do what is necessary—then get to a phone.

Probably it's unnecessary to note that once you've made an off-airport landing, you *do not* take off again, but will have your instructor or somebody come to the scene and fly the airplane out (or dismantle it for shipping home). There have been cases of pilots making off-airport landings with low fuel and/or weather problems with no damage to the airplane or themselves, and then when the weather improved, attempting to take off with a resulting—sometimes fatal—accident. Short-field *landings* are useful to a student or low-time pilot, but this is no time to practice short-field *takeoffs*.

Weather

The best maneuver when in doubt about the weather ahead is a 180° turn while you still have visual references.

In the warmer months you may encounter isolated thunderstorms or fast-moving lines of thunderstorms called "squall lines."

In the case of the single thunderstorm (cumulonimbus cloud), you can circumnavigate, or fly around it. The vertical currents within a thunderstorm are able to tear an airplane apart. While you will not fly into the cell, it should be noted that violent vertical currents are also found in the areas close to the storm. Stay plenty wide of the cell, remembering these currents and the fact that hail sometimes falls out of the anvil-shaped overhang of the cloud.

If you are blocked by a squall line that is too long to fly around, there's nothing to do but go back (Figure 25-7).

Occasionally a squall line will have a break, through which the sun can be seen shining brightly on the other side. This is one version of what is known as a "sucker hole." If, in trying to go through the gap, the turbulence doesn't get you, the closing of the hole will probably do the trick.

In winter, snow and snow showers will be a problem. Visibility goes to nothing in snow, and snow areas can spread rapidly.

When the visibility is well down and you are flying a strange area, don't bore along at full cruise, but slow the airplane down. This isn't as critical now in the comparatively slow trainer you're flying, but later when you are flying that fast retractable it could make quite a difference. The radius of turn of an airplane for a given bank angle is a function of the square of the velocity, so if you are traveling twice as fast as you need to be when you see that ridge suddenly appear, your radius of turn will be four times as great. This doesn't mean you'd put the airplane right on the edge of a stall, but you would reduce airspeed to a value that would still give you safe control but would not maintain full-out cruise. (Trim the

airplane.) Trying to remain VFR while the ceiling and visibility are getting below VFR minimums is an exotic form of Russian roulette and is called "scud running."

If you are approaching for a landing and there's a thunderstorm in the near area, be prepared for very strong and shifting winds. Sometimes the thunderstorm may beat you to the airport. Usually they move on in a few minutes, but you will have to make the decision to wait it out or go on to another airport.

Engine Problems

If you have a partial power failure and can maintain altitude without overheating the engine, head for an alternate airport, but look for fields on the way. If possible, fly around poor landing areas. Usually if you get a partial power failure, a complete power failure is not far away.

The problem of dropping (or no) oil pressure was discussed in Chapter 3; as noted there, the instrument can be wrong, but you'd turn toward the nearest good landing area (preferably an airport) and watch the oil temperature gauge for a rise. If it starts to go up, reduce power to get more time from the engine to make that field.

If the engine starts overheating, head for an alternate airport. If the power loss is severe, remember that the least power is required at a speed about 1.2 times the stall speed. Conserve altitude. With such emergencies as power loss or overheating, the engine could quit at any time. This means that you'd be in a bad spot if it quit during a power approach or when dragging

Figure 25-7. An airplane should fly the dashed-line route, staying safely away (at least 10 miles) from the cloud and overhang, or complete the 180° turn well before getting to the squall line. Note that the turkey who tried to go through lost some feathers.

the area. When you reach the alternate, circle it within gliding distance. If it's a controlled field and you have a transmitter and receiver, before you get there tell them in plain language what's happening; the tower will clear traffic out of your way. If the engine is in danger of quitting, an emergency situation exists and you will have the right of way. For non-tower fields, keep your eyes open and land. (Contact UNICOM if available.)

Carburetor ice (discussed in Chapter 4) may ease in while you're looking for checkpoints or have your attention diverted from engine operations. If the rpm (on a fixed-pitch prop) starts creeping back, you'd better check on this. If you're using a constant-speed prop, the best indication of carburetor ice is a decrease in manifold pressure—if you are at a constant altitude and haven't moved the throttle. Follow your instructor's recommendations on use of carburetor heat (full or partial heat).

You may inadvertently fly into such heavy rain that, in addition to the expected visibility problems, it may partially block the carburetor intake screen and the engine will lose much of its power. Use carburetor heat or alternate air. Talk to your instructor and check the *Pilot's Operating Handbook* for recommendations for your airplane.

Engine fires in flight are very rare, and while you'll follow the instructions of your particular *Pilot's Operating Handbook* and/or instructor, generally you'll want to shut off fuel controls (mixture and fuel selector) and sources of sparks (ignition and master switches). This naturally would mean a forced landing, but that is not *immediately* the big problem. Sometimes the fire can be put out by diving. After the fire is out, you can keep your mind occupied with picking a field (Chapters 11 and 18).

You may be so absorbed in navigation that you run a tank dry enroute. The sudden silence will certainly grab your attention and for a couple of seconds your mind will be blank. Throttle back and switch to the fuller tank and then reset power after the engine is running property again. (It will take about 5 minutes after operations are normal for *you* to settle down again.) If you have been so remiss as to have flown out *all* of your fuel and have no other tank to switch to, you can get practice in picking a field (Chapters 11 and 18). Check the *POH ahead of time* for specific procedures when a tank runs dry. This may require use of electric fuel pump, richening the mixture, etc., as you switch.

Electrical Problems

Your instructor will go over possible electrical problems on the cross-country (or local flights, for that matter). If you smell burning insulation, better turn off the electrical master switch. If you don't need radios, etc., leave the switch off for the rest of the flight. If things are tight and you need radios and/or other electrical equipment, you might turn off the master switch to stop the immediate problem (kill the electrical system) and then turn off all the radios and other electrical equipment. After the fire's out, open cabin ventilators to get rid of residual smells or smoke. One method of isolating the troublemaker is to turn the master switch back ON, and turn ON the individual systems one by one until you smell the culprit. Of course, what you will do in such a situation will actually depend on your airplane's electrical system, the *POH*, and your instructor's recommendations, based on your hours of experience. Your instructor may prefer to have you turn the master switch OFF and leave it that way and land at an airport as soon as practicable in case of "funny smells." (Remember that the electrical system has nothing to do with *keeping* the engine running; it only furnishes the power for starting.)

There have been cases of a popped circuit breaker or of inadvertently turning the master switch OFF ("somebody's" knee hit it), and the pilot looks up to see the fuel gauges on *empty*. This usually happens over water or the worst terrain in a 700-mile radius. Pilots have landed or ditched airplanes, thinking that there must have been a sudden and complete fuel leak because they should have had 2 (or 3, etc.) hours of fuel left at the expected consumption. This is not to say that a fuel leak should not be considered, but you might first check the master switch and circuit breaker(s) or fuses before landing in a strange place. If the master switch and circuit breaker(s) are okay (and the fuel gauges still indicate empty), a turn toward better terrain and airports should be in order.

Take a took at Figure 3-26 in this book, the electrical system for a light trainer. Note that the oil *temperature* gauge for that airplane has a circuit breaker. People generally don't get as excited about *no* oil *temperature* as they do about an indication of *no* fuel (understandably).

Probably after reading this section you're wondering if the cross-country flight will be nothing less than a hazardous operation. That isn't the case at all; it's highly unlikely that you will ever have a real problem on the cross-country. You may have to avoid bad weather or may find yourself off course temporarily, but you can minimize the chances of trouble by *careful preflight planning*. The flight is usually a success or failure before leaving the ground. The cross-country is just like the rest of flying—*a matter of headwork*.

Introduction to Night Flying
Private Pilot

You will probably face your first session of night flying with some trepidation but will find that, once you get started, it can be even more enjoyable than daytime operations. It will increase your confidence in your daytime flying, too.

Usually the air is smoother, and you can see cities and towns at greater distances because of their lights. You'll also be able to see more airborne traffic for this same reason.

There's one factor that you will likely encounter, and that is *Zilch's Law*. Zilch's Law basically states that as you get out of gliding range of the airport at night, the engine starts running rough. Zilch's Law is also applicable in the daytime when flying over mountainous terrain or well out over the water (in a land plane). "The roughness of the engine is directly proportional to the *square* of the roughness of the terrain and the *cube* of the pilot's imagination." This phenomenon is also known as *automatic rough* (Figure 26-1).

You'll get 3 hours of dual instruction including at least 10 takeoffs and landings to a full stop. You'll fly

a dual night cross-country of over 100 NM total distance. The instructor will probably also have you fly in the local area at a good altitude before having you come back into the pattern for the 10 dual takeoffs and landings.

Cones and Rods

Owls and cats (and other night predators) do better than people at night because their eyes are designed for it.

The retina, or layer of cellular structure at the back of the eyeball, electrochemically converts the light of the optical image into nervous impulses flowing to the brain. This conversion takes place in light-sensitive cells (millions of them), which are of two distinct types: (1) The rods (highly sensitive, activated by a minimum of light intensity) enable only black and white (but no color) perception and are mostly useful for night vision. (2) The cones, considerably less light sensitive than the rods, require higher light intensities to get activated, enable color perception as well as black and white, and are mostly useful for daylight vision.

The human retina contains both types of cells; the animal retina contains only rods. A bull gets excited by the movements of the bullfighter's muleta, not by its red color, which he is unable to perceive.

Your top visual acuity occurs by focusing your eyes on an object, in which case its optical image is projected on a tiny portion of the retina called the *fovea*. Foveas are very useful for the details needed in say, "girl or guy watching."

You will never make out visual details at night as well as by daylight because the human fovea contains exclusively the less sensitive color-distinguishing cones and in the dark becomes much less sensitive than the rest of the retina, which contains only rods. The resulting differences in the visual perception is, in principle, illustrated in Figure 26-2, which shows an identical scene visualized by the human eye by day

Figure 26-1. Zilch's Law makes the engine run rough and "sound funny" over bad terrain or when out of gliding distance of the airport at night. This phenomenon starts to make itself known when darkness approaches and you are still some distance from the airport.

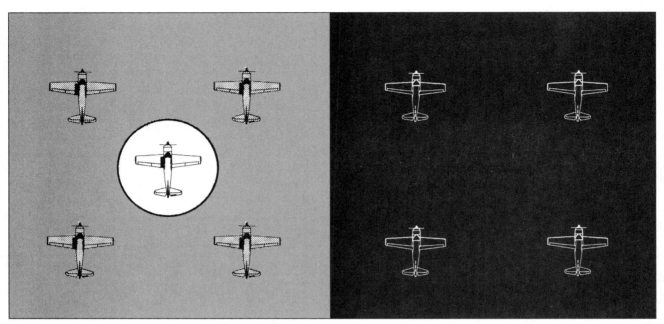

Figure 26-2. Different views of a flight of five airplanes as seen by day and night. The vision is focused in the center of the formation in both cases. At night a blind spot exists in the center; in order to see that airplane, you would focus on one of the outer airplanes. *Scan* slowly at night.

light and at night. Owls, cats, etc. don't have this kind of visual problem (they have other visual problems). Their retinas, containing only rods, are uniformly relatively highly sensitive in the dark.

Figure 26-3 gives an idea of the physical makeup of the human eye. The light reflected from the objects in your visual field enters the eyeball; the amount of the light admitted is constantly being adjusted by the changes in diameter of the iris (which is comparable to the diaphragm of a camera). The light rays go through the optical media (lens, etc.), form an optical image of those objects, and project it on the retina (which is comparable to the film in a camera).

The optical nerves of both eyes are interconnected in a crossover and transmit the light-generated impulses to the optical centers in the brain.

The final visual perception results from interactions between the transferred image from the retina and the activity of the optical brain centers and is therefore different from the real optical image. In other words, the eyes can lie to you about what's really going on. You could have an eye disease characterized by a blind sector in the retina and not be aware of it. The brain simply fills in what it feels should be there. A blind spot exists in the normal eye where the optical nerve leaves the retina; you can find it in your own eye by the following experiment: Figure 26-4 is a section from this book with a cross and large dot marked in it. Hold the figure approximately 6 inches from your eyes—eyes perpendicular to the page—and focus with your right eye on the cross. When you cover or close your left eye, the dot will disappear because its image will fall on that eye's blind spot. You may have to adjust the distance from your eye to the figure. The experiment can be repeated with the left eye (right eye closed) focusing on the dot. You'll get the impression that you can see the printing that's covered by the dot or cross because the brain "fills it in." Think about that when you stare fixedly from the airplane (day or night). Another

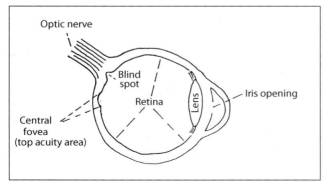

Figure 26-3. A look at the human eye.

There's one factor that you will likely encounter, and that is *Zilch's Law*. Zilch's Law basically states that as you get out of gliding range of the airport at night, the engine starts running rough. Zilch's Law is also applicable in the daytime when flying over mountainous terrain or well out over the water (in a land plane). "The roughness of the engine is directly proportional to the *square* of the roughness of the terrain, and the *cube* of the pilot's imagination." This phenomenon is also known as

Figure 26-4. A test for checking the blind spot in each eye.

airplane might be in your blind spot and the brain fills in background details (horizon or blue sky) because it can't "see" that area and assumes that it's landscape like the rest. Of course, using two eyes tends to cover possible blind spots and the idea of two-eye *scanning* is even better—day or night.

You'll never be able to see as well at night as in the day, and Figure 26-2 is merely given to show the comparative areas of coverage.

The shift from cones to rods is gradual, as the light decreases, more and more of the rods take over. The rods require a certain period of adaptation to the dark. That's why you sat down on that person's lap in the movie theater—your eyes weren't dark-adapted.

It takes about 30 minutes to become night-adapted. The rods are not as sensitive to red lights, so night fighter pilots are briefed in a room with red lights or wear red-lensed goggles before a flight.

Adaptation to the dark actually occurs in two steps: (1) The first rise in sensitivity, due to the cones, is completed in 4–5 minutes. (2) The second rise is due to rods and is completed in 40 minutes, making a *total* time of about 45 minutes. But, as noted, you'll be about as dark-adapted as practical after a total time of 30 minutes. That last 15 of the 45 minutes raises adaptation only a little.

While a theoretical look at the eyes' reactions to darkness might warrant the program of red lighting just mentioned (as well as having all cockpit and instrument lights red), for practical purposes in civil aviation, white lighting is used in many of the newer airplanes.

If you are night-adapted, a bright flash of white light will ruin your careful work, and the whole adaptation procedure has to begin again.

It's impractical and unnecessary for you to wear red goggles for 30 minutes before the flight, but you should have an idea of what to do for night vision:

1. Avoid *brilliant* white lighting before flying if possible.
2. Under normal flying conditions keep the instrument and cockpit lighting as low as practicable.
3. If you are over a brightly lighted city or other bright outside lights, turn the instrument lights up in intensity.
4. When looking for objects at night, scan, don't stare. Remember that center blind spot.
5. *Always* carry a flashlight when night flying. It can be very difficult to fly while holding a cigarette lighter or matches to check the instruments. Older instruments had luminous paint on the numbers and hands that could be "excited" by shining a flashlight on each instrument for a few seconds. The flashlight could be turned off and the hands and numbers would continue to glow for several minutes. This was helpful when cockpit lighting was lost. On the downwind leg the instruments could be "energized." You wouldn't need the flashlight any more and would have both hands free for the rest of the approach and landing. You might order a "cold" light stick that can be stored in the map compartment until needed. It can be taken out of its wrapper and energized by bending it and shaking it, it then gives several hours of constant light for chart or instrument reading. Since the light is "cold," it can be put in a pocket or back in the compartment when light is not needed.
6. Don't stare at the instruments; it tires your eyes quickly.

Oxygen helps night vision, but it's doubtful that you would have it or want to use it. Alcohol and tobacco hurt night vision. If you were a night fighter, you could set up a daily routine (including a diet to ensure that there was sufficient vitamin A in your system) to help improve your night vision, and all of your cockpit lighting would be red, including your flashlight lens. (If you need to convert your flashlight to a red light type, a round piece of red cellophane placed inside the lens is an inexpensive way.)

Airplane Lighting

Following are requirements for night lighting and equipment, in addition to the required equipment discussed in Chapter 3 (14 CFR §91.205):

1. Approved position lights.
2. An approved aviation red or aviation white anticollision light system.
3. If the aircraft is operated for hire, one electric landing light.
4. An adequate source of electrical energy for all installed electrical and radio equipment.
5. One spare set of fuses, or three spare fuses of each kind required.

The airplane's navigation (or position) lights, like a lot of other aviation equipment and terminology, are arranged similarly to those of ships. The lighting arrangement (red light on the left wing, green on the right, and white light on the tail) can tell you approximately what that other airplane is doing.

Suppose that you see the red and green wing lights of an airplane dead ahead and on your altitude. Is it coming or going? One clue that it is moving toward you is the fact that the white taillight is very dim or not showing. The final touch would be if the red light is on your right and the green is on your left—it is headed your way!

Remember the term, "Red, right, returning," meaning that when you see the red and green lights of another airplane and the red light is on the right, the other airplane is headed toward you—not necessarily on a collision course but at least in your general direction.

The airplane's position lights must be on *any time the airplane moves after sunset*—taxiing or flying. Also, the lights must be on if the airplane is parked or moved to within dangerous proximity of the portion of the airport used for or available to night operation if the area is not well lighted.

The red rotating beacon (or a white anticollision strobe, as applicable) is required for all airplanes flying at night. The anticollision light can be seen many miles away in good atmospheric conditions. Many pilots also turn on this light in the daytime when visibility is down.

The landing light is a great aid but not as necessarily vital to night operation on a lighted field as you might think. If you find yourself at night with the landing light on the blink, you'll still have no trouble at all making a good landing by watching the runway lights and using a little power in the landing.

Don't fly without adequate cockpit lighting. If you fly into hazy conditions, it's possible that you may lose all visual references and have to go on instruments to get out of that area. You may also fly into clouds or fog before realizing it. You'd be in pretty sad shape if you couldn't see the instruments.

If you inadvertently get on solid instruments, turn off the anticollision light. The "flashing" effect as it rotates can lead to disorientation. After you've completed the 180° turn and are back out in VFR conditions, turn it on as you go back home.

Airport Lighting

Taxiing is one of the toughest parts of night flying when going into or out of a strange, large airport. This is especially rough if you haven't been there in the daytime. Even a familiar airport is strange the first time you try to taxi at night. The only thing to do is to get help from ground control if it's available. Otherwise just take it slow and easy until you find your destination on the field. One private pilot, on his first night taxi, was too proud to ask directions and managed to taxi out the airport gate and onto the freeway. He was last seen taxiing at 60 miles an hour, trying to keep from being run over by traffic (auto type). He didn't know that taxiway lights are blue. Figure 26-5 shows

Figure 26-5. Taxiway and runway lighting.

taxiway and runway lighting. Some bigger airports have small lights embedded in the taxiway centerline for guidance.

The runway edge lights are white lights of controlled brightness and are usually at the lowest brightness compatible with atmospheric conditions. The runway lights in some airports may be nearly flush with the runway; others may be on stands a foot or two high. The lights marking the ends of the runway are green (Figure 26-5). Runway end lights are red on the runway side to warn pilots on the roll-out that The End Is Near.

Airport beacons flash alternating green and white. This is because they are rotating and have the different-colored lights on opposite sides of the beacon head. The following should be noted:

1. Civilian airport beacons—green-white-green, etc.
2. Military airport beacons—green-white-white-green, etc.

The military airport beacon has a dual-peaked white flash between the green flashes to differentiate it from the civilian. Remember this because the beacons can be seen from a great distance and are used to help the pilot locate the airport at night. It would cause plenty of excitement if you were talking to a civilian tower and landed at a nearby military base by mistake (Figure 26-6).

If an airport beacon is on during the day in Class B, C, D, or E surface areas, it often means that the weather conditions at the airport are less than 3 miles visibility and/or 1,000 feet of ceiling. It's no longer VFR.

All dangerous obstructions near the airport are marked by red lights. High-intensity flashing white lights identify tall structures (chimneys, etc.) and overhead structures of transmission lines going across rivers, gorges, etc.

Figure 26-6. Know the difference between military and civilian rotating beacons.

Pilot Controlled Airport Lighting

Radio control of lighting is available at selected airports to provide airborne control of lights by keying the aircraft's microphone. Pilot control of lighting systems is sometimes available at airports where there is no control tower or FSS or when those facilities are closed. All lighting systems that are radio controlled at an airport, whether on a single runway or multiple runways, operate on the same radio frequency.

The control system consists of a 3-step control response to 7, 5, and/or 3 microphone clicks.

The suggested use is to always initially key the mike 7 times, this ensures that all controlled lights are turned on to the maximum available intensity. You can make an adjustment to lower the intensity by keying 5 and/or 3 times. You may have to be fairly close to the airport to get the service, and it will last for 15 minutes after activation. You may want to key again as you get closer to ensure that the time doesn't run out just as you are on final or flaring for landing.

The *Airport/Facility Directory* contains the types of lighting, runway, and the frequency that is used to activate the system under "Airport Remarks." (*See* Appendix A in this book.) Airports with this service are also shown on the sectional chart in each airport information cluster with an *L indicating that there is some limitation to the runway lighting (not full time). Pull out a sectional of your area, check the legend and see what airports nearby have this service. Your instructor will also be a source of information on this.

The system works like this:
1. *Key mike*—7 times within 5 seconds—*Function:* Highest intensity available.
2. *Key mike*—5 times within 5 seconds—*Function:* Medium or lower intensity—lower REIL (Runway End Identifier Lights) or REIL-off.
3. *Key mike*—3 times within 5 seconds—*Function:* Lowest intensity available—lower REIL (Runway End Identifier Lights) or REIL-off.

The *Aeronautical Information Manual* has detailed information of the various types of approach light and runway light systems.

Tips for Night Flying

You might consider the following when you are about to start night flying.

Starting

Be doubly careful in starting at night. The darkness could result in your starting the engine when someone was in the propeller arc. Turn on the position (navigation) lights and rotating beacon before starting. Granted, this won't help the battery, but it will serve to warn people on the ramp that you are going to start. If other airplanes' engines are running-up close by, no one can hear your "CLEAR." Keep all other equipment off while starting, particularly the taxi and landing lights and radios. If you can possibly work it, have someone standing outside as you start. If it's all clear, that person will give you a signal that consists of moving one of the wands or flashlights in a rotary motion and pointing to the engine to be started with the other wand (in your case, at this stage, pointing to the *only* engine).

Taxiing

After the engine (or engines) is started, turn on other needed equipment but leave the taxi or landing lights off until you are released by the taxi director. The taxi signals shown in Figure 6-8 still apply at night. The director will hold a lighted wand or flashlight in each hand.

A signal normally used at night but not shown in Figure 6-8 is crossed wands or flashlights, meaning "stop" or "hold brakes."

Taxi slowly at all times and very slowly in congested areas at night. You'll find that judgment of distances is harder when you first start night operations. Your visibility is limited to the area covered by the taxi light and you don't want to have to suddenly apply brakes while moving at a high speed.

Run-Up

Once you have reached the run-up position and have stopped, turn the taxi or landing lights off to conserve electrical power. Turn off the strobes to avoid distracting other pilots. Use a flashlight to check controls and switches not readily seen by normal instrument or cockpit lighting. Make a pretakeoff check carefully, as you should always do—day or night.

When you are ready to go, call the tower; or if you have no transmitter, turn on the landing lights and turn toward the tower. (You would arrange by phone before flying in such a rare situation.) If you are at a nontower airport, clear the area carefully before taxiing out onto the runway. Make sure the cockpit lighting is at the proper level and that the navigation lights and strobes or rotating beacon are on.

Takeoff

You will normally use the landing light(s) during the takeoff roll, but the instructor will probably have you make several takeoffs and landings without it during one or more of the dual sessions. You'll find that the runway edge lights and the landing light will be more than sufficient to help you keep the airplane straight. Don't just stare into the area illuminated by the landing lights. Scan ahead, using the runway edge lights as well. Your first feeling will be that of a great deal of speed because of your tendency to pick references somewhat closer than during daytime takeoffs. Because of this, make sure that you have reached a safe takeoff speed before lifting off, don't try any short- or soft-field takeoff techniques for the first few times. Actually, only in an emergency would you attempt taking off from a very short or soft field at night.

Retract the gear (if applicable) when you are definitely airborne and can no longer land on the runway ahead. Establish a normal climb and turn off the landing light(s). Turn off the boost pump (if applicable) at a safe altitude.

Airwork

You'll find that you are referring more to the flight instruments at night than in the daytime because of the occasional lack of a definite horizon in sparsely populated areas.

On a hazy night with few scattered lights, the ground lights may appear as a continuation of the stars and you could talk yourself into a good case of disorientation. If you're in doubt, rely on the instruments.

You may have a tendency to fumble for controls in the cockpit at first. It's wise to spend extra time sitting on the ground in the cockpit until you can find any control blindfolded. At night you may suddenly encounter IFR conditions. Make a 180° turn as discussed in Chapter 15.

Figure 26-7 shows some night lighting combinations for various relative airplane positions and headings. If you see the *Super Cub* (the bottom airplane) at this position and relative size, you could be in a little trouble.

Approach and Landing

The landing checklist should be carefully followed, taking even more time than in daylight, to ensure that you make no mistakes.

Make the downwind leg farther from the runway than in the daytime. Plan on a wider, more leisurely pattern. Since judging distances also is more difficult, plan on a pattern that requires the use of power *all* the way around. Figure 26-8 shows three views of the lighted runway after turning final.

Turn the landing lights on after turning onto final. You will notice that if the night is hazy, your visibility

Figure 26-7. Some of the light combinations of other airplanes you might see on a night flight.

Figure 26-8. From left to right: a too-high, too-low, and proper final approach as seen from the cockpit.

will be less during the early part of the final approach with the landing lights on but will improve as you get to the round-off height. When you are using landing lights, the landing technique should be very close to that used in daytime landings (power-off). If the landing lights are not used, make the touchdown still carrying some power. Those first few landings will seem to be a speeded-up process. Figure 26-9 shows how that first night landing might seem to you.

The common tendency is to carry too much airspeed on night landings; watch for it.

The landing light is important, but the amount of light reflected varies with the atmospheric conditions for a particular runway and will vary from airport to airport. The runway lights may be the essential reference.

Your instructor will probably have you shoot takeoffs and landings without the landing lights and may also have you shoot one or two without cockpit lighting so that you can see the difficulty of handling a flashlight and flying the airplane. The instructor will also review emergency procedures such as partial power loss, or total engine failure, and electrical problems with special attention to your particular airplane and local terrain.

Summary

You'll find that after the slight confusion of the first flight has passed, you'll be sold on night flying and Zilch's Law won't be such a big factor. If you get caught away from the airport after dark, it won't be a crisis situation after you've had instruction. Night flying is like everything else: familiarity and experience ease your worry.

Figure 26-9. On your first night landing, things will seem to be moving more rapidly than in the daytime.

Part Five **5**

The Knowledge and Practical (Flight) Tests

The Knowledge Test Review

The purpose of your flight and ground instruction is to make you an efficient and safe pilot, not to specifically prepare you for passing tests. However, in order to use all of that good training and to fly passengers to those vacation spots you have in mind, you'll have to pass the knowledge and practical tests.

Before going up for the practical test, you'll have to have passed the FAA knowledge test with a score of 70 percent or better. Some people sweat the knowledge test more than the practical test, particularly if they've been out of school and haven't taken any examinations for more years than they'd like to remember. As often happens, however, they have better self-discipline than recent high school or college graduates (applying their studying time better) and they do better on the knowledge test than expected. This doesn't ease that initial nervousness when sitting down face to face with a blank answer sheet or in front of a computer screen.

Home Study

You may have an opportunity to attend a formal ground-school or you may prefer to study on your own; either is a legitimate way to get ready for the knowledge test. However, you'll want to get some advice on areas to study from your instructor, who can then review your work and make a written statement that you have successfully completed the requirements so that you can take the test. Your instructor will suggest sections of the Federal Aviation Regulations (Parts 61, 91, and NTSB 830) to study.

Review

Following is a list of chapters in this book with suggestions for home study that apply especially to the knowledge test:

Chapter 2—Know the four forces and how they work. Remember that lift doesn't make the airplane climb, but the axis of reference is the airplane's flight path and the forces are measured *parallel* and *perpendicular* to the flight path. Make sure that you know how the trim tabs move to get the required control (elevator, etc.) reaction.

Chapter 3—Review the actions of the various flight instruments, noting what could cause erroneous indications. (Know the various types of airspeeds and altitudes.) Be sure that you know what airplane document must be *displayed* and whether the logbooks must be kept in the airplane at all times. Know the requirements for 100-hour and annual inspections.

Chapter 4—Know *why* you check the various items in the preflight check. It will make it much easier to remember. In fact, in all of your ground instruction study, try to tie all of the information with your experiences in the airplane. You should be getting ready for the knowledge test as you fly; don't wait and cram just before the test. It's best to take the test after you've had at least one solo cross-country and had a chance to pin down in your mind that area of the training, because many of the questions are based on a typical cross-country trip.

Chapter 5—Review the mixture control, general starting and shutdown, and procedures for cold or hot engines or different outside air temperatures. Remember that the airplane should not be hand propped by anyone who has not had proper instruction in the art; there must be a competent operator inside the airplane during this effort.

Chapter 6—You may run into a question on the test about how the controls should be held when taxiing in winds from various directions relative to the airplane. Confirm that you know the various airport wind indicators and can read them properly (and know what indicates a right-hand traffic pattern).

Chapter 7—Here in the pretakeoff or cockpit check, know why items are checked. (What are you looking for in the mag check or carb heat check, etc.?)

Chapter 8—Know the three axes of the airplane and how the flight controls (and trim) work.

Chapter 9—Know the Four Fundamentals, and the effects of bank on the stall speeds. Understand torque and the forces and moments that operate on the airplane at lower airspeeds and higher power settings.

Chapter 12—The stall is a function of angle of attack, not airspeed, although the calibrated airspeed at the stall depends directly on the square root of the weight of the airplane. Know the effects of flaps and power on the stall speed (CAS) at a given weight. For light general aviation trainers, altitude has no effect on the calibrated airspeed (CAS) at the stall if flaps, weight, power used, and bank angle are the same. Check Figure 12-13 for a review of power required in relation to CAS.

Chapter 13—Check with your instructor about the demonstrated maximum crosswind component for your airplane and also get the word on avoiding wake turbulence. If the *Pilot's Operating Handbook* has a crosswind chart, you should review its use.

Chapter 14—Reaffirm that the stall is the result of a too-high angle of attack, not airspeed. Review accelerated stalls.

Chapter 15—Be able to look at diagrams of flight instruments and describe what actions the airplane is taking (Figures 15-1, 15-3, 15-4, 15-5, and 15-12).

Chapter 16—Note that in turns around a point and eights around pylons, the angle of bank, as in S-turns across the road, is proportional to the ground speed. Be able to look at any diagram of these maneuvers (with wind direction shown) and pick the point of steepest or shallowest bank.

Chapter 17—Look over Figures 17-10, 17-11, 17-12, 17-13, and 17-14 to make sure you can use the different types of takeoff and landing performance charts. Review the atmospheric factors that affect the performance (e.g., moist air, if factors of temperatures and pressure are equal, gives *poorer* performance than dry air). Temperature changes affect the density-altitude more than pressure changes.

Chapter 18—Know the significance of charts such as Figure 18-4.

Chapter 19—Review this chapter thoroughly and be able to work from true to magnetic to compass directions and back, using isogonic lines and a compass correction card (Figure 19-5). When working from CAS to IAS on an airspeed correction table, you may have a tendency to add when you need to subtract, and vice versa (check Figure 19-8). You may want to have your instructor give you some sample problems in "different approaches." For example, you may be given the pressure altitude and density-altitude and required to find the outside air temperature. In other words, pin down your knowledge and use of the computer.

When measuring courses with the plotter, double check the figures you get. You might measure a number of courses between points on your sectional chart and ask the instructor to confirm their accuracy.

Be able to locate geographic points when given latitude and longitude.

Chapter 20—Sit down one evening for a few minutes with your sectional chart and look it over for symbols you might not have encountered in your cross-country planning.

You'll be expected to be able to use the *Aeronautical Information Manual* and the *Airport/Facility Directory* on the knowledge and the practical test, so you should review all parts. You won't be expected to memorize any of the *AIM*, but a fairly brief review of what information is available and how to use the *Airport/Facility Directory* could save you some fumbling around during the knowledge test. (Such information is furnished but it's better if you've looked it over before taking the test.)

Chapter 21—Review the uses of the VOR and ADF and their advantages and limitations. One question sometimes used on the knowledge test includes a diagram showing several airplanes at various positions around a VOR station, and you are required to match the proper VOR received indication with the airplane at a particular position. (One hint is to "turn" the airplane in your mind to the OBS given and see whether the needle is pointed toward the selected radial.) Your instructor will want to review this with you.

Know the basics of ATIS and VASI.

Chapter 22—Confirm the circulation around low- and high-pressure areas, the symbols, and weather associated with warm, cold, occluded, and stationary fronts. Be able to read hourly reports, forecasts, and wind information. Brush up on converting local time to UTC (Zulu time) and back. Know what weather information services are available to the pilot.

Chapter 23—Know the significance of maneuvering speeds and the effects of turbulence on the airplane. Brush up on the steps of running a weight and balance calculation and remember that the basic empty weight includes full operating fluids and unusable fuel and full oil. Be able to use both types of cruise charts as shown by Figures 23-12 and 23-14.

Chapter 24—Go over in your mind the steps involved in navigation planning, including filling out a flight log and filing a VFR flight plan. Ask your instructor to review with you the procedure for reporting an accident or an overdue aircraft.

Chapter 25—Fly one of your own cross-countries again in your mind and think of the items you had to consider on the trip, including (as applicable) taxi director signals and runway markings, as you review this chapter.

Take another look at procedures used in helping to locate yourself by use of VOR cross bearings and what FAA ground facilities are available to help.

Chapter 26—Hit this chapter for aircraft and airport lighting and the physiological aspects of night vision.

Review the AIM sections "Wake Turbulence" and "Medical Facts for Pilots." There will be questions on the knowledge test about these subjects; as a pilot you should be aware of the factors discussed.

The Knowledge Test Guide

The following is from the Private Pilot Knowledge Test Guide.

Introduction

The FAA has available hundreds of computer testing centers nationwide. These testing centers offer the full range of airman knowledge tests including military competence, instrument foreign pilot, and pilot examiner predesignated tests.

The knowledge test guide provided by the FAA was developed to be used by applicants preparing to take a knowledge test for the Private Pilot—Airplane, Single-Engine, Land.

This is not offered as a quick and easy way to obtain the necessary information for passing the knowledge tests. There is no quick and easy way to obtain this knowledge in addition to the skills needed to transform a student into a pilot capable of operating safely in our complex national airspace system. Rather, the intent of the guide is to define and narrow the field of study, while directing the applicant to the required knowledge for obtaining a private pilot certificate.

Eligibility Requirements

An applicant for a private or sport pilot certificate should review 14 CFR §61.83, Eligibility requirements: Student pilots, for detailed information pertaining to eligibility.

An applicant for a private pilot certificate should review 14 CFR §61.103, Eligibility requirements: General, for additional detailed information pertaining to eligibility. (Sport pilot: see 14 CFR §61.305.)

Knowledge Areas on the Tests

The tests are comprehensive because they must test an applicant's knowledge in many subject areas.

An applicant for a private pilot certificate should review 14 CFR §61.105, Aeronautical Knowledge, for the knowledge areas on the tests (14 CFR §61.309 for sport pilots).

Description of the Tests

All test questions are the objective, multiple-choice type, with three choices of answers. Each question can be answered by the selection of a single response. Each test question is independent of other questions, that is, a correct response to one does not depend upon, or influence, the correct response to another.

The maximum time allowed for taking the test is based on previous experience and educational statistics. This amount of time is considered adequate for applicants with proper preparation and instruction.

The Private Pilot–Airplane Test currently contains 60 questions.

Communication between individuals through the use of words is a complicated process. In addition to being an exercise in the application and use of aeronautical knowledge, a knowledge test is also an exercise in communication because it involves the use of the written language. Since the tests involve written rather than spoken words, communication between the test writer and the person being tested may become a difficult matter if care is not exercised by both parties. Consequently, considerable effort is expended to write each question in a clear, precise manner. Make sure you carefully read the instructions given with each test, as well as the statements in each test item.

When taking a test, keep the following points in mind:

1. Answer each question in accordance with the latest regulations and procedures.

2. Read each question carefully before looking at the possible answers. You should clearly understand the problem before attempting to solve it.

3. After formulating an answer, determine which choice most nearly corresponds with that answer. The answer chosen should completely resolve the problem.

4. From the answers given, it may appear that there is more than one possible answer. However, there is only *one* answer that is correct and complete. The other answers are either incomplete, erroneous, or represent common misconceptions.

5. If a certain question is difficult for you, it is best to mark it for RECALL and proceed to the next question. After you answer the less difficult questions, return to those that you marked for recall and answer them. The recall marking procedure will be explained to you prior to starting the test. Although the computer should alert you to unanswered questions, make sure every question has an answer recorded. This procedure will enable you to use the available time to the maximum advantage.

6. When solving a calculation problem, select the answer nearest your solution. The problem has been checked with various types of calculators; therefore, if you

have solved it correctly, your answer will be closer to the correct answer than any of the other choices.

Taking a Knowledge Test by Computer

You must determine what authorization requirements are necessary before contacting or going to the computer testing center. Testing center personnel cannot begin the test until you provide them with the proper authorization, if one is required. A limited number of tests require no authorization. In the case of retesting, you must present either a passed, expired passed (24 months old), or failed test report for that particular test. This policy is covered in FAA Order 8080.6, Conduct of Airmen Knowledge Tests via the Computer Medium. However, you should always check with your instructor or local Flight Standards District Office if you are unsure of what kind of authorization to bring to the testing facility.

The next step is the actual registration process. Most computer testing centers require that all applicants contact a central 1-800 phone number. At this time you should select a testing site of your choice, schedule a test date, and make financial arrangements for test payment.

You may register for tests several weeks in advance of the proposed testing date. You may also cancel your appointment up to 2 business days before test time, without financial penalty. After that time, you may be subject to a cancellation fee as determined by the testing center.

You are now ready to take the test. Remember, you always have an opportunity to take a sample test before the actual test begins. Your actual test is under a time limit, but if you know your material, there should be sufficient time to complete and review your test. Within moments of completing the test, you will receive an airman test report, which contains your score. It also lists those subject matter knowledge areas where questions were answered incorrectly. *The total number of subject matter knowledge codes shown on the test report is not necessarily an indication of the total number of questions answered incorrectly.*

Your instructor is required to review each of the knowledge areas listed on your airman test report with you and complete an endorsement that remedial study was conducted in these deficient areas. The examiner may also quiz you on these areas of deficiency during the practical test.

The airman test report, which must show the computer testing company's embossed seal, is an important document. DO NOT LOSE THE AIRMAN TEST REPORT, for you will need to present it to the examiner prior to taking the practical test. Loss of this report means that you will have to request a duplicate copy from the FAA in Oklahoma City. This will be costly and time consuming.

Cheating or Other Unauthorized Conduct

Computer testing centers follow rigid testing procedures established by the FAA. This includes test security. When entering the test area, you are permitted to take only scratch paper furnished by the test administrator and an authorized aviation computer, plotter, etc., approved for use in accordance with the FAA. The FAA has directed testing centers to stop a test any time a test administrator suspects a cheating incident has occurred. An FAA investigation will then follow. If the investigation determines that cheating or other unauthorized conduct has occurred, any airman certificate that you hold may be revoked, and you may not be allowed to take a test for 1 year.

Retesting Procedures

If the score on the airman test report is 70 or above, in most cases the report is valid for 24 calendar months. You may elect to retake the test, in anticipation of a better score, after 30 days from the date your last test was taken. Prior to retesting, you must give your current airman test report to the computer testing administrator. Remember, the score of the latest test you take will become the official test score. The FAA will not consider allowing anyone with a passing score to retake a test before the 30-day remedial study period.

A person who fails a knowledge test may apply for retesting providing that person presents the failed test report and an endorsement from an authorized instructor certifying that additional instruction has been given, and the instructor finds the person competent to pass the test.

Summary

The questions on the Knowledge Exam will not be difficult with thorough preparation. You'll recognize many of the things you did for the cross-country such as using performance charts, computer and plotter. One of the key points to remember is this: thoroughly read each question and all the answers. There are often answers that seem the right choice if read too quickly. Reviewing the areas noted at the beginning of this chapter and following your instructor's advice should take you through the test smoothly.

28

The Practical (Flight) Test

Introduction

After you've passed the knowledge test, you'll fly more dual and solo flights to review any particular problems and bring your skill up to private pilot level. As noted in Chapter 27, you should take the knowledge test sometime after the first solo cross-country so that you'll have the procedures well in mind; but allow a few days and some flying time after getting your passing grade back before taking the practical test. (This chapter is for the Airplane, Single-Engine Land test.)

Figure 28-1 is a recommended checklist to use when going to take the practical test; it wouldn't look too good, for instance, if the examiner (check pilot) found that the airplane was lacking required papers.

Following are areas of knowledge necessary for you to safely perform the privileges of a private pilot. The chapter numbers in parentheses after the various procedures/maneuvers are from this book, *The Student Pilot's Flight Manual (SPFM)*, that apply to the private pilot practical test. There has been some personal advice added, plus some paraphrasing of the various elements of the test. *For full details get the latest issue of the FAA Practical Test Standards.*

References (in addition to *this* book) upon which this practical test is based include

14 CFR Part 43 Maintenance, Preventive Maintenance, Rebuilding, and Alteration
14 CFR Part 61 Certification: Pilots, Flight Instructors, and Ground Instructors
14 CFR Part 91 General Operating and Flight Rules
14 CFR Part 97 Standard Instrument Approach Procedures
NTSB Part 830 Notification and Reporting of Aircraft Accidents and Incidents
AC 00-2 Advisory Circular Checklist
AC 00-6 Aviation Weather
AC 00-45 Aviation Weather Services
FAA-H-8083-1 Aircraft Weight and Balance Handbook
FAA-H-8083-3 Airplane Flying Handbook
FAA-H-8083-15 Instrument Flying Handbook
FAA-H-8083-25 Pilot's Handbook of Aeronautical Knowledge
AC 61-65 Certification: Pilots and Flight and Ground Instructors

---

APPLICANT'S PRACTICAL TEST CHECKLIST

APPOINTMENT WITH EXAMINER:

EXAMINER'S NAME_____

LOCATION _____

DATE/TIME _____

ACCEPTABLE AIRCRAFT

☐ Aircraft Documents:
    Airworthiness Certificate
    Registration Certificate
    Operating Limitations
☐ Aircraft Maintenance Records:
    Logbook Record of Airworthiness Inspections
    and AD Compliance
☐ Pilot's Operating Handbook, FAA-Approved
    Airplane Flight Manual
☐ FCC Station License, if applicable

PERSONAL EQUIPMENT

☐ View-Limiting Device
☐ Current Aeronautical Charts
☐ Computer and Plotter
☐ Flight Plan Form
☐ Flight Logs
☐ Current AIM, Airport Facility Directory, and Appropriate
    Publications

PERSONAL RECORDS

☐ Identification - Photo/Signature ID
☐ Pilot Certificate
☐ Current and appropriate Medical Certificate
☐ Completed FAA Form 8710-1, Airman Certificate and/or
    Rating Application with Instructor's Signature (if
    applicable)
☐ AC Form 8080-2, Airman Written Test Report, or
    Computer Test Report
☐ Pilot Logbook with Appropriate Instructor Endorsements
☐ FAA Form 8060-5, Notice of Disapproval (if applicable)
☐ Approved School Graduation Certificate (if applicable)
☐ Examiner's Fee (if applicable)

Figure 28-1. Practical test checklist.

AC 61-67   Stall/Spin Awareness Training
AC 61-84   Role of Preflight Preparation
AC 90-48   Pilot's Role in Collision Avoidance
AC 91-69   Seaplane Safety for 14 CFR Part 91
            Operators
AC 120-51   Crew Resource Management
            Training
    AIM   Aeronautical Information Manual
    AFD   Airport/Facility Directory
NOTAMs   Notices to Airmen
Pilot Operating Handbooks
FAA-Approved Flight Manuals

Some More Ideas to Consider

You may encounter the term AREA OF OPERATION in the practical test. Areas of operation are phases of flight arranged in a logical sequence within the guide. They begin with the flight's preparation and end with its conclusion. The examiner, however, may conduct the practical test in any sequence that results in a complete and efficient test. Certain demonstrations may be impractical (for example, night flying), so your knowledge may be checked by oral testing.

TASKS are procedures and maneuvers appropriate to an area of operation. PREFLIGHT PREPARATION, for example is an area of operation; one task in that area would be an explanation of the certificates and documents pertaining to you and the airplane.

Each task is broken down into OBJECTIVES. The objectives of all tasks must be demonstrated and evaluated sometime during the practical tests.

As an example of an area of operation on the practical test:

VIII. SLOW FLIGHT AND STALLS (AREA OF
      OPERATION)
   A. Maneuvering During Slow Flight (Task)
      Objectives: (Gives expected performance
      criteria for 8 listed requirements)
   B. Power-Off Stalls (Task) (Objectives follow)
   C. Power-On Stalls (Task) (Objectives follow)
   D. Spin Awareness (Task) (Objectives follow)

Consistently exceeding the tolerances noted before taking corrective action will be considered unsatisfactory. Any procedures, or lack thereof, that require the examiner to take over will be disqualifying. If you don't look around and clear the flight area adequately during the practical test, you could be failed.

The examiner will be looking for safe performance as a pilot; you won't be expected to fly like an ace, but the main thing is to use good clearing procedures,

checklists, and other techniques and aids in avoiding accidents and incidents. There also will be emphasis on coping with spatial disorientation and wake turbulence hazards.

You'd better know the meaning and significance of airplane performance speeds, including:

V_{S0}—the stalling speed or minimum steady flight speed in landing configuration.

V_Y—the speed for the best rate of climb.

V_X—the speed for the best angle of climb.

V_A—the maneuvering speed.

V_{NE}—the never exceed speed.

V_{NO}—max normal operating speed (max structural cruising speed).

V_{FE}—max flaps extended speed.

V_{S1}—the stalling speed, or the minimum steady flight speed obtained in a specific configuration (normally with flaps and landing gear retracted).

The examiner will emphasize stall/spin awareness, spatial disorientation, wake turbulence avoidance, runway incursion avoidance, and as noted earlier, checklist usage.

You'll hear the term "stabilized approach," which is not to be construed in the same context as the term used in large aircraft. As used for the practical test guide, it means that the airplane is in a position where minimum output of all controls will result in a safe landing. Excessive control input at any point could be an indication of improper planning.

When you're doing simulated emergency procedures, consideration will always be given to local conditions, including weather and terrain. If safety will be jeopardized, the examiner will simulate that part of the task.

General Procedures for Practical Tests

Satisfactory Performance

You'll be judged on your ability to safely:

1. Perform the approved *areas of operation* for the certificate or rating sought within the approved standards.
2. Demonstrate mastery of the aircraft, with the successful outcome of each *task* performed never seriously in doubt.
3. Demonstrate satisfactory proficiency and competency within the approved standards.
4. Demonstrate sound judgment.
5. Demonstrate single-pilot competence if the aircraft is certificated for single-pilot operations.

Unsatisfactory Performance

If you fail any of the required tasks, you fail the practical test. The examiner or you may discontinue the test at any time when the failure of a required task makes you ineligible for the certificate or rating sought. If the test is discontinued, you are entitled to credit for only those pilot operations, or tasks, that you have successfully performed. At the discretion of the examiner any task may be reevaluated, including those previously passed.

Typical areas of unsatisfactory performance and grounds for disqualification are:
1. Any action or lack of action by you that requires intervention by the examiner to maintain safe flight.
2. Failure to use proper and effective visual scanning techniques to clear the area before and while performing maneuvers.
3. Consistently exceeding tolerances stated in the *objectives*.
4. Failure to take prompt corrective action when tolerances are exceeded.

Practical Test Prerequisites

As an applicant for the practical test, you are required by the Federal Aviation Regulations to have (1) passed the appropriate private pilot knowledge test within 24 calendar months before the date you take the practical test; (2) completed the applicable instruction and aeronautical experience prescribed for a private pilot certificate; (3) obtained a first-, second-, or third-class medical certificate issued within the past 24 months; (4) reached at least 17 years of age; and (5) have a written statement from an appropriately certificated flight instructor certifying that you have been given flight instruction in preparation for the practical test within 60 days preceding the date of application, that you are competent to pass the test, and that you have a satisfactory knowledge of the subject areas in which you were shown to be deficient by the Airman Knowledge Test Report.

Aircraft and Equipment Required

You're required to provide an appropriate, airworthy, certificated aircraft for the practical test. The aircraft must be equipped for, and its operating limitations must not prohibit, the performance of all tasks required on the test. As a practical suggestion aircraft should have the following:

1. A two-way radio suitable for voice communications with aeronautical ground stations.
2. A radio receiver that can be utilized for available radio navigation facilities (it may be the same radio used for communications). Private pilot.
3. Appropriate flight instruments for the control of the airplane during instrument conditions. Appropriate flight instruments are considered to be those required by Part 91 for flight under instrument flight rules. Private pilot.
4. Engine and flight controls that are easily reached and operated in a normal manner by both pilots.
5. A suitable view-limiting device that is easy to install and remove in flight, for simulating instrument flight conditions (private pilot only).
6. Operating instructions and limitations. You should have an appropriate checklist, a *Pilot's Operating Handbook (POH)*, or, if required for the airplane used, an FAA-approved airplane flight manual. Any operating limitations or other published recommendations of the manufacturer that are applicable to the specific airplane will be observed.

A good question on the oral part of the test is: Does this particular airplane require a propeller spinner to be legal to fly? In some cases the spinner is required to smooth airflow into the cowling for cooling, and the airplane has been flight tested and is certificated *on that basis*. It's possible that without the spinner, the engine could run hot. Look at the equipment list in the *POH* or pertinent airplane papers to see if the letter designating required equipment is by the spinner listing.

Take time to go through the *POH* well beforehand so that you'll at least know where to look for information.

Use of Distractions During Practical Tests

It's been noted that many accidents occur when the pilot's attention is distracted during various phases of flight. Many accidents have resulted from engine failure during takeoffs and landings under conditions in which safe flight would have been possible had the distracted pilot only used proper techniques.

Distractions that have been found to cause problems are:
1. Preoccupation with situations inside or outside the cockpit.
2. Maneuvering to avoid other traffic.
3. Maneuvering to clear obstacles during takeoffs, climbs, approaches, or landings.

The examiner may provide realistic distractions during the practical test, which could include:

1. Simulating engine failure.
2. Simulating radio tuning and transmissions.
3. Identifying a field suitable for emergency landings.
4. Identifying features or objects on the ground.
5. Reading the outside air temperature gauge.
6. Removing objects from the glove compartment or map case. (This could start an avalanche of objects you didn't even know were in there, including the ham sandwich you misplaced while on that cross-country flight last month.)
7. Questioning by the examiner.

Preflight Preparations

Certificates and documents—You'll be required to present your pilot and medical certificates and locate and explain the airplane's papers (including airworthiness directives) and other records including your and the airplane's logbooks. Locate and explain the operating limitations, placards, instrument markings, and *POH (Pilot's Operating Handbook)* and *AFM (Airplane Flight Manual)*. Review the airworthiness and registration certificates and weight and balance documentation and be able to explain them (Chapter 3).

Airworthiness requirements—You will need to know the required instruments and equipment for day/night VFR (check 14 CFR §91.205). Know the procedures and limitations for determining airworthiness of the airplane with inoperative instruments and equipment with or without an MEL (Minimum Equipment List). Be aware of the requirement for obtaining a special flight permit (14 CFR §§91.313, 91.315, 91.317, and 91.319). Be able to locate and explain ADs (airworthiness directives), compliance records, maintenance/inspection requirements, and appropriate record keeping (Chapters 3 and 23).

Weather information—You'll have to exhibit knowledge of the elements related to weather information by analyzing weather reports, charts, and forecasts from various sources, with emphasis on the METAR, TAF, and FA; surface analysis chart; radar summary chart; winds and temperatures aloft chart; SIGMETs, AIRMETs, and the significance of AWOS, ASOS, and ATIS reports. You'll make a competent GO/NO GO decision based on available weather information (Chapter 22).

Cross-country flight planning—You'll show that you know the elements related to cross-country flight planning by explaining a preplanned VFR cross-country flight as assigned by the examiner. On the day of the practical test, the final flight plan shall be to the first fuel stop, based on the maximum allowable passengers and baggage and/or cargo loads, using realtime weather. Use appropriate and current aeronautical charts and properly identify airspace, obstructions, and terrain features while you select easily identifiable en route checkpoints. Watch out for prohibited areas or those that are less restrictive but still hazardous to fly through. Select the most favorable altitudes considering weather conditions and equipment capabilities. Compute headings, flight time, and fuel requirements and select appropriate navigation systems/facilities and communication frequencies. You'll be expected to apply pertinent information from NOTAMs, TFRs, *Airport/Facility Directories*, and other flight publications. You'll then complete a navigation log and simulate filing a VFR flight plan (Chapters 23, 24, and 25).

National airspace system—Know the basic VFR weather minimums for all classes of airspace. Be sure that you also know the airspace classes—their boundaries, pilot certification, and airplane equipment requirements for Classes A, B, C, D, E, and G. How's your knowledge of special-use airspace and other airspace areas? (*See* Chapter 21.)

Performance and limitations—You may be quizzed on performance capabilities, approved operating procedures, and limitations of your airplane. Know the power settings, placarded speeds, and fuel and oil requirements. You may be asked to demonstrate the application of the approved weight and balance data for your airplane to determine if the weight and CG locations are within limits for various passenger, fuel, and/or baggage combinations. What are the effects of adding, removing, or shifting weight? Use the manufacturer's charts and graphs for performance figures. (Review Chapter 23.)

Know what could happen if you exceed various limitations, such as loading, so that the CG is out of the envelope. What are the effects of frost or ice on the airplane's takeoff performance? (*See* Chapter 22; review Chapters 17 and 23 also.)

Operations of airplane systems—You'll be expected to be knowledgeable about the following items; some of the factors are discussed in various parts of the book, but the chapters (or other references) cited are the major sources of information:

1. Primary flight controls and trim (Chapters 8 and 9).
2. Wing flaps and leading edge devices (Chapters 12, 13, and 17).
3. Flight instruments, pitot-static and vacuum/pressure systems (Chapters 3 and 15).
4. Landing gear (Chapter 14—*The Advanced Pilot's Flight Manual*).
5. Engine (Chapters 4, 5, 7, and Appendix B).

6. Propeller (Chapters 2, 4, 5, 7, and 23).
7. Fuel system (Chapters 3, 4, 5, 7, and 23).
8. Hydraulic system (Chapter 14 — *The Advanced Pilot's Flight Manual*).
9. Electrical system (Chapters 3 and 25).
10. Environmental system (Chapter 19 — *The Advanced Pilot's Flight Manual*).
11. Oil system (Chapters 4, 7, and 23).
12. De-ice and anti-ice systems (Chapter 7 — *The Instrument Flight Manual*).
13. Avionics (Chapter 21).

Aeromedical factors — You'll be expected to have knowledge of the aeromedical factors, including symptoms and the effects of and corrective action for hypoxia, hyperventilation, middle ear and sinus infection, spatial disorientation, motion sickness, and carbon monoxide poisoning. Review the effects of alcohol and over-the-counter drugs, plus scuba diving as factors in creating flying hazards. (Check the AIM.)

Preflight Procedures

Preflight inspection — Be able to explain why you are checking various items on the airplane (and use the checklist). You'll be expected to determine if the airplane is safe for flight; if you try to take the airplane when one wing is lying flat on the ground, certain questions (and eyebrows) might be raised. Know the colors of the various fuels and the type of fuel and oil used (and also be able to find all fuel and oil filler points). Know where the battery and other components are located. Check for fuel contamination and be able to explain what you are looking for and when it is most likely to occur. Know capacities of fuel and oil tanks and where to look for leaks in these systems. (This also goes for the hydraulic and brake systems.) Check and explain the flight controls and look at the balance weights on the rudder, elevator, and ailerons, as applicable. (You should know by now that in normal operations when one aileron goes up, the other goes down.) Check for structural damage (hangar rash) as you go around, and for Pete's sake, don't try to taxi off with the airplane tied down, control lock(s) in place, or chocks under the wheels. Again, you should know that ice and frost are detrimental to takeoff operations. See to the security of baggage, cargo, and equipment. You are acting as pilot-in-command and will be checked on your judgment of the airplane's readiness to fly safely (Chapters 4 and 23).

Cockpit management — You are expected to have an adequate knowledge of cockpit management and be able to explain the related safety factors. In other words,

you'll be expected to organize your material and equipment in a manner that makes them readily available. (Taking off with the charts and other navigation equipment well out of reach in the far corner of the baggage compartment could cost you several points.) Make sure that the safety belts and harnesses are fastened (with you and the examiner *inside* them). Your seat should be adjusted — and locked — in the proper position. Be sure that the controls are free and have full and proper movement. Since the examiner is a "passenger," you should brief him or her (and any others on board) on the use of the belts and any emergency procedures. Use an appropriate checklist (Chapter 4).

Engine starting — You'll be expected to explain the starting procedures, including starting under various conditions. *Use the checklist — all items — for prestart, start, and poststart procedures. You'll be expected to be safe, with emphasis on (1) positioning the airplane to avoid creating hazards (don't blast people or airplanes behind you), (2) making sure that the propeller area is clear, and (3) ensuring that the engine controls are properly adjusted (for instance, a wideopen throttle with a cold engine, a mixture left in idle cutoff, or a fuel selector OFF could cause problems). Set (or better yet, *hold*) the brakes before, during, and after start, and don't let the airplane *inadvertently* move after the start. *Don't* let the engine roar up after the start; keep the rpm under control. Check the engine instruments after start. (Read Chapter 5 — now — not while starting the engine on the check flight.)

Check the *Pilot's Operating Handbook (POH)* of your airplane to confirm the proper procedures for using an external power source. (Some airplanes require the battery master switch to be OFF and others require it to be ON during a start using an external power source.)

Taxiing — You'll be expected to explain and use safe taxiing procedures. Check the brakes for effectiveness as you move out of the parking spot. You'll be checked on safe ground operations, your use of brakes and power to control taxiing speeds, and proper positioning of the flight controls for the existing wind conditions. You'll be expected to be aware of ground hazards and comply with taxiing procedures and instructions. (Review Chapter 6.) (As one applicant said to the check pilot after sideswiping two airplanes, nearly running over a flight instructor, and ending up with the airplane's nose sticking into the flight office, "I suppose this means that I've flunked the surface operations part of the test.")

Don't abuse the brakes by carrying too much power and using them to keep the taxi speed down. This is a common error.

Before takeoff check—Review Chapter 7. During the flight test, as anytime, you should be able to explain the reasons for checking the items. Don't create a hazard during the runup. Don't stick your head down in the cockpit and keep it there; divide your attention. Touch each control or switch as you *follow the checklist* and call out each item as you check it. Give the instrument reading, if applicable, after checking it on the list. Make sure, again as always, that the airplane is in a safe operating condition, emphasizing (1) flight controls and instruments, (2) engine and propeller operation, (3) seats adjusted and locked, (4) belts and harnesses fastened, and (5) doors and windows secured. If there is any discrepancy, you'll be expected to determine if the airplane is safe for flight or requires maintenance. Know the takeoff performance—airspeeds and takeoff distances (Chapter 17)—and be able to describe takeoff emergency procedures (Chapter 13). You'll handle the takeoff and departure clearances and will note the takeoff time. Make sure that there's no traffic conflict when you taxi into takeoff position.

Airport Operations

Radio communication and ATC light signals—Be at ease using the radio, including knowing pertinent frequencies. You are required to interpret and comply with ATC light signals (*see* Figure 21-21). Use prescribed procedures following radio communications failure. Make sure you comply with traffic pattern procedures instructions.

Traffic pattern—You'll be expected to explain traffic pattern procedures at controlled and nontower airports. You'll be expected to follow prescribed traffic patterns, using proper arrival and departure procedures. Watch your wind drift corrections, spacing with other aircraft and altitudes, airspeeds, and ground traffic. Know the factors of runway incursion, collision avoidance, wake turbulence, and wind shear. Better hold altitudes within ±100 feet and airspeeds within ±10 K of those required. Prompt corrections will be expected. Complete the **prelanding** checklist.

You are expected to maintain orientation with the runway in use, perform the prelanding cockpit check on the downwind leg, and have a final approach leg at a stabilized airspeed (Chapter 13).

Airport and runway marking and lighting—Review Chapters 25 and 26.

Takeoffs, Landings, and Go-Arounds

Normal takeoff and climb—Be able to describe the elements of a normal takeoff and climb, including airspeeds, configurations, and emergency procedures. The examiner will watch for safe operations in normally anticipated conditions. Align the airplane on the runway center line and open the throttle *smoothly* to max power—don't ram it open. Check the engine instruments as the run commences and watch your directional control. Rotate at the *POH*-recommended speed and establish the pitch attitude for V_Y +10/-5 K during the climb. Retract the flaps (and gear, if applicable) at a safe point and altitude. (Keep the landing gear extended until you can no longer land on the runway.) Use the takeoff power until at a safe altitude and don't forget to maintain a straight track on the climbout. Comply with noise abatement procedures, if any. Use the checklist (Chapter 13).

Crosswind takeoff and climb—Know and be able to explain the crosswind takeoff and climb, including airspeeds, configurations, and emergency procedures. For normal takeoffs, apply power smoothly after you are well lined up on the center line. Use full aileron deflection (in the proper direction) and check the engine instruments as the takeoff run starts. Stay on the center line and adjust the aileron deflection pressure as the run progresses. (Note: For some runways with center-line lighting, you may want to keep the nosewheel slightly to the left or right of the line.) Again, you'll rotate at the *POH*-recommended speed and establish and maintain V_Y +10/-5 K. Get the gear and flaps up as applicable at a safe point and altitude during the climb. Maintain the takeoff power to a safe maneuvering altitude and don't drift over into the next county during the straight portion of the climbout. You'll be judged on power application, smoothness, and wind drift correction (make sure the airplane doesn't skip and drift during the takeoff and climb). Comply with noise abatement procedures and use a checklist. (Review Chapter 13.)

Normal approach and landing—Know what elements affect a normal approach and landing, including airspeed and configuration. Be aware of wind conditions, landing surface, and obstructions. Keep a good straight track on final at the proper approach and landing configuration and power, maintaining the recommended airspeed but not more than 1.3 V_{S0} +10/-5 K with a gust factor applied. You'll be expected to make smooth, timely, and correct control applications during the final approach and the transition to landing. You should touch down smoothly on the main gear (tricycle gear) or three-point gear (tailwheel landing gear) at the approximate stalling speed, beyond and within 400 feet of a specified spot, with no drift and the longitudinal axis aligned on the runway center line. Maintain directional control during the roll-out. You could be asked to make landings at different flap configurations (Chapter 13).

Crosswind approach and landing—You'll be expected to show adequate knowledge by explaining crosswind approach and landing techniques, limitations, and recognition of excessive crosswind. You'll be expected to establish the approach and landing configuration and power and to maintain a straight track on final. Keep the airspeed as recommended but not more than 1.3 V_{S0} +10/-5 K and make smooth, timely, and correct control application through the approach to landing attitude. The airplane is to touch down smoothly (it says here) on the upwind main gear (tricycle gear) or upwind main gear and tailwheel at approximately the stalling speed, beyond and within 400 feet of a specified point, with no drift and the longitudinal axis aligned along the runway center line. Maintain directional control after touchdown, increasing aileron deflection into the wind as necessary (Chapter 13).

Soft-field takeoff and climb—You should be able to describe the elements and possible emergency situations of the soft-field takeoff and climb, noting that attempting to climb at airspeeds of less than V_X can be fraught with peril. Select the proper flap setting and keep rolling as you turn onto the takeoff surface, but don't make a full-power, hairy, tire-ruining turn onto the runway. Set the pitch attitude to get the weight off the wheels as soon as possible and maintain directional control. (Here's where problems might occur at the slow speed and blocked forward view.) If obstructions are a problem, maintain V_X +10/-5 K until you've cleared them, then V_Y +10/-5 K. Lift off at the lowest possible airspeed and use ground effect to help acceleration. The same rules apply in this maneuver concerning when to retract flaps (and gear) and tracking straight after takeoff (Chapter 17).

Soft-field approach and landing—Know airspeeds, configurations, and operations on various surfaces. Check out the obstructions, landing surface, and wind condition; establish the recommended softfield approach and landing configuration and recommended airspeed. If no approach speed is recommended, make it at not more than 1.3 V_{S0} +10/-5 K with a gust factor applied. Keep it lined up on final; touch down with a minimum descent rate and groundspeed, with no drift and the airplane lined up with the landing area. Maintain directional control after touchdown and maintain sufficient speed to taxi on a soft surface (Chapter 17).

Short-field takeoff and climb—Know and be able to describe the procedure and the expected performance for the existing conditions. Review Chapter 17 and the *POH* for your airplane and be able to use the takeoff performance charts. Select the proper wing flap setting, line up with the center line, and smoothly apply power. Keep your directional control. (Taking off across the runway won't cut it.) Set up the proper pitch attitude to get the best acceleration and rotate the airplane at the recommended airspeed. Accelerate to V_X and maintain within +10/-5 K until at least 50 feet above the surface or until the "obstacle" is cleared; then assume V_Y +10/-5 K. Don't suddenly pull up the flaps and settle back in; retract the flaps and the landing gear at a safe point and altitude, as noted in the earlier takeoff procedures. Keep full power on until the "obstacle" is cleared and check back occasionally during the straight part of the climbout to see that you are tracking properly. Don't forget to comply with noise abatement procedures on all takeoffs cited here. Airspeed control is a big factor for best climb performance. (*See* Chapter 17.)

Short-field approach and landing—You'll be expected to explain short-field approach and landing procedures, including airspeeds, configurations, and performance data. You'll be asked to evaluate obstructions, landing surface, and wind condition and to select the most-suitable touchdown point. Be prepared for a go-around if necessary. You are to establish the recommended configuration and airspeed or use a speed of not more than 1.3 V_{S0} +10/-5 K, if no other information is available. Maintain precise control of the descent rate along the extended runway center line. There should be little float, and you should touch down beyond and within 200 feet of a specified point, lined up with the runway center line, with no side drift. Keep the airplane directionally straight after landing. Brake as necessary to stop in the shortest distance consistent with safety (no squared-off tires, please). Holding the control wheel or stick full back while braking and upping the flaps (*not the gear*) will give more-efficient braking (Chapter 17).

Forward slip to landing—You should have a good grasp of the principles involved and be aware of technique, limitations, and effect on the airspeed indicator. Be aware of any manufacturer's limitations on slips with flaps. You are to demonstrate a forward slip at a point from which a landing can be made in a desired area, using the recommended configuration. Remember that if there's a crosswind, you drop the wing that's into the wind (Figure 13-23). Keep the airplane's track straight with the runway and maintain an airspeed that results in little floating during the landing. The requirements for touchdown point (at or within 400 feet beyond a specified point), with no side drift and good directional control, are the same as for the normal landing just cited (Chapter 13).

Go-around/rejected landing — You may have to demonstrate the procedure for go-around on an approach (balked landing). You'll be expected to make a timely decision, fly the recommended airspeeds, and cope with any undesirable pitch and yaw tendency (keep up with the trim requirements). Apply takeoff power, attain the proper pitch attitude (airspeed), and retract the flaps as recommended at a safe altitude. If the airplane has retractable gear, pull it up after a rate of climb has been established and you can't land on the remaining runway if the engine fails. Trim the airplane, climb at V_Y +10/−5 K, and track a good traffic pattern for the next landing (Chapter 13).

Performance Maneuver

Steep turns — Review this maneuver in Chapter 10. Be able to explain the requirements involved, including increased load factors, additional power, and other elements. Stay above 1,500 AGL. Establish the airspeed at the manufacturer's recommended speed or one designated by the examiner, not to exceed the airplane's maneuvering speed (V_A) and set up a bank angle of 45° ±5°, maintaining coordinated flight for 360° of turn, as directed, then roll out and do a 360° turn in the opposite direction. Divide your attention between airplane control and orientation, keep the bank ±5° of that required, and rollout with ±10° of the desired heading. Keep the altitude within ±100 feet and the airspeed within ±10 K.

Ground Reference Maneuvers

Rectangular course — Know the principles of wind drift correction in straight and turning flight and the tie-in between the rectangular course and airport traffic patterns. You'll be expected to pick the field or fields, set up the maneuver, and enter at the proper distance from the boundary at a 45° angle to the downwind leg at traffic pattern altitude (600–1,000 feet AGL). (No, you aren't allowed to fly up and down between those altitudes; keep the altitude within ±100 feet of that selected.) Keep your flight path parallel to the sides and be prepared to fly it with both left or right turns. You'll be expected to be able to divide your attention between airplane control and the ground track. Check your coordination and maintain airspeed within ±10 K.

Avoid excessive maneuvering (keep the bank angle to a maximum of 45° and airspeed to ±10 K — writer's suggestion) and stay above the minimum legal altitude for local obstructions. You'll reverse course as directed by the examiner. Exit at the point of entry at the same airspeed and altitude the maneuver was begun. Watch for other airplanes (Chapter 10).

S-turns — Be able to expound on the principles of this maneuver. Select a long, straight reference perpendicular to the wind (know its approximate direction and speed) and fly it at a selected altitude of 600–1,000 feet AGL. Keep the turns with a constant radius (*see* Figures 10-6 and 10-7), divide your attention between airplane control and the ground, and keep the maneuver coordinated. Reverse the turns directly over the reference line and keep the altitude within ±100 feet of that selected. The airspeed should stay within ±10 K of that desired; it is suggested that you don't exceed a bank of 45° at the steepest point of the turn. (Not mentioned in the PTS, but it is suggested in this book as a maximum bank.) Keep it legal as far as obstructions are concerned and don't have a midair collision. Also, don't take the examiner on a cross-country but reverse the turns as directed.

Turns about a point — Pick the point promptly and enter, checking your heading by the heading indicator or a geographic reference. The practical test guide requires two turns and the examiner will ask for such, so you'd better get in the habit of knowing where you are during practice sessions. As Chapter 16 notes, be prepared to do the turns in either direction, but most folks start out with left turns. (The examiner will probably call for reversal of the turns after the first two turns.) The altitude, airspeed, and max bank (45°) limitations are the same as for the S-turns just covered (*see* also Chapter 10).

Navigation

Pilotage and dead reckoning — You should be able to give the examiner the straight information on piloting and dead reckoning techniques and procedures. You'll demonstrate that you are able to follow the preplanned course solely by reference to landmarks and identify these landmarks by relating the surface features to chart symbols.

You also must be able to navigate by means of precomputed headings, groundspeed, and elapsed time and *combine* pilotage and dead reckoning with a verification of the airplane's position within 3 NM of the flight-plan route at all times. You're expected to hit enroute checkpoints within 5 minutes of the initial or revised ETA and make your destination within 5 minutes of the ETA. Be aware of the remaining fuel at all times. Make corrections for differences between preflight groundspeed and heading calculations and those determined enroute (and record them). Keep your altitude within ±200 feet. You'd better maintain the desired heading within ±15°. Use those climb, cruise, and descent checklists. Don't get lost (Chapters 24 and 25).

Navigation systems and radar services (private pilot) — Be able to explain radio navigation equipment, procedures, and limitations. You'll be required to select, tune, and identify the desired radio facility and locate the airplane's position relative to that facility. Better practice using VOR and NDB facilities and be able to intercept and track a given radial or bearing. Know how to locate the airplane's position using cross bearings (*see* Figure 25-4). Recognize station passage and/or be able to describe it. Check with your flight instructor to find out the best method of recognizing signal loss and how best to regain the signal, as applied to the equipment you're using. While you're doing the radio navigation, stay within ±200 feet of the altitude chosen. Use proper communications procedures when dealing with ATC radar services. (Be aware of the radar services available.) Check on your local sectional chart legend (control tower frequencies) to see what facilities have ASR (airport surveillance radar) for approaches. You'll be expected to follow verbal or radio navigation guidance and determine the minimum safe altitude. Maintain altitude within ±200 feet and heading ±15° (Chapters 21 and 25).

Diversion — The examiner will want to see how you cope with having to change your plans during flight. You'll be expected to recognize the conditions that require a diversion (such as unexpected headwinds, lowering ceilings and visibilities, or other factors). At the examiner's prompting, you'll select an alternate airport and route and proceed to it without delay. Make an accurate estimate of heading, groundspeed, arrival time, and fuel required to get there. Use pilotage, dead reckoning, or radio navigation aids and ATC assistance. Keep the altitude within ±200 feet during the trip off the preplanned course. Keep the heading within ±15 once you're established on course (Chapter 25).

Lost procedures — Make sure that you know and can explain lost procedures, including the following items:

1. Maintaining the original or appropriate heading, identifying landmarks, and climbing if necessary (Chapter 25).
2. Rechecking the calculations. ("Ah, Igor, it's really 110 K groundspeed not 1,100!")

3. Proceeding to and identifying the nearest concentration of prominent landmarks. ("Is that the Atlantic or the Pacific Ocean over there?")
4. Using available communications and navigation aids for contacting the appropriate facility for assistance. ("Jonesville approach control, I'd like a *practice* vector to the airport.")
5. Planning a precautionary landing if deteriorating visibility and/or fuel exhaustion is imminent. Use your skills at dragging the area and short- and softfield landings. (One pilot inadvertently made a precautionary landing in the middle of a nudist colony in 1985 and has not yet gotten over it.)

You'll be expected to *select the appropriate course of action* when given a "lost" situation. (*See* Chapter 17, and take another good look at Chapter 25.)

Slow Flight and Stalls

Maneuvering during slow flight — Know the background of this requirement and why it is an important part of flight training. Stay above 1,500 feet AGL. Establish and maintain an airspeed at just above a stall +10/-0 K while (1) in coordinated straight and turning flight in various configurations and bank angles as established by the examiner and (2) in coordinated climbs and descents in various configurations as specified by the examiner. Maintain the specified angle of bank ±10° in level flight and maintain the specified angle of bank ±10° in climbing or descending flight. Roll out on the specified heading ±10°. You'll be expected to maintain the desired altitude within ±100 feet, when a constant altitude is specified, and level off from climbs and descents within ±100 feet. Your heading during straight flight must be maintained within ±10 of that specified in coordinated flight (Chapter 12).

Power-off stalls — These are basically the approach to landing stalls covered in Chapter 12, but you might want to review Chapter 14 also. You'll be expected to explain the aerodynamics of the stall and know the flight situations that result in power-off stalls, including the proper recovery procedures. Know the hazards of stalling during slips and skids. Recover above 1,500 feet AGL or the recommended altitude, whichever is higher. Set up the normal approach or landing configuration and airspeed with the throttle closed or at a reduced power setting. Establish a straight glide (±10° heading) or gliding turn of (suggested) 20°, ±10° in coordinated flight as required to induce the stall. Maintain good coordination, establish a landing pitch attitude, and keep it there to induce a full stall. You'll be expected to recognize the indications of a stall and promptly recover by decreasing the angle of attack, simultaneously leveling the wings, and advancing the power to max allowable to regain the normal flight attitude. Retract the flaps (if extended) and landing gear (if retractable) and establish a climb. Accelerate to V_X or V_Y before the final flap retraction. Return to the altitude, heading, and airspeed specified by the examiner. Don't get a secondary stall, build up excessive airspeed, lose excessive altitude, spin, or get below 1,500 AGL at any time.

Power-on stalls—The examiner will want to know that you understand the principles of these stalls and what can contribute to aggravating them (slips and skids) and will look at your recovery effectiveness. Again, don't get below 1,500 AGL at any time during the demonstration. Basically, these stalls are the *takeoff and departure stalls* covered in Chapter 12. Set the airplane up in the takeoff or normal climb (departure) configuration and establish the takeoff or climb airspeed before applying takeoff or climb power. (You may have to use reduced power to avoid excessive pitch-up during the entry, but then apply more power as things progress.) Set the power to no less than 65 percent. You'll smoothly set up and maintain a pitch attitude that will induce a stall in both wings when they are level ($\pm10°$ constant heading) and in 20° ($\pm10°$) banks. "Torque" may tend to skid and turn the airplane to the left; watch your coordination during the entry. Increase elevator (stabilator) back pressure smoothly until the stall occurs, as indicated by (1) a sudden loss of control effectiveness, (2) buffeting, or (3) uncontrollable pitching.

The required recovery will be to promptly and positively reduce the angle of attack (pitch altitude), simultaneously level the wings, and regain normal flight attitude with coordinated use of flight and power controls. (Always use full power when recovering from stalls unless the examiner asks for a power-off recovery as a demonstration of your knowledge that reducing the angle of attack is the main action in stall recovery; remember that the use of power reduces the altitude loss.) After recovery, clean up the airplane and establish a climb. Accelerate to V_X or V_Y before the final flap retraction and return to the altitude, heading, and airspeed specified by the examiner. Again, if the examiner has to take over to keep you from spinning or having other problems, such as going below 1,500 feet AGL, or if you get a secondary stall during recovery, you will be disqualified (Chapters 12 and 14).

Spin awareness—You'll be expected to explain flight situations where unintentional spins may occur. (A good all-round answer is "when the pilot is distracted.") Review Chapter 12 for the aerodynamics and your *POH*, and discuss with your instructor ways to recover from unintentional spins, with particular emphasis on the spin recovery procedure for the airplane you're using on the practical test.

Basic Instrument Maneuvers

(Private practical test)

Straight and level flight—Know why you are looking at the various instruments in your scan (crosscheck) and how you control the airplane when flying by reference to instruments. (It's exactly the same as when using outside references.) Your control application should be smooth, timely, and coordinated; if the ball in the turn indicator leaves the cockpit, you may be in a little trouble. You are to maintain straight and level flight keeping the heading within $\pm20°$, the assigned altitude within ±200 feet, and the desired airspeed within ±10 K. Use all flight instruments available (Chapter 15).

Constant-airspeed climbs—You should be able to explain what you are doing and what makes the airplane climb. Establish the climb pitch attitude and power setting on an assigned heading. You'll be asked to make turns to headings. The heading must be maintained within: $\pm20°$ (watch that "torque" effect) and the airspeed maintained within ±10 K; you are to level off and maintain flight within ±200 feet of the desired altitude (Chapter 15.)

Constant-airspeed descents—Again, know what you're doing and be able to talk about it. Set up the airspeed and power (*see* Chapter 15 for some suggestions) for about a 500-fpm descent and be smooth and coordinated. The heading should be within: $\pm20°$ and airspeed limits within ±10 K; level off and maintain flight within ±200 feet of the desired altitude. You'll make turns to a specific heading.

Turns to headings—These are constant-altitude turns. Use standard-rate turns and don't make the examiner sick with your rough control. Keep the altitude within ±200 feet and airspeed within ±10 K, maintain a standard-rate turn, and roll out within $\pm10°$ of the assigned heading (Chapter 15).

Recovery from unusual flight attitudes—You'll be expected to demonstrate that you can cope with the situation when it's necessary to recover from a "nonstandard" flight situation. You should recognize the critical attitudes promptly; interpret the instruments; and recover by prompt, smooth, coordinated controls applied in the proper sequence. If you bend something, go too fast, spin the airplane, and/or make the examiner's voice rise a couple of octaves while he's saying

"I've got it," you aren't doing a satisfactory job of flying (Chapter 15).

Radio communications, navigation systems/facilities, and radar services—Know how to use the NAV/COMM system to help yourself if you get caught in instrument conditions. Follow verbal instructions and/or navigation systems/facilities for guidance. Determine the minimum safe altitude. Maintain altitude within ±200 feet, heading within ±20°, and airspeed within ±10 K.

Emergency Operations

Emergency descent—An emergency descent is a matter for urgency, and you should have checked out the procedure in the *POH*. Know the emergency descent configuration and airspeed (and establish it within ±5 K). Keep oriented, use proper planning, and divide your attention between the proper procedure and flying the airplane. Don't forget to use the emergency checklist (Chapter 18). *Note:* This is no longer listed in the latest PTS but was kept here for training purposes.

Emergency approach and landing—Get to that best-glide attitude, configuration and airspeed (±10 K). Be sure to pick a suitable emergency landing area *within gliding distance.* (This is important!) You should set up and follow a flight pattern to that area, considering altitude, wind, terrain, and obstructions. When you're set up, try to figure out the reason for the malfunction and correct it, if possible. (But *fly the airplane*, don't spin it while distracted—or anytime for that matter.) Don't forget the appropriate emergency checklist (Chapter 18).

Systems and equipment malfunctions—You better know what problems are possible with your airplane. The examiner will set up simulated malfunctions and/or emergencies such as partial or complete power loss, engine roughness or overheat, carburetor or induction icing, loss of oil pressure, fuel starvation, electrical or flight instruments malfunction (including pitot/static problems), landing gear or flap troubles, inoperative trim, inadvertent door or window opening, structural icing, smoke/fire engine compartment fire, and any other emergency appropriate to the airplane being used for the practical test. Use the emergency checklist.

Emergency equipment and survival gear—Know the location, method of operation, or use for all emergency equipment and survival gear. Check the servicing requirements and method of safe storage; be aware of the equipment and survival gear appropriate for operation in various climates and topographical environments. Use that emergency checklist.

Night Flight Operations

(Private practical test)

Preparation and equipment—You may be asked how you would go about preparing for a local cross-country night flight. Be able to answer questions on airport lighting and the airplane lights and their operation. Know what equipment you'd need; a flashlight or another kind of backup would be essential. Weather factors are particularly pertinent to night flight (such as the relationship of temperature and dewpoint and the possibility of ground fog forming during night flights). Be aware of the possible need for reference to the flight instruments (1) over unlighted areas and (2) if actual instrument conditions are unexpectedly encountered. Understand the factors of night vision, including the effects of changing light conditions, coping with illusions, and how the pilot's physical condition affects visual acuity. If you don't meet night flying experience requirements, this area won't be evaluated and your certificate will bear the limitation, "Night Flying Prohibited" (Chapter 26).

Night flight—If the demonstration of night flight is impracticable, your competency may be determined by oral testing. If night navigation is required by the examiner, you will follow procedures similar to those described earlier under "Cross-Country Flying." Be aware of night flying procedures, including safety precautions and emergency action. *Use a checklist.* You should be sharp at explaining (and demonstrating, if required) the starting, taxiing, and pretakeoff check. Use good operating practices for night takeoff, climb, approach, and landing. Know the factors in navigation and orientation for night flight under VFR conditions. Don't forget your flashlight and checklist (Chapter 26).

Postflight Procedures

After landing—Know what should be done after the landing and taxi to the parking/refueling area, using the proper wind control technique and obstacle avoidance procedures. Complete the appropriate checklist. Be aware of runway hold lines and other surface control markings and lightings.

Parking and securing—You'll be expected to know the parking hand signals and understand the factors for deplaning passengers. (Shutting the engine(s) down is *always* the safest procedure before people enplane or deplane.) Park the airplane *properly*, considering the other aircraft and the safety of nearby persons and property on the ramp. Use the recommended procedure for engine shutdown and secure the cockpit and the airplane. Perform a satisfactory postflight inspection and complete the appropriate checklist.

Aeronautical Decision Making (ADM)

Analysis of aviation accidents over the past years shows that a large percentage are caused by a lack of judgment or the pilot's lack of aeronautical decision making. Airplanes land short of destination airports, killing or injuring occupants because pilots decide to skip that interim refueling stop, figuring they "can make it." Or perhaps the weather was not checked or weather warnings were ignored by the pilot, resulting in a fatal accident.

More and more emphasis is being placed on aeronautical decision making (ADM) during the practical tests by examiners. Review each TASK indicated in this chapter and see how *your* good or bad ADM could affect the outcome. For instance, a superficial preflight check (or *no* preflight check), not using a checklist, failing to clear the area before starting a maneuver, or not continuing to look around as you proceed are some instances of poor judgment or poor ADM. A very large portion of flying is headwork, and the examiner will be interested in your grasp of this. If you are careless on a check ride that you've been preparing for, the examiner will wonder how your mind will work after you get out on your own and meet unforeseen situations head-on.

It's been estimated that approximately 80 percent (or more) of aircraft accidents are caused by human factors. The Advisory Circular 60-22, *Aeronautical Decision Making*, lists five hazardous attitudes and the antidotes for them.

1. *Anti-Authority*—"Don't tell me." This pilot resents rules and thinks regulations and procedures are silly and unnecessary.
   Antidote: Follow the rules. They are usually right.
2. *Impulsivity*—"Do it quickly." These people don't stop to consider what they are about to do, but do the first thing that comes to mind.
   Antidote: Not so fast. Think first.
3. *Invulnerability*—"It won't happen to me." It's always the other guy who's going to have an accident.
   Antidote: Hey, it could happen to me.

4. *Macho*—"I can do it." This is probably a good attitude (if controlled) for a fighter pilot but could cause serious problems for a low-time private pilot (and other more experienced pilots, also).
   Antidote: Taking chances is foolish.
5. *Resignation*—"What's the use?" This pilot will leave the action to others, for better or worse.
   Antidote: I'm not helpless. I can make a difference.

Checkitis

Checkitis is a mysterious disease that strikes just before a practical test. The victims are usually of at least average intelligence, but as soon as this malady hits, they are lucky to remember their own names. It is characterized by shaking knees, a knotted stomach, sweating, and loss of memory. You may not get checkitis—if this is the case, you're one of the chosen few.

The examiner probably has also had it and will make allowances. The good thing about checkitis is that as soon as you get busy in the practical test, its symptoms lessen or fade completely. The best insurance against it is to know what you're doing beforehand. If you don't do too well on the oral, it may hurt the entire flight because of added nervousness. Learn all you can about the plane and flying in general and then don't worry about checkitis.

You may feel that the check pilot is indeed a sinister figure (Figure 28-2).

Figure 28-2. As shown here, the check pilot is just an ordinary human being like yourself—with no ax to grind.

THE AIRPLANE NUMBERS

PAPERS AND LOGBOOKS

1. Logbooks

   Date of last annual inspection _____

   Date of last 100-hour inspection _____

   Next 100-hour inspection due (tachometer reading) _____ hours

2. Airworthiness Certificate—Standard

   Issued to (number of plane) _____

3. Certificate of Registration

   Issued to (name) _____ on (date) _____

4. Operation Limitations

   Up-to-date? _____

5. Weight and balance form

   Is it up-to-date, or has a major repair and alteration form superseded it?

   Latest information on equipment list and empty weight (date) _____

STATISTICS

1. Basic Empty Weight

   _____ pounds

2. Empty Weight Center of Gravity

   _____ inches aft of datum; or empty weight moment _____ pound-inches

3. Maximum Certified (Gross) Weight

   Normal category _____ pounds

   Utility category _____ pounds (either or both may apply)

4. Fuel

   Total capacity _____ gallons

   Usable _____ gallons (fuel weighs 6 pounds per gallon)

5. Oil

   Total capacity _____ quarts

   Minimum for flight _____ quarts (oil weighs 7 pounds per gallon)

   Brand name and viscosity—winter _____; summer _____

6. Baggage

   Maximum weight _____ pounds

PERFORMANCE

   (All figures are for maximum certified weight)

1. Range

   At 65% power, _____ NM, _____ gallons per hour

   Max range: At _____ % power, _____ K, _____ NM

2. Rate of Climb at Sea Level

   _____ feet per minute

   Best rate-of-climb speed: _____ K at sea level

   Max angle-of-climb speed: _____ K at sea level, _____° flaps

3. Takeoff Distance at Sea Level (run):
   _____ feet
   Total distance over 50-foot obstacle: _____ feet
4. Landing Roll
   _____ feet
   Total distance over 50-foot obstacle: _____ feet (sea level)
5. Service ceiling
   _____ feet. (The service ceiling is the altitude at which the airplane's maximum rate of climb is 100 feet per minute.)

MANEUVERS

1. Slow Flight
   _____ K (clean). 20°–30° banked turns, climbs and guide, cruise and landing configurations
2. Takeoff and Departure Stalls
   Reduce power and slow to _____ K, then apply climb power (a) straight ahead and (b) 10°–20° banked turns
3. Approach to Landing Stalls
   Start at _____ K and full flaps. Slow to stall. Gliding turns (20°–30° banks) and straight ahead (trim set)
4. Accelerated Stalls
   Cruise configuration: No flaps, 45° bank, _____ rpm, slow to _____ K (bottom of green arc plus 10 K)

CLEAR THE AREA BEFORE DOING STALLS

5. Emergency Flying by Reference to Instruments
   Climbs: Full power and best rate of climb speed _____ K
   Descents: At _____ K and _____ rpm (to give approximately 500 fpm descent)
6. Turns Around a Point and Other Ground Reference Maneuvers
   Note heading of entry
   Altitude for maneuver _____ feet MSL,
   or _____ feet above the local surface
7. Short-Field Takeoff
   Flap setting _____°
   Climb speed to clear obstacle _____ K
8. Short-Field Landing
   Flap setting (usually full flaps) _____°
   Approach speed _____ K
9. Soft- or Rough-Field Takeoff
   Flap setting _____°
10. Soft-Field Landings
    Flap setting _____°
    Approach speed _____ K

Figure 28-3. Important airspeeds.

After the Practical Test

It seems that immediately after getting the certificate and getting out on his or her own, the average new pilot sets about developing as many bad habits as possible. Actually, it's not a deliberate move, but sometimes it seems so. More about this later.

The training, while intended to be realistic, can't cover all of the problems that can be encountered in a long-term flying career.

High, Hot, Humid, and Heavy

For instance, the chances are that you haven't flown a loaded four-place airplane (with people and baggage) from a high density-altitude airport. Probably you took your flight training in that same fourplace airplane with only you and the instructor (and then only you, solo). And maybe your flying was in low density-altitude conditions. Be prepared for a loss of performance when you take those three friends and their baggage out of a high, hot, and humid airport. Give yourself plenty of time and distance. You may have to (1) wait overnight for a cooler, early morning takeoff, (2) fly your passengers one or two at a time to a lower elevation airport, or (3) have somebody drive them to that airport.

Preflight Check, Slackening of

The preflight check you so carefully learned and used during the flight training (and particularly during the practical test!) is oftentimes like memory as a person gets older, the first or second thing to go. This is particularly a problem in extreme temperature conditions. It's too hot on the ramp, and the pilot moves around the airplane at a rate closely approximating Indians riding around a circled wagon train. When the temperatures are nudging zero, it's tough to get a good fuel check (gasoline is cold), shortcuts are established, and the overall preflight check suffers as well. *Your habit pattern should be so established for a thorough preflight check that you wouldn't take off without one because you'd feel uncomfortable during the entire flight.* You'll have to stop or slow down from time to time, and *really* look at the airplane as you preflight it.

Shortcuts

One shortcut is the one just mentioned about the preflight check. Another is the lack of use of a checklist for starting and the pretakeoff and prelanding checks. There are a couple of ways to use checklists: (1) Take it step by step, item by item as it appears on the list or (2) use the checklist after the fact to confirm that the items are covered. The first choice seems to work better for most people, but be sure that you don't skip an item as you go through it. (This is the most common mistake.) If a checklist is interrupted, you should start it over from the beginning.

Another common shortcut is to use less than the full runway even when there is no pressure for a quick take-off. Plenty of pilots whip out on the runway, leaving a couple of hundred feet (or more) behind them. You might need that unused runway to brake to a stop if a takeoff has to be aborted for one reason or another.

It's been noted that many accidents and incidents aren't caused by a catastrophic occurrence but a series of "minor" upsets and delays.

You're leaving with your family on that long-planned flying vacation:

If you don't get off by a certain time the weather will preclude going VFR. (You don't have an instrument rating yet.) The car has a flat tire. This takes time to fix. There's more luggage than you'd counted on. Traffic is heavy (and slow) on the way to the airport. The airplane's master switch was left ON by the other airplane owner yesterday, requiring the use of a battery charger before *you* can fly today.

The weather has moved in, but after all this trouble you've decided that you can be out of it with only a "little" scud running.

So you take off.

You're nervous and upset and this detracts from your judgment of the weather problem and also in flying the airplane. If you make it, you'll swear you'll never do that again.

If there is one thing that could sum up your flying attitude after you get out on your own, it is to never be pressured into flying when you don't want to. (Many pilots have sat a number of days on the ground at remote airports because the weather was worse than they or the airplane's equipment could cope with.) On every flight (local or otherwise) *always*, repeat, *always* have an alternative plan of action.

There's an old, old truism, "If you have time to spare, go by air." There'll be times when you have to rent a car to get home and then have the hassle of going back and getting the airplane later. *So welcome to the club.*

Another shortcut is to not oversee the fueling of your airplane at a strange airport. (Sure, you're in a hurry to get to the motel.)

Currency

After a layoff for several weeks (or months) you'll feel unsure of yourself about flying again. The longer the layoff, the more unsure you'll be about even going out to the airport.

Even experienced pilots don't feel quite as at home with the airplane, and it may take them 30 minutes or an hour to get back to where "things feel right," even in an airplane they have flown for many hours.

Get some dual at selected intervals. Discuss this with your instructor. Too many private pilots think that dual is now a check ride. Of course, you'll get a Flight Review as necessary, but additional dual as you (or your instructor) feel necessary doesn't hurt. For instance, you might get instruction on some of the commercial maneuvers such as chandelles, lazy eights, and eights-on-pylons. You'll be learning new items. Who knows, you may want to go on to the commercial anyway. When done in a properly certificated airplane and with an experienced instructor, aerobatics and spin training is a great confidence builder. (Like everybody else, you'll approach such training with trepidation that first time but will find that your other areas of flying will profit after you've completed it.)

Work on a higher certificate or rating. Just flying around the local area is expensive and can get boring after a while. Working on a new certificate or rating doesn't mean that you have to fly *every* flight with that in mind, but at least you have a long-term goal. For instance, the instrument rating would be a good goal to work on right after the private certificate. Probably by the time you get the private you'll have around 66 hours total (this is the national average). Fifty hours of cross-country experience is required including the hours solo you got as a student pilot. You can be flying some long cross-countries with family and friends, interspersed with instrument instruction and practice—with a qualified instructor or safety pilot, of course.

Another way for you to keep flying fresh is to get a good checkout in an airplane type or model you haven't flown before. Perhaps you would like to fly a tailwheel airplane and so you would contact a school that specializes in this. Or maybe you have an eye on that four-place with the constant-speed propeller, which would be good for those long cross-country trips with the family.

It's been said that a long cross-country flight is no more than a series of short cross-country segments stuck together. That's true to a certain extent, but fatigue and weather become more important factors on the long ones. After flying 7 or 8 hours and several hundred miles, you'll find that many times both have put a certain amount of added pressure on you. Your weather judgments may be decayed by fatigue; "get-home-itis" has caused more than one bad accident near the end of

a long flight home. Don't push weather beyond your capabilities; as said earlier, there will be times when you'll have to leave the airplane at a distant airport and find other means to get home. Remember that there is weather in which *nobody* flies (airlines, corporate or military), and your minimums should be appreciably higher at this early stage of your flying career.

As time goes on, get a night checkout and some local solo night time. This is a good confidence builder. Later you'll want to extend your night flights to cross-countries to nearby airports and then farther. (A tip for night cross-countries—keep up with the lighted towns on the sectional chart as you come to them; it's easier than goofing off and trying to figure if that's Smithfield down there, or whether you've passed it, or not.) Of course, airport rotating beacons and their relative position to a town are a good aid in identifying a particular town or city, but it's best to keep up with things as you go rather than, for instance, needing VOR cross bearings to finally locate yourself.

Bad Habits

Earlier it was mentioned that (probably inadvertently) you'll start to acquire some bad habits, maybe subtly starting on the day after the private pilot check ride.

For instance, your approaches and landings start getting faster and faster. You'll start landing that tricycle-gear airplane in a flatter attitude until you'll touch down with all three wheels at once, using much more runway than necessary and finding that the brakes are often abused.

Another bad habit is to let your traffic pattern flying deteriorate, with too-far or too-close downwind legs, imprecise turns at all "four corners" of the pattern, and poor wind drift correction on the legs. Some pilots even start flying straight-in approaches and non-standard patterns at uncontrolled airports.

Some private pilots still are leery of crosswind landings; if this is the situation for you, get some dual in crosswind conditions a little stronger (but still safe) than you had during training. That's a very good confidence builder and breaker of bad habits.

If your time and money are limited, you'll get the best recurrent training per dollar or per hour if you shoot an hour or so of landings every so often. Don't shoot all touch-and-go's, but break it up with full stops and taxiing back for another go. If you don't want to get dual instruction during some of these sessions, you might have a more experienced friend or a flight instructor, who's sitting out in front of the airport office, critique your takeoffs, patterns, and landings (from the ground).

Summed Up

Don't let yourself grow stale; regularly scheduled dual, both on the basics and new areas of flying, will increase your safety and hold your interest as you gain experience.

No matter how skilled or experienced you are in your line of work, flying is comparatively new to you at this point. Stay within your own limitations and never let yourself get pressured to fly.

Part Six
Syllabus 6

Private Certificate Syllabus

Contents

*If an approved flight simulator or other approved flight training device and authorized instructor are available, 14 CFR §§61.4 and 61.109 permit them to be used for these units.

Training Records **S–3**

Hourly Breakdown: Ground Instruction and Flights **S–4**

Books and Equipment **S–6**

Introduction **S–7**

Stage 1   Presolo **S–9**

   Unit 1   Introduction of Effects of Controls and the Four Fundamentals S–9

   Unit 2   Review and Repeat of Unit 1 . . . . .S–13

   Unit 3   Introduction of Steep Turns, Slow Flight, Rectangular Courses,
             and S-turns Across a Road S–16

   Unit 4   Introduction to Stalls S–18

   Unit 5   Emergency Procedures S–20

   Unit 6   Pattern Work: Normal Takeoffs and Landings and
             Introduction to Recoveries from Bad Situations S–23

   Unit 7   Takeoffs and Landings and a Review of Recoveries from Bad Situations S–25

   Unit 8   Review of High-Altitude Emergencies; Introduction to Forward
             and Sideslips; Pattern Work at Another Airport S–26

   Unit 9   Shooting Takeoffs and Landings S–28

   Unit 10   Presolo Knowledge Test — Stage 1 Written Test 1.0 Hour S–29

   Unit 11   First Solo S–31

   Unit 12   Summary S–32

Stage 2   Immediate Postsolo **S–33**

   Unit 1   Postsolo Flight Check and Supervised Solo S–33

   Unit 2   Solo in the Pattern S–35

   Unit 3   Review of Stalls, Introduction to Incipient Spins and Recoveries S–36

   Unit 4   Solo in the Practice Area and Pattern I S–38

Unit 5   Solo in the Practice Area and Pattern II S–39

Unit 6   Introduction to Emergency Instrument Flying* S–40

Unit 7   Dual Review of Previous Instruction S–41

Unit 8   Solo in the Practice Area and Pattern III S–42

Unit 9   Dual: Short- and Soft-Field Takeoffs and Landings. S–43

Unit 10   Solo in the Practice Area and Pattern IV S–44

Unit 11   Emergency Instrument Flying* S–45

Unit 12   Solo Takeoffs and Landings in the Local Pattern. S–47

Unit 13   Stage 2 Written Test S–48

Stage 3   Cross-Country **S–49**

Unit 1   Solo Flight to a Nearby Airport S–49

Unit 2   Use of NAVAIDs and Communications Procedures S–50

Unit 3   Introduction to Night Flying S–52

Unit 4   Navigation Ground School: Preparation for Dual and Solo Cross-Countries S–54

Unit 5   Dual Cross-Country to Two Other Airports S–57

Unit 6   Solo Cross-Country S–59

Unit 7   Stage Check after the First Solo Cross-Country S–61

Unit 8   Emergency Instrument Flying* S–62

Unit 9   Solo Triangular Cross-Country S–64

Unit 10   Dual Night Cross-Country and Local Pattern Work S–65

Unit 11   Solo in the Practice Area and Pattern V S–67

Unit 12   Dual and Solo Flight to a Tower-Controlled Airport (VFR-Day) S–69

Unit 13   Weather Theory and Weather Services. S–70

Unit 14   Solo Long Cross-Country Flight S–73

Unit 15   Stage 3 Written Test S–74

Stage 4   Preparation for the Knowledge Test **S–77**

Stage 5   Private Pilot (ASEL) Practical (Flight) Test **S–85**

Unit 1   Review and Introduction to the Practical Test S–85

Unit 2   Student Practice S–87

Unit 3   Student Practice S–87

Unit 4   Navigation S–88

Unit 5   High Work and Emergency Instrument Flying S–89

Unit 6   Systems and Equipment Malfunctions, Emergency Equipment,
               Survival Gear, and Night Operations S–91

Unit 7   Stage Check: Practical Test S–92

Unit 8   FAA Practical Test S–93

Training Records

Reference: 14 CFR §141.101 (paraphrased)

Each holder of a pilot school or provisional pilot school certificate shall establish and maintain a current and accurate record of the participation and accomplishment of each student enrolled in an approved (141) course of training. (The student's logbook is not acceptable for this record.)

A copy of this syllabus and all required information should be kept for each student. This page should be filled out and the approved school authority, upon request of a student, should make a copy of this record available to the student.

Student's Name _____

Date of Enrollment _____

Date of Termination (Student Drop-Out) _____

Date of Transfer to Another School _____

Date and Grade of School Stage 1 Presolo Knowledge Test _____

Date and Grade of School Stage 2 Written Test _____

Date and Grade of School Postsolo Cross-Country Knowledge and Practical Test

_____

Date and Grade of School Stage 3 Written Test _____

Date and Grade of School Stage 4 Written Test _____

Date and Grade of FAA Knowledge Test _____

Date and Grade of School Final Practical Test _____

Date of Certification/Graduation and Result of FAA Practical Test

Date_____ Pass_____ Fail_____

Signature of Chief, or Other Authorized, Instructor

DATE _____ SIGNED _____

Certificate No./Expiration _____

Hourly Breakdown: Ground Instruction and Flights

Stage 1 – Presolo

Unit	Ground	Dual	Solo
1	2.0	1.5	-
2	1.0	1.5	-
3	1.0	1.0	-
4	2.0	1.0	-
5	1.0	1.0	-
6	1.0	1.0	-
7	1.0	1.0	-
8	1.0	2.0	-
9	1.0	1.0	-
10	1.0 (Presolo Test)	1.0	1.0
Stage Sub-Total	*12.0 Hours*	*12.0 Hours Minimum*	*1.0 Hour*

Stage 2 – Immediate Postsolo

Unit	Ground	Dual	Solo
1	0.5	1.0	1.0
2	-	-	1.0
3	1.0	1.0	1.0
4	1.0	-	-
5	0.5	-	1.5
6	1.0	1.0 (Hood work)	-
7	1.0	1.0	-
8	0.5	-	1.0
9	1.0	1.5	-
10	0.5	-	1.5
11	1.0	1.5 (Hood work)	-
12	1.0	-	1.0
13	1.0 (Stage 2 Test)	-	-
Stage Sub-Total	*10.0 Hours*	*7.0 Hours*	*8.0 Hours*

Stage 3 – Cross-Country

Unit	Ground	Dual	Solo
1	2.0	-	2.0
2	3.0	-	-
3	1.5	1.0 (Night)	-
4	3.0	-	-
5	1.5	2.5 (XC)	-
6	1.0	-	3.0 (XC)
7	-	1.5	-
8	1.0	1.5 (Hood work)	-
9	1.0	-	3.0 (XC)
10	1.0	2.5 (Night)	-
11	1.0	-	1.0
12	1.0	2.0 (XC)	1.0
13	6.0	-	-
14	1.0	-	4.0 (XC)
15	1.0 (Stage 3 Test)	-	-
Stage Sub-Total	*25.0 Hours*	*11.0 Hours*	*14.0 Hours*

Stage 4 - Preparation for the Knowledge Test

Ground Instruction	9.0	
School Knowledge Test	2.0	
FAA Test	3.0	
Stage Sub-Total	*14.0 Hours*	

Stage 5 - Practical Test Preparation

Unit	Ground	Dual	Solo
1	3.0	2.5	-
2	-	-	1.0
3	-	-	1.0
4	1.0	1.5	-
5	1.0	1.0	-
6	2.0	-	-
7	1.0	2.0 (Final Stage Check)	-
8	2.0	2.0 (FAA Check)	-
Stage Sub-Total	*10.0 Hours*	*9.0 Hours*	*2.0 Hours*

	Ground	Dual	Solo
Total Hours	***71.0 Hours***	***39.0 Hours***	***25.0 Hours***

Books and Equipment

This syllabus is based on use of the following books and equipment (which are referred to by the titles' initials in italics, as shown below). They should be available for study and use by the student pilot and instructor during this course:

- *The Student Pilot's Flight Manual, Tenth Edition (SPFM)*

- *The Flight Instructor's Manual, Third Edition (FIM)* for use by the flight instructor to cross-reference with *SPFM.*

- *Pilot's Operating Handbook (POH)*

- Plotter

- Flight computer (E6-B or electronic type)

- *FAR/AIM*, published by ASA *(FAR)* and *(AIM)*

- *Aviation Weather (AW)* AC 00-6

- *Aviation Weather Services (AWS)* AC 00-45

- Current sectional chart(s) for the cross-country flights and the local area

- *Airport/Facility Directory (A/FD)* for the airports in the training course

- Pilot logbook

- Practical Test Standards (latest) for Private Pilot, ASEL *(PTS)*

The flight school or instructor should have available a library of Advisory Circulars that apply to student and private pilots.

Introduction

This syllabus is written to meet the requirements of 14 CFR Parts 61, 141, and 142, and is intended to be used primarily as a checklist, reference, guide, and record for the flight instructor and the student from the first flight through the private pilot (ASEL) Knowledge and Practical Tests and Certification.

By design this is a summary, in order, of the steps the aspiring private pilot must take to successfully complete the course of ground and flight instruction and is to be used by the flight instructor as a checklist. For each subject reference is made to the more detailed information in *The Student Pilot's Flight Manual (SPFM)* or *The Flight Instructor's Manual (FIM)* so that both the student and instructor may read more details about a particular subject or flight maneuver. *However, this is intended to be more than a bare-bones syllabus with reminders, so memory joggers (cryptic comments) are included to help the flight instructor review what was learned from SPFM, FIM, and the other references cited here.*

This syllabus is broken down into Units rather than flights or hours because of the variations in student progress, which may be a function of schedule. For instance, bad weather, illness, or other factors may cause a large time gap between flights, requiring extra flight or ground school review. The instructor using this syllabus will in some cases divide the Units into several sessions for easier handling; some suggested "break" points have been included (Stage 3, Unit 4 is one example).

As the elements of each Unit are completed to the satisfaction of both the student and instructor, the next Unit should be introduced. In some cases the instructor may have the student go on to a following Unit in the same Stage because of weather problems and, for instance, do pattern work rather than fly to the practice area. The incomplete Unit then should be completed as soon as possible.

Certain maneuvers are referred to in several Units and the user may think, "This was mentioned earlier." Yes, it was; but as a memory jogger and review, those items are repeated.

The time noted for each Unit, ground instruction or flight, is an estimate since one flight school may be at a non-tower airport and have its practice area very close, while another school may be located at a busy airport with a tower, thus, much more time is needed to complete the Unit. Suggested ground instruction time for each Unit includes pre- and postflight briefings.

By checking off the items covered, the instructor and student each can review the syllabus to confirm the areas completed (or those that need to be reviewed). The student should initial each Unit to confirm its completion.

There will not be a repeat of "completion standards" with each Unit. The standards for the various Units will be complete when the student has performed the requirements for that Unit to the satisfaction of the flight or ground instructor, as applicable.

At the end of each Unit the Assigned Reading is in preparation for the next Unit.

The minimum requirements for a Part 141 school are 35 hours of ground instruction and 35 hours of flight training, with 20 hours of flight training from a CFI. The minimum requirements for Part 61 operations are 40 hours flight time, including at least 20 hours of flight instruction from a certified flight instructor and 10 hours of solo flight with the breakdowns as listed in §61.109.

Note that the minimum of 20 hours dual and 10 hours solo do not add up to the total minimum of 40 hours. The flight instructor may, for instance, use the extra 10 hours of total time for dual as required for a student, or have a combination of dual and solo for that time.

The average flight time for the certification of a private pilot (Airplane SEL) in the United States is approaching 75 hours, and this syllabus is intended to cover more than the bare minimums as cited by either Part 61 or 141. This syllabus requires a *minimum* of 12 hours of dual before solo (the average student will need more time than this); with the five Stages included, the course is set up for a total of 71 hours of ground instruction or oral exams, 39 hours of dual flight (including check flights), and 25 hours of solo flight, for a combined total of 135 hours. These times can be modified to fit a particular airplane or local condition but still must meet the minimum number of hours of ground instruction, dual or solo. The goal of the program is not to just provide a minimum number of hours of instruction but to train a safe and competent pilot, and it is up to the instructor(s) to assure that flight times and more-than-minimum performance standards are met.

The cross-country requirements cited in Stage 3 are a case in point. *This writer believes there is not enough solo cross-country, both in times and distances, required by Part 61 and so has expanded the requirements in this area of instruction. The instructor/user, of course, may limit the experience to that currently required by Part 61.*

Note that up to 2.5 hours of instruction may be given in a flight simulator or flight training device representing an airplane from an authorized instructor and credited toward the total hours required by §61.109. A maximum of 5 hours of instruction in a simulator or flight training device representing an airplane may be credited toward the total hours required by §61.109 if the instruction is accomplished in a course conducted under Part 142. The instruction flights that may use a flight simulator are so indicated in this syllabus.

The various tasks and maneuvers are aimed for the flight instructor's action or are general suggestions unless the student is specifically cited. For instance, such items as "Discuss the power-off stall" or "Demonstrate a forward slip" are for the flight instructor's use. "Student practices forward slips" is obviously for the student's actions. This syllabus, as indicated earlier, serves as a checklist for both parties to confirm that various requirements have been completed.

Much thanks is owed to Paul A. Craig, author of several aviation textbooks and chief instructor of a major flight school, for his keen eye and ability to find gaps in the material required. His comments and suggestions were most valuable. I also want to thank Ellen Roberts, a flight instructor whose techniques and methods should be copied by more of us. James E. Perkins, Aviation Safety Inspector at the Nashville FSDO, was most helpful with his review of the manuscript and comments and suggestions. My son, Bill, who flies for American Airlines and is a flight instructor, reviewed the manuscript and made valuable suggestions also. Thanks to editor Lynne Bishop, whose humor and always good help is much appreciated. And, as with my other books, my wife Betty gave most invaluable typing and editing help.

I would appreciate comments and suggestions to make this syllabus more useful to the flight instructor and to the student.

William K. Kershner

This stage of the syllabus is more detailed at the beginning, gradually tapering off as the student approaches solo. In the last few flights before solo, the instructor acts more or less as a check pilot, with occasional comments or instruction, as needed. By the tenth flight, most of the necessary instruction has been given and only reviews and reminders are necessary as the student gains confidence and develops the skills for taking the airplane around the airport solo.

Unit 1
Introduction of Effects of Controls and the Four Fundamentals

Ground Instruction, 2.0 Hours

The instructor should discuss the following topics in the office or classroom before flying. The amount of detail before the first flight will depend on the student's background and time elements. The instructor may set aside more time for this first ground session and may not fly at this first meeting. Some points may be reserved for Units 2 or 3. The student should already have read *SPFM*, Chapters 2–9. The instructor's reference is *FIM*, Chapters 4 and 5.

_____ Effects of Controls (*SPFM*, Chapter 8).

    _____ Elevators.

        _____ Pitch control.

        _____ Control angle of attack and airspeed.

        _____ Use of elevator trim in various phases of flight. The importance of trimming to relieve pressure on the control. The trim tab is the "poor man's autopilot," and its primary purpose is to maintain certain attitudes/airspeeds without the pilot having to continually exert control pressure. Some more-advanced airplanes have trim available for rudder and ailerons.

        _____ Change of elevator effectiveness with airspeed. Slow flight or flight at minimum airspeeds or maximum angles of attack (*SPFM*, Chapter 2, "Angle of Attack") will be covered again later in the course.

    _____ Ailerons.

        _____ Roll control.

        _____ Why and how an airplane turns; the horizontal lift vector.

        _____ Adverse yaw; why rudder is used with ailerons in starting or completing turns.

    _____ Rudder.

        _____ Yaw control.

_____ Use in turns.

_____ Use in slips. Covered in more detail in *SPFM*, Chapter 13, "Slip."

_____ Correction for the left-turning forces in a climb or slow flight.

_____ Primary use for steering on the ground for some airplanes. Introduction of nosewheel or tailwheel steering in taxiing.

_____ Adverse yaw. A review, as given in the aileron discussion.

_____ Rudder tab or rudder trim use.

_____ Throttle.

_____ Power control.

_____ How it works: Move it forward (open) for more power, retard it (close) for less power.

_____ The climb and descent control.

_____ Flaps.

_____ Why they are used.

_____ Lift and drag effects.

_____ Stall speed effects.

_____ Approach angle changes with flaps.

_____ Four Fundamentals: Turns, Climbs, Straight and Level, and Glides (*SPFM*, Chapter 9).

_____ Turns.

_____ Entering the turn; application of ailerons and rudder.

_____ Why is back pressure required in the turn?

_____ Three aspects of the turn (ailerons, rudder, and elevator).

_____ Load factors in the turn.

_____ Rolling out of the turn; the need for relaxing back pressure. The three aspects of the roll-out (ailerons, rudder, and elevator).

_____ Climbs. To enter, use 3 steps:

_____ 1. Ease the nose up to climb attitude.

_____ 2. Increase power to climb value.

_____ 3. Correct for "torque."

_____ Ensure that climb attitude is for V_Y, the airspeed for maximum rate of climb. Check instruments; trim off control pressures. The rate of climb is the result of *excess* thrust horsepower existing at the pre-chosen airspeed and power setting. Thrust horsepower is that horsepower actually being used to fly the airplane.

_____ Straight and level (from a climb). Use 3 steps:

_____ 1. Ease nose over to level flight, maintain climb power.

_____ 2. Allow airspeed to build up, ease off right rudder.

_____ 3. Adjust power to cruise setting as cruise airspeed is reached.

_____ Maintain the straight and level attitude; check altitude and heading and relieve pressure with trim.

_____ Glides (Descents).

    _____ Carburetor heat ON or as a check for presence of carburetor ice, as recommended by the manufacturer.

    _____ Close throttle smoothly.

    _____ Hold airplane's nose in level flight attitude until airspeed reaches recommended glide value.

    _____ Assume glide attitude; check airspeed indicator.

    _____ Trim.

_____ Straight and level (from glide).

    _____ Lead the selected altitude by about 50 feet for most trainers (it depends on the rate of descent).

    _____ Add cruise power. Add enough power to stop descent, then adjust as necessary.

    _____ Stop nose from rising with forward pressure of wheel or stick.

    _____ Trim.

    _____ Carburetor heat OFF (if applied).

    _____ Maintain level flight attitude; check with instruments.

    _____ Adjust power as needed.

_____ Climbing turns.

    _____ Differences in left and right climbing turns ("torque" includes all left-turning tendencies of the airplane).

    _____ Why the banks are kept shallow.

_____ Descending (gliding) turns.

    _____ The airspeed is close to that of climb, but the rudder is comparatively weak because of a lack of slipstream (coordination problems).

    _____ Banks should be kept shallow at this point of training.

Flight Instruction: Dual, 1.5 Hours

(Including preflight check and cockpit checkout). The following should be discussed in the airplane on the ground or in flight, as applicable.

_____ The flight.

    _____ Preflight check. Use the manufacturer's checklist. Instructor should discuss the flight controls (which controls yaw, pitch, and roll) and why each item is checked on the airplane.

    _____ Cockpit familiarization. Affirm that the student is comfortable and check seat security and adjustment to assure the ability to see out and move all controls. The sight-picture should be discussed.

    _____ Instruments and controls including trim tabs. Briefly review the Four Fundamentals, with the student moving and watching the flight controls to simulate entry and recovery from each.

    _____ Start engine (using the checklist) and explain the procedure. The instructor handles the tower communications.

    _____ Taxi technique and brake system. Demonstrate and explain.

    _____ Pretakeoff check, using checklist. Explain *why* for each item but don't go into detail.

_____ Takeoff. Make and explain the takeoff. The student's hand should be kept on the throttle during climb-out.

_____ Max rate-of-climb attitude. Demonstrate and explain.

_____ Level-off procedure. Demonstrate use of trim and leaning of mixture, noting that a full explanation will come later.

_____ Effects of controls.

_____ Student uses roll, pitch, and yaw controls (ailerons, elevators, and rudder), and also notes the effect of power changes.

_____ Turns. Demonstrate medium 30° bank and shallow turns with ailerons, rudder, and elevators. Student practices and checks for other traffic before turning. (Say, "Clear right, clear left"; use outside references.)

_____ Climb entry. Demonstrate and identify sight-picture attitude. Student practices. Note that right rudder is required to correct for "torque."

_____ Straight and level from a climb. Demonstrate and identify sight-picture attitude.

_____ Student climbs straight ahead and levels off.

_____ Student turns plane while climbing (with proper rudder), then levels off.

_____ Normal glide. Demonstrate and identify sight-picture attitude. Student practices setting up glide, then leveling off at a prechosen altitude.

_____ Return to airport. Instructor operates the radio and, with the student observing, goes through the checklist. Student flies and makes the turns in the pattern with instruction. Instructor handles power and flaps and takes over on final. Cover the use of the postflight checklist and explain postlanding, shutdown, and parking procedures.

_____ Postflight instruction.

_____ Evaluation.

_____ Critique.

_____ Review.

Make and Model _____ Airplane N-No. _____

Ground Instruction _____ Flight Time: Dual _____ Solo _____

Comments _____

_____

_____

Instructor _____ No. _____ Exp. _____

Date _____ Student Initials _____

Assigned Reading—Student: _SPFM_ (Chapters 2–9). Instructor: _FIM_ (Chapters 4 and 5).

Unit 2
Review and Repeat of Unit 1

(New Material is Added as Necessary.)

Ground Instruction, 1.0 Hour

The following will be covered in the classroom or in the parked airplane as applicable:

_____ Review of Four Fundamentals.

_____ Airplane stability. The airplane wants to maintain equilibrium when trimmed. Briefly discuss nontechnical longitudinal, lateral, and directional stability.

_____ Local traffic patterns and traffic patterns in general. Introduction of the wind indicators (wind sock, tetrahedron, wind tee). If the airport is tower controlled, the communications procedures and transponder, as well as airport taxi and runway signs, should be briefly discussed. The instructor will handle the radio during this flight if at a controlled field, otherwise, the student will use UNICOM or Multicom communications under supervision.

_____ Taxi (establish forward motion before attempting to turn). Check brakes as taxi begins. There is no emphasis on crosswind taxiing and control positions at this point.

    _____ Brake system.

_____ Pretakeoff checklist.

    _____ Magnetos check. Expected rpm drop; the ignition system.

    _____ Carburetor heat check. Expected rpm drop; source of warm air.

    _____ Ammeter and suction gauge. Cover their importance briefly.

    _____ Idle rpm check.

_____ Use of trim.

_____ Wind drift correction theory. Introduction of the concept of crabbing and the rectangular course.

_____ Radio procedures to be used on this flight.

_____ Posttakeoff checklist.

_____ Climb straight ahead or as directed by ATC.

_____ At pattern altitude or as locally recommended, make a 45° left turn or climb straight out to exit airport traffic pattern (non-tower field).

_____ Electric fuel pump (if so equipped) is turned off at 1,000 feet AGL or higher. Affirm by the fuel pressure gauge that the engine-driven pump is providing fuel pressure. Briefly explain use of electric fuel pump.

_____ Use shallow climbing turns to clear the area ahead.

_____ Review Four Fundamentals and effects of controls.

_____ Landing checklist.

_____ Descend to pattern altitude at least 2 miles out (non-tower airport). Do not descend into the pattern itself.

_____ Before entering the pattern:

    _____ Check brake pedal(s) pressures.

    _____ Fuel on fullest tank. Turn ON electric fuel pump, if so equipped. For Cessna C172 and C182, check fuel selector on BOTH; for C150/152 check that fuel selector is properly seated ON.

_____ Undercarriage coming down if not already welded in place.

_____ Mixture RICH. Short discussion of mixture control.

_____ Make traffic call.

_____ Enter downwind leg from 45° angle, if pattern calls for this.

_____ When established on downwind:

    _____ If POH procedure, pull carb heat ON; leave ON for at least 10 seconds to clear out any ice that has formed. Leave either ON or OFF as required by manufacturer. Repeat why carburetor heat is used.

    _____ Report position to tower or UNICOM, as applicable.

    _____ Perform G-U-M-P-P check. Reconfirm:

        _____ *G*as is on fullest tank.

        _____ *U*ndercarriage: check DOWN indications, if retractable.

        _____ *M*ixture RICH.

        _____ *P*ump: electric fuel pump ON, if so equipped, and POH indicates its use.

        _____ *P*ropeller: set pitch (if equipped).

_____ Abeam landing point, reduce power to approximately 1,600 rpm (or to the particular training airplane requirements). Maintain altitude and let speed dissipate.

_____ When the airspeed is below V_{FE} (within white arc), lower flaps 2 notches (20° on C172/C152 and 25° on PA-28-l61 Warrior). This procedure is to be modified to fit a particular airplane.

_____ Stabilize airspeed at recommended approach speed. Trim. Check prop again for go-around as recommended by the *POH* if the airplane has a constant-speed propeller.

_____ Student turns base (30° bank) and final (20° bank) as directed. Start the turn onto base when the touchdown area is 45° behind the wing. Set final landing flaps on base. This may be modified to setting landing flaps on final, depending on the airplane.

_____ Take over on final and land airplane, explaining procedure.

Flight: Dual, 1.5 Hours (including preflight check)

_____ Review controls and instruments, with student seated in cockpit. Assure again that the

student's seat is adjusted properly for height and fore and aft position.

_____ Preflight. Use checklist. Brief introduction to servicing airplane.

_____ Student uses prestart checklist, starts airplane, checks brakes as the airplane starts to move, and taxis to run-up position under instructor's supervision.

_____ Pretakeoff check. Use checklist.

    _____ In addition to items on the checklist, explain that it is a good operating procedure to check idle RPM with carb heat ON or OFF (as the particular POH requires for approach and landing).

_____ Check traffic. Student uses radio under supervision.

_____ Student makes takeoff under supervision.

_____ Assume climb attitude; check airspeed indicator; trim.

_____ Explain scanning pattern when checking for other traffic. Use definite climbing turns to clear area. (Don't wander.)

_____ Climb to practice altitude.

_____ Level off, using the 3 steps.

_____ Turns, left and right (15–30° bank). Student practices.

_____ Glides. Student practices.

_____ Nose drops when power is reduced, requiring back pressure or nose-up trim.

_____ Level off from the glide. Emphasize pitch-up effects of nose-up trim when the power is added during the recovery from the glide.

_____ Exercise. (Limits are ±100 feet altitude and ±10° heading in the straight and level portion.)

    _____ Climb: 1,000 feet.

    _____ Straight and level: 2 minutes.

    _____ Descend: 1,000 feet.

    _____ Straight and level: 2 minutes, then 180° turn.

    _____ Repeat sequence.

_____ Demonstrate airplane longitudinal stability (phugoid oscillations–*SPFM*, Chapter 12; and *FIM*, Chapter 4).

_____ Demonstrate approach attitude with/without flaps, as applicable. (Refer to the *POH* for the airspeeds at various flap settings.)

_____ Student handles communications, under supervision, and enters traffic pattern, performs landing checklist, handles throttle and flaps, with help. Check brake pedal pressure. Instructor takes over on short final, and lands airplane while describing the process.

_____ Student taxis to ramp and shuts down, under supervision. (Instructor checks magneto ground wires for proper operation at idle by turning ignition OFF, then ON.) Student then runs up engine for a few seconds and shuts down the engine with the mixture, uses postlanding, shutdown, and postflight checklist, and secures the airplane. *Note: This is to be done for each flight without repeated instruction, but will be noted from time to time throughout this syllabus.*

_____ Postflight instruction.

    _____ Evaluation.

    _____ Critique.

    _____ Review.

Make and Model _____ Airplane N-No. _____

Ground Instruction _____ Flight Time: Dual _____ Solo _____

Comments _____

_____

_____

Instructor _____ No. _____ Exp. _____

Date _____ Student Initials _____

Assigned Reading— Student: *SPFM* (Chapters 10, 12, 13, and 21). Instructor: *FIM* (Chapters 6 and 7).

Unit 3
Introduction of Steep Turns, Slow Flight, Rectangular Courses, and S-turns Across a Road

Ground Instruction, 1.0 Hour

_____ Review Units 1 and 2 as necessary, with added emphasis on communications procedures at a controlled, or uncontrolled (non-tower) airport, as applicable. If controlled, briefly cover ATIS, clearance delivery, ground control, tower, departure and approach controls, and the frequencies required and *why* of each (*SPFM*, Chapter 21).

_____ Resolve questions relative to assigned reading material.

_____ Introduce 45°-banked power turns (360° and 720° turns) (*SPFM*, Chapter 10) and cover the following:

　　_____ Forces acting on airplane.

　　_____ Elevator, aileron, rudder, and power requirements.

　　_____ Pick a good reference on the horizon.

　　_____ Roll into 45°-banked turn (coordinated); then neutralize ailerons and rudder.

　　_____ Add power as bank increases.

　　_____ Add back pressure as bank increases.

　　_____ Continually check pitch and bank attitudes and check with altimeter.

　　_____ Roll out on original reference on horizon after one and two complete turns, as planned. As bank decreases, ease off back pressure and reduce power to cruise.

　　_____ Note correction for "torque" in left and right turns.

　　_____ The airplane may encounter its own wake turbulence.

_____ Introduce the Power required/Drag curve in simplified terms on chalkboard. (*SPFM*, Figure 12-13).

　　_____ Induced drag (brief explanation).

　　_____ Parasite drag (brief explanation).

_____ Slow flight. Flight at minimum controllable airspeed (*SPFM*, Chapter 12; *FIM*, Chapter 6.) Slow flight is flight at such an airspeed that any further increase of angle of attack, decrease in airspeed, added g forces, or reduction of power would result in indications of a stall.

　　_____ Decay of effectiveness of aileron, elevator, and rudder control at low airspeeds.

　　_____ The relationship of stall speed to angle of bank. With the airspeed close to stall at straight and level flight attitude, make all turns shallow because stall speed increases with bank, if back pressure is held.

　　_____ Control airspeed with pitch (elevators); altitude control with power (throttle).

　　_____ Note pitch changes necessary with addition or retraction of flaps during slow flight.

　　_____ Realistic distractions during slow flight. Scanning for other airplanes, etc.

　　_____ Straight and level altitude ±100 feet, heading ±10°.

_____ Review (if covered earlier) or introduce the concepts of wind correction.

_____ Procedures for flying over and parallel to a road.

_____ Rectangular course.

_____ S-turns across a road.

_____ Review radio and transponder procedures.

Flight: Dual, 1.0 Hour

_____ Student performs preflight, taxi, run-up, and takeoff, with supervision, and handles communications. Introduce flight control positions for various wind conditions.

_____ After takeoff, student assumes V_Y attitude with attitude indicator covered; check the airspeed indicator.

_____ Climb to practice area and altitude.

_____ Demonstrate 45°-banked power turn for 720°.

_____ Student practices both right and left.

_____ Demonstrate slow flight, with shallow turns left and right.

_____ Student practices.

_____ Student establishes glide (carburetor heat as necessary) and levels off at approximately 600–1,000 feet above the ground.

_____ Student flies over and also parallel to a road.

_____ Demonstrate rectangular course.

_____ Student practices.

_____ If time permits, demonstrate S-turns across a road.

_____ Student practices.

_____ Listen to ATC. Student calls approach control for return to airport (controlled field). Student calls UNICOM or uses communications procedures as required (non-tower field).

_____ Student performs prelanding checklist, checks brake pedal pressure, enters normal traffic pattern, or as instructed by ATC, performs GUMPP check as a back-up; assumes approach attitude, and flies airplane to short final.

_____ Land the airplane, again describing the process.

_____ Student retracts flaps after clearing runway. Verify, as applicable, that the flap, not the gear handle, is being moved.

_____ Student taxis to ramp and performs shutdown and postflight checklist, under supervision.

_____ Postflight instruction.

    _____ Evaluation.

    _____ Critique.

    _____ Review.

Make and Model _____ Airplane N-No. _____

Ground Instruction _____ Flight Time: Dual _____ Solo _____

Comments _____

_____

_____

Instructor _____ No. _____ Exp. _____

Date _____ Student Initials _____

Assigned Reading—Student: *SPFM* (Chapters 4–7, 10–12). Instructor: *FIM* (Chapters 9 and 11).

Unit 4
Introduction to Stalls

Ground Instruction, 2.0 Hours (May be done in two sessions.)

_____ Review earlier flights as necessary.

_____ Resolve questions relating to assigned reading material, etc.

_____ Review use of mixture control.

_____ Review carburetion, carb ice, and carb heat.

_____ Discuss the following items relative to aerodynamics:

    _____ Four Forces.

    _____ Airfoils (wings and propellers).

    _____ Chord.

    _____ Angle of incidence.

    _____ Relative wind.

    _____ Angle of attack.

    _____ Lift as it relates to angle of attack and airspeed:

    _____ Critical angle of attack.

    _____ More about flaps and why they are used.

    _____ Stall as a function of angle of attack, not airspeed.

    _____ The stall-warner leads the stall by a few knots (1-g stalls).

    _____ Elevators as they relate to stall entry and recovery. To recover from a stall, point the airplane in the direction it's going.

    _____ Power is used during a stall recovery *to minimize altitude loss*.

    _____ To recover from the stall, simultaneously move the wheel or stick forward enough to break the stall (lower the angle of attack) and add full power to minimize altitude loss.

_____ Presolo stalls.

    _____ Takeoff and departure stalls.

    _____ Approach-to-landing stalls.

    _____ Stalls as an aid to landings.

    _____ Approach to, or partial (imminent), stalls.

    _____ Recovery at the first indication of a buffet.

_____ Review concepts of wind correction.

_____ Review rectangular courses and S-turns as necessary, citing common errors.

_____ Turns about a point (optional discussion).

_____ Another look at the traffic pattern with added emphasis on pattern departures and entries.

_____ Normal approach and landing:

_____ Flap use.

_____ A stabilized approach is established by gradually reducing power, with elevator pressures trimmed off. Close throttle when runway is made.

_____ On final, at a height of approximately 20 feet (about hangar height), the transition is started from approach attitude to landing attitude. Gradually ease the wheel back. The transition must be gradual.

_____ About 19 of the 20 feet are used in the transition; the airplane is slowing up during this period.

_____ When the airplane is about 1 foot above the ground, it should be in the landing attitude – slightly nose high. The pilot will not be able to see directly over the nose in most airplanes. The pilot should look out along the left side of the nose, not over the nose, to line up with the runway. If the pilot can see over the nose, some airplanes won't have the proper landing attitude and will fly into the ground.

_____ Once in the landing attitude (about 1 foot above the ground):

    _____ That attitude should be held. (The student should try to keep the airplane from landing.) As the airplane approaches the stall, back pressure on the wheel or stick is increased as necessary.

    _____ Eyes should be focused about 10° left of the nose and far enough ahead so the ground is not blurred. Don't stare at one spot. Scan the surface.

    _____ The airplane should be lined up with the runway and have wings level at touchdown (assuming no crosswind).

_____ During ground roll, back pressure should be held. The nosewheel should come down by itself.

_____ Brake as necessary. If the runway is long enough, the pilot may want to save brakes and turn off at a taxiway farther down the runway.

Flight: Dual, 1.0 Hour

_____ The student performs preflight, taxi, run-up, takeoff, and posttakeoff checklist. Student makes climbout at V_Y, and handles communications including transponder, under supervision.

_____ Climb to practice area and altitude. Use clearing turns.

_____ Student practices 45°-banked power turns 360° left and right.

_____ Check 121.5 MHz for ELT transmissions every flight, then immediately return to primary frequency.

_____ Practice slow flight without flaps.

_____ While in slow flight, demonstrate simple stall and recovery without addition of power.

_____ Set up again for student to practice.

_____ Student establishes approach attitude with landing flaps. Demonstrate a full-stall landing at altitude.

_____ Student practices several, then cleans up airplane for climb.

_____ Student climbs at V_Y and levels off at a predetermined altitude.

_____ Demonstrate departure stall and recovery.

_____ Student practices departure stall.

_____ Demonstrate approach-to-landing stall (straight flight) and recovery.

_____ Student practices.

_____ Instructor demonstrates approaches to stalls.

_____ Student practices.

_____ Student executes descending turn(s) to an assigned heading and altitude for low work.

_____ Return to airport; listen to ATIS; check heading indicator with magnetic compass; call approach control (controlled airports). Call UNICOM for airport advisory (non-tower airports).

_____ *Check brake pedal pressure at this point in every flight.*

_____ Student uses checklist; handles controls, using gradual reduction of power during the approach, and "lands" the airplane under supervision.

_____ Student retracts flaps after clearing runway (verifying that his hand is on the flap handle, not the landing gear handle).

_____ Student taxis to ramp and performs shutdown and postflight checklists.

_____ Postflight instruction.

      _____ Evaluation.

      _____ Critique.

      _____ Review.

Make and Model _____ Airplane N-No. _____

Ground Instruction _____ Flight Time: Dual _____ Solo _____

Comments _____

_____

_____

Instructor _____ No. _____ Exp. _____

Date _____ Student Initials _____

Assigned Reading—Student: *SPFM* (Chapters 11–13 and 18). Instructor: *FIM* (Chapter 8), *POH* Emergency Procedures.

Unit 5
Emergency Procedures

Ground Instruction, 1.0 Hour

_____ Review previous flights as necessary.

_____ Resolve questions relative to assigned reading material, etc.

_____ Wake turbulence and wind shear avoidance procedures.

_____ Collision avoidance procedures.

_____ Briefly discuss maximum performance climbs, V_X and V_Y.

_____ Review stall series.

_____ Introduction of emergency procedures. Use checklist.

_____ Simulated engine failure at cruise altitude. Close throttle, do not use mixture control.

    _____ Carb heat ON as best glide is being set up.

    _____ Establish best glide attitude and check with airspeed indicator. Trim to maintain.

    _____ Pick a landing area and turn toward it.

    _____ Mixture RICH.

    _____ Electric fuel pump ON, and switch tanks, if so equipped.

    _____ Confirm surface wind direction.

    _____ After switching tanks, wait a few seconds to let the pump get fuel from new tank.

    _____ The propeller normally will be windmilling; so if the fault (carb ice or a dry fuel tank) is remedied, the engine will start again. Do not try to use the starter.

_____ If engine starts, climb while circling the field until you are sure the problem is corrected before turning toward the airport.

_____ If the engine will not restart, the following must be done before landing. Emphasize that these are all secondary to the primary need to keep the airplane under control at the best glide speed and make a safe landing.

    _____ Declare an emergency on frequency 121.5, or if in contact with approach control or UNICOM, stay on that frequency.

    _____ Set transponder to 7700.

    _____ Mixture to IDLE CUTOFF.

    _____ Fuel selector OFF.

    _____ Use flaps, as necessary, to land on chosen spot. It is best to use flaps in increments, but the first requirement is to make the field.

    _____ After (electric) flaps have been extended and committed to landing, turn OFF master and ignition switches.

    _____ Unlatch doors just prior to touchdown.

    _____ Land nose high, tail low; touch down as slowly as possible.

    _____ THE FIRST RESPONSIBILITY IS TO CONTROL AND FLY THE AIRPLANE TO A SAFE LANDING. _Note that with low-altitude emergencies, line-of-sight factor (and distance), and time limits may preclude use of transponder or transmitter(s)._

_____ Engine running rough.

    _____ Carb heat ON.

    _____ Try individual mags.

    _____ Mixture RICH.

    _____ Fuel pump ON.

    _____ Switch tanks.

    _____ Primer locked?

    _____ If problem is apparently solved, stay over "friendly" terrain and continue the lesson or return to the airport, depending on the problem.

    _____ If immediate return to the airport is necessary, maintain altitude as long as safely practicable.

    _____ Instructor introduces the concept of forced landing procedures while in descents and in the traffic pattern.

_____ Review the normal landing process for return to the home airport. Emphasize that the transition from approach attitude to landing attitude must be done carefully to avoid ballooning or flying into the ground.

Flight: Dual, 1.0 Hour

_____ Student performs all pretakeoff functions and executes the takeoff using appropriate checklists.

_____ Student climbs at V_Y, establishes pitch attitude, then maintains that attitude with airspeed indicator (ASI) covered.

_____ Student levels off at practice altitude, then performs shallow (15°-bank) and medium (30°-bank) turns.

_____ Student does stall series (approach to and full stalls), in both straight and turning flight.

_____ Simulate power failure at altitude, by closing the throttle.

    _____ Pull carb heat immediately to take advantage of engine's residual heat as the best glide airspeed is being set up.

    _____ Electric fuel pump ON, switch tanks (if so equipped). Use the emergency checklist discussed during ground instruction.

    _____ Pick a landing area. Check wind direction.

_____ Student glides toward landing spot. (Instructor takes over at safe altitude.)

_____ Set up rectangular course and/or S-turns across a road. Student practices.

_____ Return to the airport. Student handles the radio, flies the pattern, approach, and lands the airplane with supervision. Review the landing process during the return.

_____ The instructor may elect to have the student taxi back to shoot one or more patterns and fullstop landings before returning to the ramp.

_____ Student handles radio and flaps (flaps up after the airplane is off the runway) and taxis to the ramp. Student shuts down the airplane and uses postflight and shutdown checklist.

_____ Postflight instruction.

    _____ Evaluation.

    _____ Critique.

    _____ Review.

Make and Model _____ Airplane N-No. _____

Ground Instruction _____ Flight Time: Dual _____ Solo _____

Comments _____

_____

_____

Instructor _____ No. _____ Exp. _____

Date _____ Student Initials _____

Assigned Reading—Student: *SPFM* (Chapters 12 and 13). Instructor: *FIM* (Chapters 9 and 10).

Unit 6
Pattern Work: Normal Takeoffs and Landings and Introduction to Recoveries from Bad Situations

Ground Instruction, 1.0 Hour

_____ Review earlier Units as necessary.

_____ Resolve questions relative to assigned reading.

_____ Normal takeoff.

　　　_____ Check for traffic. Do not blindly trust the tower at a controlled airport; emphasize that not all airplanes landing at an non-tower field have, or use, radios.

　　　_____ Importance of lining up with center line of the runway.

　　　_____ Smoothly apply full power, keep hand on throttle; emphasize that right rudder is needed to maintain runway alignment.

　　　_____ Check engine instruments.

　　　_____ Airspeed comes "alive."

　　　_____ As controls become firm, back pressure (tricycle gear) is used to obtain proper angle of attack on takeoff. Note that larger airplanes may use "numbers" for takeoff steps.

　　　_____ Let the airplane fly itself off the runway; add right rudder as necessary as the nosewheel or tailwheel lifts off runway.

　　　_____ Assume V_Y attitude (unless V_X is needed); check with ASI.

　　　_____ Climb out straight ahead; student's hand is on throttle; continue correcting for torque as necessary.

_____ Review traffic pattern (including departures and entries); prelanding checklist, both the initial and following power reduction; flap settings; establish approach attitude; and negotiate the approach down to the point of transition to a normal landing.

_____ Review landing process from breaking the glide to touchdown and roll out to taxi speed.

_____ The power-off approach.

_____ Introduction of the go-around or aborted landing procedure. Emphasize early decision and performance.

　　　_____ Add full power to stop the descent. Forward pressure on wheel or stick as needed to keep nose from pitching up. Carburetor heat OFF if used.

　　　_____ Trim.

　　　_____ When there is a positive rate of climb, retract the flaps in 10° increments (or by notches, as applicable).

　　　_____ Trim.

　　　_____ Slight right turn then climb out parallel to runway (watch for traffic taking off).

　　　_____ Trim.

　　　_____ Landing gear retracted (if applicable).

_____ Discuss recoveries from bad situations during approach and the landing itself.

　　　_____ Too high on final. Take it around.

_____ Too low on final. *Do not drag* the airplane up to the runway using minimum power (*see FIM*, Figure 10-26).

_____ Flying into the ground (resulting in a bounce): *Ease* nose over. Add power *as the airplane descends* (if bounce is estimated 5 feet or more). If the bounce is higher, or if the runway is short, add full power and go around.

_____ Dropping it in. Add full power to lessen impact effects *as the airplane descends*.

Flight Instruction: Dual, 1.0 Hour

_____ Preflight.

_____ Taxi.

_____ Normal takeoff.

_____ Practice full-stop takeoff and landings.

_____ Demonstrate a power-off approach, explaining the difference in the downwind abeam position.

_____ Demonstrate an aborted approach/go-around.

_____ Student practices one or more as time allows.

_____ Postflight instruction.

_____ Evaluation.

_____ Critique.

_____ Review.

Make and Model _____ Airplane N-No. _____

Ground Instruction _____ Flight Time: Dual _____ Solo _____

Comments _____

_____

_____

Instructor _____ No. _____ Exp. _____

Date _____ Student Initials _____

Assigned Reading—Student: *SPFM* (Chapters 12, 13, and 21). Instructor: *FIM* (Chapter 10).

Unit 7
Takeoffs and Landings and a Review of Recoveries from Bad Situations

Ground Instruction, 1.0 Hour

_____ Review earlier flights as necessary.

_____ Resolve any questions relative to assigned reading.

_____ Traffic pattern, approach, and normal landing procedures.

_____ Introduce attitude flying in the pattern (loss of ASI).

_____ Communications requirements.

_____ Review recoveries from bad situations.

     _____ Flying into the ground (bouncing).

     _____ Dropping it in.

     _____ Too low in the approach.

     _____ Too high in the approach.

_____ Discuss emergencies on takeoff.

     _____ Power failure while on runway.

     _____ Power failure on climbout. Discuss the hazards of turning back.

     _____ Partial power failure after lift-off.

     _____ Door open during takeoff roll or after lift-off. Fly the airplane!

     _____ Seat belt hanging outside. Describe sound. Fly the airplane!

     _____ Emphasize that there are times when a takeoff must be aborted during the early part of the roll. Hold the wheel or stick full back while braking.

_____ Instructor briefly reviews forced landing procedures in cruise, descent and in the pattern.

_____ Introduce the crosswind takeoff.

     _____ Taxiing in a strong crosswind. Flight control positions for various relative winds.

     _____ Maintaining directional control in a strong crosswind (holding full ailerons into the wind and decreasing deflection as airspeed increases).

_____ Introduce the crosswind landing.

     _____ Crabbing as a drift correction maneuver in the pattern.

     _____ Sideslip as a drift correction maneuver on final and through touchdown.

     _____ Crab approach and sideslip correction during the landing process.

_____ Introduce the effects of gusty air and wind gradients.

_____ Discuss loss of directional control; causal factors and recovery techniques.

_____ Review go-around procedure.

     _____ During turns to base or final.

_____ From final approach.

_____ During landing flare.

_____ Clean up procedure.

_____ Cover wake turbulence avoidance procedures as necessary.

_____ Review scanning and collision avoidance procedures.

Flight: Dual, 1.0 Hour

_____ Student performs preflight check under supervision.

_____ Normal takeoffs and landings.

_____ Student climbs (at V_Y) and sets up approach attitudes with ASI covered for at least two patterns.

_____ Intersperse full-stop and touch-and-go landings, as appropriate for the training situation.

_____ Simulate engine failure on climbout after takeoff and demonstrate procedure. (Get nose down immediately and make only shallow turns, depending on altitude.)

_____ Postflight instruction.

_____ Evaluation.

_____ Critique.

_____ Review.

Make and Model _____ Airplane N-No. _____

Ground Instruction _____ Flight Time: Dual _____ Solo _____

Comments _____

_____

_____

Instructor _____ No. _____ Exp. _____

Date _____ Student Initials _____

Assigned Reading—Student: *SPFM* (Chapters 11–13 and 18). Instructor: *FIM* (Chapters 8 and 10).

Unit 8
Review of High-Altitude Emergencies; Introduction to Forward and Sideslips; Pattern Work at Another Airport

Ground Instruction, 1.0 Hour

_____ Review earlier flights as necessary.

_____ Resolve any questions relative to assigned reading material.

_____ Review simulated engine failure at altitude. This is a refresher only and will not be done in flight this Unit.

_____ Carburetor heat ON while establishing best glide speed.

_____ Picking a field.

_____ Restoring power if possible.

_____ Pattern procedures at field.

_____ Using voice or transponder procedures.

_____ Immediate prelanding steps.

_____ Postlanding procedures.

_____ Forward slip. As a means to lose altitude without picking up airspeed. Does the manufacturer allow slips with flaps? (Optional.) Note: Airplane and airport conditions may require that the student be proficient in forward slips before solo.

_____ Sideslip. As a means to correct for wind drift in a crosswind landing (if not covered in Unit 7).

_____ Crab approach and wing-down landing (if not covered in Unit 7).

_____ Landings with various flap settings (including no-flaps) in particular situations for later use.

_____ Review procedures for being too high or too low on final and for bounce or high level-off on landing.

_____ Steps in a go-around or aborted landing procedure.

_____ If time permits, draw the course to another airport on the sectional chart and briefly introduce the concept of pilotage.

_____ Note pattern altitudes, entry procedures, and radio communication requirements at the nearby practice airport.

_____ Traffic patterns, approaches, and landings applicable to varying environments of different airports.

Flight: Dual, 2.0 Hours

_____ Student executes preflight, run-up, and normal or crosswind takeoff. Crosswind work should be avoided if the student does not have a complete grasp of normal takeoffs and landings.

_____ Fly to another airport between 25 and 40 NM distance (if available) to practice takeoffs and landings.

_____ Review enroute to the practice airport:

_____ Climb attitudes and airspeeds at V_Y and V_X.

_____ Leveling-off procedures.

_____ Student descends to and enters the traffic pattern at the other airport for takeoffs and full-stop landings.

_____ Demonstrate procedures for too-high or too-low approaches, bounce recoveries, and throttle use if drop-in is imminent or occurring.

_____ Demonstrate go-around procedure.

_____ Set up a too-high and/or too-low approach and turn the airplane over to the student to check reaction and use of proper procedures.

_____ Student makes a go-around under direction.

_____ Crosswind takeoff and landing demonstration; practice if indicated, or not already practiced by airport and operating requirements.

_____ Return to home airport and shoot two or three landings (full-stop) as time and/or student fatigue permits.

_____ Postflight instruction.

_____ Evaluation.

_____ Critique.

_____ Review. Introduce briefly the required airplane papers and logbooks.

Make and Model _____ Airplane N-No. _____

Ground Instruction _____ Flight Time: Dual _____ Solo _____

Comments _____

_____

_____

Instructor _____ No. _____ Exp. _____

Date _____ Student Initials _____

Assigned Reading—Student: _SPFM_ (Chapters 12 and 13). Instructor: _FIM_ (Chapter 10).

Unit 9
Shooting Takeoffs and Landings

Ground Instruction, 1.0 Hour

_____ Review previous flights with emphasis on problem areas. Depending on the student's progress, the emergencies on takeoff and in the pattern should be reviewed. The emergencies should be reviewed a flight or two before solo but not emphasized in the briefing just before the solo flight, to avoid creating anxiety.

_____ Resolve questions concerning the traffic pattern: altitudes, departures, entries, etc.

_____ Review collision avoidance and wake turbulence.

_____ Briefly introduce cockpit resource management (CRM) and aeronautical decision making (ADM) concepts.

Flight: Dual, 1.0 Hour

The last few flights should not require the instructor to say much, as noted in the text of _The Flight Instructor's Manual_, but the student's actions should be monitored. The instructor will be beginning to get a sense of when the student is ready to solo. See the introductory paragraph at the beginning of this STAGE. It's best to shoot full-stop-and-taxi-back landings as the student approaches solo. This will make the transition to solo easier than if he has previously been shooting touch-and-go's.

_____ Shoot full-stop landings.

_____ On at least one landing, set up a bounce condition from which the student must recover (if this hasn't already been practiced inadvertently during the previous takeoff and landing sessions). Also check the student's response to an imminent or actual drop-in.

_____ Student makes a go-around or aborted landing during the session.

_____ Depart and reenter the traffic pattern at least once during the period.

_____ Student makes _at least_ one pattern with ASI _and_ altimeter covered.

_____ Some instructors have the student depart the pattern and go to the practice area for stalls or slow flight to break up the continuous landing practice. (Students can lose progress by too much concentration on pattern work.)

_____ Postflight instruction.

      _____ Evaluation.

      _____ Critique.

      _____ Review.

Make and Model _____ Airplane N-No. _____

Ground Instruction _____ Flight Time: Dual _____ Solo _____

Comments _____

_____

_____

Instructor _____ No. _____ Exp. _____

Date _____ Student Initials _____

Assigned Reading—Student: *SPFM* (Chapter 13). Instructor: *FIM* (Chapter 10).

Unit 10
Presolo Knowledge Test — Stage 1 Written Test 1.0 Hour

Before solo, the student must pass a knowledge test on the FAA regulations, operation of the airplane being used, and general safety practices. The test should be made up based on the airplane, local conditions, and regulations and review it with the student after testing to assure a full understanding of missed questions. Some suggestions for the flight instructor:

I. The Airplane
  A. *Fuel system.*
    1. Usable fuel (gallons).
    2. Weight of fuel per gallon.
    3. Expected average fuel consumption (gph) for cruise at the power setting used in the practice area.
    4. Minimum octane fuel to be used.
    5. Color of fuel used.
    6. Electrical auxiliary fuel pump operations, if applicable; when and why it is used.
    7. Preflight fuel check items and order of checking them.
  B. *Oil system.*
    1. Brand and viscosity number of oil currently in use in the airplane.
    2. Total capacity and minimum operational volume (quarts).
  C. *Electrical system.*
    1. Equipment and instruments (flaps, oil temperature, fuel gauges, etc.) that are electrically controlled.
    2. Effects of turning off the master (electrical) switch on the running of the engine in flight (none).
    3. Steps to be used in a suspected, or real, electrical fire.
  D. *Instruments.*
    1. The instrument(s) that would be affected if the static port is totally closed.
    2. Location of the static port.

3. Significance of each of the following airspeed markings:
   a. Green arc.
   b. White arc.
   c. Yellow arc.
   d. Red radial line.
4. The max rate (V_Y) and max angle (V_X) climb airspeeds. Note that these values change with density-altitude but have the student give the numbers for sea level.
5. The number of seconds for the oil pressure to come up to normal in moderate ambient temperatures.
6. The normal fuel pressure (if applicable), in psi (green arc)
7. Steps to follow if the low-voltage light comes on in flight. Discuss several options with the student. If in the traffic pattern, continue the approach and land, terminating the flight. If some distance from the airport, recycle the master (electrical) switch, etc.

E. *Airplane papers.* (The flight instructor will have introduced the airplane papers during one or more of the presolo sessions.)
   1. Airworthiness certificate. Must be displayed. For how long is it valid?
   2. Registration certificate. When must it be replaced?
   3. Weight and balance information (*SPFM*, Chapter 23).
   4. Logbooks for airframe, engine, and propeller. Annual and 100-hour inspections.
   5. Operating limitations. Performance charts and how to use them for finding required runway lengths.

F. *Emergency procedures and equipment malfunctions.*
   1. Approaches to a landing area with an engine malfunction.
   2. Loss of airspeed indicator.
   3. Flaps inoperative.
   4. Rough-running engine—symptoms.
      a. Magneto problems.
      b. Carburetor ice.
      c. Fuel starvation.

II. Traffic Pattern and Practice Area Operations

A. *Pattern.*
   1. The student should sketch the traffic pattern for the home airport for all runways. (If some patterns are right hand, this should be shown.) The altitudes (MSL) for the first turn after takeoff and the downwind leg(s) for normal approach should be shown.
   2. The student should sketch the approximate practice area showing towns and other landmarks that would help pin down the boundaries.
   3. The student should list airports in the area that can be used as alternates should weather or other factors preclude the return to the home base. (The student may have already shot landings at one or more of these airports, but should review them here.)

B. *Discuss the following situation with the student:* You are solo and doing a takeoff and departure stall in a right-climbing turn at the break and the airplane rolls abruptly to the left. The nose is down and the airplane is rotating. The wheel is full back but is not bringing the nose up. You should immediately do which of the following?
   1. Hold the control wheel full back and make sure the engine is at full power to try to stop the altitude loss.
   2. Close the throttle, apply full rudder opposite to the rotation, and immediately move the control wheel forward. (This is the correct answer for a spin recovery, but the POH procedure should be the determining factor.) Briefly discuss spins.
   3. Apply rudder into (with) the rotation, maintain full power and stop the nose from getting farther down with full-back wheel.

III. Airspace and Regulations

    A. *Airspace.* The instructor should be sure that the student is aware of taxi and runway signs and airspace that would be a factor in solo operations in the pattern and practice area. The instructor should cover local airways and Class B, C, D, E, and G airspace; prohibited and restricted areas; plus Military Operations Areas (MOAs) and Military Training Routes, *but only* as they would affect the student at this stage of his local training. To ask about operations in Class B airspace 200 miles away does nothing but clutter the student's mind with trivia.

    B. *Regulations.*

        1. The instructor's questions on 14 CFR Parts 61 and 91 should also be applicable to the current situation. For instance, the requirement of 30 minutes minimum fuel reserve for VFR flight (14 CFR §91.151) has probably been superseded by your, or the school's, hour or more fuel reserve requirement.

        2. The instructor should apply questions to what is required at this point in his training, both general and local. For instance, there may be local restrictions such as, "Don't fly below 3,000 feet AGL over the Veterans' Hospital" and other rules that would only apply to your operations.

        3. While it's not required, the instructor might later want to make up a written test for the student to take before going on that first solo cross-country. Ask general questions on FARs and airspace; the trip itself, with emphasis on the destination airport facilities, traffic patterns, etc.; plus alternate plans for weather and other factors. The instructor might not want to bother with tests for each of the following solo cross-countries if he or she is satisfied with the student's judgment on the first one.

        4. The instructor should keep the presolo written test and any others on file for future reference for at least 3 years (§61.189).

        5. To repeat: The point of the instructor making up test(s) rather than getting a "canned" quiz from commercial publishers is twofold: First, he or she knows more about local operations and requirements than somebody sitting at a desk a thousand miles away. Second, making up such a test will add knowledge of the requirements for a safe postsolo period for the student and will also help gain experience in this area for the instructor's ground school instructing.

Presolo Aeronautical Knowledge: 14 CFR §61.87(B)

I certify that Mr./Ms. _____ has satisfactorily completed the presolo aeronautical knowledge exam as of paragraph 61.87(b)

for the _____ (make and model airplane). Grade _____

Signed_____ Date_____

(Print name)_____ CFI No._____ Expiration date_____

Unit 11
First Solo

Flight: Dual/Solo, 1.0 Hour

This Unit, while numbered 11, will occur for most students between the 12th and 20th hours, depending on the student and frequency of flights. Be sure that the presolo knowledge test has been completed, graded, and reviewed and is on file; the following should be checked:

_____ All areas of the presolo syllabus have been covered.

_____ Any special local rules and procedures are clear to the student.

_____ Emergencies and go-around procedures are clear to the student.

_____ The wind and weather conditions are good for a pattern solo for this particular student.

_____ The student will shoot three full-stop landings. Full-stop landings are always best for the first solo (*FIM*, Chapter 10).

_____ Air traffic is such that no conflict should occur while the student is in the pattern.

_____ The student's pilot/medical certificate is in order and is signed before the solo takes place.

_____ Logbook endorsement.

Endorsement for Presolo Flight Training: 14 CFR §61.87(c) and (d)

I certify that Mr./Ms. _____ has received the required presolo training in

a _____ (make and model aircraft).

I have determined that he/she has demonstrated the proficiency of Paragraphs 61.87 (c) and (d)

and is proficient to make solo flights in _____ (make and model aircraft).

Signed_____ Date_____

(Print name)_____ CFI No._____ Expiration date_____

Debriefing:(Fill out logbook.)

Number of takeoffs and landings_____ Dual_____ Solo_____

Flight time_____ Dual_____ Solo_____

Comments_____

_____

Instructor_____ Date_____

CFI. No._____ Expiration Date_____

Student Initials_____

Unit 12
Summary

As noted earlier, the 10th and following Units until solo are essentially a review of the previous instruction, with the instructor doing less flying and less talking as the student becomes more proficient. Again, most students solo between the 12th and 20th hours, depending on consistency of schedule, airplane type, and airport environment (traffic density, tower control, crosswinds, length and width of runways, and other factors).

To repeat, the term "Unit" rather than "Flight" has been used in the syllabus because the items in a Unit may need more than one flight to complete. For instance, on the third flight the student may still need work on the Four Fundamentals in the first and second units. A timid student shouldn't be introduced to emergency procedures (in Unit 5) as early as the fifth flight; he's still worried about banking over 10° at that point. Certainly an instructor would not want to get into crosswind takeoffs and landings if the student doesn't understand the no-wind or wind-down-the-runway techniques. Under certain conditions, a delay until after solo for the student to begin crosswind procedures, or slips, may be wise, but the instructor should discuss and demonstrate these maneuvers before solo (*see* Units 7 and 8).

While the suggested order of introduction is listed here, it may need to be modified for a particular student and/or local requirements.

Stage 2
Immediate Postsolo

For many student pilots, the first solo is the high point, something that has been looked forward to for the past several hours of flying, but a letdown is often experienced in the following hours. Most dropouts occur in Stage 2.

The immediate postsolo syllabus material is intended to keep up the student's interest and to continue progress toward achieving the experience and skills required to safely exercise the private certificate. Early in Stage 2 and throughout, work in dual flights to cover crosswind takeoffs and landings for the student when local conditions allow.

Unit 1
Postsolo Flight Check and Supervised Solo

Ground Instruction, 0.5 Hour

_____ Review first solo flight.

_____ Review traffic pattern and collision avoidance.

_____ Review traffic communications.

_____ Review go-arounds, bounce recoveries, being too high or too low on final, and crosswind techniques.

_____ Plan at least three dual takeoffs and landings followed by solo patterns as time and weather permit.

Flight: Dual, 1.0 Hour

Pick the time, weather and wind conditions. The conditions for any crosswind operation during the solo portion of this Unit should be carefully considered.

_____ Preflight inspection.

_____ Start and taxi.

_____ Run-up.

_____ Takeoff, and depart the pattern for the practice area.

_____ Check the student on the following maneuvers by the chief, or another, instructor (some of these maneuvers may not be done because of instructors' decisions and/or time limitations):

    _____ 720° power turns.

    _____ Slow flight.

    _____ Stalls in all configurations.

    _____ Simulated high-altitude emergency.

_____ Rectangular course.

_____ S-turns across the road.

_____ Introduce turns around a point (demonstration).

_____ Return and traffic pattern entry.

_____ Crosswind takeoff and landing instruction as conditions allow.

_____ Three takeoffs, traffic pattern and landings, with review and instruction as necessary for safe solo landings.

Flight: Supervised Solo, 1.0 Hour

Following the postsolo flight check, the student should shoot at least six solo takeoffs and landings to a full stop at the home airport. Touch-and-go's are not recommended for this flight. The flight instructor should be present at the airport during this period, preferably at a position where critiques of each pattern may be made. A table, such as given in Figure 10-39 of *The Flight Instructor's Manual*, should be used for critique. The following items should be noted for the critique:

_____ Takeoff.

_____ Climb.

_____ Crosswind leg.

_____ Downwind leg.

_____ Base leg.

_____ Final.

_____ Forward slips to landings if the student has had dual in the procedure during the presolo stage.

_____ Go-arounds (as applicable).

_____ Roundout or flare.

_____ Touchdown.

_____ Rollout.

_____ Crosswind corrections (as applicable).

_____ Taxi.

_____ Parking.

_____ Shutdown.

_____ Postflight check.

_____ Postflight instruction.

_____ Evaluation.

_____ Critique.

_____ Review.

Make and Model _____ Airplane N-No. _____

Ground Instruction _____ Flight Time: Dual _____ Solo _____

Comments _____

_____

_____

Instructor _____ No. _____ Exp. _____

Date _____ Student Initials _____

Assigned Reading — Student: *SPFM* (Chapters 13, 18, and 21). Instructor: *FIM* (Chapter 10).

Unit 2
Solo in the Pattern

Flight: Solo, 1.0 Hour

No ground instruction for this Unit, unless the student has questions. If the first solo takeoffs, patterns, and landings are satisfactory, the student should be scheduled for an hour in the pattern under selected wind and weather conditions. The instructor is aware of the time, place, and weather conditions of this flight and has briefed the student on the time in the pattern. The student will shoot full-stop landings.

_____ Postflight instruction.

_____ Evaluation.

_____ Critique.

_____ Review.

Make and Model _____ Airplane N-No. _____

Ground Instruction _____ Flight Time: Dual _____ Solo _____

Comments _____

_____

_____

Instructor _____ No. _____ Exp. _____

Date _____ Student Initials _____

Assigned Reading — Student: *SPFM* (Chapters 10, 12, and 13). Instructor: *FIM* (Chapters 6, 7, and 10).

Unit 3
Review of Stalls, Introduction to Incipient Spins and Recoveries

Before the student is sent out to practice solo slow flight and stalls he or she should have demonstrated an understanding of stalls and incipient spin recognition and recovery.

Ground Instruction, 1.0 Hour

Discuss the following:

_____ Stalls.

     _____ Slow flight.

     _____ Theory of stalls. *Why* the stall occurs.

     _____ Stalls as a function of angle of attack, not airspeed.

     _____ Accelerated stalls.

_____ Review of straight-ahead and turning stalls introduced before solo. (Takeoff and departure, approach-to-landing stalls, clean and dirty.)

_____ Stall recoveries: at first indication and when stall has broken.

_____ Approach to stalls: recognition and recovery.

_____ Spins.

     _____ Spin theory. *Why* an airplane spins.

     _____ Autorotation and the incipient spin.

     _____ Developed spin.

_____ Spin recovery procedure (refer to *POH*) but cover generally:

     _____ Close the throttle.

     _____ Neutralize the ailerons.

     _____ Ensure that the flaps are up.

     _____ Opposite rudder. Discuss different methods for detecting rotation direction.

     _____ Brisk forward wheel or stick applied after rudder has reached stop.

     _____ When rotation stops, neutralize the rudder to avoid a progressive (opposite) spin.

     _____ Pull out of dive.

     _____ Immediate response necessary when high angle of attack and yaw are occurring.

     _____ Neutralize rudder and ailerons.

     _____ Wheel forward if spin is impending and confusion exists as to direction (to avoid using the wrong rudder).

     _____ No solo spin practice!

     _____ Cross-control (skidding) stall. Where and when it is most likely to happen. If the situation is pending on the turn to final, get off the rudder, relax the excessive back pressure, the wings should be rolled level and a safe go-around executed.

     _____ Discussion of trim tab stalls and recovery.

     _____ Review of high-altitude emergencies.

     _____ Return to airport. Student handles all communications.

Flight Instruction: Dual, 1.0 Hour

_____ Preflight, start, and taxi.

_____ Use of checklist.

_____ Taxi, takeoff, climb, and flight to practice area.

_____ Practice takeoff and departure and approach-to-landing stalls. Recover after the stall has broken.

_____ Approaches to stalls and recoveries at the first indication of impending stall.

_____ Incipient spin entries and recoveries, left and right. Ensure that Parts 91.303 and 91.307 are respected, and the airplane is certified for spins.

_____ Demonstrate cross-control (skidded) stalls.

_____ Demonstrate accelerated stalls (depending on airplane and student).

_____ High-altitude emergency. Instructor points out suitable areas for landing and takes over at safe altitude.

_____ Return to airport. Student handles all communications.

This Unit is an "active" flight, so frequent breaks should be made for the student's comfort. There should be an open "comfort bag" under the instructor's seat—just in case.

_____ Postflight instruction.

     _____ Evaluation.

     _____ Critique.

     _____ Review.

Make and Model _____ Airplane N-No. _____

Ground Instruction _____ Flight Time: Dual _____ Solo _____

Comments _____

_____

_____

Instructor _____ No. _____ Exp. _____

Date _____ Student Initials _____

Assigned Reading—Student: *SPFM* (Chapters 10, 12, and 13). Instructor: *FIM* (Chapters 6, 7, and 9).

Unit 4
Solo in the Practice Area and Pattern I

Ground Instruction, 1.0 Hour

The following should be reviewed:

_____ Pattern departure and entry.

_____ Practice area.

_____ Collision avoidance procedures.

_____ Steep turns.

_____ Descents. Use of carburetor heat and suggested airspeeds.

_____ S-turns.

_____ Turns around a point.

_____ Return to traffic pattern.

_____ Communications procedures.

Flight: Solo, 1.0 Hour

_____ Climb to altitude and complete a 720° power turn (45° bank) in each direction.

_____ Slow flight.

_____ Descend to the altitude for rectangular course in practice area (use carb heat). NO SIMULATED EMERGENCIES SOLO!

_____ S-turns.

_____ Turns around a point.

_____ Return to traffic pattern and shoot at least three takeoffs and landings (full stop preferred). *No stall practice on this flight.*

_____ Postflight instruction.

    _____ Evaluation.

    _____ Critique.

    _____ Review.

Make and Model _____ Airplane N-No. _____

Ground Instruction _____ Flight Time: Dual _____ Solo _____

Comments _____

_____

_____

Instructor _____ No. _____ Exp. _____

Date _____ Student Initials _____

Assigned Reading—Student: *SPFM* (Chapters 12 and 14). Instructor: *FIM* (Chapters 6, 11, and 12).

Unit 5
Solo in the Practice Area and Pattern II

Ground Instruction, 0.5 Hour

A review and briefing for solo practice of steep turns, stalls, slow flight, wind drift correction maneuvers, and takeoffs and landings.

Flight: Solo, 1.5 Hours

As many of the following maneuvers should be done as time allows.

_____ Steep turns (45°-banked 720° power turns). PTS (Practical Test Standards) limits are 45°- banked ±5°, airspeed ±10 knots, altitude ±100 feet, and rollout on the entry heading ±10°.

_____ Slow flight. Maintain the specified altitude ±100 feet, specified heading ±10°, and specified airspeed +5/-0 knots.

_____ Stalls; straight ahead and turning stalls, power-on and power-off (clean).

_____ Rectangular course. Maintain altitude ±100 feet, airspeed ±10 knots. Look around!

_____ S-turns. Altitude ±100 feet, airspeed ±10 knots.

_____ Turns around a point. Fly turns in both directions; exit at the same altitude and heading as the entry.

_____ Normal or crosswind takeoffs and landings.

_____ Review flight with instructor.

_____ Postflight instruction.

      _____ Evaluation.

      _____ Critique.

      _____ Review.

Make and Model _____ Airplane N-No. _____

Ground Instruction _____ Flight Time: Dual _____ Solo _____

Comments _____

_____

_____

Instructor _____ No. _____ Exp. _____

Date _____ Student Initials _____

Assigned Reading — Student: *SPFM* (Chapters 3 and 15). Instructor: *FIM* (Chapters 12 and 24).

Unit 6
Introduction to Emergency Instrument Flying

Ground Instruction, 1.0 Hour

_____ Answer any questions that may have arisen since the solo flights in the practice area and pattern.

_____ Introduction to flying by instruments.

     _____ Aviate, navigate, communicate.

     _____ The pitot-static instruments (briefly).

     _____ The gyro instruments (briefly).

     _____ Instrument scan.

     _____ Bank instruments.

     _____ Pitch instruments.

     _____ Control and performance instruments.

     _____ Attitude plus power equals performance.

     _____ Primary and supporting instruments (briefly).

_____ Four Fundamentals and the instrument indications.

     _____ Straight and level.

     _____ Climbs.

     _____ Descents.

     _____ Turns.

Flight: Dual, 1.0 Hour

The student will do all flying except when instructor demonstration may be required. This Unit may use a flight simulator or flight training device (and authorized instructor) per Parts 61.4 and 61.109.

_____ Preflight with added checks on instrument factors (antennas, pitot heat, and other IFR equipment). No detailed discussion at this point.

_____ Start.

_____ Taxi.

_____ Pretakeoff check.

_____ Takeoff.

_____ Climb, referring to flight instruments, not hooded.

_____ Level off, power and trim.

_____ Straight and level using all flight instruments but not hooded.

_____ Straight and level, hooded.

_____ Climbs, using all instruments, hooded.

_____ Turns, using all instruments, not hooded.

_____ Turns to headings, hooded.

_____ Straight descents, all instruments, not hooded.

_____ Straight descents to a prechosen altitude, hooded.

_____ Alternating straight climbs, straight and level, and descents, hooded.

_____ Constant altitude turns to prechosen headings, hooded.

_____ Break from hood work for 5 minutes or more.

_____ Descend to traffic pattern altitude, hooded, if the student is not fatigued.

_____ Visual pattern entry and landing: emphasize use of prelanding checklist.

_____ Shutdown procedures.

_____ Postflight instruction.

        _____ Evaluation

        _____ Critique

        _____ Review

Make and Model _____ Airplane N-No. _____

Ground Instruction _____ Flight Time: Dual _____ Solo _____

Comments _____

_____

_____

Instructor _____ No. _____ Exp. _____

Date _____ Student Initials _____

Assigned Reading—Student: *SPFM* (Chapters 10, 15, 16, and 18). Instructor: *FIM* (Chapters 6–12).

Unit 7
Dual Review of Previous Instruction

Ground Instruction, 1.0 Hour

_____ Review stalls, slow flight, and spin recoveries.

_____ Review Four Fundamentals and instrument flying.

_____ Review high-altitude emergencies.

_____ Review rectangular course and S-turns.

_____ Review turns around a point.

_____ Review crosswind takeoff and landing techniques.

Flight: Dual, 1.0 Hour

_____ Preflight, start, and taxi.

_____ Use of check list.

_____ Taxi, takeoff, climb, and flight to practice area.

_____ Four Fundamentals, using all instruments, hooded.

_____ High-altitude emergency, not hooded, naturally.

_____ S-turns and turns around a point.

_____ Return to airport. Student handles communications and enters traffic pattern by approach control/tower clearance, or UNICOM, as applicable.

_____ Student shoots crosswind takeoff(s) and landing(s) if conditions allow.

_____ Demonstrate no-flaps landing.

_____ Student shoots no-flaps landing.

_____ Postflight shutdown and check.

_____ Postflight instruction.

      _____ Evaluation.

      _____ Critique.

      _____ Review.

Make and Model _____ Airplane N-No. _____

Ground Instruction _____ Flight Time: Dual _____ Solo _____

Comments _____

_____

_____

Instructor _____ No. _____ Exp. _____

Date _____ Student Initials _____

Assigned Reading—Student: *SPFM* (Chapters 10, 12, and 13). Instructor: *FIM* (Chapters 6 and 7).

Unit 8
Solo in the Practice Area and Pattern III

Ground Instruction, 0.5 Hour

_____ Review of preceding dual flight.

_____ Brief on slow fight and stalls.

_____ Stalls, clean and dirty. (Only takeoff and departure and approach to landing stalls to be practiced on this flight.)

_____ Steep turns (720° power turns at 45° banks).

_____ Emphasis on clearing the area and collision avoidance procedures.

_____ Review of wake turbulence avoidance.

_____ Rectangular course and turns around a point.

Flight: Solo, 1.0 Hour

_____ Slow flight and stalls.

_____ 720° power turns.

_____ Descend to practice rectangular course, S-turns, and turns around a point.

_____ Return to airport. Shoot at least three takeoffs and landings (full stop).

_____ Postflight instruction.

      _____ Evaluation.

      _____ Critique.

      _____ Review.

Make and Model _____ Airplane N-No. _____

Ground Instruction _____ Flight Time: Dual _____ Solo _____

Comments _____

_____

_____

Instructor _____ No. _____ Exp. _____

Date _____ Student Initials _____

Assigned Reading—Student: *SPFM* (Chapter 17; review Chapters 13, 15, 16, and 18). Instructor: *FIM* (Chapter 11).

Unit 9
Dual: Short- and Soft-Field Takeoffs and Landings

Ground Instruction, 1.0 Hour

_____ Dragging the area for an off-airport landing (emergency only).

_____ Short-field takeoffs.

_____ Max angle and obstacle-clearance climbs.

_____ Soft-field takeoff techniques.

_____ Soft-field postliftoff procedures.

_____ Comparison of short- and soft-field takeoff configurations and procedures.

_____ Short-field approach and landings; airspeed control, use of power, 1.3 V_{S0} approach speed.

_____ Braking techniques.

_____ Soft-field approach and landing techniques.

_____ Comparison of short- and soft-field landing configurations and procedures.

_____ Crosswind takeoff and landing review.

_____ High density-altitude takeoffs (restricted RPM to simulate conditions).

Flight: Dual, 1.5 Hours

_____ Student preflights, starts, performs pretakeoff check and takeoff.

_____ Climb to practice area and altitude; emphasize clearing turns in climb.

_____ Steep turns.

_____ Slow flight.

_____ High-altitude emergency.

_____ Instructor demonstrates dragging the area at a field in the practice area.

_____ Return to airport; pattern entry. Emphasize airspeed and altitude control on approach.

_____ Instructor demonstrates at least one short-field approach and landing.

_____ Instructor demonstrates at least one short-field takeoff and climb.

_____ Student does at least one short-field takeoff and landing.

_____ Instructor demonstrates at least one soft-field approach and landing.

_____ Student performs at least one soft-field approach and landing.

_____ Instructor has student perform one or more high density-altitude takeoffs (restricted RPM).

_____ Postflight instruction.

      _____ Evaluation.

      _____ Critique.

      _____ Review.

The instructor may elect to follow this flight with another dual on the special takeoff and landing techniques before having the student practice them solo.

Make and Model _____ Airplane N-No. _____

Ground Instruction _____ Flight Time: Dual _____ Solo _____

Comments _____

_____

_____

Instructor _____ No. _____ Exp. _____

Date _____ Student Initials _____

Assigned Reading—Student: *SPFM* (Chapters 13 and 17). Instructor: *FIM* (Chapters 6, 7, 9, 10, and 11).

Unit 10
Solo in the Practice Area and Pattern IV

This Unit will combine Parts I, II, and III of "Solo in Practice Area and in the Pattern," plus short- and soft-field and crosswind takeoffs and landings (dual in Unit 9).

Ground Instruction, 0.5 Hour

The instructor will review special takeoff and landing techniques with the student and may elect to give another Unit of dual in these procedures before solo work.

Flight: Solo, 1.5 Hours

_____ Short-field takeoff and obstacle climb. Use proper flap configuration and obstacle-clearance airspeed, or V_X, as required.

_____ Steep turns 45° bank ±5°, airspeed ±10 knots, altitude ±100 feet; rollout on the entry heading ±10°.

_____ Slow flight. Altitude ±100 feet, heading ±10°, and airspeed +5/-0 knots.

_____ Stalls. Takeoff and departure and approach-to-landing stalls.

_____ Rectangular course, ±100 feet, ±10 knots.

_____ S-turns, ±100 feet, ±10 knots.

_____ Turns around a point; turns in both directions, exit at the same altitude and heading as the entry, ±100 feet, ±10 knots.

_____ Return to airport using proper communications, pattern entry, and pattern.

_____ Short- and soft-field takeoffs and landings to a full stop. No touch-and-go's.

_____ Instructor should fill out critique sheet (_FIM_, Figure 10-39) if takeoffs and landings were observed.

_____ Review flight with instructor.

Make and Model _____ Airplane N-No. _____

Ground Instruction _____ Flight Time: Dual _____ Solo _____

Comments _____

_____

_____

_____

Instructor _____ No. _____ Exp. _____

Date _____ Student Initials _____

Assigned Reading—Student: _SPFM_ (Chapters 12 and 15). Instructor: _FIM_ (Chapter 12).

Unit 11
Emergency Instrument Flying

Ground Instruction. 1.0 Hour

_____ Review Four Fundamentals.

    _____ Straight and Level.

    _____ Climbs.

    _____ Glides (descents).

    _____ Turns.

_____ Six Basic Maneuvers.

    _____ Straight and level ±10° of heading.

    _____ Left and right 180° constant-altitude turns ±10° on rollout.

    _____ Shallow, climbing, constant-airspeed turns to a predetermined altitude and heading.

    _____ Shallow, descending turns to a predetermined altitude and heading.

    _____ Recovery from the start of a power-on spiral.

    _____ Recovery from the approach to a climbing stall.

Flight: Dual, 1.5 hours

This Unit may use a flight simulator or flight training device (and authorized instructor) for Parts 61.4 and 61.109.

_____ Takeoff and climb to the practice area and safe altitude.

_____ Four Fundamentals, hooded.

_____ Six Basic Maneuvers, hooded.

    _____ Straight and level ±10° of heading.

    _____ Left and right 180° constant-altitude turns ±10° on rollout.

    _____ Shallow, climbing, constant-airspeed turns to a predetermined altitude and heading.

    _____ Shallow, descending turns to a predetermined altitude and heading.

    _____ Recovery from the start of a power-on spiral.

    _____ Recovery from the approach to a climbing stall.

_____ Introduction to hooded tracking with VOR or homing to an NDB (if equipment is available).

_____ Return to vicinity of airport. Student flying, hooded, with instructor acting as radar.

_____ Simulated ASR or PAR if traffic permits.

_____ Short- or soft-field approach and landing, visual!

_____ Postflight instruction.

    _____ Evaluation.

    _____ Critique.

    _____ Review.

Make and Model _____ Airplane N-No. _____

Ground Instruction _____ Flight Time: Dual _____ Solo _____

Comments _____

_____

_____

Instructor _____ No. _____ Exp. _____

Date _____ Student Initials _____

Assigned Reading—Student: *SPFM* (Chapters 13 and 17). Instructor: *FIM* (Chapters 6, 7, 9, 10, and 11).

Unit 12
Solo Takeoffs and Landings in the Local Pattern

Ground Instruction, 1.0 Hour

The instructor should review normal, crosswind, soft- and short-field takeoffs and landings and assure that the student has a full understanding of each of the requirements. A check and confirmation of the strength of a crosswind component should be made before sending the student solo; this is particularly important for short- and soft-field takeoffs and landings. The student may leave and reenter the pattern for practice and a "break," traffic permitting.

Flight: Solo, 1.0 Hour

_____ Preflight check.

_____ Special takeoff and landing procedures.

     _____ Short-field takeoffs and landings.

     _____ Soft-field takeoffs and landings.

     _____ Crosswind takeoffs and landings.

     _____ Slips to landing, if approved.

_____ Debriefing by flight instructor (review of flight with student).

     _____ Evaluation.

     _____ Critique.

     _____ Review.

Make and Model _____ Airplane N-No. _____

Ground Instruction _____ Flight Time: Dual _____ Solo _____

Comments _____

_____

_____

Instructor _____ No. _____ Exp. _____

Date _____ Student Initials _____

Assigned Reading— Student: _SPFM_ (Chapters 19–25, in preparation for Stage 3 Cross-Country Flying).

Unit 13
Stage 2 Written Test

The student will be given a multiple-choice test made up by the flight school or instructor to cover the ground and flight instruction given in STAGE 2. The questions should cover at least the following areas:

_____ Preflight inspection, possible problem areas.

_____ Pretakeoff checks, possible problem areas.

_____ Traffic pattern and communications.

_____ Go-around procedures.

_____ Bounce recoveries.

_____ Crosswind takeoff and landing techniques.

_____ Turns around a point.

_____ Flight by reference to instruments.

   _____ The Six Basic Maneuvers.

_____ Takeoff and departure stalls.

_____ Approach-to-landing stalls.

_____ Slow flight.

_____ High-altitude emergencies.

_____ Airplane "numbers." Max rate and max angle climb airspeeds, max distance glide, etc.

_____ Wake turbulence avoidance.

_____ Collision avoidance.

_____ Soft- and short-field takeoffs and landings.

_____ Postlanding procedures.

Grade_____

Instructor_____

Date_____ Ground Instruction Time_____

Student Initials_____

Stage 3
Cross-Country

This Stage introduces and completes the dual and solo cross-country requirements for the private certificate for 14 CFR Parts 61 or 141. If possible, a dual flight to a public-use airport with a grass runway should be accomplished sometime during the course so that the student can have experience taking off and landing on a nonpaved surface.

Unit 1
Solo Flight to a Nearby Airport

Ground Instruction, 2.0 Hours

Note that this is an introduction to "real" cross-country. The following items should be covered:

_____ Brief for a solo flight to another (non-tower) airport within 25 NM, or more than 25 NM but not more than 50 NM, if the flight instructor and student have flown to that airport and the student is competent and proficient to enter and depart the traffic pattern and to make those landings or takeoffs. The student pilot's logbook must be endorsed with an authorization for one or more flights (§61.93[b]). *See* Stage 1, Unit 8.

_____ Ground servicing, including fuel and oil.

_____ Use of external power (as available) for starting.

_____ Sectional chart, use of plotter (courses and distance) to and from the airport previously flown to dual at a distance of 40 NM (as an example).

_____ Introduction to weather and other services available for cross-country flights.

    _____ Hourly weather reports (METARs).

    _____ Terminal forecasts (TAFs).

    _____ Area forecasts.

    _____ Winds aloft forecasts.

    _____ Pilot reports (PIREPs).

    _____ NOTAMs.

_____ Check weather. Suggested ceiling/visibility minimums of 6,000 feet/8 statute miles for solo flight with a forecast of this minimum or better for the next 4 to 6 hours. Student calls FSS or AFSS with flight instructor on the phone extension (or speaker) so that a student-instructor conference may be made during and/or after the briefing. Check surface winds at destination airport.

_____ Alternate plans available in case of weather change on outbound and inbound legs.

_____ Review student's paperwork and sign the logbook.

Flight: Solo, 2.0 Hours

_____ Student does normal full-stop takeoffs and landings at the other airport.

_____ Postflight debriefing.

    _____ Review solo flight to the other airport; ask and answer questions and discuss any problems the student may have encountered enroute.

    _____ Evaluation.

    _____ Critique.

    _____ Review.

Make and Model _____ Airplane N-No. _____

Ground Instruction _____ Flight Time: Dual _____ Solo _____

Comments _____

_____

_____

Instructor _____ No. _____ Exp. _____

Date _____ Student Initials _____

Assigned Reading—Student: *SPFM* (Chapters 19–21). Instructor: *FIM* (Chapters 14, 15, and 25).

Unit 2
Use of NAVAIDs and Communications Procedures

Ground Instruction, 3.0 Hours (may be done in two or three sessions)

It is suggested that this Unit be taught at a formal ground school or one-on-one, with no plans to fly immediately following. Certain parts will be repeated as part of the preflight briefings in this STAGE, but the student should have a thorough introduction to communications and navigation aids available early on. Some of this Unit will have been covered, earlier as needed, but should be "pulled together" here.

_____ VOR VHF, Omni-Directional Range.

    _____ The major components (omnibearing selector [OBS], course deviation indicator [CDI], and TO-FROM indicator).

    _____ Theory of how the VOR works (*SPFM*, Figure 21-4).

    _____ Frequencies in use. Compare with communications frequencies already used.

    _____ Advantages (VHF, OMNI—selection of bearings).

    _____ Disadvantage, line of sight (*SPFM*, Figure 21-8).

    _____ Selecting the proper frequency (identify!) and setting up the VOR receiver to track TO or FROM a station.

    _____ Discussion of tracking directly TO or FROM the station.

_____ 180° ambiguity. The CDI needle reads in reverse if the OBS is set opposite to the desired course.

_____ Brief mention of tracking to the station on a desired bearing but emphasize, at this point, that tracking directly to a VOR is the recommended procedure if lost or "uncertain."

_____ Principles of locating by cross-bearing (*SPFM*, Figure 25-4).

_____ Station crossing. Indications.

_____ Airplane may not always cross directly over the station; the needle may be slightly to one side or the other for an acceptable station passage.

_____ NDB, non-directional beacon.

_____ Components of the automatic direction finder equipment in the airplane.

_____ Frequencies. Discuss AM radio frequencies and compare with NDB frequencies.

_____ Advantage of ADF, *not* line of sight. Signals may be picked up when station is over the horizon.

_____ Disadvantages. Thunderstorms "attract" the needle; precipitation and storm static may make reception weak or impossible.

_____ Homing to the NDB. (*Tracking* will not be covered at this point.)

_____ Always confirm that the proper station has been selected; identify.

_____ Station passage. The airplane may not go directly over the station but can be a few hundred yards to either side for an acceptable passage.

_____ Transponder.

_____ Theory of operation.

_____ 4096 codes available.

_____ VFR code is 1200 for *all altitudes* (the student probably has been using the transponder since starting flying, but the equipment should be reviewed at this point).

_____ Emergency (7700) and loss of communications (7600) codes and when they should or should not be used.

_____ Practice setting codes while sitting in the airplane with engine shutdown and master switch OFF.

_____ Communications procedures to radar facility if lost; Confess, Climb, Communicate, Comply, Conserve, and Cool, keeping your (*SPFM*, Chapter 25).

_____ Frequencies to use if lost. Call FSS, towers, or approach controls, check sectional chart for possibilities within a 100-NM radius.

_____ Use of radar services for locating the aircraft.

_____ Frequencies to be used, FSS, tower, or approach control. If unsure of frequencies, call "nearest Flight Service Station on this frequency": 122.0 (at selected stations, Flight Watch), 122.2, 122.3, 122.6, 123.6, Emergency 121.5 MHz. FSS will listen on 122.05, 122.1, 122.15, and 123.6, and the pilot can receive on the affiliate VOR frequencies. Confirm these frequencies. Assure the student/private pilot that if lost or "uncertain" contact should be made on the listed frequencies and let those folks carry the ball from there. They will give location and all help possible, a successful on-airport landing is assured if the fuel situation has not passed the critical point. *Emphasize that the sooner the steps are taken, the better.* The student will probably be asked to switch frequencies to a radar facility for vectoring. The frequency-switching procedure should be well understood so that communications aren't lost. Student pilots should have all these frequencies available on a card (clipboard, wallet, etc.) when on a cross-country flight.

_____ VHF/DF services. This is a disappearing service and may not be available for some parts of the country. The student/private pilot should contact the FSS, tower, or approach control for any help available.

_____ ATC light signals. Review in the classroom (*SPFM*, Figure 21-21).

_____ Review communications procedures.

    _____ UNICOM. Frequencies used at different locations.

    _____ Multicom. When is this frequency used?

    _____ Air-to-air frequencies.

    _____ FSS. Position reports, weather data, or local advisory service.

    _____ Communications steps flying into a tower-controlled airport.

    _____ Communications steps in departing a tower-controlled airport.

Assigned Reading—Student: *SPFM* (Chapters 21 and 16); *AIM* (Chapters 2 and 8). Instructor: *FIM* (Chapter 13).

Comments _____

_____

_____

Instructor _____

Date _____ Ground Instruction Time _____

Student Initials _____

Unit 3
Introduction to Night Flying

At least one night dual should be completed before the student flies the first day triangular solo cross-country (50 NM leg).

Ground Instruction. 1.5 Hours

Cover the following areas before the first night dual:

_____ Airplane equipment.

    _____ Required equipment (§91.205) and lighting (§91.209) for VFR night flying.

    _____ Personal equipment, flashlight, charts, checklist.

    _____ Procedures in the event of loss of electrical power.

_____ Physiology of night flying.

    _____ Rods and cones.

_____ How to effectively scan for other aircraft.

_____ Visualizing the position and course of another aircraft by its position lights.

_____ Vertigo.

_____ Indications of flying into fog or mist (haloes around lights).

_____ Illusions in flight.

　　　_____ The need to rely more on the flight instruments at night.

　　　_____ Sparse ground lights and disorientation.

　　　_____ Landing errors and illusions. Use of VASI and electronic glide slopes.

　　　_____ Runway up- or down-slopes and narrow and wide runways.

　　　_____ Atmospheric illusions. Rain on windshield, landing in fog.

　　　_____ Don't land on a road or parking lot, use the runway. It has happened!

　　　_____ "Leans."

　　　_____ Acceleration after takeoff. An illusion of nose-up attitude.

_____ Cockpit lighting. Variable controlling for different night conditions.

_____ Airport lighting.

　　　_____ Airport rotating beacons, civilian, military, and water airports. Rotating beacons may be on in the daytime for Class B, C, D, and E airspace when conditions are below VFR.

　　　_____ Runway edge lights.

　　　_____ VASI. Various types available.

　　　_____ Runway end lighting.

　　　_____ Approach light systems.

　　　_____ Taxiway and other surface lights.

　　　_____ Pilot control of runway lighting systems.

_____ Discuss short cross-country to nearby town and return.

_____ Takeoffs and landings.

_____ Discuss go-arounds at night.

Flight: Dual, 1.0 Hour

This first night flight should start in twilight so that a gradual transition to darkness occurs; however, a minimum of 1.0 hour in legal night flight should be accomplished, so that the total flight time could be up to 2 hours in some cases.

_____ Preflight check of all exterior and interior lighting. Flashlight and other personal equipment within easy reach.

_____ Prestart and starting procedures. Navigation (position) lights ON before engaging starter. All other electrical equipment OFF. Other lights (rotating beacon, taxi) ON after start.

_____ Taxi.

_____ Run-up (taxi and/or landing lights OFF).

_____ Takeoff. Using landing light(s).

_____ Climb.

_____ Departure pattern.

_____ Short cross-country, using pilotage (and VOR, and nondirectional beacon [NDB] as available).

_____ Reenter pattern.

_____ Shoot at least five takeoffs and landings to a full stop, using landing lights and interior lights.

_____ Demonstrate go-around procedure.

_____ Shutdown and secure the airplane.

_____ Postflight check and security of the airplane.

_____ Postflight instruction.

    _____ Evaluation.

    _____ Critique.

    _____ Review.

Make and Model _____ Airplane N-No. _____

Ground Instruction _____ Flight Time: Dual _____ Solo _____

Comments _____

_____

_____

_____

Instructor _____ No. _____ Exp. _____

Date _____ Student Initials _____

Assigned Reading—Student: *SPFM* (Chapters 19–25); *AIM* (Chapters 3 and 4). Instructor: *FIM* (Chapters 14 and 15).

Unit 4
Navigation Ground School: Preparation for Dual and Solo Cross-Countries

Ground Instruction, 3.0 Hours (This should be given in two or more sessions.)

_____ Types of navigation.

    _____ Pilotage.

    _____ Dead (deduced) reckoning.

    _____ Celestial navigation, briefly.

    _____ Radio navigation.

_____ Meridians and parallels.

    _____ Meridians run north/south and converge at the true North and South Poles.

        _____ Prime meridian runs through Greenwich, England.

        _____ Lines of longitude run north and south; longitude is measured from the prime meridian east and west.

        _____ Time zones/universal coordinated time.

    _____ Parallels (lines) run east/west.

_____ Prime parallel runs through the equator.

_____ Latitudes are measured north and south of the equator.

_____ Degrees of latitude.

_____ 60 minutes = 1 degree.

_____ 1 minute = 1 nautical mile (NM) or 1.152 statute miles (SM).

_____ True North. Courses are measured clockwise from True North.

_____ Magnetic North Pole is in Canada.

_____ Magnetic variation = difference between Magnetic North and True North. This is not necessarily the _geometric_ angle between the two poles since the isogonic lines "meander."

_____ Isogonic lines = lines of equal magnetic variation.

_____ Agonic line.

_____ East is least, West is best. Subtract from the true course or heading for easterly variation; add for westerly.

_____ Compass deviation.

_____ Swinging or correcting a compass.

_____ TVMDC. (True + Variation = Magnetic course + Deviation = Compass course)

_____ Plotter.

_____ Measuring the true course on the midmeridian.

_____ Mileage scales. Sectional and other charts; nautical and statute miles.

_____ Wind triangle.

_____ Vector system.

_____ Wind directions (winds aloft) are given in true directions and in knots.

_____ Selecting VFR cruising altitudes (above 3,000 feet AGL).

_____ 0°–179° = odd thousands plus 500 feet.

_____ 180°–359° = even thousands plus 500 feet.

_____ Selecting the altitude with most-favorable winds.

_____ Draw a True North/South line on a blank sheet of paper for reference.

_____ Use a plotter to measure and lay out the true course line through some point on the north/south line. Draw this line of indefinite length.

_____ Using the nautical mile scale on the plotter, draw the wind vector in the proper direction and length from some point on the course line.

_____ From the head of the wind arrow, swing a line the length of the true airspeed value (use the nautical mile scale on the plotter) until it hits the true course line.

_____ Discuss the meaning of each line in the triangle.

It is suggested that this might be a good break point for this Unit.

_____ Using the E6-B and other computers.

_____ Finding true airspeed.

_____ Checking fuel consumption and speed.

_____ Finding density-altitude.

_____ Finding groundspeed and estimated time of arrival (ETA).

_____ Finding fuel consumption.

_____ Correcting indicated or pressure altitude for temperature.

_____ Converting the true course to true heading to compass heading and back.

_____ Sectional chart.

_____ Aeronautical symbols.

_____ Chart coverage and scale.

_____ Topographical symbols.

_____ Radio aids to navigation and airspace information.

_____ Data on obstruction symbols.

_____ List of ATC frequencies.

_____ Prohibited, restricted, warning, military operations, and alert areas.

_____ A, B, C, D, E, and G classes of airspace.

_____ _Aeronautical Information Manual (AIM)_ — Basic flight information and ATC procedures.

_____ _Airport/Facility Directory (A/FD)._

_____ Review legend and check information for airports on the first dual and solo cross-country flights.

_____ Notices to Airmen (NOTAMs). TFR, D, and the FDC publication.

Another suggested break point for Unit 4.

_____ National Transportation Safety Board Part 830.

_____ The airplane.

_____ Performance factors for takeoffs and landings.

_____ Systems.

_____ Weight and balance.

_____ Seesaw principle.

_____ Datum moments and CG positions.

_____ Empty weight CG and moment.

_____ Basic empty weight.

_____ Useful load.

_____ Fuel and oil weights.

_____ Effects of adding, subtracting or moving weights.

Use the following as a checklist.

_____ Airplane papers required on board (A ROW):

_____ Airworthiness certificate (A).

_____ Registration certificate (R).

_____ Operations limitations (O).

_____ Weight and balance (W).

_____ Emergency procedures.

_____ Weather information sources.

    _____ Hourly reports.

    _____ Forecasts.

    _____ Weather charts.

    _____ Winds aloft.

    _____ In-flight advisories.

_____ Filing flight plans.

    _____ Advantages of filing. Procedures for opening and closing a VFR flight plan.

    _____ Use of transponder in emergency situations.

    _____ Review cockpit resource management (CRM) and aeronautical decision making (ADM) as applied to student and low time private pilots.

Assigned Reading—Student: *SPFM* (Chapters 19–25); *AIM*; *A/FD*. Instructor: *FIM* (Chapters 14 and 15).

Comments _____

_____

_____

Instructor _____

Date _____ Ground Instruction Time _____

Student Initials _____

Unit 5
Dual Cross-Country to Two Other Airports
(One of Which is More Than 50 NM from the Airport of Origin)

Ground Instruction, 1.5 Hours

_____ Sectional chart.

    _____ Measure the true course and distances for the three legs and mark the chart. (It is suggested that markers be placed every 10 NM.)

    _____ Plan at least one leg on a federal airway.

    _____ Track on a VOR or home on NDB on one leg, if ground and airborne equipment is available.

    _____ Check alternate airports.

    _____ Set up flight log (*SPFM*, Figure 24-19)

    _____ Select enroute check points and mark on chart.

    _____ Operational problems associated with different terrain features.

    _____ Operations at high density-altitude airports, including leaning of fuel mixture for best power for takeoff.

_____ Estimating visibility while in flight, tips.

_____ Check for restricted, prohibited, or special-use airspace on the routes or at the destinations.

_____ Review chart legends, including listings of control tower frequencies and Class B, Class C, and selected radar-approach control frequencies.

_____ Airport/Facility Directory.

_____ Check facilities at destination. Review with student the airports and Fixed Base Operators (FBOs), location of wind indicators, UNICOM, or approach control/tower frequencies.

_____ Review radio navigation aids available at destination and enroute.

_____ Flight Service Station. Personal visit or the student calls, with the instructor on the phone extension.

_____ Current weather enroute and at the two destination airports.

_____ Area and terminal forecasts (if available for destination airports or if not, get at closest airports). Obtain area forecasts and terminal forecasts for trip time plus 2 hours. Write them down.

_____ Winds aloft forecast.

_____ Check NOTAMs, enroute and at destination airports.

_____ Compute climbs, fuel used, enroute times, and headings. Decide on refueling points.

_____ File flight plan, agree on activation procedures. Leave plenty of time prior to ETD for student to complete flight log.

Flight: Dual, 2.5 Hours

_____ Checklist for personal equipment, charts, logs, computers, plotters, and a reliable timepiece.

_____ Preflight check (full fuel and oil).

_____ Airplane servicing requirements.

_____ Start.

_____ Taxi.

_____ Pretakeoff check.

_____ Takeoff.

_____ Fly over the airport enroute, start timing.

_____ Checkpoints and times.

_____ Estimating visibility while in flight.

_____ Alternate airport procedures.

_____ Track VOR or home on NDB.

_____ Flight under the hood on part of one or more legs.

_____ Locating position by VOR cross-bearings.

_____ Traffic pattern at destination airports.

_____ Close flight plan(s). If possible always close flight plan after landing at destination (but don't forget).

_____ Refuel at one or both airports, for student training purposes.

_____ Return to home airport.

_____ Postlanding procedures. Postflight check and securing of airplane.

_____ Fill out logbook for completion of dual cross-country.

Note: The instructor may elect to fly a second dual cross-country to the same airports before sending the student on the solo cross-country.

_____ Postflight instruction.

      _____ Evaluation.

      _____ Critique.

      _____ Review.

Make and Model _____ Airplane N-No. _____

Ground Instruction _____ Flight Time: Dual _____ Solo _____

Comments _____

_____

_____

Instructor _____ No. _____ Exp. _____

Date _____ Student Initials _____

Assigned Reading— Student: *SPFM* (Chapters 19–25); *AIM* (Chapters 24, 25). *A/FD* (Legends). Instructor: *FIM* (Chapter 15).

Unit 6
Solo Cross-Country

Ground Instruction, 1.0 Hour

Review first dual cross-country and work with student to plan a solo cross-country to those same airports.

_____ Review airplane servicing requirements.

      _____ Fueling and proper grounding of the airplane.

      _____ Oil.

      _____ Starting the engine with external power (if the airplane has an external starting system) and when not to use external power (when the battery is completely dead).

      _____ Proper windshield cleaner.

      _____ Special requirements for a particular airplane.

_____ Weather (current and forecast), enroute and destinations.

_____ Winds aloft. Student chooses altitudes (odd +500, even +500 as applicable) for each leg.

_____ Student prepares flight log.

_____ If student lands at an airport (or other point) other than the destination airports he is to call a flight instructor at home base and not depart until cleared.

_____ Review VOR or NDB, communications frequencies, and lost aircraft procedures.

_____ Alternate airports.

_____ Student files flight plan with FSS for each separate leg or a round robin under instructor agreement and supervision.

_____ Discuss advantages and disadvantages of filing for the full trip versus filing for each leg.

_____ Checklist for charts, computers, timepiece, and logbook.

_____ Pilot logbooks and pilot/medical certificates.

_____ Money or credit card(s) for refueling.

_____ Review paperwork and sign student pilot certificate and logbook, describing the allowed crosscountry.

Flight: Solo, 3.0 Hours

(4.0–5.0 hours total elapsed time; allow more time than for the dual cross-country.)

_____ Preflight check (*full* fuel and oil).

_____ Activate flight plan after takeoff.

_____ Student flies to first destination airport, closes flight plan, and gets logbook signed.

_____ Refuels at first airport, if planned. Files flight plan for second airport.

_____ Departs for second airport without undue delay.

_____ Opens flight plan.

_____ Closes flight plan, refuels at second airport (if planned or necessary), and gets logbook signed.

_____ Files flight plan for home airport as required.

_____ Departs for home airport.

_____ Opens flight plan.

_____ Closes flight plan after arrival.

_____ Postflight procedures.

_____ Instructor and student review and debrief the flight.

     _____ Evaluation.

     _____ Critique.

     _____ Review.

Make and Model _____ Airplane N-No. _____

Ground Instruction _____ Flight Time: Dual _____ Solo _____

Comments _____

_____

_____

Instructor _____ No. _____ Exp. _____

Date _____ Student Initials _____

Assigned Reading—Student: *SPFM* (Chapters 21–25). Instructor: *FIM* (Chapters 13 and 14).

Unit 7
Stage Check after the First Solo Cross-Country

A flight test is to be given at the completion of the first solo flight, at the completion of the first solo cross-country flight, and at the conclusion of the course.

For this postsolo cross-country stage check, the check pilot will have the student pilot plan and fly a short cross-country, utilizing current weather and forecasts, including winds aloft information, NOTAMs, Airport/Facility Directory, and latest sectional chart(s). The check pilot may, during the flight, require that the student divert to another airport to cope with various simulated inflight problems and emergencies, such as engine overheating, partial power failure, electrical failure, carburetor ice, and unforecast deteriorating weather. The flight will return to home base without landing at other airports unless the check pilot feels it is necessary for a particular student. The use of VOR and/or NDB will be checked, as applicable.

Flight: Dual, 1.5 Hours

_____ Weather planning.

    _____ Current weather enroute and at destination.

    _____ Forecast weather enroute, destination, and home airport for the proposed flight period plus 2 hours.

    _____ Winds aloft forecasts for the terminal(s) nearest to the route.

_____ Preflight navigation planning.

    _____ Drawing course line(s).

    _____ Using a plotter.

    _____ Computer.

    _____ Expected fuel consumption.

    _____ ETAs to checkpoints, destination, and home base.

_____ Preflight check.

_____ Cockpit management.

_____ Pretakeoff check.

_____ Procedures to climb and get established on course.

_____ Follow the preplanned course by use of landmarks; verify position within 3 NM.

_____ Altitude control (±100 feet).

_____ Heading control (±10°).

_____ Enroute checkpoints and destination ±5 minutes.

_____ Landmark identification.

_____ On-course accuracy.

_____ Correct and record differences between preflight fuel, groundspeed, and heading.

_____ Diversion to an alternate airport.

_____ Use of VOR or NDB for bearing, tracking, or homing to get to an alternate airport.

_____ Emergencies. Choose one of the following to be simulated:

    _____ Complete power failure.

    _____ Partial power failure.

_____ Electrical failure.

_____ Overheating engine.

_____ Weather deterioration.

_____ Procedures, including communications, when lost.

_____ Return to home airport.

    _____ Checklist.

    _____ Communications.

    _____ Traffic pattern.

    _____ Landing.

    _____ Postlanding procedures. This is necessary after every flight as was noted in STAGE 1.

        _____ Checklist.

        _____ Postflight inspection.

        _____ Security of the airplane.

    _____ Postflight instruction.

        _____ Evaluation.

        _____ Critique.

        _____ Review.

Make and Model _____ Airplane N-No. _____

Ground Instruction _____ Flight Time: Dual _____ Solo _____

Comments _____

_____

_____

Instructor _____ No. _____ Exp. _____

Date _____ Student Initials _____

Assigned Reading— Student: *SPFM* (Chapter 15). Instructor: *FIM* (Chapter 12).

Unit 8
Emergency Instrument Flying

Ground Instruction, 1.0 Hour

_____ Review Four Fundamentals.

_____ Instrument scan.

_____ Six Basic Maneuvers. Brief on using both full and emergency panels.

_____ Straight and level flight, ±10° of heading.

_____ Left and right 180° turns, ±10° on rollout.

_____ Shallow climbing turns to a predetermined altitude and heading.

_____ Shallow descending turns to a predetermined altitude and heading.

_____ Recovery from the start of a power-on spiral.

_____ Recovery from the approach to a climbing stall.

_____ Tracking to a VOR, hooded at a constant altitude.

_____ Homing to an NDB, hooded at a constant altitude.

_____ Radar vectors, hooded to an ASR approach. The instructor may simulate ATC.

Aviate, Navigate, Communicate!

Flight: Dual, 1.5 Hours

This Unit may use a flight simulator and authorized instructor if available (14 CFR §§61.4 and 61.109).

_____ Student puts on hood during climbout and flies specified headings (full panel).

_____ Climb to safe altitude and fly to practice area, vectored by instructor.

_____ Six Basic Maneuvers, hooded full panel, followed by emergency panel practice.

_____ Tracking to a nearby VOR, full panel.

_____ Homing to an NDB (if aircraft and ground equipment is available), full panel.

_____ Use of communications while flying the airplane, hooded and full panel.

_____ "Radar" vector by instructor to home airport.

_____ Evaluation.

_____ Critique.

_____ Review.

Assignment for the next Unit: Plan a triangular solo cross-country to two airports not previously visited.

Make and Model _____ Airplane N-No. _____

Ground Instruction _____ Flight Time: Dual _____ Solo _____

Comments _____

_____

_____

Instructor _____ No. _____ Exp. _____

Date _____ Student Initials _____

Assigned Reading— Student: *SPFM* (Chapters 22–25). Instructor: *FIM* (Chapters 14 and 15).

Unit 9
Solo Triangular Cross-Country
(A solo cross-country to two airports not previously visited.)

Ground Instruction, Preflight Briefing, 1.0 Hour

_____ Airplane papers. Review fuel and oil requirements.

_____ Review student's sectional chart planning and checkpoints on log, refueling procedures, and alternate courses of action.

_____ Check *Airport/Facility Directory* for the destination airports plus alternate airports and communications procedures.

_____ Weather check (current and forecasts) by student, with instructor review.

_____ Winds aloft information checked, then enroute altitudes chosen.

_____ NOTAMs, enroute and at airports.

_____ Student completes the flight log.

_____ Check flight log and ETAs.

_____ Student files flight plan to first destination.

_____ Instructor signs logbook for this specific flight route and date. (Double check student pilot certificate for the cross-country sign-off.)

_____ Review collision avoidance and wake turbulence avoidance procedures.

_____ Check that student has money and/or credit cards for fuel.

Flight: Solo, 3.0 Hours

(4.5 hours elapsed time for the trip.) The student completes the following:

_____ Preflight.

_____ Departure.

_____ Navigation to first destination.

_____ Traffic pattern and landing.

_____ Close flight plan.

_____ Logbook signed.

_____ Fuel as necessary.

_____ Check second destination weather and forecast.

_____ File flight plan to second destination.

_____ Depart and open flight plan, or open flight plan just before departure. Note that Flight Following Service on student cross-countries is discouraged.

_____ Navigate to second destination, using pilotage (and radio navigation as available).

_____ Traffic pattern and landing.

_____ Close flight plan.

_____ Logbook signed.

_____ Fuel as necessary.

_____ Review route to home airport.

_____ File flight plan: check enroute and home airport weather.

_____ Depart and open flight plan.

_____ Navigation to home airport using pilotage and radio navigation.

_____ Land at home airport and close flight plan.

_____ Instructor reviews the flight and, after the airplane is fueled, compares actual fuel used with predicted fuel consumption.

_____ Instructor signs logbook for arrival at home.

      _____ Evaluation.

      _____ Critique.

      _____ Review.

Make and Model _____ Airplane N-No. _____

Ground Instruction _____ Flight Time: Dual _____ Solo _____

Comments _____

_____

_____

Instructor _____ No. _____ Exp. _____

Date _____ Student Initials _____

Assigned Reading—Student: *SPFM* (Chapters 22–26); *AIM* ("Lighting"). Student prepares a flight log and reviews the sectional and *A/FD* for dual night cross-country flight to an airport 50+ NM distant. Instructor: *FIM* (Chapters 13, 14 and 15).

Unit 10
Dual Night Cross-Country and Local Pattern Work
(Initiate actual flight in full darkness)

Ground Instruction, 1.0 Hour

_____ Preflight briefing for a dual night cross-country for a total of 100 NM distance including performing take-offs and landings (full stops) at one or more airports; return to home airport for more practice landings (if time and student fatigue allow). If possible, fly to an airport with pilotcontrolled lighting during one of the night flights.

_____ Check weather, current and forecast, for destination and home airports.

_____ Check charts, *Airport/Facility Directories*, and NOTAMs.

_____ Review student's flight log previously prepared for this flight (except for winds aloft information).

_____ Assure that personal equipment (flashlight, timepiece, etc.) are available.

_____ File round-robin flight plan, including time for takeoffs and landings at the other airport and at home, as desired.

Flight: Dual, 2.5 Hours (More time may be required, depending on the situation.)

_____ Preflight check.

    _____ Airplane's interior and exterior lighting.

    _____ Discuss problems of preflight checking at night with a flashlight versus full daylight preflighting.

_____ Prestarting procedures. Master switch and interior lights ON. Flashlight is needed for hard-to-see items, such as fuel selectors and other controls.

_____ Navigation (position) lights ON, indicating that pilot is onboard and ready to start.

_____ After start, all necessary exterior lights ON.

_____ Taxi. Taxi/landing lights ON. Use extreme caution.

_____ Run-up. Taxi/landing lights OFF. Use flashlight to check controls (ailerons, elevator, rudder) for proper movement and for interior hard-to-see switches or controls.

_____ Takeoff. Check area for other airplanes. Landing light(s) ON before taking the runway.

_____ Open the flight plan.

_____ Depart for destination airport(s), noting relative position of nearby towns while enroute.

_____ Contact approach control, tower, UNICOM or broadcast in the blind on the CTAF as applicable.

_____ Enter traffic, using proper communications and utilizing collision avoidance procedures.

_____ Shoot at least one full-stop landing, depending on the size of the airport or other factors.

_____ Return to home airport.

_____ Shoot first two patterns (full stop) with full cockpit lighting and landing/taxi light.

_____ Shoot at least two patterns (full stop) without landing/taxi light. Use landing/taxi light for taxi back.

_____ Two patterns (full stop) with landing/taxi lights but interior lights OFF. (Use exterior references and red lensed flashlights.)

_____ Two patterns with landing/taxi lights and interior lights OFF. Keep navigation/position lights and rotating beacon ON.

_____ One pattern (full stop) with full interior lights restored.

_____ Go-around by student, followed by full-stop landing and securing of the airplane.

_____ Close flight plan.

_____ Instructor debriefs after flight and fills out logbook.

    _____ Evaluation.

    _____ Critique.

    _____ Review.

Make and Model _____ Airplane N-No. _____

Ground Instruction _____ Flight Time: Dual _____ Solo _____

Comments _____

_____

_____

Instructor _____ No. _____ Exp. _____

Date _____ Student Initials _____

Assigned Reading—Student: *SPFM* (Chapters 10 and 13). Instructor: *FIM* (Chapters 14, 15 and 25).

Unit 11
Solo in the Practice Area and Pattern V

This flight is to assure that the student maintains proficiency in the maneuvers previously discussed and flown. It provides a "break" from the night and cross-country work and maintains student confidence in slow flight, stalls, wind drift correction maneuvers, and normal and special takeoffs and landings. The briefing is to review the maneuvers and resolve any questions; it may be longer than earlier briefings for practice area and pattern work.

Ground Instruction, 1.0 Hour

_____ Pattern and departure.

_____ Slow flight, clean.

_____ Takeoff and departure stalls.

_____ Approach-to-landing stalls.

_____ 360° and 720° power turns.

_____ Descent to wind drift maneuver altitude (600 to 1,000 feet AGL).

_____ Carburetor heat, as needed.

_____ Rectangular course.

_____ S-turns across the road.

_____ Turns around a point.

_____ Return to airport.

    _____ Checklist.

    _____ Communications.

    _____ Pattern entry.

_____ Normal takeoffs and landings (full stop).

_____ Crosswind takeoffs and landings, as applicable.

_____ Short-field takeoffs and landings, full stop.

_____ Soft-field takeoffs and landings, full stop.

_____ Postlanding procedures.

_____ Postlanding checklist.

_____ Securing the airplane.

Flight: Solo, 1.0 Hour

_____ Preflight and pretakeoff checklists.

_____ Depart traffic pattern and climb to practice area.

_____ 360° and 720° power turns.

_____ Slow flight, clean.

_____ Takeoff and departure stalls.

_____ Approach-to-landing stalls.

_____ Descend to the altitude required for wind drift correction maneuvers, airspeed ±10 knots of best glide speed. Use carburetor heat as directed by the POH.

_____ Wind drift correction maneuvers (time may not allow practice of all three listed), airspeed ±10 knots, altitude ±100 feet.

    _____ Rectangular course.

    _____ S-turns.

    _____ Turns around a point.

_____ Return to pattern.

_____ Normal or crosswind takeoffs and landings, as applicable.

_____ Short-field takeoffs and landings, full stop.

_____ Soft-field takeoffs and landings, full stop.

    _____ Postlanding procedures.

    _____ Postlanding checklists.

    _____ Securing the airplane.

_____ Postflight review by instructor.

Make and Model _____ Airplane N-No. _____

Ground Instruction _____ Flight Time: Dual _____ Solo _____

Comments _____

_____

_____

Instructor _____ No. _____ Exp. _____

Date _____ Student Initials _____

Assigned Reading—Student: *SPFM* (Chapters 21 and 24); *AIM* (Chapter 4 and parts assigned by instructor). Instructor: *FIM* (Chapters 14 and 15).

Unit 12
Dual and Solo Flight to a Tower-Controlled Airport (VFR-Day)

The outline of this unit assumes that the home airport does not have an approach control/tower and that this is the student's first experience with a controlled airport. In this case the instructor may elect to shoot at least three dual takeoffs and landings to a full stop with taxi-back at the big airport so that the student feels comfortable with operations and communications. It's suggested that time be set aside during this lesson for a visit to the approach control/tower facilities to allow the student to meet the personnel and to feel more comfortable in operations at that airport. A student pilot who has been operating out of a controlled airport will have already met the requirements of 14 CFR §61.109, which requires three solo takeoffs and landings to a full stop at an airport with an operating control tower.

Ground Instruction. 1.0 Hour

_____ Steps when approaching and landing at a controlled airport.

_____ ATIS (Airport Terminal Information Service).

_____ Approach control. Assigns a discrete transponder code on initial contact.

_____ Tower.

_____ Ground Control.

_____ Procedures during takeoff and landing operations in the pattern.

_____ Ground control; contact when directed by the tower.

_____ Tower.

_____ Steps when departing the controlled airport.

    _____ ATIS.

    _____ Clearance delivery. Indicate that Information Delta, etc., has been received.

        _____ Heading and altitude are given.

        _____ Departure control frequency (and discrete transponder code) given here. Set the code but keep the transponder on standby.

    _____ Ground control.

    _____ Tower.

    _____ Transponder ON at start of takeoff.

    _____ Contact departure control when directed by tower on climb-out.

    _____ Transponder, 1200 after release by departure control.

_____ Wake turbulence avoidance.

_____ Light signals—Review. Ensure that light signals card is in the aircraft.

_____ Describe layout of taxiways and location of FBOs at the large airport.

    _____ Have diagram of the airport, if available.

_____ Confirm available sectional charts (IFR approach charts also, if available) are current.

_____ Check log of the trip.

_____ Check destination airport information in the *A/FD*. Discuss any special requirements for that particular airport.

_____ Check *AIM* for airport markings and signs. Take copy of *AIM* on flight for reference to "unusual" markings.

Flight: Dual, 2.0 Hours; Solo, 1.0 Hour

_____ Student conducts preflight check, pretakeoff check, takeoff, and climb.

_____ Navigate to tower-controlled airport.

_____ Student listens to ATIS, confirms information, and contacts approach control at proper time and position.

_____ Student sets transponder code as given by approach control.

_____ Student communicates, lands, taxies to destination on airport, and secures airplane, under supervision.

_____ Fuel as necessary.

_____ Tower visit.

_____ Student returns to airplane and shoots at least three solo takeoffs and landings to a full stop. Instructor may elect to stay in tower cab during the takeoffs and landings.

_____ Returns to FBO to pick up instructor *before* departing for home airport. This is very important!

_____ Navigates directly to home airport. It's suggested that no side trips or alternate routes be taken since the student is probably fatigued by this "busy" session.

_____ Postlanding procedures.

_____ Review with instructor all parts of trip after landing.

     _____ Evaluation.

     _____ Critique.

     _____ Review.

Make and Model _____ Airplane N-No. _____

Ground Instruction _____ Flight Time: Dual _____ Solo _____

Comments _____

_____

_____

Instructor _____ No. _____ Exp. _____

Date _____ Student Initials _____

Assigned Reading—Student: *SPFM* (Chapters 22 and 23); read selected portions of the latest copies of *Aviation Weather Services (AWS) AC* 00-45 and *Aviation Weather (AW) AC* 00-6.

Unit 13
Weather Theory and Weather Services

Meteorology

This Unit will consist of ground instruction on basic meteorology and weather services available. Particular attention will be paid to hazards to flight and how to recognize them both on the ground and in flight. These subjects should be covered in three or more ground school sessions, but they should be completed before the long cross-country.

Ground Instruction, 6.0 Hours

_____ Basic meteorology *Aviation Weather (AW)*.

    _____ Heat and circulation.

    _____ Coriolis effect in Northern and Southern hemispheres.

    _____ Moisture: temperature and dewpoint effects on the atmosphere's ability to produce or hold moisture.

    _____ Relative humidity.

    _____ Lapse rates: normal, dry, and wet.

    _____ Clouds, families.

        _____ How clouds are formed.

        _____ Clouds, cumulus and stratus forms.

    _____ Fog: advection, radiation, upslope, precipitation, and ice fog.

    _____ Precipitation: rain, hail, sleet, and snow.

    _____ Fronts: Warm, cold, occluded, and stationary; the clouds and visibilities (and precipitation) expected with each.

        _____ Cold front: type of clouds and weather, turbulence, area covered, and precipitation. Cross-section of the front.

        _____ Warm front: expected clouds and weather and extent of area covered. Freezing rain in winter may occur. Cross-section.

        _____ Occluded front: may contain weather of both warm and cold fronts.

        _____ Frontogenesis and frontolysis.

Suggested break point.

_____ Hazards to flight.

    _____ Thunderstorms.

        _____ How thunderstorms are formed; the three requirements are instability, lifting force, and moisture.

        _____ Cumulus clouds. Mature and dissipating stage, updrafts, downdrafts, and precipitation. Mature stage is the most hazardous.

        _____ Dissipating stage, the anvil head. *Do not* fly under the anvil head; stay *at least* 5 miles away (10 miles is even better).

    _____ Hail. How it is formed.

    _____ Icing. Clear, rime, and mixed.

    _____ Freezing rain: When it may occur.

    _____ Lightning.

    _____ Turbulence.

    _____ Windshear (loss of airspeed).

    _____ Microbursts.

    _____ Fog: A 4°F (2°C) temperature and dewpoint spread could indicate that fog formation may start.

_____ Major hazards of fog to the student and private pilot.

_____ Microbursts. How they occur.

_____ Turbulence in clear air conditions (*SPFM*, Chapter 23).

Break point.

_____ *Aviation Weather Services (AWS).*

    _____ Review a typical hourly routine weather report (METAR).

    _____ TAFs (Terminal Aerodrome Forecasts).

    _____ Area forecasts.

    _____ Inflight advisories.

        _____ EFAS (enroute flight advisory service).

        _____ SIGMETs (significant meteorological information).

        _____ AIRMETs (meteorological phenomena that are potentially hazardous to aircraft).

        _____ Convective SIGMETs.

        _____ AWOS (automated weather observation system).

        _____ ASOS (automated surface observation system).

    _____ PIREPs (pilot reports).

    _____ Wind information.

        _____ Winds aloft forecasts.

        _____ Winds aloft charts.

    _____ Other services.

        _____ TIBS (telephone information briefing service).

        _____ HIWAS (hazardous inflight weather advisory service).

        _____ Flight watch, 122.0 MHz.

Break point.

    _____ Weather charts.

        _____ Surface analysis chart.

        _____ Weather depiction chart.

        _____ Radar summary chart.

        _____ Weather prognostic chart.

_____ Evaluation.

_____ Critique.

_____ Review.

Make and Model _____ Airplane N-No. _____

Ground Instruction _____ Flight Time: Dual _____ Solo _____

Comments _____

_____

_____

Instructor _____ No. _____ Exp. _____

Date _____ Student Initials _____

Assigned Reading—Student: *SPFM* (Chapters 21–25); *FAR* (Parts 61 and 91). Instructor: *FIM* (Chapters 14, 15, and 25).

Unit 14
Solo Long Cross-Country Flight

Ground Instruction, 1.0 Hour

This flight is suggested to be a cross-country of about 300 NM total distance with landings at a minimum of 3 airports, one of which is greater than 100 NM from the point of origin. The basic requirements are for 150 NM total distance with full-stop landings at 3 airports and one leg being greater than 50 NM straight-line distance. The instructor should tailor the flight based on the student, flight time required and conditions of training, of course, but the longer distances ensure that the student feels he or she has definitely left the local area (versus being only 30 or so minutes cruise flight from home base). The instructor will ensure that the flight will be completed well before dark.

_____ Review sectional chart(s) and initial navigation log with student. Check for restricted and prohibited areas.

_____ Flight instructor and student together complete weather briefing with current weather and forecasts (terminal and area) and check NOTAMs for enroute and destinations.

_____ Instructor and student check winds aloft and times enroute to complete the navigation log.

_____ Assure that the airplane papers are in order and that a credit card or cash is available for fueling at pre-chosen destination airport(s). Suggested: refueling at each airport recommended.

_____ Recheck student pilot certificate for initial endorsement; sign logbook for this route and date.

_____ Confirm that the student logbook has latest 90-day endorsement.

_____ Student pilot has phone number(s) where CFI can be located during the time period of the trip.

_____ Student files flight plan for the first leg and will file for the other two legs in order.

_____ Flight instructor will be available at airport to debrief the student upon return.

Flight: Solo, 4.0 Hours

_____ Student flies the cross-country.

_____ Review the cross-country flight with student upon return.

Make and Model _____ Airplane N-No. _____

Ground Instruction _____ Flight Time: Dual _____ Solo _____

Comments _____

_____

_____

Instructor _____ No. _____ Exp. _____

Date _____ Student Initials _____

Assigned Reading—None.

Unit 15
Stage 3 Written Test

Ground Instruction Credit, 1.0 Hour

A written test made up by the school or instructor will be given on the cross-country phase to check that the student fully understands the requirements for a safe VFR cross-country. The test should cover the following areas as a minimum:

_____ Weather services available.

_____ Preflight weather briefing.

_____ FAA flight plans.

_____ Sectional chart.

_____ Navigation.

      _____ Pilotage.

      _____ Radio navigation.

_____ Communications with the FSS and/or tower.

_____ Emergency procedures.

      _____ Weather encounters.

      _____ Carburetor ice.

      _____ Diversion to other airports.

      _____ Electrical failure or fire.

      _____ Rough-running engine.

      _____ Lost procedures.

            _____ Communications.

            _____ Precautionary off-airport landing.

                 _____ Dragging the area.

                 _____ Postlanding procedures.

Grade _____

Date _____ Instructor Signature _____

Cert. No. _____ Exp. _____

Stage 4
Preparation for the Knowledge Test

Private Pilot, ASEL

Ground Instruction, 9.0 Hours

This ground instruction preparation for the Knowledge Test session may be broken up into eight 1-hour or four 2-hour sessions or reviews, plus one 1-hour session for summary and questions. The subject matter is broken up and arranged to fit the student's and instructor's schedule: because of this, the sequence may not exactly match the order listed here. Depending on the student, it may be recommended that the Knowledge Test be taken anytime during the postsolo period, but it is suggested that at least the first solo cross-country be completed before taking the test. It's hoped that this STAGE will not be just for preparation for the Knowledge Test but will present information to be used throughout the pilot's career. The following topics should be reviewed:

_____ Federal Aviation Regulations 1, 61, 71, and 91 and NTSB 830, as applicable to student and private pilots.

_____ Categories and classes, as indicated for certification of pilots and aircraft.

_____ Definition of night time.

_____ V speeds. V_A, V_{FE}, V_{LE}, V_Y, V_X.

_____ Preventive maintenance.

_____ Pilot documents required in flight and requirements for presentation.

_____ Duration of medical certificates.

_____ Requirements for flying a high-performance airplane.

_____ Flight reviews.

_____ Recent flight experience. Day, night, and in tailwheel airplanes.

_____ Change of address.

_____ Glider towing.

_____ Private pilot general limitations.

_____ Federal airways dimensions.

_____ Final authority for aircraft operations.

_____ Inflight emergencies and pilot authority. When is a report of a deviation required?

_____ Aircraft limitations information sources.

_____ Dropping objects from an aircraft.

_____ Consumption of alcohol by pilot or passenger.

_____ Preflight action required of the pilot.

_____ Seatbelts and shoulder harnesses.

_____ Formation flight.

_____ Aircraft rights-of-way.

_____ Maximum airspeeds in, or underlying, Class B airspace.

_____ Minimum safe altitudes.

_____ Altimeter settings.

_____ ATC clearance deviations.

_____ Tower light signals and taxi and runway signs and markings.

_____ Visual approach slope indicator (VASI) systems.

_____ Non-tower airport traffic patterns.

_____ Fuel requirements, VFR day and night.

_____ VFR cloud clearances and visibility requirements for operations below and above 10,000 feet MSL.

_____ VFR cruising altitudes.

_____ Papers required to be onboard the aircraft.

_____ Emergency locator transmitter (ELT) battery requirements.

_____ Instrument and equipment requirements. VFR day and night.

_____ Inoperative equipment.

_____ Aircraft position lights. When required to be ON.

_____ Supplemental oxygen requirements; altitudes and times.

_____ Transponders (and encoding altimeters). When are they required?

_____ Aerobatic flight, airspace and altitudes; parachute repacking requirements.

_____ Restricted and experimental aircraft limitations.

_____ Aircraft inspections and repairs. Annual and 100-hour inspections.

_____ Airworthiness directives.

_____ Aircraft accidents and incidents.

Suggested break point for the review.

_____ Aerodynamics and airplane systems. *SPFM*, Chapters 2, 3, 4, 5, 7, 23, and 25 and Appendix B.

_____ Four Forces.

_____ Angles of attack and incidence.

_____ Four Forces in straight and level flight.

_____ Wing frost and its effect on takeoff performance.

_____ Torque and P-factor.

_____ Airplane stability.

_____ Rudder.

_____ Load factors in turns.

_____ Wing flaps, operations and purpose.

_____ Engine operations, temperatures and mixture effects.

_____ Ignition system.

_____ Running a tank dry in flight, carburetor or fuel-injected engines.

_____ Carburetors, fuel injection, and mixture controls.

_____ Carburetor icing. Conditions favorable for, and indications of, carburetor icing.

_____ Carburetor heat or alternate air (fuel injection). Effect on fuel/air mixture.

_____ Minimum fuel grades for an engine.

_____ Detonation.

_____ Fuel tanks. Moisture condensation.

_____ Oil system.

_____ Density-altitudes and propeller efficiency.

_____ Pitot-static system: airspeed, altimeter, and vertical speed indicator.

_____ Altimeter and various altitudes.

_____ Setting the altimeter.

_____ Altitude effects on indicated airspeed at stall.

_____ Airspeed markings. White Arc, Green Arc, Yellow Arc, and Red Line.

_____ Maneuvering airspeed. V_A, not marked on airspeed indicator.

Suggested break point.

_____ Aircraft Instruments. *SPFM*, Chapters 3, 15, 19, and 25.

_____ Determining flight conditions from illustrations of instruments.

_____ Magnetic compass.

_____ Deviation.

_____ Compass reactions to turns.

_____ Compass reactions to acceleration or deceleration.

_____ When is the magnetic compass accurate?

_____ Gyro instruments: types and theory of operations.

_____ Airplane operations, performance and stability: *SPFM*, Chapters 2, 3, 6, 9, 12, 17, 19, and 23.

_____ CG position and effects on longitudinal stability.

_____ Density-altitude effects on takeoff, climb, and landing.

_____ Temperature, relative humidity, and pressure-altitude effects on performance.

_____ Finding the effects of temperature on density-altitude from performance charts.

_____ Correcting from indicated to pressure altitude by computer.

_____ Correcting from indicated to pressure altitude using the chart.

_____ What force makes an airplane turn?

_____ Flight control positions for taxiing in varying wind directions.

_____ What causes a spin?

_____ Stall condition of wings in a developed spin.

_____ Stall angle of attack.

_____ Ground effect, performance and stability.

_____ Load factor effect on stall speed.

_____ Angle of attack, what is it?

Suggested break point.

_____ Weather. *SPFM*, Chapter 22; *AW* AC 00-6; and *AWS* AC 00-45.

_____ Physical process of weather.

_____ Earth pressure variations.

_____ Temperature inversion.

_____ Standard temperature and pressure.

_____ Altitudes. True, absolute, density, pressure, and indicated.

_____ Altimeter. Flying from high to low pressure and vice versa.

_____ Altimeter. Temperature effects.

_____ Coriolis and friction effects on wind.

_____ Clouds and moisture.

_____ Frost formation and its effect on flight.

_____ Dew.

_____ Atmospheric stability.

_____ Cloud formation associated with stable or unstable air masses.

_____ Finding cumulus cloud bases. (Temperature minus dewpoint in degrees C, divided by 2.2 or 2.5, depending on source.)

_____ Cloud families.

_____ Lenticular clouds.

_____ Fronts and their characteristics.

_____ Windshear.

_____ Aircraft structural icing.

_____ Requirements for formation of cumulonimbus clouds.

_____ Thunderstorm stages and their characteristics.

_____ Squall lines.

_____ Flight in turbulence.

_____ Fog types.

Suggested break point.

_____ Weather information and briefings available.

_____ Transcribed weather broadcasts.

_____ Types of weather briefings.

_____ METARs, as applicable.

_____ PIREPs.

_____ TAFs, as applicable.

_____ Area forecasts.

_____ SIGMETs, AIRMETs, and Convective SIGMETs.

_____ Winds-aloft forecasts.

_____ Weather depiction charts.

_____ Surface analysis charts.

_____ Significant weather prognostic charts.

_____ Radar summary chart.

_____ Steps in getting a weather briefing.

Suggested break point.

_____ Sectional chart: *SPFM*, Chapters 19, 20, 21, 24, 25, and chart in back of book.

_____ Wildlife refuges.

_____ Airspace and cloud clearance requirements.

_____ Recognizing airspaces by color and symbols.

_____ Airport legends for tower and non-tower airports.

_____ Terrain elevations. Colors and symbols.

_____ Services available at various airports on the chart.

_____ Obstacles and safe obstacle clearances.

_____ Recognizing various navigation aids by the symbols.

Suggested break point.

_____ Engine operations. *SPFM*, Chapters 4, 5, 7, 23, and Appendix B.

_____ Engine cooling. Mixture and airspeed effects.

_____ Throttle, mixture, and prop control for a constant-speed propeller.

_____ Constant-speed propeller. Sequence of control usage for adding and reducing power.

_____ Preflight inspections.

_____ Starting. Handpropping or using the starter.

_____ Starting in cold or hot weather.

_____ Using an external power source.

_____ Special preflight checks after aircraft storage.

_____ Weight and balance: *SPFM*, Chapter 23.

_____ Fuel and oil weight.

_____ Empty weight, standard and basic.

_____ Useful load.

_____ Computing aircraft CG positions by using tables and charts.

_____ Computing moments when aircraft is empty and loaded.

_____ Calculating weight and CG positions to determine the category, Normal or Utility.

_____ Effects of shuffling passengers and baggage around.

_____ Estimating weight and balance for landing.

_____ Cruise control and fuel consumption. *SPFM*, Chapter 23.

_____ Use of power setting charts.

_____ Determining fuel consumption.

_____ Takeoff and landing performance. *SPFM*, Chapter 17.

_____ Use of tabular and graphical takeoff and landing charts.

_____ Crosswind component graph use. Calculating headwind and crosswind components.

Suggested break point.

_____ Safety in flight. *SPFM*, Chapters 10, 13, and 25.

_____ Clearing the area before starting a maneuver.

_____ Power failure after takeoff.

_____ Aircraft and airport lighting. *SPFM*, Chapter 26, *AIM*.

_____ Scanning at night.

_____ Determining another aircraft's path by its position lights.

_____ VFR approaches at night.

_____ Precision approach path indicator.

_____ VASI. Two- and three-light types and indications.

_____ Pulsating approach slope indicators.

_____ Runway high-intensity lights.

_____ Pilot-controlled lighting.

_____ Airport rotating beacons.

_____ Civilian.

_____ Military.

_____ Use during daylight hours.

_____ Airport markings: *SPFM*, Chapter 25, *AIM*.

_____ Precision runways.

_____ Nonprecision runways.

_____ Closed runways.

_____ Displaced thresholds.

_____ Taxi lines and taxi-holding-position markings.

_____ Chevrons (runway unusable for landing, takeoff, or taxiing).

Suggested break point.

_____ Class B, C, D, E, G, and special use airspace: *SPFM*, Chapter 21, *FAR*, and *AIM*.

    _____ Special VFR requirements.

    _____ Class B. Minimum pilot and equipment requirements.

    _____ Class C. Vertical and horizontal limits.

    _____ Class C. Satellite airport operations.

    _____ Class D. Lateral dimensions.

    _____ Class D. Non-tower satellite airports.

    _____ Airport Advisory Area Operations (Flight Service Stations).

    _____ Automatic Terminal Information Service (ATIS).

    _____ Alert areas.

    _____ Military operations area (MOA).

    _____ Radar advisories about other traffic and where to look.

    _____ Radar traffic information service.

    _____ Transponder use and codes.

_____ Airport operations: *SPFM*, Chapters 6, 21, 24, and 25, and *AIM*.

    _____ Communications failure. Procedures when landing at a controlled airport.

    _____ Traffic patterns.

        _____ Wind indicators.

        _____ Segmented circles.

_____ Ground control procedures after landing and during taxi.

    _____ Special VFR. Who to contact?

_____ Flight Plans. *SPFM*, Chapters 24 and 25; and *AIM*.

    _____ Filing.

    _____ Estimated time enroute (ETE).

    _____ Closing the flight plan. With what FAA facility?

    _____ Extending a flight plan – the procedure.

Suggested break point.

_____ Emergency locator transmitter (ELT): *SPFM*, Chapter 21, *FAR*.

    _____ Transmitting frequencies.

    _____ Battery replacement.

    _____ Testing the ELT. Time frame.

    _____ Monitoring the ELT on 121.5 MHz.

_____ Wake turbulence and wing tip vortices. *SPFM*, Chapter 13.

    _____ Creation.

    _____ Actions.

_____ Worst wind and atmospheric conditions.

_____ Departing or landing behind a large aircraft.

_____ Flight Physiology: *SPFM* and *AIM*.

_____ Carbon monoxide symptoms and effects.

_____ Scanning for other aircraft.

_____ Collision course detection.

_____ Hypoxia.

_____ Hyperventilation.

_____ Spatial disorientation.

_____ Night vision adaptation.

_____ FAA advisory circulars.

_____ General numbers for Airmen (60), Airspace (70), and General Operations (90).

_____ How to obtain them (U.S. G.P.O.).

The Knowledge Test.

The instructor or school should make up a Knowledge Test of 60 sample questions from the Internet and other sources, assuring that each area reviewed in this STAGE is covered. Allow 2 hours for this test. A minimum grade of 80 should be required to pass; the missed answers should be reviewed and cleared before endorsing the student to take the FAA Knowledge Test after which the instructor will arrange an appointment with a nearby Computer Testing Designee and sign the endorsement for taking the FAA Knowledge Test.

Endorsement for Aeronautical Knowledge Test: 14CFR §§61.35(a)(1), 61.103(d), and 61.105

I certify that _____ has received the required training of §61.105. I have determined that he/she is prepared for the Private Pilot (ASEL) Knowledge Test.

Signed_____ Date_____

(Print name)_____ CFI No._____ Expiration date_____

Unit 1
Review and Introduction to the Practical Test

At least 3 hours of flight instruction (in preparation) are required within 60 days of the practical test.

Ground Instruction, 3.0 Hours

Review *SPFM*, Chapter 28, and lay out the program for preparation for the practical test, clearing up any questionable areas so that no bad habits have been "set." This review may be done in two or more sessions and should cover the oral portion of the practical test in particular.

Flight: Dual, 2.5 Hours

This Unit will be an introduction to a portion of the flight section of the Practical Test Standards and the instructor will spend as much time as necessary on each maneuver/flight requirement to assure exceeding the standards set out by the PTS. All of the subjects are covered in detail in *SPFM*, Chapter 28.

_____ Preflight check. Use of the manufacturer's checklist is required.

_____ Cockpit management.

_____ Start. Review cold and hot starting and safety procedures. Use of an external power source.

_____ Taxi.

_____ Pretakeoff check. Use checklist.

_____ Radio communications and ATC light signals.

_____ Airport and runway markings and lighting.

_____ Pattern work.

    _____ Normal and crosswind takeoff and climb.

    _____ Normal and crosswind approach and landing.

    _____ Soft-field takeoff and climb.

    _____ Airspeed control after takeoff.

    _____ Soft-field approach and landing.

    _____ Airspeed control.

    _____ Short-field takeoff and climb.

    _____ Airspeed control after takeoff.

    _____ Short-field approach and landing.

    _____ Airspeed control.

_____ No-flaps approach and landing.

_____ Forward slips to landing.

_____ Airspeed control.

_____ Pattern departure.

_____ Performance and ground reference maneuvers.

     _____ Steep turns.

     _____ High-altitude emergency.

     _____ Rectangular course.

     _____ Turns around a point.

     _____ Low-altitude emergency.

_____ Return to traffic pattern.

     _____ Radio communications. UNICOM, MULTICOM, or ATC.

     _____ Prelanding checklist.

     _____ Pattern entry.

     _____ Collision avoidance procedures.

     _____ Downwind.

     _____ Base.

     _____ Final.

     _____ Touchdown and rollout.

_____ Postlanding and shutdown procedures.

_____ Postflight inspection.

_____ Parking and securing.

_____ All takeoffs. Directional control.

_____ All landings. Touchdown and directional control.

_____ Evaluation.

_____ Critique.

_____ Review.

Make and Model _____ Airplane N-No. _____

Ground Instruction _____ Flight Time: Dual _____ Solo _____

Comments _____

_____

_____

_____

Instructor _____ No. _____ Exp. _____

Date _____ Student Initials _____

Assigned Reading—Student: _SPFM_ (Chapter 28); _PTS_ (most current). Instructor: _FIM_ (Chapter 16).

Unit 2
Student Practice

Flight: Solo, 1.0 Hour

The student should practice solo material and maneuvers covered in Unit 1 with a discussion and debriefing by the instructor.

_____ Evaluation.

_____ Critique.

_____ Review.

Make and Model _____ Airplane N-No. _____

Ground Instruction _____ Flight Time: Dual _____ Solo _____

Comments _____

_____

_____

Instructor _____ No. _____ Exp. _____

Date _____ Student Initials _____

Assigned Reading. Student: _SPFM_ (Chapters 10, 12, 14, and 28); _PTS_.

Unit 3
Student Practice

Flight: Solo, 1.0 Hour

The student should practice the Practical Test maneuvers assigned by the instructor, based on performance of Units 1 and 2 of this STAGE. Particular attention should be paid to airspeed and altitude control and remaining within the PTS limits. The following should be practiced:

_____ Steep turns.

_____ Slow flight. Straight and level and turns to headings, ±10°, ±100 feet, +10/-5 knots.

_____ Approach-to-landing stalls; straight ahead and turning.

_____ Takeoff and departure stalls; straight ahead and turning.

_____ Descent for turns around a point.

_____ Turns around a point.

_____ Takeoffs and landings. Normal, crosswind, short- and soft-field, as applicable.

_____ Postlanding, shutdown, and airplane securing procedures.

_____ Review and discussion with instructor.

Make and Model _____ Airplane N-No. _____

Ground Instruction _____ Flight Time: Dual _____ Solo _____

Comments _____

_____

_____

Instructor _____ No. _____ Exp. _____

Date _____ Student Initials _____

Assigned Reading—Student: *SPFM* (Chapters 19–25); *PTS*. Instructor: *FIM* (Chapters 14 and 15).

Unit 4
Navigation

Ground Instruction, 1.0 Hour

_____ Pilotage and dead reckoning. Student plans a short cross-country calculating groundspeed, times, and fuel required.

_____ Review of navigation systems and radar services.

_____ VOR bearings and cross-bearings and/or ADF homing to a station.

 _____ Proper communications procedures when using ATC radar services.

_____ Diversion. Discuss diversions to alternate airports for the planned trip.

_____ Procedures when lost.

 _____ Confess; climb; communicate; comply; conserve; cool, keeping your.

 _____ Use all ATC communications available.

 _____ Dragging the area.

Flight: Dual, 1.5 Hour

Particular attention should be paid to the student's understanding of the following items:

_____ Preflight. Know and be able to explain why the various components of the airplane are checked.

_____ Use and understanding of checklist for prestart, start, and poststart procedures.

_____ External power source use and hot and cold weather starting.

_____ Cockpit management.

_____ Taxi, takeoff, and departure.

_____ Staying within altitude and heading limits during the cruise portion (*SPFM*, Chapter 28; *PTS*).

_____ VOR or ADF operations.

_____ Brief demonstration of procedures when lost.

_____ Awareness of geographical position.

_____ Communications with ATC or Unicoms.

_____ Return to airport.

    _____ Checklist.

    _____ Traffic pattern.

    _____ Airspeed control.

    _____ Landing. Touchdown and directional control.

_____ Postlanding and shutdown procedures.

_____ Evaluation.

_____ Critique.

_____ Review.

Make and Model _____ Airplane N-No. _____

Ground Instruction _____ Flight Time: Dual _____ Solo _____

Comments _____

_____

_____

Instructor _____ No. _____ Exp. _____

Date _____ Student Initials _____

Assigned Reading—Student: *SPFM* (Chapters 12, 14, 15, and 28); *PTS*. Instructor: *FIM* (Chapters 10, 12 and 24).

Unit 5
High Work and Emergency Instrument Flying

Ground Instruction, 1.0 Hour

_____ Review Unit 3, as necessary.

_____ Maneuvering during slow flight. Brief review of the power curve (*SPFM*, Figure 12-13).

_____ Power-off stalls.

_____ Power-on stalls.

_____ Spin awareness.

_____ Six Basic Instrument Maneuvers, hooded.

    _____ Straight and level flight.

    _____ Constant airspeed climbs.

    _____ Constant airspeed descents.

    _____ Turns to headings.

    _____ Recovery from unusual flight attitudes (spirals and approach to stalls).

    _____ Radio communications, navigation systems/facilities, and radar services.

Flight: Dual. 1.0 Hour

The student should practice the following:

_____ Slow flight.

_____ Power-off (approach-to-landing) stalls, straight and turning.

_____ Power-on (takeoff and departure) stalls, straight and turning.

_____ Instrument maneuvers, hooded (full or partial panel).

       _____ Straight and level.

       _____ Constant airspeed climbs.

       _____ Constant airspeed descents.

       _____ Turns to headings.

       _____ Recoveries from unusual flight attitudes (spirals and approach to stalls).

_____ Simulated procedures when lost, with VOR tracking or ADF homing.

_____ Simulate (for a few hundred feet) an emergency descent (maintain airspeed ±10 knots).

_____ Orientation, division of attention and proper planning.

_____ High-altitude emergency approach and landing. Break off at a safe altitude unless it is planned for a landing at the home airport. Use proper communications and collision avoidance procedures in that case.

_____ Selection of suitable emergency landing area within gliding distance.

_____ Use of emergency checklist.

_____ Best glide attitude. Configuration and airspeed (±10 knots).

_____ Judgment of wind direction.

_____ Determine the reason for a malfunction and correct if possible.

_____ Flight pattern to selected landing area, considering altitude, wind, terrain, and obstructions.

_____ Positive control of the airplane at all times.

_____ Postflight instruction.

       _____ Evaluation.

       _____ Critique.

       _____ Review.

Make and Model _____ Airplane N-No. _____

Ground Instruction _____ Flight Time: Dual _____ Solo _____

Comments _____

_____

_____

Instructor _____ No. _____ Exp. _____

Date _____ Student Initials _____

Assigned Reading—Student: _SPFM_ (Chapter 28); _PTS_ (most current).

Unit 6
Systems and Equipment Malfunctions, Emergency Equipment, Survival Gear, and Night Operations

Ground Instruction, 2.0 Hours

Review these subject items as indicated in *SPFM*, Chapter 28, and the PTS. Make sure that the following items have been covered and checked off:

_____ Partial or complete power loss.

_____ Engine roughness or overheating.

_____ Carburetor or induction icing.

_____ Loss of oil pressure.

_____ Fuel starvation.

_____ Electrical system malfunction.

_____ Flight instruments malfunction.

_____ Landing gear or flap malfunction.

_____ Inoperative trim.

_____ Inadvertent door or window opening.

_____ Structural icing.

_____ Smoke/fire/engine compartment fire.

_____ Emergency descent.

_____ Any other emergency appropriate to the airplane provided for flight test.

_____ Emergency equipment and survival gear.

    _____ Location in airplane.

    _____ Operation or use.

    _____ Servicing requirements.

    _____ Method of safe storage.

    _____ Equipment and survival gear appropriate for operation in various climates and topographical environments.

    _____ Emergency checklist.

_____ Night flying.

    _____ Physiology. Rods, cones, and other factors.

    _____ Lighting. Airplane, airport, and obstruction.

        _____ Pilot-controlled airport lighting.

    _____ Personal equipment essential.

    _____ Night orientation. Navigation and chart reading techniques.

    _____ Safety precautions and emergencies peculiar to night flying.

_____ Review general CRM and ADM as required for the private pilot.

_____ Evaluation.

_____ Critique.

_____ Review.

Make and Model _____ Airplane N-No. _____

Ground Instruction _____ Flight Time: Dual _____ Solo _____

Comments _____

_____

_____

Instructor _____ No. _____ Exp. _____

Date _____ Student Initials _____

Assigned Reading—None.

Unit 7
Stage Check: Practical Test

This flight is the final stage check in preparation for the student's FAA Practical Test. The check pilot will cover as much of the oral and flight portions as possible in the time allowed. Particular attention should be given to those weak areas as shown by the preparatory dual flights in this STAGE. The check pilot may, after this flight, call for extra time and a recheck.

Check Flight: Ground, 1.0 Hour; Flight Time, 2.0 Hours

_____ Evaluation.

_____ Critique.

_____ Review.

    _____ Headwork.

    _____ Air discipline.

    _____ Attitude toward flying.

_____ Recommendation for the Practical Test.

_____ Recommendation for extra time and recheck.

Comments _____

_____

_____

Endorsement for Flight Proficiency/Practical Test: 14 CFR §§61.102(f), 61.107(b), and 61.109

I certify that _____ has received the required training of paragraphs 61.107 and 61.109. I have determined that he/she is prepared for the Private Pilot (ASEL) Practical Test.

Signed_____ Date_____

(Print name)_____ CFI No._____ Expiration date_____

Unit 8
FAA Practical Test

Checklist. Allow 2.0 Hours ground and 2.0 Hours flight for the Practical Test

_____ Student pilot certificate current, plus medical certificate, if required.

    _____ Student certificate properly endorsed for solo and cross-country.

_____ Logbook. All endorsements correct, including presolo written, solo, solo cross-country, stage checks, and recommendations for Knowledge and Practical Tests.

_____ Knowledge Test results.

_____ Charts, *Airport/Facility Directory*, sectional and approach charts, as needed.

_____ Airplane papers and logbooks in order.

_____ Examiner's fee.

_____ Graduation certificate, if applicable.

_____ Application for practical test correctly filled out and signed.

Date _____

PASSED _____ Temporary Certificate Issued _____

FAA Inspector or Examiner _____

FAILED _____ Recheck required.

NOTES AND COMMENTS _____

_____

_____

Student Initials _____

A/FD Excerpts and Legend

TENNESSEE

SEWANEE
FRANKLIN CO (UOS) 1 E UTC−6(−5DT) N35°12.24' W85°53.92' **ATLANTA**
1953 B **FUEL** 80, 100LL **L−14H**
RWY 06−24: H3300X50 (ASPH) S−15, D−25 LIRL
RWY 06: VASI(V2L)—GA 3.5°TCH 28'. Trees. RWY 24: VASI(V2L)—GA 4.0° TCH 31'. Trees.
AIRPORT REMARKS: Attended 1400−2300Z‡. Sporadic crosswinds and turbulence. Deer on and invof rwy. Rwy 06
effective gradient up 0.9%. Portion exceeds 1.8%. Rwy 06−24 pavement cracking. Rotating bcn located on top of
hangar.
COMMUNICATIONS: CTAF/UNICOM 122.8
NASHVILLE FSS (BNA) TF 1−800−WX−BRIEF. NOTAM FILE BNA.
RADIO AIDS TO NAVIGATION: NOTAM FILE BNA.
SHELBYVILLE (L) VOR/DME 109.0 SYI Chan 27 N35°33.72' W86°26.35' 130° 34.1 NM to fld. 810/01W.
SEWANEE NDB (MHW) 275 UOS N35°12.26' W85°53.75' at fld. (VFR only).

COLUMBIA/MOUNT PLEASANT
MAURY CO (MRC) 2 NE UTC−6(−5DT) N35°33.25' W87°10.74' **ATLANTA**
681 B S4 **FUEL** 100LL, JET A OX 1,2 **H−4H, L−14G**
RWY 06−24: H6003X100 (ASPH) S−28, D−43, DT−70 MIRL **IAP**
RWY 06: PAPI(P4R). Trees. RWY 24: ODALS. PAPI(P4L). Trees.
RWY 17−35: 2000X200 (TURF)
RWY 17: Trees. RWY 35: Trees.
AIRPORT REMARKS: Attended continuously. PAEW invof rwys 1300−2300Z‡. Rwy 17−35 surface is rough and
unmarked. ACTIVATE ODALS Rwy 24—CTAF.
WEATHER DATA SOURCES: AWOS−3 128.625 (931) 379−0844.
COMMUNICATIONS: CTAF/UNICOM 122.8
JACKSON FSS (MKL) TF 1−800−WX−BRIEF. NOTAM FILE MKL.
Ⓡ MEMPHIS CENTER APP/DEP CON 125.85
RADIO AIDS TO NAVIGATION: NOTAM FILE MKL.
GRAHAM (L) VORTAC 111.6 GHM Chan 53 N35°50.04' W87°27.11' 138° 21.4 NM to fld. 770/03E.
NDB (MHW) 365 PBC N35°36.49' W87°05.48' 234° 5.4 NM to fld.
SDF 108.7 MRC Rwy 23.

ALABAMA

HUNTSVILLE
HUNTSVILLE INTL−CARL T JONES FLD (HSV) 9 SW UTC−6(−5DT) **ATLANTA**
N34°38.43' W86°46.39' **H−4H, L−14H**
629 B S4 **FUEL** 100LL, JET A OX 1, 2, 3, 4 LRA ARFF Index C **IAP**
RWY 18L−36R: H10000X150 (ASPH−GRVD) S−90, D−200, DT−350, DDT−850 HIRL
RWY 18L: MALSR. PAPI(P4R)—GA 3.0° TCH 70'. Pole.
RWY 36R: REIL. VASI(V4L)—GA 3.0° TCH 55'. Thld dsplcd 200'. Pgt tfc.
RWY 18R−36L: H8000X150 (ASPH−GRVD) S−90, D−200, DT−350, DDT−850 HIRL CL
RWY 18R: ALSF2. TDZL. Rgt tfc. RWY 36L: MALSR
RUNWAY DECLARED DISTANCE INFORMATION
RWY 18L: TORA−10000 TODA−10000 ASDA−9800 LDA−9800
RWY 36R: TORA−10000 TODA−10000 ASDA−10000 LDA−9800
AIRPORT REMARKS: Attended continuously. Migratory birds wild life refuge S and W of arpt. PAEW W of General
Aviation apron. Twy X and Twy 'ONAN' CLOSED indef. Approximately 300 ft of Twy J south of the terminal;
southeast portion of Twy G where it enters the air carrier apron; and approximately 75 ft of Twy E between Twys
E5 and E6 are not visible from the twr. Intersection of Twy J and svc road is uncontrolled. 24 hr PPR for
unscheduled air carrier ops with more than 30 passenger seats call arpt manager 256−461−1116 extension
265. Rwy 18L−36R CLOSED to air carrier ops with more than 30 passenger seats. When twr clsd; ACTIVATE
HIRL Rwys 18R−36L and 18L−36R and Twy lgts—CTAF. Flight Notification Service (ADCUS) avbl.
WEATHER DATA SOURCES: ASOS (256) 772−8074. LLWAS.
COMMUNICATIONS: CTAF 127.6 ATIS 121.25 UNICOM 122.95
ANNISTON FSS (ANB) TF 1−800−WX−BRIEF. NOTAM FILE HSV.
RCO 122.2 (ANNISTON FSS)
Ⓡ APP CON 125.6 (360°−179°) 118.05 (180°−359°)118.75 (1200−0600Z‡)
Ⓡ DEP CON 125.6 (359°−179°) 118.05 (180°−358°) 120.35 (1200−0600Z‡)
MEMPHIS CENTER APP/DEP CON 120.8 (0600−1200Z‡)
TOWER 127.6 (1200−0600Z‡, other times by NOTAM) GND CON 121.9 CLNC DEL 120.35
AIRSPACE: CLASS C svc 1200−0600Z‡ other times CLASS E.
RADIO AIDS TO NAVIGATION: NOTAM FILE DCU.
DECATUR (L) VORW/DME 112.8 DCU Chan 75 N34°38.90' W86°56.37' 094° 8.3 NM to fld. 590/01W.
HIWAS.
CAPSHAW NDB (MHW) 350 CWH N34°46.42' W86°46.74' 179° 8 NM to fld. NOTAM FILE HSV.
ILS 109.3 I−HSV Rwy 18R.
ILS 108.5 I−ELL Rwy 36L.
ILS 111.9 I−TVN Rwy 18L.
ASR

GENERAL INFORMATION
TABLE OF CONTENTS

General Information..
Abbreviations ....
Legend, Airport/Facility Directory ....
Airport/Facility Directory ....
Seaplane Landing Areas ....
Notices ....
Land and Hold Short Operations (LAHSO)..................................
FAA and National Weather Service Telephone Numbers.......................
Air Route Traffic Control Centers/Flight Service Station Communication Frequencies...............
FSDO Addresses/Telephone Numbers ....
Preferred IFR Routes/VFR Waypoints ....
VOR Receiver Check ....
Parachute Jumping Areas ....
Aeronautical Chart Bulletin ....
National Weather Service (NWS) Upper Air Observing Stations ....
Enroute Flight Advisory Service (EFAS) ....

ABBREVIATIONS

The following abbreviations are those commonly used within this Directory. Other abbreviations may be found in the Legend and are not duplicated below. The abbreviations presented are intended to represent grammatical variations of the basic form. (Example—"req" may mean "request", "requesting", "requested", or "requests").

abv	above	lgts	lights
acft	aircraft	med	medium
AER	approach end rwy	MSL	mean sea level
AFSS	Automated Flight Service Station	MSAW	minimum safe altitude warning
AGL	above ground level	NFCT	non-federal control tower
apch	approach	ngt	night
arpt	airport	npi	non precision instrument
avbl	available	NSTD	nonstandard
bcn	beacon	ntc	notice
blo	below	opr	operate, operator, operational
byd	beyond	ops	operations
clsd	closed	OTS	out of service
ctc	contact	ovrn	overrun
dalgt	daylight	PAEW	personnel and equipment working
dsplcd	displaced	p-line	power line
durn	duration	PPR	prior permission required
eff	effective	req	request
emerg	emergency	rgt tfc	right traffic
extd	extend	rqr	require
FBO	fixed—base operator	RSRS	reduced same runway separation
FCT	FAA Contract Tower	rwy	runway
fld	field	SPB	Seaplane Base
FSS	Flight Service Station	SR	sunrise
hr	hour	SS	sunset
indef	indefinite	svc	service
ints	intensity	tfc	traffic
invof	in the vicinity of	thld	threshold
LAA	Local Airport Advisory	tkf	take-off
ldg	landing	tmpry	temporary
lgtd	lighted	twr	tower
		twy	taxiway

GENERAL INFORMATION

This Airport/Facility Directory is a Civil Flight Information Publication published and distributed every eight weeks by the National Ocean Service, NOAA, Department of Commerce, Silver Spring, Maryland 20910. It is designed for use with Aeronautical Charts covering the conterminous United States, Puerto Rico and the Virgin Islands.

It contains an Airport/Facility Directory of all airports, seaplane bases and heliports open to the public, communications data, navigational facilities and certain special notices and procedures.

CORRECTIONS, COMMENTS, AND/OR PROCUREMENT

CRITICAL information such as equipment malfunction, abnormal field conditions, hazards to flight, etc., should be reported as soon as possible to the nearest FAA facility, either in person or by reverse charge telephone call.

FOR REVISIONS/UPDATES/CORRECTIONS TO THIS PUBLICATION:
Forward changes to:
Federal Aviation Administration
Aeronautical Information Services, ATA—100
800 Independence Ave. S.W.
Washington, D.C. 20591
Toll Free 1-800-457-6656
FAX (202) 267-5322

DIRECTORY LEGEND
SAMPLE

CITY NAME
AIRPORT NAME (ORL) 4 E UTC–5(–4DT) N28°32.72′ W81°21.17′ **JACKSONVILLE**
200 B S4 **FUEL** 100, JET A OX 1, 2, 3 TPA—1000(800) AOE ARFF Index A Not insp. **COPTER**
H–4G, L–19C
IAP

18 → **RWY 18–36:** H12004X300 (CONC–GRVD) HIRL
RWY 18: LDIN. ALSF1. TDZL. REIL. PAPI(P2R)—GA 3.0° TCH 36′.
Thld dsplcd 300′. Trees. Rgt tfc. Arresting device. 0.3% up.
RWY 36: ALSF1. 0.4% down.
RWY 09–27: H6000X150 (ASPH-PFC) S–90, D–160, DT–300–PCN
80 R/B/W/T HIRL CL 0.4% up E
RWY 09: ALSF1. Trees. **RWY 27:** REIL. Rgt tfc.
RUNWAY DECLARED DISTANCE INFORMATION
RWY 09: TORA–6000 TODA–6700 ASDA–5700 LDA–5500
RWY 27: TORA–6000 TODA–6000 ASDA–6000 LDA–5700
19 → **AIRPORT REMARKS:** Special Air Traffic Rules—Part 93, see Regulatory
Notices. Attended 1200-0300Z‡. Parachute Jumping. CAUTION:
Cattle and deer on arpt. Acft 100,000 lbs or over ctc Director of
Aviation for approval 305–894-9831. Fee for all airline charters,
travel clubs and certain revenue producing acft. Flight Notification
Service (ADCUS) available.
20 → **WEATHER DATA SOURCES:** AWOS-1 120.3 (202) 426-8000. LLWAS.
21 → **COMMUNICATIONS: CTAF** 118.7 **ATIS** ARR 127.25 DEP 134.025
(303) 342–0820 **UNICOM** 122.95
NAME FSS (ORL) on arpt. 123.65 122.65 122.2.
TF 1–800–WX–BRIEF. NOTAM FILE ORL. **← 22**
NAME RCO 112.2T 112.1R (NAME FSS)
Ⓡ NAME APP/DEP CON 128.35 (1200–0400Z‡)
TOWER 118.7 NFCT (1200–0400Z‡) **GND CON** 121.7 **GCO** 135.075 (ORLANDO CLNC) **CLNC DEL** 125.55
PRE TAXI CLNC 125.5
23 → **AIRSPACE: CLASS B** See VFR Terminal Area Chart.
24 → **RADIO AIDS TO NAVIGATION:** NOTAM FILE MCO. VHF/DF ctc FSS.
(H) ABVORTAC 112.2 MCO Chan 59 N28°32.55′ W81°20.12′ at fld. 1110/8E.
TWEB avbl 1300–0100Z‡. VOR unusable 050°–060° byd 15 NM blo 5000′.
HERNY NDB (LOM) 221 OR N28°37.40′ W81°21.05′ 177° 5.4 NM to fld.
ILS 109.9 I–ORL Rwy 18. LOM HERNY NDB.
ASR/PAR (1200–0400Z‡)
25 → **COMM/NAVAID REMARKS:** Emerg frequency 121.5 not avbl at twr.
• •
HELIPAD H1: H100X75 (ASPH)
HELIPAD H2: H60X60 (ASPH)
HELIPORT REMARKS: Helipad H1 lctd on general aviation side and H2 lctd on air carrier side of arpt. **1**
• •
187 TPA 1000(813)
WATERWAY 13–31: 5000X300 (WATER)
SEAPLANE REMARKS: Birds roosting and feeding areas along river banks. Seaplanes operating adjacent to NE side of
arpt not visible from twr and are required to ctc twr.

All Bearings and Radials are Magnetic unless otherwise specified.
All mileages are nautical unless otherwise noted.
All times are UTC except as noted.
The horizontal reference datum of this publication is North American Datum of 1983 (NAD83), which for charting purposes
is considered equivalent to World Geodetic System 1984 (WGS 84).

DIRECTORY LEGEND

⑧ SKETCH LEGEND

RUNWAYS/LANDING AREAS

Hard Surfaced . . . .

Metal Surface . . . .

Sod, Gravel, etc. . . . .

Light Plane, ...
Ski Landing Area or Water

Under Construction . . . . .

Closed . . . .

Helicopter Landings Area . . . . (H)

Displaced Threshold . . . .

Taxiway, Apron and Stopways . .

MISCELLANEOUS BASE AND CULTURAL FEATURES

Buildings . . . .

Power Lines . . . .

Fence . . . .

Towers . . . .

Tanks . . . .

Oil Well . . . .

Smoke Stack . . . .

Obstruction . . . .   5812 ∧

Controlling Obstruction . . . .   +5812

Trees . . . .

Populated Places . . . .

Cuts and Fills . . . . . .   Cut   Fill

Cliffs and Depressions . .

Ditch . . . .

Hill . . . .

RADIO AIDS TO NAVIGATION

VORTAC . . .   VOR . . . .

VOR/DME . .   NDB . . . .

TACAN . . . .   NDB/DME . . . .

MISCELLANEOUS AERONAUTICAL FEATURES

Airport Beacon . . . .   ✩

Wind Cone . . . .

Landing Tee . . . .

Tetrahedron . . . .

Control Tower . . . .   ᵇ

APPROACH LIGHTING SYSTEMS

A dot ' • ' portrayed with approach lighting letter identifier indicates sequenced flashing lights (F) installed with the approach lighting system e.g. (A₁) Negative symbology, e.g., ● indicates Pilot Controlled Lighting (PCL).

Runway Centerline Lighting . . . . .

(A) Approach Lighting System ALSF-2 . .

(A₁) Approach Lighting System ALSF-1 . .

(A₂) Short Approach Lighting System SALS/SALSF . . . .

(A₃) Simplified Short Approach Lighting System (SSALR) with RAIL . . . . .

(A₄) Medium Intensity Approach Lighting System (MALS and MALSF)/(SSALS

(A₄) and SSALF) . . . .

(A₅) Medium Intensity Approach Lighting System (MALSR) and RAIL . . . . . .

Ⓧ Omnidirectional Approach Lighting System (ODALS) . . . .

(D) Navy Parallel Row and Cross Bar . . .

(I) Air Force Overrun . . . .

(V) Visual Approach Slope Indicator with Standard Threshold Clearance provided

(V₂) Pulsating Visual Approach Slope Indicator (PVASI)

(V₃) Visual Approach Slope Indicator with a threshold crossing height to accomodate long bodied or jumbo aircraft

(V₄) Tri-color Visual Approach Slope Indicator (TRCV)

(V₅) Approach Path Alignment Panel (APAP)

(P) Precision Approach Path Indicator (PAPI)

DIRECTORY LEGEND
LEGEND

This Directory is an alphabetical listing of data on record with the FAA on all airports that are open to the public, associated terminal control facilities, air route traffic control centers and radio aids to navigation within the conterminous United States, Puerto Rico and the Virgin Islands. Airports are listed alphabetically by associated city name and cross referenced by airport name. Facilities associated with an airport, but with a different name, are listed individually under their own name, as well as under the airport with which they are associated.

The listing of an airport in this directory merely indicates the airport operator's willingness to accommodate transient aircraft, and does not represent that the facility conforms with any Federal or local standards, or that it has been approved for use on the part of the general public.

The information on obstructions is taken from reports submitted to the FAA. It has not been verified in all cases. Pilots are cautioned that objects not indicated in this tabulation (or on charts) may exist which can create a hazard to flight operation.

Detailed specifics concerning services and facilities tabulated within this directory are contained in Aeronautical Information Manual, Basic Flight Information and ATC Procedures.

The legend items that follow explain in detail the contents of this Directory and are keyed to the circled numbers on the sample on the preceding pages.

① CITY/AIRPORT NAME

Airports and facilities in this directory are listed alphabetically by associated city and state. Where the city name is different from the airport name the city name will appear on the line above the airport name. Airports with the same associated city name will be listed alphabetically by airport name and will be separated by a dashed rule line. All others will be separated by a solid rule line. (Designated Helipads and Seaplane Landing Areas (Water) associated with a land airport will be separated by a dotted line.)

② LOCATION IDENTIFIER

A three or four character code assigned to airports. These identifiers are used by ATC in lieu of the airport name in flight plans, flight strips and other written records and computer operations.

③ AIRPORT LOCATION

Airport location is expressed as distance and direction from the center of the associated city in nautical miles and cardinal points, i.e., 4 NE.

④ TIME CONVERSION

Hours of operation of all facilities are expressed in Coordinated Universal Time (UTC) and shown as "Z" time. The directory indicates the number of hours to be subtracted from UTC to obtain local standard time and local daylight saving time UTC–5(–4DT). The symbol ‡ indicates that during periods of Daylight Saving Time effective hours will be one hour earlier than shown. In those areas where daylight saving time is not observed that (–4DT) and ‡ will not be shown. All states observe daylight savings time except Arizona, Hawaii and that portion of Indiana in the Eastern Time Zone and Puerto Rico and the Virgin Islands.

⑤ GEOGRAPHIC POSITION OF AIRPORT

Positions are shown in degrees, minutes and hundredths of a minute and represent the approximate center of mass of all usable runways.

⑥ CHARTS

The Sectional Chart and Low and High Altitude Enroute Chart and panel on which the airport or facility is located. Helicopter Chart locations will be indicated as, i.e., COPTER.

⑦ INSTRUMENT APPROACH PROCEDURES

IAP indicates an airport for which a prescribed (Public Use) FAA Instrument Approach Procedure has been published.

⑧ AIRPORT SKETCH

The airport sketch, when provided, depicts the airport and related topographical information as seen from the air and should be used in conjunction with the text. It is intended as a guide for pilots in VFR conditions. Symbology that is not self-explanatory will be reflected in the sketch legend. The airport sketch will be oriented with True North at the top. Airport sketches will be added incrementally.

⑨ ELEVATION

The highest point of an airport's usable runways measured in feet from mean sea level. When elevation is sea level it will be indicated as (00). When elevation is below sea level a minus (–) sign will precede the figure.

⑩ ROTATING LIGHT BEACON

B indicates rotating beacon is available. Rotating beacons operate dusk to dawn unless otherwise indicated in AIRPORT REMARKS.

⑪ SERVICING

S1: Minor airframe repairs.

S2: Minor airframe and minor powerplant repairs.

S3: Major airframe and minor powerplant repairs.

S4: Major airframe and major powerplant repairs.

DIRECTORY LEGEND

⑫ FUEL

CODE	FUEL
80	Grade 80 gasoline (Red)
100	Grade 100 gasoline (Green)
100LL	100LL gasoline (low lead) (Blue)
115	Grade 115 gasoline
A	Jet A—Kerosene freeze point–40° C.
A1	Jet A-1—Kerosene freeze point–47°C.
A1+	Jet A-1—Kerosene with icing inhibitor, freeze point–47° C.
B	Jet B—Wide-cut turbine fuel, freeze point–50° C.

CODE	FUEL
B+	Jet B—Wide-cut turbine fuel with icing inhibitor, freeze point–50° C.
J8	(JP–8 Military specification) Jet A–1, kerosene with icing inhibitor, freeze point–47°C.
J8+100	(JP–8 Mil spec) Jet A–1, Kerosene with FS–II (Fuel System Icing Inhibitor), FP (Freeze Point) minus 47°C, with fuel additive package that improves thermo stability characteristics of JP–8.
MOGAS	Automobile gasoline which is to be used as aircraft fuel.

NOTE: Automobile Gasoline. Certain automobile gasoline may be used in specific aircraft engines if a FAA supplemental type cetificate has been obtained. Automobile gasoline which is to be used in aircraft engines will be identified as "MOGAS", however, the grade/type and other octane rating will not be published.

Data shown on fuel availability represents the most recent information the publisher has been able to acquire. Because of a variety of factors, the fuel listed may not always be obtainable by transient civil pilots. Confirmation of availability of fuel should be made directly with fuel dispensers at locations where refueling is planned.

⑬ OXYGEN

OX 1	High Pressure
OX 2	Low Pressure

OX 3	High Pressure—Replacement Bottles
OX 4	Low Pressure—Replacement Bottles

⑭ TRAFFIC PATTERN ALTITUDE

Traffic Pattern Altitude (TPA)—The first figure shown is TPA above mean sea level. The second figure in parentheses is TPA above airport elevation.

⑮ AIRPORT OF ENTRY, LANDING RIGHTS, AND CUSTOMS USER FEE AIRPORTS

U.S. CUSTOMS USER FEE AIRPORT—Private Aircraft operators are frequently required to pay the costs associated with customs processing.

AOE—Airport of Entry—A customs Airport of Entry where permission from U.S. Customs is not required, however, at least one hour advance notice of arrival must be furnished.

LRA—Landing Rights Airport—Application for permission to land must be submitted in advance to U.S. Customs. At least one hour advance notice of arrival must be furnished.

NOTE: Advance notice of arrival at both an AOE and LRA airport may be included in the flight plan when filed in Canada or Mexico, where Flight Notification Service (ADCUS) is available the airport remark will indicate this service. This notice will also be treated as an application for permission to land in the case of an LRA. Although advance notice of arrival may be relayed to Customs through Mexico, Canadian, and U.S. Communications facilities by flight plan, the aircraft operator is solely responsible for insuring that Customs receives the notification. (See Customs, Immigration and Naturalization, Public Health and Agriculture Department requirements in the International Flight Information Manual for further details.)

⑯ CERTIFICATED AIRPORT (FAR 139)

Airports serving Department of Transportation certified carriers and certified under FAR, Part 139, are indicated by the ARFF index; i.e., ARFF Index A, which relates to the availability of crash, fire, rescue equipment.

FAR—PART 139 CERTIFICATED AIRPORTS
INDICES AND AIRCRAFT RESCUE AND FIRE FIGHTING EQUIPMENT REQUIREMENTS

Airport Index	Required No. Vehicles	Aircraft Length	Scheduled Departures	Agent + Water for Foam
A	1	<90'	≥1	500#DC or HALON 1211 or 450#DC + 100 gal H_2O
B	1 or 2	≥90', <126'	≥5	Index A + 1500 gal H_2O
		≥126', <159'	<5	
C	2 or 3	≥126', <159'	≥5	Index A + 3000 gal H_2O
		≥159', <200'	<5	
D	3	≥159', <200'	≥5	Index A + 4000 gal H_2O
		>200'	<5	
E	3	≥200'	≥5	Index A + 6000 gal H_2O

> Greater Than; < Less Than; ≥ Equal or Greater Than; ≤ Equal or Less Than; H_2O–Water; DC–Dry Chemical.

NOTE: The listing of ARFF index does not necessarily assure coverage for non-air carrier operations or at other than prescribed times for air carrier. ARFF Index Ltd.—indicates ARFF coverage may or may not be available, for information contact airport manager prior to flight.

DIRECTORY LEGEND

⑰ FAA INSPECTION

All airports not inspected by FAA will be identified by the note: Not insp. This indicates that the airport information has been provided by the owner or operator of the field.

⑱ RUNWAY DATA

Runway information is shown on two lines. That information common to the entire runway is shown on the first line while information concerning the runway ends are shown on the second or following line. Lengthy information will be placed in the Airport Remarks.

Runway direction, surface, length, width, weight bearing capacity, lighting, slope and appropriate remarks are shown for each runway. Direction, length, width, lighting and remarks are shown for sealanes. The full dimensions of helipads are shown, i.e., 50X150.

RUNWAY SURFACE AND LENGTH

Runway lengths prefixed by the letter "H" indicate that the runways are hard surfaced (concrete, asphalt). If the runway length is not prefixed, the surface is sod, clay, etc. The runway surface composition is indicated in parentheses after runway length as follows:

(AFSC)—Aggregate friction seal coat	(GRVD)—Grooved	(RFSC)—Rubberized friction seal coat
(ASPH)—Asphalt	(GRVL)—Gravel, or cinders	(TURF)—Turf
(CONC)—Concrete	(PFC)—Porous friction courses	(TRTD)—Treated
(DIRT)—Dirt	(PSP)—Pierced steel plank	(WC)—Wire combed

RUNWAY WEIGHT BEARING CAPACITY

Runway strength data shown in this publication is derived from available information and is a realistic estimate of capability at an average level of activity. It is not intended as a maximum allowable weight or as an operating limitation. Many airport pavements are capable of supporting limited operations with gross weights of 25-50% in excess of the published figures. Permissible operating weights, insofar as runway strengths are concerned, are a matter of agreement between the owner and user. When desiring to operate into any airport at weights in excess of those published in the publication, users should contact the airport management for permission. Add 000 to figure following S, D, DT, DDT, AUW, etc., for gross weight capacity:

S—Single-wheel type landing gear. (DC-3), (C-47), (F-15), etc.
D—Dual-wheel type landing gear. (DC-6), etc.
T—Twin-wheel type landing gear. (DC-6), (C-9A), etc.
ST—Single-tandem type landing gear. (C-130).
SBTT—Single-belly twin tandem landing gear (KC-10).
DT—Dual-tandem type landing gear, (707), etc.
TT—Twin-tandem type (includes quadricycle) landing gear (707), (B-52), (C-135), etc.
TRT—Triple-tandem landing gear, (C-17)
DDT—Double dual-tandem landing gear. (E4A/747).
TDT—Twin delta-tandem landing gear. (C-5, Concorde).
AUW—All up weight. Maximum weight bearing capacity for any aircraft irrespective of landing gear configuration.
SWL—Single Wheel Loading. (This includes information submitted in terms of Equivalent Single Wheel Loading (ESWL) and Single Isolated Wheel Loading). SWL figures are shown in thousands of pounds with the last three figures being omitted.
PSI—Pounds per square inch. PSI is the actual figure expressing maximum pounds per square inch runway will support, e.g., (SWL 000/PSI 535).

Quadricycle and dual-tandem are considered virtually equal for runway weight bearing consideration, as are single-tandem and dual-wheel. Omission of weight bearing capacity indicates information unknown.

The ACN/PCN System is the ICAO method of reporting pavement strength for pavements with bearing strengths greater than 12,500 pounds. The Pavement Classification Number (PCN) is established by an engineering assessment of the runway. The PCN is for use in conjunction with an Aircraft Classification Number (ACN). Consult the Aircraft Flight Manual or other appropriate source for ACN tables or charts. Currently, ACN data may not be available for all aircraft. If an ACN table or chart is available, the ACN can be calculated by taking into account the aircraft weight, the pavement type, and the subgrade category. For runways that have been evaluated under the ACN/PCN system, the PCN will be shown as a five part code (e.g. PCN 80 R/B/W/T). Details of the coded format are as follows:

(1) The PCN NUMBER—The reported PCN indicates that an aircraft with an ACN equal or less than the reported PCN can operate on the pavement subject to any limitation on the tire pressure.

(2) The type of pavement:
   R — Rigid
   F — Flexible

(3) The pavement subgrade category:
   A — High
   B — Medium
   C — Low
   D — Ultra-low

(4) The maximum tire pressure authorized for the pavement:
   W — High, no limit
   X — Medium, limited to 217 psi
   Y — Low, limited to 145 psi
   Z — Very low, limited to 73 psi

(5) Pavement evaluation method:
   T — Technical evaluation
   U — By experience of aircraft using the pavement

NOTE: Prior permission from the airport controlling authority is required when the ACN of the aircraft exceeds the published PCN or aircraft tire pressure exceeds the published limits.

DIRECTORY LEGEND

RUNWAY LIGHTING

Lights are in operation sunset to sunrise. Lighting available by prior arrangement only or operating part of the night only and/or pilot controlled and with specific operating hours are indicated under airport remarks. Since obstructions are usually lighted, obstruction lighting is not included in this code. Unlighted obstructions on or surrounding an airport will be noted in airport remarks. Runway lights nonstandard (NSTD) are systems for which the light fixtures are not FAA approved L-800 series: color, intensity, or spacing does not meet FAA standards. Nonstandard runway lights, VASI, or any other system not listed below will be shown in airport remarks.

Temporary, emergency or limited runway edge lighting such as flares, smudge pots, lanterns or portable runway lights will also be shown in airport remarks. Types of lighting are shown with the runway or runway end they serve.

NSTD—Light system fails to meet FAA standards.
LIRL—Low Intensity Runway Lights.
MIRL—Medium Intensity Runway Lights.
HIRL—High Intensity Runway Lights.
RAIL—Runway Alignment Indicator Lights.
REIL—Runway End Identifier Lights.
CL—Centerline Lights.
TDZL—Touchdown Zone Lights.
ODALS—Omni Directional Approach Lighting System.
AF OVRN—Air Force Overrun 1000' Standard Approach Lighting System.
LDIN—Lead-In Lighting System.
MALS—Medium Intensity Approach Lighting System.
MALSF—Medium Intensity Approach Lighting System with Sequenced Flashing Lights.
MALSR—Medium Intensity Approach Lighting System with Runway Alignment Indicator Lights.

SALS—Short Approach Lighting System.
SALSF—Short Approach Lighting System with Sequenced Flashing Lights.
SSALS—Simplified Short Approach Lighting System.
SSALF—Simplified Short Approach Lighting System with Sequenced Flashing Lights.
SSALR—Simplified Short Approach Lighting System with Runway Alignment Indicator Lights.
ALSAF—High Intensity Approach Lighting System with Sequenced Flashing Lights.
ALSF1—High Intensity Approach Lighting System with Sequenced Flashing Lights, Category I, Configuration.
ALSF2—High Intensity Approach Lighting System with Sequenced Flashing Lights, Category II, Configuration.
VASI—Visual Approach Slope Indicator System.

NOTE: Civil ALSF-2 may be operated as SSALR during favorable weather conditions.

VISUAL GLIDESLOPE INDICATORS

APAP—A system of panels, which may or may not be lighted, used for alignment of approach path.

PNIL	APAP on left side of runway	PNIR	APAP on right side of runway

PAPI—Precision Approach Path Indicator

P2L	2-identical light units placed on left side of runway	P4L	4-identical light units placed on left side of runway
P2R	2-identical light units placed on right side of runway	P4R	4-identical light units placed on right side of runway

PVASI—Pulsating/steady burning visual approach slope indicator, normally a single light unit projecting two colors.

PSIL-	PVASI on left side of runway	PSIR-	PVASI on right side of runway

SAVASI—Simplified Abbreviated Visual Approach Slope Indicator

S2L	2-box SAVASI on left side of runway	S2R	2-box SAVASI on right side of runway

TRCV—Tri-color visual approach slope indicator, normally a single light unit projecting three colors.

TRIL	TRCV on left side of runway	TRIR	TRCV on right side of runway

VASI—Visual Approach Slope Indicator

V2L	2-box VASI on left side of runway	V6L	6-box VASI on left side of runway
V2R	2-box VASI on right side of runway	V6R	6-box VASI on right side of runway
V4L	4-box VASI on left side of runway	V12	12-box VASI on both sides of runway
V4R	4-box VASI on right side of runway	V16	16-box VASI on both sides of runway

NOTE: Approach slope angle and threshold crossing height will be shown when available; i.e., —GA 3.5° TCH 37'.

PILOT CONTROL OF AIRPORT LIGHTING

Key Mike	Function
7 times within 5 seconds	Highest intensity available
5 times within 5 seconds	Medium or lower intensity (Lower REIL or REIL-Off)
3 times within 5 seconds	Lowest intensity available (Lower REIL or REIL-Off)

Available systems will be indicated in the Airport Remarks, as follows:

ACTIVATE MALSR Rwy 07, HIRL Rwy 07–25–122.8 (or CTAF).
or
ACTIVATE MIRL Rwy 18–36–122.8 (or CTAF).
or
ACTIVATE VASI and REIL, Rwy 07–122.8 (or CTAF).

Where the airport is not served by an instrument approach procedure and/or has an independent type system of different specification installed by the airport sponsor, descriptions of the type lights, method of control, and operating frequency will be explained in clear text. See AIM, ''Basic Flight Information and ATC Procedures,'' for detailed description of pilot control of airport lighting.

RUNWAY SLOPE

Runway slope will be shown only when it is 0.3 percent or more. On runways less than 8000 feet: When available the direction of the slope upward will be indicated, ie., 0.3% up NW. On runways 8000 feet or greater: When available the slope will be shown on the runway end line, ie., RWY 13: 0.3% up., RWY 21: Pole. Rgt tfc. 0.4% down.

RUNWAY END DATA

Lighting systems such as VASI, MALSR, REIL; obstructions; displaced thresholds will be shown on the specific runway end. ''Rgt tfc''—Right traffic indicates right turns should be made on landing and takeoff for specified runway end.

DIRECTORY LEGEND

RUNWAY DECLARED DISTANCE INFORMATION

TORA—Take-off Run Available
TODA—Take-off Distance Available
ASDA—Accelerate-Stop Distance Available
LDA—Landing Distance Available

⑲ AIRPORT REMARKS

Landing Fee indicates landing charges for private or non-revenue producing aircraft, in addition, fees may be charged for planes that remain over a couple of hours and buy no services, or at major airline terminals for all aircraft.
Remarks—Data is confined to operational items affecting the status and usability of the airport.
Parachute Jumping.—See "PARACHUTE" tabulation for details.
Unless otherwise stated, remarks including runway ends refer to the runway's approach end.

⑳ WEATHER DATA SOURCES

ASOS—Automated Surface Observing System. Reports the same as an AWOS-3 plus precipitation identification and intensity, and freezing rain occurrence (future enhancement).
AWOS—Automated Weather Observing System
    AWOS-A—reports altimeter setting.
    AWOS-1—reports altimeter setting, wind data and usually temperature, dewpoint and density altitude.
    AWOS-2—reports the same as AWOS-1 plus visibility.
    AWOS-3—reports the same as AWOS-1 plus visibility and cloud/ceiling data.
    See AIM, Basic Flight Information and ATC Procedures for detailed description of AWOS.
HIWAS—See RADIO AIDS TO NAVIGATION
LAWRS—Limited Aviation Weather Reporting Station where observers report cloud height, weather, obstructions to vision, temperature and dewpoint (in most cases), surface wind, altimeter and pertinent remarks.
LLWAS—indicates a Low Level Wind Shear Alert System consisting of a center field and several field perimeter anemometers.
SAWRS—identifies airports that have a Supplemental Aviation Weather Reporting Station available to pilots for current weather information.
SWSL—Supplemental Weather Service Location providing current local weather information via radio and telephone.
TDWR—indicates airports that have Terminal Doppler Weather Radar.

㉑ COMMUNICATIONS

Communications will be listed in sequence in the order shown below:
Common Traffic Advisory Frequency (CTAF), Automatic Terminal Information Service (ATIS) and Aeronautical Advisory Stations (UNICOM) along with their frequency is shown, where available, on the line following the heading "COMMUNICATIONS." When the CTAF and UNICOM is the same frequency, the frequency will be shown as CTAF/UNICOM freq.
Flight Service Station (FSS) information. The associated FSS will be shown followed by the identifier and information concerning availability of telephone service, e.g., Direct Line (DL), Local Call (LC-384-2341), Toll free call, dial (TF 800-852-7036 or TF 1-800-227-7160), Long Distance (LD 202-426-8800 or LD 1-202-555-1212) etc. The airport NOTAM file identifier will be shown as "NOTAM FILE IAD." Where the FSS is located on the field it will be indicated as "on arpt" following the identifier. Frequencies available will follow. The FSS telephone number will follow along with any significant operational information. FSS's whose name is not the same as the airport on which located will also be listed in the normal alphabetical name listing for the state in which located. Remote Communications Outlet (RCO) providing service to the airport followed by the frequency and name of the Controlling FSS.
FSS's provide information on airport conditions, radio aids and other facilities, and process flight plans. Local Airport Advisory Service is provided on the CTAF by FSS's located at non-tower airports or airports where the tower is not in operation.
(See AIM, Par. 157/158 Traffic Advisory Practices at airports where a tower is not in operation or AC 90 - 42C.)
Aviation weather briefing service is provided by FSS specialists. Flight and weather briefing services are also available by calling the telephone numbers listed.
Remote Communications Outlet (RCO)—An unmanned air/ground communications facility, remotely controlled and providing UHF or VHF communications capability to extend the service range of an FSS.
Civil Communications Frequencies—Civil communications frequencies used in the FSS air/ground system are now operated simplex on 122.0, 122.2, 122.3, 122.4, 122.6, 123.6; emergency 121.5; plus receive-only on 122.05, 122.1, 122.15, and 123.6.
    a. 122.0 is assigned as the Enroute Flight Advisory Service channel at selected FSS's.
    b. 122.2 is assigned to most FSS's as a common enroute simplex service.
    c. 123.6 is assigned as the airport advisory channel at non-tower FSS locations, however, it is still in commission at some FSS's collocated with towers to provide part time Local Airport Advisory Service.
    d. 122.1 is the primary receive-only frequency at VOR's. 122.05, 122.15 and 123.6 are assigned at selected VOR's meeting certain criteria.
    e. Some FSS's are assigned 50 kHz channels for simplex operation in the 122-123 MHz band (e.g. 122.35). Pilots using the FSS A/G system should refer to this directory or appropriate charts to determine frequencies available at the FSS or remoted facility through which they wish to communicate.
Part time FSS hours of operation are shown in remarks under facility name.

Emergency frequency 121.5 is available at all Flight Service Stations, Towers, Approach Control and RADAR facilities, unless indicated as not available.
Frequencies published followed by the letter "T" or "R", indicate that the facility will only transmit or receive respectively on that frequency. All radio aids to navigation frequencies are transmit only

DIRECTORY LEGEND

TERMINAL SERVICES

CTAF—A program designed to get all vehicles and aircraft at uncontrolled airports on a common frequency.

ATIS—A continuous broadcast of recorded non-control information in selected areas of high activity.

UNICOM—A non-government air/ground radio communications facility utilized to provide general airport advisory service.

APP CON —Approach Control. The symbol ® indicates radar approach control.

TOWER—Control tower.

GND CON—Ground Control.

GCO—GROUND COMMUNICATION OUTLET—An unstaffed, remotely controlled, ground/ground communications facility. Pilots at uncontrolled airports may contact ATC and FSS via VHF to a telephone connection to obtain an instrument clearance or close a VFR or IFR flight plan. They may also get an updated weather briefing prior to takeoff. Pilots will use four ''key clicks'' on the VHF radio to contact the appropriate ATC facility or six ''key clicks'' to contact the FSS. The GCO system is intended to be used only on the ground.

DEP CON—Departure Control. The symbol ® indicates radar departure control.

CLNC DEL—Clearance Delivery.

PRE TAXI CLNC—Pre taxi clearance.

VFR ADVSY SVC—VFR Advisory Service. Service provided by Non-Radar Approach Control.

   Advisory Service for VFR aircraft (upon a workload basis) ctc APP CON.

TOWER, APP CON and DEP CON RADIO CALL will be the same as the airport name unless indicated otherwise.

22 NOTAM SERVICE

All public use landing areas are provided NOTAM ''D'' (distant dissemination) and NOTAM ''L'' (local dissemination) service. Airport NOTAM file identifier is shown following the associated FSS data for individual airports, e.g. ''NOTAM FILE IAD''. See AIM, Basic Flight Information and ATC Procedures for detailed description of NOTAM's.

23 AIRSPACE

CLASS B—Radar Sequencing and Separation Service for all aircraft in CLASS B airspace

TRSA—Radar Sequencing and Separation Service for participating VFR Aircraft within a Terminal Radar Service Area

Class C, D, and E airspace described in this publication is that airspace usually consisting of a 5 NM radius core surface area that begins at the surface and extends upward to an altitude above the airport elevation (charted in MSL for Class C and Class D).

When CLASS C airspace defaults to CLASS E, the core surface area becomes CLASS E. This will be formatted as: **AIRSPACE: CLASS C** svc ''times'' ctc **APP CON** other times CLASS E.

When Class C airspace defaults to Class G, the core surface area becomes Class G up to but not including the overlying controlled airspace. There are Class E airspace areas beginning at either 700' or 1200' AGL used to transition to/from the terminal or enroute environment. This will be formatted as: **AIRSPACE: CLASS C** svc ''times'' ctc **APP CON** other times CLASS G, CLASS E 700' (or 1200') AGL & abv.

NOTE: AIRSPACE SVC ''TIMES'' INCLUDE ALL ASSOCIATED EXTENSIONS. Arrival extensions for instrument approach procedures become part of the primary core surface area. These extensions may be either Class D or Class E airspace and are effective concurrent with the times of the primary core surface area.

(See CLASS AIRSPACE in the Aeronautical Information Manual for further details)

24 RADIO AIDS TO NAVIGATION

The Airport Facility Directory lists by facility name all Radio Aids to Navigation, except Military TACANS, that appear on National Ocean Service Visual or IFR Aeronautical Charts and those upon which the FAA has approved an Instrument Approach Procedure. All VOR, VORTAC ILS and MLS equipment in the National Airspace System has an automatic monitoring and shutdown feature in the event of malfunction. Unmonitored, as used in this publication for any navigational aid, means that FSS or tower personnel cannot observe the malfunction or shutdown signal. The NAVAID NOTAM file identifier will be shown as ''NOTAM FILE IAD'' and will be listed on the Radio Aids to Navigation line. When two or more NAVAIDS are listed and the NOTAM file identifier is different than shown on the Radio Aids to Navigation line, then it will be shown with the NAVAID listing. NOTAM file identifiers for ILS's and their components (e.g., NDB (LOM) are the same as the identifiers for the associated airports and are not repeated. Hazardous Inflight Weather Advisory Service (HIWAS) will be shown where this service is broadcast over selected VOR's.

NAVAID information is tabulated as indicated in the following sample:

TACAN/DME Channel   Geographical Position   Site Elevation

NAME (L) ABVORTAC 117.55   ABE   Chan 122(Y)   N40°43.60' W75°27.30'   180° 4.1 NM to fld.   1110/8E. **HIWAS.**

Class   Frequency   Identifier   Bearing and distance   Magnetic Variation   Hazardous Inflight
                                            facility to center of airport   Weather Advisory Service

VOR unusable 020°-060° byd 26 NM blo 3,500'

Restriction within the normal altitude/range of the navigational aid (See primary alphabetical listing for restrictions on VORTAC and VOR/DME).

   Note: Those DME channel numbers with a (Y) suffix require TACAN to be placed in the ''Y'' mode to receive distance information.

DIRECTORY LEGEND

HIWAS—Hazardous Inflight Weather Advisory Service is a continuous broadcast of inflight weather advisories including summarized SIGMETs, convective SIGMETs, AIRMETs and urgent PIREPs. HIWAS is presently broadcast over selected VOR's and will be implemented throughout the conterminous U.S.

ASR/PAR—Indicates that Surveillance (ASR) or Precision (PAR) radar instrument approach minimums are published in the U.S. Terminal Procedures. Only part-time hours of operation will be shown.

RADIO CLASS DESIGNATIONS

VOR/DME/TACAN Standard Service Volume (SSV) Classifications

SSV Class	Altitudes	Distance (NM)
(T) Terminal	1000' to 12,000'	25
(L) Low Altitude	1000' to 18,000'	40
(H) High Altitude	1000' to 14,500'	40
	14,500' to 18,000'	100
	18,000' to 45,000'	130
	45,000' to 60,000'	100

NOTE: Additionally, (H) facilities provide (L) and (T) service volume and (L) facilities provide (T) service. Altitudes are with respect to the station's site elevation. Coverage is not available in a cone of airspace directly above the facility.

The term VOR is, operationally, a general term covering the VHF omnidirectional bearing type of facility without regard to the fact that the power, the frequency protected service volume, the equipment configuration, and operational requirements may vary between facilities at different locations.

AB	Automatic Weather Broadcast.
DF	Direction Finding Service.
DME	UHF standard (TACAN compatible) distance measuring equipment.
DME(Y)	UHF standard (TACAN compatible) distance measuring equipment that require TACAN to be placed in the ''Y'' mode to receive DME.
GS	Glide slope.
H	Non-directional radio beacon (homing), power 50 watts to less than 2,000 watts (50 NM at all altitudes).
HH	Non-directional radio beacon (homing), power 2,000 watts or more (75 NM at all altitudes).
H-SAB	Non-directional radio beacons providing automatic transcribed weather service.
ILS	Instrument Landing System (voice, where available, on localizer channel).
IM	Inner marker.
ISMLS	Interim Standard Microwave Landing System.
LDA	Localizer Directional Aid.
LMM	Compass locator station when installed at middle marker site (15 NM at all altitudes).
LOM	Compass locator station when installed at outer marker site (15 NM at all altitudes).
MH	Non-directional radio beacon (homing) power less than 50 watts (25 NM at all altitudes).
MLS	Microwave Landing System.
MM	Middle marker.
OM	Outer marker.
S	Simultaneous range homing signal and/or voice.
SABH	Non-directional radio beacon not authorized for IFR or ATC. Provides automatic weather broadcasts.
SDF	Simplified Direction Facility.
TACAN	UHF navigational facility-omnidirectional course and distance information.
VOR	VHF navigational facility-omnidirectional course only.
VOR/DME	Collocated VOR navigational facility and UHF standard distance measuring equipment.
VORTAC	Collocated VOR and TACAN navigational facilities.
W	Without voice on radio facility frequency.
Z	VHF station location marker at a LF radio facility.

AND SOME ADDED-ON A/FD INSERTS...

FLIGHT SERVICE STATION COMMUNICATION FREQUENCIES

NASHVILLE AFSS 122.1R 122.2 **122.55**
- BRISTOL RCO 122.2
- CHATTANOOGA RCO 122.2 123.65
- CROSSVILLE RCO 122.2 122.5
- HINCH MOUNTAIN VORTAC 117.6T 122.1R
- HOLSTON MOUNTAIN VORTAC 114.6T 122.1R
- LIVINGSTON VORTAC 108.4T 122.1R
- MCGHEE TYSON RCO 122.2 122.3
- NASHVILLE VORTAC 114.1T
- SHELBYVILLE VOR/DME 109.0T 122.1R
- VOLUNTEER VORTAC 116.4T 122.1R

LAHSO

LAND AND HOLD SHORT OPERATIONS (LAHSO)

LAHSO is an acronym for "Land and Hold Short Operations." These operations include landing and holding short of an intersection runway, an intersecting taxiway, or other predetermined points on the runway other than a runway or taxiway. Measured distance represents the available landing distance on the landing runway, in feet.

The hold–short point, marked by an asterisk (*), represents the predetermined points on the runway other than a runway or taxiway.

Specific questions regarding these distances should be referred to the air traffic manager of the facility concerned. The Aeronautical Information Manual contains specific details on hold-short operations and markings.

CITY/AIRPORT	LDG RWY	HOLD–SHORT POINT	MEASURED DISTANCE
ALABAMA			
BIRMINGHAM/BHM	06	18/36	8,700 feet
	36	06/24	5,150 feet
DOTHAN/DHN	14	18/36	6,750 feet
	18	14/32	3,150 feet
MONTGOMERY/MGM	10	03/21*	6,000 feet
FLORIDA			
DAYTONA BEACH/DAB	07L	16/34	7,950 feet
	16	07L/25R	2,900 feet
FORT LAUDERDALE/FXE	26	13/31	3,000 feet

FSDO

FLIGHT STANDARDS DISTRICT OFFICES (FSDO)

Below is a list of FSDO's in the area of coverage of this directory. These offices serve the aviation industry and the general public on matters relating to certification and operation of general aviation aircraft. Address letters to Manager, Flight Standards District Office–Federal Aviation Administration.

ALABAMA

Municipal Airport
6500 43rd Ave. North
Birmingham, AL 35206
Telephone: 205–731–1557

MISSISSIPPI

Jackson Intl. Airport
120 North Hanger Dr., Suite C
Jackson, MS 39208
Telephone: 601–965–4633

Added Notes on Engines and Other Systems

Added Notes on Engine Theory, Construction, and Operations

There have been cases of certificated private and commercial pilots who have never fully seen the engine of the airplane they've been flying for many hours. (They open the small access door to check the oil and only get a glimpse of the top of the engine crankcase.) The cowlings of many airplanes are designed so that it is impractical for the pilot to open them before every flight; probably the only time the engine is fully seen is when a 100-hour or annual inspection is done.

The point is that you should have a basic understanding of how various things work, so that a lot of the mystery disappears and you aren't sweating out some unknown and unexplained failure. You might avoid a bad situation such as loss of electrical power at night, for instance, by noting that the belt that drives the alternator is getting frayed and should be replaced before it breaks. If you didn't know the function of the belt, you might not be so concerned about replacing it before that long night flight over the Louisiana swamps.

Engine Operation

In order to know what to look for in the preflight check or how to analyze engine problems in flight, you should have some basic knowledge of how an engine works. Most general aviation airplane engines are horizontally opposed and air cooled. The horizontally opposed engine is "flat" and has an equal number of cylinders on each side of the crankcase (Figure B-1).

Figure B-1. The Lycoming 0-235 L2C four-cylinder, horizontally opposed, air-cooled engine. This is used in current two-place trainers. (Courtesy of Avco Lycoming)

The engine uses the "Otto cycle" in operation and works this way: The pistons, enclosed in the cylinders, move *in* and *out* within a limited distance. The burning of the fuel-air mixture pushes the piston in, and it is attached by a connecting rod to an offset section of the crankshaft. Because of that offset section, the back and forth motion of the piston is translated to a rotary motion of the crankshaft, which in turn rotates the propeller either directly or through a gearing system. Most lighter airplane engines have direct drive; that is, the propeller is directly attached to and rotates at the same speed as the engine crankshaft. Higher horsepower engines may have gears that reduce the propeller rotation speed. The engine has four strokes (Figure B-2):

1. *Intake stroke*—The piston moves toward the base of the cylinder with the intake valve open (exhaust valve closed), pulling the fuel-air mixture into the cylinder.

2. *Compression*—As the crankshaft rotates, the piston moves away from the base of the cylinder with both valves closed so that the fuel-air mixture is compressed.

1. Intake   2. Compression   3. Power   4. Exhaust

Figure B-2. The four strokes. The cylinder is shown as upright rather than horizontal here.

3. *Power stroke*—The fuel-air mixture is *ignited* in its compressed state, which gives greater power than if it was not compressed. Combustion moves the piston downward (or inward), rotating the crankshaft and thus turning the propeller.

4. *Exhaust stroke*—As the crankshaft turns, the piston moves up (out) with the exhaust valve open, purging the burned gases out through the exhaust system.

The crankshaft has to make two full revolutions for each cylinder's power stroke, as you can see by analyzing Figure B-2. This sequence is happening in other cylinders at different times, and each power stroke turns the crankshaft and provides for the intake, compression, and exhaust strokes as needed for the other cylinders.

Engine Components

The pistons, which in most cases are made from aluminum alloy forgings, have rings that fit into grooves that are cut in them. The rings are made from a good stock of cast iron and have a slightly larger outside diameter than the piston (Figure B-3).

Compression rings are designed to prevent the escape of the fuel-air mixture or exhaust gases into the crankcase. There are usually two or more of these per piston, and they are replaceable if worn or broken. The barrel of the cylinder is forged steel; for a certain number of hours from the time the new engine is first started, the rings will be considered to be "seating," or fitting to the cylinder walls. (An operating time of 50 hours is considered a reasonable period for this.) The manufacturer usually recommends that straight mineral oil, which has no additives, be used because this

Figure B-3. A — Piston and components: (1) piston, (2) compression rings, (3) oil regulating or oil scraper ring, (4) piston pin (sometimes called "wrist pin"), (5) piston pin plugs, (6) connecting rod (from piston to crankshaft), (7) bushing, (8) connecting rod bolts, (9) connecting rod nuts, (10) connecting rod bearings (replaceable). The line C-C shows where the connecting rod joins the crankshaft. B — Two views of a cylinder. Note the cooling fins. Look at Figure B-2 again.

allows more friction so that the slight wear needed for seating is speeded up. Once the rings are seated, ashless dispersant oils are normally used to keep friction to a minimum.

One possible later problem, as the hours pile up on the engine, is that these piston rings get worn or may break, allowing oil from the crankcase to get into the combustion chamber and burn with the fuel-air mixture. That's what was happening in that car in front of you the other day; the driver was laying a smoke screen because oil as well as gasoline was burning. Not only was too much oil being burned, but the residue was fouling the spark plugs and gumming up the valves so that they didn't close properly.

Mechanics run compression checks on the 100-hour and annual inspections to check for valve and ring problems. If the airplane you're flying isn't developing the power it should or the oil consumption has gone up radically, rings may be the problem. This can also be checked by an experienced pilot or the mechanic, who (after making sure the ignition is off, the mixture is at idle cutoff, and the airplane is chocked or tied down) pulls the prop through and checks for a cylinder (or cylinders) that doesn't resist the pulling through like the others. Extreme caution is suggested when pulling the prop through, even though the mag switch "says" OFF.

The oil control rings are below the compression rings and regulate the thickness of the oil coating on the cylinder walls.

The camshaft is geared to the crankshaft at the rear of the engine. The camshaft has nodes or cams that are offset around the shaft; as it rotates, the cams move up against pushrods that open the spring-loaded exhaust or intake valves for the various cylinders in the proper sequence. A pushrod extends from the camshaft to the rocker arm, which pushes the valve (exhaust or intake) down and opens it (Figure B-4).

Engines are classified by the cubic-inch displacement in the cylinders or the volume of air in all cylinders if the pistons are in the bottom dead center or "withdrawn" position. For example, suppose the *diameter* of each piston (with rings) of a four-cylinder engine is 5.4 inches (its *bore*) and it *travels* 3 inches (its *stroke*) from full up to full down (or in a horizontally opposed engine, full out to full back) (Figure B-5). One cylinder's displacement is the volume of that travel. Volume (V) or displacement = area × distance. (Area = πr^2.)

Radius (r) = 2.7 inches; $r^2 = (2.7)^2 = 7.3$ square inches; $\pi r^2 = 22.9$ square inches = area

Stroke = 3 inches; displacement = $3 \times 22.9 = 68.7$ cubic inches

There are four cylinders, so the total displacement is $4 \times 68.7 = 274.8$ cubic inches, and this fictitious engine would have a designation of O-275 because it is a horizontally opposed type. If it had fuel injection, the designation would be IO-275; if it was also turbocharged, the designation would be TIO-275. Another letter G would be included (TGIO-275) if the engine was geared and not a direct drive. It's likely that an engine with this small amount of displacement would not have all the refinements mentioned, but it's an example. The term "compression ratio" is used for reciprocating engines to indicate the ratio of the amount of volume of the mixture when the piston is at the bottom dead center

Figure B-4. Crankshaft, camshaft, and other parts: (1) crankshaft, (2) camshaft, (3) crankshaft bearing (same item as 10 in Figure B-3), (4) magneto gears, (5) starter ring gear.

position (fully withdrawn down or back in the cylinder) to top dead center (at the greatest compression). Figure B-6 gives an idea of the relative volumes for a compression ratio of 7 to 1.

Time Between Overhauls

You'll hear the expression *time between overhauls* (TBO) as you progress as a pilot, and the tendency is to think that this is a definite time required by regulation until a complete major overhaul of the engine. Also, you might think there would be an immediate failure if the engine was secretly operated past that limit. Not so. The manufacturer sets a *recommended* limit based on

Figure B-5. Piston displacement.

Figure B-6. Compression ratio. In moving from the bottom dead center point (A), the piston compresses the fuel-air mixture to one-seventh of its original volume at (B); the compression ratio is 7 to 1. Low-compression engines are considered to be those from 6.5 to 1 to 7.9 to 1. Above that they are considered high-compression type.

inputs of users from around the world and its own experience in overhauling engines returned for that purpose. An engine having a recommended TBO of 2,000 hours, for instance, may need overhauling at 1,200 hours (if abused and the manufacturer's recommendations for operations neglected), or it may go 2,500 hours or more if properly operated and maintained, but you'd be smart to adhere to the TBO.

Another term you'll hear is *top overhaul*, and this usually consists of removing only the cylinders so that piston rings may be replaced and valves may be replaced or reseated. This is done by some operators between *major* overhauls (in which the engine is totally disassembled). Some manufacturers feel that if the engine is properly maintained and operated, it should go to at least the recommended TBO without the need for a top overhaul. However, local conditions, need for special operations, and use of higher lead content fuels may necessitate a top overhaul.

Carburetion

The engine has a way to get the fuel-air mixture in, compress it, fire it, and exhaust it, so the next step is to design a method of mixing the fuel and air in the proper amounts. Figure B-7 shows a carburetor, which for horizontally opposed engines is located beneath the crankcase.

The carburetor has a float chamber that stores a small amount of fuel for use in mixing with the incoming air. As the fuel in the chamber is depleted, the float moves down, opening a valve to let in more fuel. This is a repeating process as the engine runs.

The fuel is vaporized by the main discharge nozzle and mixes with the incoming air (as shown in Figure B-7) just past the venturi (which speeds up the airflow

Figure B-7. Float-type carburetor.

like the upper camber of an airfoil). As you move the throttle forward, the throttle valve opens more and allows a greater amount of fuel and air to enter the engine and provide more power. The temperature is decreased in the venturi discharge nozzle and throttle valve area by two events: (1) the pressure of the air moving through the venturi is lowered, lowering the temperature, and (2) the vaporization of the fuel lowers the temperature so that a drop of up to 60°F is possible. If the incoming air contains moisture, it may freeze in that area and eventually shut off the air (and fuel) flow, with engine stoppage resulting. Look again at Chapter 4 for the background of carburetor heat and for diagrams of how it works.

Fuel Injection

The fuel injection system is now being used for some trainers and you may have a chance to fly an airplane so equipped. The advantage of this system is that the fuel is injected into the air just as it enters the cylinder, resulting in less chance of induction ice and a better fuel distribution.

When you lean a carburetor-equipped engine, it will become rough (you can feel it), since the air and fuel are mixed at the carburetor and the mixture will vary between cylinders because of the distances involved. One or more cylinders may be leaner than the others, and as you move the mixture control out to lean the engine, those cylinders start losing power earlier. The engine runs rough, so you move the mixture control forward just enough to smooth it out.

Because of the better fuel distribution, the fuel injection normally can't be leaned by feel and you'll use a fuel-flow gauge or an EGT (exhaust-gas temperature) gauge. Fuel-injected engines don't use carburetor heat as such but have an alternate air source (usually from inside the cowling) if induction icing (icing in the air intake area) occurs. One trainer, with a 125-horsepower engine and fixed-pitch prop uses fuel injection, and has, instead of carburetor heat, the alternate air source as just mentioned. The pilot uses a cockpit control to select the alternate air. Other airplanes of higher horsepower have a spring-loaded door that will open automatically by engine suction when an alternate air source is needed; the pilot has no cockpit control for the system and the Information Manual (for one such airplane) warns that at full throttle the open alternate air door will result in an approximate 10 percent power loss. (But that's a lot better than a 100 percent power loss!)

As *The Pilot's Handbook of Aeronautical Knowledge* (FAA) indicates the pros and cons of fuel injection are summed up as follows:

PRO
a. Reduction in evaporative icing
b. Better fuel flow
c. Faster throttle response
d. Precise control of mixture
e. Better fuel distribution
f. Easier cold weather starts

CON
a. Difficulty in starting a hot engine
b. Vapor locks during ground operations on hot days
c. Problems associated with restarting an engine that quits because of fuel starvation.

If a tank is run dry in a carburetor system, it normally takes 1–2 seconds for power to be restored after the tanks are switched; a fuel injection system may require 8–10 seconds and special techniques to get power back. It's best never to deliberately run a tank dry with any system. Check your *Pilot's Operating Handbook* now for the procedure if you should inadvertently run a tank dry.

Ignition

Magnetos

There must be a system to ignite the mixture when it's been compressed in the cylinder. The magneto is used in an airplane because it is self-sufficient, as noted in Chapter 4. Two magnetos are used for two reasons: (1) there is one remaining to keep the engine going if one fails, and (2) two spark plugs provide a smoother burning of the mixture in the cylinder. With one magneto and one spark plug, the ignition would start in one corner of the combustion chamber and proceed across, taking some time (milliseconds), whereas two separate sparks can each set off a portion of the fuel-air mixture and make for smoother and more efficient combustion. That's one reason why you get a drop in rpm in the mag check when going from BOTH to just LEFT or RIGHT.

The magneto is "timed" so that the spark plug gives ignition to its cylinder at a time that would result in the most efficient burning and best power. The initial thought would be that the spark should occur just at the instant the piston reaches its farthest point up (or out) in the cylinder when the compression is greatest (*top dead center*, or TDC). The problem in that case is that by the time the burning reached its peak, even though it's burning fast, the piston would have already started down and the peak power wouldn't result. The idea is to time the spark so that the maximum effect of combustion results. Since it takes time for the combustion to propagate, the ignition should be started *before* the piston reaches TDC so that the best "push" is obtained. The mechanic "times" the magneto by setting it to fire at some point, say 25° of crankshaft rotation before TDC, as recommended by the manufacturer. Magnetos get out of time and mechanics have to check them. Timing is critical to smooth operation; for instance, you can imagine what would happen if the timing was accidentally set too early (for instance, 90° before TDC) so that the piston was still moving up when the full force of combustion occurred. There would be pandemonium in the powerhouse.

It's possible that in flight one of the magnetos might slip out of timing and the engine would run very rough. You might go from BOTH to LEFT or RIGHT to find the magneto that is acting properly. Since the airplane is now running on one mag, it would be best to get on to the nearest safe airport for repairs.

In some cases, the magnetos may be timed slightly apart. One is set to give the word to the spark plug at 25° before TDC, and the other fires its plug in the same cylinder slightly later, at 23° before TDC. This may be done to get an even smoother operation; it depends on the engine.

If you get a chance, go out into the hangar or shop some day between flights and observe some of the engine work being done. Most mechanics don't mind good questions as long as they don't interfere with the work. There's a sign that mechanics show to airplane owners:

MAINTENANCE CHARGES

1. Our mechanic alone $30.00/hr
2. If you stand around and
     offer suggestions $35.00/hr
3. If you help $40.00/hr

The pilots come back with a sign that says:

IT TAKES SIX PEOPLE TO WORK

ON AIRPLANES HERE:

ONE MECHANIC

AND FIVE MORE TO HOLD THE PILOT BACK

Most engines have each magneto separately geared to the engine accessory section, but some newer models use a common engine drive with both magnetos in the same housing. Advantages of this are a decrease in weight and freeing of one magneto drive that might be used for other accessories. Some argue against having a *single* drive for *both* mags and prefer a separate one for each.

The magnetos and plug leads ("leeds") must be shielded to prevent ignition noise from coming through the radio receivers. If you hear a repetitive crackling noise coming through the radio, you might try checking to see which mag and its ignition components (plugs, leads, etc.) are causing the problem. You can tell the mechanic which is the guilty system and save time in analysis.

Spark Plugs

Spark plugs are seemingly simple pieces of equipment, but they can affect the performance of the engine to a great extent. They are subjected to extremely high temperatures when the engine is running.

A great deal depends on the plug "gap" or gaps, that is, how far apart the electrodes are. The spark has to "jump" a certain length to get the optimum ignition—the wider or narrower the gap from that recommended by the manufacturer, the less efficient the result.

Spark plug electrodes are subjected to temperatures of over 3,000°F, gas pressures of up to 2,000 pounds per square inch, and electrical pressures of up to 15,000 volts.

It's noted in Chapters 4 and 7 that each magneto furnishes ignition (through the spark plugs) to each cylinder, and the wiring route may vary between makes and models. The ignition wiring on one four-cylinder engine used in a current trainer is established so that the right magneto fires the two lower right and two upper left plugs and the left magneto fires the lower left and upper right (Figure B-8). Usually though not always, the lower plugs foul more easily, so if you had a bad permanent drop on the left mag, under the arrangement just described you'd probably start a maintenance check, looking at those bottom left plugs first. Of course, the mechanic would know the wiring arrangement, but you should have an idea of the general layout of your airplane ignition system.

Problems occurring in the combustion chamber are *preignition* and *detonation*, and sometimes people get confused between the two.

Preignition, as defined by the *Lycoming Flyer*, is a situation in which the combustion takes place within the cylinder before the timed spark occurs. Usually it's

Figure B-8. In this particular installation the left magneto (1) fires the bottom plugs on the left two cylinders (2) and the top plugs on the right cylinders (not shown). The right mag (not shown) fires the bottom right (not shown) and top left (3). While it's not a part of the ignition system, (4) shows the ground-service plug receptacle for use of an external electrical power source.

caused by combustion deposits, such as lead, which cause local hot spots. It can be caused by a cracked valve or piston or a broken spark plug insulation that sets up a local glow spot. The mixture is not fired at the proper time, the engine runs rough and backfires, and a sudden increase in cylinder-head temperature is noted if you have a CHT (cylinder head temperature) gauge. Older airplanes without mixture control had to be shut down by turning off the ignition, and if the engine was hot it continued running. Also, some model-airplane engines use the principle of preignition by electrically preheating a certain type of plug, which is then kept hot by combustion.

Preignition is a serious condition that can cause burned pistons and damaged valves and is similar to early timing of the spark.

Detonation results when limits of compression and temperature are exceeded; this is most likely at higher power settings. Leaning the mixture at high power settings and abrupt opening of the throttle can cause detonation.

Unless the detonation is heavy, the pilot doesn't know it's happening. Light to medium detonation may not cause noticeable roughness, observable oil temperature or CHT increase, or loss of power. But after an engine has been detonating, a teardown shows damage to valves, pistons, and cylinder heads.

In *normal combustion* the piston is pushed smoothly down (or in, in a horizontally opposed engine); with

detonation the piston acts as if it was being hit by a sledgehammer.

The best temporary in-flight methods for correcting preignition and detonation are to retard the throttle, richen the mixture, open cowl flaps if available, or do all three.

You might remember the causes of detonation by the following three "too's":

Too lean—mixture too lean for higher power settings.

Too hot—climbing at too slow an airspeed and/or too lean a mixture.

Too cheap—lower grade fuel than recommended.

Oil System

The engine operation would be short-lived without lubrication. The oil used in the engine has three major purposes: (1) to maintain a film between moving parts so that they do not actually make metal-to-metal contact, (2) to carry off heat from the various internal parts as it circulates, and (3) to pick up foreign particles for depositing in a filter.

The oil used in the airplanes you are flying is designed to take care of the three items just mentioned. Without going into laborious details about the theory of oil viscosity (or flow rate ability), the higher the commercial aviation number or SAE (Society of Automotive Engineers) number, the higher the viscosity (thickness). The viscosity of oil varies inversely with heat—the colder the temperature, the thicker the oil. If you choose a low-viscosity (thin oil) for use in hot weather, the viscosity gets even lower as the engine heats up, and metal-to-metal contact results. The use of high-viscosity oil in cold climates would mean that it would be like grease, making the engine difficult to start, and the oil circulation would be very poor. Your *Pilot's Operating Handbook* will note the oil grades to be used for various ambient temperature ranges and, as indicated earlier, will probably note that after the first 50 hours of operation, ashless dispersant oil meeting certain criteria is to be used. It may recommend use of multiviscosity oils.

Some typical light-trainer oil system components are shown in Figure B-9. This is a wet-sump system, meaning that the oil is contained in the lower part of the engine (the sump), as in most automobiles.

The carburetor for this engine is located as shown in Figure B-9 and gets warmth from the warm oil in the sump. Because of this, the engine is less susceptible to carburetor ice than the dry-sump type, which has the oil in a container separate from the engine and not close to the carburetor. The wet-sump engine can have carb ice troubles, and carb heat should be used to check for the presence of ice before the throttle is retarded to lower power settings, such as when starting an approach.

With less availability of 80-octane fuel and more use of 100 low-lead, it's important that the oil be changed more often when using higher-grade fuels with their attendant higher lead contents. The old oil, when drained, will carry off impurities, thus lengthening the engine life.

Your instructor may show you the engine oil breather, which is an attachment and hose designed to release pressures that build up in the crankcase because of the high temperature there. The breather usually comes out the top of the crankcase, with the hose running down and out the bottom of the cowling (item 9, Figure B-9). During the preflight check in the winter, be sure that the breather is not closed by ice (the warm water vapor from the engine will freeze at the breather outlet).

Since lighter airplanes don't have a cylinder-head temperature gauge, the oil temperature gauge becomes very important in indicating whether the engine is being abused in a too-slow climb or a too-lean setting for the flight condition. As noted at the beginning of this section, part of the job of the oil is to remove heat from the engine components. The *Airframe and Powerplant Mechanics Powerplant Handbook* (DOT–FAA) indicates that the thermal distribution of the heat released by combustion in an engine is approximately as follows:

1. 25–30 percent is converted into useful power.
2. 40–45 percent is carried out with the exhaust.
3. 5–10 percent is removed by the oil.
4. 15–20 percent is removed by the cylinder cooling fins.

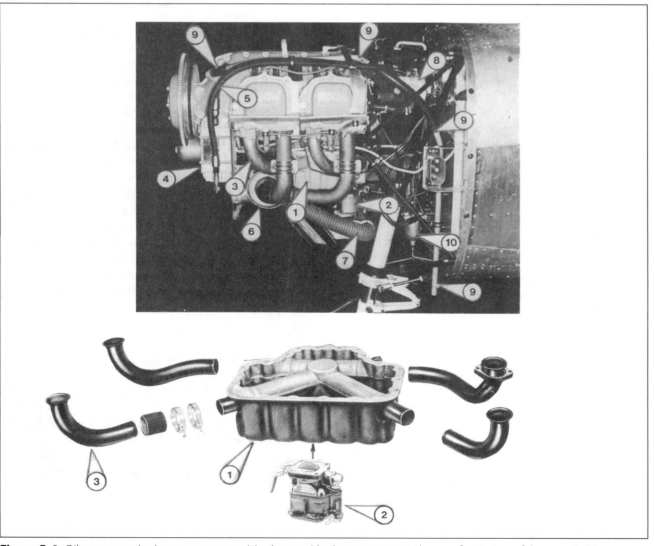

Figure B-9. Oil system and other components: (1) oil sump (the bottom picture shows a front view of the sump), (2) carburetor (note its position in relation to the oil sump), (3) intake pipe, (4) oil cooler (radiator), (5) oil line, (6) carburetor heat/ cabin heat muff, (7) carburetor heat hose, (8) oil filter, (9) breather pipe, (10) fuel strainer.

Engine Cooling

The principle of the cylinder cooling fins is radiation of heat from the cylinder into the air moving past the engine. The fins present a large surface area and are oriented so that the air moves around and between them, thus removing heat. In a preflight inspection you may note that some of the fins are broken off; this should call for a discussion with your instructor or mechanic because if enough cooling fin area is missing, serious heat problems could arise and the cylinder should be changed.

In the spring, birds may build a nest in the cowling, with the result that the cooling flow is shut off or redirected and a hot spot exists, leading to serious damage. Baffles are shaped aluminum plates attached to the engine or cowling to help direct the airflow for best engine cooling. These should be checked for security and proper alignment during the preflight if possible.

Your current light trainer may not have cowl flaps (which are normally located at the bottom rear of the cowling), but probably one or more of the airplanes you fly later will have them.

Engine cooling, from a pilot's standpoint, results from two main sources: (1) rich mixture and (2) airflow past the cylinders. Looking at the airflow, there's usually no problem at cruise, and a small opening at the bottom-rear of the cowling is sufficient for the warmed ram air to escape; there is a large volume of air moving over the engine each second, carrying off engine heat. Also, the power is back to cruise, so there's a comparatively low heat problem and plenty of air passing by to take care of it.

When the airplane is sitting on the ground with the engine running, there is comparatively little air moving across the cylinders, and the cowl flaps should be fully open to allow the greatest amount of heat escape possible. Some airplanes require that the cowl flaps be set fully open for takeoff and not quite fully open for a cruise climb. After cruise is established, the cowl flaps are closed to cut down on aerodynamic drag and also, particularly in cold weather, to keep the engine from running too cool. You may also fly an airplane using exhaust augmenters, which use exhaust gas velocity to draw air over the engine. The simpler types do not require cowl flaps or other controls to be adjusted by the pilot. The system is automatic; as the exhaust gases are released through the ejector, the hot air is pulled from the engine compartment and sent out with the exhaust.

Exhaust Systems

The exhaust system should seem simple enough; all that is apparently needed is a pipe to let the burned gases out. The most efficient (and noisiest) system was that of the short-stacks type used earlier on radial engines; it consisted of a short, curved exhaust pipe for each cylinder. This meant that there would be little back pressure in the "system." When the exhaust system requires long pipes or collector rings (as for bigger, cowled radial engines), it is less efficient because of the resistance of the burned gases in the longer system. The exhaust gas just emerging from the exhaust port has to push against this mass to get out. The exhaust system must provide a method of getting the hot waste safely out of the cowling and away from the airframe; this may require a long crossover exhaust pipe system in some airplanes.

The metal of the exhaust system must withstand very high temperatures without burning through at a critical place in the engine compartment. Exhaust systems on each side of horizontally opposed engines may be joined to a single final exhaust stack (Figure B-10).

Exhaust Gas Temperature Gauge

The exhaust gas temperature (EGT) gauge measures the relative change in the exhaust gas temperature with change in mixture and gives an indication of the best economy and best power mixtures.

Figure B-10. Exhaust system. The exhaust stacks (1) join to one outlet (2). The other end of the carburetor heat/cabin heat muff and the other two stacks can be seen in Figure B-9. The cabin heat hose is shown at (3). Item (4) is the oil filler cap, admittedly not a part of the exhaust system, but there it is anyway.

One simple system consists of the gauge, wiring, and a probe into one of the exhaust stacks at a point 1.5 inches, or slightly more, from the cylinder head. The gauge may be calibrated in 25°F increments (with no fixed numbers shown) or in a range of 1,200°–1,750°F. One manufacturer's engines normally operate in the 1,200°–1,600°F EGT range.

Peak EGT—As you slowly lean the mixture from full rich, the fuel-air ratio decreases and the cooling effect of the fuel is lessened. Watching the EGT gauge, you can see the gradual increase in the temperature until at some point it peaks and further leaning will cause a decrease in temperature. The peak EGT is where the maximum utilization of the fuel and air occurs; it's a chemically correct mixture. As the leaning continues, the ratio of air to fuel increases and power will be lost, and the exhaust temperature will decrease for that one examined cylinder. If the mixture control is moved forward, richening the mixture from peak, the EGT will drop again as fuel cooling takes place. More expensive EGT systems have a probe for each cylinder, with a selector to check each.

Operating at peak EGT is only practical in *fuel injected* engines of over 250 horsepower.

Remember the earlier discussions pointing out that the fuel distribution was more even in fuel-injected engines because it was injected at the intake port of each cylinder? It was also noted that the carburetor did not allow this good distribution, and an engine so equipped can be leaned by ear or feel, since the leanest cylinder would start complaining first as the mixture control was moved out and the rough-running engine tells you to richen it forward just a tad. Some pilots are afraid that this roughness means detonation and so hesitate to lean. If leaning is done at the manufacturer's recommended top cruise power setting or below, no detonation can occur. Leaning in climb or other high power settings can cause detonation. Peak EGT operations are limited to 75 percent rated power or below in some direct drive, normally aspirated (nonsupercharged) engines.

Best *economy mixture*—For practical purposes, the best economy for some engines starts at the peak temperature. Expect a slight loss of horsepower and a loss of 2–3 knots at cruise if you use this. Other engines may use a temperature drop of 125°F on the rich side of peak.

Best *power mixture*—This is sometimes referred to as *maximum power range*, which is in the range of a temperature drop of 100–150°F from the peak on the rich side. (Remember that the temperature will drop from the peak when the mixture is either leaned or richened.) This provides a safe mixture for higher than cruise power settings (except for takeoff). A rule of thumb compromise between best economy and best power mixtures has been a mixture setting of 50°F on the rich side of the peak. The *Pilot's Operating Handbook* for a particular airplane is the final word on this as well as for other operations.

Electrical System

As a pilot, the electrical system may be a mystery to you (that is, how the electrons move through it), but you should know how to check it in the preflight and know what procedures to use in case of problems. Note the electrical system in Figure 3-26. Maybe it doesn't make sense with all the symbols, but at least you can tell what components of the airplane are electrically powered by looking at the circuit breakers. Maybe you didn't know that the oil temperature gauge depended on electrical power for indication (the oil *pressure* gauge does not). The oil pressure switch seen at the left of the electrical system diagram energizes the flight hour recorder when the engine starts, and thus oil pressure is available.

Note that the ignition switch is in the electrical system, not because the magnetos are battery powered, but because the spring-loaded starter position is part of that switch.

The Alternator

The airplane's alternator is like that of your automobile. It is engine-driven by gears or a belt, and it has more than enough capacity to keep the battery charged when working properly. If an overvoltage occurs, the system will automatically turn off the alternator and you are warned by a red light or other indication. Check with your instructor concerning procedures in event of overloading and alternator loss. Procedures will differ among airplane types.

The alternator has replaced the generator in airplanes and cars because it develops electrical power at lower engine rpm and is more efficient in the idle power range. (While it's working at lower rpm or down to idle, it still may not be keeping up with the electrical requirements, so run the engine up a little if in doubt.) The older generators required 1,200 rpm or more even to "cut in," and the battery could be discharged when the situation called for low rpm and large electrical requirements (such as taxiing at night with taxi and navigation lights and radios on). Figure B-11 shows components of the electrical system for a light trainer. This system is protected by circuit breakers (which can be *reset* in the event of an electrical overload) except for the clock, flight hour recorder, and external power plug, which are protected by fuses that are replaced if an overload burns them out. In other words, the circuit breakers and fuses are deliberately established "weaker" spots so that if an electrical overload in the system occurs, the circuit breaker will "pop" or an inexpensive fuse will burn out rather than damaging such components as radios or other expensive electrically operated items. Of course, you should have all unnecessary electrical items off for starting, particularly radios that could be damaged by surges of transient voltages during the start.

Ammeter

The ammeter indicates the current flow in amperes from the alternator through the battery to the system. If the ammeter shows a discharge, it means that either the alternator is not keeping up with the load being placed on the system or it's out of action and the battery is being discharged at the rate shown (amperes). For instance, if the battery in your airplane is rated at 32 amp-hours, it means that the battery, when fully charged without alternator input, should produce an electric current flow of 16 amps for 2 hours, or 8 amps for 4 hours, etc. However, at high usage the battery loses power at a higher rate; if 32 amps were being used with a 32 amp-hour battery, it might last only 30 minutes or less rather than the hour indicated by the earlier arithmetic. If you have an alternator overvoltage problem and have to pull it from the system (turn that ALT half of the switch OFF), you'd lengthen the battery power availability by turning off unnecessary electrical components. For instance, landing and taxi lights are usually

the biggest users of current. The cigarette lighter takes a great deal of current, and you shouldn't be smoking in the airplane anyway; it's bad for the vacuum-driven gyro instruments (attitude indicator and heading indicator), as will be shown shortly.

Vacuum System

Older airplanes used a venturi, shown in Figure 3-17, but the drawback with that system is that the airplane had to be moving for some time before the suction got the instruments up to speed. Now, even the smaller trainers have an engine-driven vacuum pump to operate the gyro instruments. As noted in Chapter 3, the usual procedure is to have the attitude and heading indicators run by the vacuum system and the turn and slip or turn coordinator electrically driven. Figure B-12

Figure B-12. Vacuum system schematic. The overboard vent line shown here can be seen in Figure B-11 behind and above the oil filler cap; it's that aluminum tube with two 90° bends. If you look closely, you can see that the vacuum pump, which is behind the oil filler tube, is a black drum with a light metallic band around it. You also might look just above item 8 in Figure B-9 to see the pump and overboard vent line. (The pump is almost hidden by part of the engine mount.)

Figure B-11. Electrical components: (1) alternator, (2) belt drive of alternator, (3) battery box (the battery is inside), (4) fuses for the clock and flight hour recorder and external power receptacle. (*See* item 4, Figure B-8.)

shows a vacuum system installation for a light trainer. (Larger airplanes have "pressure" systems.)

The vacuum pump is at the rear of the engine (at the accessory section) and pulls air from the cockpit area through the gyro instruments and discharges it into the engine compartment.

Note in Figure B-12 that a suction gauge is a part of the system, and for this airplane the normal range is 4.6–5.4 inches of mercury. These figures indicate the drop in pressure in the system as compared with atmospheric pressure and give the suction available to the instruments.

The air filter is located on the aft side of the firewall and, as just noted, takes air from the cockpit area. This is a good reason for not smoking in the airplane, since tars and other contaminants will clog the filter and cut down the accuracy and dependability of the gyro instruments.

The more you know about the systems, the better able you will be to avoid or correct problems in flight. Most systems are based on simple principles and are presented here from a pilot's standpoint. The Bibliography contains references for further reading.

Review Questions

Okay, answer the following questions on this section of Appendix B, and after finding out those you missed (if any), read Chapter 4 and this section again.

01. The four strokes of an Otto-cycle airplane engine are

1 — thrust, rotary, power, and exhaust.
2 — intake, power, thrust, and exhaust.
3 — intake, compression, power, and exhaust.
4 — intake, thrust, compression, and power.

02. Which of the following would most likely result in a sudden increase in oil consumption in the engine of an airplane? (There are no outside leaks in evidence.)

1 — Eroded spark plug electrodes.
2 — Worn or broken piston rings.
3 — A poorly adjusted carburetor.
4 — A coagulated frammis.

03. A horizontally opposed six-cylinder, direct drive, nonturbocharged engine with fuel injection has a bore of 5 inches and a stroke of 4 inches. Its designation by the manufacturer would be

1 — GO-470.
2 — IO-470.
3 — IO-540.
4 — TIO-470.

04. The addition of carburetor heat

1 — leans the mixture.
2 — has no effect on the mixture.
3 — richens the mixture.
4 — causes oil pressure fluctuations.

05. An advantage in the fuel injection system over the carburetor is that it

1 — has better fuel distribution to the cylinders.
2 — does not require an alternate air system.
3 — can be used best with fixed-pitch propellers.
4 — has a simpler oil system.

06. As an all-around procedure you should

1 — deliberately run a tank dry to use all the fuel only if it is a fuel injection system.
2 — expect a delay of 1–2 seconds in power after the selector is switched from an empty to a usable tank with the fuel injection system.
3 — deliberately run a tank dry only at altitudes above 1,500 feet MSL.
4 — never deliberately run a tank dry.

07. During the pretakeoff check after checking the mags, you pull the carburetor heat ON at 1,800 rpm (or the manufacturer's recommended number). There is no change of rpm (plus or minus) when you pull it ON or for 30 seconds thereafter. This is a sign that

1 — carburetor ice was present before the heat was applied.
2 — there was no carburetor ice present before the heat was applied.
3 — the carburetor is not getting heat from the system.
4 — you did not leave the heat on long enough to get an effect.

08. Smoking in an airplane

1 — is useful in finding out the wind direction by blowing the smoke out a window.
2 — may cause you to be thrown overboard by a nonsmoker.
3 — can cause clogging of the vacuum system air filter.
4 — can clog the carburetor heat.

Questions 09–17 are based on Figure B-13.

09. Item A is the

1 — carburetor air filter.
2 — oil cooler.
3 — alternator.
4 — carburetor heat muff.

10. If item B is ruptured, you would

1—expect a rapidly rising oil temperature.
2—lose use of the carburetor heat.
3—have ignition problems on the vacuum pump.
4—lose tire pressure.

11. Item C is the

1—magneto overflow simplex routing system (MOSRS).
2—air line to the nosewheel, used for filling the tire in flight.
3—carburetor heat hose.
4—oil breather line.

12. Item D is a component of which system?

1—Oil.
2—Fuel.
3—Electrical.
4—Ignition.

13. Item G is important in the event of

1—low oil pressure.
2—electrical overload.
3—carburetor ice.
4—alternator failure.

14. Item H is

1—a magneto.
2—the alternator.
3—the carburetor.
4—the oil reservoir.

15. Item I is

1—an intake manifold.
2—a fuel line.
3—an oil line.
4—an exhaust manifold.

16. If item J was severed, the result would be

1—a drop in oil pressure.
2—an ignition problem.
3—a fuel leak.
4—an alternator failure.

17. Items E and F, respectively, are part of which systems?

1—Oil and fuel.
2—Electrical and fuel.
3—Oil and electrical.
4—Oil and brake.

Answers

01. 3. See the text at the beginning of Appendix B.
02. 2. As indicated in this chapter, worn or broken piston rings may allow oil to get into the combustion chamber and be burned. A coagulated frammis (4) is not the answer because it is a factor that makes dentures slip and also may cause the heartbreak of psoriasis.
03. 2. IO-470. The engine is opposed (O) and has fuel injection (I). The bore of 5 inches would mean a piston surface area of πr^2 or $(2.5)^2 \times \pi$. Using 3.1416 for π, the area is 19.635 square inches. The stroke (piston movement) is 4 inches so that each cylinder displaces $4 \times 19.635 = 78.54$.

Figure B-13. Engine and system components for questions 09–17.

There are six cylinders, so that the total displacement is 471.24 cubic inches. The engine is direct drive (not geared), so a "G" wouldn't be part of the numbers. Your numbers may differ slightly from the above answers, depending on how far you take the decimal points.

04. 3. Chapter 4. The warmer air is less dense, so for the same weight of fuel being metered the mixture is richened. If, say at cruise, you need to use carburetor heat (and in trainers you should use *full* heat if you use *any*), you'll have to re-lean the mixture to get smooth running.

05. 1. The fuel injection system has better fuel distribution because the mixing is done just before it enters the cylinders. Because of this, the system is less susceptible to carburetor ice. Induction icing (caused by visible moisture freezing in the intake area) can still occur however.

06. 4. Because of possible restart problems, a good all-around philosophy is never to deliberately run a tank dry, particularly with a fuel injection system.

07. 3. The carburetor is not getting heat. In this book it is noted that the warmer air is less dense and a slight power loss would result. (A figure of 100 rpm is given as an average, but it could vary among airplanes.) If no ice was present, the rpm would stay at the lower value as long as the heat was ON. If ice had been present when the heat was applied, the rpm would drop initially because of the warmer air and then pick up above the first setting as the ice cleared out. This question ties in with question 13 in that there is a good possibility that the heat hose is detached at one or both ends. (*See* item G in Figure B-13 and also *see* Figure 4-2.) You may have missed this in the preflight check but might catch it here, since that's the purpose of pulling the heat ON. Don't pull the carburetor heat ON and quickly shove it OFF. Leave it ON for 10 seconds to check an initial drop in rpm and to see if it has cleared out ice. As the answer to question 13 notes, without an operating carburetor heat you might get into icing conditions that could cause a forced landing. Taxi back to have the problem checked if the heat isn't working properly during the pretakeoff check.

08. 3. Students fall into categories. Some students have fallen out of airplanes (or were pushed) when they smoked and contributed to vacuum-system air-filter problems.

09. 2. That's the oil cooler.

10. 1. If item B ruptures, you can expect to have a large oil leak, a rapidly rising oil temperature, and possible engine stoppage.

11. 4. That's the oil breather line. If you picked the first choice, it's possible that you are overwhelmed by technical gobbledygook. (A magneto overflow simplex routing system?) As far as filling the nosewheel tire in flight is concerned, when you get the private certificate you can send out that passenger who is always making sneering comments about your landings.

12. 1. Item D is the oil sump where the engine oil is stored.

13. 3. That's the carburetor heat hose, and during your preflight you should check it for attachment at the heat muff *and* at the carburetor. If it is off at either point, you could find yourself in a bad icing situation with no heat available.

14. 1. It's the right magneto.

15. 4. Exhaust manifold. In the picture, you might initially mistake it for an intake manifold, but look at it disappearing into the carburetor heat muff. When looking at an actual engine, you could readily see evidence of prior heating, whereas the intake manifold usually stands (or sits) in unheated glory.

16. 2. That's an ignition lead going to the bottom plug of the right front cylinder. The engine would still run on BOTH with that lead cut, but a mag check would show a problem. This particular installation has the right mag firing the lower right and upper left plugs. Selecting the right mag would show a prodigious drop, since on that mag one cylinder would be totally out of action. Remember that different engines have different ignition wire routings.

17. 2. E is the alternator and F is the carburetor.

More Notes on Brakes

The brakes in smaller airplanes are an independent hydraulic system; that is, they have their own reservoir, separate from a main hydraulic system that might actuate the landing gear and flaps. On some airplanes the brakes are the only hydraulic system on board.

Hydraulics for brakes, flaps, or landing gear work because liquid, unlike gas, is incompressible. Any force transmitted at one end goes directly to the other end of the system. (Purists will argue that liquids are compressible, but compared with air, not much.) If the lines had been filled with air, there would be little action at the far end because the air would allow itself to be compressed before passing on some of the forces. An analogy might be pushing against the back of a toy wagon with an iron bar (liquid) and a rubber hose (air). The iron bar will send your force directly and get the wagon rolling, but the rubber hose may bend and flex before transmitting part of your force to get the same (or lesser) result.

You may run into the problem of air in the brake lines in the airplane. The air is compressible, so as you press the pedal(s) there is no immediate response to pedal pressure because the air compresses rather than sending a direct message as the liquid brake fluid would do. A small amount of air in the system would mean a relatively small amount of "sponginess" of the pedals, but if the pedals start feeling this way, you'd better check with the mechanic who will "bleed" the system of air and check for loose connections or tighten up the system to stop the further encroachment of air. More about this later.

One type of light-airplane brake system consists of a master cylinder for each brake pedal, with its own reservoir of hydraulic fluid. Additional components consist of a mechanical linkage from each pedal to its cylinder, with required fluid lines to a brake assembly on each main wheel. In other words, each wheel has its own separate brake system.

Airplanes with a brake handle (no toe brakes) have a single master cylinder that transfers pressure to both main wheels at the same time.

Other systems may have a separate reservoir in the engine compartment, and the fluid level should be checked during each preflight inspection (if you can get to it).

During the preflight check you should look at the brake lines and at the surface under each main wheel to check for signs of brake fluid leaks. The wheel covers (speed fairings) on some airplanes make it difficult to check the condition of the brake disks and cylinders. Incidentally, if your airplane is such that the disks and brakes can be seen—and touched—don't put your hand on the disk if the airplane has just come in from a flight. A painful burn could result because the disks will remain hot for a while.

The parking brake is essentially a valve that locks pressure in the wheel cylinders. You'll press on the pedals and then set the parking brake, which (it says here) will hold the pressure exerted until released.

The parking brake generally should not be trusted. The pressure may bleed off, and the brakes would no longer hold. More than one pilot has set the parking brake for the engine run-up and looked up from a checklist to find that the airplane was moving rapidly toward some expensive object.

If the parking brake is set in the morning, rising temperatures during the day can cause fluid expansion and destroy seals in the system. Chocks or tiedowns are more dependable for an airplane that is to be left sitting for more than a few minutes.

Brake Problems

Probably one of the most common problems you'll run into is "soft brakes" or air in the system. The pedal or pedals may go easily to the limit with little or no brake effectiveness. If you unexpectedly encounter such a problem (you've taxied into the ramp too fast and suddenly realize that a very expensive mistake is about to be made), *pump* the brake pedals. This will build up temporary pressure for braking. It's a good idea to press the brakes—and release them—before coming in to land, so that you'll know whether the pedals feel normal. If they are soft, you might plan on pumping the brakes during roll-out or consider that you may not have *any* braking effectiveness and should make a short-field approach or fly to another airport with longer runways.

If on roll-out you discover that one brake of your tricycle-gear airplane isn't working, press the other brake gently and use rudder pedal pressure on the failed brake side to help keep the airplane straight.

People have opened doors on the roll-out after brake failure; the air drag of the door(s) can definitely help slow a smaller airplane.

Another problem is that of "hard" brakes. The brake pedals feel like they are solid and not hinged, and braking effectiveness is very low. You should get a mechanic on this also, as soon as practicable.

Dragging brakes (you can hear them sometimes) can cause tire wear on touchdown, brake heating problems, and longer takeoff runs. You can sometimes see the effects of a brake dragging by looking at a main wheel (high-wing airplane) as the airplane is taxied on a smooth surface; one landing gear shakes while the nondragging side moves smoothly.

Older airplanes have mechanical brakes in which a cable is used instead of the hydraulic line. When the pedal (usually a heel brake) was pressed, the cable moved the brake pad against the disk. A disadvantage of this type of system was that one of the cables would wear and break, usually at an "inopportune time." (*See* Figure 6-10 to check their use.) Press the brake pedals *before* starting the engine and also check their effectiveness just as the airplane starts to move for taxi.

You aren't expected to be a mechanic, and these problem descriptions are presented so you'll know that people in maintenance should be consulted and you can give them an idea of what to look for, thus saving time (and money).

Sport Pilot — Airplane, Single-Engine Land (ASEL)

The Sport Pilot is a day/VFR certificate that allows for easier entry into aviation. Reduced flight time requirements allow less training time and lower costs than the Private Pilot certificate, but bring restrictions on types of aircraft and flight conditions. It should be noted that the airmanship needed to fly the required Sport Pilot practical test maneuvers is the same as for the Private flight test. It is not a lower quality certificate.

A sport pilot (Land) is restricted to flying Light Sport Aircraft (LSA). LSAs have a maximum weight of 1,320 pounds (600 kg), a maximum level speed of 120 KCAS (knots calibrated airspeed), and a maximum stall speed without "lift-enhancement devices" (flaps) of 45 KCAS. In addition, LSAs must have fixed gear, a fixed or ground adjustable propeller, a single reciprocating engine, no more than two seats (including pilot) and be unpressurized. Under the LSA heading is a wide range of aircraft, from modern composite airplanes with glass cockpits to the classic Aeronca Champ and Piper Cub.

LSAs are divided into two large groups based on Vh (maximum level speed): Vh lower than or equal to 87 KCAS and Vh higher than 87 KCAS. These groups are divided into "sets" based on the landing gear type (tricycle, tailwheel or ski). A sport pilot may fly a different type of airplane so long as it is in the same set or the pilot has had training and a logbook sign-off for the new set. The training and logbook endorsement for the high-speed LSAs is a onetime requirement. An additional endorsement and training is required to fly in B, C or D airspace or airspace with an operating control tower.

For example, if a pilot trains at a controlled field in a fast tricycle gear LSA, the >87 KCAS (61.327) and the class B, C, D (61.325) sign-offs would be complete. The pilot would need a sign-off to fly the tailwheel version of the same trainer (61.323 – different set).

Figure E-1 shows the flight time differences between the Private and the Sport Pilot certificates. Other obvious differences are the omission of instrument and night training for the sport pilot, no requirement for controlled field (tower) take-offs and landings and a shorter solo cross-country with no minimum hours for solo cross-country.

A thorough reading of the Student Pilot's Flight Manual will prepare a student for the Sport Pilot certificate. Chapters 15 and 26 cover areas not required for the Sport Pilot, but they contain useful information for later certificates and ratings. Privileges and limitations are covered in 14 CFR §61.315.

The Sport Pilot Practical Test is very much like the Private Pilot checkride with the same altitude, heading and airspeed tolerances. Instrument and night flying are not covered. Although "Navigation Systems and Radar Services" is not required on the Sport Pilot checkride, you should be familiar with any equipment installed in your test airplane.

	Private (14 CFR §61.109)	Sport (14 CFR §61.313)
Total time	40 hours	20 hours
Instruction	20 hours	15 hours
Solo	10 hours	5 hours
Cross-country instruction	3 hours	2 hours
Solo cross-country	5 hours with 1 flight 150 nm total length	No minimum 1 flight 75 nm total length
Instrument training	3 hours	—
Night instruction, cross country	3 hours with 1 flight >100 nm total length 10 full stop landings	—
Controlled field	3 T/O & landings to a full stop with patterns	— can get sign-off (61.325)
Practical test preparation	3 hours	3 hours

Figure C-1. Comparison of the Aeronautical experience requirements of the Private versus the Sport certificates.

Bibliography
and Recommended Reading

FAA publications:

Federal Aviation Administration, *Aeronautical Information Manual*. Washington, D.C.,
U.S. Government Publishing Office (GPO). Electronic version online at http://www.faa.gov/atpubs

Aviation Weather (Advisory Circular 00-6A). Washington, D.C., U.S. GPO

Aviation Weather Services (Advisory Circular 00-45). Washington, D.C., U.S. GPO

Practical Test Standards for Private Pilot Single-Engine Land & Sea (FAA-S-8081-14)

Practical Test Standards for Sport Pilot (FAA-S-8081-29, FAA-S-8081-30)

Practical Test Standards are available at www.faa.gov/training_testing/, and also printed and published by Aviation Supplies & Academics, Inc.

Other publications:

Kershner, William K., *The Advanced Pilot's Flight Manual, 7th Edition*. Newcastle, WA, Aviation Supplies & Academics, Inc. 2006.

Langewiesche, Wolfgang, *Stick and Rudder*. New York, McGraw-Hill, 1944.

Information received from companies and POHs referred to:

Bendix/King, General Aviation Avionics Division, Olathe, KS 66082.

Castleberry Instruments and Avionics, Inc., Austin, TX; *Aircraft Instruments*.

Cessna Aircraft Co., Wichita, KS; *Pilot Operating Handbooks*.

Preface to the Ninth Edition
Printing History and Acknowledgments

This manual is a gathering of material used in preflight and postflight briefings and in-flight instruction. The maneuvers are written in the probable order of introduction to the student. The spin was included because the writer felt that students should have some idea of just what this maneuver entails, even if they would never be required to practice one. No attempt was made to set up a rigid schedule of maneuvers because such a schedule is precluded by variation in student ability.

This book is not intended to just help the reader "get past" the FAA knowledge and practical (flight) tests but includes information for use in the day-to-day process of learning to fly airplanes. There is emphasis on making judgment calls in various areas of flying (formally known as aeronautical decision making) to help the student pilot start setting up individual methods of coming to the right decision for a go or no-go situation.

At various points in the book, judgment factors are included to achieve this end.

I would like to thank the following for help on this manual for the first five editions:

Colonel E. F. Quinn, Professor of Air Science at Iowa State University, whose encouragement and backing got the book started.

Major J. W. Carothers and Captain H. E. Fischer also of the Iowa State University Air Science Department, who reviewed the first manuscript and made suggestions and comments.

Dr. M. L. Millett of the Department of Aeronautical Engineering at Iowa State University, who reviewed both the first and final drafts of the first manuscript, with particular attention to the aerodynamics and instrument theory, and who made comments and suggestions that improved the book.

The Army Aviation School personnel at Fort Rucker, Ala., who reviewed and made many valuable suggestions.

The Air Force ROTC Headquarters personnel at Maxwell Field, Ala., who reviewed and encouraged the completion of the manual.

A. J. Prokop, who checked the first manuscript; Eugene Anderson, also of the Des Moines Aviation Safety District Office, who checked the manuscript with particular emphasis on emergency recovery by instruments; and Glen Bower, flight instructor of Ames, Iowa, who reviewed and commented on the manual.

The FAA General Operations Branch Office personnel in Washington, D.C., who made several pertinent corrections and suggestions.

J. M. Bennett of Morgantown, W.Va., who furnished reports on the instrument training program at the University of West Virginia.

Particular thanks must go to K. R. Marvin, former head of the Department of Technical Journalism at Iowa State University, who backed the effort.

John Murray, of the Weather Bureau Airport Station at Williamsport, Pa., for his review and suggestion for revision of the chapter on weather.

Jerome Bosworth and John Leck of the Williamsport, Pa., Flight Service Station for their help in obtaining the latest material about the functions of the FSS.

Delbert W. Robertson of the Chattanooga, Tenn., Weather Bureau Airport Station for answering questions and furnishing weather data.

James D. Lee of the Crossville, Tenn., Flight Service Station for furnishing FSS information.

Colonel Leslie McLaurin, flight instructor and manager of the airport here at Sewanee, for suggestions and ideas that were used in the book.

W. D. Thompson, Chief, Flight Test and Aerodynamics, Commercial Aircraft Division of Cessna Aircraft Company, for furnishing data on Cessna airplanes.

I've had many good suggestions for improving the book from student and private pilots and flight instructors. I would especially like to mention Allen Hayes of Chartair, Inc., Ithaca, N.Y., and Robert S. Woodbury of Massachusetts Institute of Technology.

Again, I've been lucky in having knowledgeable individuals helping with this book over the years. Any errors are mine, though. I would especially like to thank the following people:

William Thompson, who sent me data on Cessna airplanes with dispatch and with valuable personal comments on the aerodynamics of flight.

Thanks must also go to Cessna and Grumman for allowing me to use information of their airplanes as examples.

Appreciation is expressed to Dr. A. V. Ray of Burlington, Ontario, for suggestions on improving the section in Chapter 26 on the physiology of the eye.

Special thanks must go to Elizabeth Motlow, who flew the example cross-country with me and took pictures of the checkpoints.

The people at the Chattanooga Weather Service Office, as always, were most cooperative and came through with actual material and, more importantly, simple explanations for the computerized methods of weather reporting and forecasting. In particular, I would mention Ed Higdon and W. R. Wright. Others who helped are Ray R. Casada, Hugh Pritchard, Jr., Delbert Robertson, M. H. Smith, Jack Phillips, and Sam DeLay.

Thanks to Jules Bernard of Tullahoma, Tenn., for help.

David F. Shaw, of Penn Yan, N.Y., gave good suggestions for later printings.

Thanks to Larry Crawford, of the Nashville Flight Service Station, for furnishing actual weather information.

Kermit Anderson, formerly of the FAA at OKC, gave much appreciated and valuable help.

My wife encouraged me, as always, and gave practical help by typing the rough copies of the manuscript in the first four editions. Mrs. Barbara Hart typed the smooth copy for the fourth edition.

For the sixth edition, I would add:

Thanks to Margaret Puckette of Corvallis, Ore., and Tim Keith-Lucas of Sewanee for suggestions that would make the book more useful to the student and low-time private pilot.

Eleanor Ulton of Sewanee did her usual outstanding job of translating my scribbling into understandable English.

Nancy Bolen, my astute editor at ISU Press, kept a sharp eye on my grammar and helped ensure that female pilots were given proper recognition. Her efforts have made my books much better over the years of our association.

Thanks to Lynne Bishop, also an editor at ISU Press, for her patience, humor, and ability to catch my mistakes in this edition.

My son, Bill, currently flying for a major airline, gave much help.

Special thanks to Kathleen Schlachter, meteorology instructor at the FAA Academy at OKC, for translating weather presentations to the METAR/TAF format.

To Hap's Air Service, Ames, Iowa, for donating the airplane, fuel, and air time used during the photo session for the cover. Thanks also are expressed to James Kurtenbach for piloting the plane, to Kristen Krumhart for being the student pilot, and to Peter Krumhart for taking the photograph.

This book is aimed at the individual who is working directly for the private pilot (airplane, single-engine, land) certificate; therefore, other certificates and ratings (recreational pilot or private pilot, seaplane, etc.) are not emphasized here. The basics of flying an airplane are covered, so people working on those other certificates/ratings will still find it useful.

Thanks to Jim Oliver, training specialist at the Nashville Flight Service Station, for answering my questions and furnishing material to update the weather services and NOTAM materials.

Thanks to Charles Knowles for helping in updating this printing.

Thanks to Bob Salton, Diamond Aircraft Industries of London, Ontario, Canada, for information on the DA 20-C1 and DA40-180 airplanes.

The eighth edition contained 621 questions and the answers and explanations for the private pilot (airplane ASEL) knowledge test; these have been removed and replaced with the syllabus for the private certificate. The printing of a book with additions and updates is made to cover several months to a year. However, during this time a number of the questions on the actual FAA knowledge test may be changed—the wording may be changed, questions may be deleted, or additions may be made. The reader now has the ability to get the latest questions on the computer and from other up-to-date sources and should use these in preparation for the knowledge test.

As a textbook, a general approach must be taken here in discussing maneuvers and flight areas such as weather services and other rapidly changing information services. Some airplanes may require specific techniques in, for instance, use of flaps, carburetor heat, alternate air, or recommended spin entries and recoveries. Do not use any of the navigation or performance charts; they are samples only. The procedures for a particular airplane as outlined in the Pilot's Operating Handbook, Airplane Flight Manual, or the equivalent information for your airplane will naturally be the final guide for operations. And, as noted in Chapter 3, your flight instructor will also have suggestions for your airplane and operating conditions.

William K. Kershner
Sewanee, Tennessee

Index

180° turns 15-5
720° power turn 10-1

A

abbreviations, weather report 22-8
accelerated stalls 14-3
accelerating pump 5-2
adiabatic lapse rate 22-5
ADIZ (Air Defense Identification Zone) 24-16
advection fog 22-7
aeronautical decision making (ADM) 28-12
Aeronautical Information Manual (AIM) 20-1
ailerons 8-3
ailerons, inspection 4-7
ailerons, pretakeoff check 7-1
ailerons, used in slips 13-12
aileron tab 2-7
aircraft documents 3-17, 23-1
aircraft registration 23-1
air density 2-4
air discipline 1-2
airfoil 2-1
AIRMETs (WA) 22-12
airplane categories and load factors 23-1
Airplane Flight Manual 3-18, 23-1
airplane lighting 26-3
Airport/Facility Directory 20-3, 24-1
airport lighting 26-4
airports, non-tower 6-1
airport traffic pattern 13-8
airspace 20-1
airspace classification 21-14
airspeed 3-6
airspeed control 8-2
airspeed correction table 19-6
airspeed indicator 3-5
airspeed indicator, pretakeoff check 7-2
airspeed limitations 3-18
air traffic control 20-1
Airworthiness Certificate 3-17, 23-1
alternate airports 24-5
alternator B-10
alternator, inspection 4-4
altimeter 3-3, 15-2, 15-3, 15-4, 19-8

altimeter, pretakeoff check 7-2
altimeter setting 3-5
amended forecast 22-9
ammeter 3-16, B-11
angle of attack 2-3, 12-1, 12-12, 12-13
angle of bank 12-8
angle of incidence 2-3
approaches 13-9–13-26
approaches, to stall 12-3
Area Forecast (FA) 22-11
artificial horizon 3-13
ASR (airport surveillance radar) 15-11
ATIS (Automatic Terminal Information Service) 6-1
attitude 2-3
attitude indicator 3-13
attitude indicator, pretakeoff check 7-2
attitude, in stalls 12-5
attitude, toward flying 1-2
audio console 3-2
automatic direction finder (ADF) 3-2
Automatic Terminal Information Service (ATIS) 21-10

B

ballooning 13-5, 13-16
bank 8-3
bank angle 10-5
barometric pressure 3-3
base key 13-22
Bernoulli's theorem 2-1
bounce, recovery from 13-15
brake horsepower 2-5
brakes 6-6
brakes, airplane B-14
brakes, inspection 4-2
braking effectiveness B-15

C

cabin air control 3-2
cabin heat, inspection 4-3
calibrated airspeed (CAS) 3-7, 19-6
canting 2-6
carburetion B-4
carburetor 5-2
carburetor heat 9-8

carburetor heat, inspection 4-3
carburetor heat, pretakeoff check 7-4
carburetor ice 25-9
carburetor icing 4-3
carburetor intake fire 5-2
carburetor intake screen, inspection 4-6
celestial navigation 19-1
center of gravity (CG) 23-3
center of gravity moment envelope 23-7
centripetal force 8-4
Certificate of Aircraft Registration 3-17
checkitis 28-12
checkpoint 25-1
CHT (cylinder head temperature) gauge B-7
circuit breaker panel 3-2
Class C airspace 21-13
clear ice 22-6
climbing stall 15-4
climbing turn 9-6
climbing-turn stall 12-7
climb, maximum angle of 17-1
cloud types 22-4
cockpit instruments 3-1
cockpit of trainer, illustrated 3-1
coefficient of lift 2-3
cold front 22-1, 22-2, 22-21
common traffic advisory frequency (CTAF) 21-9
compass 3-8, 19-2
compass correction card 19-4
compass deviation 19-4
compass locators 21-1
compass variation 19-2
compression rings B-2
computer 19-5
computing time and fuel 24-11
cones and rods 26-1
constant-speed propeller 23-15
controls, effects of 8-1–8-4
control tower 21-9
convective SIGMETs 22-14
coordinated universal time (UTC) 19-2
coordination exercises 9-4
cowling, inspection 4-6
crab 10-3, 10-4
crab method of correction 13-20
cross-control stall/skidding 14-1

cross-country flight 24-1
cross-country, flying 25-1
cross-country, planning 23-1–23-16
crosswind component 13-19
crosswind landing 13-19
crosswind takeoffs and landings 13-17–13-21
cruising flight 23-9
cumulus clouds 22-4
currency 28-15
cylinder cooling fins B-9
cylinders B-3

D

datum 23-6
dead (deduced) reckoning 19-1
density-altitude 3-5, 17-8, 19-8
density altitude chart 3-4
descending turns 16-8
detonation B-7
distance measuring equipment (DME) 21-6
diving spiral 15-2
documents required on aircraft 3-19
downwind key 13-22
drag 2-7, 9-1
drift correction 13-8, 13-14

E

eights around pylons 16-4
electrical problems 25-9
electrical switches 3-2
electrical system, engine B-10
electrical system, pretakeoff check 7-3
electrical systems 3-16
electric flap control 3-2
elevators 8-1
elevators, inspection 4-7
elevator trim tab 8-2
elevator trim tab, pretakeoff check 7-1
emergencies 25-4
emergencies, high-altitude 18-1
emergency instrument flying 15-1–15-11
emergency landings 11-1–11-2
emergency locator transmitter (ELT) 21-18
emergency maneuvers 15-1
engine 5-1, 5-3, 5-4
engine compartment, inspection 4-3
engine-cooling openings, inspection 4-6
engine fires 25-9
engine instrument cluster 3-2
engine, pretakeoff check 7-4
engine problems 25-8
engine theory, construction, and operations B-1–B-11
en route 25-1
equivalent airspeed (EAS) 3-7
estimated time of arrival (ETA) 19-7
exhaust gas temperature (EGT) gauge B-9
exhaust system B-9

F

Federal Aviation Administration 1-1, 3-17
Federal Aviation Regulations 3-10, 12-1, 27-1
fields, for emergency landings 11-1
fin, offset 2-6
flaps 13-11
flaps, pretakeoff check 7-2
flight controls, in taxiing 6-3
flight log 24-13
flight plan 21-7, 25-2
flight plan, closing 25-3
flight plan, filing 20-2, 24-15
flight planning 24-1
Flight Service Station (FSS) 21-7, 22-7, 24-15, 25-2
FLIGHT WATCH (Enroute Flight Advisory Service—EFAS) 22-16
flooding engine 5-1–5-2
fluid leaks 4-1
flying straight and level 15-10
fog 22-6
force 2-4
forced landings 18-1
forward slip 13-13
four forces, the 2-1–2-8
four main directions, use of in turns 15-6
frontal systems 22-1
frost 22-6
fuel and oil information 23-8
fuel consumption 19-8
fuel injection system B-5
fuel management 23-12
fuel, pretakeoff check 7-3
fuel pump 3-2
fuel selector valve 3-3
fuel strainer drain, inspection 4-4
fuel system schematic 23-14
fuel tanks 4-3
fuselage, inspection 4-2

G

glass cockpit 3-20
glide airspeed 11-1
glide ratio 18-2
gliding turn 9-9, 11-1
gliding turns, in landing 12-8
global positioning system (GPS) 21-18
graveyard spiral 15-2
gravity 2-8
Greenwich Mean Time 19-2
ground effect 17-3
ground loop 13-8
groundspeed 3-6, 3-7
groundspeeds, finding 19-7
gusty winds 13-26
gyro instruments 3-10
gyroscopic precession 2-7, 13-3

H

hazards to flight, weather 22-5
heading indicator 3-14, 15-6
heading indicator, pretakeoff check 7-2
headwork 1-1
heel brake 6-6
high-altitude emergencies 18-1
high- and low-pressure systems 22-1–22-2
holding position markings 6-7
horsepower 9-5
hourly weather report (METAR) 22-8

I

ICAO (International Civil Aviation Organization) 22-10
icing 22-6
ignition 4-1
ignition switch 3-2
ignition system 3-17
indicated airspeed (IAS) 3-7, 19-6
induced drag 2-8, 12-12
in-flight weather advisories 22-12
instrument panel, pretakeoff check 7-2
isobars 22-2, 22-16
isogonic lines 19-3, 19-4

K

key position 18-1
knowledge test guide 27-3
knowledge test review 27-1

L

land and hold short operations (LAHSO) 21-18
landing attitude 13-5
landing checklist 26-6
landing, dragging the area 17-7
landing gear, inspection 4-6
landing, normal 13-4
landings, approaches 13-16
landings, forced 11-1–11-2
landings, recoveries 13-14–13-16
landing stalls 12-8
lapse rate 3-7
latitude 19-1
lift 2-1, 9-1
lift equation 2-3
light signals 21-17
light sport aircraft (LSA) C-1
load factors 9-2, 23-1
loading graph 23-7
local airport advisory 21-8
logbooks 3-19, 23-1
longitude 19-1
low-level prognostic chart 22-19
low-level significant weather prognostic chart 22-20
lubber line 3-10

M

magnetic compass 3-9, 15-10
Magnetic North Pole 3-8, 19-2
magneto, inspection 4-3
magneto, pretakeoff check 7-3
magnetos 4-1, B-5
maintenance record 3-19
maneuvers, precision 16-1–16-8
manual flap control 3-3
map work 24-1
master switch 3-2
mean sea level (MSL) 3-3
meridians and parallels 19-1
METAR (Meteorological Aviation Routine
    Report) 22-8
microphone 3-2
minimum controllable airspeed 12-9–12-10
mixture control 5-2, 23-11
moment 23-4
MULTICOM 21-7

N

National Weather Service 22-1
nautical mile 19-1
NAV/COMM 3-2
navigation 19-1
navigation planning 24-1
Newton's law 2-2
night flying 26-1
night flying tips 26-5
night vision 26-1
nondirectional radio beacons (NDB) 21-1
normal climb 9-5
normal glide 9-7, 11-2
normal landing 13-4
normal stall 12-4–12-5
normal takeoff 13-1
NOTAMs (Notices to Airmen) 20-3, 21-7,
    24-1

O

occluded front 22-3
oil 23-8
oil check 4-6
oil control rings B-3
oil, inspection 4-4
oil pressure 5-4
oil pressure gauge 3-8
oil pressure, pretakeoff check 7-2
oil system B-7
oil temperature gauge 3-8
oil temperature, pretakeoff check 7-3
Otto cycle B-2

P

parasite drag 2-7, 12-12
parking brake 6-7, B-15
PAR (precision approach radar) 15-11
P factor 2-7

phugoid oscillations 12-6
pilotage 19-1, 19-5, 24-8, 25-7
pilot briefing service 21-7
pilot reports 22-16
pilot reports (PIREPs) 21-7, 22-16
Pilot's Operating Handbook 3-8, 3-18, 24-2
pistons B-2
pitot-static system 3-5
pitot-static tube 4-6
P-leads 13-28
plotter 19-5
power 2-4, 23-9
power approaches 17-2
power curve 12-12
power-on spiral 15-2
power versus airspeed 12-12
practical (flight) test 28-1
practical test checklist 28-1
precession 3-10
precipitation fog 22-7
precision landings 17-2
precision maneuvers 10-1–10-7
precision maneuvers, postsolo 16-1
preflight check 4-1–4-8
preflight preparations, practical test 28-4
preflight procedures, practical test 28-5
preignition 5-3, B-7
pressure 22-1
pressure altitude 3-5, 19-7
pretakeoff check 7-1–7-4
primer 5-2
progressive stall 12-4
propeller 2-5, 2-6, 2-7
propeller, inspection 4-6
propping a plane 5-3
propwash 2-5, 7-1

R

radar 25-6
radar summary chart 22-19
radiation fog 22-7
radio beacons 21-1
radio equipment 3-20
radio frequencies 21-1
radio navigation 19-1
radio navigation aids 21-1
radios, pretakeoff check 7-2
range and endurance profile 23-12
rate of climb 9-5
rate of climb indicator 3-15
rectangular course 10-4
relative wind 2-1, 2-3, 12-14
repair and alteration forms 23-1
rheostat 3-2
ridge 22-1
rime ice 22-6
roll 12-7
roll-out 9-4, 10-2, 10-3
rudder 2-6, 8-2
rudder control, pretakeoff check 7-2
rudder, inspection 4-7

rudder pedals 6-2
rudder tab 2-6–2-7
rudder trim 8-3
run-up 7-1
runway markings 25-3
runway numbering 6-2
runways 25-3

S

sectional chart 20-1, 24-1
segmented circle 6-2
shaft horsepower 2-5
short-field landing 17-2
short-field takeoff 17-1
sideslip 13-13
SIGMETs (WS) 22-12
simulated high-altitude takeoffs 17-9
simulated radar advisories 15-11
skid 3-11, 9-2
slip 3-11, 9-2, 12-7, 13-12
slipping turn 3-11
slipstream effect 2-5, 9-7
slow flight 12-9–12-10
slow flight, instrument indications 12-10
soft-field landing 17-5
soft-field takeoff 17-5
solo 13-29
solo cross-country 24-1
spark plugs B-6
spin and spiral, instrument indications
    12-16
spin recovery 12-14
spins 12-13, 12-17
spirals 12-16, 16-8
Sport Pilot Practical Test C-1
squall lines 25-8
stabilator 14-5
stabilizer, inspection 4-7
stall 2-3, 13-4
stall break 12-7, 12-9
stalling speed 9-3
stall, power-off 12-3
stall, power-on 12-3
stall recovery 12-17
stalls 14-1
stalls, accelerated 14-3
stalls, and flaps 12-9
stalls and slow flight 12-1
stalls, approaches to 12-3
stalls, as landing aid 12-2
stalls, climbing turns 12-7
stalls, instrument indications 12-4
stalls, normal 12-4–12-5
stalls, straight-ahead 12-4
stall strips 12-2
stall warning indicator 12-17
stall warning light 4-1
standard-rate turn 3-11, 3-13, 3-14, 15-7
standard sea level pressure 22-1
starter 5-3, 5-4
starting procedures 5-1–5-4

static port 13-14
static tube 3-6
stationary front 22-4
station models 22-16
steep turn 10-1
straight and level flying 9-9, 15-10
stratus clouds 22-4
stress raiser 4-6
S-turns across a road 10-6
suction gauge 3-2
suction gauge, pretakeoff check 7-3
surface analysis chart 22-16, 22-18
switch off 4-1

T

tab adjustment 2-6
TACAN (tactical air navigation) 21-6
tachometer 3-8
tachometer, pretakeoff check 7-2
tailwheel, inspection 4-7
takeoff and departure stall 12-7
takeoff, normal 13-1
takeoffs and landings 13-1, 17-1
takeoffs and landings, crosswind 13-17–13-21
takeoffs and landings, emergencies 13-16
takeoffs and landings, performance 17-8–17-11
takeoffs and landings, traffic pattern 13-8
takeoff, tailwheel airplanes 13-2
takeoff, tricycle-gear 13-1
taxi 13-28
taxiing 6-1–6-7
taxi signals 6-5
Terminal Aerodrome Forecast (TAF) 22-9
tetrahedron 6-2
three-point landing 13-6
throttle 2-5, 12-13
thrust 2-4
thrust horsepower 2-5
thunderstorms 22-5
thunderstorm, stages of 22-6

TIBS 22-16
time 19-2
time between overhauls (TBO) B-4
timed turn 15-6
time, fuel, and distance 23-9
tires, inspection 4-2
toe brake 6-6
torque 2-5
torque effect 2-6
touch-and-go's 13-9
tricycle-gear airplanes 6-2
trim tab, inspection 4-7
trim tab stall 14-5
trough 22-1
true airspeed (TAS) 3-6, 19-6
turn 9-1–9-4
turn and slip indicator 3-11, 3-12
turn coordinator 3-12
turn coordinator, pretakeoff check 7-2
turning stalls 12-7
turns around a point 16-1
turns, precision 16-1
turns, shallow-climbing and descending 15-7–15-9

U

UNICOM 3-20, 21-7, 25-2
upslope fog 22-7

V

vacuum system B-11
venturi 3-12
vertical speed indicator 3-15
vertical speed indicator, pretakeoff check 7-2
VHF omnirange (VOR) 21-3
visual approach slope indicator (VASI) 21-17
VOR airways 20-2
VORTAC stations 21-6
VOR (VHF omnirange) 21-3

W

wake turbulence 13-26
warm front 22-3, 22-21
washout 12-2
weather 25-8
weather charts 22-16–22-21
weathercock 6-3, 13-17
weather depiction chart 22-18, 22-19
weather forecasts 22-9–22-11
weather information sources 22-7–22-21
weather patterns 22-1–22-5
weight 2-8, 9-1
weight and balance 23-3–23-7
weight and balance envelope 23-4
wheel landing 17-6
wind conditions 6-3
wind direction 18-1
wind drift correction 10-3–10-7
wind effects on takeoffs and landings 13-17–13-26
wind indicators 6-1
wind information 22-15
winds aloft chart 22-15
windsock 6-1
wind tee 6-1
wind triangle 19-9, 19-11
wing, inspection 4-6
wing-low flying 9-10
wing tanks, inspection 4-2
wing tip vortices 2-8, 13-26
work 2-4

2022
On 8-15-19
8-25-14 only copy